£ 13-66

Au

Ti

Ac

John Keats

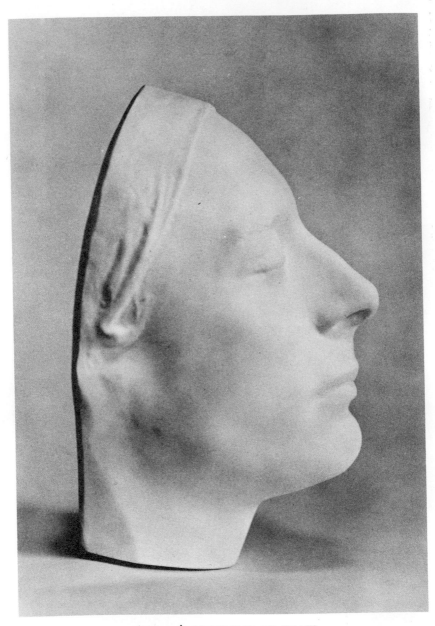

HAYDON'S LIFE MASK OF KEATS

John Keats

by

WALTER JACKSON BATE

THE BELKNAP PRESS OF
HARVARD UNIVERSITY PRESS
Cambridge, Massachusetts

© Copyright 1963 by the President and Fellows of Harvard College
All rights reserved

Third Printing, 1972

Distributed in Great Britain by Oxford University Press, London

Library of Congress Catalog Card Number 63-17194

SBN 674-47800-2

Designed by Burton L. Stratton

Printed in the United States of America

To

Douglas Bush

Preface

THE LIFE OF KEATS provides a unique opportunity for the study of literary greatness and of what permits or encourages its development. The interest is thus deeply human and moral, and in the most capacious sense of both of these words. For, to begin with, we have to do with a type of poetic genius that—whatever the handicaps or restrictions with which Keats starts—quickly acquires a personal relevance to a wide variety of readers. We find the steady growth of qualities of both mind and character that are equally appropriate to other forms of achievement, and that are at the same time being practically and dramatically tested in Keats's daily experience from the age of twenty-one to the end of his short life. The development of his technical craftsmanship as a poet proceeds simultaneously, a growth that interests us all the more because it is not something separate but, as it were, partly a by-product—at least an organically related accompaniment—of his larger, more broadly humane development. This is one of the reasons why, for over a century, Keats has continued to strike so many readers—and writers—as the most Shakespearean in character of all poets since Shakespeare himself.

The story of his development has the further interest that it takes place in a relatively modern setting. We are thus able to find out at least something to help us in considering two problems that puzzle many of us. The first is that (again as with Shakespeare, about whose life we know so little) not much is apparently given at the start—very little indeed when compared with the education and what are ordinarily called "advantages" that have been lavished on some millions of people (many of them highly gifted) even in the relatively short period since 1800. We naturally wonder how it was done: how so much was done in so many different ways—what helped and what hindered. Aside from this broad educational interest, there is a special one that grows sharper with each generation. It is a commonplace that poetry and indeed all the arts have seemed to become increasingly specialized or restricted throughout the last two hundred and fifty years, and especially during the twentieth century. We face even more directly the problem that was widely discussed throughout the fifty years before Keats was born and also throughout his lifetime: where are the Homers and Shakespeares, the "greater genres"—the epic and dramatic tragedy—or at least reasonable equivalents? How much of this is to be explained by the modern premium on originality—by the vivid awareness of what the great art of the past has achieved, and by the poet's or artist's embarrassment before that rich amplitude? The pressure of this anxiety and the variety of reactions to it constitute one of the great unexplored factors in the history of the arts since 1750. And in no major poet, near the beginning of the modern era, is this problem met more directly than it is in Keats. The question of the way in which Keats was somehow able, after the age of twenty-two, to confront this dilemma, and to transcend it, has fascinated every major poet who has used the English language since Keats's death and also every major critic since the Victorian era.

Finally, if we want to make use of it, there is an available knowledge of Keats's life, once he reaches the age of twenty-two, quite as detailed as that for any major poet in any language at a comparable age. There are in fact times, after his most creative period begins, when we can follow him week by week if we really want to do so. Though the material for the earlier years is relatively meager, even here we have one advantage. For at least his early poetry survives almost complete, whereas longer-lived poets have had a chance to suppress or dispose of their first trials. Few of us care to exhibit the awkwardnesses of our adolescence either to ourselves or to others. Admittedly most of Keats's earlier poetry is interesting as poetry only to the specialist in the psychology of styles, including the styles of stock expressions, or to the fellow writer, healthfully reassured that an imaginative and mental endowment so impressive should itself have begun as haltingly as many of us secretly do and then try to forget. But the story quickly picks up afterwards. And shortly after Keats has reached the age of twenty-two (Chapters X and XI) we find ourselves on a level of thinking (and, within another year, a level of expression) habitual to only the very greatest writers.

All of these more general interests have been active concerns of this particular biography, however inadequately any one of them has been pursued. There was also some thought that the justification for still another book on Keats existed even if one merely tried to bring together the new biographical material that has become known since the second World War. The last really full-length biography was that of Amy Lowell, published a generation ago (1925), although since that time other books, including the more condensed biography by Dorothy Hewlett, have incorporated further details. Moreover, in the years that followed the biography by Amy Lowell, discussions and reconsiderations of Keats have often mirrored an unhappy characteristic of our specialized generation: those concerned with biographical details are often less interested in the criticism of the writer's principal works. Conversely the more specialized studies of Keats's writing—indeed of any major author's work—have often been written with far less interest in the biography, or even in the general drama of the human achievement, than in particular aspects of his individual works (sources, recurring themes, psychoanalytic preoccupations, or the various forms of stylistic analysis). The present writer, however much he prizes amplitude and diversity as ideals, could hardly hope to present the fruits of every previous analysis of the poems or argue the possible inferences at every stage. But I have made an effort to retain a reasonable openness of approach to most of them, especially after the greater writing of Keats finally begins.

A note may be added about the discussion of particular poems—not the casual mention of the earlier verse, which it can be assumed is necessarily brief (perhaps not brief enough), but the discussion of the major poems beginning with *Hyperion,* and especially of the poems from the odes to the *Fall of Hyperion.* These poems have for years been the subject of the most detailed analyses. When one loves a thing, one is always tempted to discuss it as fully as one can, especially when the very essence of the appeal of the subject is its own amplitude and debatability, its diversity and richness of implication. But the attempt to discuss the poems here, within the confines of a biography—though these are the poems that have interested me most over the past twenty-five years—has naturally had to be limited. Such poems could not be fully explicated as though each one, or a group of them, were the sole concern of the book. For much of the context of Keats's life and writing that is most relevant to each major poem has necessarily, in a biography, been already dealt with in a chronological way and to that extent separately. To summarize it again when every important work is considered would lead to an intolerable amount of repetition. Even so I have doubtless been guilty of too much repetition when a major poem or a particular period of Keats's life is being considered. The only excuse—or explanation if not an excuse—is that Keats's development, however rapid, is by no means linear. Linear developments exist only to a perception in which diagnosis is hurried by the heat of argument or kept simple by lack of all but a few obvious facts. Keats's development naturally circles and eddies. He constantly goes back, even in his short life, to premises and values, or to the challenges or impressions, of a year before—or two or three years before—and then reconsiders, ramifies, and begins again, as indeed we all do, though often in a slower progression.

In order to reduce the number of footnotes, I have simply referred in the text, whenever it could be done easily, to the dates of Keats's letters. The date, in each case, is that assigned the letter in Hyder Rollins' authoritative edition; the reader can refer immediately to the appropriate letter in Rollins by means of the date. Keats's hurried and idiosyncratic spelling and punctuation are followed in almost every case. The text used for the poems is in general the standard edition by H. W. Garrod (1939). Exceptions are made in the case of poems quoted directly from the *Letters*.

Acknowledgments are numerous if a writer frankly hopes to include or distill material from earlier works. Since the standard biographies of Sir Sidney Colvin (1917) and Amy Lowell (1925), a great deal of material has been made available. Of special value is the material published by my late colleague Hyder Rollins in the *Keats Circle* (1948), which printed hitherto unpublished manuscripts from the Houghton Library at Harvard, from the Morgan Library, and from other collections. Later publications of Rollins, culminating in his memorable edition of Keats's *Letters* (1958), published just after his death, help fill out the picture further, especially in the redating of some of Keats's letters. I have hoped to take advantage of this material, while supplementing it with whatever might be gained from a free access to Rollins' sources in the Houghton Library and elsewhere.

Since this biography was planned as a companion publication to Rollins' edition of the *Letters,* the endpapers of that edition, which provide helpful maps of London and the London area of Keats's time, are reproduced here.

I should also express my debt to the writings and in many cases the kind personal encouragement of the following: Professors Willard Pope of the University of Vermont, Claude Finney of Vanderbilt University, Earl Wasserman of Johns Hopkins, J. C. Stillinger of Illinois, Harold Bloom of Yale, Miss Dorothy Hewlett, the late Professors H. W. Garrod of Oxford and Clarence Thorpe of Michigan, and the late Mr. Louis Holman of Boston, to whose collection and careful chronology of Keats, now at Harvard, every writer on Keats's life during the last forty years has been indebted either directly or indirectly. Thanks are also due to Professor Geoffrey Tillotson and to Miss Carol Landon of the University of London, for helping me to find out a little more about the finances of the Keats family; to Professors David Owen and Alex Gerschenkron of Harvard, and Professor Albert Imlah of Tufts University, for help in estimating the cost of living in Keats's time as compared with the present day; and to Signor Gino Doria, Chairman of the Art Galleries of the Naples area, for giving me some details relevant to Keats's final months in Italy.

The curators of the three principal Keats collections have been especially generous in their help: Miss Mabel Steele, of the Keats Collection of the Houghton Library at Harvard; Signora Vera Cacciatore, of the Keats-Shelley Memorial House in Rome; and Mr. William R. Maidment, of the Keats Memorial House, Hampstead. I also wish to thank them, as well as the authorities of the National Portrait Gallery and the Dedham Historical Society, for permission to reproduce the illustrations.

Among many colleagues and former teachers at Harvard who have befriended my effort to understand Keats over the last twenty-five years, I should mention in particular the late Professor John Livingston Lowes; the late Professor Hyder Rollins, to whose definitive editions I have already mentioned my obligation (and that of any student of Keats henceforth) ; Professor Herschel Baker, whose authoritative work on Hazlitt has recently appeared; Professor Harry Levin, who has taught me much about the history of critical theory, and Professors Archibald MacLeish and I. A. Richards, to whose writings and general conversation over the years I owe so much. My use of the fine study of the major romantic poets by Professor David Perkins is mentioned in the discussion of Keats's odes as well as elsewhere; and I also thank him for the care with which he went over many of the chapters of this book. To Professor Douglas Bush my debt was already large when I was a beginning student and attempted a small undergraduate thesis, published under the title of *Negative Capability* (1939), on Keats's conception of the poetic character. However jejune that youthful effort, the aspirations that had led me to try to write it in the first place were encouraged by him in the years that followed, during most of which I was occupied with a variety of tasks and, occasionally, with writing on different subjects. Now, after almost twenty-five years, I wish I could better express what I owe to this humanist whose range and vision, in approaching literature from the Greeks to the present day, subsume so close a knowledge of detail that even the specialist, restricting himself to a single period, still turns to it for authority. The only way in which I can express my own thanks, however inadequately, is by inscribing this book to him.

W. J. B.

Cambridge, Massachusetts
January 1963

Preface to the Third Printing

Typographical errors and some statements of fact were corrected in the second printing (1964) and a few more in this printing. Since the publication of this book, further light has been thrown on the finances of the Jennings and Keats families by Robert Gittings, in *The Keats Inheritance* (1964). A few changes have been made to bring the short discussion here more closely in line with new details discovered by Mr. Gittings, and I also use this occasion to refer the reader generally to his detailed study of the subject.

Contents

✳︎✥❀✥✳︎✥❀✥✳︎✥❀✥✳︎✥❀✥✳︎✥❀✥✳︎✥❀✥✳︎✥❀✥✳︎✥❀✥✳︎✥❀✥✳︎✥❀✥✳︎✥❀✥❀

xiv Contents

Illustrations

✳↝☯↝✳↝☯↝✳↝☯↝✳↝☯↝✳↝☯↝✳↝☯↝✳↝☯↝✳↝☯↝✳↝☯↝✳↝☯↝✳↝☯

Frontispiece

HAYDON'S LIFE MASK OF KEATS
From a cast belonging to the author

Following page 44

1. THE CLARKE SCHOOL AT ENFIELD
A drawing (about 1840) in the Holman Collection, Harvard

2. DR. HAMMOND'S SURGERY, EDMONTON
*A photograph by Sir William Hale-White (about 1920) in the
Holman Collection, Harvard*

3. EDMONTON IN 1806
An engraving in the Holman Collection, Harvard

4. THE BOROUGH AROUND 1820
A print in the Holman Collection, Harvard

5. THE NORTH FRONT OF GUY'S HOSPITAL IN KEATS'S TIME
A print in the Holman Collection, Harvard

6. MARGATE IN KEATS'S TIME
An engraving in the Holman Collection, Harvard

Following page 108

7. CHEAPSIDE, SHOWING THE KEATS BROTHERS' LODGINGS AT NO. 76
A print in the Holman Collection, Harvard

8. SILHOUETTE OF KEATS BY CHARLES BROWN
In the Keats Memorial House, Hampstead

9. JOHN KEATS
The miniature by Joseph Severn in the National Portrait Gallery

10. GEORGE KEATS
The miniature by Joseph Severn in the Keats-Shelley Memorial House, Rome

ABBREVIATED TITLES

References merely to volume and page numbers, without title, are to *The Letters of John Keats,* ed. Hyder E. Rollins, 2 vols. (1958). In cases where there might be some ambiguity, the word *Letters* is included in the reference.

Brawne
Letters of Fanny Brawne to Fanny Keats, ed. F. Edgcumbe (1937).

Brown
Charles Armitage Brown, *Life of John Keats,* ed. Dorothy Bodurtha and Willard B. Pope (1937).

Colvin
Sir Sidney Colvin, *John Keats, His Life and Poetry, His Friends, Critics, and After-Fame,* 3rd ed. (1920).

Finney
Claude Lee Finney, *The Evolution of Keats's Poetry,* 2 vols. (1936).

Garrod
The Poetical Works of John Keats, ed. H. W. Garrod (1939).

Gittings
Robert Gittings, *John Keats: The Living Year* (1954).

Hampstead Keats
The Poetical Works and Other Writings of John Keats, ed. Harry Buxton Forman, revised by Maurice Buxton Forman, 8 vols. (1938–1939).

Haydon, *Diary*
The Diary of Benjamin Robert Haydon, ed. Willard B. Pope, 5 vols. (1960–1963).

Hewlett
Dorothy Hewlett, *A Life of John Keats,* 2nd ed. (1949).

KC
The Keats Circle, ed. Hyder E. Rollins, 2 vols. (1948).

KSMB
Keats-Shelley Memorial Bulletin (Rome).

Lowell
Amy Lowell, *John Keats,* 2 vols. (1925).

Recollections
Charles and Mary Cowden Clarke, *Recollections of Writers* (1878).

Sharp
William Sharp, *The Life and Letters of Joseph Severn* (1892).

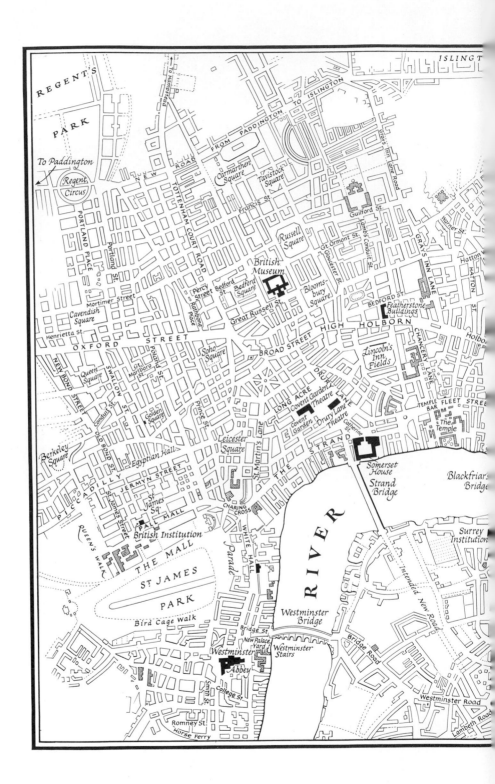

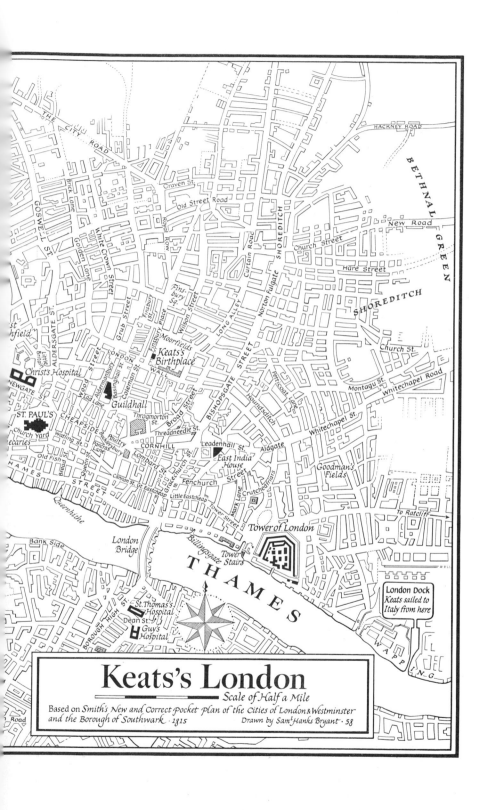

Keats's London

Scale of Half a Mile

Based on *Smith's New and Correct Pocket Plan of the Cities of London & Westminster and the Borough of Southwark* · 1815   Drawn by Saml Hanks Bryant · 58

THE CITY ROAD

HACKNEY ROAD

BETHNAL GREEN

New Road

Craven St.

Old Street Road

Royal Row

SHOREDITCH

Church Street

Curtain Road

Hare Street

SHOREDITCH

GOSWELL ST.

Brick Lane

Golden Lane

White Crown Street

Fins-bury Place

Finsbury St.

Grub Street

Finsbury Sq.

Moorfields

Wilson Street

LONG ALLEY

Norton Fulgate

Church St.

ALDERSGATE ST.

Little Britain

Keats's Birthplace

LONDON WALL

Coleman St.

BISHOPSGATE STREET

Montagu St.

Whitechapel Road

hfield

st

Christ's Hospital

NEWGATE

Wood Street

Lad Lane

Aldermanbury

Basinghall St.

Guildhall

Throgmorton St.

Broad Street

Threadneedle St.

Houndsditch

Petticoat Lane

Whitechapel St.

ST. PAUL'S

CHEAPSIDE

Poultry

CORNHILL

Leadenhall St.

Aldgate

Church Yard

Watling St.

St Pancras Lane

Newbury

Lombard St.

East India House

Goodman's Fields

caries

Old Fish St.

Bread St.

Queen St.

Cannon St. Gt. Eastcheap

Grace Church

Fenchurch Street

Little Eastcheap

Mark Lane

Crutchedfriars

To Ratcliff

THAMES STREET

Queenhithe

Bank Side

London Bridge

Billingsgate

Tower Street

Tower Stairs

Tower of London

London Dock
Keats sailed to Italy from here

BOROUGH HIGH ST.

St. Thomas's Hospital

Dean St.

Guy's Hospital

T H A M E S

WAPPING

Road

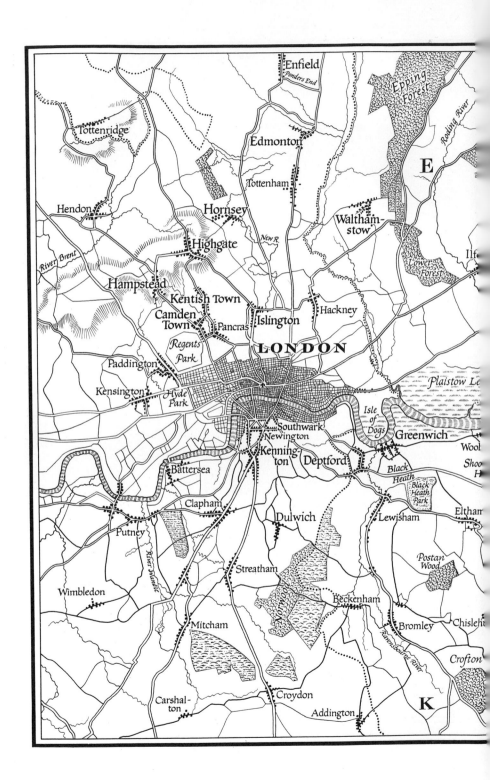

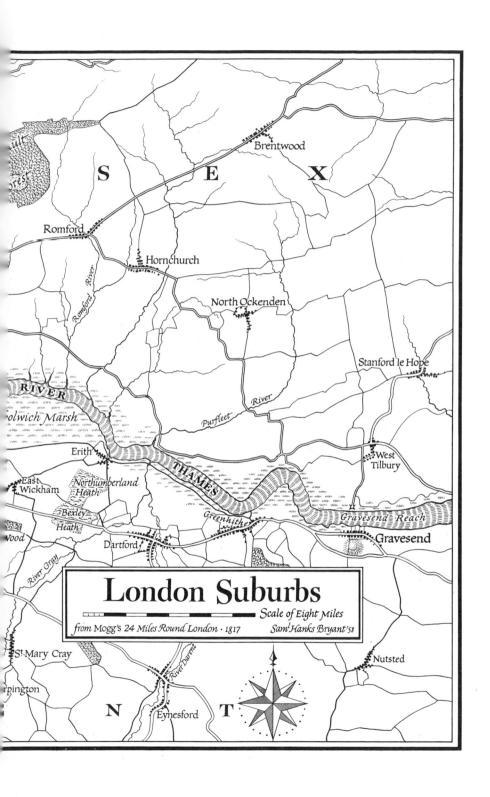

London Suburbs

Scale of Eight Miles

from Mogg's 24 Miles Round London · 1817   Sam¹ Hanks Bryant '58

John Keats

The First Years

❋⚘❋⚘❋⚘❋⚘❋⚘❋⚘❋⚘❋⚘❋⚘❋⚘❋⚘❋⚘❋⚘❋⚘

1795–1810

JOHN KEATS was born on the 31st of October, 1795, the first of a family of five children, one of whom died shortly after birth. His young parents had just begun to manage the livery stables that the father of Mrs. Keats, John Jennings, had built into a fairly prosperous business. The stables, which bore the name of the "Swan and Hoop," were in Finsbury (24 Moorfields Pavement Row), then on the northern outskirts of London. They served northeastern London and the adjacent villages, providing horses for hire and possibly even a few coaches.

London had been expanding more rapidly than at any time since the period of Elizabeth. In fact it was now beginning the extraordinary growth that, within a century and a half, was to engulf surrounding areas and transform it from a city of about eight hundred thousand to one of ten million or more. People from all parts of England were arriving every week. Mrs. Keats's mother was an example: Mrs. Jennings had come from the village of Colne in Lancashire, next to the Yorkshire border. Thomas Keats himself, Keats's father, was no Londoner by origin. Keats's sister, Fanny, remembered hearing that her father had come as a boy from Cornwall, near Land's End.[1] He almost certainly came from some part of the west country.

2

Though so much is known of Keats from the time he was seventeen or eighteen until his death, comparatively little can be discovered about his very earliest years, and especially about his parents and their origin. Yet the life of no writer of the last hundred

[1] See Appendix I.

and fifty years has been more carefully combed for details. The reason for that close study is the always heartening union of achievement with the familiar. We have a natural hunger to learn what qualities of mind or character, and what incidents in a man's life, encourage—or at least permit—an achievement so compelling when, at the same time, so little is apparently given at the start. This same appeal explains the fascination with which the life of Lincoln, to jump to a superficially different realm, still continues to be scanned and reinterpreted. Whatever our usual preoccupations, in approaching such figures we become more open to what Johnson thought the first aim of biography—to find what can be "put to use." That direct interest, so broad in its appeal, continues just as strongly for the professional writer who, like the poets of Keats's own day, has wrestled darkly with the fear that there is little left for the poet to do—little that will permit the large scope or power of the poetry of more confident, less self-conscious eras in the past. He may not wish to divulge that anxiety; but it is very much on his mind. Hence, despite the most radical changes in taste during the last hundred years, no English or American poet (however widely he may swing away from any of his other predecessors since the death of Shakespeare) fails to drop the usual querulousness over poetic idiom or other details when he comes to Keats, and to look quietly, closely, and perhaps with a suspended, secret hope.

At the same time, the life of Keats—even at first reading—has always seemed haunted by a feeling of familiarity. It reads like something we have read before, and are eager to hear again. At least one explanation is not far to seek. Of no major writer, in any language, have the early years more closely paralleled the traditional folktales of the orphan forced to seek his own fortune. No self-conscious fear of sentimentality, no uneasy wriggle backward into the sophistications or timidities of detachment, can minimize this moving and unexpected beginning. Again Lincoln offers a parallel: we wonder how someone who subsumes, with large honesty, so many of our modern aspirations—who attained so much more than most other statesmen (or, in the case of Keats, than most other writers)—should have begun life as characters in an older allegory do. For a century and a half we have prated of folklore, tried to resurrect it, moaned the loss of its simplicities, and condemned our own lives as humdrum in comparison. We have praised the psychological clairvoyance of the traditional myth, and appeared to rejoice over its complex use, and reuse, in fiction, while, for all our talk, we have not seriously expected to match it in real life; and indeed, if we do encounter it there, we may even feel embarrassed for a moment unless we can put it at arm's length while we get our bearings: we ourselves are genuinely moved, but fear that others may think us simple. Dickens, whose own early life is something of a counterpart to that of Keats, understood our divided natures. The affectations by which we complicate life for ourselves and others, feel that we ought to shun the familiar, and mince (in our approach either to art or social life) into what Johnson calls "the habitual cultivation of the powers of dislike," and "elegance refined into impatience," all appear on the large comic stage of Dickens. Against this plays the simple motif of the orphan of folklore, and we all respond to it.

Recalling the drama of Keats's life, the thought of Dickens grows upon one as the years pass. It has a special, local relevance as well. For no writer knew more closely than he, at least none has put so well, the London in or near which the four Keats children were to find themselves. The difference is that these orphans did not stumble into the unknown, waiting family that Dickens' warm heart compelled him to provide for his foundlings. This is a very large difference. But the beginning of the story would not have been unfamiliar to him.

3

Somewhat more is known of the Jennings family, into which Thomas Keats married at so early an age, than about Thomas Keats himself. Frances Jennings was the eldest of three children. Her mother, Alice Whalley, seems to have been a mature woman when she came to London, for she was thirty-seven when she married John Jennings.[2] But the most detailed account we have of the Jennings household is far from reliable. The source is the prim,

[2] She was born November 1, 1736, the daughter of John and Alice (née Haworth) Whalley, of Doughty Pasture, Colne. Her marriage, recorded in the register of St. Stephen, Coleman Street, took place on February 15, 1774. The baptismal dates of their three children were: Frances, January 29, 1775; Midgley John, November 21, 1777; and Thomas, January 4, 1782. (See Phyllis Mann, *KSMB*, No. 11 [1960], 33.)

captious tea merchant, Richard Abbey, to whom the young Keats children, by an almost insane irony of circumstance, were entrusted by their grandmother, Mrs. Jennings, after the early death of their parents. A few years after John Keats died at twenty-five, his generous-natured publisher, John Taylor, thought of writing a biographical memoir. He naturally turned at once to Abbey for any light that Abbey could throw on Keats's early years and the family background.

Richard Abbey, like Mrs. Jennings, had come down to London from the north. He had known Alice Jennings before her marriage, when he himself was a boy in Colne. During his interview with the conventional, well-meaning Taylor, Abbey was instinctively on his guard. The Keats child for whom he had the least use (who had seemed to him, in fact, either "Mad or a Fool") was, to Abbey's complete surprise, about to become the subject of a biography. What few remembrances he may still have had about the dead youth were inhibited. He had next to nothing to say of Keats himself. He preferred to scurry around the subject, and to suggest, under the disguise of frankness and garrulity, that the family background had something of a bad odor about it. Startled by this interview with a publisher of some standing, he could hardly wish that his own stern, repressive conduct to the Keats children, and the way he had sat on the money they inherited, should become public knowledge. He could excuse it to himself. Yet his handling of the estate had recently been questioned. Moreover, he had refused to advance a penny when Keats, plainly dying, left for Italy. Inevitably, Abbey's impulse was to justify indirectly where he could, and, where he could not, to denigrate. There is also a peculiar mixture of attraction and resentment in his attitude toward Keats's mother (who occupies a full third of the brief reminiscences he dictated).

4

The attractive, impetuous Frances Jennings was nineteen when she married Thomas Keats, slightly more than a year (October 9, 1794) before John, reputedly a seven-months child, was born. Thomas Keats himself was only twenty. The young couple arranged to be married not in their own neighborhood but at St.

George's, Hanover Square, in the fashionable West End. This youthful, somewhat naive gesture is typical of their eagerness to better themselves—an eagerness which may have shown itself in the "remarkably fine horse" that, according to Abbey, Thomas Keats kept for "his own Riding," [3] but which also appears in their hope, mentioned by George Keats, of sending the boys to Harrow. Ten years later, when Frances Keats remarried shortly after the death of her husband, this unhappy second wedding also took place at St. George's in Hanover Square.

If there was any thought of sending the Keats boys to Harrow, it was by no means impossible before the death first of Thomas Keats and then of John Jennings, Frances' father. Jennings, however he began life, was a man of some property. At his death, his estate amounted to at least £13,000, a sum which could be safely multiplied by five in order to judge its equivalent value now, and which, invested at a conservative three percent, would bring an amount now equal to £2,100 a year. In addition to the daughter, Frances, the Jennings family had two sons, both younger than Frances, and both educated at the school in Enfield to which the three Keats boys were later sent. Of the younger son, Thomas, nothing is known except that he died in 1796 at the age of fourteen. The other, Lt. Midgley John Jennings (who became a captain shortly before his own death in 1808), was a tall, kindly man, who is said by Charles Cowden Clarke to have served with distinction on Admiral Duncan's flagship in the Battle of Camperdown. Whether or not he did so,[4] he saw active service, and was later something of a hero to the Keats boys when they went to school.

George Keats speaks of his grandfather as an "extremely generous and gullible" man, a description we have no reason to doubt. The means by which Jennings tried to realize his good fortune seem to have been innocent if not inspired. He fancied himself, says Abbey, to be "a complete Gourmand," and "for 4 Days in the Week" Mrs. Jennings and the family were kept busy "preparing

---

[3] Abbey continues with irritation: Thomas Keats "on Sundays would go out with others who prided themselves in the like Distinction, to Highgate, Highbury, or some other places of public Entertainment for Man & Horse" (KC, I.304). Abbey's inaccurate account of Thomas Keats's death, in falling from a horse, occurs immediately afterwards, and suggests a feeling on Abbey's part that the accident was poetic justice.

[4] Louis Holman (Lowell, I.18) found no mention of a Midgley Jennings in the roster of Duncan's flagship, the *Venerable*.

for the Sunday's Dinner." Abbey was probably irked as much by what he considered the pretentious style in which Jennings lived as by anything else. But his immediate reason for dwelling on it to Taylor was to make a direct transition to the sensuousness of the daughter, and to suggest the amount of bad blood carried by the troublesome, unappreciative grandchildren with whom he later had to deal. This portion of the account, though now readily available, is best quoted in full; for by revealing so much about Abbey himself, it makes one wary in interpreting his other remarks. Moreover, Abbey is later so important in the lives of the Keats children that an early sense of his character is helpful. "His Daughter in this respect"—the fondness of Jennings for "the pleasures of the Table"—

> somewhat resembled him, but she was more remarkably the Slave of other Appetites, attributable probably to this for their exciting Cause.—At an early Age she told my Informant, Mr. Abby, that she must & would have a Husband; and her passions were so ardent, he said, that it was dangerous to be alone with her.—She was a handsome, little woman—Her features were good & regular, with the Exception of her Mouth which was unusually wide. A little Circumstance was mentioned to me as indicative of her Character—She used to go to a Grocers in Bishopsgate Street, opposite the Church, probably out of some Liking for the Owner of the Shop,—but the Man remarked to Mr. Abby that Miss Jennings always came in dirty Weather, & when she went away, she held up her Clothes very high in crossing the Street, & to be sure, says the Grocer, she has uncommonly handsome Legs.—He was not however fatally wounded by Cupid the Parthian—
>
> But it was not long before she found a Husband, nor did she go far for him—a Helper in her Father's Stables appeared sufficiently desirable in her Eyes to make her forget the Disparity of their Circumstances, & it was not long before John [sic] Keats had the Honor to be united to his Master's Daughter.—He did not possess or display any great Accomplishments.—Elevated perhaps in his Notions by the sudden Rise of his Fortunes he thought it became him to act somewhat more the Man of Consequence than he had been accustomed to do.

Warming to his subject, Abbey pauses to speak maliciously of the accidental death ("riding very fast, & most probably very much in liquor") of Thomas Keats, to whom, by an interesting slip, he gives the name of his troublesome son, John. Then, discussing

Mrs. Keats's second marriage ("Mrs. Keats again being determined to have a husband"), he states that she

> became addicted to drinking and in the love of the Brandy Bottle found a temporary Gratification to those inordinate Appetites which seem to have been in one Stage or other constantly soliciting her.— The Growth of this degrading Propensity to liquor may account perhaps for the strange Irregularities—or rather Immorality of her after-Life.[5]

If Abbey's hope was to impress Taylor with the undesirable background of the Keats children, he succeeded. For a moment, Taylor hesitated, wondering whether Abbey's vindictive story might not suggest that Abbey himself had enjoyed an irregular relationship with Frances Jennings before her marriage: "As he spoke of the Danger of being alone with Miss Jennings I looked to see if I [could] discern any of the Lineaments of the young Poet in his Features, but if I had heard the whole of his Story I should have banished the Thought more speedily than it was conceived.— Never were there two people more opposite than the Poet & this good Man." Whether or not he felt that Abbey was trustworthy, Taylor was a little shocked. He sent the account to Keats's good friend, Richard Woodhouse, with whom Taylor had thought of writing the memoir of Keats. But he added a brief note: "These are not Materials for a Life of our poor Friend which it will do to communicate to the World . . . How strange it seems that such a Creature of the Element as he should have sprung from such gross Realities.—But how he refined upon the Sensualities of his Parents!" The Abbey account was quietly put away, its existence almost forgotten until a century later.

5

Soon after his daughter's marriage, Jennings seized the opportunity to retire. He handed over the management of the business at the Swan and Hoop to his son-in-law, and went with his wife to live in Ponder's End, a small cluster of houses near the village of Enfield. Jennings may have been only too glad to have Thomas Keats succeed him. Though still in his mid-sixties, he seems to

[5] *KC*, I.303–305.

have been unwell in his last years. His surviving son, Midgley, plainly preferred being an officer in the navy to his father's business.

Thomas Keats appears to have managed the Swan and Hoop capably. He may well have hoped to buy the property eventually or to acquire the lease (Jennings' own lease was to expire in two years).[5a] At the start, the couple apparently lived at the Swan and Hoop. Here their first two, possibly their first three, children were born: John on October 31, 1795, baptized at the nearby St. Botolph's Church, Bishopsgate, on December 18; George on February 28, 1797; and Thomas on November 18, 1799. Shortly after the birth of the third boy, if not before, the family felt prosperous enough to move away from the stables to a separate house a little more than half a mile north, on Craven Street, just off City Road. There were born Edward (April 28, 1801), who died in infancy, and, on June 3, 1803, Frances Mary—the endearing Fanny Keats.

No significant anecdotes of Keats's infant years survive. Benjamin Robert Haydon, the painter, records two that are always quickly mentioned. An old lady, who had lived near the children, met George Keats on the street years later, and asked about John. Told that John wanted to be a poet, she remembered that, as a small child, he had answered questions with remarks that would rhyme with the last word of the question asked. If the story really survived transmission through George and then Haydon, it is only the sort of remark, as Amy Lowell said, that "old ladies always recollect of children in after years." The second story is that when Mrs. Keats became ill, and had been told that complete quiet was necessary, John, who was almost five, secured an old sword and stood guard before her bedroom door, even to the extent, according to Haydon, of forbidding his mother to leave her room.

The household seems to have been an affectionate one for the short time it existed as a unit. From the beginning the children felt a strong loyalty to each other. Of their mother George Keats, writing in 1828, said that he could recall very little; but he did remember, and emphasized, "her prodigality, and doting fondness for her children, particularly John, who resembled her in the face." The remark about her facial similarity with John may seem

---

[5a] Robert Gittings, *The Keats Inheritance* (1964), p. 7.

to conflict with the impressions of Charles Cowden Clarke, who stated that "John was the only one resembling [his father] in person and feature, with brown hair and dark hazel eyes," while the two brothers "were like the mother, who was tall,[6] of good figure, with large, oval face, and sensible deportment." But Clarke could hardly be expected to remember Mrs. Keats's face as closely as George did. Clarke's memory when he wrote his account (over forty years later) may have been influenced by the difference in height and form: John Keats, like his father, was unusually short and fairly stocky, whereas the brothers were at least of normal height. In any case, all the Keats children, to judge from the later portraits, showed a strong facial resemblance, particularly the two youngest, Tom and Fanny. Keats, when dying, asked his friend Charles Brown to write for him to George and to Fanny, "who walks about my imagination like a ghost—she is so like Tom." And eight years later George wrote to Fanny, from Kentucky, that his wife, just returned from England, "says you are a female edition of Tom." [7]

6

When John was approaching eight, his parents decided that the two older boys should be sent to school. The nearby academy at the country village of Enfield, only ten miles from London, seemed desirable. There was already a family connection since the two Jennings brothers had gone there. Moreover, its gentle headmaster, John Clarke, who had originally intended to enter the law, was known as a gifted teacher.[8] The small academy at Enfield, with

[6] Whereas Clarke speaks of Mrs. Keats as "tall," Abbey described her to Taylor as a "handsome, little woman." That he did not mean it in merely an affectionate sense may perhaps be shown by the fact that Taylor, at first, wrote "a handsome, but not a tall, little woman," and then crossed out "but not a tall." However, Abbey could possibly have meant to say "a handsome, but not at all little woman"; and because of the apparent incongruity, as he took it down ("not a tall"), Taylor later deleted the puzzling phrase. In any case, Abbey, who had seen her more often (and observantly), could be expected to have a better idea of her height than Clarke, unless, so many years after her death, he was thinking of her only as a young girl.

[7] *More Letters and Poems of the Keats Circle*, ed. Hyder E. Rollins (1955), p. 52. Rollins also cites (p. 53) Dilke's annotation to the 1848 Milnes biography: Tom "was very like Mrs. Llanos [Fanny Keats]—so like that John spoke of it as most painful to him."

[8] While articled to a lawyer in Northampton, Clarke had been forced to run the risk—according to his daughter-in-law—of "having to hang a man, in consequence of being deputed to fulfill the sheriff's office . . . The whole night was spent in such an

almost seventy-five students, was not thought of as a preparatory school for scholars any more than for sons of the aristocracy. The intention was to offer a fairly liberal education to students whose families were in trade or in the less affluent professions, and who were not necessarily looking forward to entering a university. One of the prizes Keats later won was Kaufmann's *Dictionary of Merchandize . . . for the Use of Counting Houses* (1803). Some mathematics and science were taught; and the grounding in Latin was good, at least by present-day standards. Greek was probably not taught, or we could otherwise assume that Keats, when he was reading so avidly in his final year or two, would certainly have studied it. French was taught, and Keats learned to read it fluently. If Enfield lacked the advantages of the great Public Schools, it had compensations. There was no fagging. There even seems to have been little or no physical punishment. The school was small enough so that the enlightened influence of John Clarke was constantly felt.

The building is often mentioned because of its varied history and because a fragment of it survives in an unlikely place. Erected for his own use in 1717 by a West India merchant, it was also the house where Isaac Disraeli was later born. Early in Victoria's reign it was bought and used as a railway station for a branch line to Enfield. Finally, in 1872, it was demolished. But because its elaborate façade was regarded as a good example of its kind, the top central portion was preserved and placed in that vast collection of memorabilia, the Victoria and Albert Museum, where it can still be seen. The rooms were spacious. Those used as a dormitory could hold six to eight beds. The large schoolroom was constructed in the area once occupied by the stables and the coach house. The courtyard between the schoolroom and the main house had been turned into a playground. Adjoining the playground, said Cowden Clarke, there was

---

agony of mind by John Clarke while endeavouring to find a substitute for the task so inexpressibly repugnant . . . he resolved then and there to leave a situation that had subjected him to so horrible a chance, and at once renounced the legal profession, for which he had never felt any liking, and adopted that of schoolmaster, for which he was eminently fitted." (Mary Cowden Clarke, *My Long Life* [1896], pp. 54–55.) Clarke (b. 1757) took a position in a school conducted by his father-in-law, John C. Ryland, in Northampton. When Ryland moved his school to Enfield (1786), Clarke was put in charge—the Jennings boys were among his first pupils. Around 1815 he retired to Ramsgate, and died December 22, 1820, only two months before the death of his most famous student.

a garden, one hundred yards in length, where in one corner were some small plots set aside for certain boys fond of having a little garden of their own, that they might cultivate according to their individual will and pleasure; and farther on was a sweep of greensward, beyond the centre of which was a pond, sometimes dignified as "The Lake" . . . at the far end of the pond, beneath the iron railings which divided our premises from the meadows beyond, whence the song of the nightingales in May would reach us in the stillness of night, there stood a rustic arbour, where John Keats and I used to sit and read Spenser's "Faery Queene" together, when he had left school, and used to come over from Edmonton, where he was apprenticed to Thomas Hammond the surgeon. On the other side of the house lay a small enclosure which we called "the drying-ground," and where was a magnificent old morella cherry-tree against a wall well exposed to the sun. Beyond this, a gate led into a small field, or paddock, of two acres,—the pasture-ground of two cows that supplied the establishment with fresh and abundant milk.[9]

The first formative influence on Keats, aside from that of his family, came from John Clarke and his son, Charles Cowden Clarke. The son, whose steady and honorable character is something of a tribute to his father's teaching, was eight years older than Keats. In his function as usher, or assistant, he was later to know Keats unusually well, and to offer encouragement at a time when it was desperately needed. Naturally, when he wrote his recollections many years later and so many people were eager for every detail of Keats's years at school, Clarke could remember very little of the boy of eight, "the youngest individual in a corporation of between seventy and eighty youngsters." He even assumed that John's younger brother, George, was the older of the two, probably because George was already taller; apparently he never discovered his mistake. It is Keats about five years afterwards, when he turned so strongly to study, that is really the main subject of Clarke's account. But Clarke could still remember, he said, the frequent visits that Thomas Keats would make during the first few months: "I can remember that my own father always spoke of him with respect, on account of his excellent natural sense, and total freedom from vulgarity and assumption . . . I have a clear recollection of his lively, and energetic countenance, particularly when seated in his gig, and preparing to drive his wife home, after visiting his sons at school."

9 Clarke's "Note on the School-House . . . at Enfield," in H. Buxton Forman's edition of Keats's *Works* (1883) , V.343–344.

7

Suddenly, on April 15, 1804, when John was still eight and had been at Enfield for less than half a year, Thomas Keats had a fatal accident. It was Sunday, and he had gone on a visit, said Clarke, to the Keats boys at Enfield, and then had a late dinner at Southgate, so called because it had once been the southern gate into Enfield Chase. As he neared home, his horse slipped, as horses only too frequently did on cobblestones, and in the accident his skull was fractured. The account in the *Times* (Tuesday, April 17) reads:

> On Sunday, Mr. Keats, livery-stable keeper in Moorfield, went to dine at Southgate; he returned at a late hour, and on passing down the City-Road, his horse fell with him, when he had the misfortune to fracture his skull. It was about one o'clock in the morning when the watchman found him, he was at that time alive, but speechless; the watchman got assistance, and took him to a house in the neighbourhood, where he died about 8 o'clock.

Other periodicals confirm the details. Abbey's account to Taylor, twenty-three years later, differs in the way one might expect.[10]

The chaos into which the family was thrown by this accident could be illustrated only by a detailed account of the next fifteen years or more. Aside from any steadying influence Thomas Keats could have provided, and aside from the fact that, if only he had lived, the children would never have lost their inheritance, there was the unfortunate effect during the next few years on his wife, and hence indirectly on the children. The Swan and Hoop demanded active management; and whatever else can be said for the widow, she was not the sort to conduct such a business by herself, though other women had done so. London abounded with men who, because of the laws affecting women's property, were only too willing to take over their responsibilities and fortunes. The marriage of Murdstone with the mother of David Copperfield is the classic account in fiction of the situation: the widow pines away, and the child is fleeced. There was, however, no Aunt Betsey Trotwood.

---

[10] Abbey, as mentioned above, states that Thomas Keats was "returning with some of his jolly Companions from a Carouse"; he was "riding very fast, & most probably very much in Liquor, when his Horse leaped upon the Pavement opposite the Methodist Chapel in the City Road, & falling with him against the Iron Railings so dreadfully crushed him that he died as they were carrying him Home" (*KC*, I.304).

William Rawlings, a minor clerk in the company of Smith, Payne, and Smiths of George Street, a banking firm, was doubtless able to impress Mrs. Keats with his business sense. To Mrs. Jennings, the grandmother, Rawlings was plainly a fortune hunter. (According to Fanny Keats, Rawlings had no property of his own before he married her mother.) But in desperation Mrs. Keats went ahead with the marriage, which took place on June 27, 1804. Mrs. Jennings immediately took responsibility for the children, whose home was henceforth with their grandmother. "We never lived with them" (her mother and Rawlings), said Fanny Keats, "but went at once to my grandmother who disapproved of this marriage." We have no way of knowing what went on between Rawlings and the unhappy widow he married. But not long afterwards—the exact time is uncertain—she left Rawlings (Abbey said he died, and that she then lived for a while with another man) [11] and returned to her mother. The disillusion of this emotional, impetuous woman must have been enormous. For, by leaving Rawlings, she also left with him, as she certainly knew she would have to, the property she had inherited from her former husband. Rawlings seems to have accepted the situation agreeably. From now on, Frances Keats Rawlings, far from well, was anything but self-confident. We hear little about her, except her progressive decline in health.

8

Within a year after the accident that killed Thomas Keats, John Jennings, the kindly grandfather and original proprietor of the Swan and Hoop, died, on March 8, 1805. A few weeks before —obviously ill, to judge from the signature—he had made his will.

The story of the Jennings will and of the financial complications that followed it during the next twenty years is sufficiently confused and unhappy in its results to have justified Dickens' mention of it as an episode in *Bleak House*. The opening comment by the Court of Chancery was ominous: "This Will is very obscure." All that emerges clearly is that, because there was no concerned and competent person to represent them, the Keats children received little—at least not until well after two of them, Tom and John, had been dead for some time.

[11] *KC*, I.305.

To begin with, by their mother's hasty remarriage, the children had lost whatever Rawlings had pocketed. Far more serious, the Jennings will proved to have been poorly drafted. Exemplifying George's remark that his grandfather was "gullible" as well as "generous," Mr. Jennings had neglected to employ a lawyer, naively trusting a neighboring land surveyor, Joseph Pearson, to draft his will. As a result, the vague phrasing permitted disputes that distracted attention, and no one appeared much concerned about the grandchildren. About £2,500 (at the very least, £1,200) that he never received—and this in pounds with the purchasing power they had then, at a time when it was possible to live on £50 a year and to live reasonably well on £200—would otherwise have come to Keats.[12]

The main outlines of the will can be quickly summarized. (1) Mrs. Jennings was given £200 a year, together with personal effects. The Court allowed her more than the appropriate amount of capital (£7,364). All of this later came under the control of Richard Abbey, whom she appointed trustee and guardian of the grandchildren. (2) The son, Midgley John Jennings, received the lifetime use of the income from £3,900.[11a] The phrasing is unclear at this point. But the intention was plainly that, if the son should die without issue, his widow, at his death, should receive only £500, "the remaining part to return to my family." Midgley asked the Court for clarification. The Court postponed a decision until there should be children. In 1811, three years after Midgley's death, by which time he had three and possibly four children, his widow and children received a full half of the £2,900, the balance reverting to his mother. (3) For whatever reason, Mr. Jennings left his daughter, Mrs. Rawlings, a lifetime annuity of only £50 a year (for which the Court allotted the capital). The money was to be divided after her death among her children. Unquestionably the children were simply not informed of this sum,[13] and the money, after it had

[11a] Mr. Gittings (*The Keats Inheritance*, p. 11) has shown that Jennings overestimated by £1,000 the amount of stock he left his son. The total bequest therefore amounted to £2,900.

[12] For discussion of the wills of John and Alice Jennings, the amount of the children's inheritance, and related matters, see Appendix III.

[13] There was probably no one to inform them, after 1810, except Abbey, Mrs. Jennings having left their affairs in his hands. The former Mrs. Keats, returning to her mother's home after her unfortunate marriage with Rawlings, had no special need of it, and may have even hoped to keep it a secret from Rawlings. She did not touch the money in her own lifetime. The accumulated income, after her death, became

legally passed to the children, lay uncollected in Chancery until two years after the death of John Keats. (4) There was also a sum of £200 due the children both as arrears on their mother's annuity before her death and for maintenance for her children from 1805 to 1810, allowed from interest on the bequest they received outright. This particular sum was still in Chancery in 1888, when Fanny, the sole remaining child, was eighty-three and Keats himself had been dead for sixty-seven years. Then it was discovered by a solicitor, Ralph Thomas, and claimed for Fanny. (5) To the four Keats grandchildren Jennings left £1,000 "to be equally divided amongst them as they become of age with the accumulating interest thereon." The question, of course, is whether Jennings intended the money to be awarded to each individual child as he became of age, or whether the division should be made only after they had all become of age. There is every reason to assume that he meant what he said—that the money should be allotted to each child on reaching twenty-one. George Keats discovered the existence of the fund in 1823. (6) To his sister, Mary Sweetingburgh, Jennings left a life annuity of £30 a year, the capital to revert to the estate. (7) An amount remained after all bequests. Understandably hurt, Frances Rawlings, joined by her husband, started an unsuccessful Chancery suit claiming not only a third share of the unspecified residue but that her father had died intestate and that she was entitled to a third of what was left to her mother and, in case of Midgley's death, to half of what was left to him. The suit was unsuccessful; and even the unspecified residue was divided between the widow and her son.

9

Mrs. Jennings, now almost seventy, tried to face the new situation with courage and good sense. Her income was about half the amount she and her husband had been in the habit of receiving. Far from reassured of her daughter's business sense, she was doubtless already hoping to save what she could for the grandchildren. Within a few months she left the country home in Ponder's End and took a house, presumably smaller, in Church Street, Lower Edmonton, a village nine miles north of London and very close to Enfield.

---

legally the property of Rawlings. Whether because of ignorance or change of heart, he did not claim it. George and Fanny finally received the money in 1823–24, after George had discovered its existence.

Here Mrs. Jennings attempted to offer a home. It was, in fact, the last real home that the family was to have. There was no question but that Tom, now seven, should be given the same opportunity as his brothers, and he was sent to join them at Enfield. With Tom away, the household was exclusively feminine—the two widows, grandmother and mother, the baby Fanny, now three years old, and a maid; and we can understand the excitement with which the three boys were welcomed in the holidays. While the boys, said George, "were always devising plans" to amuse Fanny, jealous lest she "prefer either of us to the other," they in turn appear to have been as much indulged. Keats, years later, when Fanny was fifteen, could joke with her about the numerous pets he used to inflict on the family. Asking her what she would like as a present, he went on: "anything but live stock. Though I will not now be very severe on it, remembering how fond I used to be of Goldfinches, Tomtits, Minnows, Mice, Ticklebacks, Dace, Cock salmons and the whole tribe of the Bushes and Brooks: but verily they are better in the Trees and water." And in one of the letters written during his walking trip through Scotland in 1818, after making up for her a ballad about the old gypsy woman, Meg Merrilies, he suddenly offers her a "song about myself." Plunging at once into doggerel, he jokes of his restlessness, his trip, his knapsack, his "scribbling," and then stops to mention the years at Edmonton:

> There was a naughty boy
>   And a naughty boy was he,
> He kept little fishes
>   In washing tubs three
>   In spite
>   Of the might
>   Of the Maid
>   Nor afraid
>   Of his Granny-good—
>   He often would
>   Hurly burly
>   Get up early
>   And go
>   By hook or crook
>   To the brook
>   And bring home
>   Miller's thumb,
>   Tittlebat

Not over fat,
Minnows small
As the stall
Of a glove,
Not above
The size
Of a nice
Little Baby's
Little finger—
O he made
'Twas his trade
Of Fish a Pretty Kettle
A Kettle—
A Kettle
Of Fish a Pretty Kettle
A Kettle!

Meanwhile, at the school in Enfield, the boys were enthusiastically liked. John in particular caught the imagination of his schoolfellows. Their accounts stress an appealing combination of qualities rarely found together—courage, sensitivity, and generosity. Exactly this same union of qualities, in later, very different contexts, was to capture the loyalty of others. Biographies follow the early memoirs, and always mention his love of fighting as a boy. "He would fight any one," said one of his schoolfellows, Edward Holmes,

> morning, noon, or night; his brothers among the rest. It was meat & drink to him. Jennings their sailor relation was always in the thoughts of the brothers & they determined to keep up the family reputation for courage; George in a passive manner, John & Tom more fiercely. . . . The generosity & daring of his character . . . in passions of tears or outrageous fits of laughter always in extremes will help to paint Keats in his boyhood.

The war with France was going on, of course, and Napoleon, who had crowned himself Emperor in 1804, had been boasting that he would soon invade England. The South Coast was fortified. Drills were taking place in and near London. All this may have enlivened the atmosphere of the school, at least for the younger students, of whom Holmes was one, heightening the admiration of physical courage common among boys. Yet we should keep in mind that these instances of Keats's courage did not result from quarrelsomeness, the desire to dominate, or sheer obliviousness except of what is admired by the group. Instead, they were a by-product of an engaging selflessness, though doubtless sharpened now and then by his awareness of his small size (he was never to be more than five feet and three-quarters of an inch tall) .

It was this same capacity for selflessness that later permitted his rapid development as a writer, a development unparalleled in literary history. One thinks ahead to the evening years afterward—he was then twenty-two—when he at last had the opportunity of meeting some real "literary" men. He had been reading Shakespeare, and these men, intent on "saying things that make one start" and highly self-conscious, were not quite what he had expected. "They talked of fashionables," and, in everything they said or did, fell into pose. He thought about it as he walked home, and then, as he wrote his brothers (December 21, 1817) , "at once it struck me, what quality went to form a Man of Achievement especially in Literature & which Shakespeare possessed so enormously—I mean *Negative Capability.*" The ability to negate one's own identity, to lose it in something larger or more meaningful than oneself, is what he has in mind, the thought coming almost as self-discovery. The raw materials were already present in his own temperament long before the age of twenty-two. Hence, as Clarke says of his early years at school,

> He was not merely the "favourite of all," like a pet prize-fighter, for his terrier courage; but his high-mindedness, his utter unconsciousness of a mean motive, his placability, his generosity, wrought so general a feeling in his behalf, that I never heard a word of disapproval from any one, superior or equal, who had known him.[14]

Not long before Clarke first began to write out his recollections, George Keats, who had emigrated to Kentucky, stressed similar qualities in a letter to Charles Dilke:

> John was open, prodigal, and had no power of calculation whatever. John's eyes moistened, and his lip quivered at the relation of any tale of generosity of benevolence or noble daring, or at sights of loveliness or distress—he had no fears of self thro interference in the quarrels of others, he would at all hazzards, without calculating his power to defend, or his reward for the deed, defend the oppressed.[15]

And there was something picturesque, almost comic, in this ardent selflessness, this readiness to plunge, which is so characteristic of Keats's early poetry and which was later to mature into resolu-

[14] *Recollections,* p. 123.   [15] *KC,* I.325.

tion and steadiness of understanding. His pugnacious spirit, said Clarke,

> when roused, was one of the most picturesque exhibitions—off the stage—I ever saw. One of the transports of that marvellous actor, Edmund Kean—whom, by the way, he idolized—was its nearest resemblance; and the two were not very dissimilar in face and figure. Upon one occasion, when an usher, on account of some impertinent behaviour, had boxed his brother Tom's ears, John rushed up, put himself in the received posture of offence, and, it was said, struck the usher—who could, so to say, have put him into his pocket. His passion at times was almost ungovernable; and his brother George, being considerably the taller and stronger, used frequently to hold him down by main force, laughing when John was in "one of his moods," and endeavouring to beat him.

What most puzzled Keats's schoolfellow Edward Holmes, writing when Keats's reputation was becoming established, was that as a child Keats showed so little of what is conventionally expected of a future poet. Keats "was a boy whom any one . . . might easily have fancied would become great—*but rather in some military capacity than in literature.*" The reactions of Holmes are worth having. He was far from being a naive outsider to the arts: by the time he wrote his account, he was already a distinguished music critic; moreover, he was interested in the biography of genius, and had just published, the year before, his *Life of Mozart* (1845). If the two boys shared a love of horseplay and broad mimicry (Holmes remembered Keats's fondness for schoolmates who had "a sort of grotesque and buffoon humour. I recollect . . . his delight at the extraordinary gesticulations and pranks of a boy named Wade who was celebrated for this"), they could both be touched by other things. In the evening, when Clarke would be playing the piano, the door was occasionally left open, and the sound of the music could be heard above. Holmes would rush from bed in his nightgown and stand at the top of the stairs. Keats, two years older, would listen quietly in his bed. Clarke remembered, long after the death of both Keats and Holmes, Keats reading to him in 1819 from the *Eve of St. Agnes* and saying, when they came to the passage where Porphyro listens to the midnight music in the castle hall below, that the last line of it "came into my head when I remembered how I used to listen in bed to your music at school":

> The boisterous, midnight, festive clarion,
> The kettle-drum, and far-heard clarinet,

Affray his ears, though but in dying tone:—
The hall-door shuts again, and all the noise is gone.

When he wrote his own account in 1846, Holmes had been reading a short memorandum of Clarke's, which was later expanded in
the *Recollections of Writers* (1878). Clarke had stressed the
amount of reading Keats did at school. But this active interest,
Holmes said, did not appear until shortly before he left the school.
As a younger contemporary, Holmes had seen a side of Keats that
Clarke, eight years older than Keats, might not have glimpsed:
Holmes wanted to emphasize, as he said near the start of the account he wrote for Keats's first biographer, R. M. Milnes, that
"Keats was not in childhood attached to books." The emphasis
keeps recurring. Keats was at first "noted for his indifference to
lessons"; "The point to be chiefly insisted on is that he was *not*
Literary":

> his love of books & poetry manifested itself chiefly about a year be-
> fore he left school. In all active exercises—he excelled. The gener-
> osity & daring of his character—with the extreme beauty & anima-
> tion of his face made I remember an impression on me—& being
> some years his junior I was obliged to woo his friendship—in which
> I succeeded but not till I had fought several battles. This violence &
> vehemence—this pugnacity and generosity of disposition—in passions
> of tears or outrageous fits of laughter always in extremes will help to
> paint Keats in his boyhood.[16]

10

Meanwhile the situation at home quickly changed. Keats's
mother, who had been increasingly confined to bed, took a rapid
change for the worse. She probably had consumption—the disease
that was henceforth to prove such a nightmare to the Keats children and had probably killed her two brothers. Keats, however
open in other ways, froze into reticence before calamity, hated
peevishness and complaint, and rarely mentioned the unhappy history of his family, even in his letters to his brothers and his sister.

At least by the Christmas holidays in 1809, when the three boys
(aged ten to fourteen) came back from Enfield, their mother was
gravely ill. But, partly because she had been so often confined to
bed by what had been diagnosed as severe rheumatism or arthritis

[16] *KC*, II.164–165.

but may have been something more serious, the younger children were hardly aware of the extent of their mother's sudden decline. It is possible that even their grandmother did not completely appreciate it, though she had already lost much of her family and could be expected to feel at least uneasy. But John—the oldest child and possibly the closest to the mother—was obviously distressed. Jolted into a sudden sense of responsibility, he sat up with his mother, according to Haydon, for nights on end, giving her medicine, even trying to cook food for her, and "read novels to her in her intervals of ease."

Not knowing precisely what was happening, the boys went back to Enfield. Within less than three months (by the middle of March, 1810) their mother died. Death could perhaps be taken more for granted by a child at that time than it is now. Still, the board was being cleared rather swiftly. The father was gone, the uncles, the grandfather, and now the mother. No great amount of empathy is needed to grasp Keats's feelings. Moreover there was the "doting fondness" that George always remembered in his mother. A child does remember such things with some poignance. George and Fanny, the only two who lived even into middle age, might later be fairly dispassionate about their mother. Fanny, who was only six at the time and who lived to eighty-six, could especially be so. Upon John, however, the death of the mother struck powerfully. The full implication would appear in what happened to him at school, where, though merely fourteen, he was to have only one more year. But now there was only the stunning sense of loss. Inevitably there was the momentary retreat that we all experience, and the strong but confused sense that a large responsibility had fallen on him. For he was now the oldest male in the family, and except for his grandmother the oldest person. The boy of fourteen who could plunge like a terrier against injustice now crept, said Edward Holmes, into "a nook under the master's desk" in the schoolroom at Enfield; and anyone who saw him, in this "impassioned and prolonged" sense of loss, felt the "liveliest pity & sympathy." In that desire to hide grief, that retreat of the small child beneath the desk of the kindly schoolmaster, John Clarke—there was no one else—we have a hint of the future. The home or refuge to which he gradually turns will have something to do with the sort of world John Clarke represented.

11

Whatever else can be made of Keats's early years, in any hope we may have of understanding what happened in the next decade, one fact takes obvious and overwhelming precedence: the sense of loss and bewilderment that the four Keats children felt in being so early orphaned. Moreover, the children were not only orphans, but orphans in a large city. They were without relatives—except for their elderly grandmother—who either could or would be of much help.

In addition to the loss of whatever security, through affection, the parents might have offered, there is the tantalizing cruelty of the financial situation—tantalizing because there was at least some money, if only they had been allowed to receive it, and cruel because it could later have been of such enormous help. Finally, there were the ambitions that the children had already caught from their parents. If these were a fruitful legacy, they were not without some pain; for all the external means of attaining them seemed completely lacking.

This at least can be said of the children: they were all, in their independence and capacity for commitment, what was once praised in an earlier New England as "Come-Outers"; and the ultimate geographical spread of the story adds a further symbolic poignance. The kindly, clear-eyed Tom, whom Keats nursed through his final illness, died early; but he was far from conventional. George emigrated to Kentucky at the age of twenty-one, meeting and surmounting obstacles he had never imagined; Fanny married a Spaniard, and went to live in Spain; and John, with perhaps the greatest poetic endowment England has witnessed since the death of Milton, died at twenty-five in Rome.

Abbey's Wards

1810–1815

FOR A WHILE, the Keats children at least had each other. There is a certain novelty, even surprise, in the fact that of the finest letters left by any poet a good portion (including those in which, as T. S. Eliot says, there is hardly a statement about poetry that will not be found to be true) were written not by one man of letters to another but by the young Keats to his still younger brothers George and Tom. As far as we can tell, neither George nor Tom had any vivid interest in poetry. Their sympathy was more personal; it included a loyalty so strong that it was unthinkable not to try to share an interest that so absorbed their brother. That Keats could so freely open his mind to them offers a graphic illustration of the simple closeness and trust they shared.

But their sturdy, north-country grandmother, now almost seventy-four, was naturally worried. With husband, sons, daughter, and son-in-law dead, she may have become rather frightened about the future of these four children. Always practical, she immediately tried to find a way to ensure for them whatever she could. Perhaps affection and a home could not be guaranteed. But there was at least some money. A trustee, or better two of them, could protect the money for the children, and possibly give helpful advice. Her acquaintance with people qualified for this position was small, especially now in her age. She found herself thinking of the Lancashire lad, Richard Abbey, who years before had come down to London from her own village. Abbey was now perhaps a man of fifty (he died in 1837, twenty-seven years later, sixteen years after the death of John Keats). Having survived her own children, Mrs. Jennings might naturally feel that the north-country stock was stronger. Moreover, Abbey had in a sense done very well—at least he had made his way practically—in this quickly growing world of London.¹ His office (Abbey, Cocks, and Company, Tea-Dealers) was at 4 Pancras Lane, in the Poultry. He appears to have lived on the premises during much of the winter, spending the rest of the year in Walthamstow, only four miles southeast of Edmonton. Mrs. Jennings finally decided to select Abbey.

In her cautious hope of finding a second trustee, Mrs. Jennings had little to help her. On whatever advice, she chose John Nowland Sandell, described in her will as a merchant in Broad Street Buildings. At the time she and her husband had the Swan and Hoop, Sandell had an office nearby. But we know little else about him. He took a very small part, if any, in the trusteeship. He does not seem to have been an unkindly man. A few months before his death at the age of forty-six (April 1816), Fanny Keats—then twelve and a half years old—was allowed by Abbey to visit Mrs. Sandell. A little note Sandell gave her still survives in the Keats House at Hampstead:

> This is to certify to whom it may concern, that Frances Mary Keats during the time she was on a Visit to Mrs. Sandell, was a very good Girl.
>
> J.S. 14 Jany. 1816

2

By July 1810, four months after the death of their mother, Mrs. Jennings had made over to the trustees a large part of what she had inherited from her husband, and her will confirmed the appointment of Abbey and Sandell as guardians.² Though it was

¹ Mrs. Jennings had also seen, at first hand, something that could hardly fail to impress her. A girl from their small village in Lancashire had come to London, married, and then lived in Edmonton itself. The girl was murdered by her husband. As a neighbor who had been kind to the wife, Mrs. Jennings was sent for, and she found two children—a girl of two, and a boy of three months. At a loss, she immediately asked Richard Abbey, as a fellow townsman, for help. Abbey took in the children, Mrs. Jennings offering to assist with the expense. An aged grandmother came down from Colne to get the children. Mrs. Abbey appeared to like the little girl so much that the grandmother willingly left her and took back only the boy. Mrs. Jennings was naturally touched by this affection for the little girl, and doubtless felt that Abbey, in addition to his other merits, might even be willing to offer a home of sorts. John Taylor, years later, hearing the skeleton of this story from Abbey, noted that this girl was "going into a Decline." The decline, in view of Abbey's treatment of the Keats children, does not come as a surprise.

² At least something was also set aside for the children of Midgley Jennings; for her will (July 31) mentions this as having already been done without specifying the amount. The deed does not seem to have survived. Abbey and Sandell were also the trustees for this amount. We can assume that Mrs. Jennings felt Midgley's children were far less in need. What they were to get in 1811 from their father (see Chap-

assumed that the guardianship would become active only after her death, she was certainly open to any suggestions that Abbey in particular might make. The status quo was actually kept for a short while. The three boys remained in school. Fanny stayed with her grandmother. But Abbey had definite plans about what should be done with the children.

The reading Keats pursued so actively during his last two years at school had already begun. John Clarke, at the end of each term, would award prizes to the boys who did the most voluntary work; and "such was Keats's indefatigable energy," said Cowden Clarke, "for the last two or three successive half-years of his remaining at school, that, upon each occasion, he took the first prize by a considerable distance." Though the first class was at seven in the morning, Keats had begun to study well before then. He worked on Latin and French translation during play hours and holidays, and took no recreation until Clarke or others would drive him out of the schoolhouse for exercise. He read at meals. "Thus, his *whole* time," said Clarke,

> was engrossed. He had a tolerably retentive memory, and the quantity that he read was surprising . . . In my "mind's eye," I now see him at supper (we had our meals in the school-room), sitting back on the form, from the table, holding the folio volume of Burnet's "History of his Own Time" between himself and the table, eating his meal from beyond it. This work, and Leigh Hunt's *Examiner*— which my father took in, and I used to lend to Keats—no doubt laid the foundation of his love of civil and religious liberty. He once told me, smiling, that one of his guardians, being informed what books I had lent him to read, declared that if he had fifty children he would not send one of them to that school.

By his last few months at Enfield, Keats had exhausted the school library, which consisted, said Clarke,

> principally of abridgments of all the voyages and travels of any note; Mavor's collection, also his "Universal History;" Robertson's histories of Scotland, America, and Charles the Fifth; all Miss Edgeworth's productions, together with many other works equally well calculated for youth. The books, however, that were his constantly

---

ter I, section 8), who had died a year and a half before, may not have been very much. But the family of Midgley's widow apparently had some money. In any case, their son, also named Midgley John (born 1806), had no difficulty securing an education. He went to Cambridge (B.A., 1829; M.A., 1832), entered the Church, went to India in the Delhi Mission, and was killed in the Indian mutiny.

recurrent sources of attraction were Tooke's "Pantheon," Lempriére's "Classical Dictionary," which he appeared to *learn,* and Spence's "Polymetis." This was the store whence he acquired his intimacy with the Greek mythology . . . for his amount of classical attainment extended no farther than the "Æneid;" with which epic, indeed, he was so fascinated that before leaving school he had *voluntarily* translated in writing a considerable portion. And yet I remember that at that early age—mayhap under fourteen—notwithstanding, and through all its incidental attractiveness, he hazarded the opinion to me (and the expression riveted my surprise), that there was feebleness in the structure of the work.[3]

The modest prizes Keats won included at least two books: in 1809 Kaufmann's *Dictionary of Merchandize . . . for the use of Counting Houses,* which we noticed before, and Bonnycastle's *Introduction to Astronomy,* given him in 1811.[4] There may have been another book awarded in 1810; a silver medal bearing that date is probably not genuine.[5]

[3] Pages 123–124.

[4] Miss Lowell (I.41) wonders whether Keats was ever tempted to read in Kaufmann's *Dictionary.* But the book, far less forbidding than its title, is merely a readable description, in alphabetical order, of articles of commerce—woods, fruits, grains, spices, manufactures. Kaufmann had a predilection for the exotic, and the descriptions are by no means irreconcilable with some of the imagery and references of some of Keats's verse (e.g., the articles on "alabaster," "dates," the "Cedars of Lebanon," the sentences about the pearl-divers, under "pearls"; or, under "silk," of the caravans crossing Asia, throughout the centuries, to the seacoasts of Syria). No one questions that Keats read the much better-known *Introduction to Astronomy* by John Bonnycastle. In this engaging book, which contains many excerpts from poems, particularly *Paradise Lost,* is a final chapter "Of the New Planets, and Other Discoveries." As Sir Ifor Evans noted, the discussion of Herschel's discoveries has some relevance to the famous lines in the sonnet "On First Looking into Chapman's Homer":

> Then felt I like some watcher of the skies
> When a new planet swims into his ken.

[5] For a photograph of the medal, which is in the Harvard Keats Collection, see Lowell, I.42. It is stamped with the words "Rev. Wm. Thomas's Academy Enfield." At the bottom is the date 1810, and around the lower edge is engraved "Awarded to Master J. Keats." On the reverse side, surrounding a Latin inscription, are the smaller words, "Audivit Clarkenem." Miss Lowell wondered whether Thomas might not be the previous proprietor of the school, Clarke simply using an old die with the words "Audivit Clarkenem" added. But Thomas came later, though we are not certain when. Miss Lowell was convinced the medal was genuine; for a great-granddaughter of George Keats (Mrs. John Whiting) had told Louis Holman that she remembered seeing it at her grandmother's house. (It had been sent, with other articles, to John Gilmer Speed, the grandson of George Keats, when he was preparing his edition of Keats's *Letters;* and Speed later sold these articles when he became financially pressed.) Holman (ms. note, Harvard Keats Collection) shrewdly guessed that the medal was a fraud, pointing out that the medal was obviously never designed to include the name either of Clarke or of a recipient. Presumably someone got hold of the medal after Thomas took over the academy, had the date 1810 engraved on the space as well as the names of Clarke and Keats, and then either sold

The date of the first prize is a helpful reminder. Without it, we should be tempted to make a rather neat pattern: the time at which Keats began to read so eagerly (during the last three terms he was in school, as Clarke said) would start almost exactly after the death of his mother in March 1810. Unquestionably this final loss, coming after others, had much to do with his sustained commitment to study, to reading, and to all that was represented by the school of the kindly John Clarke. Two years is a long time for a youth of fourteen or fifteen to continue working with such single-minded absorption. And there is Keats's own memorable statement in a letter seven years later (May 10, 1817): "I must think that difficulties nerve the Spirit of a Man—they make our Prime Objects a Refuge as well as a Passion." But this presupposes that, before the "Prime Objects" or aims become "a Refuge," they are already a "Passion"; and the "Prime Objects"—if one can apply the concept to school activities—had begun to manifest themselves a year or so earlier, as the little prize of Kaufmann's *Dictionary of Merchandize* suggests. Moreover, before one explains Keats's strenuous effort in the last years at school solely by his mother's death, one should remember the obvious—there were other children. George, less than two years younger and physically larger, shared the same family background, the same losses and possible challenges.

3

The particular interest of these last two years at Enfield is that Keats, who had by no means been bookish before, was not really bookish now, in any usual sense of the word. What we have is rather another illustration of the qualities of character that we have already noticed: a union of energy, courage, and absorption in something outside himself. It is this generous capacity for commitment, for imaginative identification, that underlies the "highmindedness" that Holmes and Clarke keep stressing, and it was to take many forms in the rapid march to maturity that began a few years later in this virile and by no means precocious young poet.

The microscopic scrutiny that a full century has given to every detail of his reading, now and for the next three or four years, is

---

it directly to Georgiana Keats—who could not have known much about Enfield—or more probably sold it to a friend of the Keats or Wylie families who then sent it in good faith as a gift to Georgiana and her children.

easily justified. What he read from fourteen to eighteen is relevant for understanding the later life of any writer; and it becomes more so if the life is short. Nevertheless, it would be less important if Keats had continued at school and then gone on to a university. But to note the titles and search for phrases that might be later echoed in his poetry does not provide the answer when the details are still, at this point, so meager. The larger gain in this reading was simply that a door was opened—that its opening was sensed so powerfully that henceforth the open door, the open window, became a haunting metaphor to Keats. For it brought the vital discovery (though there might be a few years before he realized it) that we are not completely the creatures of the environment in which we are placed—that we need not be imprisoned by the room where we are, by the stock responses we pick up from those about us, but that there are openings to something more spacious through the large written record of the past that we call literature.

This discovery was to prove formative in the highest degree. Take, as an example, the commonplace that Keats is the most purely "literary" of the great nineteenth-century poets. This has always seemed a paradox in one so unbookish, and above all in a poet who left school at fifteen. The nineteenth and twentieth centuries are filled with poets who have been academically steeped in literature. But in the case of Keats, the introduction to literature did not come passively, by imperceptible degrees. It came suddenly; it also came in such a way that it was partly—perhaps largely—self-found. Deprived, as he was so soon to be, of the resources of further education, he fell into naivetés that would have been surprising in the youth of a poet with a tenth his talent. But there was at least the gain that finally, after these four or five years of plunging about, he was freer, bolder, in turning to the large simplicities of the greater literature of the past. Hence this literature could be used creatively (and remembered in the days after he left school as "a Refuge as well as a Passion").

But even more important was the concrete experience of actually having taken things into his own hands, and the healthful discovery—for which there is no substitute—that "activity," as Johnson once said, carries within itself "the seeds of its own reformation." Granted that there is such a thing as useless "bustle"—as Johnson was the first to admit ("getting on horseback in the midst of a ship"); yet, to paraphrase a favorite image of his, if it is necessary to go north, the man who is walking south is more likely to end up going north than the man who merely sits in an armchair. So, after his first long poem, *Endymion,* Keats could justly say (October 9, 1818) that if he had been nervous about it,

> & trembled over every page, it would not have been written . . . I have written independently *without judgment*—I may write independently *& with judgment* hereafter. . . . In Endymion, I leaped headlong into the Sea, and thereby have become better acquainted with the Soundings, the quicksands, & the rocks, than if I had stayed upon the green shore, and piped a silly pipe, and took tea & comfortable advice.

4

By the summer of 1811, a year after he had become their trustee and guardian, Abbey decided that the two oldest boys should learn to support themselves. Given Abbey's premises, the decision is understandable. Given the premises of most people, we can find their decisions at least understandable. Abbey, who had gone to no Enfield, could—and doubtless did—point to himself as a result of the conduct he advocated. His house at nearby Walthamstow was imposing compared with the cottage he had left as a boy at Colne. There were four servants in the house. Mrs. Abbey prided herself on her freedom from any housework—something Mrs. Jennings could not do. Abbey also had a coachman and a carriage. Both Mr. and Mrs. Abbey flaunted their rudimentary sense of propriety. When little Fanny Keats came to live with them, she was not allowed to keep her dog. She was sternly forbidden to talk or laugh at dinner. Abbey prided himself on wearing at his countinghouse the clothes fashionable a generation before. His motives are made questionable by exactly this assertive self-righteousness. The energy with which he pushed his elementary opinions was matched— as concave is by convex—by a powerful, innate suspicion of others. To paraphrase a Greek epigram: he who will never believe another's oath knows himself to have perjured.

Suspicion was indeed the dominant trait of Abbey. Resenting the oppressive, lower-middle-class conventions through which his own success had been strained, he naturally sought to even the balance by imposing them, with militant fervor, on others. The eagerness with which he would chat with the grocer about the mother of the Keats children and about the way in which she lifted her skirts to cross the muddy puddles of the street; the deeper dislike both of her and of her generous "gourmand" father, with his naive love of a good table, a dislike that stemmed from Abbey's instinctive hatred of amplitude and openness; the malicious readiness to say that Thomas Keats had been killed when "most probably in liquor"—all betray Abbey as much as the old-fashioned dress that he insisted on wearing with the prim bravado of the man who takes it for granted that only externals matter. Inevitably hypocrisy was a part of the way in which he went through life. When he was talking to John Taylor, he could speculate salaciously—and self-righteously—about Mrs. Keats's looseness. But with George Keats, the only child who seemed to him passable, he curried favor and praised the mother's virtues. Long afterwards, George could write: "Mr. Abbey used to say that he never saw a woman of the talents and sense of my grandmother, except my mother."

It was probably at the end of the midsummer term of 1811 that Abbey withdrew the two eldest boys from Clarke's school.[6] John, in two months, would be sixteen. George was fourteen and a half. Tom, still twelve, was allowed to remain at Enfield for a while. Abbey placed George in his countinghouse. He was less eager to have John on the premises. Whether the decision was made entirely by Abbey or with the encouragement of Mrs. Jennings, who may have been struck by the boy's reading and may also have felt it desirable for him to remain nearby, John was apprenticed to a nearby surgeon and apothecary, Thomas Hammond. Apparently the customary fees were paid Hammond,[7] and the term of the apprenticeship was expected to be the usual one of five years.

Because we have no first-hand knowledge of the way Keats himself felt, it has often been assumed that he found the change agreeable. It is incredible that Keats, after what had happened to him at Clarke's school during his last two years, could have left Enfield without an almost desperate reluctance, however quiet he may have been about it. A sentence of Cowden Clarke's is always

---

[6] The date may have been earlier. See Appendix II.

[7] George Keats, in a letter to Dilke (see below, p. 709, n. 6), stated that Hammond was paid a premium of "two hundred Guineas and expenses." In the first printing of the present book (1963), I wrongly described this as an exaggeration. Mr. Gittings has since shown that George was almost certainly right (*The Keats Inheritance*, pp. 45–47).

quoted. "This arrangement [with Hammond] evidently gave him satisfaction, and I fear that it was the most placid period of his painful life; for now with the exception of the duty he had to perform in the surgery—by no means an onerous one—his leisure hours were employed in indulging his passion for reading and translating." But, in the first place, Clarke is not speaking of Keats's frame of mind at the start of the apprenticeship with Hammond. He is thinking of the general situation after it came to be accepted as inevitable, and comparing it not with Keats's school-days but with the tragic course of Keats's later life. If Clarke is to be used as the source for Keats's reactions at this time, the appropriate material is his account of Keats's frequent visits to Enfield to borrow books and to talk. Moreover, loathing complaint as he did, Keats would hardly have whined to Clarke, or to anyone else. A boy of fifteen is especially on his mettle with a young man of twenty-three. One can imagine the self-assured maturity, the shared sophistication, with which Keats had mentioned to Clarke the year before ("smiling," said Clarke) Abbey's disapproval of the books he read. That Keats should not have enjoyed speaking to his later friends of his apprentice days is understandable. The only graphic reference we have is therefore important. Mentioning, in a letter to George (September 21, 1819) the constant change in the tissues of the body, he said, "seven years ago it was not this hand that clench'd itself against Hammond." [8] Seven years before would bring us back to the first year of the apprenticeship.

Still, the choice of surgery was understandable. It at least offered an assured standing and income. Socially it stood between the lower or middle ranks of trade and those professions, like medicine itself, that involved university study. As compared with "physicians," "surgeons" at this time were still only a step from barbers. The position had to do with the simpler functions of the general practitioner of medicine and dentistry now—setting bones, pulling teeth, serving as apothecary and general medical adviser. Given the extent of Keats's education, and the modest financial position of the family, it might seem a desirable solution—provided he

[8] It is of course possible that Keats was referring to one of Hammond's two sons (Henry or Edward) rather than to Hammond himself, or to one of his nephews (*KSMB*, No. 12 [1961], 25).

could not remain at school much longer. The provision is a large one. Finally, he would still be close to his grandmother's house. Hammond's own house, which stood until 1931, was at 7 Church Street, only down the way. A garden and also an orchard stretched behind it. Next to the garden was the surgery, and above it the room, with an outer staircase, where Keats lived.

5

If the details of the next three or four years are even more meager, the explanation is simple. Before the apprenticeship with Hammond, Keats at least was at school. Some knowledge of the school, and remarks of those who remembered him, can be put together. But no one who saw much of Keats now, with the single exception of Cowden Clarke, was to be able to pass on much information about him. Fanny Keats was too young; Mrs. Jennings was dead by 1814, Tom by 1818, and Hammond by 1817. George, who had seen John daily while at Enfield, was now in Abbey's countinghouse in the midst of the city.

Hence, for these crucial years, we have little more than the brief paragraphs of Cowden Clarke, written half a century later. What emerges from them is that Keats tried to continue something of the life he had known before. Rather touchingly, not knowing what else to do, he worked at first during his spare hours on the prose translation of the *Aeneid* he had begun at school. Apparently it was finished within a few months. Moreover, Keats, now so alone, was inevitably drawn back to the school. He would walk over from the small Edmonton surgery, says Clarke,

> five or six times a month on my own leisure afternoons. He rarely came empty-handed; either he had a book to read, or brought one to be exchanged. When the weather permitted, we always sat in an arbour at the end of a spacious garden . . .
>
> It were difficult, at this lapse of time, to note the spark that fired the train of his poetical tendencies; but he must have given unmistakable tokens of his mental bent; otherwise, at that early stage of his career, I never could have read to him the "Epithalamion" of Spenser; and this I remember having done, and in that hallowed old arbour, the scene of many bland and graceful associations—the substances having passed away.

After they had read Spenser's "Epithalamion," Clarke, before Keats left that night, lent him the first volume of the *Faerie*

Queene. Keats's reaction has passed into legend. He went through the poem, said Clarke,

> as I formerly told his noble biographer [Monckton Milnes, Lord Houghton] "as a young horse would through a spring meadow—ramping!" Like a true poet, too—a poet "born, not manufactured," a poet in grain, he especially singled out epithets, for that felicity and power in which Spenser is so eminent. He *hoisted* himself up, and looked burly and dominant, as he said, "what an image that is—*'sea-shouldering whales!'*" [9]

Clarke's account of the experience was confirmed by what Keats himself later told his friend, Charles Brown.[10] Clarke shows his own perception in noting at once the nature of the appeal: Keats's immediate response to intensity and felicity of epithet and image. Clarke plainly had not observed it before, when Keats was at school (he was now, says Clarke, almost sixteen—in the first year, that is, of the apprenticeship with Hammond); otherwise he would certainly have mentioned it.

What is particularly significant about the two passages [11] Clarke remembers (or else singles out) is that they are not merely good examples of felicity of language or image. There are many ways, needless to say, in which happiness of phrase can be attained. The significance is that both passages are characterized by the sort of empathy—the adhesive, imaginative identification—that increasingly marked Keats's own poetry and that later deepened in his clairvoyant understanding of Shakespeare. The reaction Clarke remembers—the young apprentice entering into the image of the whales, feeling the weight on his own shoulders of the parting billows, and looking "burly" as he "hoisted himself up"—reminds us of another description, of Keats telling about a bear and instinc-

---

[9] Pages 125–126.

[10] "It was the 'Faery Queen' that awakened his genius. In Spenser's fairy land he was enchanted, breathed in a new world, and became another being; till, enamoured of the stanza, he attempted to imitate it, and succeeded. This account of the sudden development of his poetic powers I received from his brothers, and afterwards from himself" (Brown, p. 42).

[11] The second (p. 126) follows: "Once, when reading the 'Cymbeline' aloud, I saw his eyes fill with tears, and his voice faltered when he came to the departure of Posthumus, and Imogen saying she would have watched him—

> 'Till the diminution
> Of space had pointed him sharp as my needle;
> Nay follow'd him till he had *melted from*
> *The smallness of a gnat to air;* and then
> Have turn'd mine eye and wept."

tively imitating it, moving slowly about, with his paws dangling as he reared backward. One also thinks of Keats's puckish statement to his friend Richard Woodhouse, a few years later, that he could enter into a billiard ball as it rolled about, feeling "a sense of delight from its own roundness, smoothness, volubility, & the rapidity of its motion."

It is easy to understand the gratitude to Clarke that Keats always felt. No teacher could receive a higher tribute than the early verse letter, timidly written and surrounded with long apologies for writing at all, that Keats sent to Cowden Clarke three or four years later. The key statement, of course, is:

> Ah! had I never seen,
> Or known your kindness, what might I have been?

But before this come the famous lines. They are youthful and are perhaps memorable largely because of the context. But one cannot say "only because of the context": "only" is hardly appropriate when the context is a poetic development as unparalleled as his. If Keats feels diffident—something not in the least characteristic— in writing this verse letter, the reason is that he has written nothing remotely comparable to the works to which Clarke introduced him. He tries to offer this tribute only because "you first taught me all the sweets of song":

> Who read for me the sonnet swelling loudly
> Up to its climax and then dying proudly?
> Who found for me the grandeur of the ode,
> Growing, like Atlas, stronger from its load?
> Who let me taste that more than cordial dram,
> The sharp, the rapier-pointed epigram?
> Show'd me that epic was of all the king,
> Round, vast, and spanning all like Saturn's ring?

As Keats closes the verse letter we almost seem to have something that anticipates the end of the last letter he was to write (to Charles Brown, November 30, 1820) : "I can scarce bid you good bye even in a letter. I always made an awkward bow." Now he speaks of his reluctance to leave during these meetings with Clarke. Their talk, he says, would go on until nightfall, until after supper, "when reluctantly I took my hat." And if Clarke should walk halfway to Hammond's surgery, Keats lingered after they parted until he could no longer hear Clarke's footsteps on the gravel path. "In those still moments I have wished you joys," he says, and have thought, "It cannot be that aught will work him harm."

6

Three years after Keats left Enfield, and perhaps a year or two after the day he and Cowden Clarke first read Spenser, the apprentice at Edmonton wrote his first poem, an "Imitation of Spenser." He was eighteen, approaching nineteen. It was dated variously during the nineteenth century from 1812 to 1814. We can accept the conventional opinion at the present time that Keats wrote it in 1814. Four or five other short poems among those that have come down to us (and we probably have most of them) were also written before the end of the same year.[12]

These shy beginnings as well as the poems written during the next year or two have interested writers since they were first discovered. For, if we lack details of Keats's life before he was twenty, we are unusually fortunate in having not only his earliest poems but a large proportion of the immature verse that follows. Poets who live longer have the opportunity to sweep their earliest verse under the rug: no one loves to see his tentative gropings advertised. For this reason alone the naked exposure of Keats's first writing is valuable, and has carried a reassurance to later writers so strong that it reminds one of the last phrase in Johnson's famous remark to Edmund Malone on the uses of biography:

> If nothing but the bright side of characters should be shewn, we should sit down in despondency, and think it utterly impossible to imitate them in *any thing*. The sacred writers (he observed) related the vicious as well as the virtuous actions of men; which had this moral effect, that it kept mankind from *despair*.[13]

A second interest is that between these beginnings in 1814–15 and the great poetry of 1818–19 is a development of only four years. A

---

12 When Clarke in 1816 was to introduce him to Leigh Hunt, Keats copied out a few of his poems in preparation. In looking over "a sheet or two of Verses which I composed some time ago," he found so much "to blame in them that the worst part will go into the fire" (I.113). This does not mean they actually went into the fire. Moreover, he is thinking of poems composed the previous year, not of the very earliest poems (it would not have occurred to him to show those to Hunt). In any case, he is referring to "a sheet or two."

13 Boswell, *Life,* ed. Hill-Powell (1934–1940), IV.53.

final interest is that the poetry is so far from being gifted (not merely the very first poems—that is taken for granted—but the poetry that follows for some time) , and that the start comes fairly late: Keats is surprisingly, refreshingly remote from precocity.

What we generally think of as Keats's early poetry—poetry that actually begins in the winter of 1815–16 and continues another two years through the writing of *Endymion*—is characterized by the same energy, the same uninhibited readiness to commit himself, that his schoolmates noted in him at Enfield. Hence the quiet, careful tone when he first begins to write may come as a surprise. The four Spenserian stanzas that make up the first poem may have taken some time to complete. They are inlaid with phrases from Spenser, Milton, and eighteenth-century versifiers that looked back to both; and the structure of the stanza carefully follows that of the eighteenth-century imitations of Spenser rather than that used by Spenser himself.[14] Partly because the lines were so diligently labored, Keats still thought them good enough to include in his volume three years later.

After this first poem, at least five others survive that were written before the end of 1814, and, like the "Imitation of Spenser," all are essentially exercises in conventional late eighteenth-century forms. A sonnet "On Peace," in the irregular Shakespearean rhyme scheme common in the 1790's, presumably celebrates the hope for peace after Napoleon's exile to Elba. In August Keats tried to vary his vein by writing a series of octosyllabic couplets, "Fill for me a brimming bowl," with its amusing implication of a practiced taste in women ("the fairest form / That e'er my reveling eyes beheld") .[15] A couplet catches interest as the first expression of a thought that is to recur much later in the mature poems:

> I want as deep a draught
> As e'er from Lethe's waves was quaft.

14 The amplest discussion of sources for all the earliest poems is that of Finney, I.29–114, *passim;* on versification, see also my *Stylistic Development of Keats* (1945) , pp. 8–10, 19–20, 189–197.

15 The sight of an actual woman, however, was the immediate occasion of these lines, and, in fact, remained in his mind for some years. In his Book of Transcripts (p. 222) , Woodhouse wrote: "On p. 28 will be found a sonnet ["Time's Sea," written February 4, 1818] alluding to the same lady—Keats mentioned the circumstances of obtaining a casual sight of her at Vauxhall, in answer to my inquiry—Feb. 1819. See also p. 64." Page 64, in Woodhouse's transcripts, contains the sonnet, "When I have fears," with the lines referring to the "Fair creature of an hour."

In December he wrote a sonnet "To Byron," which deserves a few sentences.[16] For the conventions used in the other beginning poems help to float them along, whereas here they prove an insurmountable handicap; and yet something is retrieved. The elegiac or "plaintive" sonnet had for twenty years or more been used indiscriminately by lesser poets—and especially poetesses—for praise, grief, meditation, and mere description. Working alone, he might understandably take for granted—however he felt about his reading in Spenser and other earlier poets—that this was an appropriate idiom for poetry now: for poetry, at least, that hoped to be published. He himself found it moving. The stock props were new to him; and he uses a few of them ("plaintive lute," "amber rays," "dying swan") and the gentle contrarieties that were fashionable ("sweetly sad," "pleasing woe"). Timidly he inserts one example (a coined adverb "beamily") of the pseudo-bold diction through which he later had to pass, as through an obstacle course, before he hit his stride:

> thou thy griefs dost dress
> With a bright halo, shining beamily.

In reading the absurd close of the sonnet ("Still warble, dying swan!")—the awkward expression of a boyish sympathy wanting to praise, and doing so in a way that his reading had taught him was a compliment—one ironically thinks ahead almost five years to the scene on the ship, the *Maria Crowther,* when Keats, who was actu-

---

16 Byron! how sweetly sad thy melody!
    Attuning still the soul to tenderness,
    As if soft Pity, with unusual stress,
Had touch'd her plaintive lute, and thou, being by,
Hadst caught the tones, nor suffer'd them to die.
    O'ershadowing sorrow doth not make thee less
    Delightful: thou thy griefs dost dress
With a bright halo, shining beamily,
As when a cloud the golden moon doth veil,
    Its sides are ting'd with a resplendent glow,
Through the dark robe oft amber rays prevail,
    And like fair veins in sable marble flow;
Still warble, dying swan! still tell the tale,
    The enchanting tale, the tale of pleasing woe.

The sonnet has sometimes been said to have been written after the death of Keats's grandmother in the same month because of the line and a half beginning "O'ershadowing sorrow." But Keats, of course, is referring not to himself but to Byron's "griefs."

ally dying, was on his way to Italy. He had been reading Byron's *Don Juan,* said Severn, and suddenly

> threw the book down & exclaimed "this gives me the most horrid idea of human nature, that a man like Byron should have exhausted all the pleasures of the world so compleatly that there was nothing left for him but to laugh & gloat over the most solemn & heart rending [scenes] of human misery . . . the tendency of Byron's poetry is based on a paltry originality, that of being new by making solemn things gay & gay things solemn." [17]

Yet when all these handicaps are taken for granted—misapplication of conventions, stock diction, and the rest—the sonnet is fairly neat and compact for so early a performance. A few qualities even remind us of Keats two or three years hence. The phrase "fair veins in sable marble" is reasonably condensed. More important, the poem lingers with the subject, continually returning to details and increasingly amplifying the conception (as the "Ode on a Grecian Urn" and "To Autumn" were to do in so massive a way) : it takes a thought, contemplates it in a tranquil pause, and ends where it began, the "pleasing woe" in the last line recurring to the "sweetly sad . . . melody" at the start. Unlike so much of the poetry written under the influence of Hunt, but like the later poems, it is, in its own way, self-contained.

7

In the middle of December, 1814, Mrs. Jennings died at the age of seventy-eight. Winter and early spring could understandably seem a trying time to Keats as the years passed. Members of the family always seemed to die in the months from December through March; and the summer, before the end of Keats's life, became invested with more hope than it holds for most of us. A few days after his grandmother's death, Keats wrote a sonnet.

On deeply personal matters, at least when the feeling was one of loss or hurt, he always seems to have grown reticent. It was years before anyone learned the occasion of this particular sonnet. His friend Richard Woodhouse, in February 1819 (the year of Keats's greatest writing) , asked him whether it had been written "on the death of a person . . . and he said he had written it on the death of his grandmother, about five days after; but that he had never told any one, not even his brother, the occasion on which it was

[17] *KC,* II.134.

written; he said he was tenderly attached to her." Since the elegiac tone is at least appropriate to the occasion, the sonnet is free from the radical incongruity that cripples the lines "To Byron" from the start. But there is less to it otherwise,[18] since he has no subject but only an occasion. It would have been unlike him to devote the poem to his own sense of loss; and even if he could have been expected from his own reading to think that he might dwell more specifically on his grandmother herself, he had neither the experience nor the detachment to do so with what he would feel a dignified propriety. The alternatives were limited: to picture his grandmother in a conventional heaven, or to write more generally of life after death. Keats apparently tried both. The sonnet itself attempts the former: his grandmother is seen with other "happy spirits, crowned with circlets bright," singing in "the immortal quire," or else (with Keats introducing a Miltonic phrase in the hope of imparting energy) "cleaving the air" when sent "on holy message." A Spenserian archaism is added to the descriptive touches: the angels are "gloriously bedight." Possibly because he was dissatisfied with the sonnet, he may have written at this time also the more effective lines in the eighteenth-century elegiac stanza:

> Can death be sleep, when life is but a dream,
>   And scenes of bliss pass as a phantom by?
> The transient pleasures as a vision seem,
>   And yet we think the greatest pain's to die.
>
> How strange it is that man on earth should roam,
>   And lead a life of woe, but not forsake
> His rugged path; nor dare he view alone
>   His future doom which is but to awake.[19]

18 As from the darkening gloom a silver dove
    Upsoars, and darts into the Eastern light,
    On pinions that nought moves but pure delight,
So fled thy soul into the realms above,
Regions of peace and everlasting love;
    Where happy spirits, crown'd with circlets bright
    Of starry beam, and gloriously bedight,
Taste the high joy none but the blest can prove.
There thou or joinest the immortal quire
    In melodies that even Heaven fair
Fill with the superior bliss, or, at desire
    Of the omnipotent Father, cleavest the air
On holy message sent—What pleasures higher?
    Wherefore does any grief our joy impair?

19 The lines, first printed by H. Buxton Forman (1883), were found in what is generally called the Keats-Wylie Scrapbook, kept by George Keats and his wife. Garrod (p. xlv) doubted that they were written by Keats, for "the piece is unsigned,

8

After Mrs. Jennings died in December, the house in Edmonton that had been home to the Keats children for almost nine years was closed. Tom, now fifteen, was removed from Enfield probably at the close of the winter term—at the latest by summer 1815—and put with George in Abbey's countinghouse in Pancras Lane. John, at Hammond's surgery down the street from his grandmother's house, was without even the semblance of a family nearby. If only because he had left it three years before, the school at Enfield was receding as a possible substitute.

Perhaps because of the loneliness, he began after a few weeks to spend more time writing. Of the four to twelve poems [20] that survive from the remaining nine months of his apprenticeship with Hammond, three are dated February. A fourth was probably written about the same time: a sonnet "To Chatterton," the boy poet who had committed suicide in 1770 at the age of seventeen, and to whose memory Keats was to dedicate *Endymion*. Needless to say, sentimentalists during the half century after Keats's death were tempted to interpret his early fondness for Chatterton as a prescient identification.

---

nor does anything in the book either indicate or suggest that Keats wrote these weak verses." That the verses are weak, of course, means nothing. That they are weak in a slightly different way from Keats's other poems of the time could conceivably mean something. But we have nothing to help us except internal evidence; and in dealing with a poet so far from being formed, who in fact is experimenting with more than one of the conventional eighteenth-century styles, there is no internal evidence that can be used. Hence editors have generally followed Forman in assigning the poem, however uneasily, to Keats. I myself can see nothing in these quiet, tame lines that conflicts with the sonnet ("As from the darkening gloom") that Keats wrote after the death of his grandmother: in fact they seem rather similar in mood.

[20] "To Hope," the "Ode to Apollo," "Written on the Day that Mr. Leigh Hunt Left Prison," all discussed above, are dated. So are the liberal-spirited lines (May 29) attacking the anniversary of Charles II's restoration. The sonnet "To Chatterton" is simply dated 1815 by Woodhouse. It is so close in temper to the sonnet "To Byron" that we are justified in placing it in January or at least the early spring of 1815. The stanzas "To Some Ladies" and "On Receiving a Curious Shell," the first addressed to the Misses Mathew and the second to their cousin, G. F. Mathew, were probably written in the summer of 1815, when the Mathews were at the seaside in Hastings. The song in the same anapestic meter but in couplets rather than quatrains, "O come, my dear Emma," may very well date from the spring or summer. From Mathew's later enthusiastic endorsement of them (see below, Chapter VII), we can conclude that the "Three Sonnets on Woman" were written while he and Keats were seeing each other most frequently (March to December, 1815). A twelfth poem, "Stay, ruby-breasted Warbler," could have been written by George Keats (see the discussion in Finney, I.69–70); if it is by Keats himself, it was probably written before the autumn of 1815.

Of these various poems, those actually dated February come the nearest to justifying mention: a poem of eight stanzas, rather touchingly addressed "To Hope"; an "Ode to Apollo"; and the sonnet entitled "Written on the Day that Mr. Leigh Hunt Left Prison." That they again fall into typical eighteenth-century modes can be taken for granted. The interest of the jejune lines "To Hope" is that, at so trying a moment, Keats should have attempted to write a poem of this length (forty-eight lines) on this particular abstraction. Moreover, something of his actual situation filters through the conventional imagery: in the first lines, for example ("When by my solitary hearth I sit"), and in the sort of thing he believes he must find strength to meet (despondency "at the fall of night," the feeling that the "bare heath of life presents no bloom," the sorrow at "the fate of those I hold most dear"). In the same February, trying to capture the strong clang and vigor of the odes of Dryden, he wrote his "Ode to Apollo" ("In thy western halls of gold"). Here for the first time he tries to mount on stilts and move in the declamatory rather than the sentimental style of the eighteenth century.

Given his reticence on matters about which he most cared, it is natural that he told none of his friends—not even Clarke—that he was trying to write poetry. It was more than two months after his grandmother's death before he admitted it, and the poem he then handed to Clarke was a sonnet (February 2, 1815) "Written on the Day that Mr. Leigh Hunt Left Prison." Hunt and his brother John had been prosecuted without success three times between 1808 and 1811 for advocating liberal reforms in their periodical, the *Examiner*. Finally, in 1812, a bold attack by the Hunts on the Prince Regent ("a violator of his word, a libertine," a man who has lived "half a century without one claim on the gratitude of his country, or the respect of posterity") led to a successful prosecution for libel; and the brothers were each fined £500 and sentenced to a prison term of two years.

Even now the poem Keats showed Clarke—and Keats handed it to him with "hesitation" and only when they parted—had to be one that was prompted by a special occasion, and an occasion that had to do with one of Clarke's own heroes. It was in walking to London, said Clarke,

to see Leigh Hunt, who had just fulfilled his penalty of confinement in Horsemonger Lane Prison for the unwise libel upon the Prince

Regent, that Keats met me; and, turning, accompanied me back part of the way. At the last field-gate, when taking leave, he gave me the sonnet entitled, "Written on the day that Mr. Leigh Hunt left Prison." This I feel to be the first proof I had received of his having committed himself in verse; and how clearly do I recall the conscious look and hesitation with which he offered it! [21]

9

With George and Tom at Abbey's countinghouse, and with Fanny herself living either above or near it until Abbey, in the warm months, moved with his family to his country place in Walthamstow, Keats was inevitably drawn to London. Moreover, he obviously felt that if George and Tom were put to work he himself, as the oldest of the children, should be making more of a start than he seemed to be doing at Edmonton. Probably at Keats's own urging, Hammond was persuaded to cut the five-year term of apprenticeship to four years. Abbey seems to have agreed, although he himself, twelve years later, gave a different explanation: he told John Taylor that Hammond had been lax in his duties, and that Abbey himself therefore removed Keats from Hammond's charge. For several reasons, Abbey's account is at this point especially unreliable.[22]

In the following summer, arrangements were made for Keats, now nineteen, to register at Guy's Hospital for further study as a

[21] *Recollections,* p. 127.

[22] Abbey's story is as follows (*KC,* I.307): "John was apprenticed to a Surgeon at Edmonton, who did not however conduct himself as Mr. A. conceived he ought to have done to his young Pupil, & partly to punish him by the Opposition,—partly because Mrs. Jennings was known & respected in the Neighbourhood, on which Acct. her Grandson had a better Introduction there than elsewhere, it was Mr. Abbey's advice that John should commence Business at Tottenham as a Surgeon. He communicated his Plans to his Ward but his Surprize was not moderate, to hear in Reply, that he did not intend to be a Surgeon." Then follows the passage, quoted in full in Chapter VI, section 6, where it is more relevant, in which Keats states that he is going to try to "gain his living" by poetry, and Abbey dismisses him. Plainly Abbey is thinking of the period after Keats left Guy's Hospital. Keats could under no circumstances have set up as a surgeon after a mere four years of apprenticeship. It is well over a year later that Keats decided to devote himself wholly to poetry. Moreover, Abbey states that "not long after" this interview Keats brought him "a little Book which he had got printed." This, of course, would be the *Poems* published in 1817. Abbey is telescoping the summer of 1815 with the autumn or winter of 1816. The distrust we should normally feel for what Abbey says of Hammond is thus strengthened. The remark about Hammond seems to be a typical example both of his disapproval of most people and also of his desire to impress himself as well as Taylor with the assurance that he was no one's fool, completely in charge of things, and zealous for the well-being of the orphans.

surgeon. Hammond, who seems to have been a kindly, hard-working man (he himself was to die within two years at the age of fifty-three), signed Keats's application papers. On October 1, 1815, when he lacked a month of being twenty, Keats was registered at Guy's Hospital as a student for one term (six months) .[23] Here he was to remain until the middle of July, 1816, when he passed his examinations and then became licensed to practice as a surgeon and an apothecary.

[23] He paid the office fee of £1.2.0, and the next day the sum of £25.4.0. Abbey advanced the money. On the same day John White Webster, of Boston, Massachusetts, was entered as a surgeon's dresser, immediately below the name of Keats. This was the Webster who later taught at Harvard Medical School, and was involved in the most famous murder in Harvard history (the Webster-Parkman murder of 1849). Webster was at Guy's Hospital throughout Keats's stay there.

Guy's Hospital

✻⇝۞⇗✻⇝۞⇗✻⇝۞⇗✻⇝۞⇗✻⇝۞⇗✻⇝۞⇗✻⇝۞⇗✻⇝۞⇗✻⇝۞⇗✻⇝۞⇗✻⇝۞⇗✻⇝۞

1815–16

THE CHANGE from the quiet rural village of Edmonton to any busy section of London would have been dramatic. The change to Southwark, or the "Borough," was far more so.

Guy's and St. Thomas's Hospitals, across the street from each other, were close to the southern edge of London Bridge. Immediately west of them ran the High Street, the principal artery from London to the south of England. Nearly three hundred coaches a week left or arrived at Southwark itself; and this does not include the number that passed through it on the way to and from the City. Vast numbers of wagons and carts bearing produce also entered through the High Street. The winding, narrow streets on either side, together with their adjacent alleys and courtyards, were lined with tenements; and parts of the Borough were a principal haunt of the large underworld of London. The open ditches used for both sewage and garbage were considered the worst in England; at least there were far more of them for the area. One of the constant grievances of the prisoners at the Marshalsea was the large fetid ditch nearby, to which they attributed the fevers and "putrid sore throat" that afflicted them.

The Borough was known for its prisons as well as its hospitals. Two or three minutes' walk to the right, after one crossed London Bridge, was Deadman's Place, Bankside, where the famous prison of the Clink had stood until it was burned in the riots of 1780. St. Thomas's and Guy's Hospitals were on one's left as one went south along the High Street, which still, in 1815, had many houses with half-timbered, overhanging stories. About two hundred yards south of Guy's was the old Marshalsea Prison. The new Marshalsea—that of Dickens' *Little Dorrit*—had been begun in 1811, on the site of the old White Lyon Prison. Across the High Street from

1. THE CLARKE SCHOOL AT ENFIELD

2. DR. HAMMOND'S SURGERY, EDMONTON

3. EDMONTON IN 1806

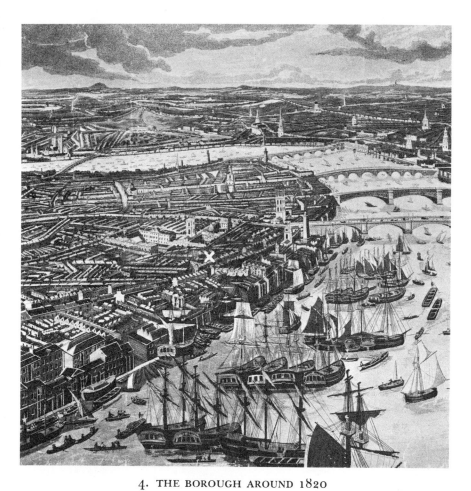

4. THE BOROUGH AROUND 1820

The cross marks the approximate location of 8 Dean Street, where Keats lived.

5. THE NORTH FRONT OF GUY'S HOSPITAL IN KEATS'S TIME

6. MARGATE IN KEATS'S TIME

The bathing machines may be seen in the water.

the Marshalsea Prisons was the disreputable area called the Mint, and below it the King's Bench Prison.

Most of the buildings between Guy's Hospital and the river were to be torn down and some of the streets themselves to be arched over during the 1860's when the railroad and the London Bridge station were built. Keats himself gives a brief description of the area in the first letter of his that we have. He is telling Cowden Clarke (October 9, 1816) how to find the spot to which he later moved:

> Although the Borough is a beastly place in dirt, turnings and windings; yet No. 8 Dean Street [1] is not difficult to find; and if you would run the Gauntlet over London Bridge, take the first turning to the left and then the first to the right and moreover knock at my door which is nearly opposite a Meeting [a Baptist chapel], you would do me a charity.

And his first published poem—a sonnet written shortly after he entered the Hospital in October—begins:

> O Solitude! if I must with thee dwell,
> Let it not be among the jumbled heap
> Of murky buildings.

The rest of the sonnet then turns for contrast to the countryside he had known at Edmonton.

2

There were compensations, however. To begin with, he was not far from his brothers. A walk of fifteen or twenty minutes across London Bridge and toward the Poultry would take him to Abbey's countinghouse in Pancras Lane, where George and Tom were working. Moreover, within a few days after he arrived, he made at least one friend, John Spurgin, a youth considerably different from those he had met thus far; and within a few months he was to acquire several more friends.[2] Spurgin, two years younger than Keats,

---

[1] One of the streets arched over. What is left of the street, together with a new extension of it, was renamed Stainer Street.

[2] In addition to those mentioned below, he was also on friendly terms with Charles Butler, who had entered Guy's Hospital the day before he did and was later a relative by marriage of Keats's friend John Hamilton Reynolds (I.235); Daniel Gosset, originally from Edmonton; Frederick Leffler, who was also a friend of G. F. Mathew; and especially Charles Severn—apparently no relation of Joseph Severn—who later became a well-known physician. Keats may have visited Severn's home, for his sister Emma (KC, II.256) also knew Keats.

was leaving Guy's Hospital within a week or two in order to study at Caius College, Cambridge. A year before, he had become a follower of Swedenborg. The two youths talked about religion: Keats, skeptical yet open-natured, struck the serious-minded Spurgin as a receptive soul who might be touched. A long letter survives from Spurgin, written in December from Cambridge, in which—following their talks when they first met—Spurgin tried to outline the ideas of Swedenborg as he understood them.[3] Keats, when he and Spurgin met, had been full of talk about poetry and the great poets of the past; and in his letter Spurgin states that, with a knowledge of "the Life which actuates and animates Nature," Keats would also be better able to judge "what can give the brightest and most lucid Flame to the Fire of Poetry even, and wander in Paths amid the Geniuses of old which I know you so much admire." Though Spurgin says that he will be seeing Keats in a fortnight, we know nothing more of their acquaintanceship. Because of the address of the letter, we know that Keats was already living—and probably had been living since he arrived—at St. Thomas's Street, which ran between Guy's and St. Thomas's Hospitals, continuing east until it met the street called "The Maze."

It was also something new to the village youth to crowd with three hundred other students into the amphitheater—with scores sitting on the stairs or standing in the passages—when Astley Cooper lectured. For almost fifty years the medical schools of Guy's and St. Thomas's had been combined; and the students flocked back and forth across St. Thomas's Street, as they went to lectures or followed the surgeons through the various wards of either hospital. The lectures Keats attended are listed in the Register of Apothecaries' Hall [4] as follows:

2—COURSES on ANATOMY and PHYSIOLOGY
2—THEORY and PRACTICE of MEDICINE
2—CHEMISTRY
1—MATERIA MEDICA

A small leather notebook survives containing notes to lectures by the famous Astley Cooper, already at the head of his profession.[5]

[3] Spurgin's letter (Harvard Keats Collection) is printed in E. B. Hinckley, *Keats-Shelley Journal*, IX (1960), 15–25.
[4] Printed in Lowell, I.154.
[5] Keats Museum, Hampstead; printed in *John Keats: Anatomical and Physiological Note Book*, ed. M. B. Forman (1934); Sir William Hale-White, *Keats as Doctor and Patient* (1938), pp. 20–22.

Warm-natured, brilliant, and immensely hard-working, he was also one of the great medical teachers of the nineteenth century. His personal kindliness to students was proverbial. He even, among the hundreds of students he had at the time, noticed Keats. Sensing the youth's loneliness, he asked one of his "dressers," George Cooper (no relation of his own) to help look after him. George Cooper and Frederick Tyrrell, both near the end of their course at Guy's Hospital and living at the house of a tallow chandler named Markham in St. Thomas's Street, invited Keats to share their lodgings.

At first glance, Keats would seem to have taken his lecture notes on whatever page fell open, and then, when the book was filled, to have started to insert further notes between the lines of those made earlier: the inference being that he was either completely indifferent or hopelessly confused. From a comparison of two volumes of careful notes taken by a contemporary at Guy's Hospital, Joshua Waddington, Miss Mabel Steele has explained the apparent lack of order.[6] Keats first neatly copied out a syllabus for the forthcoming lectures. He obviously assumed that the syllabus was the important thing—perhaps all that was really necessary—though he left space here and there throughout it, as well as before and after, in case anything crucial needed to be inserted. Then, showing up at the lectures in the crowded amphitheater, he finally started to write because he saw others writing. He may even have begun as late as Lecture IV, the notes for which appear on the first page of the notebook, and then afterwards, using the notes of other students, have tried to get something down for the earlier lectures. In time, as the separate pages filled, notes were written in the margin of the syllabus, and others even between the lines of it. Hence the confusion. We can infer that the whole procedure of lectures and note taking puzzled him at first. Later, the fullness of the notes varies according to subject. Lectures on bone setting he seems to have found dull. Next to them he sketched little pictures of flowers and fruits. The notes to the lectures on physiology are more detailed.

After he had been at the hospital for a month, on October 29, 1815, Keats himself became a "dresser."[7] Before the use of anti-

6 In an unpublished ms. Miss Steele kindly allowed me to read. Cf. also G. A. R. Winston, "John Keats and Joshua Waddington, Contemporary Students at Guy's Hospital," *Guy's Hospital Reports,* XCII (1943), 101–110.

7 At this point the records at Guy's show that six guineas are refunded from his

septics, wounds almost always became infected. They had to be cleaned and bandaged at least daily by the dresser, who thus had a responsible position. The task, of course, was hardly pleasant. The dresser went his rounds with a tin plaster box containing bandages and implements for cleaning the wounds. He also handled routine cases in the outpatient department, pulling teeth, dressing wounds, or setting bones. The surgeon to whom Keats was assigned as dresser—at least for part of the time—was William Lucas, described by John Flint South, a fellow pupil of Keats, as a "tall, ungainly man, with stooping shoulders and a shuffling walk, as deaf as a post, not over-burdened with brains, but very good-natured and easy. His surgical acquirements were very small, his operations generally badly performed, and accompanied with much bungling, if not worse."

The mention of operations, which were daily witnessed by the students, can recall what they were like before the use of anesthetics. South himself gives a vivid account: the patient held down, often screaming with pain; the pupils packed in the operating theater, pressed from behind by others; the surgeon with hardly room to operate. There is a story told of Astley Cooper when he was about to operate on a child. The child, as it was lifted to the operating table, looked up at Cooper and smiled; and seeing the smile, Cooper turned aside and burst into tears.

3

Two accounts of Keats while he was at Guy's Hospital, both written over thirty years later, help to fill out what little we know of him at the age of twenty: one by Henry Stephens,[8] a fellow student who also shared rooms with Keats for several months, and another by George Felton Mathew, a languid, somewhat peevish youth with literary aspirations. Stephens, a direct, energetic man, became a successful physician by early middle age, and published two books on medical subjects. Having an inventive turn of mind, he also developed a popular ink.

---

previous fee in return for the services he will perform as a dresser. The following March 3 (1816) he is entered in the list of "Dressers to the Surgeons" for twelve months at the fee of £1.1.0.

8 Stephens' account was written as a letter to Mathew (March 1847), who had been trying to gather information for Milnes to use in his biography. It is printed in full in KC, II.206–214. Other remarks of Stephens' were published by Stephens' friend Sir Benjamin Richardson, in the *Asclepiad*, April 1884.

Stephens and another student, George Wilson Mackereth, shared lodgings in the same house in St. Thomas's Street where Keats lived with George Cooper and Frederick Tyrrell. At some time during Keats's first half-year at the Hospital (October 1815 to March 1816) , Cooper and Tyrrell finished their course and left. It was customary, as Stephens said, for "two or three students to hire a joint Sitting room and separate bed Rooms in the same House." Keats, "being alone, & to avoid the expense of having a Sitting room to himself, asked to join us, which we readily acceded to." A fourth student, named Frankish, also appears to have joined the group for a while.[9] In any room where Keats happened to be, he tended to sit at the window, looking out, "so that the window-seat was spoken of by his comrades as Keats's place." His two brothers visited him frequently: "They seemed to think their Brother John was to be exalted, & to exalt the family name." Stephens naturally felt that Keats was somewhat confined in his interests—meaning not only that Keats was much more interested in literature than in medicine but that he was ready to become quite argumentative in defense of his tastes in poetry, and may well have bruised Stephens' feelings in the process:

> Poetry was to his mind the zenith of all his Aspirations—The only thing worthy the attention of superior minds—So he thought—All other pursuits were mean & tame. He had no idea of Fame, or Greatness, but as it was connected with the pursuits of Poetry, or the Attainment of Poetical excellence. The greatest men in the world were the Poets, and to rank among them was the chief object of his ambition.—It may readily be imagined that this feeling was accompanied with a good deal of Pride and some conceit, and that amongst mere Medical students, he would walk, & talk as one of the Gods might be supposed to do, when mingling with mortals. This pride had exposed him, as may be readily imagined, to occasional ridicule, & some mortification,—
>
> Having a taste & liking for Poetry myself, though at that time but little cultivated, he regarded me as something a little superior to the rest, and would gratify himself frequently, by shewing me some lines of his writing, or some new idea which he had struck out. We had frequent conversation on the merits of particular poets, but our tastes did not agree. He was a great admirer of Spencer. His Fairy Queen was a great favorite with him, Byron was also in favor, Pope he maintained was no poet, only a versifier. I was fond of the bold, nervous & declamatory kind of Poetry. He was fond of Imagery, The

9 According to the daughter of Henry Stephens, Mrs. Martha Walsh (letter to Louis Holman, April 20, 1913; Holman mss., Harvard) .

most trifling Similes appeared to please him, Sometimes I ventured to show him some lines which I had written, but I always had the mortification of hearing them—condemned, indeed he seemed to think it presumption in me to attempt to head along the same pathway as himself, at however humble a distance.

If Stephens is to be taken at face value, Keats at this time was somewhat self-defensive "unless among those who were of his own tastes, & who would flatter him," as Stephens said Keats's brothers did. Hence when Stephens later took him to the country for a visit and stopped for a day or two at the home of some of his own friends, with whom Keats apparently had little in common, Keats failed to make a "favorable impression": "He could not well unbend himself & was rather of an unsocial disposition." Relations improved if the discussion could be turned to something besides poetry. For he was really "gentlemanly in his manners . . . a steady quiet and well behaved person"; and "when he condescended to talk upon other subjects he was agreeable & intelligent."

If Keats spoke unappreciatively of the verses Stephens wrote, he was more than repaid in kind by a friend named Newmarch, or possibly Newmarsh, a student at St. Bartholomew's Hospital who was also something of a classical scholar. Newmarch dropped in frequently, and would talk with Keats about classical poets. Stephens was not wholly displeased that when Keats

> showed Newmarch any of his Poetry it was sure to be ridiculed, and severely handled.—Newmarch was a light hearted, & merry fellow, but I thought he was rather too fond of mortifying Keats, but more particularly his brothers, as their praise of their Brother John amounted almost to idolitry, & Newmarsh & they frequently quarrelled.

By Keats's second half year at the Hospital, lectures had become less intimidating. During them, said Stephens, Keats would occasionally scribble some doggerel rhymes on his own syllabus or that of a friend. At least Stephens himself had one such specimen:

> Give me women, wine and snuff
> Until I cry out "hold enough!"
> You may do so sans objection
> Till the day of resurrection;
> For bless my beard they aye shall be
> My beloved Trinity.[10]

10 Stephens in his own account (*KC*, II.210) omits several words. The lines above, printed by Garrod, are from the leaf now in Trinity College, Cambridge. A

4

There were other friends outside the Hospital. For George had an enviable gift for getting to know people easily; and he quickly introduced his brother to them. Before the end of 1814 George had become acquainted with the Wylie family, which consisted of the widow of a marine officer, James Wylie; two sons, Henry and Charles; and a daughter, Georgiana, whom George Keats married in May 1818, before he left for America. By the later months of 1814 or early in 1815 George had also introduced John to Caroline and Anne Mathew, daughters of a yeast merchant, Felton Mathew, who lived in Goswell Street. At their house he soon met their cousin, George Felton Mathew (the son of Richard Mathew, a mercer in Oxford Street, with a house in Regent's Park), who became a friend of Keats for at least a year or two, and Mary Frogley, whom George Keats liked but who seems to have had something of a crush on John and secured copies of his poems through the good offices of George. Finally, it was George who introduced his brother to William Haslam, a young solicitor who was later to prove one of Keats's most dependable friends; and through Haslam, in the spring of 1816, Keats met Joseph Severn, who enters the Keats story so prominently near its close, and whose portraits of Keats—largely posthumous—are still reproduced.[11]

Despite his direct openness, Keats—at least for another two or three years—appears to have been shy in making acquaintances by himself.[12] With few exceptions, his friends came to him through George or Cowden Clarke, either directly or indirectly, and later

former student at St. Thomas's, Walter Cooper Dendy, who may possibly have still had some connection with it in 1815–16, wrote in his *Philosophy of Mystery* (1841) that "Even in the lecture-room of St. Thomas's, I have seen Keats in a deep poetic dream; his mind was on Parnassus with the muses. And here is a quaint fragment which he one evening scribbled in our presence, while the precepts of Sir Astley Cooper fell unheeded on his ear." The fragment, a prose account in pseudo-medieval spelling of Alexander meeting an Indian maid, is reprinted in Colvin, App. I. Dendy, who often mingled fact with fiction and later wrote an imaginary account of Keats and Hazlitt meeting at Box Hill, may possibly have made up the fragment himself. A summary of the circumstances is in Finney, I.90–91.

11 It is sometimes assumed that Haslam and Keats were schoolfellows. But this rests on a tentative statement of Charles Brown to Milnes years later (1841): "I believe they were schoolfellows" (*KC*, II.52). On Severn's portraits of Keats, see below, Chapter VI, section 4.

12 Cf. Keats's remark to George (October 14, 1818): "I know not how it is, but I have never made any acquaintance of my own—nearly all through your medium my dear Brother" (I.392).

through John Hamilton Reynolds. It was Clarke, for example, who later introduced him to Hunt (October 1816) and through Hunt Keats then quickly met Haydon and Reynolds. Within a few more months, Reynolds was to introduce him to most of the other friends he was to have—James Rice, Benjamin Bailey, the publishers Taylor and Hessey, and later Charles Brown and Charles Dilke. Yet, despite Keats's comparative reserve on first acquaintance, most of the people just mentioned preferred Keats to each other and to the majority of their other friends. A corollary interest is that the friends to whom he was most devoted, at one time or another, were, almost without exception, older than himself. Hunt was eleven years older, Haydon nine, and Clarke eight; his friendly publishers, Taylor and Hessey, fourteen and ten years older. For his other friends, a comparison of the year of their birth with that of Keats himself, 1795, quickly suggests the difference: Charles Brown, 1787; Richard Woodhouse, 1788; Charles Dilke, 1789; Benjamin Bailey, 1791; James Rice, 1792; Joseph Severn, 1793; and John Hamilton Reynolds, 1794. Of all who were really close to Keats, only his brothers and sister, possibly William Haslam, and Fanny Brawne (five years younger) were not older than himself. Felton Mathew was only a few months older, but he could hardly be called a close friend for any length of time. We need not dally with the interpretation that would see this as the need of the orphan for older people, though this may enter the picture. The principal explanation, of course, is that the entire career of Keats, after the summer of 1816, represents so rapid a development that— however unprecocious he had been as a child—he now took on one of the familiar qualities of the "gifted child": an instinctive predilection for older people, with whom he could share what was important to him, and who in turn were naturally abler to sense his promise.

5

George Felton Mathew has a fairly important place in what we can learn about Keats's life in 1815. This is not so much because of the short account of Keats he wrote for Monckton Milnes thirty years later: that tells us far more about Mathew than it does about Keats. But in Mathew Keats met, for the first time, someone who at least pretended to be a poet of sorts.

There now took place a comedy of enthusiasm, with most of the enthusiasm coming from Keats. Though Mathew's mental endowments were light, Keats at once invested him with every virtue of heart and imagination (together with the liberal political sentiments that Keats, from his acquaintance with Clarke, thought common to all literary men, but that Mathew actually disliked). Mathew's own verses must be seen to be believed. But fired and assured by this youth's pretensions, Keats wrote a poem to him a few months later (his verse letter "To George Felton Mathew," written in November 1815, patterned after the epistles of Michael Drayton) expressing his delight in this new poetic "brotherhood":

> Sweet are the pleasures that to verse belong,
> And doubly sweet a brotherhood in song.

At once he thinks of the partnership of the seventeenth-century dramatists, Beaumont and Fletcher. Everything "high, and great, and good" appears in the ideal exemplified by those "brother Poets":

> The thought of this great partnership diffuses
> Over the genius-loving heart, a feeling
> Of all that's high, and great, and good, and healing.

The phrase "the genius-loving heart" is crucial in what it tells of Keats, however mistaken he may be in assuming that Mathew shares the ideal. The poem continues with a plea—"Mathew lend thy aid"—that they may "humanity put on," "think on Chatterton" and "warm-hearted Shakespeare": "With reverence would we speak of all the sages." To Mathew's disgust ("He was of the . . . republican school," said Mathew thirty years later, "An advocate for the innovations which were making progress . . . A fault-finder with everything established. I, on the contrary, hated controversy"), Keats trots out the patriotic heroes of Cowden Clarke and Clarke's father:

> We next could tell
> Of those who in the cause of freedom fell;
> Of our own Alfred, of Helvetian Tell.

With excessive generosity, he ends by picturing Mathew as "Close to the source" of the Pierian Spring; and the final eighteen lines praise the wonders Mathew must know, the envied secret delight.

While attributing to Mathew ideals of his own or of John and Cowden Clarke, Keats did for a while actually catch some of

Mathew's own interests. The quiet, meditative care of the very first poems—"Imitation of Spenser," "On Peace," even "To Byron"— is replaced throughout the spring and summer of 1815 by verses of what Mathew called "sentiment," whether of the light complimentary sort or of a more earnest variety. The latter particularly appealed to Mathew, who was to praise the "Three Sonnets on Woman" as an example of what Keats might have continued to do had he not strayed from Mathew's influence and gone on to write such specimens of "unseemly hyperbole" as the sonnet "On First Looking into Chapman's Homer." Mathew was especially moved by the following lines:

> God! she is like a milk-white lamb that bleats
> For man's protection. Surely the All-seeing,
> Who joys to see us with his gifts agreeing,
> Will never give him pinions, who intreats
> Such innocence to ruin,—who vilely cheats
> A dove-like bosom.

But the jingling, anapestic quatrains of Tom Moore also appealed to Mathew and his cousins, and Keats was ready to oblige. When Mathew and the two girls went to the seaside during the summer of 1815, Anne and Caroline sent Keats a shell and a copy of Moore's "Golden Chain." Keats responded with two poems: one to the girls themselves ("To Some Ladies") and one, despite its title, to Mathew ("On Receiving a Curious Shell, and a Copy of Verses, from the Same Ladies"). Mathew is addressed as a knight, "valiant Eric," and the first sixteen lines consist wholly of rhetorical questions:

> Hast thou a steed with a mane richly flowing?
>   Hast thou a sword that thine enemy's smart is?
> Hast thou a trumpet rich melodies blowing?
>   And wear'st thou the shield of the fam'd Britomartis? [13]

During the preceding month or more, Keats had been reading the famous German poem *Oberon* (1780), by Wieland, in the transla-

[13] For Anne and Caroline, who wanted new words for a tune they liked, he wrote some more anapestic stanzas ("O come, dearest Emma, the rose is full blown"). Since it also survives in the scrapbook left by George Keats and his wife as "Stanzas to Miss Wylie," and begins, "O come, Georgiana," we can infer that George may have later used it when he began to court Georgiana Wylie. The following February, Keats did actually write a valentine (though in a different meter) for George to send to Mary Frogley, "Hadst thou liv'd in days of old." According to Richard Woodhouse, Keats wrote two other valentines on the same occasion. One may have been the sonnet, "Had I a man's fair form," possibly addressed to Mary Frogley or one of the Misses Mathew. See Finney, I.97–98.

tion by William Sotheby. Mathew may have introduced him to it; they probably read parts of it together. The poem struck Keats at once. As Werner Beyer has shown,[14] the echoes from *Oberon* begin with the "shell stanzas" and continue in Keats's poetry for another four years.

Mathew enjoyed his chivalric role as Sir Eric, as well as the leaping anapests, which he himself found easier to write than iambics. Mathew replied in verses "To a Poetical Friend," filled with phrases and images from Sotheby's translation of *Oberon*. The beginning catalogue illustrates his vein:

> Oh thou, who delightest in fanciful song,
> And tellest strange tales of the elf, & the fay;
> Of Giants tyrannic, whose talismans strong
> Have power to charm the fair ladies astray.
>
> Of courteous knights, & of high mettled steeds,
> Of forests enchanted, and marvellous streams,
> Of bridges, & castles, & desperate deeds,
> Of magical curses, & fair ladies' screams.

He ends by saying that Keats need not feel so disconsolate about the long hours at the Hospital, amid "Nature's decays," and the lack of opportunity to write verse. There is often spare time at night in which to write:

> When evening shall free thee from Nature's decays,
> And free thee from study's severest controul,
> Oh! warm thee in Fancy's enlivening rays,
> And wash the dark spots of disease from thy soul.

6

By the 1840's Mathew was struggling to support a family of twelve children on a small salary earned by working for the Poor Law Board. He would have been a somewhat touching figure had he not acquired an ingrown self-righteousness that makes his earlier sentimental affectations seem almost pleasant by contrast. Milnes, preparing his biography of Keats, discovered his whereabouts and wrote for information. Mathew's reply, asking for a few weeks' delay, shows the spirit in which his account was written a month later: we catch the self-congratulatory note ("It will always

[14] In his *Keats and the Demon King* (1947).

be a great pleasure . . . to remember that I at any time contributed to the happiness of his short life by introducing him to my
father's family, and exercising toward him hospitable intentions")
and also his ability to disguise, at least from himself, an obvious
resentment within a frame of kindly inquiry and interest: "Do you
happen to know whether George Keats is living, and in what part
of the world he is located?—his affection for his brother John was
really more remarkable than even his brother's poetic genius."
Mathew's long grudge may be explained partly by his awareness
that Keats, after Cowden Clarke reappeared on the scene and after
Keats came to know Hunt, Haydon, and others, had lost interest in
Mathew's own guidance. When Keats's first volume of poems appeared the following year, Mathew wrote a pettish review of them
for the *European Magazine,* singling out the worst poems—those
written during Keats's acquaintance with him—as "of superior
versification," and attacking most of the others for savoring too
much of "the foppery and affectation of Leigh Hunt." [15]

If these reservations are kept in mind, we can get some objective
impression, from Mathew's account, of Keats's character and interests at age nineteen and twenty. To begin with, we have Keats's
eager interest in language itself—in imagery and metaphor. To
Mathew, who equated poetry with outright sentiment, preferably
of the more languid sort, this imaginative interest seemed cold—
an attention to the "external decorations" rather than "the deep
emotions of the Muse." In addition to Keats's growing concern for
the medium of expression, which Mathew found "more critical
than tender," there is an indirect revelation of his virility, good
humor, and also a certain reserve—indirect because Mathew implies that these were limitations to the poetic temperament. An almost comic moment occurs as he speaks of Keats reading aloud.
Mathew thought tears and a broken voice appropriate. (Clarke
says that, in reading *Cymbeline,* "I saw [Keats's] eyes fill with
tears, and his voice faltered." But then they were reading Shakespeare; and Clarke, with whom Keats was reading, was not
Mathew, and had a far less restricted conception of poetry.)
Mathew states:

> His eye was more critical than tender, and so was his mind. He ad-
> mired more the external decorations than felt the deep emotions of

15 See Chapter IX, section 14.

the Muse. He delighted in leading you through the mazes of elaborate description, but was less conscious of the sublime and the pa-
thetic. He used to spend many evenings in reading to me, but I
never observed the tears in his eyes nor the broken voice which are
indicative of extreme sensibility. These indeed were not the parts of
poetry which he took pleasure in pointing out. Nevertheless he was
of a kind and affectionate disposition, and though his feelings might
not be so painful to himself, they would perhaps be more useful to
others.

Keats and I, though about the same age, and both inclined to literature, were in many respects as different as two individuals could
be. He enjoyed good health—a fine flow of animal spirits—was fond
of company—could amuse himself admirably with the frivolities of
life—and had great confidence in himself. I, on the other hand, was
languid and melancholy—fond of repose—thoughtful beyond my
years—and diffident to the last degree. But I always delighted in ad-
ministering to the happiness of others: and being one of a large
family, it pleased me much to see him and his brother George enjoy
themselves so much at our little domestic concerts and dances.[16]

Finally, Mathew reveals that the liberal political principles Keats
had imbibed at Enfield were still very much on his mind. Doubtless Keats's energy in espousing them now was quickened in opposition to the passive languor of Mathew. The republican expressions in his verse letter "To George Felton Mathew" may actually
have been a puckish attempt to tease Mathew. Their differences in
approaching poetry, said Mathew, were equaled by their variance on

the gravest subjects of human interest. He was not one who thought
it better to bear the ills we have, than fly to others which we know
not of. He was of the sceptical and republican school. An advocate
for the innovations which were making progress in his time. A fault-
finder with everything established. I, on the contrary, hated controversy and dispute—dreaded discord and disorder—loved the institu-
tions of my country—believed them founded in nature and truth
—best calculated to uphold religion and morality—harmonising on
the one hand with the Theocracy of heaven, and on the other with
the paternal rule at home. But I respected Keats' opinions, because
they were sincere.

[16] This and the other citations from Mathew are from his letter to Milnes (February 3, 1847), printed in *KC*, II.184–188; cf. II.180–181, 192, 202–204, 214–215, 240–
247. Cf. also J. M. Murry's perceptive essay on Mathew (*Studies in Keats* [1930],
Ch. I). For Mathew's use of the opportunity to appeal to the influence of Milnes
in securing a better position, an appeal repeated in four successive letters, see *KC*,
II.204, 215, 240–247.

Yet Mathew was "ever ready with some caution to repress the ardour of his temperament"; and "it is pleasing to recollect that while I had opportunity, I aided him to the utmost of my power." Mathew concludes this letter to Milnes—to be followed by others requesting help in finding a better job—by discussing Keats's verse epistle to himself and explaining the more complimentary remarks.[17]

7

By the spring of 1816, though he had been at the Hospital only since October, Keats began to think of taking the examination in July that would allow him to practice as an apothecary and surgeon. His fellow lodger, George Mackereth, was also intending to take it. Henry Stephens apparently decided to wait for another year. If Keats passed the examination, he need not begin practice at once. He could not in any case begin it until his twenty-first birthday, on October 31; and even after that he could perhaps satisfy Abbey for a while by simply remaining at the Hospital as a dresser and gaining experience. At the same time, with the examination out of the way, there would be less pressure to study and attend lectures (which began at eight in the morning and were staggered throughout the day, the last being at eight in the evening); and there would be more time left in which to try to write.

The thought of past poets increased its hold on his imagination. Far from intimidating him when he tried to write seriously, it gave him encouragement. In March he wrote a sonnet on the subject, one of his two or three best poems thus far, and felt satisfied

17 Mathew received a jolt when he wrote to his cousin Caroline (late 1846 or early 1847), who with Anne had left London long before (1819), for any information about Keats that he might pass on to Milnes. She had changed in thirty years far more than he. After saying she remembers that Keats met Mathew at their house, she goes on: "My recollection of those days is perhaps very different from yours, I cannot reflect on them with any degree of pleasure or satisfaction, they were worse than useless, and the idols we were then worshiping were self and the world . . . I never refer to them but to magnify the grace of God . . . in not having cut us off in the midst of those days of folly and in awakening both Ann and myself to a sense of our danger ere it was too late." As for Keats, if it were possible for him to return, surely "he would not direct our attention to his own works, beautiful as I believe many of them are," but to "that Book which . . . warns us to prepare for that awful day which it tells us will come as a thief in the night." The remainder of her letter is in the same admonitory vein, and concludes by expressing the hope that Mathew "may at the last great day be found among the happy number of those who have washed their robes" (KC, II.189–191).

enough with it to send it to Cowden Clarke.[18] But the real "test of invention," as he said a year later, is a "long Poem." This, of course, meant a narrative poem. The verse letter to Mathew, despite its length, was not the answer. If it turned out to be something of a prototype for much of Keats's writing throughout the next year, it was not through choice. When his experience failed to provide him with other subjects, it was always possible to write about poetry itself. The limitations of doing so were obvious, and his later struggle against them is a significant part of his development. The effort of trying to meet them also gradually opened unpredictable paths, and the sincerity of his preoccupation gave a further momentum. But the desire to face up to the demands of a narrative poem was already strong. Here the problem of finding a subject could not be avoided. And so harassing a problem was it, and so constant his frustration, that within another year the project into which he threw himself, with pent-up desperation, was nothing less than to "fill" four thousand lines of a narrative poem, however far he was from a clear idea of what to put in it.

In February 1816, Clarke's admired Leigh Hunt published his romance *The Story of Rimini*. Everything about it encouraged Keats to try an imitation. He was prepared to admire anything Hunt wrote, political or poetic. When he thought of longer poems, he was used to thinking of romances. Here was a romance. Yet it was modern in tone: its idiom was new; and the story moved briskly. In energy, dispatch, fluency, originality, it far excelled the verse of such writers as Mary Tighe and James Beattie. At the same time *Rimini* had the immense virtue for a model of seeming within the realm of possibility. The verse form, too, was familiar: Keats had used it, though far more cautiously than Hunt, back in November in his epistle to Mathew. Though he had written poems

18 How many bards gild the lapses of time!
  A few of them have ever been the food
  Of my delighted fancy,—I could brood
Over their beauties, earthly, or sublime:
And often, when I sit me down to rhyme,
  These will in throngs before my mind intrude:
  But no confusion, no disturbance rude
Do they occasion; 'tis a pleasing chime.
So the unnumber'd sounds that evening store;
  The songs of birds—the whisp'ring of the leaves—
The voice of waters—the great bell that heaves
  With solemn sound,—and thousand others more,
That distance of recognizance bereaves,
  Make pleasing music, and not wild uproar.

for less than two years, and principally only within the last six or eight months, he could justifiably feel that a quarter to a third of the lines he had written thus far could equal (as mere lines of verse) the average quality Hunt maintained.

8

In late spring he made a start, and put down sixty-eight lines of descriptive introduction to a tale, afterwards entitling it, when no story evolved, a "Specimen of an Induction to a Poem." He may, of course, have intended it as only a preliminary exercise before making an actual beginning. But this would have been unlike his usual practice, which was to plunge into a poem, see what evolved as he wrote it, and, if he was dissatisfied with the way it progressed, discard it.[19] He had no one to advise him persuasively of the advantages of blocking out a longer poem in advance. When, late in the summer, he was to set off to Margate in order to see what he could really do if he had free time, he had no definite plan in mind, but trusted to what the occasion might prompt; and it was because those weeks were free, and because he had no other work to blame as a distraction, that he felt, for the first time, rather frightened when nothing came. For *Endymion,* the following year, he did have a fable as a framework, but a thin one indeed for four thousand lines. Only with *Isabella* (in the spring of 1818) was his story clearly in mind in advance.

Given the large provision that the lack of subject would not paralyze effort—and it did not—two large advantages accrued throughout this apprenticeship. For one thing, the more prudential and cautionary lessons of writing were learned actively through self-discovery. They were earned acquisitions. Moreover, the need to develop incident through the actual process of writing also tended to develop the general fluency and the habit of readiness that proved so valuable later when discouragements, otherwise unnerving, rapidly increased. One thinks especially of his most productive year, beginning in September or October, 1818: one brother had left for America; the other was dying; Keats had returned from his northern walking tour with the ominous sore throat that gradually becomes worse from then on; the vicious personal attacks on *Endymion* were appearing. The opportunities for

[19] See his remark to Woodhouse, below, p. 234.

self-pity and paralysis were unrivaled. And yet the great poetry for which he has been preparing begins to appear steadily, month after month.

What he completed of his primitive "Specimen of an Induction" falls roughly into two parts, the first of which consists of variations on the opening lines:

> Lo! I must tell a tale of chivalry;
> For large white plumes are dancing in mine eye.
> Not like the formal crest of latter days:
> But bending in a thousand graceful ways.

A few lines later he begins again:

> Lo! I must tell a tale of chivalry;
> For while I muse, the lance points slantingly
> Athwart the morning air.

The images that cluster around his basic line—repeated once again ("Yet must I tell a tale of chivalry")—tend to be more vivid than the others: the line, significantly an expression of intention, may well have been the only specific detail he had in mind before he began.

Midway through the fragment it is plain that no tale is to come. The assertions begin to give way to the questionings, the self-doubt alternating with moments of hope or trust, that create the main interest of "Sleep and Poetry" eight or nine months later: "Ah! shall I ever tell . . . No, no! this is far off . . ." But then comes a suggestion of what, within less than two years, was to prove so unpredictably valuable—the trustful, imaginative approach to great writers of the past (the "genius-loving heart," to go back to the phrase in the epistle to Mathew) that Longinus advocated: "Spenser! thy brows are archèd, open, kind." Hence Keats does not call "so fearfully . . . on thy gentle spirit to hover nigh / My daring steps." (One thinks ahead to his remark to Haydon, a year later, after he set off to begin *Endymion:* "Is it too daring to Fancy Shakespeare this Presider?")

But after these confident lines, nothing remains to be said, at least at the moment. "Libertas" Hunt's *Rimini* still stands unrivaled, even unimitated. He has not even been able to catch the rapid slipper-shuffle of Hunt's versification: his own couplets in comparison are rather self-contained, even sedate. Keats has been overbold after all. Should Spenser be startled

that the foot of other wight
Should madly follow that bright path of light
Trac'd by thy lov'd Libertas; he will speak
And tell thee that my prayer is very meek;
That I will follow with due reverence,
And start with awe at mine own strange pretence.
Him thou wilt hear.

In "Calidore," over twice the length of the "Specimen of an Induction," Keats made a fresh start, possibly within a few days. This
time he definitely intended to complete a tale—or at least to get
some sort of action into the poem. Calidore, whose name Keats
takes from the *Faerie Queene,* is pictured as a youth whose knight-
hood is yet to win: the adventures, in other words, lie ahead and
will presumably be traced. Keats is now determined that there shall
be no delay in getting to the action; and in the very first line (recalling the start of the *Faerie Queene,* "A gentle knight was prick-
ing on the plaine") "Young Calidore is paddling o'er the lake."
Unfortunately, while he paddles, Calidore is also enjoying the scenery, and the door is immediately opened for description. Another
fifty lines pass before the action resumes. Then it returns in a burst
of incredible speed. Hearing a trumpet announcing the arrival of
friends at a castle across the lake, Calidore darts over the water,
dashes into the castle, and actually hops along the halls:

Nor will a bee buzz round two swelling peaches
Before the point of his light shallop reaches
Those marble steps that through the water dip:
Now over them he goes with hasty trip,
And scarcely stays to ope the folding doors:
Anon he leaps along the oaken floors
Of halls and corridors.

But then he hears horses arriving outside. Back at once into the
courtyard he springs. Two ladies have come. "What a kiss, / What
gentle squeeze he gave each lady's hand." Keats now, for a full
twenty-five lines, pauses to draw out the one characteristic of Hunt
he has been able to capture, aside from a more open, slangy couplet: the peculiar union of languor with a sort of twitching nervousness by which Hunt, in his love scenes, hoped to give dash and
verve to sentiment. While helping the ladies to dismount during
these twenty-five lines, "whisperings of affection" make Calidore
"delay to let their tender feet / Come to the earth." Moisture

touches his cheek: it may be dew, or it may be "tears of languishment." At all events, he "blesses" it with "lips that tremble," while the "soft luxury" nestles in his arms. Sir Clerimond appears and introduces Calidore to another knight, "the far-fam'd" Gondibert. They all go into the castle and sit down. Calidore burns to "hear of knightly deeds." Everyone looks placidly or smilingly at the others. Immediately evening comes: some lines are given to the song of the nightingale, the rising of the moon. Keats forgets to have his company served dinner. He ends abruptly: "Sweet be their sleep." The poem was then dropped and subtitled "A Fragment." The hundred and sixty lines were discouraging. Despite his efforts to start with action and maintain it, description was always breaking in and smothering it; and the attempt to bring action back resulted only in the ludicrous speed with which people moved when they did move.

9

If he was to write a longer poem of the kind he had in mind—or of any kind—he plainly needed more time than he had. Though nothing came of these first two attempts, the month of May brought some consolation. One of his poems was being published, and by Hunt himself in the *Examiner* (May 5) : the sonnet beginning "O Solitude! if I must with thee dwell," which he had written back in November when he first came to the Borough and, in the solitude in which he at first lived there, had thought by contrast of the open fields

> where the deer's swift leap
> Startles the wild bee from the fox-glove bell.

The sonnet had still seemed good enough to Keats in the spring to venture to send to Hunt, who knew nothing of Keats at this time.

He was naturally tempted now to write other versions of his first published poem, especially since it expressed a desire that was returning so strongly. The line in *Paradise Lost* (IX.445) , "As one who long in populous city pent," may often have struck home to him since he had come to the crowded Borough. With a slight adaptation of it he began a new sonnet in June. The line blends unobtrusively with the rest of the poem; and the final quatrain helps to neutralize the echo—by now very close—of the smiling,

offhand casualness of Hunt ("a debonair / And gentle tale of love
and languishment"—the tale referred to doubtless being Hunt's
own *Story of Rimini*).[20]

Three other poems of June and early July walk the same or
similar ground. From Charles Wells, a bouncing, red-haired youth
of seventeen, addicted to practical jokes, and a former schoolfellow
of Tom Keats, he received a gift of roses either as an impish tribute
to an aspiring poet, or as a peace offering, or as both.[21] Keats, at all
events, accepted them in good spirit, and thanked Wells in a sonnet ("To a Friend Who Sent Me Some Roses," June 29) where he
makes a point of saying that the gift suggests "friendliness un-
quell'd," and otherwise uses the opportunity for more descriptive
mention of countryside walks. Not until after Tom's death, when
he was going through his brother's papers, did he learn the details
of another prank begun by the precocious Wells within two or
three months after whatever led to the gift of the roses. Probably
with the help of an accomplice, Wells wrote Tom a series of long
letters supposedly from a girl, "Amena Bellafila," who had fallen
in love with Tom. Of the surviving letter (September 1816), part
is written in pseudo-Spenserian language with occasional echoes
of Keats's own less happy phrases.[22] Still another sonnet ("Oh! how

20 To one who has been long in city pent,
   'Tis very sweet to look into the fair
   And open face of heaven,—to breathe a prayer
Full in the smile of the blue firmament.
Who is more happy, when, with heart's content,
   Fatigued he sinks into some pleasant lair
   Of wavy grass, and reads a debonair
And gentle tale of love and languishment?
Returning home at evening, with an ear
   Catching the notes of Philomel,—an eye
Watching the sailing cloudlet's bright career,
   He mourns that day so soon has glided by:
E'en like the passage of an angel's tear
   That falls through the clear ether silently.
21 Richard Hengist Horne (author of *Orion*, 1843, and a student at Enfield when
Wells and the Keats brothers were there) said the roses were sent as an apology
after Wells had offended Keats; but he may possibly have confused the incident
with the later quarrel mentioned above. Wells, it should be added, became a friend
of Hazlitt, and wrote an imitation of Italian novelettes, *Stories after Nature* (1822),
and a poetic drama, *Joseph and His Brethren* (1823), to which no attention was
paid until it was resurrected by Rossetti.
22 Keats, when he learned what Wells had done, was convinced that the discovery of the hoax may have shaken Tom's health further. From the surviving letter
(Hewlett, pp. 377–381) it seems incredible that Tom should have been deluded. He
may not have been for long; and Keats, despondent after his brother's death as
well as piqued by the allusions to his own early verse, may have jumped too quickly

I love") pictures a rural "reprieve" from the Hospital during which he can also turn to poetry. But by this third rewriting of his published "Solitude" sonnet, Keats is sinking into flaccid repetition. Though he inserted the others in his first volume, he omitted this. Finally he jotted down some descriptive lines—perhaps fifty to a hundred—for a fourth poem, later expanded into the verses beginning "I stood tip-toe upon a little hill." They were suggested, Leigh Hunt later learned, "by a delightful summer-day, as [Keats] stood beside the gate that leads from the Battery on Hampstead Heath into a field by Caen Wood."

10

Cowden Clarke, who talked with Keats at this time, had been taking it for granted that he had entered his work at the Hospital quite voluntarily. Keats had hitherto refrained from making any complaint. But noting the "total absorption . . . of every other mood of his mind than that of imaginative composition, which had now evidently encompassed him," Clarke began to inquire more closely "what was his bias of action for the future." Keats then

> made no secret of his inability to sympathize with the science of anatomy, as a main pursuit in life; for one of the expressions that he used, in describing his unfitness for its mastery, was perfectly characteristic. He said, in illustration of his argument, "The other day, for instance, during the lecture, there came a sunbeam into the room, and with it a whole troop of creatures floating in the ray; and I was off with them to Oberon and fairyland." And yet, with all his self-styled unfitness for the pursuit, I was afterwards informed that at his subsequent examination he displayed an amount of acquirement which surprised his fellow-students.[23]

And Clarke goes on to emphasize the clarity and "technical precision" with which Keats could talk of surgery if he chose.

The thought of getting away from the Borough for at least a while was indeed becoming obsessive. His impatience to get away

---

to the conclusion he did. On the parody of Keats's phrases (e.g., "& thou shouldst wear the Sword that the high Britomartis wielded" echoing Keats's "And wear'st thou the shield of the fam'd Britomartis" in the lines to Mathew quoted above), see Gittings, pp. 120–122. Until Tom's death Keats and Wells were on good terms, despite Wells's bumptious manner. Keats inserted the sonnet to Wells in his *Poems* (1817), and gave him a copy of the book with a gently pointed inscription: "From J. K. to his young friend Wells."

[23] *Recollections,* pp. 131–132.

might take the form—as in the sonnets he had been writing—of nostalgia for the countryside. This was understandable. Most of his life since he was eight had been spent in or near it. Of course if he went to the country he would be alone. But there was no alternative if he really wanted to write. To move in with George and Tom over Abbey's countinghouse was hardly the solution: it was crowded, noisy, distracting; and Abbey would be hanging over him. In any case, loneliness was not at the moment what was uppermost in his mind.

An Adventure in Hope

✻❦✻❦✻❦✻❦✻❦✻❦✻❦✻❦✻❦✻❦✻❦✻❦✻❦✻❦✻❦✻❦✻❦❦

Summer 1816

ON JULY 25, 1816, Keats went to Apothecaries' Hall and took the examinations that would allow him, as soon as he was twenty-one, to practice as an apothecary.[1]

Almost immediately afterwards he left for the coastal town of Margate, about seventy miles southeast of London. He would be twenty-one by the end of the following October. Except for more fortunate youths who had gone on to a university, most men of his age and position would either have made a start in a trade or would be preparing to do so in a profession. Keats, of course, had himself been preparing for such a start for almost five years; he had even finished his examinations at Apothecaries' Hall before time. He could hardly think of poetry as a real alternative. The few poems he had composed amounted to nothing. On the other hand, he had two months or so that were completely free; he could not practice as apothecary or surgeon anyway until October 31, when he came of age. Abbey was willing to advance him enough to take a vacation during this interlude.

He doubtless selected Margate because he had heard of it as a resort and because it was on the sea. It would be altogether new. But he could scarcely be expected to know what a fashionable sea resort was like; and Margate had become just that, though the population was still little more than six thousand. Along the shore were seven "Bathing Rooms." From these rooms, as a guide book of the year before states, one entered the four-wheeled "bathing machines" that were "afterwards driven out two or three hundred yards into the sea, under the conduct of careful guides. There is a

---

[1] The entry in the Register of Apothecaries' Hall is printed in Lowell, I.154. The list of successful candidates was published at the end of the year in the *London Medical Repository*, VI (1816) , 345. Keats was one of seventy-one. Keats's examiner was Everard Brande, brother of the famous chemist, William Thomas Brande (Hale-White, p. 32) .

door in each bathing machine, which being opened the bathers
descend into the water, by means of a ladder: an umbrella being, at
the same time, let down to the surface of the water, which conceals them from public view." [2] A theater had been built in 1787.
Wherever Keats may have stayed, the high ground above the
town to the north, which was noted for its extensive views, was
plainly one of the spots he most frequented.

After unpacking his books and taking his first look around, he
quickly became homesick and thought of his brothers. Without
doubt he wrote to them, if only to tell them where he was, and to
encourage Tom to visit him. Probably because Tom came within
two weeks or so to join him for at least a while, he addressed the
two poems he wrote during August (or at least the only two that
we know he wrote) to his brother George—a sonnet and a long
verse letter (of 142 lines) written in couplets.

The sonnet "To My Brother George" is perhaps the best that
Keats had yet written. He is not now writing to Byron, whom he
has never seen and does not at this point even begin to understand.
He is not writing an exercise on an abstraction, as in the sonnet
"On Peace." Instead the Margate sonnet is closer to the two descriptive sonnets ("O Solitude" and "To one who has been long in
city pent") written in reaction to the crowded alleys of the Borough and the traffic on London Bridge. The difference is that it is
not nostalgia for the remembered countryside of Middlesex that
now stirs him but an immediate, new experience, though an experience of limited possibilities. The first line is typical—"Many the
wonders I this day have seen." And then follows, with cleaner economy of phrase than the earlier sonnets show, a quick list of sights:
the sunrise at Margate, the ocean with all it suggests (its "vastness,"
"Its ships, its rocks, its caves, its hopes, its fears," and its "mysterious" power to suggest the past and the future). The closing six
lines, attempting to make a neat, conventional break from the preceding octave, turn to the night in which he is writing—obviously
lonely—and then end:

> But what, without the social thought of thee,
> Would be the wonders of the sky and sea?

[2] *Crosby's Complete Pocket Gazetteer* (1815), pp. 324–325. Cf. the more detailed
description in Edward Brayley, *The Beauties of England and Wales* (1808),
VIII.956–966.

2

In all the poetry written at Margate we note a deliberate attempt to find a subject. Subjects do not crowd into his head; and of course there is no reason why they would. With the natural hope that two months of leisure time would now give him the chance to try himself, and with the confidence that change of place could excite him to effort or at least free him from the clog of habitual and stale associations, he is at last in a position where, as he might very well feel, he would have only himself to blame if he could not produce something. Margate might offer some new subjects. But once he had enumerated the "wonders," he began to discover that the possibilities of mere enumerative description are limited. One thinks ahead to the doggerel verses he wrote his young sister Fanny from Scotland two years later (July 3, 1818), some of which we have already noticed. The verses end:

> There was a naughty Boy,
>   And a naughty Boy was he,
> He ran away to Scotland
>   The people for to see—
>   There he found
>   That the ground
>   Was as hard,
>   That a yard
>   Was as long,
>   That a song
>   Was as merry,
>   That a cherry
>   Was as red—
>   That lead
>   Was as weighty,
>   That fourscore
>   Was as eighty,
>   That a door
>   Was as wooden
>   As in England—
>   So he stood in
>   His shoes and he wonder'd,
>   He wonder'd
>   He stood in his
>   Shoes and he wonder'd.

The real task at Margate was still ahead of him, and as the days passed he began to get a little frantic. This brave trip, carrying with it a hope we can all understand, had a special urgency in his case: it was a decisive time for Keats, or at least it could be. A sense of urgency may stimulate, of course, but it can also paralyze. It particularly tends to paralyze if we lack a fairly clear goal. Invention does not spring from a vacuum; the friction of specific contexts and aims is usually necessary. To change the metaphor: if we have no harbor in mind, as Coleridge said, then no wind can seem favorable. And the mere general ideal of "writing poetry" is not a harbor. It could—and perhaps should—involve going in many directions. Hence, as Keats said a month later in the verse letter he wrote to Cowden Clarke,

> With shatter'd boat, oar snapt, and canvass rent,
> I slowly sail, scarce knowing my intent;
> Still scooping up the water with my fingers.

Inevitably, therefore, the poetry Keats now wrote at Margate turned upon poetry itself—turned upon the vocation of writing poetry, its justifications and its aims. Moreover, it is poetry about trying to write poetry, as though he were unconsciously trying to tie down the ideal he has in mind. Significantly, the poems he was now to compose, before returning to London, were two epistles, first to his brother George (written in August), and then to Cowden Clarke (written in September). It is virtually impossible for anyone to write successfully without at least some imaginary audience in mind. We are gregarious animals, and we cannot, while sane, talk about urgent matters solely to ourselves. So young and untried a poet was particularly in need of this imagined audience. Hence he addresses his first poem to one of the two closest members of his family—the oldest (aged 19) other than himself—and then his second poetic letter to the bluff, kindly, rather confused man who had helped him just before he left school and especially in the lonely years in Edmonton. Without them—or without someone like them—he would probably have been unable to write very much, if at all, in this brave excursion to Margate.

3

After the first breathless sonnet to his brother—the catalogue of "wonders"—the epistle "To My Brother George" reveals the true state of affairs. It begins with a rather frank confession, the first line echoing in reverse the first line of his sonnet ("Many the wonders") :

> Full many a dreary hour have I past,
> My brain bewilder'd, and my mind o'ercast
> With heaviness.

The bewilderment, the despair, arise from the fear that nothing "could e'er be caught" from these new surroundings. He could look at the sky to "the far depth where sheeted lightning plays," or lie on this grass, so removed from the crowded alleys near Guy's Hospital, and, with the stars above, "strive to think divinely." But nothing much leaps to mind, and he is beginning to fear that this long-anticipated change will never produce anything after all (he has doubtless spent a good week or two in waiting) —that he will "never hear Apollo's song," that the country sights will "never teach a rural song to me."

The verse letter falls roughly into four parts. The first, as we noticed, disarmingly presents his situation to his friendly audience, and thus gives him a subject of sorts. The second now summarizes remarks about poetry that he had read or heard Clarke make: that a poet may see "wonders strange." He is able to fill forty-seven lines here. (Keats would be the first to allow the frankness of the expression; he was soon to speak of the desirability, as a "test" of invention, of being forced to "make 4000 Lines of one bare circumstance [in *Endymion*] and fill them with Poetry.") To envision "wonders strange"—a possibility confirmed by no less an authority than Leigh Hunt, alias "Libertas" ("For knightly Spenser to Libertas told it") —provides "the living pleasures of the bard." But what of the benefits the "bard" can bestow on posterity? Having launched this third theme, Keats pictures a dying poet who, throughout thirty-nine lines, sees that his verses will benefit mankind in every way. The political liberalism that the epistle "To George Felton Mathew" had already mingled with mythological and neoclassic elements now re-emerges. The "patriot" is fired by poetry and by means of it is brought, "in the senate," to

> thunder out my numbers
> To startle princes from their easy slumbers.
> The sage will mingle with each moral theme
> My happy thoughts sententious.

And, as a sort of icing to the cake, there will also be "lays" to warm the lover, or to read to the child; and, dying, the poet can rejoice

> while thus I cleave the air,
> That my soft verse will charm thy daughters fair,
> And warm thy sons!

This is a far cry from the powerful questionings raised three
years later, in the *Fall of Hyperion*. There the poet is altogether
on the defensive, and a sense of the urgent simplicities of experience cuts through everything else:

> What benefit canst thou do, or all thy tribe,
> To the great world? Thou art a dreaming thing.

But given such questionings at the start, nothing would have been
done at all. Johnson mentions how close all of us are, especially
writers, to Don Quixote—exaggerating and coloring both importance and rewards, and living in the future: "our hearts inform us
that he is not more ridiculous than ourselves, except that he *tells*
what we have only thought." "The natural flights of the human
mind are not from pleasure to pleasure, but from hope to hope."
But on the other hand, as Johnson reminds us, few enterprises
would ever be undertaken unless we could magnify the importance
of what we are doing and imagine the extent to which it might
"fill the minds of others." If only, says Keats in this poem, he could
smother his "mad ambition," he would be happier. He realizes that
the ambition is "mad": he has done nothing before, and to his own
mind is doing nothing very important now. He is not only being
modest but trying to accept fact when he says to George:

> As to my sonnets, though none else should heed them,
> I feel delighted, still, that you should read them.

And here in Margate he can at least say that there has been a
"calm enjoyment" in "scribbling lines for you." The fourth part of
the letter (lines 123–142) echoes the sonnet ("E'en now, dear
George, while this for you I write") ; it begins:

> E'en now I'm pillow'd on a bed of flowers
> That crowns a lofty cliff, which proudly towers
> Above the ocean-waves.

And from here to its close, seventeen lines later, the poem is essentially a rewriting, in couplet form, of the "Many the wonders" sonnet to his brother.

4

The reason for lingering on this crucial poem is that now, for the first time, we are at least touching on the central problem that Keats himself increasingly faced. Granted, the problem was to become far more complex within another three years, and his sense of it far more perceptive, even clairvoyant. But however elementary the considerations are at the start, the problem is all of a piece.

With all his frank misgivings, and with virtually no other subject than how it feels to lack subjects, Keats still manages to make a breakthrough of sorts. It is the kind of breakthrough that he was to make constantly throughout his career, and as an example has some relevance to the whole poetic effort of the past two centuries. For the primary inspiration of this virile, relatively unbookish poet is intensely literary—the ideals, the criteria, the experience (what little he has) . The inevitable corollary is the sense by contrast of how little he himself has to offer. This is the fearful legacy that the great writers of the eighteenth century had seen coming to themselves and, even more, to their successors. The burdens of government, as Pliny said, become more oppressive to princes when their predecessors are great. We shall be coming back increasingly to this large, often paralyzing embarrassment, which accompanied the rise of romanticism, which intimidated the Victorian poet, and which was to threaten the vitality and range of poetry even more in the twentieth century. The embarrassment is that the rich accumulation of past poetry, as the eighteenth century had seen so realistically, can curse as well as bless. So, in a moment of despondency two years later, Keats was to tell his friend Richard Woodhouse that he felt "there was now nothing original to be written in poetry; that its riches were already exhausted,—& all its beauties forestalled." [3]

Whether we want it or not, the massive legacy of past literature is ours. We cannot give it away. Moreover, it increases with each generation. Inevitably, we must work from it, and often by means of it. But even if we resist paralysis and do try to work from and by means of it, the question at once arises, does the habitual (and almost sole) nourishment of the imagination by the great literature of the past lead to the creation of more poetry of equal value?

[3] I.380.

As Hazlitt said, the Aristotelian *katharsis* of tragedy "substitutes an artificial and intellectual interest for real passion"; and, if so, then

> Tragedy, like Comedy, must therefore defeat itself; for its patterns must be drawn from the living models within the breast, from feeling or from observation; and the materials of Tragedy cannot be found among a people, who are the habitual spectators of Tragedy, whose interests and passions are not their own, but ideal, remote, sentimental, and abstracted. It is for this reason chiefly, we conceive, that the highest efforts of the Tragic Muse are in general the earliest; where the strong impulses of nature are not lost in the refinements and glosses of art.[4]

Keats, to whom Hazlitt's critical insights were one of the "three things to rejoice at in this Age," [5] was to feel such apprehensions only too keenly. For the moment, we are only stressing that, much as Keats might wish to face common experience imaginatively and vividly throughout the next three years, his principal impetus, like that of most poets of the past century, was literary; and that still—with all the liabilities that this self-consciousness might imply—he managed to make headway, and at a sure pace. The magnetic appeal of Keats to every later poet is that somehow the dilemma is constructively put to use.

During Keats's two months at Margate, what he attempted could seem to an older poet refreshingly easy. His first large effort, after all, is written only to his young brother of nineteen, working in a countinghouse in Pancras Lane: the audience is far from unfriendly or sophisticated. In the poem he merely sets down his despair, his self-admonitions, his self-encouragements about poetry, or what he thinks is poetry; and many of the ideas have come from people like Leigh Hunt or Cowden Clarke. Finally, he concludes the poem by simply going back and, in effect, redoing his "Many the wonders" sonnet to his brother. Yet given the facts that he had written so little before, that he had no real subject, and that this deliberate, self-conscious trial could have had an immensely intimidating effect on invention, he had still written a poem of some size. "Did our great Poets," as he said two years later (October 28, 1817), "ever write short pieces?" The suppositions behind this question were to remain with him until the end. Now, however, he had filled one hundred and forty-two lines. One of the two or three greatest critics of modern times would have immediately un-

4 "On Modern Comedy," final paragraph.   5 I.203.

derstood the achievement. In speaking of his somber, powerful poem, "The Vanity of Human Wishes," which, as Sir Walter Scott said, "has often extracted tears from those whose eyes wander dry over pages professedly sentimental," Johnson admitted that, as he wrote, he ran his finger down the margin to count the number of lines completed and the number he had yet to do.

5

Encouraged by the achievement, Keats naturally, while the iron was hot, struck again, and in September wrote the verse letter "To Charles Cowden Clarke" mentioned earlier. This letter is, in a sense, a redoing of the epistle to his brother, this time with far less anxiety. The descriptive verve that we find primarily at the end of the epistle to George now begins this letter. The poem has at least two other obvious qualities that the verse letter of the previous month lacks. Though Keats may trot out, for the third time, references to

> the patriot's stern duty;
> The might of Alfred, and the shaft of Tell,

and interplay them with various allusions from the coyer corners of classical mythology, he has here a better opportunity for a gymnastic exercise in concreteness. He is able to be more specifically concrete, that is, about what really presses upon his mind: the poetry he has read—poetry that Clarke has also read, and in fact first showed him. Hence the new felicity of phrase, as in

> Spenserian vowels that elope with ease,
> And float along like birds o'er summer seas;

or in the lines cited before:

> Who read for me the sonnet swelling loudly
> Up to its climax and then dying proudly?
> Who found for me the grandeur of the ode,
> Growing, like Atlas, stronger from its load?

In addition to this possibility of concreteness (however literary) there is also a personal drama which, however undeliberately, is being used. It is the personal—but, by implication, universally relevant—drama of the discovery that there are open doors—doors that, as we mentioned, Clarke had helped to open for him. Exactly this same sense was to recur vividly in the sonnet, written only a few weeks later, "On First Looking into Chapman's Homer."

6

It remains to speak briefly of the more external qualities of style that we find in these two verse essays, and to some extent in the poetry of the following year. What matters to our purpose at the moment is that Keats should have been so much attracted to writing in longer, non-lyric forms. No poet of his period—perhaps no poet since Milton—was to match Keats in the more massive, richly laden forms of the lyric. Yet at the very time he wrote the odes, and even more in the months that followed, he was moving, at least in hope, toward what the eighteenth century called the "greater genres"—above all the poetic drama. And even at the start, in the year of which we are speaking and the year after, he felt the need for a larger form than the lyric. The need was not, of course, sophisticatedly felt or expressed at this point. But there was a pressing sense of the scope of past poetry, and the problem of what one is to do with that challenge; and the presence of lengthy, talky forms (such as the verse letter, inherited from the sophisticated, self-conscious writers of the previous century) was a boon.

So energetically has Keats's craftsmanship been studied during the past half century that no one can hope to imitate the biographies of a generation ago—those of Sir Sidney Colvin and Amy Lowell—and offer in a biography what he feels to be a detailed or capacious discussion of Keats's stylistic development at every stage. Only the barest summary is possible. This is particularly so when we are concentrating on the various styles of Keats's early verse— the poetry written before his great Miltonic fragment, *Hyperion,* which in the autumn of 1818 ushers in his most productive year. For the earlier poetry, by and large, is rather remote in idiom and versification from the more serious interests of the twentieth century. The poetry of Leigh Hunt, and of others who served as a model to the early Keats, means little to most of us. In fact, to the early twentieth century it typified almost everything that poetry should avoid: looseness, sentimentality, escapism, and obviousness of idiom. But there is a perennial relevance, at a higher critical level; and from that level mere differences of idiom—in poetry of such limited quality—appear less significant ("nothing," as Sainte-Beuve said, "so much resembles a hollow as a swelling") .

For most beginning poets, the fashionable models—at least among their own contemporaries—have usually been no better than those followed by Keats, however different they might be in kind. It is exactly this common experience, and Keats's ability to move through and beyond it, that lends interest to his early poetic style or styles. For as soon as the tepid, juvenile poems in later-eighteenth-century forms are finished, one principal characteristic of his early writing, from now through *Endymion* in 1817, is the extent to which he tries to exploit one device after another in order to depart from the various eighteenth-century norms of style. He does almost everything that Hunt does, but he carries it further. In a sense, the sort of style that Hunt and his school adopted is analogous to the more routine attempts of the early twentieth century to be as unlike the Victorians or Edwardians as possible. In every major transition of poetic style, there are side-skirmishes—often indistinguishable from the main battle—where the procedure is essentially negative. The ideal of poetry becomes, at least in part, the reverse of what was conventional fifty years before. Throughout the later eighteenth century, slow, massively indirect changes had taken place. But Hunt and his followers still fought against Pope, and, as usual in such cases, the dispute was largely about trivia. One thinks of Johnson's remark about Thomas Warton—that by saying "evening gray" instead of "gray evening," Warton thought something was gained: "that not to write prose is certainly to write poetry." In the present case what most interests the student of poetic styles is that Keats shared, at the start, what every youthful poet begins with if he is writing in an era of militant transition, a procedure largely negative; that he did so with gusto, at least by the time he wrote "Sleep and Poetry" and *Endymion;* that he became increasingly positive, and inevitably creative; and that within another year and a half—by the autumn of 1818—he had almost completely transcended the parochialism with which he began.

7

Any discussion of the early poetic style, or styles, of Keats—however perfunctory—must linger for a moment on Leigh Hunt, though the influence of Hunt on the early Keats has long been one of the elementary clichés in the history of English poetry. Many other influences, needless to say, are clear in Keats's early verse.[6] The sonnets, except for a trace here and there of Milton, tend to follow recent models—the later eighteenth-century sonneteers generally. The longer poems in heroic couplets, especially the verse letters, jump the eighteenth century and go back to the late sixteenth and early seventeenth centuries: they show his reading in Michael Drayton's epistles and William Browne's *Britannia's Pastorals*.

But the major influence on much of the poetry before the summer of 1816, and especially on the poetry from this summer at Margate through *Endymion* and the poetry of 1817, is still that of Hunt. And because it was not just a literary influence in the ordinary sense of the term, but something psychologically more important, we linger on it for the moment, though our concern is primarily with the life of Keats. In at least one way it is analogous to the later influence of Milton and Shakespeare (and in a way that the influence of Spenser, for example, was not—however strong it might have been in other respects) ; for it had a great deal to do with encouraging him to write—with giving him an active model, felt empathically, with which for a while he was creatively identified. In this respect, the influence of Hunt was obviously valuable.

That Hunt's unpleasing mannerisms are found everywhere in Keats's early verse is no real misfortune. It is common to say that they disfigure it. But this implies that the early poetry of Keats could stand by itself—that we should be returning to it even if it were not by Keats; that it is good enough in its own right so that we could feel it to be "disfigured" by these mannerisms. Fundamentally we must evaluate influences to the degree that they release energies, and allow one to go ahead on one's own feet. It is thus that most teachers are ultimately judged. The enormous benefit Keats derived from Hunt was that Hunt as a model did not inhibit but in fact encouraged fluency. Moreover, he was a model who could in time be surpassed—something, in other words, was left to the powers of the student. Granted, he encouraged a certain excess in the youthful Keats; but, as Johnson said, "excess" is usu-

6 The most extensive study is still that of C. L. Finney, I.28–322. More specialized studies would include Werner Beyer, *Keats and the Daemon King* (1947) , and, on versification, *Stylistic Development*, Pt. I.

ally preferable to "deficiency." For it is easier "to take away super-
fluities than to supply defects"; "timidity is a disease of the mind
more obstinate and fatal"; and he who "has passed the middle
point . . . is a fairer object of hope, than he who fails by falling
short." Keats himself was to say much the same in speaking of his
leap "headlong into the sea" when he wrote *Endymion,* through
which he learned more than if he had "stayed upon the shore" and
taken "tea and comfortable advice."

At the time that he wrote his three epistles, to Mathew, to
George, and to Clarke, Keats had not met Leigh Hunt. But back
at Enfield the liberal John Clarke had taken the *Examiner;* he and
his son, as we have noted, were admirers of Hunt; and the first
poem Keats showed Cowden Clarke was the sonnet "Written on
the Day that Mr. Leigh Hunt Left Prison." A confidence counterbalanced his shyness when he handed him the sonnet, for a common liberalism was taken for granted in the young Keats and his
mentor, Clarke. A year and a half after writing that sonnet, when
he was at last to meet Hunt, the admiration was solidified by personal friendliness; and the first volume of Keats's poems was to be
dedicated to Hunt. Something of Hunt's poetic style is illustrated
by the way in which he went through life in other respects. A picturesque—and probably an unfair because extreme—example is
what happened when he was sent to prison for the attacks in the
Examiner on the Prince Regent. Hunt was allowed to have his wife
and children with him, and was visited by sympathetic artists and
writers. He was also allowed his library; and he put it to good use,
devoting much of his time to translating the Italian poets. Spending far more than he could afford, he had the walls of his prison
room covered with paper picturing roses twined about trellises; the
ceiling of this artificial bower was painted to look like the sky. The
small adjoining yard was turned into a flower garden. There was a
Micawberlike quality about Hunt, especially in his earlier years,
and the good cheer, the jaunty optimism, carried over into his
poetic style. Because of it, the plaintive sentimentality that had
been common in English poetry—and usually found only in more
languid temperaments—is given a novel manner by Hunt. Languor and sentiment become brisk; they are shown in rapid magic-
lantern slides with colloquially phrased commentary to accompany
them. Pastoral conventions from the seventeenth-century Spenserians, chivalric images and sentiments from the Italian romances, are

in the *Story of Rimini* put into heroic couplets that consciously try to by-pass the closed couplets of Pope. Varied pauses, feminine and double rhymes, any variation that was not common in Pope, stud the verse.

Hunt's aim, in short, was deliberate sentiment put with easy sprightliness. Hence the coy terms ("a clipsome waist," "with tip-toe looks," "with thousand tiny hushings") ; the distinctive way in which he makes adjectives of verbs ("scattery light") , or adjectives of nouns ("flamy heart's-ease," "One of thy hills gleams bright and bosomy") ; adverbs made from participles ("crushingly," "trem-blingly") ; and the other mannerisms that Keats took over and used far more excessively than Hunt. There are also the stock words, usually nouns ("luxury") or adjectives ("The birds to the *deli-cious* time are singing") . Finally there is what one can only call a certain would-be smartness that comes in the attempt to be collo-quial, and is most glaring when the subject is serious. An example from the *Story of Rimini* is always quoted. Francesca's father knew that, though she was

> prepared
> To do her duty, where appeal was barred,
> She had stout notions on the marrying score.

Two other couplets will quickly illustrate the tone:

> He kept no reckoning with his sweets and sours;—
> He'd hold a sullen countenance for hours
>
> .   .   .   .   .   .
>
> He read with her, he rode, he went a-hawking,
> He spent still evenings in delightful talking.

We are not, of course, concerned with a rounded estimate of Hunt—even if this were possible in a page or two. We are merely noticing quickly those aspects of style that spread through the early verse of Keats more energetically than they ever did in Hunt, and that had this large value: they gave him a vocabulary, an idiom, that permitted him to be fluent, and then, in the process of being fluent, to become constructively self-critical and increasingly self-directive. There are the *y*-ending adjectives, far more even than in Hunt ("lawny," "sphery," "bloomy," "surgy") ; the adverbs made from participles ("cooingly," "lingeringly") ; the favorite words, but with more of a tendency—caught from George Chapman—to use abstract nouns than we find in Hunt ("languishment," "soft ravishment"); the use of what Hunt would call "luxuries" as stock props ("Pink robes and wavy hair"; the "soul" being "lost in pleasant smotherings"). And as for the jaunty, colloquial smartness, there are plenty of similar examples in the pupil, from the early "Three Sonnets on Woman" ("God! she is like a milk-white lamb that bleats") through the writing of *Endymion* and even *Isabella*.

8

It is in versification that Keats's relation to Hunt, from the early couplets through *Endymion,* is most surprising. For it is one of the most graphic examples in literary history of a pupil's imitating not what the master actually did so much as what the master intended to do.

The same empathic quickness of mind that enabled Keats, when he turned to Milton, to grasp the essence of Milton's versification, and to write, within little more than two months, the most genuinely Miltonic verse since Milton himself, here adhesively identified itself with the hope and purpose of Hunt. For until Hunt's *Story of Rimini* appeared, in February 1816, Keats had no actual model for handling the couplet in the way Hunt had been advocating; and even the *Story of Rimini* was only a mild exercise in what Hunt had been theoretically preaching. In the *Feast of the Poets,* Hunt had devoted far more space to the notes than to the poem; and the message of these notes was the need to pry open the couplet as it was used by Pope, and, in effect, to do everything that Pope had avoided. In the poetry of 1816 and the next year, Keats followed the prescription to an extent that may have been contemplated by Hunt but was never practiced by him.[7] The one respect in which Keats did actually duplicate his model was in the use of the caesura.[8] This was always to be the case in Keats's use of models; it tells us something about his remarkable awareness of pace in poetry. Hunt attacked Pope for putting the pause so frequently after the fourth or fifth syllable:

See! from the brake (x) the whirring pheasant springs,	(4th syllable)
And mounts exulting (x) on triumphant wings:	(5th syllable)
Short is his joy; (x) he feels the fiery wound,	(4th syllable)
Flutters in blood, (x) and panting beats the ground.	(4th syllable)

7 *Stylistic Development,* pp. 19–23, 196–197.
8 *Ibid.,* pp. 13–15, 26–28, 203–209.

The practice obsessed Hunt. Mainly because of Pope's "want of variety" in pause, Hunt regarded him "not only as no master of his art, but as a very indifferent practiser, and one whose reputation will grow less and less." Hunt himself made a point of using a pause later in the line, preferably after a weak syllable—

> The throng of life has strengthened (x) without harm;
> You know the rural feeling, (x) and the charm—

and this gave a falling, sometimes limp, cadence to the line. A few lines from Keats's sonnet, "To one who has been long in city pent," will also illustrate the effect:

> Returning home at evening, (x) with an ear
> Catching the notes of Philomel,— (x) an eye
> Watching the sailing cloudlet's (x) bright career.

Versification is far less interesting to the early and middle twentieth century than it was to the eighteenth and early nineteenth centuries. If we become technical about style now, we concentrate merely on metaphor and imagery, and then relax our pretentious analytic rigor. But the style of the romantic poets—not only the greater ones but even writers like Hunt—cannot be considered apart from the interest in versification that became so strong in English poetry and criticism after the middle of the eighteenth century. This is especially true of Keats, who within two or three years was to develop a theory of vowel interplay that anticipates far more exclusively formalistic poets of a much later date.

9

In these brief remarks about style we have naturally been anticipating. We know in advance that Keats was to become a poet—and a poet of the first rank; and our rapid notice of the style has inevitably carried us ahead through the following year. But Keats himself, of course, was anything but certain of this in September 1816, when he left Margate and returned to the Borough and Guy's Hospital. The fortunate experiences of the next two or three months were needed to give him confidence.

Yet if he went to Margate as an adventure in hope, it was already ending in commitment; and the experiences that followed, in the autumn of 1816, were as fruitful as they were only because of the momentum already generated. Even the first sight of the sea was to remain as an active association with discoveries and beginnings. A half year later, in his next important trial, he again went off—this time to the Isle of Wight—in order to find out whether he could begin *Endymion,* a poem with which he needed to leap "headlong into the Sea" in order to learn "the soundings, the quicksands, & the rocks." He felt unable to write. He was "all in a tremble," he says, "for not having written any thing"; and "the passage in Lear—'Do you not hear the Sea?'—has haunted me intensely." He then wrote his sonnet "On the Sea" (which "did me some good"). Finally, in a few days, he gave up, and left. A little embarrassed about his desperation (as the playful "forsooth" and the casual reference merely to his "old Lodging" show), he "set off pell mell for Margate, at least 150 Miles—because forsooth I fancied that I should like my old Lodging here, and could contrive to do without Trees."

The Commitment to Poetry:
Chapman's Homer, Hunt, and Haydon

✳⥽❂⥼✳⥽❂⥼✳⥽❂⥼✳⥽❂⥼✳⥽❂⥼✳⥽❂⥼✳⥽❂⥼✳⥽❂⥼✳⥽❂⥼✳⥽❂⥼✳⥽❂⥼✳⥽❂

Autumn 1816

AT THE END OF SEPTEMBER 1816, Keats returned from his Margate excursion. He took lodgings near Guy's Hospital, at 8 Dean Street. In this "beastly place" of "dirt, turnings, and windings," as he called it, he stayed for only a few weeks. There was no real need for him to come back to the hospital at all. He had paid a fee on March 3 that would allow him to remain there for a year as "dresser to the surgeons"; but since he had passed his examinations in July, he was already licensed to practice independently as an apothecary as soon as he became twenty-one.

If Keats went back to the Borough, therefore, it was only because no other place occurred to him at first. It was a natural result of his general homelessness. He at least knew the neighborhood. In fact, except for Hammond's surgery at Edmonton, he had lived nowhere else since his Enfield days. The loneliness may have oppressed him.[1] There was no reason why he and his brothers could not share lodgings near Abbey's countinghouse, and within a month or so they made plans to do this. Keats could still walk down to the hospital and do enough work there to satisfy Abbey for a while and to mark time until he had a better idea of what to do next.

Shortly after Keats returned to the Borough in September, he looked up Cowden Clarke, who had left Enfield in August and was now living in London at the house of his brother-in-law, John Towers, a chemist (6 Little Warren Street, Clerkenwell). The reunion, as Clarke said fifty years later, was "a memorable night . . . in my career." A folio edition of Chapman's translation of Homer had been lent him; and he and Keats, as the night got under way,

---

[1] There is no basis for the belief that Tom lived with him at Dean Street. Even if Tom had ceased working at the countinghouse, it is still probable that he was living with the Abbey family. Moreover, Clarke speaks of Keats as "solitary" at this time (*Recollections*, p. 128).

began to read aloud some of the famous passages that they had read long before in Pope's Homer. Clarke quotes two passages, and then concludes:

> One scene I could not fail to introduce to him—the shipwreck of Ulysses, in the fifth book of the "Odysseis," and I had the reward of one of his delighted stares, upon reading the following lines:—
>
> > Then forth he came, his both knees falt'ring, both
> > His strong hands hanging down, and all with froth
> > His cheeks and nostrils flowing, voice and breath
> > Spent to all use, and down he sank to death.
> > *The sea had soak'd his heart through . . .*[2]

In this "delighted stare" we have the sudden perception, the long prepared-for recognition, that climaxes the restless, uneasy weeks at Margate—the weeks of hoping that the resort town and the surrounding area would give him the stimulus that the "jumbled heap" of "murky buildings" in the Borough, he thought, had not; of trying to write to George about the "wonders" he had seen—only one of which, the sea, proved to be very lasting; of ending by writing poetry not only about poetry, but about trying to write poetry. The sonnet he was now to write in the four or five hours that followed is also—like the verse letters to George and to Clarke—about poetry. But all self-consciousness is forgotten. The large concern of two months is suddenly transmuted into actual discovery, and not stretched out in thought, hopes, and misgivings about the possibility of making discoveries. *"The sea had soak'd his heart through."* The virile, penetrating idiom of this poetry was not completely new to him. He had read some Shakespeare at Enfield and probably later. But it was new to him as an actively writing poet, however amateur, whose reading, notions, and models had for a year been very different. It was far from the eighteenth-century Spenserians—Mrs. Tighe, James Beattie, and others. In a sense it was even far from Spenser himself as Keats had viewed him—the Spenser of sensuous and elaborate ornament. The masculine strength of this language was in another world entirely from G. F. Mathew and his tastes, or even from Leigh Hunt. Homer was a name that obviously meant something: it represented, to a youth who possessed common sense as well as impetuosity, a necessary field to be explored—but at some later time when

[2] Page 130.

he might be able to learn Greek. Now, however, through Chapman, the poetry was speaking out "loud and bold."

Looking ahead, we see repeatedly that formative influences on the greater poetry of Keats are always bold, and that their immediate effect on him is toward spirit and vigor. The "delighted stare" on hearing Homer in Chapman's translation is one instance. Soon afterwards he felt a personal influence of the most salutary, liberating sort: that of the hapless, grandiose, but certainly bold painter, Benjamin Haydon, who, whatever his defects, did more than anyone else in the crucial year ahead to jolt Keats out of the restricted and coy approach to art with which he had inevitably been tempted—inevitably because then as now the first levels of influence from contemporaries were of a sort to make any young poet confined and modish. For the external mannerisms of a style, always the easiest to copy, are more nakedly obvious in the mediocre contemporary, and are not embarrassed by disruptive honesties. Two years later, the powerful influence of Milton suddenly lifted Keats to the high plateau on which he henceforth proceeded. The clairvoyant perception of Longinus, when he speaks of the value of great models in freeing our own aspirations and energy, is relevant to no major poet so much as to Keats. After Milton, the vigor of Dryden was to catch his imagination; and at all times from early 1818 until the end, there was the gradual, pervasive effect on him of Shakespeare.

2

At daybreak Keats parted from Clarke and walked the two miles back to Dean Street, through the City and over London Bridge. He may have reached his lodgings in half an hour of brisk walking; he could easily have taken an hour. He at once began to write down the lines of which he had been thinking. Naturally he used the sonnet form, to which he was accustomed. Moreover, the form had the advantage of being short; if one really had something to say, it compelled economy. But the sonnet has little in common with the earlier ones—even with "O Solitude," of which, as his only published poem, he was still naturally proud. Perhaps the nearest parallel among the sonnets is the one he had written to George at Margate, "Many the wonders." But the sense of wonder was now more genuine.

Within two hours at most—possibly from six or seven o'clock that morning to eight or nine—the sonnet, except for one important change (in the seventh line) , was finished. They parted, said Clarke, "at day-spring, yet he contrived that I should receive the poem from a distance of, may be, two miles *by ten o'clock.*" The haste in which the sonnet was written is illustrated by one of those

On the first looking into Chapman's Homer

Much have I travell'd in the Realms of Gold, —
And many goodly States, and Kingdoms seen;
Round many Western islands have I been,
Which Bards in fealty to Apollo hold.
Of one wide expanse had I been told.
Which deep brow'd Homer ruled as his Demesne:
Yet could I never judge what Men could mean,
Till I heard Chapman speak out loud and bold.—
Then felt I like some Watcher of the Skies
When a new Planet swims into his Ken,
Or like stout Cortez, when with wond'ring eyes
He star'd at the Pacific, and all his Men
Look'd at each other with a wild surmise —
Silent upon a Peak in Darien —

Ms. in the Harvard Keats Collection

extraordinary lapses that we find in Keats's manuscripts when he composes rapidly. "Deep-brow'd Homer" is at first written "low-brow'd Homer": the "low" is almost immediately crossed out, and "deep" put above it. Moreover, in the right-hand margin, he has drawn lines to mark the rhyme scheme for the octave of the Petrarchan sonnet—a rhyme scheme with which he has been familiar for some time. Plainly he is tired, writing in the early morning after this memorable night; and however rapidly he is coalescing thoughts or aspirations of the past few months, he is checking himself now in the first draft. For what is probably the first draft reads:

On the first looking into Chapman's Homer

Much have I travell'd in the Realms of Gold,
   And many goodly States, and Kingdoms seen;
   Round many western islands have I been,
Which Bards in fealty to Apollo hold.
Oft of one wide expanse had I been told,
   Which ⟨low⟩ deep brow'd Homer ruled as his Desmesne:
   Yet could I never judge what Men could mean,
Till I heard Chapman speak out loud, and bold.
Then felt I like some Watcher of the Skies
   When a new Planet swims into his Ken,
Or like stout Cortez, when with wond'ring eyes
   He star'd at the Pacific, and all his Men
Look'd at each other with a wild surmise
   Silent upon a Peak in Darien.[3]

The poem represents as much a summing up as an anticipation. The anticipation is in an idiom and mastery of phrase that foreshadow the greater poetry of a year and a half later. The summing up is in the materials and preoccupations that have long been accumulating. The sonnet subsumes the two months at Margate—the effort to write poetry by invoking past poetry and trying to use it (and there is the vivid sense of the "vastness" of the sea—"its rocks, its caves, its hopes, its fears," and the association of this first sight of the sea with self-discovery); but the sonnet also reaches beyond the previous summer to much that had been forgotten in the verse Keats wrote in 1815 and early 1816—back to the formative days at Enfield, when, after the death of his mother, he had read through most of the small school library. There are the books Clarke mentioned ("abridgements of all the voyages and travels of any note"; Robertson's *History of America*), and those mentioned by his schoolmate Edward Holmes ("Robinson Crusoe and something about Montezuma & the Incas of Peru"). And in the prize book given him at Enfield in 1811, Bonnycastle's *Introduction to Astronomy*, there is the vivid description of Herschel's discovery of the new planet Uranus. Every possible echo in this sonnet of Keats's reading has been exhaustively traced. We need note simply the way in which so much is now being swept up, not only

[3] The seventh line, said Clarke, struck Keats as "bald, and too simply wondering." Later, using a fairly conventional eighteenth-century phrase that he probably read in Coleridge's "Hymn before Sun-rise," Keats altered it to "Yet never did I breathe its pure serene." In the eleventh line, Keats later changed "wond'ring eyes" to "eagle eyes," with its suggestion of far-seeing, almost predatory eagerness.

from the preceding months but also from those vivid glimpses of discovery, five years before, at the little academy of Enfield. What is significant for the later writing is not so much the discovery in Chapman of economy and condensation of language as the discovery, through actual experience, that he himself could attain it. Earlier, whatever condensation he had achieved was in isolated phrases or lines. Here it is sustained throughout the whole of a fourteen-line poem.

The principal gain to Keats himself was a new confidence. Given his rapidly maturing critical sense, he could hardly be unaware of the achievement, however much the desire to write something other than a "short piece" was always to prod him. There were at least two other gains. The subject that was pressing upon him so strongly—the sense of the great poetry of the past, and what there was left to do—was successfully met by being turned into something else. He also half-discovered that poetry could after all be written in London. Change of place was always to attract him. Even if he sometimes came close to laughing at himself for doing so, he continued to move about (though within a very short radius until the final trip to Italy). But he quickly realized that, if there was any gain in these short trips, it was not because of a desperate need to find subjects. Instead, the trips were tokens of his decision sometimes to detach himself and at other times to spur himself forward. So dependent was he on his own efforts that these innocent gestures of resolution that anyone might make were particularly necessary to a youth who had been homeless since fourteen, and, after the death of Tom and the departure of George, was to be largely homeless until the end.

3

Everything seemed to be happening this October, on the last day of which Keats was to become twenty-one. Besides writing the sonnet on Chapman's Homer, he was introduced to three men who, in different ways, were to have a large effect on his life: Leigh Hunt, who had already been a vivid model in poetic style; Benjamin Robert Haydon, the painter; and a young writer, John Hamilton Reynolds, to whom Keats was later to send some of his most thoughtful letters and through whom he was to meet most of the other friends he was to have.

Clarke, in late September or early October, had been showing a few of Keats's poems to Hunt, who was altogether enthusiastic.[4] Hunt now lived in a cottage on Hampstead Heath in the Vale of Health, which had been given its hopeful name a few years before when the marsh previously there had been drained. He invited Clarke to bring Keats out to the cottage, and Clarke at once told Keats of the invitation. Keats excitedly wrote to Clarke, in the first surviving letter (October 9) except for the verse epistles: "The busy time has just gone by" (possibly he was making some half-hearted arrangements for continuing at Guy's Hospital; more probably he was using every spare moment to go over his poems carefully) ; and he can now, he says, "devote any time you may mention to the pleasure of seeing Mr. Hunt—'twill be an Era in my existence." He admits that in preparation he has been copying out "a sheet or two of Verses," and finds "so much to blame in them that the best part [he then appears to stop, and puts "worst" above "best" without crossing out the latter word] will go into the fire—those to G. Mathew I will suffer to meet the eye of Mr. H. notwithstanding that the Muse is so frequently mentioned." Unquestionably the meeting with Hunt took place soon after October 9.[5]

It was indeed "a 'red-letter day' in the young poet's life," said Clarke, "and one that will never fade with me while memory lasts." They walked much if not all of the way out to Hampstead— about five or six miles from Clerkenwell:

> The character and expression of Keats's features would arrest even the casual passenger in the street; and now they were wrought to a tone of animation that I could not but watch with interest,

[4] "I could not but anticipate," said Clarke, "that Hunt would speak encouragingly . . . but my partial spirit was not prepared for the unhesitating and prompt admiration . . . Horace Smith happened to be there on the occasion, and he was not less demonstrative . . . The piece which he read out was the sonnet, 'How many bards gild the Lapses of Time!' marking with particular emphasis and approval the last six lines . . . Smith repeated with applause the line in italics ['That distance of recognizance bereaves'], saying, 'What a well-condensed expression for a youth so young!' After making numerous and eager inquiries about him personally, and with reference to any peculiarities of mind and manner, the visit ended in my being requested to bring him over to the Vale of Health." (*Recollections,* pp. 132–133.) Hunt, of course, had published Keats's sonnet, "O Solitude," in the *Examiner* the previous May 5, but at the time, as he said, he knew nothing of Keats personally.

[5] The date of the meeting, so often disputed, and placed as late even as December, is resolved, as Rollins points out, by the doggerel-verse invitation Haydon sent in October to J. H. Reynolds to have dinner with him and Keats; for it was at Hunt's that Keats had met Haydon (*KC,* I.4–6) .

knowing what was in store for him from the bland encouragement, and Spartan deference in attention, with fascinating conversational eloquence, that he was to encounter and receive. As we approached the Heath, there was the rising and accelerated step, with the gradual subsidence of all talk. The interview, which stretched into three "morning calls," was the prelude to many after-scenes and sauntering about Caen Wood and its neighbourhood; for Keats was suddenly made a familiar of the household, and was always welcomed.[6]

Hunt, for his part, could never forget

the impression made upon me by the exuberant specimens of genuine though young poetry that were laid before me, and the promise of which was seconded by the fine fervid countenance of the writer. We became intimate on the spot, and I found the young poet's heart as warm as his imagination. We read and walked together, and used to write verses of an evening upon a given subject. No imaginative pleasure was left unnoticed by us, or unenjoyed; from the recollection of the bards and patriots of old, to the luxury of a summer rain at our window, or the clicking of the coal in wintertime. Not long afterwards, having the pleasure of entertaining at dinner Godwin, Hazlitt, and Basil Montague, I showed them the verses of my young friend, and they were pronounced to be as extraordinary as I thought them. One of them was that noble sonnet on first reading Chapman's Homer, which terminates with so energetic a calmness, and which completely announced the new poet taking possession.[7]

The friendship, as Hunt himself implied, was almost immediate. Hunt was the first established poet Keats met, and Keats had looked up to him ever since he was thirteen or fourteen. What is more, he found Hunt kindly, warm-natured, interested. Hunt, for his part, was understandably glad to find so devoted a disciple; he had been rather bruised, not merely by imprisonment for his liberal principles (this he could view as a sort of martyrdom), but also by snubs of which this eager disciple knew nothing. Nor was it just that. Hunt was a generous man.

4

Leigh Hunt's father, Isaac, came originally from Barbados, where his own father served as a vicar. Settling in Philadelphia, he married a Quakeress. Because of the strong feelings that preceded

[6] *Recollections*, p. 133.
[7] *Lord Byron and Some of His Contemporaries* (1828), I.409–410.

the American Revolution, his loyalty to George III subjected him to harsh treatment from his neighbors and even to prison. In time he made his way to England; and though he became a popular preacher, he was often harassed by debt and spent time in prison as a debtor. Leigh Hunt, like his father, had the courage of his principles. When he and his brother John, after their attack in the *Examiner* on the Prince Regent, were sentenced for libel, they were told that both the fine and the prison term would be remitted if they pledged themselves to abstain from future attack. But they rejected the proposal.

This winning, kindly man, always spontaneously courteous, has often been treated rather roughly by admirers of Keats.[8] The difference between Keats's early verse and the poetry written after the summer of 1818 is so striking that the Keatsian takes it for granted that the blame ought to be shared, so to speak; and Leigh Hunt serves as the obvious scapegoat. But if we approach Hunt solely in this way, we simply follow what Keats himself, unconsciously and understandably, was tempted to do during the next two years. It was natural enough that Keats should yield to this temptation, though it is not entirely to his credit. But his later need to disengage himself from a strong identification and the remarks he makes in the process are far from an objective guide in any approach that we ourselves—with no such excuse—make to Hunt.

Within a few weeks, Keats was walking out to Hampstead constantly. Hunt, even more fluent in conversation than in writing, was "matchless," said Charles Lamb, "as a fireside companion." His eloquence came in short breaths. It was softened by general amiability, and diversified by what Clarke justly called his "Spartan deference of attention." Moreover, the rather higgledy-piggledy state of the household, which was later to distress Keats, was now immensely welcome. He did not object to the playful nickname Hunt bestowed on him, in which "John Keats" was telescoped into "Junkets"; with so few encouraging relationships in the past, he could even have been mildly pleased for a while by the interest it showed, though no one else felt the nickname appropriate enough to use it. Whatever was to happen later in Keats's own feeling about Hunt and the Hunt family, the warmth of his welcome became permanently, and in time unconsciously, imprinted on him. When the Keats brothers left their lodgings in Cheapside a few

8 A notable exception is the biography by Edmund Blunden (1930).

months later, though Keats himself was by then beginning to question much that Hunt seemed to stand for, they went, with John undoubtedly taking the lead, to Hampstead. That Hampstead is forever associated with Keats is owing to Hunt's welcome and all that Hunt's welcome would naturally mean. There is another tribute, perhaps more moving. So deeply did these first happy months become a part of him that long afterwards, in June 1820, when Keats was mortally ill, he went to the Hunts, who by this time were living in Kentish Town. There was a difference by this time: the noise and confusion bothered him; there had been a long estrangement, and an unhappy accident soon occurred that ended the visit. But it is still a fact that near the end, as at the beginning, Hunt was present.

Very soon after Keats's first meeting with Hunt a bed of sorts was made up for him on a sofa in the library of the Hunt cottage. Here, as Clarke said, "he composed the frame-work and many lines of the poem on 'Sleep and Poetry'—the last sixty or seventy lines being an inventory of the art garniture of the room." Keats's excitement and his vivid sense of reassurance are put in a sonnet of November 1816 written, as Clarke says, "shortly after his installation at the cottage, and on the day after one of our visits." The walk back from Hampstead to Cheapside was long, and in November it was cold. But as he goes along, he scarcely notices it; for he is

> brimfull of the friendliness
> That in a little cottage I have found;

and brimful as well of the talk of poetry.[9] So with a second, much poorer sonnet, written shortly after the other and called "On Leaving Some Friends at an Early Hour." To express his ecstatic state of mind he pictures himself as leaning back on "heap'd up flowers,"

[9] Keen, fitful gusts are whisp'ring here and there
   Among the bushes half leafless and dry;
   The stars look very cold about the sky,
And I have many miles on foot to fare.
Yet feel I little of the cool bleak air,
   Or of the dead leaves rustling drearily,
   Or of those silver lamps that burn on high,
Or of the distance from home's pleasant lair:
For I am brimfull of the friendliness
   That in a little cottage I have found;
Of fair-hair'd Milton's eloquent distress,
   And all his love for gentle Lycid drown'd;
Of lovely Laura in her light green dress,
   And faithful Petrarch gloriously crown'd.

calling for "a golden pen" and a "tablet whiter than a star"; and
says, while pearly cars, pink robes, and "half-discovered wings"
glide by, and music wanders "round my ears,"

> Let me write down a line of glorious tone,
> And full of many wonders of the spheres:
> For what a height my spirit is contending!
> 'Tis not content so soon to be alone.

Though the sonnet is always dismissed and occasionally ridi-
culed for piling one weak prettiness upon another, we can at least
notice an element of pathos: the elation of the long-orphaned
youth in at last being warmly welcomed by a group of people who
liked poetry—who wrote it themselves (for Reynolds and others
may have been present as well as Hunt), and thought well of what
he himself was trying to write. The "height" of enthusiasm he feels
is certainly understandable. No critic could even begin to approach
the Keats of a year later in his censure of such a poem. For Keats
himself was to turn caustically not only upon the idiom, the language, of much of the poetry of this happy, valuable time, but also
upon the whole sense of intoxication and confidence that these
months from October to March suddenly gave him. The chagrin
was to linger, giving momentum to the large inner debate on the
uses of poetry that remains so important a part of the legacy of
this poignantly allegorical life.

5

At an early visit to Hunt's in October, Keats met Benjamin Robert Haydon, the painter, a hugely energetic, bull-necked man of
thirty, nine years older than Keats and two years younger than
Hunt. Like Hunt, Haydon was a man to whom he had looked with
admiration.[10] But he could in no way have been prepared for the
immense gusto of the man, who was unlike anyone he had ever
seen. Haydon, for his part, was delighted with the generous idealism of the youth. "Keats," he wrote a few months later, "is the only

10 An undated sonnet ("Highmindedness, a jealousy for good")—possibly written immediately after he met Haydon, but just as possibly months before—expresses
exactly those qualities in Keats himself that Haydon, after a few personal meetings,
was most likely to ignite: admiration for boldness, energy, patriotism; pleasure in
seeing a "stout unbending champion" (Keats is referring to Haydon's famous battle for official recognition of the authenticity of the Elgin Marbles); and "affection
for the cause / Of stedfast genius, toiling gallantly."

man I ever met with who is conscious of a high call . . . except Wordsworth, but Keats is more of my own age." Haydon often grumbles about Hunt, whose loose religious attitudes always infuriated him. Hunt is a "flower" that may attract you "by its look of grace & colour," but "you smell it, & then cast it from you for it stinks!" By contrast, "Keats is really & truly the man after my own heart. We saw through each other *at once,* and I hope in God are friends for ever." With the touching, childlike vanity he was always showing, he reflects: "the interest I excite amongst the genius of the Country is certainly very singular. There must be something in me too." [11]

Within a few days after meeting Keats, Haydon invited him and John Reynolds to dine with him at his house in Hampstead (7 Pond Street), taking care to omit Hunt. Near the end of the month, Haydon also decided to hold a breakfast for Cowden Clarke, Keats, and perhaps others in his London studio (41 Great Marlborough Street), which was filled with paintings, sketches, and the vast canvas of "Christ's Entry into Jerusalem" on which he had been working for months. Clarke let Keats know when the day (Sunday, November 3) was settled, and Keats on October 31 excitedly replied, forgivably giddy and "literary" in the Miltonic and Shakespearean allusions at the end. "My daintie Davie," he begins, echoing a poem of Burns—

> I will be as punctual as the Bee to the Clover—Very glad am I at the thoughts of seeing so soon this glorious Haydon and all his Creation.[12] I pray thee let me know when you go to Ollier's and where he resides—this I forgot to ask you—and tell me also when you will help me waste a sullen day—God 'ield you.

The reference to Charles Ollier the publisher shows that already there had been talk in the Hunt circle—or possibly with Haydon—of publishing Keats's poems; and it was indeed Ollier and his brother James who were to bring out Keats's first volume the following March. Another invitation from Haydon followed within a week; but it turned out that Haydon was unable to be present after all—he wanted to see *Timon of Athens,* which was playing at Drury Lane. They would meet instead on November 19. In the same sportive manner in which he had dashed off the previous note

11 *Diary,* II.101, 107.
12 A pun of sorts. He is also thinking of Haydn's oratorio *The Creation.*

to Clarke, the happy Keats naively spices his letter with legal and
Shakespearean echoes:

> To C— C— C— greeting,
>   Whereas I have received a Note from that worthy Gentleman
> Mr. Haydon, to the purport of his not being able to see us on this
> days Evening, for that he hath an order for the Orchestra to see
> Timon ye Misantrophos, and begging us to excuse the same—it be-
> hoveth me to make this thing known to you for a manifest Reason
> —So I rest your Hermit—John Keats.

The evening of November 19 was memorable. For Haydon's energetic talk of power and of grandeur of conception swept Keats
again to a level of thinking toward which he had been instinctively
groping for months, reinforcing the vivid experience of reading
Chapman's Homer a few weeks before. Needing so badly the assurance that high achievement was still possible—that it was not a
thing solely of the past—and thinking of Wordsworth, of whom
they had certainly talked, and, of course, of Hunt, who was proving
to be so generous, Keats wrote another sonnet, probably composing
it on the way home that night. Wordsworth, Hunt, and Haydon, in
that order, are the "spirits" of whom he is thinking; and it is rather
sad to see that Hunt—who was soon to drop out of the trio and be
replaced by Hazlitt in the next statement, fifteen months later, of
the "three things to rejoice at in this Age"—seems to be remarkable largely for "the social smile." The next morning he wrote to
Haydon:

> My dear Sir—
>   Last Evening wrought me up, and I cannot forbear sending you
> the following—Your's unfeignedly John Keats—
>
>> Great Spirits now on Earth are sojourning
>>   He of the Cloud, the Cataract the Lake
>>   Who on Helvellyn's summit wide awake
>> Catches his freshness from Archangel's wing
>> He of the Rose, the Violet, the Spring
>>   The social Smile, the Chain for freedom's sake:
>>   And lo!—whose stedfastness would never take
>> A Meaner Sound than Raphael's Whispering.
>> And other Spirits are there standing apart
>>   Upon the Forehead of the Age to come;
>> These, These will give the World another heart
>>   And other pulses—hear ye not the hum
>> Of mighty Workings in a distant Mart?
>>   Listen awhile ye Nations, and be dumb!

Keats sent the letter by messenger, and Haydon immediately replied, saying that he would send the sonnet to Wordsworth, and suggesting that the next to the last line should stop after the words "mighty workings," thus creating a large pause before the final line. Keats, even happier, answered at once, speaking of the "proud pleasure" he feels: he will keep Haydon's letter as a "stimulus to exertion—I begin to fix my eye upon one horizon." As for the omission Haydon suggests in the next to last line, Keats—who has caught Haydon's enthusiastic habit of expression, at least for the moment—says that "My feelings entirely fall in with yours" about the change, and "I glory in it!"

With cautious modesty, he waits until the end of this short note to admit, almost brokenly, that "The idea of your sending it to Wordsworth put me out of breath—you know with what Reverence—I would send my Wellwishes to him." And on a clean sheet, which he obviously thought Haydon would forward to Words. worth, he carefully copied out the sonnet, making the change that Haydon suggested. The very day Haydon received the first draft of the poem he showed it to Reynolds; and Reynolds, not to be outdone, himself wrote a sonnet also praising Haydon's "Giant Genius"—a sonnet that bears the appended note, in Haydon's handwriting, "Wild enthusiasm." But for whatever reason, possibly because he was suddenly plunging at his painting, "Christ's Entry," with "refreshed fury"—to use a favorite expression of his—Haydon neglected for over a month to send the sonnet on to Wordsworth, and, when he finally wrote, did not enclose Keats's neatly prepared draft but copied it out himself.[13]

6

The twin influences of Hunt and Haydon were inevitably to conflict in the year ahead; they touched two different sides of Keats himself. A part of him, as he said later, was like Hunt, and what people assumed to be Hunt's influence was really himself. In a similar way, a part of him was like Haydon. Put more accurately,

---

[13] Wordsworth politely replied (January 20, 1817): "The sonnet appears to be of good promise, of course neither you nor I being so highly complimented in the composition can be deemed judges altogether impartial—but it is assuredly vigorously conceived and well expressed" (*Letters of William and Dorothy Wordsworth, the Later Years*, ed. de Selincourt [1939], III.1367f.) . For Reynolds' sonnet, see *Letters*, I.117.

a large part of him admired what Haydon—in a different way—also admired. What he was to write months later, when he saw the Elgin Marbles, puts it exactly: the power and reach of this art leave him feeling "Like a sick Eagle looking at the sky." This is the line, quite typically, that most struck Haydon himself.

Haydon stood for all that Hunt did not. He had no trace of simper, no fondness for chat. He was incapable of small talk. His vivid, simple-hearted energy was finally to collapse in his tragic last years and to end in suicide in 1846—a fearful sort of double suicide, in which, after the bullet with which he shot himself was slightly deflected in his skull, he cut his throat with a razor, and fell dead before his large unfinished canvas of a scene in the life of Alfred the Great. But these years were far ahead; and Haydon's suicide came only after a courageous battle against three decades of continual defeat.

It is only too easy for us now to think of Haydon's obsession with greatness as built on air. Unlike his contemporaries, we have his magnificently picturesque journal. A passage he had written in it a year and a half before he met Keats is often cited: "Never have I had such irresistible, perpetual, & continued urgings of future greatness. I have been like a man with air balloons under his arm pits and ether in his soul." He ends with a sincere prayer that these new "flashes of energy" he is feeling "may not be presumptuous" but "fiery anticipations." About the very time he met Keats he was again feeling the same delightful confidence. He had been away from his studio for a short while; and on his return to it he wrote:

> My Picture today struck me . . . as the most enchanting of all sights. . . . I never felt so vividly the benefit of being absent a little. It came over [me] like a lovely dream. I sat & dwelt on it like a young girl on a lover (when she is unobserved). I adored the Art that could give such sensation . . . & rode back to Hampstead musing on the delights of my glorious calling, and will return tomorrow, adequate to its noble labours. God in Heaven bless them & enable me to conclude them; in gratitude to his mercy, and with a mind fired to a greater work, Amen, in gratitude.[14]

Excess can always seem comic; and everything about Haydon, except humor, was characterized by excess.[15] His laughs might sound,

14 *Diary,* I.430, II.62.

15 A delightful example is the phrasing in a letter he sent Keats a year and a half later (March 4, 1818) when he received news that a ring possibly belonging

as Hunt said, "like the trumpets of Jericho and threaten to have the same effect." But that Haydon lacked the gift of proportion necessary for genuine humor is obvious. Take his invitation, also late in October, to John Reynolds to dine with him and his new friend Keats. It starts:

> Come thou Poet!—*free* and *brown!*
> Next Sunday to Hampstead Town
> To meet John Keats, who soon will shine
> The greatest, of this splendid time
> That e'er has woo'd the Muses nine.

Heavily it goes on for another three stanzas, and, with elephantine attempts to add to the humor, he appends a couple of notes, as if from an editor ("Quite original—'Muses nine' we never recollect having seen them in any Poet ancient or modern. Ed.").[16]

Harassed by debts and troubled with poor eyesight, Haydon met every defeat until the end by plunging with renewed energy into his vast historical paintings, all of which were too large to hang in any private house. Back in 1814, after painting "The Judgment of Solomon," he found that his debts amounted to £1,100:

> As I tottered down the Haymarket I leaned on a post and said: "What shall I do if I do not sell?" "Order another canvass," said the voice within, "and begin a greater work." "So I will," I inwardly replied and thenceforth lost all dependence.[17]

And remarks in his early letters to Keats (March and April, 1817) are in the same spirit. He thanks Keats for his "two noble sonnets—I know not a finer image than the comparison of a Poet unable to express his feelings to a sick eagle looking at the Sky! . . . You filled me with fury for an hour." "Often have I sat by my fire after a day's effort . . . and mused on what I had done and . . . would do till filled with fury I have seen the faces of the mighty

---

to Shakespeare had been found near the garden of New Place, Stratford. The letter is worth quoting in full: "My dear Keats / I shall certainly go mad!—In a field at Stratford upon Avon, in a field that belonged to Shakespeare; they have found a gold ring and seal with the initial thus—*a true WS Lover's Knot between* [he puts in a sketch of it]; if *this* is not Shakespeare who is it?—a true lovers Knott!!—I saw an impression to day, and am to have one as soon as possible—As sure as you breathe, & that he was the first of beings the Seal belonged to him—Oh Lord!—B. R. Haydon."

16 *KC*, I.4–6.

17 *Autobiography*, ed. Penrose (1927), p. 143. "The Judgment of Solomon" was a success. It was sold for £600, and the British Institution also awarded Haydon a prize of one hundred guineas.

dead crowd into my room, and I have sunk down & prayed the great Spirit that I might be worthy." *"Trust in God . . .* In all my troubles, & wants, & distresses, here I found a refuge . . . I always arose, with a refreshed fury . . . that sent me streaming on with a repulsive power against the troubles of life that attempted to stop me, as if I was a cannon shot darting through feathers." [18]

Haydon made the refreshing impact he did on so many of his contemporaries partly because of his courage. For it really was courage, even if the means by which he seemed to attain it were not those of most people. "A man," said Keats, who disliked the habit of "detracting," "ought to have the Fame he deserves." Moreover, at a time when it was feared that art had for generations been lowering its sights, it was healthful to have a man talk so energetically and firmly of "greatness." Whatever else may be said of Haydon, he scorned the comfort of smallness. Haydon might feel that Michelangelo tended at times to distort the human figure, and he fancied himself as more a follower of Raphael. But the whole spirit of his approach to the great painters of the Italian Renaissance reminds one of what Sir Joshua Reynolds, in his old age, said he would do if he had his life to live over again. Reynolds, in his last discourse as President of the Royal Academy, disowned the cautious aims of most of his own painting, pleaded openly for boldness and power, and ended by urging Michelangelo as a model. So pinched had art now become that Reynolds felt it was something even to be "capable of such sensations as [Michelangelo] intended to excite":

> It will not, I hope, be thought presumptuous in me to appear in the train, I cannot say of his imitators, but of his admirers. I have taken another course, one more suited to my abilities, and to the taste of the times in which I live. Yet however unequal I feel myself to that attempt, were I now to begin the world again, I would tread in the steps of that great master . . . and I should desire that the last words which I should pronounce in this Academy, and from this place, might be the name of—MICHEL ANGELO.

The level of conversation seemed to rise when Haydon was present. Tempers might also rise—he could become suddenly heated; but he was never niggling, and was usually more inclined to praise than to detract. The list of literary men he could call friends was impressive: Wordsworth and Keats especially, Coleridge, Hazlitt,

[18] *Letters,* I.122, 124, 135.

Lamb, Scott, and, despite temperamental differences, Hunt. The list could be extended. And one of the great events of Haydon's life was also a tribute to his courage and his unswerving dedication to what he conceived to be the heroic in art. This was his eight-year battle, in the face of immense opposition, to secure official recognition of the famous Parthenon sculptures that Lord Elgin had brought from Athens, and to persuade the nation to buy them.

In the months ahead—in a sense throughout the next two years—Haydon's influence was to be salutary, perhaps necessary, to Keats. Without it Keats could have slipped so easily, after his brave effort at Margate, back into the coy idiom, the comfortable corner-poetry, that had been his principal nourishment before he went to Margate, and that Leigh Hunt—at an admittedly higher level than G. F. Mathew—still represented. Secondly—and this was Haydon's greatest gift to Keats—he proved of immense value in helping Keats to maintain his faith in himself. Hunt, of course, also offered that help, but only up to a certain level. To the youth who was always afraid that writing only "short pieces" was a falling off from the great poetry of the past, Haydon, with his titanic canvases and his endless, booming confidence, was a sure stay against triviality. Bombast there might be: we are naturally in a better position to see it than was Keats at that time; but we need not be prim about the gift of judgment that Haydon's personal journal and a century and a half of history allow us in viewing him.

7

In Lamb's Conduit Street lived the family of George Reynolds, a writing-master, and his wife Charlotte Cox Reynolds. Their five children—four girls and a boy—were roughly the age of the Keats children. Both parents had literary interests; Mrs. Reynolds wrote verses and was later to write a novel of sorts; and they saw a few writers socially. Their son, John, a year older than Keats, had been a student at St. Paul's and had then become a clerk, when he was sixteen, in the Amicable Insurance Company. But he had been publishing poetry since he was eighteen. In fact, by the time he met Keats, he had published three small books, and a fourth was appearing.[19] He had also written critical and other essays for *The*

19 These included *Safie, An Eastern Tale* (1814), patterned after Byron's oriental verse tales; *The Eden of Imagination* (1814); and *An Ode* (1815). *The Naiad: A Tale* appeared in November 1816.

Champion and *The Inquirer*. Reynolds, though only twenty-two, could thus seem a relatively experienced writer to Keats, and, because they were so close in age, serve as a tangible symbol of hope. Much happened within the next half year or more to strengthen the rapid friendship of the two men. To begin with, each became quickly associated in the other's mind with Haydon; and this was a potentially fertile bond, at least for a while. They may have met each other through Hunt. But within a week, Haydon—who was never enthusiastic about Hunt and tended to be explosively restless around him—held the dinner for Keats and Reynolds that we noticed, and pointedly omitted to ask Hunt.[20] Both of the youths, whatever they may separately have owed to Hunt, could breathe a freer air with Haydon. Typically, when Keats during the following year began to disengage himself from Hunt, he was often franker in expression to Reynolds than to others.[21] He could assume a mutual bond—a common vocabulary, so to speak—in the ideals that Haydon had energetically and orotundly espoused and that were so rapidly to become deepened in Keats's own thinking.

Moreover, the Reynolds family—the parents, and the four sisters, as well as John Reynolds—welcomed him. They felt kindly to the orphaned youth who was aspiring to follow the lead of the son of their own family. The Reynolds household was hardly a substitute for home, as the Hunt household very nearly was for a time. Mr. Reynolds was busy. Mrs. Reynolds often talked too much. The four girls, however pleasant, tended to be chattery. At least two, possibly half a dozen, light poems were written by Keats either for or because of the Reynolds girls—Jane, who later married Thomas Hood (1825), Mariane, Eliza, and the young Charlotte, who was only fourteen.[22] In time their talk cloyed; they irri-

---

[20] In the long doggerel invitation to Reynolds, mentioned above, are the lines:
Now, Reynolds, it'll be just as well
If that, you don't do to others tell!—
and, by others, Haydon plainly meant Hunt.

[21] A provocative, undated note of Clarke's reads as follows: "Reynolds poisoned him [Keats] against Hunt—who never varied toward Keats" (see *Letters*, II.11n.). Clarke's strong language is understandable: he was always a firm friend of Hunt; and since he could hardly share the chafing uneasiness of the two young poets, but was thinking only of simple gratitude, he would naturally assume that Keats was influenced by Reynolds.

[22] For Jane he wrote the sonnet "On a Leander Gem Which Miss Reynolds, My Kind Friend, Gave Me" (mistakenly dated March 1816 by Woodhouse, and probably written in March 1817). The sonnet, "Spenser! a jealous honourer of thine" was written at the Reynolds house (February 5, 1818), and given to Eliza. The bur-

tated him by making derogatory remarks about their cousin, Jane Cox, whom he admired; and when Fanny Brawne appeared, they were even more disapproving. In another three and a half years he was to say that, except for John Reynolds himself, he felt rather prejudiced against "all that family." But all this lies a little ahead. For the time being, the Reynolds family offered a certain reassurance and pleasure; and it also gave him a chance to see more of John Reynolds.

8

Not since his days at Enfield had Keats found a friend who could so spontaneously share his own effervescent humor. There was a difference—Reynolds was far the wittier of the two. Though Keats might later tell his brothers that the talk of clever "literary" men only left him feeling "how much superior humour is to wit in respect to enjoyment," the coalescence of humor and wit fascinated him; and Reynolds had just that. Nor did it wear thin. Long afterwards, when Keats was far from well, he could still write to George's wife (January 17, 1820) that, of "three witty people all distinct in their excellence—Rice, Reynolds, and Richards," Reynolds was the "playfullest": "I admire the first, I enjoy the second, I stare at the third." Wit, of course, can be a dangerous thing to play with; and there were occasions when—goaded by a sense of real injustice—Reynolds, with brilliant readiness of mind, could put his finger quickly and unerringly on a man's weaknesses. Keats mentions an instance in a letter to George and Tom (January 13, 1818). Haydon invited some friends, including Reynolds, to meet Wordsworth. Reynolds, who could not go, forgot to answer. The volcanic Haydon (most of whose quarrels were unhappily started by himself and his unintentionally hectoring, bullying manner) then wrote, said Keats,

> a very sharp & high note to Reynolds & then another in palliation— but which Reynolds feels as an aggravation of the first—Considering all things—Haydons frequent neglect of his Appointments &c. his notes were bad enough to put Reynolds on the right side of the

lesque sonnet "To Mrs. Reynolds's Cat" was doubtless written for the girls. Charlotte, in her old age, claimed that the lyric, "Hush! hush! tread softly," was suggested by a Spanish air she played for Keats on the piano (yet see Gittings, ch. 6). It has been assumed that the song "I had a dove" (Lowell, II.141) was suggested by Charlotte's playing, and that the sonnet "To the Ladies Who Saw Me Crown'd" was addressed to Jane, Mariane, and Charlotte.

question but then Reynolds has no powers of sufferance . . . so he answered Haydon in one of the most cutting letters I ever read; exposing to himself all his own weaknesses, & going on to an excess, which whether it is just or no, is what I would fain have unsaid.

But this was an exception. In general, Reynolds' keen wit—as John Clare, the poet said—was accompanied by so much good nature that "if you looked in his face you could not be offended; and you might retort as you pleased—nothing could put him out of humour." Another friend, after Reynolds' death, spoke of his "mobile and intelligent countenance lit up by never-failing good humour, and a quiet, bland, but somewhat arch smile." [23] It was exactly this combination of good-natured archness, playful fancy, and a solid, generous common sense (it was Reynolds who persuaded Keats to alter his reckless preface to *Endymion*) that grew upon Keats. To Reynolds, more than anyone else except his brothers, he was to write without reserve of the larger hopes and misgivings he felt about himself as a poet.

The later years of Reynolds make rather sad reading. He was soon to enter the law. Gradually giving up any hope of a literary career, he felt the cruel contrast with his precocious years, and found it less easy to live with himself. Neither law nor literature could arouse much of his energy; for the first he lacked respect, and for the second he lacked confidence. Finally, often ill, tempted to drink, and shaken further by the death of his only child, he died on November 15, 1852. Only four years before Reynolds died, Richard Monckton Milnes, the first biographer of Keats, wrote to him in order to gain what information he could. About himself Reynolds could only say humbly (and it gives a refreshing contrast to the long, querulous letters of G. F. Mathew) :

My poor works have been contributions to the London Magazine when Taylor & Hessey had it—a poem published under the title of "Safie" when a Boy—(A downright imitation of Lord Byron, & who refers to it kindly in his printed Journal & letters)—an *Anticipated Parody* of Wordsworth's Peter Bell . . . a share with Hood in a work called "Odes & addresses to Great Men" . . . a little work called "The Fancy—being the Memoir & poetical works of Peter Corcoran"—and a small Volume of Poems intitled "The Garden of Florence" by John Hamilton.—Two of the poems in the little Book are from Boccacio—& were to have been published with one or two

[23] Willard B. Pope, "John Hamilton Reynolds," in the journal *Wessex*, 1935, p. 10.

more,—& Keats was to have joined me—but *he* only wrote "Isabella & the Pot of Basil."—His illness & death put an end to the work—and I referred to the circumstance in my preface. Forgive so much about that poor obscure—baffled Thing,—myself! [24]

During his last five years Reynolds served as an assistant clerk at Newport, on the Isle of Wight. By the time Reynolds died at fifty-eight, Keats was far from having the acknowledged stature that another thirty years were to grant him. Yet on the tombstone of Reynolds, in letters as large as those of his own name, are engraved the words: "The Friend of Keats." With complete conviction he had written to Milnes that Keats was not only "the sincerest Friend,—the most lovable associate,—the deepest Listener to the griefs & disappointments of all around him," but that "He had the greatest power of poetry in him, of any one since Shakespeare." [25]

That Reynolds should have ended in the Isle of Wight has a certain poignance. For only a few months after Reynolds had first met him, Keats—instinctively duplicating that first adventure in hope with which he had set off to Margate—himself went off to the Isle of Wight in order to start a real "test of Invention," *Endymion*. Then, a day or so after arriving, he begins the first of his really memorable letters (April 17 and 18, 1817); and it is to Reynolds that he writes. He tells how he unpacked his books, putting them "in a snug corner," and "pinned up Haydon"—doubtless for encouragement to boldness. He could be confident that Reynolds would immediately understand (this was almost a year before Reynolds' exasperated, cutting letter to Haydon). Then comes a more open confidence than we can see in any of the letters hitherto written to others. There is a frank confession of the complete blankness that he feels—he has become "all in a tremble for not having written anything" (though he has only just arrived). He is saying exactly what he wrote to George at the beginning of the verse letter he sent after he went to Margate. But now he is waiting even less long; he is not elevating it into verse; and he and Reynolds have a common frame of reference—they are both writing poetry, or trying to write it. With quick impulsiveness Keats goes on:

—I'll tell you what—On the 23rd was Shakespeare born . . . Whenever you write say a Word or two on some Passage in Shakespeare that may have come rather new to you; which must be continually

[24] *KC*, II.230–231.   [25] *KC*, II.173.

happening, notwithstand^g that we read the same Play forty times—
for instance, the following, from the Tempest, never struck me so
forcibly as at present,

"Urchins

Shall, for that vast of Night that they may work,
All exercise on thee—"

How can I help bringing to your mind the Line—

In the dark backward and abysm of time—

And so the letter continues. It was to Reynolds only a year later
that Keats wrote that astonishing letter in which the whole of these
vivid first months (from October 1816 through the following
spring) is caught up, subsumed, and put, page after page, with a
profundity no poet has ever begun to match in his personal letters.
This is the letter in which he speaks of what it means to enter a
"Chamber of Maiden-thought" after leaving the "infant or
thoughtless Chamber." [26] In merely mentioning it, we are jumping
ahead, and directly touching the threshold of the rapidly maturing
clairvoyance of the youth who, so short a time before, had returned
to Guy's Hospital from Margate. The point at the moment is simply the need—and the fortunate, salutary gain—of having a friend
so close to his age with whom he could feel so free, and with whom
he could make up, in his thinking and talk, for the lack of so
much in the past. There would later be small difficulties between
the two men. But such difficulties always arise; and they may have
had more to do with the reactions of Reynolds—who for all his
generosity, could scarcely help feeling that he was being out-
stripped—than with those of Keats himself.

9

In the autumn of 1816 everything seemed to be given, at least
in comparison with the six years since the death of his mother, or
the five years since he had left John Clarke's school at Enfield.
"The lamentable change," as Edgar said in *Lear*—in the play that
was increasingly to haunt Keats's imagination more than any other
—"The lamentable change is from the best." But "to be worst"—
to begin at the bottom—"Stands still in esperance, lives not in
fear." Inevitably, in the months ahead, there would be just a touch

---

[26] See below, Chapter XIII.

of swagger in his walk. But this, which would have been altogether innocent even for ten years—for twenty years—in the life of a poet who would end with a fraction of Keats's achievement, was only a matter of months with him; and even in that short time it was intermittent, casual, insignificant.

chapter vi

Completing the First Volume

✻꙰✻꙰✻꙰✻꙰✻꙰✻꙰✻꙰✻꙰✻꙰✻꙰✻꙰✻꙰✻꙰

November and December, 1816

Meanwhile the three Keats brothers (aged twenty-one, nineteen, and seventeen) had been arranging to live together, and by mid-November had taken lodgings at 76 Cheapside, only two or three minutes' walk from Abbey's countinghouse. Fanny, now thirteen, had been sent to a boarding school in Walthamstow, near Abbey's summer home, almost immediately after her grandmother's death. At this girls' academy, kept by two sisters, the Misses Tuckey, Fanny was to stay for two more years.

Because of his health, Tom had been released from work at the countinghouse. Biographers have speculated that George himself left Abbey's employ at this time, for at some point, either in the winter of 1816 or the spring of 1817, George quarreled with a junior partner of Abbey—a man named Hodgkinson, who seems to have been unbearably insolent—and withdrew from the countinghouse. But we have no way of knowing exactly when this occurred.[1] Nor is there any real basis for the general assumption that, after a "desultory search for employment and possibly a temporary position" in Wilkinson's law office, "George became the family housekeeper, the companion and nurse of Tom, the copier of poems and business agent for John's work."[2] The income from their grandmother's estate might, with careful economy, support the three brothers and also defray Fanny's expenses at the boarding

---

[1] Because Keats, on April 15, 1817, asks George to write him "particularly how you get on with Wilkinson's plan," it is assumed that by this time George had left Abbey and was either working for Wilkinson—possibly Charles Wilkinson, of Red Lion Square (I.129) —or else was about to secure a position with him. An autographed copy of the *Poems* (1817) was given "to C. Wilkinson" by Keats, who also, according to George, lent Wilkinson £40 or £50 (*More Letters and Poems of the Keats Circle*, p. 28). That the three brothers had moved to Hampstead by the middle of March may also suggest that George had by then left Abbey, though the daily walk from Hampstead to Pancras Lane would not have seemed excessive at the time.

[2] Naomi J. Kirk, "Memoir of George Keats," Hampstead Keats, vol. I, p. lxxxi.

7. CHEAPSIDE, SHOWING THE KEATS BROTHERS' LODGINGS AT NO. 76

The cross marks their sitting-room windows.

9. MINIATURE OF KEATS BY JOSEPH SEVERN

8. SILHOUETTE OF KEATS
BY CHARLES BROWN

*"Here inclosed," Keats tells his sister
(June 17, 1819), "is a very capital
Profile done by Mr. Brown."*

11. TOM KEATS

10. GEORGE KEATS

13. JOHN HAMILTON REYNOLDS

12. BENJAMIN ROBERT HAYDON

school of the Misses Tuckey. But Abbey at all times seems to have doled out this income in the most sparing fashion. Moreover, since George stayed in Abbey's good graces, we can assume that, when he left the countinghouse, he got some employment, however intermittent. Finally, though Tom might be unable to work and John tempted to gamble for a few months in the hope of beginning a literary career, nothing in George's character permits us to imagine that he would be willingly idle; and opportunities for positions as clerk were by no means hard to find. We should remember what a successful businessman George later became. Because of a good-natured gullibility, he could sometimes lose large sums in unwise investments. But he could also make money; he was very industrious; he was always able to secure the confidence of others; and by the time he was thirty-five he had become one of the wealthiest citizens of Louisville, Kentucky.

2

In a moving sonnet, called simply "To My Brothers" and written on Tom's seventeenth birthday, on November 18, we can feel the relief of the three brothers in being at last together. Whatever the poem may lack in other ways, it suggests the deep need for home always present in all of the children but especially in Keats himself after the return from Margate—a need that the Hunt family was also beginning to help fill. The contrast with the shabby, lonely room at 8 Dean Street was immensely comforting, and the poem is poignant with stock associations of home.[3] There is the hearth, so dear to the English soul—the "faint cracklings" of the fire over the coals are "whispers" of "household gods"; there

[3] Small, busy flames play through the fresh laid coals,
  And their faint cracklings o'er our silence creep
  Like whispers of the household gods that keep
A gentle empire o'er fraternal souls.
And while, for rhymes, I search around the poles,
  Your eyes are fix'd, as in poetic sleep,
  Upon the lore so voluble and deep,
That aye at fall of night our care condoles.
This is your birth-day Tom, and I rejoice
  That thus it passes smoothly, quietly.
Many such eves of gently whisp'ring noise
  May we together pass, and calmly try
What are this world's true joys,—ere the great voice,
  From its fair face, shall bid our spirits fly.

are no parents but there are at least "fraternal souls" in this small apartment in the midst of mercantile London. With some subjectivity—though indeed the brothers frequently read together—he sees George and Tom dreaming upon "lore so voluble and deep" (the lore of English poetry, of course, that has been so much in his own mind). Anxiety about Tom emerges directly for a moment, and we sense the devotion that later showed itself when he nursed Tom throughout the autumn of 1818:

> This is your birth-day Tom, and I rejoice
> That thus it passes smoothly, quietly.

This new security was to last for less than two years. But at this moment any thought of separation, as the rhetorical flourish of the close indicates, is very remote.

3

Now that Keats was twenty-one, he was of course free to make decisions about his future without Abbey's approval. He could have started practice as an apothecary at any time he wished after October 31. But the weeks were passing without any definite step to do so. As far as he knew he had only about £50 or £60 a year, and even then it would not be completely his until all the children had become twenty-one. But he might well feel that a few months of hesitation would not be fatal. Even after he moved to Cheapside in order to live with his brothers, he kept going over to the Hospital. The fee he had paid as a dresser the previous March allowed him to continue for a full year if he wished to do so; and when the year was finished, he still decided to keep his finger in surgery for a few more months. On March 17, 1817, Haydon wrote in his *Diary,* "He has gone to dress wounds, after spending an evening with me spouting Shakespeare." The position was not too demanding. Keats could arrange his own hours. To continue as a dresser at least served as a delaying action; it eased his conscience, and gave an appearance—to himself as well as to Abbey—that he was still seriously aware of the need to make a living.

Abbey was indeed becoming a little impatient. But so much had been happening—the return from Margate to the dismal lodgings in the Borough had been followed by the fortunate reunion with Clarke, the sonnet on Chapman's Homer, the warm welcome of

Hunt, Haydon, and Reynolds, all within the space of a month or six weeks. The autumn was altogether intoxicating. We may add to all this the security of the new home of the young and vulnerable brothers, reunited at last. Naturally Keats kept hesitating. Meanwhile, Hunt was preparing an article for the *Examiner* of December 1 called "Young Poets," in which he presented to his readers Shelley, Reynolds, and Keats, and, in the section on Keats, printed the sonnet on Chapman's Homer. Keats was delighted. He took the magazine over to Guy's Hospital and showed it to his former roommate Henry Stephens. The article, said Stephens, "sealed his fate and he gave himself up more completely to Poetry." [4] One thing after another continued to happen in quick succession. He met Shelley at Leigh Hunt's sometime in December. Moreover, arrangements had been made to publish his first volume of verse the following March, and in December he completed two substantial poems for it—"I stood tiptoe" and "Sleep and Poetry."

It was also in December that Haydon took the famous life mask of Keats at his studio. To do so implied a genuine compliment, for Haydon had already decided to include Keats in the huge canvas on which he was working—"Christ's Entry into Jerusalem"—and was taking the mask in preparation.[5] Like the Renaissance painters, Haydon hoped to give his picture contemporary relevance by including modern figures—Newton and Voltaire from the century before, and then his own friends, Wordsworth, Hazlitt, Lamb, and Keats. Voltaire was inserted to represent skepticism, and Haydon for a time was worried lest he was being unjust. After trying to read Voltaire carefully, he felt more than ever convinced that he had been right. The conscientious gesture and the predictable result amused his friends. Even Keats teased him, though Haydon

---

[4] "I remember the time of his first introduction to Mr. Leigh Hunt, who then Edited the Examiner, & I remember several pieces of his Poetry being inserted in that Journal, at which he was exceedingly gratified, I remember his also telling me of an introduction he had to two or three Young Poets of Promise & among them I remember well the name of Shelley—I also remember his showing me some time afterwards 'the Examiner' in which was an Article under the Title of 'the Rising Poets' or 'the Young Poets' or some such Title in which the names of several were inserted with a brief sketch of them & a Specimen of their Poetry, and the name of John Keats appeared among them, with that of Shelley.—This sealed his fate and he gave himself up more completely than before to Poetry" (*KC*, II.210–211).

[5] The picture has, interestingly enough, ended in the area of the United States associated with George Keats and his family. For a long time it hung in the Cincinnati Art Museum, and it is now at Mount St. Mary's Seminary, in Norwood, Ohio. For the life mask, see the frontispiece.

missed the joke. "Never," he writes, "shall I forget Keats, once, when looking at my Picture . . . getting suddenly up, & approaching it he placed his hand on his heart, & bowing his head, 'there is the being I will bow to,' said he—he stood before Voltaire!" [6] Constantly worked over, the picture was finally hung about three years later. In March 1820 the happy Haydon borrowed money, hired the large Egyptian Hall, and invited celebrities. The lesser figures, including the donkey,[7] secured more approval than the central figure of Christ. In fact, the face of Christ, which Haydon had been repainting for years, had unfortunately begun to show a remarkable similarity to Haydon. Keats, with the absorbed concentration Haydon thought so typical of him, was put in the upper right-hand corner, just above the bowed head of Wordsworth (which Hazlitt thought an admirable likeness) and not far from Hazlitt. Naturally flattered that Haydon took the life mask, Keats just as naturally pretended to a casual blitheness, jokingly comparing the mask to a Medusa's head when Clarke, who seems to have been present when Haydon took it, asked for a copy.[8]

4

The life mask brings up the subject of Keats's appearance. We have noticed it only in the accounts of the schooldays at Enfield and in the brief mention of his short stature.

Two difficulties tend to confuse whatever general notion readers may have of his appearance. The first and more important is that, while few writers of the period are more minutely described, the few paintings and sketches available are far from satisfactory.[9] The explanation is simple enough. Keats's reputation was almost entirely posthumous. Haydon deferred making a serious portrait: Keats was young and there always seemed to be ample time

[6] *Diary*, II.317.

[7] One viewer—sometimes said to be Samuel Rogers, and sometimes James Northcote—is reported to have remarked: "Mr. Haydon, your ass is the Saviour of the picture."

[8] He begins a letter to Clarke (December 17, 1816), "You may now look at Minerva's Aegis with impunity, seeing that my awful Visage did not turn you into a John Doree [a fish] you have accordingly a legitimate title to a Copy—I will use my interest to procure it for you." Later, when his friend Benjamin Bailey asked for copies, Keats said he would "expurgatorize" them from Haydon's studio (I.174).

[9] A detailed discussion of the portraits would be in order, were it not for Donald Parson's admirable *Portraits of Keats* (1954). References to portraits not reproduced in the present book are to the plate numbers in Parson.

ahead.[10] The sketch by Charles Brown was unknown until after the first World War.

Hence the various portraits by Severn—almost all of them posthumous, the last made almost forty years after Keats's death—moved into the vacuum during the middle and later nineteenth century and are still reproduced more through inertia than for any particular reason.[11] Unfortunately Severn was not merely a poor draughtsman but also somewhat limp in character. The worldly, experienced Barry Cornwall, after meeting Keats in 1820, thought he had "never encountered a more manly and simple young man"; and Severn himself admitted that Keats was distinguished by "a peculiarly dauntless expression, such as may be seen in the face of some seamen." But no one can find a semblance of this in the portraits Severn made. Even in his miniature, he portrayed his own notion of the way a sensitive poet ought to look. Finding his portraits were acquiring a public as Keats's posthumous fame grew, he became more dreamily self-projective as he obligingly turned out more, even going so far as to make an imaginary portrait of Keats composing the "Ode to a Nightingale." William Hilton's rival portrait, commissioned by Richard Woodhouse, understandably annoyed him. But the reason he gave for disliking it is so completely inappropriate that it tells us something of the limitations of Severn's pictures. The Hilton portrait—much manlier and closer to the life mask than any of Severn's own—made Keats look, said Severn, like "a sneaking fellow." More effective by far than the Severn portraits—perhaps the best of all the portraits of Keats—is the drawing by the businesslike Charles Brown, who had no pretensions as an artist but was at least direct and plain.[12] Two, possibly three, silhouettes by Brown are also reliable. Keats sent a copy of one—we do not know which—to his sister Fanny, speaking of it as "a very capital profile." Among the posthumous portraits, a case can be made for the painting by Hil-

10 Haydon left a few rough profile sketches (Parson, Nos. 8 and 10), but only for the very specialized pose (a darting, amazed look he wanted to suggest) in his picture "Christ's Entry." He condemned himself after Keats's death for not having made a portrait when John Taylor proposed it.

11 The only painting Severn made during Keats's lifetime is his miniature, of which there are several variants. In addition there is a charcoal sketch (Parson, No. 16) and the famous ink drawing of Keats on his deathbed, somewhat retouched and idealized in later versions. All the other Severn portraits and their variants (Parson, Nos. 38, 40, 42, 44–46, 48, 51), not to mention the several portraits attributed to Severn, were posthumous.

12 See Chapter XXI, section 1.

ton and the medallion plaque by Giuseppi Girometti (the making of which was supervised by Richard Woodhouse, with the life mask used as a basis) .[13]

Hence the importance of the life mask, supplemented by whatever impressions can be gathered from the drawing and silhouettes by Brown and a few other portraits. Yet the mask, of course, shows a face in repose; and every account stresses the mobility of the features. Most of his acquaintances also mention the large, expressive mouth Keats inherited from his mother. ("Her Features," said Abbey, "were good & regular, with the Exception of her Mouth which was unusually wide.") Clarke recalls Keats's "capacious mouth" with amusement. Everyone had something to say about the eyes. Benjamin Bailey's remarks are fairly typical:

> I was delighted with the naturalness & simplicity of his character, & was at once drawn to him by his winning & indeed affectionate manner . . . The Lady's sketch [that of Mrs. Proctor] comes very near to my own recollection . . . I do not particularly remember the thickness of the upper lip, which is so generally described, & doubtless correctly;—but the mouth struck me as too wide, both in itself, & as out of harmony with the rest of the face, which, with this single blemish, was eminently beautiful. The eye was full & fine, & softened into tenderness, or beamed with a fiery brightness, according to the current of his thoughts & conversation.[14]

If there seems to have been some disagreement about the color of the eyes (the consensus is that they were probably hazel, and that the hair was a reddish brown) [15] the explanation is that it was the general expression that caught attention, and any memory of the precise coloring was lost. Repeatedly the accounts stress the unusual combination of firmness with variability of expression. Hunt is typical when he mentions Keats's face as showing a union of "energy and sensibility"; the mouth was "not without something of a character of pugnacity," while the eyes were "glowing; large,

[13] For discussion of the Hilton painting and the Girometti plaque, see Parson, pp. 95–102, 151–152.

[14] KC, II.267–268.

[15] Mrs. Proctor told Lord Houghton that the eyes were "large and blue" and the hair "auburn." Georgiana Keats, in her copy of Houghton's Life, disagreed: "his eyes were dark brown, large, soft, and expressive, and his hair a golden red." Clarke and Severn speak of the eyes as hazel. The hair is as much disputed—the men (Clarke, Hunt, Bailey, Severn) tending to remember it as brown and the women as auburn to red. All of these people are writing several years after Keats's death. The surviving locks, despite Amy Lowell's rapt description of one as "lighter than the shade known as 'Titian red' . . . A red sunset comes nearest to the colour" (I.95), are all rather faded; but they seem to suggest a russet or reddish brown.

dark, and sensitive." We noticed before George Keats's remark about the "open, prodigal" nature of his brother: "John's eyes moistened, and his lip quivered at the relation of any tale of generosity, of benevolence or noble daring." Hunt says much the same ("At the recital of a noble action," his eyes "would suffuse with tears"), but adds that Keats "did not like these betrayals of emotion; and he had great personal as well as moral courage." There was also the look of high-mindedness. The conclusion of the description by Mrs. Proctor is often cited: Keats's face "had an expression as though he had been looking on some glorious sight." [16] Clarke quotes her account, and says of the last remark:

> That's excellent. "His mouth was full, and less intellectual than his other features." True again. But when our artist pronounces that "his eyes were large and *blue*," and that "his hair was *auburn*," I am naturally reminded of the "Chameleon" fable:—"They were *brown*, ma'am—*brown*, I assure you!" The fact is, the lady was enchanted—and I cannot wonder at it—with the whole character.[17]

The other difficulty in getting a mental picture is in remembering that his stature was only five feet and three-quarters of an inch. (This was by no means considered so short then as it is now: five feet and a half was a very good height, and Haydon writes admiringly in his diary that Wordsworth measured "5 ft. 9 In. $\frac{7}{8}$th— a very fine, heroic proportion. He made me write it down.") The people who knew him were themselves always forgetting it. Like his own father, he was broad-shouldered; and when he was sitting, one naturally noticed only the shoulders and face. Even when he stood he seemed taller than he was, said Severn, "partly from his erect attitude and a characteristic backward poise . . . and, perhaps more than anything else, from a peculiarly dauntless expression." But Keats himself was mindful enough of his height, at least at times. A few revealing remarks appear in the letters.[18] On one occasion, he was justifiably annoyed. "Mr. Lewis," he wrote George (February 14, 1819), "went a few mornings ago to

16 *KC*, II.157. Haydon makes a similar remark: Keats's eyes "had an inward look . . . like a Delphian priestess who saw visions."

17 *Recollections*, p. 153.

18 E.g., "We haven't any female friend in the house—Tom is taken for a Madman and I being stunted am taken for nothing" (June 4, 1818). Speaking of the scenery near Winander, he writes Tom: "I never forgot my stature so completely—I live in the eye; and my imagination, surpassed, is at rest" (June 27, 1818). He tells Benjamin Bailey he thinks "better of Womankind than to suppose they care whether Mister John Keats five feet [in] hight likes them or not" (July 22, 1818).

town with Mrs. Brawne they talked about me—and I heard that
Mr. L. said a thing I am not at all contented with—Says he 'O, he
is quite the little Poet' now this is abominable." Before his fatal
illness, said Clarke, Keats was "active, athletic, and enduringly
strong—as the fight with the butcher gave full attestation." [19]

We end by returning to the mask, as Fanny Keats herself did,
and by trying to remember the mobility of the face, the stockiness
of the shoulders, the shortness of height, the "dauntless expression" that Severn, despite his own paintings, tried to express in
words. The mask in its own way also suggests the strength, the res-
oluteness, the masculine good sense that almost everyone found so
abundant in him (his "common sense," said Bailey, "was a conspicuous part of his character").

5

Finally, we need to remember the ready humor—and not only
the readiness but the kind of humor—that inevitably colored
people's conception of his appearance. It could be earthy; it was
certainly direct; and it had an element of farce. There were the
"concerts" in which Keats and various friends took the part of different instruments—Keats's preference (partly because he may
have been intrigued with the word) being to imitate the bassoon.
And there was also the ready, almost unconscious mimicry that
Cowden Clarke, his oldest friend, kept recalling forty years after
Keats's death. After attending a prize fight between two skilled
lightweights of the day, Keats "in describing the rapidity of the
blows of the one, while the other was falling," began instinctively
to tap "his fingers on the window-pane." So with his "perception of
humour," said Clarke, which, "with the power of transmitting it
by imitation, was both vivid and irresistibly amusing." And Clarke
goes on to mention a bearbaiting that Keats attended:

> The performance not having begun, Keats was near to, and
> watched, a young aspirant, who had brought a younger under his
> wing to witness the solemnity, and whom he oppressively patron-
> ized, instructing him in the names and qualities of all the magnates
> present. Now and then, in his zeal to manifest and impart his
> knowledge, he would forget himself, and stray beyond the pre-

[19] The butcher's boy, who was tall and very strong, was tormenting a kitten;
Keats interfered; the butcher challenged him; the fight lasted almost an hour, with
Keats the victor (*Recollections*, pp. 143–144).

scribed bounds into the ring, to the lashing resentment of its comptroller, Mr. William Soames, who, after some hints of a practical
nature to "keep back," began laying about him with indiscriminate
and unmitigable vivacity, the Peripatetic signifying to his pupil,
"My eyes! Bill Soames giv' me sich a licker!" evidently grateful, and
considering himself complimented upon being included in the general dispensation. Keats's entertainment with and appreciation of
this minor scene of low life has often recurred to me.

Simultaneously, as Keats was acting out his description of the people present, he began to imitate the bear:

> his legs and arms bent and shortened till he looked like Bruin on
> his hind legs, dabbing his fore paws hither and thither, as the dogs
> snapped at him, and now and then acting the gasp of one that had
> been suddenly caught and hugged—his own capacious mouth adding
> force to the personation.

Even more amusing—it is so altogether unexpected—is the description of what began as a calm diagnosis on Keats's part when
Clarke complained of a stomach disorder. Keats, said Clarke, described

> the functions and actions of the organ with the clearness and, as I
> presume, technical precision of an adult practitioner; casually illus-
> trating the comment, in his characteristic way, with poetical im-
> agery: the stomach, he said, being like a brood of callow nestlings
> (opening his capacious mouth) yearning and gaping for suste-
> nance.[20]

6

It is probably about this time—between November and February—that Keats had his famous interview with Mr. Abbey. Not un-
reasonably, Abbey argued that Keats should now set up as a surgeon, and suggested that he do so in Tottenham. Abbey's account,
as recorded by John Taylor, follows:

> He communicated his Plans to his Ward but his Surprise was not
> moderate, to hear in Reply, that he did not intend to be a Surgeon
> —Not intend to be a Surgeon! why what do you mean to be? I mean
> to rely upon my Abilities as a Poet—John, you are either Mad or a
> Fool, to talk in so absurd a Manner. My mind is made up, said the
> youngster very quietly. I know that I possess Abilities greater than
> most Men, and therefore I am determined to gain my Living by ex-
> ercising them.—Seeing nothing could be done Abby called him a
> Silly Boy, & prophesied a speedy Termination to his inconsiderate
> Enterprise.

[20] *Recollections*, pp. 132, 144–145.

"Not long after," continued Abbey, Keats brought him "a little book which he had got printed"—the *Poems,* published March 3, 1817:

> I took it & said I would look at it because it was his writing, otherwise I should not have troubled my Head with any such Thing—When we next met I said, Well John I have read your Book, & it reminds me of the Quaker's Horse which was hard to catch, & good for nothing when he was caught—So your Book is hard to understand & good for nothing when it is understood. Do you know says the old Man, I don't think he ever forgave me for uttering this Opinion, which however was the Truth.[21]

Unquestionably it was the pressure Abbey applied that evoked Keats's firm response. For underneath Keats was far from certain. Every discerning acquaintance he ever had stresses his common sense; he was only too aware of the problem of making a living. He was still going to the hospital two weeks after he had taken the copy of his first volume to Abbey. It was May before he finally abandoned work as a dresser; and by then he was immersed in his long struggle with *Endymion*—his almost desperate attempt to prove himself in a poem of four thousand lines. Even so, for the next three years, he kept entertaining at least the possibility of setting up practice. Naturally the interview with Abbey, troubling him as much as it did, also steeled him in the dogged push of will that carried him through the following year. But in this interview it was not Abbey, of course, whom he wished to answer. It was himself.

7

The arrangements for the "little Book" to which Abbey refers may have been made by October or at least November. It might have been Cowden Clarke who smoothed the way between Keats and the publishers, Charles and James Ollier. The single reference we have in any of the letters of Keats occurs in a letter to Clarke, on Keats's twenty-first birthday, October 31, made with all the affected casualness of youth: "I pray thee let me know when you go to Ollier's and where he resides." But either Hunt or Haydon could have helped. Certainly their good opinion would have influenced the Olliers.[22]

21 *KC*, I.307–308.
22 It is sometimes suggested that it was Shelley who aroused the interest of the

To anyone in Keats's position the mere idea of publication would be intoxicating. Before December 1, when Hunt printed in his article on the "Young Poets" the sonnet on Chapman's Homer, the only poem of Keats that had been published was the sonnet "O Solitude." We have no reason to doubt Henry Stephens, the friend at Guy's Hospital, when he spoke of Keats's delight at the publication of these few lines, and the eagerness with which Keats showed him Hunt's article on the "Young Poets." Yet, except for the single remark about the Olliers to Clarke, back in October, nothing in the letters suggests that an entire volume—and, more than that, a first volume—is afoot. As we begin to approach the more fully documented segment of Keats's known development, we become increasingly curious about the areas of reserve and self-consciousness. The explanation for this curiosity is that we rightly feel that we are dealing with a nature remarkably unselfconscious and open. Why then, should there be these unexpected areas of reserve—and, as the next chapter suggests, of actual embarrass-ment? Granted that everyone has a need for privacy at times, still Keats could never have achieved what he did except through qual-ities that appear to be the reverse of withdrawal, secrecy, or even mere inhibition.

Keats may have been reticent partly because the volume, which the Ollier brothers were publishing largely on trust and hearsay, was likely to be appallingly thin. Probably neither Hunt nor Hay-don nor Reynolds knew how little Keats had written thus far. Par-adoxically, after having had so little access to the literary world, he was suddenly in a position where men he respected not only took for granted that he was a poet of promise, but probably as-sumed that there were more poems tucked away in the drawer than he actually had. It is possible to recognize promise, even of the highest sort, without much written evidence. But Keats him-self was only too aware that the bulk was still slight, and that much of it was not very good. Perhaps this helps explain his uneasiness around Shelley, who, in December, had advised him to defer pub-lishing. Having seen only some of Keats's writings, Shelley could not have been thinking of the potential size of the volume. What-ever his reasons—it is the sort of thing one can say without think-ing—he was doubtless well intended, though he himself was al-

Olliers; they were his publishers. But December, when he first met Keats, would have been a little late for this.

ways quick to hop into print. But the advice pressed Keats on a sensitive spot, and all the more because it came from a man ordinarily so generous in his praise.

Keats seems to have dug in quietly for the preparation of this volume. Short poems were accumulating. He wrote four more sonnets in December that he felt able to include. Three of them are rather tepid performances: a sonnet to his future sister-in-law, Georgiana Wylie ("Nymph of the downward smile") ; "To Kosciusko," the Polish patriot; and "Happy is England." On the evening of December 30 occurred one of the contests in sonnet writing that Hunt loved. Cowden Clarke and Keats were visiting him; there was some talk of the cheerful sound of the cricket at the fireside; and Hunt, said Clarke, suddenly

> proposed to Keats the challenge of writing then, there, and to time, a sonnet "On the Grasshopper and the Cricket." No one was present but myself, and they accordingly set to. I, apart, with a book at the end of the sofa, could not avoid furtive glances every now and then at the emulants. I cannot say how long the trial lasted. I was not proposed umpire; and had no stop-watch for the occasion. The time, however, was short for such a performance, and Keats won as to time. But the event of the after-scrutiny was one of many such occurrences which have riveted the memory of Leigh Hunt in my affectionate regard and admiration for unaffected generosity and perfectly unpretentious encouragement. His sincere look of pleasure at the first line—
>
> > The poetry of earth is never dead.
>
> "Such a prosperous opening!" he said; and when he came to the tenth and eleventh lines:—
>
> > On a lone winter evening, *when the frost*
> > *Has wrought a silence—*
>
> "Ah! that's perfect! Bravo Keats!" [23]

A glance at the two competing sonnets will quickly illustrate ways in which Keats is beginning to transcend not merely the Hunt idiom but also a more general form of sentimentalism common in verse of the period. Both the idiom and the sentimentalism remain with Keats for at least another year, sustained by purely literary associations—by attempts to capture the trappings of myth or chivalry (seen, admittedly, through the spectacles of Hunt). But given an occasion like this, with little time to embellish and

[23] *Recollections,* pp. 135–136.

with an unexpectedly familiar subject, his inherent taste begins to assert itself; and sentimentality, not being indigenous, does not obtrude. Hunt's sonnet, considering the time he had to write it, is by no means bad. But what he can do with it is limited from the outset by his focus on the insects themselves; and needing to fill out the lines and to make them agreeable to human feelings, he is forced to sentimentalize by personifying. The "little vaulter in the sunny grass," and the cricket—"warm little housekeeper"—are "sweet and tiny cousins." And the sonnet drives to a moral at the end: "both are sent" to carry to the thoughtful ear the salutary lesson of "mirth." [24] Keats, on the other hand, typically focuses on a psychological process rather than a moral. The generalization is disposed of at the start ("The poetry of earth is never dead") , and brought back only at the beginning of the sestet in order to introduce the cricket. A simple division in structure gives a frame; and the sonnet can thus become more freely allusive and concrete. The result is a more nearly objective empathy (the grasshopper "rests at ease beneath some pleasant weed") and finally a more genuine resolution—the blending, or continuity, of summer and winter are frankly left to the listener's imagination:

> The poetry of earth is never dead:
>   When all the birds are faint with the hot sun,
>   And hide in cooling trees, a voice will run
> From hedge to hedge about the new-mown mead;
> That is the Grasshopper's—he takes the lead
>   In summer luxury,—he has never done
>   With his delights; for when tired out with fun
> He rests at ease beneath some pleasant weed.
> The poetry of earth is ceasing never:
>   On a lone winter evening, when the frost
>   Has wrought a silence, from the stove there shrills

[24] Green little vaulter in the sunny grass
>   Catching your heart up at the feel of June,
>   Sole voice that's heard amid the lazy noon,
> When ev'n the bees lag at the summoning brass;
> And you, warm little housekeeper, who class
>   With those who think the candles come too soon,
>   Loving the fire, and with your tricksome tune
> Nick the glad silent moments as they pass;
> Oh sweet and tiny cousins, that belong,
>   One to the fields, the other to the hearth,
> Both have your sunshine; both though small are strong
>   At your clear hearts; and both were sent on earth
> To sing in thoughtful ears this natural song,—
>   Indoors and out, summer and winter, Mirth.

The cricket's song, in warmth increasing ever,
And seems to one in drowsiness half lost,
The Grasshopper's among some grassy hills.

8

But sonnets would not eke out many pages. Neither, in Keats's opinion, could they give his volume much value by themselves—"Did our great Poets ever write short pieces?" His main bid came in the two longer poems he was trying to finish. With what he doubtless thought a shrewd gesture, he decided to attract the reader by putting one of them at the start ("I stood tiptoe") and then to conclude with the second ("Sleep and Poetry"), his principal effort thus far.

The desire to write longer poems was not simply a response to the challenge of what the eighteenth century had called the "greater genres." He had an instinctive prudent sense that activity and momentum are valuable, and that longer poems provide a spacious field for exercise, tending to prevent constriction and imaginative cramp. For similar reasons, there is a help in extremely loose forms, such as the epistle. Naturally, in these two poems ("I stood tiptoe" with 242 lines, and "Sleep and Poetry" with 404) he went back to an idiom and form that he had been using for over a year: the flowing heroic couplet in which all his longer poems had been written, and the sort of idiom we noticed in the Margate poems. But there is a difference, and it reflects his growing confidence. He had previously managed to finish longer attempts only when sheltered by the artificial device of a verse letter. Now he carries through a straightforward descriptive-meditative poem in the vein so common in the eighteenth century. Only one other verse epistle was ever to be written by him, and that a mere casual effusion that he never intended to publish (to John Hamilton Reynolds, in March 1818). Otherwise, his growing gift for letters was completely diverted into the remarkable correspondence that begins in 1817.

"I stood tiptoe" had been partly written before he had gone to Margate in July. It had been suggested, says Hunt, "by a delightful summer-day, as he stood beside the gate that leads from the Battery on Hampstead Heath into a field by Caen Wood." Badly needing to fatten the forthcoming volume, Keats salvaged these lines in November and tried to expand them. He probably hoped to stumble upon a narrative theme that might be developed and might also supply a framework. He thought of using the fable of Endymion, and in fact tentatively called the poem "Endymion." On December 17 he wrote Clarke "I have done little to Endymion lately—I hope to finish it in one more attack." (He had caught from Haydon the vocabulary of energy.) But the attack was only a sally. The next day, as the date on the autograph shows, he wrote merely another twelve lines, and, in a kind of fatigued desperation, ended with a vague flourish:

> but now no more,
> My wand'ring spirit must no further soar.—

Any ideas for a narrative were deferred until, a few months later, *Endymion* was begun. At least one was of the first importance: that suggested in the line "Ah! surely he had burst our mortal bars"—the imaginative quest to participate, through myth and in other ways, in what Keats later called an "immortal free-masonry." The theme was to be central in almost all his poetry from *Endymion* through the "Ode on a Grecian Urn." But at the moment he has little more than a suggestion. Moreover, he was busily at work on his other long poem, "Sleep and Poetry," and the volume had to go to press very soon. As a result, "I stood tiptoe" simply relapses into one description after another, a sort of breathless catalogue of rural sights. Much comes from memory. The Enfield years return, the walks with Cowden Clarke, the stream near his grandmother's house in Edmonton (with the minnows "Staying their wavy bodies 'gainst the stream"). So do some of the stock images of the Felton Mathew period—maidens with "downward look," thoughts of "realms of wonderment." For generations admirers of Keats have found, in at least some of these lines, examples of "freshness," "realism," and the like. In doing so, they are unquestionably influenced by all the attendant circumstances—Keats's youth and inexperience, the hurry in writing, the massive achievement to come—and are willing to be satisfied with anything that does not imitate Hunt's worst excesses. Needless to say, we are right to be generous. But any loud admiration of these poems for their own virtues simply justifies Santayana's remark that, while "love is very penetrating," it "penetrates to possibilities rather than facts."

Moreover, the rhinocerine sighs of Johnson about the limitations of the genre apply quite as much to these couplets as to far better descriptive poems. Because "the scenes, which they must exhibit successively, are all subsisting at the same time, the order in which they are shown must by necessity be arbitrary, and more is not to be expected from the last part than the first. The attention, therefore, which cannot be detained by suspense, must be excited by diversity." The diversity, if thin, leaves the mind unengaged; if profuse enough, it only distracts. Keats himself was already aware of the limitations of the genre, and was to become more so with every half year that passed. He did not really want to write a purely descriptive poem: he was doing so now only because he lacked a subject. Within another two or three years he was to become completely weary of the attempt to elevate scenery into a central place in poetry ("Scenery is fine—but human nature is finer"; "I am getting a great dislike of the picturesque"; "descriptions are bad at all times") .

9

In the far more important "Sleep and Poetry," this bold experimenter, who was to try so many styles successfully, began once more to go over the same ground as in the three verse letters. In a sense, he was to retread that ground until the end. But because the concern was primary and universal, the return to it proved increasingly valuable. That concern was nothing less than the use of poetry itself—and it was a concern that could easily paralyze endeavor and confidence. It was precisely this large, high-minded absorption in the past monuments of literature that was to inhibit Matthew Arnold and so many who followed Arnold. Yet Keats's poetic achievement offers no greater interest than in the remarkable success with which he by-passes these inhibitions by constantly reverting to basic premises and generous ideals. He was to feel every qualm in doing so; naivetés sprouted like mushrooms; and he quickly knew them to be naivetés, and suffered accordingly. But single-mindedly in this one way (however open he was in other ways) he kept reverting to the larger aims of the great poets of the past—scorning to manicure their details, and seeking instead to recapture their spirit. This indeed had been the dream of the middle and later eighteenth century in England: it was the only way in which to rival the haunting memory of the great eras of the past. It may have proved to be little more than a dream for the eighteenth century, but it was a dream based on good sense. In his famous *Conjectures on Original Composition* (1759), the premises of which Johnson thought any intelligent man would take for granted, Edward Young had written: "He that imitates the divine *Iliad* does not imitate Homer." In our use of great predecessors, "It is by a sort of noble contagion, from a general familiarity with their writings, and not by any particular sordid theft, that we can be the better for those who went before us."

10

Now, writing largely at the Hunt cottage in Hampstead Heath, Keats picks up most of the thoughts in the verse letters to Mathew, to George, and to Clarke, but he tries to sharpen them. He gives them the rather loose frame suggested by his title ("Sleep and Poetry"). This is at least not a verse letter. In fact he is beginning to grope toward a general premise that becomes prominent in the final year of his writing: the Januslike character of the human imagination, turned as it is to the inner life, on the one hand, and the concrete objective world, on the other. But the attempt to make "sleep" an integral part of the poem does not go very far. If we look forward to the later poems, of course, the use of "sleep" takes on some importance. But here, in effect, he uses it as a vestibule to something very different. Quickly Keats summarizes the attractions of what can only be called "revery"—an appeal that continued to obsess or tease poetry and music throughout the entire century, and well after the nineteenth century.

In this poem of 404 lines (quite the longest poem he had written thus far) Keats doubtless intended to put the claims of revery sympathetically and persuasively. His thought was obviously to begin with this subject and then move on to other functions and approaches to poetry—to suggest that poetry could and should involve much more—and finally to return to the justifiable, pleasant results of revery, thus offering, he thought, an effective if not too neat a close. But we find him already beginning to anticipate the split that, within two years and a half, was to become essential and dramatic in his greatest poetry: the question, for example, that ends the "Ode to a Nightingale"—"Was it a vision"—a true insight—"or a waking dream?"; or the strong, mocking skepticism of *Lamia;* or the powerful indictment in the *Fall of Hyperion:*

> The poet and the dreamer are distinct,
> Diverse, sheer opposite, antipodes.

For after only eighteen lines Keats quickly drops all thought of mere revery. There is the abrupt question: "But what is higher beyond thought than thee?"—that is to say, sleep and revery. Swans, doves, green islands, are forgotten. There is a sudden sense, in the living world, of a meaning that is always astir to the receptive ear (like "low rumblings" before the storm). He probably recalls Wordsworth's sonnet to his daughter:

> Listen! the mighty Being is awake,
> And doth with his eternal motion make
> A sound like thunder—everlastingly.

To the open heart, the low rumblings, and the sense that something "breathes about us in the vacant air," are hints, suggestions leading to the thought of what, following Wordsworth, he later called "the burden of the mystery."

Then suddenly Keats makes the plunge into what is to serve as the fluid basis of his poem—fluid because it consists so entirely of a welter of floating ideals, hopes, ambitions, intentions. Frank, altogether naked confidences are jotted down, and always with the misgivings he feels about himself:

> O Poesy! for thee I hold my pen
> That am not yet a glorious denizen
> Of thy wide heaven—should I rather kneel
>
> .   .   .   .   .   .
>
> O Poesy! for thee I grasp my pen
>   . . . yet, to my ardent prayer,
> Yield from thy sanctuary some clear air.

He is stirred with a dim sense that amplitude and realism (amplitude working from and through the realistic awareness of fact) are what is wanted: the ultimate ideal would be to

> Write on my tablets all that was permitted,
> All that was for our human senses fitted.
> Then the events of this wide world I'd seize
> Like a strong giant.

Then come the famous lines where youthfully, not at all pom-
pously, he begins:

> Stop and consider! Life is but a day:
> A fragile dew-drop on its perilous way.

If the central point is the brevity of things that exist in process,
there is also the vivid, empathic sense of what Hopkins later called
"inscape": an insistence on the joy of process in sheer act, sheer fulfillment of function ("A pigeon tumbling in clear summer air").

Then follow the lines, poignant when we think of what the next
ten years were actually to bring, where he gives a sort of timetable
that would be hasty for so many poets but would actually prove
too leisurely for himself:

> O for ten years, that I may overwhelm
> Myself in poesy; so I may do the deed
> That my own soul has to itself decreed.
> Then will I pass the countries that I see
> In long perspective, and continually
> Taste their pure fountains. First the realm I'll pass
> Of Flora, and old Pan . . .
>
> .   .   .   .   .   .
>
> And can I ever bid these joys farewell?
> Yes, I must pass them for a nobler life,
> Where I may find the agonies, the strife
> Of human hearts.

The bold question follows that he was to continue to pose—and
meet:

> Is there so small a range
> In the present strength of manhood, that the high
> Imagination cannot freely fly . . . ?

Some rather silly talk, routinely echoing Hunt with halfhearted
smartness, fills out fifty lines: remarks about the eighteenth century's having failed to continue the great Renaissance tradition.
These are the lines at which Byron and others were later to scoff.
Using an image he remembered from Hazlitt, Keats dismisses the
whole neoclassic tradition, and its fondness for closed couplets:

> with a puling infant's force
> They sway'd about upon a rocking-horse,
> And thought it Pegasus.

Here we have the Keats that Hunt, and perhaps others of the
Hunt circle, fondly called "Junkets." And "Junkets" goes on, with

blithe abandon and jerky bravado, to say that this "ill-fated, impious race" has "blasphemed" Apollo. Jauntily he speaks of the past century as having straggled about with a "decrepid standard" bearing in large "The name of one Boileau." Of course he had probably never read a word of Boileau. Within two and a half years he was to think far differently, and to begin his poem *Lamia* only after a respectful study of Dryden's versification.

11

The heart of the poem (lines 230–312) follows; and a divided heart it is at this time. For we have a twofold ideal of poetry, to begin with; and it alternates with confessional uncertainties about himself. In neither respect does this ideal have anything to do with escapism, sleep, or revery. Clairvoyantly it suggests a debate that, within less than two years, was to declare itself in his greatest poetry and further complicate the still larger debate between the escapist and the more essential functions of poetry. In one respect, this ideal can be called sculpturesque: a prizing of power and grandeur of conception firmly restrained; an ideal of poetry as

> the supreme of power;
> 'Tis might half slumb'ring on its own right arm.

It is this side of Keats that was to respond so eagerly to the influence of Milton, within a year and a half, and to be expressed with a firmness unique in modern poetry in the fragment of *Hyperion* and in the great odes of 1819. But there is also the humanitarian aspect of this ideal: a conception of poetry as directly human, reassuring, personal, and potentially dramatic (though still far from the Shakespearean depth it was later to begin to reach) ; an ideal of poetry as

> a friend
> To soothe the cares, and lift the thoughts of man.

In the "Ode on a Grecian Urn" he was to achieve one possible resolution. In this most sculpturesque of English poems, of power kept in reserve ("half slumb'ring on its own right arm") , the conclusion of the drama of the heart's response to this ideal is the extent to which a trust in it can itself be "a friend to man." Each of the odes, in its own way, offers a different resolution. But the reso-

lution was still tentative, precarious; and the whole matter was to
be reopened again, three months after the odes, in the revised fragment, the *Fall of Hyperion*.

Against this many-sided "vast idea" of the "end and aim of
Poesy," Keats can scarcely help counterpointing his own meager
achievement and almost ludicrous lack of qualification. Would it
not be "better far to hide my foolish face"? Should this "whining
boyhood" that is he as he now is—and may never get beyond other
than physically—do anything before such an ideal except bow with
"reverence"? Again one glances ahead to the final rewriting of this
poem—and of almost all the longer poems—the *Fall of Hyperion*,
and especially the lines beginning, "What am I that should so be
saved from death?"

Yet he refuses to be inhibited. With transparent frankness he
states where he has placed and will be placing his trust. He has no
sophisticated sense at this time that an ideal of greatness can be
immensely formative, that it can free endeavor provided it be felt
with a vividness that obliterates thought of self: he has not read
Longinus' *On the Sublime*, or, perhaps, even heard of it. But his
answer is prophetic. Despite his lacks,

> yet there ever rolls
> A vast idea before me, and I glean
> Therefrom my liberty.

The freedom in reverting to the basic and primary, and the freedom caught in turning to the great partly because the great subsumes the basic and primary, is usually learned too late. But from
the beginning this trust has been instinctive in Keats. Inevitably it
is crossed by moments of self-doubt and fatigue. Now, having put
the matter, he has little more to say. He feels like an Icarus flying
near the sun with waxen wings. He mentions again the enormous
task ahead in the exploration of the "widenesses" of the ideal that
haunts him:

> Ah, what a task! upon my bended knees,
> I could unsay those—no, impossible!
> Impossible!

He has indeed run out, except to assert that it is impossible for
him to retract what he has just been saying. Lamely, and with engaging frankness, he returns to the insipidities of sleep ("For sweet
relief I'll dwell / On humbler thoughts"). The poem has to be

ended. After some hesitancy and mere filler, he turns to the room in the Hunt cottage where he is staying for the night on a sofa— the living room or parlor, with its busts and pictures, "The glorious features of the bards who sung / In other ages." He also refers to the "cold and sacred busts" Hunt loved. It is rather sad to find Keats writing to George two years later that, because Hunt makes "fine things petty," one becomes tired of marble or plaster busts and even "indifferent to Mozart." But all this lies ahead.

The Laurel Crown
and the Vision of Greatness

❋↩☸↱❋↩☸↱❋↩☸↱❋↩☸↱❋↩☸↱❋↩☸↱❋↩☸↱❋↩☸↱❋↩☸↱❋↩☸↱❋↩☸↱❋↩☸↱❋↩☸

December 1816 to March 1817

THIS VIVID AUTUMN and winter were to haunt Keats until the end. No period of comparable length in his short life so much affected him in retrospect. He was still serving part-time as a dresser at Guy's Hospital. Despite this gesture toward prudence, he began to go about—as his former fellow lodger, Henry Stephens, said— "with his neck nearly bare à la Byron. The collar turned down & a ribbon tied round his neck without any neckerchief. He also let his moustachios grow occasionally." [1] The printer for the firm of Taylor and Hessey, Henry C. Reynell, took it into his head a few months later that Keats was wearing "some sort of sailor costume." A loose coat, rather baggy trousers, a handkerchief around the neck, and hair longer than usual were all typical of the British sailor's appearance. Any combination of these could have explained the puzzled impression of the cautious Reynell. John Taylor himself, when he met Keats in March, was apparently enough struck by Keats's dress to describe it in a letter to his brother, Henry.[2]

Shortly after Taylor's first meeting with Keats, Haydon mentions an amusing episode in his journal, unfortunately deleting the most revealing part of it: "Keats said to me today as we were walking along 'Byron, Scott, Southey, & Shelley think they are to lead the age, but [*the rest of the sentence, consisting probably of eight or ten words, has been erased.*]' This was said with all the con-

---

[1] *KC*, II.211.

[2] Henry Taylor was not impressed, and wrote back to his brother (March 26): "Your interesting description of Mr. Keats gave me great pleasure, he must be a bold young man to affect such a singular style of dress. Cowley's dress was agreeable to the costume of the day but Mr. Keats's violates all decorum and can only excite ridicule and pity. His Poetry will not suit the old-fashioned taste of mine" (Edmund Blunden, *Keats's Publisher: A Memoir of John Taylor* [1936], p. 41).

sciousness of Genius; his face reddened." [3] Much that took place
during these months made his face redden—partly at the time but
much more in the year or two that followed. "The most unhappy
hours in our lives," he wrote a year later to his friend Reynolds
(April 27, 1818), "are those in which we recollect times past to
our own blushing—If we are immortal that must be the Hell." If
there is immortality, he hopes he will first be able to drink a little
of the waters of Lethe "in order to forget some of my schoolboy
days & others since." His later chagrin, of course, arose principally
from the quality of his writing. But the embarrassment also spread
to other things—to innocent mannerisms, to mild statements he
had made, and to what he had admired at the time. Some sense of
this helps to explain one of the puzzling qualities of the great poetry of two and three years later: the extent to which so much of it
(such as *Lamia* and the *Fall of Hyperion*) appears to be trying to
answer, modify, and compensate for what Keats felt to be the fool-
hardiness and excessive confidence (the necessary confidence) of
these valuable months. One especially thinks ahead to the bitter
passages of the *Fall of Hyperion,* where the poet is asked

> What benefit canst thou do, or all thy tribe,
> To the great world?

And not long before the *Fall of Hyperion* he wrote the line (so often applied to these months from October 1816 through the following spring), "A pet lamb in a sentimental farce," and in a letter (June 1819) mentioned his hope that he is "a little more of a
Philosopher than I was, consequently a little less of a versifying
Pet-lamb." The interest is to find this sharp, long-remembered embarrassment—and one quite without justification—in a talent so
generally free from self-consciousness. As we study these few
months in the context of what went before and what followed, we
are tempted to raise the question, what are the possible by-products of holding strongly to the Longinian ideal of greatness, when
at the same time this ideal is proving formative in the highest degree? Possibly our legacy from Freud and from the historical approach of the nineteenth century encourages us to concentrate too
exclusively on what we conceive to be origins and to neglect the
psychological effects of efforts and ideals. "Our notions," said Coleridge, "resemble the index and hand of the dial; our feelings are

[3] April 7, 1817, *Diary,* II.106–107.

the hidden springs which impel the machine." Yet there is this essential difference: that "notions and feelings react on each other reciprocally."

2

On Sunday evening, December 22, Keats wrote a sonnet in a few minutes and gave it the title "Written in Disgust of Vulgar Superstition." It never occurred to him to print it. Not only was its poetic value meager, but he may have felt it a poor thing in other ways. We know the length of time Keats took. For Tom, who was with him that evening, wrote in his copybook: "Written by J. K. in fifteen minutes." Yet here we glimpse for the first time—at least in any really graphic way—the youthful, almost absent-minded agnosticism with which he began his adult life. "Agnosticism" is the most positive word we can justifiably use.

It is easy to see why the whole subject of Keats's religious attitudes should for so long have been left relatively unpursued.[4] Yet the subject, however elusive, has a considerable importance. For within another year and a half Keats was to begin to think independently—with little help from others—about the larger issues of religion. This brave, persistent grope toward meaning makes up a substantial portion of the drama of Keats's development. Then, after all this, condensed within so short a time, come the final months when, bewildered, ill, often helplessly delirious, and constantly questioning why everything should be torn from him, the early agnosticism—the product of sheer accident and environment —returns in the cruelest way.

But at the moment of Keats's writing this sonnet, at twenty-one, there is a youthful bravado that tells us something of the atmosphere he had been breathing during these crucial months as well as the previous five or ten years. Without this self-revelatory son-

---

[4] The principal explanation, of course, is that the poetry itself is so largely untouched by any direct interest in religion, either one way or another. Hence admirers of Keats's work, if they themselves were devout, could conscientiously leave the subject undisturbed. Others felt contented that the subject did not obtrude. One senses uneasiness among some of the Victorians; but this was based solely on a few remarks in the letters, and more particularly on what little was known of his protesting, questioning, bewildered last months. In the earlier part of the twentieth century, the subject was dropped: it seemed (and in a sense was) irrelevant to the poetry. More recently, those interested in the letters of Keats and the actual life per se have wisely felt that the subject cannot be taken up in isolation; there is too little to go on, and that little is meaningful only if it is carefully considered in a context in which much else must be taken into account.

net we might be tempted into a flat, run-of-the-mill generalization about the liberal, agnostic spirit of the times. We could find ourselves saying that just as Shelley rebelliously equated priests and tyrants, ministers of religion and ministers of state, so Keats, influenced by the liberal periodicals taken by John Clarke at Enfield, imbibed a revolutionary spirit, and was encouraged by Hunt. Naturally all this enters as part of the picture. But other ingredients also enter. To begin with, the orphaned Keats boys were certainly not imbued with a militantly antireligious spirit. Left to shift for themselves, they were relatively untouched by religion.[5] Clarke, in his own school, was merely trying to be undoctrinaire. When Keats first came to Guy's Hospital at twenty and met the earnest youth John Spurgin, the confirmed Swedenborgian who was about to leave for Cambridge, he appears to have confronted his new friend not with argumentative skepticism so much as indifference. If Spurgin talked of Swedenborg, Keats talked of the great poets of the past. Spurgin was so far from thinking Keats a convinced agnostic that he wrote the letter we have already noticed. In the sonnet Keats wrote on December 22 there is a slight difference in attitude. He has been seeing much of Hunt for two and a half months. More important, he has been seeing Hunt in the company of Shelley for about two weeks. Had he not, there is little likelihood that the sonnet would ever have been written at all.

Shelley's descent on the Hunt cottage in early December was followed by a series of parties to at least some of which Keats was invited. Shelley carried his ideas with him wherever he went; and if Hunt had thus far avoided the subject of religion in Keats's presence (or more likely found it uninteresting to talk about with a youth so completely absorbed in other subjects), Keats now found the Hunt cottage very different. Hunt, who took time to write two sonnets "To Percy Shelley on the Degrading Notions of the Deity," had personal motives for encouraging Shelley to talk freely on anything he wished (although anyone who knew Shelley —Hunt had only just met him—was aware that no amount of disagreement seemed to bother him): for Hunt was financially pressed, and Shelley, always generous with money, was advancing him £1,500. We can catch something of the atmosphere from Haydon's outraged account of a dinner in January to which Hunt, unable to resist the chance of teasing the fiercely orthodox Haydon,

5 See Benjamin Bailey's remarks, below, Chapter IX, section 12.

had encouraged Horace Smith to invite him. Haydon entered a little late and innocently sat down

> right opposite Shelley himself, as I was told after, for I did not then
> know what hectic, spare, weakly yet intellectual-looking creature it
> was carving a bit of broccoli or cabbage in his plate, as if it had been
> the substantial wing of a chicken. —— and his wife and her sister,
> Keats, Horace Smith, and myself made up the party.
>
> In a few minutes Shelley opened the conversation by saying in
> the most feminine and gentle voice, "As to that detestable religion,
> the Christian—." I looked astounded, but, casting a glance round the
> table, easily saw by ——'s expression of ecstasy and the women's sim-
> per, I was to be set at that evening *vi et armis*. No reply, however,
> was made to this sally during dinner, but when the dessert came,
> and the servant was gone, to it we went like fiends —— and ——
> were deists. I felt exactly like a stag at bay, and resolved to gore with-
> out mercy. . . .
>
> Neither Smith, Keats, nor —— said a word to this; but still Shel-
> ley, —— and —— kept at it till finding I was a match for them in
> argument, they became personal, and so did I. We said unpleasant
> things to each other, and when I retired to the other room for a mo-
> ment I overheard them say, "Haydon is fierce." "Yes," said ——, "the
> question always irritates him." [6]

Despite the title, despite the occasion, despite the dinner talk of
Shelley and Hunt, the "Vulgar Superstition" sonnet is particularly
revealing because it by-passes these recent promptings, or at most
turns them into something very different, something almost com-
ically typical of Keats at this time. The language of the sonnet is
indeed strong, some of it doubtless echoing Shelley and Hunt.
"The church bells," it begins, "toll a melancholy round," calling
people to evening prayer in order to listen again

[6] *Autobiography*, pp. 220–221. Haydon on returning home wrote in his *Diary:*
"I have known Hunt now *10 years*, during which we have scarcely ever met without
a contest about Christianity. . . . After such perpetual contests without effect on
either side . . . one would think he as well as myself must see the uselessness of tormenting each other on a subject in which we cannot from the constitution of our
Minds ever come to a similar conclusion. Of this I have been long since convinced
and therefore never began it, but of late my resolution to put in Voltaire's head into
my picture [see Chapter VI, section 3] seems to have brought up all Hunt's bile . . .
My only refuge now is in personal insult, and that I will make a point of inflicting
whenever I meet him" (II.80–82) . A temporary reconciliation took place two months
later. "March 17. Leigh Hunt called & caught me reading [Hunt's poem] Rimini.
Old associations crowded on us, & we soon forgot our irritations, in talking about
Raffaello & Shakespeare. He saw Voltaire's head in, but said not a word. I was ready
with a broadside for the dog if he had. . . . There is no resisting him, I got as delighted as ever by his wit, his poetry, his taste, his good humour. . . . I would never
have called again if he had not called on me. I'll now go and see him as usual"
(II.101) .

> to the sermon's horrid sound.
> Surely the mind of man is closely bound
> In some black spell; seeing that each one tears
> Himself from fireside joys, and Lydian airs,
> And converse high of those with glory crown'd.

The heart of the hasty sonnet—the extraordinary naiveté—lies in the assumption that those attending evening prayer are tearing themselves away not only from "fireside joys" but also from "Lydian airs," and from "converse high of those with glory crown'd." Here we have the essence of the matter. The weak sestet of the sonnet repeats it—for it is the only thing he has to say: fortunately all these traces of "vulgar superstition" are "dying like an out-burnt lamp." In their place,

> fresh flowers will grow
> And many glories of immortal stamp.

3

Nothing could show more strikingly the subjective absorption in poetry into which Keats has fallen than the unintentional transference to poetry—or rather to *poets* (for it is with his powerful empathic identification with the great poets of earlier eras that we are dealing)—of terms, values, even symbols conventionally associated with religion. Established religion will be replaced by "many glories of immortal stamp"; and the "glories" will plainly be those of poetry and art. Again, going to church is contrasted with "converse high of those with glory crown'd." And the touching comedy of the whole thing is that there is no intentional irony at all. He is not thinking even remotely of the crown of thorns: this is no "metaphysical" poem; to be oversubtle is to miss the point completely. He is virtually incapable during these months of thinking of any crown other than "laurel crowns." All during December he has been writing his longest poem thus far—"Sleep and Poetry." Almost at the start he begins to speak of an ideal in almost religious terms ("The thought thereof is awful, sweet, and holy, / Chasing away all worldliness"); and what that ideal is becomes plain very quickly. For the awakened heart, sensing

> some wond'rous thing
> That breathes about us in the vacant air,

begins to look around it, perhaps

> To see the laurel-wreath, on high suspended,
> That is to crown our name when life is ended.

Increasingly, as the poem goes on, we realize that we have to do with an astonishing seriousness (whatever Keats himself was later to think of his state of mind at this time). Poetry is viewed as a temple; it is his "ardent prayer" to have access to it; he can understand the prudent advice "to hide my foolish face":

> yet there ever rolls
> A vast idea before me, and I glean
> Therefrom my liberty . . .
> The end and aim of Poesy.

He means it. With a rather awesome earnestness, he begins to speak of facing this huge challenge "upon my bended knees."

Constantly this Longinian ideal, this intoxication with the vision of greatness, has been present in the orphaned youth from the days at Enfield through the years at Hammond's surgery and Guy's Hospital. So earnest a concentration would naturally attach itself to symbols casual or even trivial to others. One of these, for at least a year or two, had been the laurel crown. Before "Sleep and Poetry" and the naive lines on "Vulgar Superstition," there was the sonnet ("Keen, fitful gusts") in which he spoke of the happiness he felt in the long walk back from Hampstead on a November night, "brimful of the friendliness" of the talk of poets in Hunt's cottage, and ended with the picture of "Petrarch gloriously crown'd." Even earlier there had been the boyish pride expressed in the sonnet "To a Young Lady Who Sent Me a Laurel Crown." There was also a line in the verse letter "To Charles Cowden Clarke," written in Margate weeks before Keats met Hunt. Timidly the young Keats mentioned his shyness in writing so openly of poetry to one who—among other enviable opportunities—had known "Libertas" Hunt, and had in fact taken

> forest walks
> With him who elegantly chats, and talks—
> The wrong'd Libertas—who has told you stories
> Of laurel chaplets, and Apollo's glories.

And about two months after Keats wrote the sonnet on hearing the bells ringing for evening prayer came the painfully embarrassing moment when he and Hunt gave crowns to each other (Hunt gave Keats a laurel crown, and Keats handed Hunt a crown of ivy). They wrote sonnets on the occasion: an occasion that burned in Keats's memory, and led to a penitent, half-playful "Ode to Apollo," in which he spoke of putting on "like a blank idiot . . . thy laurel."

4

If the incident of the laurel crown deserves more than a mere sentence or two, it is largely because of the strange extent to which it afterwards disturbed Keats himself. At first glance there is no reason at all why the incident should have rankled. For poets—or would-be poets—to exchange laurel crowns, and then write a playful sonnet or two on the occasion (with a time limit for the writing) was an innocent parlor game. Keats might be expected even less than others in the Hunt circle to feel like a fool: the dresser from Guy's Hospital was far more naive, and had actually, in fact, been looking forward to this sort of thing. But it is that greater seriousness—that wistful envy of Clarke, who had heard Hunt talk "Of laurel chaplets, and Apollo's glories"—which gives strength to the very revulsion he began to feel so soon afterwards. The emotional preparation had been too eager and too long. It is precisely because this sort of thing was not thought of as a mere game but was associated with a really serious, even high-minded, dedication that, when the dream became concretely fulfilled, he acted as he did—that he insisted, half playfully, half seriously, on keeping the crown on his head, and then, in the months afterwards, kept lacerating himself.

We know a little about the laurel crown episode because the painstaking Richard Woodhouse, who later tried to piece together what he could about the background of some of Keats's poems, left a short account. There is every indication that he got his information either from Keats, reluctantly and piecemeal, or else indirectly from Reynolds; for the account is thoroughly revised and corrected. We can assume that the incident took place in early spring—not later than the first of March.[7] Woodhouse's story follows:

---

[7] For Woodhouse's account, see Garrod, pp. 430–431. Hunt's autograph (Bodleian Library) of his sonnets on receiving an ivy crown from Keats dates them March 1, 1817. Other dates are sometimes suggested because Woodhouse, in a deleted phrase, spoke of the incident as taking place on a "summer evening afternoon," and because of the remark in the "Ode to Apollo" that the "seeds and roots in Earth / Were swelling for summer fare." Now of course the lines in the "Ode" refer to spring, not

As the author and Leigh Hunt were taking their wine together, after a dinner at the house of the latter, the whim seized them to crown themselves, after the fashion of the elder poets, with a wreath of laurel.

While they were attired, two acquaintances of Mr. Hunt called upon him:—Just before their entrance Hunt removed the crown from his own brows, and suggested to Keats that he might as well do the same.

K. however, in the enthusiasm of the moment, vowed that he would not for any human being and he accordingly wore it without any explanation thro' the visit.

He mentioned the cir.ce afterd to one or two of his friends expressing his sense how foolish he had been; and his intention of recording it, by apologetic verses suited to the occasion.—He produced shortly afterd the following fragment of an Ode to Apollo.

The sonnet Keats wrote (never published by him, and in fact not printed until 1914, ninety-three years after his death) speaks of his blankness of mind, his inability to find a subject. The fifteen minutes or so that he has in which to write, after having been crowned, are passing:

> Minutes are flying swiftly, and as yet
>   Nothing unearthly has enticed my brain
>   Into a delphic Labyrinth—I would fain
> Catch an immortal thought to pay the debt
> I owe to the kind Poet who has set
>   Upon my ambitious head a glorious gain.

He pads out the rest of the sonnet by repeating that "time is fleeting, and no dream arises / Gorgeous as I would have it." With a bravado already becoming a little shaky, he declares that at least the incident represents a triumphant "trampling down of what the

summer; and they could easily apply to early spring. Moreover, the mere fact that Woodhouse deliberately deletes his phrase "one summer evening afternoon" shows that he found he was mistaken in his own inference that Keats was speaking of summer. Finally, as Keats says in the "Ode to Apollo," "The Pleiades were up, / Watching the silent air." After the end of March, the Pleiades cannot be seen at night, and do not return to the evening sky until the autumn.

Because Keats writes of the "Ladies Who Saw Me Crown'd," and because Woodhouse refers to two men (though those references are deleted), there has been some uncertainty whether Woodhouse, in his long note to the "Ode to Apollo," refers to the same occasion. But the very fact that Woodhouse makes these deletions shows that he has learned, either indirectly through Reynolds or through a reluctant Keats, that the visitors were not necessarily men. (E.g., the deletions in brackets: Keats "vowed that ⟨for no man alive would he take off his wreath⟩ he would not for any human being and he accordingly wore it without any explanation ⟨till the gentlemen's departure, to their no small surprise⟩ thro' the visit.")

world most prizes, / Turbans and Crowns, and blank regality."
Feebly he ends, with a desperate clutch at the fine phrase ("wild
surmise") from his sonnet on Chapman's Homer:

> And then I run into most wild surmises
> Of all the many glories that may be.

Then the three girls appeared—probably the Reynolds sisters.
With embarrassed stubbornness he kept the crown on his head.
Probably only because of Keats's own chagrin, the story seems to
have persisted subterraneously until, six years after his death, *Fra-
ser's Magazine* (August 1831) printed the following account.
Thomas Love Peacock, whom Keats did not actually meet until
1818, dropped by, and found "Hunt and Keats and some others of
that coterie" crowning themselves. The account continues: " 'Do,'
said the lady [presumably Mrs. Hunt] who officiated as coronet
manufacturer, 'do, dear Mr. Peacock, let me weave you a chaplet'
. . . 'No ma'am' said Peacock, wiping his head, 'no ma'am; you
may make a fool of your husband, but there is no need of your
making a fool of me.' "

Possibly the same night, possibly a day or two later, Keats wrote
the tepid, self-conscious sonnet "To the Ladies Who Saw Me
Crown'd." It starts out asking a little defensively and awkwardly
what there is "More lovely than a Wreath from the bay tree?"—
though he is only too mindful of being watched by these faces with
"three sweet pair of lips in mirth." Nor can he get much further.
Soon afterwards he wrote the "Ode to Apollo"—or "Hymn to
Apollo"—of which Woodhouse speaks. The point is quickly put
in the lines:

> Where—where slept thine ire,
> When like a blank idiot I put on thy wreath,
> Thy laurel, thy glory,
> The light of thy story,
> Or was I a worm—too low crawling for death?

Large things, he goes on, were afoot at the time: the promise of
summer throughout the earth, and

> The Ocean, its neighbour,
> Was at his old labour,
> When, who—who did dare
> To tie for a moment thy plant round his brow,
> And grin and look proudly,
> And blaspheme so loudly?

5

By the first of January the poems were assembled for the press. He had been thinking about the arrangement. He would begin it with "I stood tiptoe," knowing that something fairly good was needed to catch the eye. This proved to be a fortunate idea. In those presentation copies that survive with underlining and marks of approval, most of the markings appear in this opening poem. But otherwise Keats thought it best to put the earliest and poorest poems first. Since all of us assume that all parts of our books will be read, he may have naively thought it wise to keep the better things in reserve and allow the reader to feel a progressive rise. Or he may have been thinking less of the reactions of others than simply of grouping the poems in a way that seemed inevitable to him—in a roughly chronological sequence. In a separate group, after the earliest minor poems, come the epistles in chronological order—to Mathew, then George, then Clarke. Seventeen of the sonnets make up the next section. They are not chronologically arranged, except in the roughest way. "Sleep and Poetry," as his credo, concludes the volume. On the title page there was to be a small vignette that looks like a head of Shakespeare but is doubtless intended to be Spenser, and above it a motto from Spenser:

> What more felicity can fall to creature
> Then to enjoy delight with liberty.

The month passed heavily. On January 20 he attended the dinner at Horace Smith's where Hunt and Shelley outraged Haydon with their light talk of Christianity. Keats and Horace Smith, said Haydon, were silent most of the evening.

In the oppressed and fatigued waiting of this month, he wrote only a few lines—a single sonnet—and then only on the last day of the month. The sonnet ("After dark vapours") is unlike anything he has written before, and strangely anticipates lines he was to write near the close of his career. This dark, long January was haunted by thoughts of spring—as all later winters were to be for him. But he was also sensing the autumn that follows the spring. "After dark vapours," he begins, "comes a day / Born of the gentle *South*," and in this January premonition of a spring there is a clearing away

From the *sick heavens* all unseemly stains.
The anxious month, relievèd of its pains,
Takes as a long-lost right the feel of *May*.

We think ahead to the mellow lines of one of the last two great
poems he was to write—the *Fall of Hyperion:*

When in mid-*May* the *sickening* East Wind
Shifts sudden to the *South,* the small warm rain
Melts out the frozen incense from all flowers,
And fills the air with so much pleasant health
That even the *dying man* forgets his shroud.

The sonnet ends, in this premonition of process, with a quick
mention of the fruition (and ultimate death) that will follow the
Spring; and the images suggest the great ode "To Autumn." There,
far more massively, the "Season of mists and mellow fruitfulness"
continues to defer the dying of the year as the fruit, in the autumn
sun, ripens slowly; and we have the unforgettable picture of autumn "sitting careless on a granary floor" or drowsing upon a
"half-reap'd furrow." Now, in this early poem, written in this
"anxious month" of waiting, there is the glance forward (after the
vivid anticipation of spring) to "fruits ripening in stillness—autumn suns . . . quiet sheaves." And finally:

The gradual sand that through an hour-glass runs,—
A woodland rivulet,—a Poet's death.

6

The proofs for the new volume were ready by early February.
Keats was altogether absorbed, if not in the proofreading itself (it
was never one of his accomplishments), in the imaginative realization that the book was tangibly there. He went out at least a
little.[8] Two sonnets were printed in the *Examiner* ("To Kosciusko" and "After dark vapours"). At a dinner of Hunt's he did
not attend—a dinner that included the Shelleys and William Hazlitt—Hunt showed the company some of Keats's poetry.
    Finally the last proof sheets were brought one evening—prob-
ably by Charles Ollier himself—and Keats was told that if he

8 He had supper with Reynolds, Hunt, and Shelley on February 5, and a week
later went out to Hunt's with George for a supper with Mrs. Shelley; and three days
after that (February 15) he called on Hunt and Mrs. Shelley.

wished to include any dedicatory verses they would have to go to the printer immediately. Several of Keats's friends were present in the room, said Clarke. Keats

> drew to a side-table, and in the buzz of a mixed conversation . . . he composed and brought to Charles Ollier, the publisher, the Dedication Sonnet to Leigh Hunt. If the original manuscript of that poem—a legitimate sonnet, with every restriction of rhyme and metre—could now be produced, and the time recorded in which it was written, it would be pronounced an extraordinary performance: added to which the non-alteration of a single word in the poem (a circumstance that was noted at the time) claims for it a merit with a very rare parallel.[9]

One cannot help feeling that, absorbed as he was in the prospect of his first book, Keats must have had a dedication to Hunt in mind, and had possibly thought over the general way in which to put it. In any case, the sonnet has a mild biographical interest when we look back over the last few months, and a stronger interest when we look forward. It suggests at least something of the spirit in which Keats himself viewed so much of the writing of the past year.

Given the hard core of common sense that so many of his friends found pre-eminent in him, he was only too aware that the stock props of his poetry—the allusions, many of the images, the tentative fingering of classical mythology (which was to become far more than fingering in the following year)—were all remote from the habitual life of the modern world. An imagination nourished too exclusively on past poetry (as Keats himself at least had been viewing that poetry) will inevitably feel that "Glory and loveliness have passed away"—and a "glory and loveliness" especially of the sort that Keats's impossible and Arcadian catalogue implies.[10]

9 *Recollections*, p. 138.
10 Glory and loveliness have passed away;
    For if we wander out in early morn,
    No wreathèd incense do we see upborne
Into the east, to meet the smiling day:
No crowd of nymphs soft voic'd and young, and gay,
    In woven baskets bringing ears of corn,
    Roses, and pinks, and violets, to adorn
The shrine of Flora in her early May.
But there are left delights as high as these,
    And I shall ever bless my destiny,
That in a time, when under pleasant trees
    Pan is no longer sought, I feel a free,
A leafy luxury, seeing I could please
    With these poor offerings, a man like thee.

When the imagination looks to any past, of course, including one's own individual past, it blends memories and images into a denser, more massive unit than ever existed in actuality. This frailty—as well as consolation—of the human imagination, occasional in all poetry, gradually became endemic in the later eighteenth century and was to continue to embarrass the literary conscience of the nineteenth and twentieth centuries. More specifically the problem sharpens to the question: how, when we have been nourished upon ideal renderings of the past, can we be faithful to the inspiration of that imagined past without turning too strongly against the present?

The great nineteenth-century wrestle against the temptations to escapism found no greater exemplar than Keats: his entire career after *Endymion* becomes a moving struggle with this large dilemma. By the time that we come to the puzzling "Ode to Psyche," two years and a quarter later, we find him developing an answer, salutary for later writers, by turning the dilemma itself into a subject for poetry.

7

A few days, perhaps a week, after he had written the dedicatory sonnet to Hunt in the room full of friends, he returned home one day (February 27) to find Clarke, who had been waiting for him, as Clarke reports,

> asleep on the sofa, with a volume of Chaucer open at the "Flower and the Leaf." After expressing to me his admiration of the poem, which he had been reading, he gave me the fine testimony of that opinion in pointing to the sonnet he had written at the close of it, which was an extempore effusion, and without the alteration of a single word.[11]

The sonnet, a light thing, was published with an enthusiastic comment by Hunt in less than three weeks: "The following exquisite sonnet . . . is from the pen of the young poet . . . who may already lay claim to that title:—'the youngest he / That sits in the shadow of Apollo's tree.' " One frankly biographical line stands out from this tepid poem: "I, that do ever feel athirst for glory." A few days later, Keats showed the poem to Reynolds. Joining in the general competition of eulogy, this stoutest of his friends at

11 *Recollections*, p. 139.

this time also wove and tossed a wreath. He wrote a sonnet "To Keats: On Reading His Sonnet Written on Chaucer." In the center occur the lines:

> Thy genius weaves
> Songs that shall make the age be nature-led,
> And win that coronal for thy young head.

Everyone who stood *in loco parentis* was warming to the occasion with the kindliest of intentions. Hunt, worried about his debts and preoccupied with his new friend and helper, Shelley; Haydon, absorbed in his vast canvas, "Christ's Entry into Jerusalem"; Horace Smith; the faithful Cowden Clarke; the Reynolds family (John Reynolds with his sonnet) : all took off time to be excited and reassuring. Shelley himself—though he had thought Keats should wait till there was more to publish—descended on the startled printer, and urged him to care and renewed zeal. The printer always remembered Shelley's "peculiar starts and gestures, and a way of fixing his eyes and whole attitude for a good while." Others, in what Keats later called, a little too sadly and caustically, a "sentimental farce," became appreciative and eager. Clarke, looking back almost sixty years later on this poignant moment, mentions that

> The first volume of Keats's minor muse was launched amid the cheers and fond anticipations of all his circle. Everyone of us expected (and not unreasonably) that it would create a sensation in the literary world; for such a first production (and a considerable portion of it from a minor) has rarely occurred. The three Epistles and the seventeen sonnets (that upon "first looking into Chapman's Homer" one of them) would have ensured a rousing welcome from our modern-day reviewers. Alas! the book might have emerged in Timbuctoo with far stronger chance of fame and approbation. It never passed to a second edition; the first was but a small one, and that was never sold off. The whole community, as if by compact, seemed determined to know nothing about it.[12]

Charles Ollier—the more literary of the two publishing brothers —also broke into song. In a stiff, Miltonic sonnet dated March 2 (the day before the book was published) , he begins:

> Keats I admire thine upward daring Soul,
> Thine eager grasp at immortality . . .

[12] *Recollections,* p. 140.

The kindly Ollier (whose brother was soon to complain of the financial loss and the "ridicule" Keats's *Poems* brought on the firm) goes on to congratulate his high-minded author for spurning, "with brow serene," the "gross controul of circumstance." Ollier ends by envisaging what he calls the "oak" of freedom entwined with Keats's "laurels." Constantly the youthful dream of Keats— the vision of the laurels that shall "crown our endeavour"—was evoked in these months. In a sense, provided the expectations were not too high, the dream was being rapidly fulfilled.

8

Keats's eagerness, though outwardly subdued, was becoming more intense. He was planning to give away a large number of copies. Probably because Charles Ollier, who was proud of the young author and had been showing up at social gatherings that Keats attended, kept prodding his brother, the firm was extraordinarily generous in the number of gift copies it allowed him. His two brothers, for their part, were excitedly sharing in what they took for granted was a joyful experience for John. Their attitude toward their brother, said Henry Stephens, "amounted almost to idolatry"; and they "seemed to think their Brother John was . . . to exalt the family name." That Charles Ollier should himself have contributed a sonnet on the forthcoming publication struck the direct and businesslike George Keats as equivalent to a guarantee of enthusiastic support. Doubtless because of this, George wrote a stern proprietary letter to the Olliers a few weeks later, when the book was not selling.

Finally, on either Saturday, March 1, or Monday, March 3, Haydon took Keats and Reynolds to see the Elgin Marbles—the great collection of sculpture from the Parthenon.[13] Immediately we are reminded again of Keats's intoxication with the ideal of greatness. But the experience was now on a far higher plane. The "genius-loving heart" (to return to his phrase in his early epistle "To G. F. Mathew") was constant in its general aim, but it was rapidly changing in its criteria.

---

[13] Probably soon afterwards, as a result of Keats's interest in the Elgin Marbles, Haydon gave him a copy of Goldsmith's *History of Greece,* inscribed "To John Keats, from his ardent friend, B. R. Haydon, 1817."

Only a year and a half had passed since Keats came down to Guy's Hospital from the Edmonton surgery and talked impulsively, said John Spurgin, of the "Geniuses of old"—showing a devotion that Spurgin, a committed and religious man, was confident could develop. Meanwhile—and particularly since Keats himself had tried independently to take things in hand, and had made his brave excursion to Margate—he had found himself on a ladder of experience that resulted in continual revision of that formative ideal.

The fine remark of Whitehead keeps recurring to us: "Moral education is impossible apart from the habitual vision of greatness." For the ideal of greatness, as the Greeks discovered, is ultimately self-corrective in its effect as well as self-impelling. This is especially true when it is presented with the compelling power of a concrete example, whether in persons we meet, or, as here, in a human achievement. We may, of course, still be naive in our approach, focusing, for a time, on accidental embellishments; but as the attraction persists, it can lead us to discover what is more fundamental. And since the example has not been merely recognized in an abstract way but is actually caught and followed through a process of identification, the further discoveries to which it persuades us are made freshly, creatively, and through our own direct experience. It is by inducing and sustaining this self-development at every stage that "alles Grosse bildet," as Goethe said—"everything great is formative."

9

When Haydon took Keats to see the Parthenon sculptures, Keats's eye was already partly self-taught. In the poem he was putting last in the new volume, "Sleep and Poetry," he had written something that anticipates much of the great poetry two years hence: poetry at its best, with a reserve of power, is "might half slumb'ring on its own right arm." Now at the sight of the great Parthenon sculptures everything came back—the thought of his inadequacy, the almost comic sense of his limitations. The sonnet written immediately afterwards sets the tone:

> My spirit is too weak; mortality
> Weighs heavily on me like unwilling sleep.

Every "imagined pinnacle," every gain in realization, such as this unrivaled sculpture provides to the open eye and the open heart, points to the fearful limitation of man and the brevity of his life:

> each imagin'd pinnacle and steep
> Of godlike hardship tells me I must die
> Like a sick Eagle looking at the sky.
>
> .   .   .   .   .
>
> Such dim-conceivèd glories of the brain
>   Bring round the heart an undescribable feud;
> So do these wonders a most dizzy pain,
>   That mingles Grecian grandeur with the rude
> Wasting of old Time—with a billowy main—
> A sun—a shadow of a magnitude.

With this sonnet he wrote another, addressed to Haydon, asking him to

> forgive me that I cannot speak
> Definitively of these mighty things;
> Forgive me that I have not eagle's wings,
> That what I want I know not where to seek.

Significantly, at the end of this second sonnet he speaks of men who could stare at the sculptures "with browless idiotism." The phase reminds us again of the half-penitent fragment of an "Ode to Apollo" that he wrote after the laurel-crowning: "like a blank idiot . . . I put on thy crown, thy glory." At the close of the sonnet one more of those extreme telescopic combinations of the religious and the poetic is made in the imagination of this youth who is fundamentally so far from being an aesthete. Only a year before he had envied George Mathew for being so close to the haunt of the muses. Haydon—he now says—has seen

> the Hesperean Shrine
> Of their star in the East, and gone to worship them.

A Trial of Invention:

Endymion

❋⇢⊛⇠❋⇢⊛⇠❋⇢⊛⇠❋⇢⊛⇠❋⇢⊛⇠❋⇢⊛⇠❋⇢⊛⇠❋⇢⊛⇠❋⇢⊛⇠❋⇢⊛⇠⊛

EXACTLY A YEAR after Keats had paid the fee that would allow him to remain for still another year as a dresser at Guy's Hospital, the volume of poems appeared, on March 3. A surprisingly large number of copies survive; and being so little thumbed, they are in good condition. The publishers had hopefully allowed him so many presentation copies that he was able to give one to almost everybody he knew personally, inscribing most of them somewhat formally. A copy was even sent to Wordsworth. "You know," he had written to Haydon a little breathlessly some months before, "with what Reverence—I would send my Well-wishes to him." And now he inscribed the copy: "To W. Wordsworth with the Author's sincere Reverence." After Wordsworth's death, the copy was found on his shelves with most of the leaves uncut.

Within three or four weeks the Olliers knew that they had something on their hands they did not want. The temptation after Keats's death to attack the Olliers for gross neglect is sentimental as well as unfair. The book was not exceptional: its interest exists almost entirely because of what came after it. As Douglas Bush has said, even the most devout modern admirer—had he been a sympathetic reviewer without the knowledge of what was to come —would have failed to discover any remarkable promise except in the one sonnet on Chapman's Homer. It was to be some months, of course, before the reviews had all appeared. Clarke, writing long afterwards, may have had a point when he said that the dedication to Hunt, who was scorned by the Tory press, made Keats a marked man. But Clarke's memory was partly affected by the hostility later shown to *Endymion*. The truth is that no one much noticed. Even Keats's new friends, after applauding the preparation and publication of the volume, became quickly absorbed in their own problems. Haydon indeed repeated his lavish praise two weeks after the book appeared: "I have read your Sleep & Poetry—it is a flash of lightning that will sound men from their occupations, and keep them trembling for the crash of thunder that *will* follow." And Haydon—so generous in praise, and so helpful in strengthening Keats's self-confidence—meant what he said. In his *Diary* he wrote: "Keats has published his first Poems, and great things indeed they promise. He is a sound young man & will be a great one. There are parts in his 'Sleep & Poetry' equal to anything in English Poetry." But with the same exuberance ("filled with fury," as he wrote to Keats) he immediately returned to his own work.

Within the Keats family, however—or what there was of it—the intensity of expectation remained at a high pitch. Keats himself typically said nothing. Moreover, much of his anxiety was already concentrating on the next step. But his brothers were deeply involved, and were enormously proud of this little book published in drab boards, with a label on the back saying "Keats's Poems, Price 6s." In April, not long after Keats left London to go to the Isle of Wight and begin *Endymion*, the stalwart, protective George, doubtless feeling that the family honor was at stake, took it upon himself to write what he thought was a businesslike letter to the Ollier brothers. His experience as a clerk in Abbey's countinghouse had really not given him the sophistication that he thought he had acquired and that he assumed would now permit him to be of service to his brother. He seems to have written the Olliers as though a business contract had been violated by them. The reply George received was certainly not written by Charles Ollier—who had joined happily though timidly in the little celebrations before the publication, and written the sonnet on the forthcoming event—but by his crusty brother, James Ollier. George and Tom, out at their new lodgings in Hampstead, waited for the response, confident that George had put the Olliers in their place. The reply was a shock:

3, Welbeck Street, 29th April, 1817

Sir,—We regret that your brother ever requested us to publish his book, or that our opinion of its talent should have led us to acquiesce in undertaking it. We are, however, much obliged to you for relieving us from the unpleasant necessity of declining any further connexion with it, which we must have done, as we think the curiosity is satisfied, and the sale has dropped. By far the greater number of persons who have purchased it from us have found fault with it in such plain terms, that we have in many cases offered to take the book back rather than be annoyed with the ridicule which has, time after time, been showered upon it. In fact, it was only on Saturday last that we were under the mortification of having our own opinion of its merits flatly contradicted by a gentleman, who told us he considered it "no better than a take in." These are unpleasant imputations for any one in business to labour under, but we should have borne them and concealed their existence from you had not the style of your note shewn us that such delicacy would be quite thrown away. We shall take means without delay for ascertaining the number of copies on hand, and you shall be informed accordingly.

Your most, &c.
C. & J. Ollier [1]

Meanwhile Keats, with Haydon as his guide, had seen the great Parthenon sculptures the very week the *Poems* were published. The little volume of poems appeared slight by contrast, and the talk with Hunt of Apollo and "Laurel chaplets" seemed ludicrous. Even without the challenge of the Elgin Marbles, there was the pressing, humbling preoccupation with the next step. As he wrote to George a month or so later, "I put on no Laurels till I shall have finished Endymion."

2

Everything in his limited experience had taught him that boldness and commitment brought rewards. But where to turn? Subjects are not plucked off a vine. In the earlier, less self-conscious eras of poetry—as the eighteenth century had kept nostalgically saying—everything was available to the receptive mind. But when so much has been written, how does one proceed? Luckily this anxiety had largely been spared Keats thus far. From the long verse letters he had written at Margate, he had learned that mere momentum often leads to the discovery of unexpected paths. When he had tried the preceding December to put into shape the lines "I stood tiptoe," he had begun to toy with the fable of Endymion. He had stopped the poem abruptly, however, in order to be able to include it in the new volume of poems, and any ideas for expanding the fable that may have occurred to him were left hanging in mid-air. But throughout January and February they

[1] Printed in the *Athenaeum*, June 7, 1873, p. 725.

began to fall into a loose pattern—a pattern into which almost everything having to do with the growth of the imagination and the heart, and with the search for the ideal, might conceivably be fitted. He wanted so large a theme not only because he hungered for grandeur, as befitted a follower of Haydon, but also to give himself room in which to develop his inventive muscles. But how was he to get started without delay? For he naturally wished to begin at once. He was a little exhausted from the excitement and from the sheer quantity of writing he had done from August through December. January had been "a long dreary season," an "anxious month," as much from uncertainties about the next step as from mere fatigue. He began to think back to the weeks at Margate, which were growing more magical in retrospect. While there he had written two sizable poems without having any real subject at all. Moreover, he had started them with far less behind him than he had now. When he went to Margate, he was nothing. Now he had met Hunt, Haydon, and Reynolds; a volume of poems was being published. There had been the whole laurel-crown episode, drawing on the expectations of a year, two years, perhaps five. He had talked with Abbey and asserted his independence. He even felt that at last he had a subject.

He began to think of going away again, just as he had deliberately gone to Margate nine months before. He talked with his brothers. On March 17 he wrote to Reynolds:

> My Brothers are anxious that I shoᵈ go by myself into the country—they have always been extremely fond of me; and now that Haydon has pointed out how necessary it is that I shoᵈ be alone to improve myself, they give up the temporary pleasure of living with me continually for a great good which I hope will follow—So I shall soon be out of Town.

3

Before Keats made definite plans to leave, the three brothers decided to move from their rooms in Cheapside out to Hampstead. The rather elfin, thin-chested Tom, who was to die of consumption in less than two years, was becoming frailer. But his laughing and kindly manner reassured his brothers and friends; they had no sense that anything was seriously wrong. The boys naturally thought that the country air would help him. George, whether he was still working in Abbey's countinghouse or as a clerk for Wilkinson, could get into the city without much effort. For John, of course, Hampstead was filled with the associations and reassurance of the past autumn and winter.

At Well Walk, in the house of a postman, Benjamin Bentley, the three youths (John, twenty-one, George, just turned twenty, and Tom, seventeen) took the last rooms they were ever to share together. This final makeshift home was a merry, noisy place. The constant shouting of the red-headed children—whom he called "the young Carrots"—wore upon Keats. The noise, in fact, became something of an obsession. He also found the smell of the children's "worsted stockings" less than pleasant. But the Bentleys were kindly. They could hardly fail to be touched by these orphaned youths. Moreover, their lodgers had their own noisy moments, less constant but at more unusual hours: for example, the loud "concerts"—accompanied by hysterical laughter—in which all present took the part of various instruments (Haydon pretending to be the organ, Keats the bassoon, and so on) .

Ironically, while the Keats brothers were thinking of moving to Hampstead, Hunt was planning to leave it. Rather shyly, Keats had given Hunt a copy of his *Poems* in a walk at Hampstead. But Hunt was altogether absorbed in Shelley, and by the end of March the entire Hunt family had left for a three months' visit to Shelley at Marlowe, Buckinghamshire. Shelley also asked Keats to come. Whatever explanation he gave to Shelley for being unable to come, his real reason was that he wished, as he told Benjamin Bailey, to have an "unfettered scope." Neither the Hunts nor the Shelleys could have given much prudent thought to this impulsively arranged and extended visit. But the high-minded Shelley was protected by the screen of his ideas, and, aptly sensing in Hunt an idealistic man in need, he was unlikely to be disturbed by details. Hunt, for his part, could hardly resist a man of family and wealth whose views were even more advanced than his own, and who was also proving to be the most generous benefactor he had ever hoped to encounter. Not until the latter part of June did Hunt return, and then he took a house at Paddington, leaving some of his family for still another month with the Shelleys. As Hunt prepared to set off on his visit, Keats and Cowden Clarke offered to look after his papers and to make arrangements for the proofs of the second edition of the *Story of Rimini*. Keats tried dutifully to celebrate the second edition by writing a sonnet on the *Story of Rimini*—a tired, flaccid poem he never thought of publishing. It was first printed in the remains (1848) collected by Lord Houghton.

If Keats had been wavering between Hunt and Haydon, everything now conspired to lead him toward Haydon. It is with Haydon that he now stayed up late at night "spouting Shakespeare." It is Haydon, with his intoxication with greatness, who urged Keats to study and restudy Shakespeare. It was to Haydon (on April 7) that he confided that "Byron, Scott, Southey, & Shelley think they are to lead the age, but . . . ," and then "his face reddened." Naturally Keats felt a slight pique at Hunt's new absent-mindedness about him, and the switch to Shelley of what Clarke called Hunt's "Spartan deference" of attention. And there is a certain irony that the move of the Keats youths to Hampstead (which would never have been made except for Keats's friendship with Hunt) should coincide with the end of Hunt's influence—of Hunt's active and personal influence, at least. Keats was often to step into a vacuum created by the ebb of previous aspirations; the poems themselves usually (not always) lag a step behind the brilliant, perceptive letters. *Endymion,* though the brief ascendancy of Hunt was ceasing now, was a kind of comet's tail to the excited autumn of 1816. But positive elements were also important in his growing attraction to Haydon rather than Hunt. The memory of his visit to the Elgin Marbles was much on his mind. And Haydon had warmly and impulsively responded to Keats's reaction. The minute he received the two sonnets—the one on the Elgin Marbles and the other to himself about the occasion—he had replied. He found the sonnets "noble": he could think of no

> finer image than the comparison of a Poet unable to express his high feelings to a sick eagle looking at the Sky!—when he must have remembered his former towerings . . . you filled me with fury for an hour, and with admiration for ever.

And with the wonderful, almost comic impetuosity of the man, he had torn open the letter in order to insert another:

> My dear Keats
>   I have really opened My letter to tell you how deeply I feel the high enthusiastic praise with which you have spoken of me in the first Sonnet [the sonnet "Forgive me, Haydon, that I cannot speak"]

—be assured you shall never *repent* it—the time shall come if God
spare my life—when you will remember it with delight—
Once more God bless you
B R Haydon [2]

4

Keats had meanwhile met John Taylor, probably through Reynolds. The Olliers might be getting impatient about the sale of his
book of poems. But now—and this was another stroke of luck,
just as one event after another during the previous autumn had
been—he was about to deal with a publisher of the sort that any
beginning writer might dream of having. Though Taylor was
fourteen years older than Keats, he was still a relatively young
man: he was thirty-five, and his partner, James Hessey, thirty-nine.
Taylor, the son of a bookseller in Nottingham, came from a large
family—he was one of eight children. He had left for London
when he was twenty-two, worked for at least two different publishers; and then in 1806, when he was only twenty-five and Hessey
twenty-nine, the two men set up at 93 Fleet Street the firm of Taylor and Hessey. For a while the youthful publishers lived at their
place of business, as was commonly done at the time. When Hessey
married, the living quarters were handed over to him, and Taylor,
liking the country, took lodgings in Hampstead. But commuting
may have become tiresome, and he moved to 91 Bond Street. Possibly by 1819, when the Hesseys felt they wanted a quieter place,
Taylor went back to the business premises in Fleet Street and
lived there; and Keats, though we are not sure of this, may have
spent his last days in England at Taylor's lodgings.

Taylor, as his biographer Edmund Blunden has shown, combined a firm business judgment with a meditative, sympathetic understanding of people and a knack for perceiving talent. Hessey,
very much the minor member of the firm, sensibly deferred to
him. Given his background, Taylor was a learned man. What
work he himself had published did him credit. He had written
some books trying to identify the author of the famous "Junius"
letters as Sir Philip Francis, and a century and a half later we can
still regard his argument as convincing. Later on, he became side-
tracked into writing on problems of currency, on theology, and on

[2] I.122–123.

antiquarian matters. His lack of confidence in his own writing was a result of genuine modesty. His education had been informal. Moreover, his imagination was healthily vicarious; the discovery and support of talent gave him more pleasure than anything else. When he was introduced to Keats, he quickly saw through the superficialities. The bizarre dress Keats affected at the time only amused him. Encouraged by Reynolds, he read the new volume of poetry carefully. The poor sale of the book did not worry him. In fact he wrote to his father late in April: "I cannot think he will fail to become a great Poet, though I agree with you in finding much fault with the Dedication [to Hunt], etc. These are not likely to appear in any other of his publications." By April 15, the firm had agreed to serve as Keats's publishers. By May 16, Taylor and Hessey had advanced him £20 (a sum, we should remember, comparable to about £100 now) ; and a month later, on June 10, Keats felt free to ask whether they could advance or "loan," as he put it, another £20. We can assume that the advance was made without impatience. Good-naturedly, the firm also took over from the Ollier brothers all the unsold copies of the *Poems* published in March, and made an effort to sell them.

5

Finally on April 14 Keats left for what we can only think of as the second Margate—the Isle of Wight. The experience was to prove rather frightening. In preparation for the trip he had bought a copy of Shakespeare in seven small volumes,[3] in the first two volumes of which he wrote his name and the date: April 1817. The book was to serve almost as a talisman or charm. When he arrived at the rooming house in the Isle of Wight, he was excited to find a picture of Shakespeare in the passage, which the landlady allowed him to remove from its place and hang over his books. "It comes nearer to my idea of him," he wrote to Haydon, "than any I have seen." Though he stayed at the rooming house only a week, the landlady "made me take it with me though I went off in a hurry—Do you not think this is ominous of good?" He kept it by him always. Two years later, after writing *Hyperion* and *The Eve of St. Agnes,* and less than three months before he wrote the

---

[3] Printed by C. Whittingham (Chiswick, 1814). The underscorings and marginal markings are discussed in Caroline Spurgeon, *Keats's Shakespeare* (1928).

great odes, he tells George and Georgiana—now in America—that as he writes he is "sitting opposite the Shakespeare I brought from the Isle of Wight." Georgiana, before she left, had woven some tassels to surround the frame. The picture was opposite him—tassels and all—when he wrote to her again in January 1820: by then he was seriously ill, with his work behind him, and with only one more year of life.

Constantly during the first few weeks of this second adventure in hope, this second Margate, he was to keep turning to Shakespeare. For he quickly fell into a despair more unnerving than any he had known since he had seriously hoped to be a poet. He himself tried to regard it as merely a sign of "a horrid Morbidity of Temperament." The phrase, which occurs in a letter to Haydon (May 11), has sometimes been interpreted as a brilliant example of self-diagnosis. But the context belies such an interpretation. When has a poet of so little experience committed himself to an assignment so mammoth (four thousand lines), without any real subject, and with a self-imposed timetable so unrealistic (the poem was to be finished by autumn)? Naturally he would rather attribute his despondency to a morbid temperament than to simple failure of nerve before an impossible demand—a demand he could not afford to think impossible. Typically he goes on, in his letter to Haydon (and the alternating despair and resort to Shakespeare for reassurance fill the letters of these weeks):

> I never quite despair and I read Shakespeare—indeed I shall I think never read any other Book much—Now this might lead to a long Confab but I desist. I am very near Agreeing with Hazlitt that Shakespeare is enough for us.

We can hardly expect this committed study of Shakespeare, which began with the writing of *Endymion* and continued throughout the year, to be reflected in the poem itself. Quick to justify any lag in growth in ourselves, we are not always prepared to allow for it in others—not because we are uncharitable but only because we hunger for neatness of pattern or wish to get on into briskness of explanation. We learn to swim in the winter, as William James said, and to skate in the summer. The result of these months of Shakespearolatry (and no milder word will do) breaks out only in the early winter, after *Endymion* itself is finished. Then for the first time we get the clairvoyant remarks about the

Shakespearean imagination and about what, in a letter to George and Tom in December, he calls "Negative Capability."

The two younger brothers, before Keats set off to the Isle of Wight, were vividly sharing this moment. It was they who had encouraged him to take the trip and to cap the success they felt was sure to come from the volume of *Poems* published March 3. They had already themselves been reading Shakespeare in the Cheapside lodgings they shared with John. After John left for the Isle of Wight, George and Tom, now in Hampstead at the house of Bentley the postman, tried loyally to keep abreast with his reading. In late May, the direct, simple George could write Joseph Severn how much he enjoyed the opportunity of reading Shakespeare in a fitting environment—in Hampstead "all in green Fields, under green Hedges, and upon green Mounts, surrounded by nature in her prettiest dress, decked in the flowers of Spring." There was some difference, of course, in what they were reading of Shakespeare. George and Tom had been reading *A Midsummer Night's Dream* and *The Tempest*. Their brother's imagination was increasingly haunted by *King Lear*.

6

April 14, when Keats set off—books and all—on the seventy-five-mile trip to Southampton, turned cold as night came. For three different stages of the journey, he sat outside, on the top of the coach. He kept glimpsing hedges, ponds, spots of wood, a cow in the fields, villages ("Barber's Pole—Doctor's Shop") ; and then he arrived at Southampton.

At the inn where he stayed in Southampton he felt a little terrified. The very morning after he arrived, he wrote to George and Tom: "I felt rather lonely this Morning at breakfast so I went and unbox'd a Shakespeare—'There's my Comfort.'" Then he ran to see when the boat would leave for the Isle of Wight; finding it left at three, he resolved to see Southampton—it was a new place, after all—and walked about noting the churches and by-streets, and an old gate with carved lions "to guard it—the Men and Women do not materially differ from those I have been in the Habit of seeing." Repeatedly he was to jest at himself in this way in the few and short trips he was to take. But immediately he goes on: "I forgot to say that from dawn till half past six I went through the most delightful Country—some open Down but for the most part thickly wooded." Always, until the end, this gifted poet was to feel free, in his letters, to fall into the innocence of exuberant simplicity as he expressed open delight in his surroundings ("a most delightful Country"; Shanklin "is a most beautiful place") ; and so the phrases keep recurring until the autumn of 1819, when, in his trip to Winchester, he could speak of the "beautiful cathedral"; "There are the most beautiful streams about I ever saw"; "you come to the most beautifully clear river."

Already homesick for his brothers and for London, though home meant no more than the new lodgings at Well Walk in Hampstead, or Haydon's crowded studio in Marlborough Street, or Reynolds' interest and understanding, he had written—still at Southampton—"you, Haydon, Reynolds &c. have been pushing each other out of my Brain by turns."

When he crossed to the Isle of Wight from Southampton, he went to Carisbrooke, and got a room at the home of Mrs. Cook, in "New Village" (a string of houses along what is now Castle Road) . At once he began to prepare for the "trial of Invention" ahead. As he wrote to Reynolds:

> I have unpacked my books, put them in a snug corner—pinned up Haydon—Mary Queen [of] Scots, and Milton with his daughters in a row. In the passage I found a head of Shakspeare which I had not before seen—It is most likely the same that George spoke so well of; for I like it extremely—Well—this head I have hung over my Books, just above the three in a row, having first discarded a french Ambassador.

7

Nothing momentous happened—no lines rushed into his head. But he was not in a hurry, he thought. He had learned to be less impetuous than when he had gone to Margate, taken a look at the "wonders," written a sonnet about them to George, and then, in a few days, fallen into despair because no epic sprang to mind—nor even the beginning of an epic. He could feel he was now something of a professional. Unpacking the books, pinning up a picture of Haydon, and getting the engraving of Shakespeare "is a good morning's work," as he said to Reynolds. He immediately set off to look at neighboring places. The place was completely new; he could afford to take time and get his bearings. Shanklin, close by, is "a most beautiful place": the "clefts" and sloping woods entrance him. But it is the memory of the sea—the memory of that discovery at Margate, caught and distilled in the Chapman's Homer sonnet—that teases his thought:

> But the sea, Jack, the sea—the little waterfall—then the white cliff—then St. Catherine's Hill—"the sheep in the meadows, the cows in the corn."—Then, why are you at Carisbrooke? say you—Because, in the first place, I sho^d be at twice the Expense, and three times the inconvenience—next that from here I can see your continent—from a little hill close by, the whole north Angle of the Isle of Wight, with the water between us. In the 3^d place, I see Carisbrooke Castle from my window . . . I intend to walk over the island east—West—North South—I have not seen many specimens of Ruins—I dont think however I shall ever see one to surpass Carisbrooke Castle. The trench is o'ergrown with the smoothest turf, and the walls with ivy—The Keep within side is one Bower of ivy—a Colony of Jackdaws have been there many years.

And then his thought, amid all this resolution, returns again to the new home he had found with his brothers and with his friends after he left Guy's Hospital. He would like, he tells Reynolds, "a sketch of you and Tom and George . . . which Haydon will do if you tell him how I want them." This open divulgence of need releases a complete frankness. For, without transition, we turn from this thought of Tom, George, and Reynolds to his readiness to commit himself in this new endeavor, and its association with the Margate excursion when he had first seen the sea. With an attempted lightness of phrase, he says that "From want of regular rest, I have been rather *narvus*—and the passage in Lear—'Do you not hear the Sea?'—has haunted me intensely." And he copies out the fine sonnet "On the Sea," which he has just written. The incident repeats the pattern started at Margate and in a sense continued throughout his career. Preparing to write a major poem, and not making the headway his timetable demands, he writes a shorter one on the side—usually an excellent one. Back in Margate he had broken the ice with the sonnet "To My Brother George," the best part of which dwells on the sea. Now, in his second Margate, troubled further by the huge, uncertain grandeur of *King Lear*, he writes another and much better sonnet, this time one openly "On the Sea." The suggestions of promise, vastness, uncertainties, again catch at him—the "eternal whisperings," the mighty swell that gluts "ten thousand caverns," the thought of the *wideness* of the sea.[4]

The next morning he goes on with his letter to Reynolds. He is obviously not getting ahead with *Endymion*. As he writes, his brothers begin to counterpoint in his imagination with Shakespeare—the new-found home with George and Tom (which after the years at Hammond's surgery and Guy's Hospital, he has had for only a few months) alternating with another home in which, as he said over a year later, "The roaring of the wind is my wife and the Stars through the window pane are my children"; where the "mighty abstract Idea" toward which he is trying to move "stifles the more divided and minute domestic happiness," and he finds that he lives not "in this world alone but in a thousand worlds." [5] "Tell George and Tom to write," he says (this is now the fourth day away from them). And then immediately, after a dash:

I'll tell you what—On the 23rd was Shakespeare born—now If I should receive a Letter from you and another from my Brothers on that day 'twould be a parlous good thing—Whenever you write say a Word or two on some Passage in Shakespeare that may have come rather new to you; which must be continually happening, notwithstand^g that we read the same Play forty times—for instance, the following, from the Tempest, never struck me so forcibly as at present,

> "Urchins
> *Shall, for that vast of Night that they may work,*
> All exercise on thee—"

How can I help bringing to your mind the Line—

> *In the dark backward and abysm of time—*

[4] It keeps eternal Whisperings around
    Desolate shores, and with its mighty swell
    Gluts twice ten thousand Caverns; till the spell
Of Hecate leaves them their old shadowy sound.
Often 'tis in such gentle temper found
    That scarcely will the very smallest shell
    Be moved for days from whence it sometime fell
When last the winds of Heaven were unbound.
O ye who have your eyeballs vext and tir'd
    Feast them upon the wideness of the Sea;
O ye whose Ears are dinned with uproar rude
    Or fed too much with cloying melody—
Sit ye near some old Cavern's Mouth and brood
    Until ye start as if the Sea Nymphs quired—
[5] *Letters,* I.403.

I find that I cannot exist without poetry—without eternal poetry—half the day will not do—the whole of it—I began with a little, but habit has made me a Leviathan.

That last desperate assertion ("I find that I cannot exist without poetry . . . half the day will not do") is partly an act of will—as was the sudden break in his letter to Haydon when he begins "I never quite despair and I read Shakespeare." For frankly, transparently, he goes on to divulge his real feelings:

> I had become all in a Tremble from not having written any thing of late—the Sonnet over leaf ["On the Sea"] did me some good. I slept the better last night for it—this Morning, however, I am nearly as bad again—Just now I opened Spencer, and the first Lines I saw [*Faerie Queene,* I.v.1] were these.—

> > "The noble Heart that harbors vertuous thought,
> > And is with Child of glorious great intent,
> > Can never rest, until it forth have brought
> > Th' eternal Brood of Glory excellent—"

. . . I shall forthwith begin my Endymion.

8

The trip to the Isle of Wight was not proving to be the answer. The problem, of course, would have been the same anywhere. He had some opening lines before he came; he had been jotting down some others. But this new solitude, the attractive ruins of Carisbrooke Castle, the eager, devout reading of Shakespeare, did not seem to be helping. Strangely enough, when he set off over two years later to write *Lamia*—his *Endymion* in reverse—he was to go back again to the Isle of Wight. Then he settled in Shanklin. The traumatic days of April 1817 were not a pleasant memory, and he began, as he said, "to dislike the very door posts here"—that is, in Shanklin, which he had thought a "most beautiful place" when he first saw it in 1817.

Now, on the first trip, he was simply bewildered and frightened. "I shall forthwith begin my Endymion," he said on April 18. But Shakespeare's birthday came five days later, on April 23. And on that very day—or more probably the day after—the abysmal distance between what little he had done and what he intended to do left him crushed. Resisting the temptation to fall into paralysis, he at once acted. He would leave the Isle of Wight. He would go back and touch base—return to Margate, bathing machines and all, and try to get the room he had taken seven months ago. At least he had been able to write something there. Moreover, Tom could come and give him company; and in eager preparation Keats bought a copy of Scott's *Marmion* to give Tom as a present.[6] As he told Hunt two weeks later (May 10) with attempted casualness:

> I went to the Isle of Wight—thought so much about Poetry so long together that I could not get to sleep at night—and moreover [he rationalizes] I know not how it was, I could not get wholesome food —By this means in a Week or so I became not over capable in my upper Stories, and set off pell mell for Margate, at least 150 Miles— because forsooth I fancied that I should like my old Lodging here, and could contrive to do without Trees. Another thing I was too much in Solitude, and consequently was obliged to be in continual burning of thought as an only resource. However Tom is with me at present and we are very comfortable. We intend though to get among some trees.

He had originally expected that John Reynolds might be joining him at the Isle of Wight. But Reynolds was too busy preparing for the law. Keats naturally felt embarrassed about the whole episode. His self-dissatisfaction turned on Margate. The lack of trees obsessed him, and became something of a symbol of the aridity he associated with the place on his second visit. Months after leaving "this treeless affair" the memory bothered him; and he found Oxford pleasant the following September because there were "plenty of Trees thank God."

It was his own good sense that led him to feel embarrassed about the way he was reacting to the Isle of Wight and then to Margate. A part of him would subscribe to Johnson's remark that a man can write anywhere or any time "if he will set himself *doggedly* to it." And Keats was working doggedly. He had been putting in eight hours a day, reading closely and writing (or trying to write), both at the Isle of Wight, after the first two or three days of sightseeing, and now at Margate. He told Hunt (May 10) that for two weeks he had "done some [writing] every day except travelling ones— Perhaps I may have done a good deal for the time but it appears such a Pin's Point to me . . . I see . . . nothing but continual uphill Journeying." He admits he has "been down in the Mouth

6 Now in the Keats-Shelley Memorial House, Rome.

lately at this Work," and that *"I have asked myself so often* [the italics are added] *why I should be a Poet more than other Men,—* seeing how great a thing it is." He wonders, in a brilliant moment of self-perception, whether "the Idea has grown so monstrously beyond my seeming Power of attainment."

Meanwhile George had been worried about the tone of his letters, and early in May called on Haydon for advice. Haydon then wrote to Keats hastily but wisely:

> I think you did quite right to leave the Isle of White if you felt no relief in being quite alone after study—you may now devote your eight hours a day with just as much seclusion as ever——Do not give way to any forebodings they are nothing more than the over eager anxieties of a great Spirit stretched beyond its strength, and then relapsing for a time to languid inefficiency——Every man of great views, is at times thus tormented . . . *Trust in God* with all your might . . . beware for God's sake of the delusions & sophistications . . . of our Friend [Hunt]—he will go out of the World the victim of his own weakness & the dupe of his own self delusions . . . God bless you My dear Keats go on, dont despair, collect incidents, study characters, read Shakespeare and trust in Providence.[7]

Keats at once replied (May 10) with grateful warmth and also with an openness he could not show to Hunt—Haydon understood so much better what he was trying to do. He declares bravely, "I must think that difficulties nerve the Spirit of a Man—they make our Prime Objects a Refuge as well as a Passion." "I suppose," he goes on, "by your telling me not to give way to forebodings George has mentioned to you what I have lately said in my Letters to him." He then breaks down and admits:

> I have been in such a state of Mind as to read over my Lines and hate them. I am "one that gathers Samphire dreadful trade" the Cliff of Poesy Towers above me—yet when, Tom who meets with some of Pope's Homer in Plutarch's Lives reads some of those to me they seem like Mice to mine. I read and write about eight hours a day. There is an old saying "well begun is half done"—'tis a bad one . . . I do begin arduously where I leave off, notwithstanding occasional depressions: and I hope for the support of a High Power while I clime this little eminence and especially in my Years of more momentous Labor. I remember your saying that you had notions of a good Genius presiding over you—I have of late had the same thought . . . Is it too daring to Fancy Shakspeare this Presider?

7 I.134–135.

He tells Haydon about the picture of Shakespeare that he found in Carisbrooke and that the landlady made him take when he left. He then puts the letter aside intending to finish it later.

But the very next day he received, he said, "a letter from George by which it appears that Money Troubles are to follow us up for some time to come perhaps for always—these vexations are a great hindrance." Whatever the financial problem, it could not have been serious—at least not serious in any novel, unexpected way. But his nerves had been so much on edge, his uncertainty about his ability so much greater than he had been admitting to himself or to anyone else, that for the first time in any of his letters he comes close to bitterness and even self-pity:

> Now I revoke my Promise of finishing my Poem by the Autumn which I should have done had I gone on as I have done—but I cannot write while my spirit is fevered in a contrary direction [by financial worries] . . . I feel that I am not in a Mood to write any to day . . . I am extremely glad that a time must come when every thing will leave not a wrack behind. You tell me never to despair—I wish it was as easy for me to observe the saying.

So acute is his self-dissatisfaction that he begins to project some of his unpleasant reactions onto Hunt. He begins by saying quite understandably (even though his letter to Hunt had been friendly) : "I wrote to Hunt yesterday—scarcely know what I said in it—I could not talk about Poetry in the way I should have liked for I was not in humor with either his or mine." But, prodded partly by Haydon's remarks about Hunt's "delusions and sophistications," he goes on with irritable smugness: "His self delusions are very lamentable they have inticed him into a Situation which I should be less eager after than that of a galley Slave."

Then with an unfairness and self-deception unmatched in Keats until some of the wretched moments near the end, when he was fatally ill, he suddenly condemns Hunt for an ambition to which Hunt never aspired but to which Keats had been completely dedicated for so long, and especially with the generous encouragement of Hunt during the last half year. And ironically he is talking about self-deception. Cringing at his own failure to produce when he has been intoxicated by so high an ideal—and has himself prated of it constantly—he says (admittedly with a qualification at the start) :

Perhaps it is a self delusion to say so—but I think I could not be deceived in the Manner that Hunt is—may I die tomorrow if I am to be. There is no greater Sin after the 7 deadly than to flatter one-self into an idea of being a great Poet—or one of those beings who are privileged to wear out their Lives in the pursuit of Honor—how comfortable a feel [a noun he has caught from Hunt] it is that such a Crime must bring its heavy Penalty?

After this transference of uneasiness and self-blame, he feels better. He goes on: "I never quite despair and I read Shakspeare," and quotes some passages from *Antony and Cleopatra* that delight him. He particularly likes moments of impatience: "Shakspeare makes Enobarb say—Where's Antony Eros—He's walking in the garden —thus: *and spurns the rush that lies* before him, cries fool, Lepi-dus!"

9

Five days after he wrote his cathartic letter to Haydon, Keats left treeless Margate and went to nearby Canterbury. He had never seen it, and the place was pleasantly associated with Chaucer. "This Evening," he wrote to Taylor and Hessey (May 16), "I go to Canterbury—having got tired of Margate—I was not right in my head when I came—At Cant^y I hope the Remembrance of Chaucer will set me forward like a Billiard-Ball." The occasion of the letter to Taylor and Hessey was to thank them for advancing £20 (probably in order to satisfy part of the debt about which George had written him a few days before and which had plunged him into such gloom). With jaunty embarrassment and pretended casualness, his letter of thanks begins:

I am extremely indebted to you for your liberality in the Shape of manufactu[r]ed rag value £20 and shall immediately proceed to de-stroy some of the Minor Heads of that spr[i]ng-headed Hydra the Dun.

Then for a full half of his letter he laboriously tries to be play-ful about the matter. "I think I could make a nice little Alegorical Poem called 'the Dun' Where we wo[u]ld have the Castle of Care-lessness—the Draw Bridge of Credit," and so on. A month later he was to write again, with less embarrassed writhing but in a similar vein, asking for another £30: "I must endeavor to lose my Maiden-head with respect to money Matters as soon as possible—and I will to[o]—so here goes—A Couple of Duns that I thought would be silent till . . . next Month . . . it would relieve my Mind if I owed you instead of these Pelican duns." He has not yet got to his point; and being unpracticed in the arts of indirection, he rightly begins to wonder whether he is being needlessly and awkwardly circuitous: "I am afraid you will say I have 'wound about with circumstance' when I should have asked plainly—However as I said I am a little maidenish or so—and I feel my virginity come strong upon me—the while I request the loan of a £20 and a £10—which if you would enclose to me I would acknowledge and save myself a hot forehead—I am sure you are confident in my responsibility." [8]

But to go back to his letter of May 16, on the evening of which he is to leave for Canterbury: he tells Taylor and Hessey that he has gone "day by day at my Poem for a Month at the end of which time the other day I found my Brain so overwrought that I had neither Rhyme nor reason in it—so was obliged to give up for a few days." He feels "all the effects of a Mental Debauch—lowness of Spirits—anxiety to go on without the Power to do so . . . However tomorrow I will begin my next Month."

When he left for Canterbury with Tom, he "had got a little way in the 1st Book." Lines 133–134 are sometimes thought to refer to his stay at Canterbury ("that I may dare, in wayfaring, / To stammer where old Chaucer used to sing"). Of the "four thousand lines," probably less than a twentieth had been written. But now the letters stop. He was devoting himself wholly to *Endymion,* and appears to have been making some progress. He may have stayed in Canterbury one week to three. We know only that he was there on May 22, six days after leaving from Margate (for George on this date wrote to Severn, "John and Tom are at Canterbury"), and that by June 10, when he wrote to Taylor and Hessey for his second advance, he was back in Hampstead at the rooms he and his brothers had taken at Well Walk. Before returning, he visited Hastings. From a letter of George to Severn we learn that he stayed at the little village of Bo Peep (now the western section of the resort St. Leonard's) and that he was alone—Tom had returned earlier. He had heard of the place from Haydon, and also of its pleasant inn, "The New England Bank." We know nothing else about the visit except that he met a woman with whom he

[8] See the far more involved letter in which he attempts to ask Taylor for money on August 23, 1819, when he is in desperate need (II.143–144).

seems to have flirted a little—a Mrs. Isabella Jones, who returns to the Keats story a year and a half later.

He had told Taylor and Hessey on May 16 that he had "some idea of seeing the Continent some time in the summer." But by mid-June, back in Hampstead, he was writing rapidly. Only two letters survive from the fifteen and a half weeks between May 16 and September 4. One (June 10) is the request for a second advance from his publishers. The second, dated simply August and probably written later that month, is a brief note to Haydon in which he is able to say "I have finished my second Book." Back on May 10 he had told Haydon the maxim he favored was "Not begun at all 'till half done." He was now "half done." The poem may be discussed at this point, for its shape was fairly well established; and in the months during which he finished it his attention was turning dramatically to other interests which are perhaps better traced without interruption.

10

The development of Keats as a poet from the autumn of 1816 through the last great poems is a development of three years. Hence our interest in it month by month, and even week by week. Yet for almost a year of this brief period of three years so little seems at first to be happening: little at least if we think of the *gradus ad Parnassum* now beginning to catch his imagination. Through most of 1817 sprawls the long, almost Haydonesque poem of *Endymion*. And that huge canvas of poetry—that alternately self-confident and inhibited filling of space—affects all but the most devoted student in the way that Haydon's room-filling paintings affected so many: it is known about; it is known to be large; and if it is once read (and most probably only in parts), it is rarely turned to again except for some special purpose. Nor have biographers and critics of Keats approached *Endymion* with much happiness, at least within the last few decades. One reason is that the accumulated commentary of the last half century forbids drastic distillation. Yet in any general discussion of Keats's life a distillation of what can be said of *Endymion* is what is needed. At the time of the first World War, Amy Lowell could devote almost a hundred and fifty pages to *Endymion*, though much of the space was concerned with details of Keats's life at the time. All possible allusions, phrasal echoes of other poets, sources of theme, interpretive speculation, could be mentioned, while following the poem book by book. To retain such a scale thirty-five years later would necessitate a volume devoted to *Endymion* alone. Uneasily the biographer begins to justify his neglect, remembering the salutary remarks of Johnson on Prior's *Solomon*—that it "wanted that [quality] without which all others are of small avail, the power of engaging attention . . . Tediousness is the most fatal of all faults."

Endymion is indeed of the first importance in the story of Keats's life. Yet two qualifications face us at the start. Each is a by-product of the very special way in which the poem was written; and in giving us this reminder, biography can possibly aid criticism, dissuading it from doomed ingenuity and the irritabilities of superfluous debate. Formalists may feel that an artist's intention is irrelevant. But form, in the concrete individual work, can never itself be explained solely by formal criteria. As Coleridge says of the doctrine of "association of ideas" in psychology, which he compares to "the term stimulus in medicine": in "explaining everything, it . . . leaves itself unexplained." "Something there must be," as he says later, "to realize the form, something in and by which the *forma informans* reveals itself." Intention—or rather intentions—not only enter, but may become burly and impelling, affecting radically the entire mode in which a poem is written. This is particularly true when the circumstances are such that the poem is written rapidly. As in the sonnets Keats wrote with a time limit, much is jotted down that is merely casual, floating, or suggested by the urgencies of rhyme.

The principal fact about *Endymion* is that it was, as Keats said, "a feverish attempt, rather than a deed accomplished." In large part, it was a "trial" of invention—an attempt to "make 4,000 lines." Moreover, it had a timetable—a timetable that would have intimidated major poets ten years older. Hence, to begin with, the real interest of the poem is psychological—and in the most elementary, obvious way. The words "elementary" and "obvious" cannot be too much stressed. For our psychological interests now tend automatically to search for the unobvious—for preoccupations, underlying obsessions, stock responses, and the like. These certainly have their place. But one of the values again of biography, as of history, is in reminding us that men are free agents: less free, perhaps, than they themselves think they are, but far freer than our academic and rather doctrinaire approaches to them assume. And in any approach to this self-imposed marathon of Keats, as in our approach to any form of gymnastics, we must resist the temptations of the sedentary theorist and remember that we are not sitting next to the couch of the helpless.

The essential, obvious psychological interest of *Endymion*—and of these crucial eight months of Keats's life—is that we have a manly intelligence, blessed with instinctive prudence as well as a trustful veneration of what the best of the past has achieved, deliberately using these months, using this long worksheet, so to speak, as a courageous exercise, confident that by such a stretch of inventive muscle he was following the examples he revered, and that the principal gain of such an exercise would appear not in the poem itself but in what he would write later—possibly much later. The following autumn (October 8), he wrote a letter to his new friend Benjamin Bailey in which he says, "You may see the whole of the case by the following extract from a Letter I wrote to George in the spring." The letter, presumably written after he left for the Isle of Wight to begin *Endymion,* was preserved by George and Tom though it has since been lost. And painstakingly Keats copies it out for Bailey:

> [*Endymion*] will be a test, a trial of my Powers of Imagination and chiefly of my invention which is a rare thing indeed—by which I must make 4000 Lines of one bare circumstance and fill them with Poetry; and when I consider that this is a great task, and that when done it will take me but a dozen paces towards the Temple of Fame —it makes me say—God forbid that I should be without such a task! I have heard Hunt say and may be asked—why endeavour after a long Poem? To which I should answer—Do not the Lovers of Poetry like to have a little Region to wander in where they may pick and choose, and in which the images are so numerous that many are forgotten and found new in a second Reading: which may be food for a Week's stroll in the Summer? Do not they like this better than what they can read through before Mrs. Williams comes down stairs? a Morning work at most. Besides a long Poem is a test of Invention which I take to be the Polar Star of Poetry, as Fancy is the Sails, and Imagination the Rudder. Did our great Poets ever write short Pieces? I mean in the shape of Tales—This same invention seems i[n]deed of late Years to have been forgotten as a Poetical excel-

lence [.] But enough of this, I put on no Laurels till I shall have finished Endymion, and I hope Apollo is [not] angered at my having
made a Mockery at him at Hunt's.

This passage had meant enough to him to wish to return to it and
to copy it out word for word. He had plainly written it as a sort
of credo (for this one poem) when he began *Endymion*. And now
as he finishes the poem, he still views that letter to George in the
same way, and wishes his new friend Bailey to understand the
principal spirit in which the poem was written.

11

A second consideration that qualifies—or at least specializes—
our interest in *Endymion* is stylistic, and in a sense that transcends
the varieties of awkwardness already familiar to us in the earlier
verse. And the style we here confront is partly a result of the intention and spirit with which the poem was written—spasmodi-
cally braced, it is true, by a quickly maturing power of conception
(it is after all, the first real poem with a *story* he has finished—and
immeasurably larger than any poem of any sort he has tried) and
heightened in spots by a deftness of phrase that we are surprised to
find in any poem written under such circumstances and with so
little experience.

We are always looking for similarities in considering the works
that mark a writer's development. This, as Bacon said, is a natural
bias of the imagination. But we should also be awake to dis-
similarities. However diversely writers, critics, readers, have approached Keats during the last century, on one quality in his writing they have been completely united. They have all been won by
an economy and power of phrase excelled only by Shakespeare. Yet
Endymion is easily one of the most diluted poems Keats wrote. In
fact, it is one of the most diluted poems in a century often given
to poetic dilution. In this one essential respect, *Endymion* is the
most atypical of Keats's major poems. For this reason more than
any other, the admirer of Keats, though prepared to be indulgent
to every awkwardness and excess, has never really found the poem
as a whole to be as interesting as he secretly thinks he should find
it. Forced to make something out of an effort that occupied so large
a portion of Keats's short career, he is tempted to trace out an elaborate and planned allegory, or, surfeited not only by the unsys-

tematic profusion of incident in the poem but also by conflicting interpretations of it, to deny any allegorical intention at all. Nineteenth-century readers were generally untroubled by any thought of allegory. Whether or not the poem was much liked, few people pretended to see much point to it. Hence Arnold's familiar remark: *Endymion,* though "undoubtedly there blows through it the breath of genius, is yet as a whole so utterly incoherent, as not strictly to merit the name of a poem at all." But after Sir Sidney Colvin's fine study of Keats, the explanation of the poem as a "parable of the poetic soul in man seeking communion with the spirit of essential Beauty in the world" (to use Colvin's words) became prevalent, and took, more often than not, a Neoplatonic coloring.[9] Allowing for wide differences in the interpretation of particular books and incidents, we can describe the general assumption as follows: Cynthia, the moon-goddess, represents ideal Beauty, for which Endymion—the human soul, the poet, or the poetic imagination—is searching. Endymion's first awareness of the ideal has come through a dream-vision. But spiritual maturing is necessary before a genuine union can take place. He must especially realize that human love and sympathy are approaches to the ideal. His pilgrimage concluded, Cynthia accepts him: he is united with "essential Beauty." Objections made to the entire approach, or to most of it, seem to fall under four headings. (1) Allegory, it is said, was foreign to Keats's mind, at least so early in his career.[10] Though advanced as an argument, the statement is hardly more than a premise. For it is supported only by reminding us that Keats had not tried his hand at allegorical verse before *Endymion;* that the next poem of any length after *Endymion* (*Isabella*) was a simple narrative; and that when he did try a major poem in an

---

[9] Interpretations in this general spirit would include those of H. C. Notcutt (1919), Clarence Thorpe (1926), Claude Finney (1936), and, with differences, the various works of J. M. Murry. Dissenting voices include Amy Lowell, the fine monograph of N. F. Ford (1951), and most recently E. C. Pettet (1957).

[10] A hidden difficulty in the discussion is the growing stock reaction to the word "allegory" since the rise of symbolism and the resurrection of Coleridge's distinction between "allegory" and "symbol." With the appropriation by "symbolism" of some of the qualities traditionally associated with "allegory" (particularly the more general, fluid, and dynamic associations), the latter term has both shrunk and hardened until it seems applicable only to a rigid, systematically arranged parable. The result is a terminological loss. For "symbol" is not a substitute: while it may suggest qualities previously associated with "allegory" (as when Keats wrote "A Man's life of any worth is a continual allegory . . . Shakespeare led a life of Allegory"), it also suggests much else that is not applicable.

allegorical vein—*Hyperion*—the procedure was so uncongenial
that he was unable to finish.[11] (2) Anything of a Platonic cast was
especially alien to so empirical a mind. Nor could he have known
much about Platonic or Neoplatonic thought anyway. Shelley, it
is true, had talked about the subject frequently in the Hunt circle
back in December. But this could not have meant much to Keats;
he was not too sympathetic with Shelley; and if there are parallels
with Shelley's *Alastor*, it can also be argued, as Leonard Brown has
said, that *Alastor* was almost an "anti-model," and that *Endymion*
was written as a sort of rebuttal. In short, if there was an allegorical intention, it was not Platonic. (3) When we come to the interpretation of particular incidents, the variety of allegorical interpretation possible is so great that the whole allegorical premise
begins to be doubted. (4) The nineteenth century was generally
satisfied to take the poem simply and directly. Along with this un-
reflective trust in the nineteenth-century view is an implied censure of the Alexandrianism of twentieth-century scholarship and
criticism: we all know that with the present-day academic premium on what Johnson calls the "epidemical conspiracy for the destruction of paper," ingenuity is stimulated more by rivalry and
the search for novelty than by the facts of the case. Granted the
Alexandrianism, many of the anti-allegorical objections are as
guilty of it as the interpretations they attack—in some cases, when
the focus is solely on the text, more so.

The very debatability of the existence or lack of allegory is a
significant comment on the form of the poem—a form (satisfying
no one, least of all the author) that cannot be understood apart
from biographical considerations. If *Endymion* were encountered
completely *in vacuo*, it would be difficult to argue that there was
an active allegorical intention (though it would also be difficult to
argue an entire lack of it). But when the poem is considered in
the context of Keats's life and the rich body of letters we have
available, we begin to sense—at the very least—an urgency of purpose aside from Keats's hurrying need to get started on something
and to stretch himself as much as he could. We begin, that is, to

11 That he had not written allegorical poetry before *Endymion* is no argument
at all (though it may be relevant to what happened to the poem as he went along).
As for the "simple" *Isabella,* there is every reason why, in reaction from *Endymion,*
he should want to try something different. The decision to give up *Hyperion* may
indicate that allegory was not basically congenial to his gift, but is certainly no argument that *Hyperion* is therefore a first rather than a second attempt.

sense an urgency of purpose in which this self-imposed stretch or exercise would not have been regarded by him as genuine or fruitful had it not also involved a search for meaning. As we go further into the letters and the context of the life, we are increasingly struck by the fundamentally moral character of this imagination. Inevitably the twentieth century, knowing so much more about the life and impressed by the moral character of the letters and the later major poems, has been tempted to enrich the poem—to fill out its large vacuities and reorder its scattered detail. It must be admitted that to try to develop a systematic Neoplatonism for the poem is a little like trying to evolve a Lockean philosophy from his frequent use of the word "sensation" in the letters. We take it for granted, when we encounter students, that youthful idealism is ardently eclectic. Yet, in approaching writers no older, our eyes begin to narrow sharply and we search for set premises and aims. But that close scrutiny must itself be eclectic, and include in its eclecticism such obvious details as the age and experience of the writer. If here and there Keats used abstractions, adjectives, or images that suggest conventional Neoplatonic poetry (he lacked even the small exposure to Plato himself that a college undergraduate might possibly have had), it is because they were emotionally welcome to the naive, untutored idealism that existed side by side with his strong empirical sense.

12

It is indeed possible to go too far in our resort to the context of the letters and his other writing. But it is also possible to fall short by neglecting it. What we are dealing with could be described simply as allegory *manqué:* not the familiar sort in which the interest of narrative, character, or even language unexpectedly becomes so assertive that the original premise is forgotten, but a form in which the allegorical intention remains, though it becomes thinned, distracted, and ultimately divided. The dilution and distraction were perhaps inevitable, given Keats's simultaneous desire to use the poem as a large, demanding "test" or "trial." He kept adding details—snatching at embellishments as mere filler—as he dashed forward. He knew only too well that this was what he was doing. Hence his desire, once he kept his timetable and finished the poem, to have it published as quickly as possible; he would not be able then to tinker with it further. Fewer weeks were spent in revising and copying out the poem freshly than months in writing it in first draft. Nor was the work of these weeks (most of which consisted of copying) nearly so concentrated an effort. He was doing many other things by then. He wished, as he candidly said in his Preface, that "this youngster should die away." "A year's castigation" would do it no good; "the foundations are too sandy." One also thinks ahead to his remark to Shelley three years later (August 1820), only six months before his death, when he counsels Shelley to curb his "magnanimity . . . and 'load every rift' of your subject with ore"; and he adds, with quick humor, "is not this extraordinary talk for the writer of Endymion? whose mind was like a pack of scattered cards—I am pick'd up and sorted to a pip."

But a fundamental division also entered as the poem progressed, further complicating or at least muddying the result. With the easy wisdom of hindsight, we can sense its presence back in the verse letters of 1816. But these epistles, because he had no story, he could break off where he wished. "I stood tiptoe," as a descriptive poem, could also break off abruptly. It ends:

> but now no more,
> My wand'ring spirit must no further soar.—

And "Sleep and Poetry," being merely descriptive and meditative, could end suddenly on a mood: these lines, he says,

> howsoever they be done,
> I leave them as a father does his son.

Calm and resolution can be asserted; they need not be depicted or evolved from the context. But narrative brings embarrassments as well as the advantages he had craved, ever since, for lack of story, he had given up the youthful "Calidore" he had written in the spring months at Guy's Hospital the year before. And a year after Endymion, when he began Hyperion—this time an epic he intended to write in "a more naked and Grecian manner"—an analogous division was to enter. But by then he was too wise to try to complete the poem. Quite understandably, throughout the later months of 1817 and even more in the year following, his eye began to turn to the drama. For until 1817 there had been only two fundamental alternatives open to him: the sort of thing represented by

G. F. Mathew and Hunt, and, on the other hand, the openly allegorical poetry of Spenser (though he was only beginning to see this side of Spenser) and also the potential allegorical uses of classical myth generally. When he began *Endymion,* he may well have had some hope of bridging the two—though "as I proceeded my steps were all uncertain."

13

    Given the situation, wanting a story for a framework on which he could stretch his four thousand lines and through which he could make some sort of union between the two kinds of poetry on which he had been nourished, he had grasped at the fable of Endymion, which he had begun to touch on the previous winter in his lines "I stood tiptoe." The love of a mortal for the ideal had been very much in his mind. It had been given a stronger context when he saw the Elgin Marbles, and felt like a "sick eagle looking at the sky." Here in the story of Endymion was a usable myth, ready-made. He could hardly be expected to think prudently of the complications. Endymion, as the mortal who pined for the moon-goddess, was a passive and pallid character; and the moon and Diana had obvious limitations as a symbol of the ideal. Whatever could be made of the situation, it was far from the "naked and Grecian" ideal he mentioned a year later, and even further from the drama of the heart's approach to the permanence of art that we find him exploring later in the great odes. But the rudiments, at least, were there in the outline. The problem of literary sources need not detain us in a general narrative of Keats's life. The subject has been exhaustively discussed. Twentieth-century scholars have been struck by the somewhat parallel plot of Michael Drayton's *Endimion and Phoebe* (1595). But the book was almost unknown; it was so rare that, as far as we know, there was only one copy to which Keats may have had access—a copy in the library at Westminster Abbey. The library, as Amy Lowell points out, could be used on application to the verger, and it is possible that Keats saw the book or talked with someone who had.[12] He

12 In considering this muddled question we are at least entitled, as Douglas Bush has said, to think that Drayton's *Endimion and Phoebe* was "not necessary" for the device of having Phoebe appear to Endymion "in the form of a mortal and winning his love away from her divine self": "if Drayton had a direct source for his own plot, none has so far turned up, and can we assume that Drayton could invent what Keats

certainly knew Drayton's revision, the *Man in the Moone;* it was
included in his own copy of Drayton. (The revision omitted the
central portions of the plot that remind one most of Keats's own
treatment of the fable.) Keats could have found some suggestions
in Lyly's *Endimion.* Mary Tighe's *Psyche* (1805), which he had
read and liked a year or two before, could have offered hints. Shelley's *Alastor,* which may indeed have been a sort of "anti-model"—
or at least a challenge—could also be listed. George Sandys's translation of Ovid provided an important source; and of course there
were the mythological handbooks he had known since his Enfield
days—Spence's *Polymetis,* Tooke's *Pantheon,* and Lemprière's
Classical Dictionary. Wieland's *Oberon* contributed suggestions,
and possibly Southey's *Curse of Kehama,* with its travels through
earth, water, and air. In diction and imagery, borrowings can be
traced throughout much of his reading—especially Spenser, Chapman, Sandys, William Browne, and, among contemporaries, Hunt
and Wordsworth.

Because of the long, wavy course of the poem, a brief summary
may tell more in the same space than categorical discussion that
must be constantly qualified. The famous introductory lines (1–62)
are transparent and relatively confident. The theme, in effect, is
the heart's hope that we can "burst our mortal bars" (to go back
to his phrase in "I stood tiptoe" when he had touched momentarily on the fable of Endymion). Keats's unpredictable response
to the Elgin Marbles, when he saw them early in March, shows
how urgent this preoccupation was becoming: before such permanence of grandeur, his attempt to frame a positive answer on the
basis of slighter experience was shaken, and his immediate feeling
was of "mortality" weighing "heavily on me," every "imagined
pinnacle" telling "me I must die." He was now to try to work out
an answer of sorts. He was to find another way of posing the question two years later when he wrote the "Ode on a Grecian Urn"—
one that avoids the "indescribable feud" that the "dim-conceivèd
glories" of the Parthenon sculptures "bring round the heart." But
at the present moment the way was yet to find. Moreover, this
youth of twenty-one was far from being a philosopher, however

---

could not? Then, if a lover of the myth of Endymion and Diana and its traditional
allegory sets out to show through that tale the ultimate identity of the real and
the ideal, is not some such device almost inevitable?" (*Mythology and the Romantic
Tradition* [1937], p. 100.)

much he might aspire to be one within another year or two. The opening line—"A thing of beauty is a joy forever"—is an assertion of trust, and the "forever" is not meant strictly.[13] The thought is primarily of the release of the human spirit during its own life-time, though hopefully for longer. At the same time, he also re-turns in this introduction to the tone of "Sleep and Poetry"—to that part of it which had suggested the health-giving power of sleep, and had tried to imply a relation between sleep and those insights that complete our daily existence and give them a finer tone, a possible unity. (The more serious poetry, two years later, is partly an attempt to get out of the difficulties he encountered by investing so much hope at the start in the uses of dream.) Hence "a thing of beauty"

> still will keep
> A bower quiet for us, and a sleep
> Full of sweet dreams, and health, and quiet breathing.

Then he at once tries to suggest the development he hopes to fol-low from this premise:

> Therefore, on every morrow, are we wreathing
> A flowery band to bind us to the earth,
> Spite of despondence, of the inhuman dearth
> Of noble natures . . .

The point, dimly conceived, is that the apprehension of what lies beyond "our mortal bars" may reconcile us to the earth—may, be-cause it reconciles us, actually "bind us to the earth." And while this prologue puts his aim, however fluid and uncertain the aim may be, it also mentions his timetable. He will begin this poem, he says, away from London ("I will begin / Now while I cannot

---

[13] The story Henry Stephens told Sir Benjamin Richardson, however hackneyed and questionable, should probably be mentioned (see Colvin, p. 176): "One eve-ning in the twilight," says Richardson, "the two students sitting together, Stephens at his medical studies, Keats at his dreaming, Keats breaks out to Stephens that he has composed a new line:—

A thing of beauty is a constant joy.

" 'What think you of that, Stephens?' 'It has the true ring, but is wanting in some way,' replies the latter, as he dips once more into his medical studies. An interval of silence, and again the poet:—

A thing of beauty is a joy for ever.

" 'What think you of that, Stephens?' 'That it will live for ever.' " Significantly Stephens did not include the story in the reminiscences he sent to Monckton Milnes.

hear the city's din") ; "as the year / Grows lusher" he will progress throughout the "many quiet hours" of the summer ("Many and many a verse I hope to write" before autumn ends) ; and

> may no wintry season, bare and hoary,
> See it half finished; but let Autumn bold,
> With universal tinge of sober gold,
> Be all about me when I make an end.

The stage is then set by the gathering of folk for the rites of Pan, and by the "Hymn to Pan" with which Keats himself justly seems to have been satisfied. In trying to write a longer poem, as we noticed before, he often paused to put masterfully in a shorter one much of what he was trying to say. In a sense he does so now. Building on the allegorical uses of Pan in Renaissance poetry, Keats here makes him, as Douglas Bush says, "the symbol of the romantic imagination, of supra-mortal knowledge." Keats's interpretation of myth in the Hymn is altogether in the spirit of Wordsworth. Hence the grim humor that Wordsworth should have responded to it as he did when Haydon praised the Hymn and asked Keats to recite it: "A very pretty piece of Paganism." [14]

The Hymn, as it works to a close, looks forward to the noble letter to Reynolds about the "Chamber of Maiden-Thought" (May 3, 1818) . As this chamber becomes darkened "at the same time on all sides of it many doors are set open—but all dark—all leading to dark passages . . . We feel the 'burden of the Mystery.' " *Endymion* itself had begun by speaking of the "o'er-darkened ways / Made for our searching." Now, in the Hymn, Pan is seen as the

> Dread opener of the mysterious doors
> Leading to universal knowledge . . .
>
> Be still the unimaginable lodge
> For solitary thinkings; such as dodge
> Conception to the very bourne of heaven.

The Hymn and the lines that precede it also anticipate, as does nothing else Keats has thus far written, the great odes of May 1819 and the later ode "To Autumn." Images, phrases, and metaphors are condensed here that persist: "globes" of flowers suggest the "globèd peonies" of the "Ode on Melancholy"; the "venerable

14 See Chapter XI, sections 1–2.

priest" and the "lowing heifers" the "Ode on a Grecian Urn"; the "musk-rose blooms" and the "rain-scented eglantine" the "Ode to a Nightingale." But it is the last great poem he was to write—the ode "To Autumn"—that is principally suggested in these opening lines. Pan is seen as presiding over the process of things—"birth, life, and death": the "enmossed realms," "ripened fruitage," "yellow-girted bees," "poppied corn," are remembered two and a half years later when the great ode touches upon the "mossed cottage-tree," and mentions autumn filling "all fruit with ripeness to the core," continuing to bring forth "later flowers for the bees," or sleeping "Drows'd with the fume of poppies" amid the half-cut corn. The "bleating" ram and, somewhat after the Hymn, the "wailful gnat" remind us of the close of "To Autumn": "Then in a wailful choir the small gnats mourn . . . And full-grown lambs loud bleat from hilly bourn." Above all there is the startling line (in which Pan "through whole solemn hours dost sit") that carries us ahead to the central stanza of the ode where autumn is seen sitting through the long day at the cider press, watching "hours by hours."

14

The opening, through the "Hymn to Pan" and for another hundred lines or so, is richer, more condensed, than any long stretch of the poem that comes later. The weeks of difficulty in getting started in *Endymion,* the nervous trips from the Isle of Wight back to Margate, then Canterbury, then home to Hampstead, were not solely a result of his struggle to overcome inertia and create a new momentum. He was trying to express those thoughts that, as his later writing shows, were most urgent. As much of his available stock was invested in this beginning as in the remaining nine-tenths of the poem. It is a beginning of four hundred lines, if we jump a hundred lines beyond the "Hymn to Pan"—three times the length of the Margate verse letters to George and Cowden Clarke of a half year before, and about equal to his longest poem thus far, "Sleep and Poetry." These were the units in which he had been thinking for "long poems"—one or two hundred up to four hundred lines. Yet now he had only begun on this ambitious self-assignment.

Endymion, a leader of his people, is melancholy and dissatisfied. Pressed by his devoted sister, Peona, who has a certain amount of practical sense (Keats may have been drawing on his own reactions to his brother George) , he discloses the explanation.[15] He has had a vision of a goddess—his account is openly, naively erotic ("madly did I Kiss / The wooing arms which held me")—and his return to the ordinary affairs of life has naturally been anticlimactic. Peona is puzzled: "Is this the cause? This all?" He has a life of action before him. Why "pierce" it "for nothing but a dream"? In his long reply, Endymion (and Keats is here somewhat autobiographical) tells how he has hungered for fame. But there is something higher—a "happiness" that includes a "fellowship with essence": an empathic openness to things, "a sort of oneness" with them. These lines (I.777–780) were added months later in a letter Keats sent to his publisher John Taylor. The previous version,[16] he tells Taylor (January 30, 1818) ,

> appears to me the very contrary of blessed. I hope this will appear to you more eligible.

> > Wherein lies Happiness? In that which becks
> > Our ready Minds to fellowship divine;
> > A fellowship with essence, till we shine
> > Full alchymized and free of space. Behold
> > The clear Religion of heaven—fold &c—

> You must indulge me by putting this in[;] for setting aside the badness of the other, such a preface is necessary to the Subject. The whole thing must I think have appeared to you, who are a consequitive Man, as a thing almost of mere words—but I assure you that when I wrote it, it was a regular stepping of the Imagination towards a Truth. My having written that Argument will perhaps be of the greatest Service to me of any thing I ever did—it set before me at once the gradations of Happiness even like a kind of Pleasure Thermometer—and is my first Step towards the chief Attempt in the Drama—the playing of different Natures with Joy and Sorrow.

[15] Before doing so, he notices that his sister is looking rather pale; and, like a conscientious student at Guy's Hospital, says—though full of his own problem—"Tell me thine ailment."

[16] After some tinkering, the passage in the revised copy (Morgan Library) sent to the printer had read:

> Wherein lies happiness? In that which becks
> Our ready minds to blending pleasureable:
> And that delight is the most treasureable
> That makes the richest Alchemy. Behold . . .

This statement to Taylor, the revised lines, and the twenty-three lines that follow [17] have been more disputed than anything else either in the poem or having to do with it. The word "essence," for example, is used to buttress the Neoplatonic interpretation. On the other hand, a strong case can be made that it is best understood in the plural (as in I.25, "Nor do we merely feel these essences," where he is referring to concrete objects and experiences); that the word is paralleled, and explained, by the question, "Feel we these *things?*" (I.795); that "essence" is for him equivalent to "existence," and that he means a sympathetic sharing in the existence of the "things" he goes on to mention. By calling the inserted lines a "regular stepping of the Imagination towards a Truth," is he implying that the whole passage about the "gradations of Happiness" pictures or symbolizes the way in which the imagination itself works upward to truth? Or, more probably, is he implying that a clearer insight into what he had been trying to say in this passage, and then adding these lines, was—in his own particular case —an example of the way in which the imagination can step toward "a Truth" (and "*a* Truth," as Keats uses the words, means not "truth"—despite the capitalization; capitalization is habitual in Keats—but a judgment, an insight, a valuable point of view)? And does the term "Pleasure Thermometer" prove that the lines (I.780–802) that follow the insert are really hedonistic—that he is measuring these adventures in participation, as has been actually

[17] Behold
The clear religion of heaven! Fold
A rose leaf round thy finger's taperness,
And soothe thy lips; hist, when the airy stress
Of music's kiss impregnates the free winds,
And with a sympathetic touch unbinds
Eolian magic from their lucid wombs:
Then old songs waken from enclouded tombs;
Old ditties sigh above their father's grave;
Ghosts of melodious prophecyings rave
Round every spot where trod Apollo's foot;
Bronze clarions awake, and faintly bruit,
Where long ago a Giant Battle was;
And, from the turf, a lullaby doth pass
In every place where infant Orpheus slept.
Feel we these things?—that moment have we stept
Into a sort of oneness, and our state
Is like a floating spirit's. But there are
Richer entanglements, enthralments far
More self-destroying, leading, by degrees,
To the chief intensity: the crown of these
Is made of love and friendship, and sits high
Upon the forehead of humanity. (I.780–802)

argued, by their "heat"? But the remark to Taylor does not apply the image of "Pleasure Thermometer" to this whole passage, though the use of it as a simile certainly indicates that he is associating pleasure with this ladder of development. "It [the argument of the inserted five lines] set before me at once the gradations of Happiness *even like* a kind of Pleasure Thermometer."

Then there is the puzzling final remark: that this insertion, which he is justifying to Taylor, "is my first Step towards the chief attempt in the Drama—the playing of different Natures with Joy and Sorrow." Does he mean that this particular sketch of the "Gradations of Happiness" is a groundwork, a premise, for what he believes to be "the chief Attempt in the Drama"? This is possible, at least as one implication. Yet it hardly describes the course of Shakespearean tragedy (and it is the great tragedies that were beginning to dominate his thought at the time he wrote to Taylor). Or does he mean, by "the chief Attempt in the Drama," the "drama" of *Endymion* itself? Indirectly he may, though this argument as a direct interpretation founders upon one large rock: given his year-long study of Shakespeare (culminating in the "Negative Capability" letter written a month before the letter to Taylor on which we are lingering), this prudent self-critic could hardly begin, except ironically, to think of "the Drama" of so undramatic a poem, a poem that not even a thorough revision could help. These inserted lines are described as "my *first* Step towards the chief Attempt in the Drama"—a step made only now, in January 1818, after the poem is finished, after he has been writing for the *Champion* on Edmund Kean's acting of Shakespeare, after he has written the "Negative Capability" letter. The autumn and winter of 1817 were by then clarifying many premises and directions that had been sensed only darkly during the happy autumn of 1816 and the first few months of writing his "test of Invention." Given the course of the poem, had Endymion really been "ensky'd"? As Keats had written near the close, addressing Endymion:

> it nigh grieves
> Me to behold thee thus in last extreme:
> Ensky'd ere this, but truly that I deem
> Truth the best music in a first-born song.

At times, forgetting the original fable and becoming himself identified with Endymion, he has "Mourn'd as if yet thou were a forester." It is only by a literal use of the *deus ex machina*—a wrench

of the story in order to get back to the fable—that the poem is
ended, and Endymion "spiritualiz'd." The new lines suggested
more of a bridge than had existed before between Endymion's hedonistic thought, as expressed in the original speech to Peona, and
the ideal he was seeking: they did so by putting that speech as an
aspiration of the heart (however impossible of complete fulfillment). Hence in the autumn of 1817 Keats was to write to his
friend Bailey, as he was trying to conclude *Endymion,* of "the ho-
liness of the Heart's affections," adding that he has "the same Idea
of all our Passions as of Love they are all, in their Sublime, creative of essential Beauty." To put this speech as a hope (to be "Full
alchemiz'd, and free of space")—a hope the poem had not genuinely fulfilled—and to see it as the expression of a character (however colorless the character)—was an inestimable "Service," and
marked a step forward in his own conception of poetry.

15

Compared with such a vision as Endymion has described to Peona, "all this poor endeavour after fame" seems thin. He is ready
to devote himself wholly to a "pilgrimage for the world's dusky
brink." In Book II he begins his search, which carries him through
the underworld. He is oppressed by loneliness as he wanders
through these passages (again we anticipate the "Chamber of
Maiden-thought" that becomes gradually darkened and discloses
passages on every side). There are moments of light. A star—like
a "sun / Uprisen over chaos"—"stuns" him, yet gives him hope.
Here Keats is touchingly autobiographical. The star—we remember the "Star in the East" that Haydon, in one of the Elgin Marble
sonnets, has "gone to worship"—is, of course, one of the great poets of the past:

> one of those
> Who, when this planet's sphering time doth close,
> Will be its high remembrancers.

The two-word rhetorical question fails disastrously:

> who they?
> The mighty ones who have made eternal day
> For Greece and England.

Naturally, caught in such solitude and without the therapeutic effect of the living world, he begins to concentrate on himself:

                                  how crude and sore
          The journey homeward to habitual self.

He refuses to remain in this situation. He starts to pray for help to
Diana—he does this blindly, with no idea that she is the dream-
goddess—and flowers begin to spring. Thus encouraged, he hastens
on and comes to the bower of Adonis, who is now being roused
from his half-year sleep by Venus. The sight gives Endymion further encouragement; for there are parallels between Adonis' situation and his own.

   Some of the worst writing in the entire poem now obtrudes. One
can go further and say that some of the worst lines Keats ever
wrote mar the last six hundred of the second book. The psychological interest is that so many of them are in the vein of Hunt—
though Hunt was never quite so bad—while, in the poem generally, Keats was earnestly trying to get away from Hunt. Granted,
the versification is substantially the same as that he had learned
largely from Hunt and used in the epistles, in "I stood tiptoe," and
in "Sleep and Poetry." This lag—using Hunt's versification while
trying to avoid his diction—was inevitable. One cannot write rapidly without falling back upon techniques that are habitual. Still
less is it possible when trying, at twenty-one, to write a work several times the length of any poem one has thus far attempted. It is
the only versification Keats has ever learned for longer poems,
though he has worked with it for only a year or so—intensively
only since the Margate epistles written eight months before he began *Endymion*.[18] It was more than enough that—distracted by so
many aims, including his timetable, his first real grapple with narrative, his attempt to make it meaningful, and his childish, bold,
and ultimately valuable obsession with size and pace—he should
also be trying to avoid the diction associated with Hunt. The
change in diction is admittedly not very striking. On quick reading
—and *Endymion* does not encourage detailed attention—the difference may appear so small as hardly to be worth the mention.
Given the Shakespearean or Miltonic standards Keats himself was
soon to apply—given neoclassic, metaphysical, or half a dozen

   18 Even so there are a few differences, and they show not a retrenchment from
Hunt but a tendency to outdo him. In his earlier couplets, he had already exceeded
Hunt in the use of run-on lines (35 per cent). But in *Endymion* he went up to
47 per cent. A better way of describing the situation is by the proportion of
couplets that are run on. About 58 per cent of the couplets in the early epistle "To
G. F. Mathew" are run on; this is close to Hunt. In *Endymion* over 75 per cent are
run on. (See *Stylistic Development*, pp. 19–28.)

other premises—the diction and imagery of most of Keats's couplets from the spring of 1816 through *Endymion* seem much of a kind. They cloy. They share a common softness and moistness: we think, as we go through the endless episodes of *Endymion,* of pastries crudely baked but abundantly topped with whipped cream. Yet Keats is really trying to get away from the jaunty briskness of Hunt's idiom, and drawing quickly and indiscriminately on Elizabethans—Chapman, to some extent, Fletcher, Drayton, Browne—with whom he was familiar. He knew beforehand that Hunt would find fault with what he was doing. He was right. When the poem was finished he wrote to his brothers (January 23, 1818) that Hunt, after looking through Book I, "allows it not much merit as a whole; says it is unnatural . . . too high-flown."

But now, writing Book II rapidly back at Hampstead in the early summer of 1817—though Hunt himself was no longer there —Keats, in the latter part of the book, began falling into something like a caricature of the sprightly, chatty style of Hunt:

>   Here is wine,
> Alive with sparkles—never, I aver,
> Since Ariadne was a vintager,
> So cool a purple: taste these juicy pears
>
>   . . . a bunch of blooming plums
> Ready to melt between an infant's gums,
>
> Rise, Cupids! or we'll give the blue-bell pinch
> To your dimpled arms . . .
>
>   . . . His poor temples beat
> To the very tune of love—how sweet, sweet, sweet.
>
>   . . O he had swoon'd
> Drunken from pleasure's nipple

So it continues: "Those lips, O slippery blisses"; "thou white deliciousness."

His heart, to say the least, was not in this large stretch. The difficulty of getting started throughout April and May, the fluency with which he was beginning to write when he joined his brothers at Hampstead in June in their new lodgings in Well Walk (with Bentley the postman and the noise of his children, "the young Carrots"), the nagging desire to finish Book II ("Not begun at all 'till half done")—all lie behind this outpouring. The stock responses, the leavings of a year's apprenticeship, are snatched as filler.

Some moments of interest punctuate this long expanse. Occasional images anticipate the empathy of the later verse (lions with "surly eyes brow-hidden, heavy paws / Uplifted drowsily, and nervy tails"). He refers to the "mighty Poets" of the past. One passage "Be ever in these arms . . . ever press . . . Why not for ever and for ever feel?" carries us forward to the "Ode on a Grecian Urn," with the repetitions of "forever" ("For ever wilt thou love, and she be fair!"; "For ever piping songs for ever new"; "for ever young"). And there is a humanitarian note at the close of the book. Meeting Alpheus and Arethusa, hearing their sad story, Endymion pities them, and prays to Diana for their happiness. Much is always made of the episode as an indication of sympathy: Endymion, it is said, is becoming aware of others. As an exercise in generosity, the pity for Alpheus and Arethusa appears rather slight (and so with the sympathy he later feels for Glaucus, and finally the Indian Maid). On the other hand, so self-absorbed has Endymion been that even a moment's kindly notice from him could be considered a triumph. We can remind ourselves, with Carlyle, that one over zero equals infinity.

16

In Book III, Endymion is wandering beneath the sea amid rotting ships, rusted anchors, and skeletons. He thinks back to the moon, and tells at some length how his heart had turned to it. Keats then brings in the figure of the aged Glaucus, about whom he had read in Sandys's translation of Ovid. By the time he wrote Book III (September), Keats was staying at Oxford with his new friend Benjamin Bailey; and Bailey thirty years later recalled Keats's "upward look" as he read aloud the description he had just written of the aged Glaucus:

> I remember very distinctly, though at this distance of time, his reading of a few passages; & I almost think I hear his voice, & see his countenance. Most vivid is my recollection of the following passage of the fine & affecting story of the old man, Glaucus, which he read to me immediately after its composition:—
>
> > "The old man raised his hoary head & saw
> > The wildered stranger—seeming not to see,

The features were so lifeless. Suddenly
He woke as from a trance; his snow white brows
Went arching up, *& like two magic ploughs*
Furrowed deep wrinkles in his forehead large,
Which kept as fixedly as rocky marge,
Till round his withered lips had gone a smile."

The lines I have italicised, are those which then forcibly struck me
as peculiarly fine, & to my memory have "kept as fixedly as rocky
marge." [19]

Glaucus, desiring something beyond what his quiet life as a fish-
erman provided, had fallen in love with the nymph Scylla, and,
when Scylla had fled him out of fear, sought help from Circe. This
"arbitrary queen of sense" enslaved him. When he discovered what
happened to Circe's victims and plotted escape, she condemned
him to a thousand years of senility before death. Returning to his
former home, Glaucus finds Scylla has been killed by Circe. Keats
here modifies Ovid's account, in which Circe has turned Scylla
into a sea monster.

Glaucus begins to live out the years. He witnesses a shipwreck,
and torn with sympathy attempts vainly to help the victims. His
effort is rewarded. He learns from a scroll in the hand of one of
the victims that, if he tries to recover all the bodies of lovers
drowned at sea, a youth will eventually appear who will help him
and also be the means of Glaucus' deliverance. Endymion, of
course, proves to be the long-awaited youth. There can be no alternative to the openheartedness now demanded of him except
death for himself and Glaucus. "The youth elect," said the scroll,
"Must do the thing, or both will be destroyed." This warning, so
weakly phrased as hardly to be noticeable in this episode, was to
return two years later in the powerful lines of the *Fall of Hyperion*
beginning:

If thou canst not ascend
These steps, die on that marble where thou art.

Endymion agrees to join Glaucus, feeling that they are "twin
brothers in this destiny." Various rites are performed; the scroll is

19 *KC*, II.270–271. Miss Lowell (I.400) thought the simile of the ploughs and
furrow "detestable . . . for ploughs connote cutting." But Keats has been reading
Shakespeare's sonnets; he has never "found so many beauties" in them, as he wrote
to Reynolds in November; and he is thinking of the various uses of the same image
there ("When forty wrinkles shall besiege thy brow, / And dig deep trenches . . .";
"carve not with thy hours my love's fair brow"; "But when in thee time's furrows I
behold"; "And delves the parallels in beauty's brow") .

torn, and the pieces, now invested with magic, bring life and youth at the touch. Glaucus loses his senility; Scylla is revived; one by one the dead lovers come to life.

Keats is now at line 806. He has been writing as many as fifty lines a day. On September 21 he tells Reynolds "I am getting on famous with my third Book—have written 800 lines thereof." Determining to continue each book until it has reached a thousand lines, he concludes by having the assembled company proceed to Neptune's palace. A hymn is sung to Neptune. Then the scene begins to whirl about the "giddy Endymion"; he swoons; and Cynthia sends a message "to his inward senses." Nothing could show more graphically the haste with which Keats is writing than this message with its unfortunate concluding rhyme:

> Dearest Endymion! my entire love!
> How have I dwelt in fear of fate: 'tis done—
> Immortal bliss for me too thou hast won.
> Arise then! for the hen-dove shall not hatch
> Her ready eggs, before I'll kissing snatch
> Thee into endless heaven.

17

With Book IV we are to reach the long-deferred climax: the union with Cynthia. The tone of the book is far from triumphant. In fact, as Sir Sidney Colvin says, it is rather "subdued and melancholy." But this could hardly come as a surprise. The fatigue of the marathon was accumulating. Moreover, Keats's critical perception had been sharpening immensely. He was already sensing that the foundations of the whole poem were too "sandy" to permit any rebuilding. Book IV begins with an apostrophe to the "Muse of my native land," long silent in her "northern grot, / While yet our England was a wolfish den." During these long centuries the great poetry of Greece and then of Italy came to flower. The English Muse was then rewarded for her patience—presumably by the Elizabethans. But that "full accomplishment" has been followed by "barren souls." A personal note—a sense of inadequacy extended to the spirit of the present time itself—concludes the passage:

> Great Muse, thou know'st what prison
> Of flesh and bone curbs, and confines, and frets
> Our spirit's wings; despondency besets
> Our pillows; and the fresh tomorrow-morn

Seems to give forth its light in very scorn
Of our dull, uninspired, snail-pacèd lives.
Long have I said, how happy he who shrives
To thee! But then I thought on poets gone,
And could not pray:—nor can I now—so on
I move to the end in lowliness of heart.

The story then proceeds. Endymion is "offering up a hecatomb of vows" when he hears a long plaint ("Is no one near to help me?"). It is an Indian Maid, lonely and hungering for human love. However hard-pressed Keats may be to find incidents to fill his four thousand lines, his central character loses no time in his transitions. The heart of the pilgrim Endymion is at once caught. He pities, he loves ("Upon a bough / He leant, wretched. He surely cannot now / Thirst for another love"). Can he surrender his search for his ideal, Cynthia? As compared with Shelley's single-minded hero Alastor, who was not to be distracted by an Arab maiden, Endymion now finds himself a divided soul.

Keats is only an eighth of the way through this book. The end must still be deferred. Understandably weary of the heroic couplet, he begins to intersperse the narrative with metrical variations. The "roundelay" that the Indian Maid now sings comes to more than a hundred and forty lines. Five short stanzas, mainly in brief chirping lines, begin it ("O Sorrow, / Why dost borrow . . ."). The decision to insert these lines came as a relief. Other metrical variations follow. Later in the book he was to try to diversify the meter again. In a choric song, anticipating Cynthia's marriage to Endymion, the couplets are interspersed every four or five lines by two-foot lines.

Following the song of the Indian Maid, Endymion addresses her. Briefly Keats falls into the slipshod idiom that, after the episode of Venus and Adonis, had marred so much of Book II ("I've no choice; / I must be thy sad servant . . . Say, beautifullest"). Taking her hand, and then reaching for her other hand ("this is sure thine other softling"), Endymion suddenly blurts out a question that would intrigue those that search for the unconscious and suspect Keats's own weariness. "Wilt fall asleep?" he suddenly asks. Ominous words, after Endymion's avowal of love, come from the woods ("Woe to that Endymion"). Mercury appears, and the two lovers are carried on winged horses into the air. The lovers sleep; Endymion dreams that he is among the gods, and learns that the goddess he has sought is really Cynthia. Naturally he feels torn. Suffering intensely, he is carried to the Cave of Quietude. In this place of desperate apathy and exhaustion, beyond sorrow or joy, he recovers peace of mind. Descending to earth, he determines to give up his long search; he has been pursuing something beyond the "natural sphere" of man:

> I have clung
> To nothing, lov'd a nothing, nothing seen
> Or felt but a great dream! O I have been
> Presumptuous against love, against the sky,
> Against all elements, against the tie
> Of mortals each to each . . .
> There never liv'd a mortal man, who bent
> His appetite beyond his natural sphere,
> But starv'd and died. My sweetest Indian, here,
> Here will I kneel, for thou redeemèd hast
> My life from too thin breathing.

They will live in the natural realm of Pan, where the breathing is not so thin. But it turns out that the Indian Maid is forbidden to accept his love. As Endymion sits unhappily on the spot where he first had his vision of Cynthia, his sister Peona appears to welcome his return to the human world. He tells her of his misfortune and announces his decision to become a hermit. Before he leaves they are to meet that evening in the grove behind the temple of Cynthia. The hour comes, and with it—in the last twenty-two lines—the rapid solution of the mystery. The Indian Maid is suddenly transformed before his eyes into Cynthia. The ideal has been discovered through the acceptance of the earthly.

18

Of course Endymion is not really "enskyed" except through the most improbable *deus ex machina*. Because of Keats's haste to conclude, the end may have been introduced more abruptly than otherwise. But another year, as he himself felt, would not have made a substantial difference in the direction of the poem. *Endymion* from the beginning had been used for too many different purposes. One use of the poem was confessional: it was used partly for self-expression in the hope of making a step in self-understanding. Hence Endymion was inevitably a victim of conflicting desires. This pallid pilgrim was merely reflecting uncertainties in Keats himself—uncertainties that were to remain with him until the end. No quick, doctrinaire solution to them could satisfy Keats's honesty. The mind, as he said much later, should be "a thoroughfare for all thoughts"; and his friend Charles Dilke, who "cannot feel he has a personal identity unless he has made up his Mind about every thing," will "never come at a truth . . . because he is always trying at it." But how does one attain this openness—more especially how does one keep it—when the heart seeks immediacy and neatness of formula? Can this honesty be preserved in poetry unless uncertainties are dramatized, and unless arguments are seen as human persuasions or hopes, presented in interaction with each other?

He hurried on to an ending now. Something had to be shown for all these months. But he was never to do this again. If a conclusion would not come more naturally, the poem was put aside. Nor was he ever again in such a hurry to publish. Copying out the poem in January, he inserted the lines we have noticed—lines, he wrote to Taylor, that were a "regular stepping of the Imagination towards a Truth." The step was a step Keats himself had made. Suddenly he had seen that Endymion's speech to Peona was an aspiration of the heart—as later with the heart's impossible longing in the great ode to join the nightingale (though the nightingale flies away) or to enter the world of the Grecian Urn (though it is only an urn). The inserted lines performed the function of a good symbol as Coleridge described it—vital in its own right and meaningful beyond itself. The new lines "set before me the gradations of Happiness"; but they were also a voice that could be heard dramatically. Rereading *King Lear* this month, and putting aside "romance"—above all his own new poem which he had insisted despite Taylor's misgivings on subtitling "A Poetic Romance"—he was grateful for this insight: so grateful in his general embarrassment about the poem that he could describe the perception as his "first Step," toward the "playing of *different* Natures with Joy and Sorrow," which is indeed the "chief Attempt in the Drama." So immense was his relief that he forgivably leapt to hyperbole, wondering whether making this step might not be "the greatest Service to me of any thing I ever did." He was free from the prison of single-mindedness, and was now to begin to turn to the theme of his greatest poetry—the drama of the heart's debate with actuality.

An Act of Will

✳↝☙↝✳↝☙↝✳↝☙↝✳↝☙↝✳↝☙↝✳↝☙↝✳↝☙↝✳↝☙↝✳↝☙↝✳↝☙↝✳↝☙↝✳↝☙

June to December, 1817

THE INCREDIBLE PROJECT Keats set for himself, with its absurd time-table, a mere six months after he had seriously decided to become a poet, could have been planned and then carried out only by an extraordinary union of naiveté and stamina. By the time he was halfway through, the naiveté was evaporating. Or we could put it another way and say that his idealism and habit of commitment were rapidly turning to other objects—and to objects quite differ-ent from the long chore he had begun. Buying the copy of Shake-speare to take with him, viewing it almost as a talisman, turning to it whenever he was depressed, wondering whether he dared to think of Shakespeare as a good genius presiding over him, could soon begin to seem hopelessly foolish and self-deluding. Goethe, far older, had rejoiced that he was not born an Englishman with the intimidating example of Shakespeare before him. Moving des-perately from place to place in April and May, Keats saw what a "pin's point" it was that he had done, and when he looked over his lines, as he told Haydon, he sometimes "hated" them. By the time he was three-quarters through, his opinion of the whole per-formance was "very low"; the most he could expect was "the fruit of experience."

In this act of will, sustained for seven months, we have some-thing almost unique in modern poetry. It has naturally intrigued all later writers, partly because of the extraordinary advance in maturity Keats showed at the end of it, and partly because of the psychological conditions under which it was written. For though invention does not need an atmosphere of hope (despair can prod it into activity quite as readily), yet some confidence in the result, the solution, is necessary if the daily renewal of invention is to continue for months on end. When this confidence is lacking, we associate a dogged and prolific output with the hack writer—usually a fairly experienced one, consoled with some hope of ulterior gain. But here we are dealing with a temperament that has not been reassured by experience and that is intoxicated with the highest aims. Moreover, as in the previous year, Keats's critical perception keeps leaping ahead of his own poetry with every month that passes. No such ratio, no such disparity between critical perception and performance, is so clearly observable in any other modern poet, at least any poet whose life we are able to follow closely.

2

By later June, when he was back in the rooms he and his brothers had taken at Hampstead, he was at last writing fluently, especially in comparison with the traumatic two months that had just passed. Only one letter survives—a letter to Haydon—from the period between June 10, when he wrote to Taylor and Hessey for the £30 advance,[1] and September 4. The inference is that he did not leave London. Finally in late August (probably the 21st), he could write happily to Haydon that he had finished Book II. Feeling a solid basis under him at last, sensing the structure rise, remembering Haydon's encouraging letter to him three months before about turning "to the great Star of your hopes," may all have suggested Milton's phrase about Shakespeare—"a star-ypointing Pyramid." At all events he signs his letter jubilantly, "your's like a Pyramid."

What social life he had was subdued; he was obviously preoccupied. Joseph Severn would "stroll over to Well Walk across the fields from smoky London," hoping to walk with Keats on Hampstead Heath and thinking he might find backgrounds for the miniatures he was now painting. Severn, speaking of Keats's absorption in whatever he saw, was especially struck by his delight in the billowing grain as the wind moved across it. As they walked, Keats

would suddenly become taciturn, not because he was tired, not even because his mind was suddenly wrought to some bewitching vision, but from a profound disquiet which he could not or would not explain. . . .

The only thing that would bring Keats out of one of his fits of seeming gloomful reverie . . . was the motion "of the inland sea" he loved so well, particularly the violent passage of wind across a

1 See Chapter VIII, section 9.

great field of barley. . . . He would stand, leaning forward, listening intently, watching with a bright serene look in his eyes and sometimes with a slight smile, the tumultuous passage of the wind above the grain. The sea, or thought-compelling images of the sea, always seemed to restore him to a happy calm.[2]

Clarke remembered a Sunday, probably in late July or early August, when Keats and Severn dropped by his place in town, "and we passed the greater part of the day walking in the neighbourhood." Keats then read to them "portions of his new poem with which he himself had been pleased." [3]

Hunt returned on June 25 from his long visit with the Shelleys, and settled in Paddington. Writing to Clarke a few days later (July 1), he said: "What has become of Junkets I know not. I suppose Queen Mab has eaten him." The first part of Hunt's review of Keats's *Poems* had appeared back in the June 1 issue of the *Examiner*. Thinking Keats might feel he had been negligent, Hunt speedily finished the review, publishing the two remaining parts on July 6 and 13. But Keats does not appear to have gone out of his way to see Hunt. He had been eager enough to walk out to Hampstead from Cheapside the previous autumn; but the effort to get from Hampstead to Paddington seemed greater now. He wished to complete *Endymion* as independently as possible. To see Hunt now would inevitably lead to complications. Hunt would expect to go over the work and would make suggestions Keats would find it embarrassing not to follow. He was able to find time, however, to see a good deal of John Reynolds and the Reynolds family. Probably at Reynolds' urging, his sonnet "On the Sea," which he had written in the Isle of Wight while preparing to begin *Endymion*, was published in the *Champion* (August 17) rather than in Hunt's *Examiner*. Hunt may possibly have been a little hurt by this. He made a kindly gesture the following month (September 21) by printing in the *Examiner* the sonnets they had written "On the Grasshopper and the Cricket" in the contest at Hunt's house last December, doubtless thinking it might remind Keats of the pleasant times they had shared.

During the spring the Keats brothers had talked of visiting

[2] Sharp, pp. 20–21.
[3] Clarke, *Recollections*, p. 141. "One of his selections was the *now* celebrated 'Hymn to Pan' in the first book. . . . And the other selections were the descriptions in the second book of the 'bower of Adonis,' and the ascent and descent of the silver car of Venus, air-borne."

France for a month or so in the summer. Abbey seemed willing to advance them a little of their own money for this purpose. They could argue that more sunlight than England offered (though the English summer actually proved to be a dry one) might help Tom. But Keats himself was unwilling to leave until he had at least finished the second book of *Endymion,* and George and Tom were apparently waiting until he was ready. July passed, and then the first half of August, before the end of Book II was well in hand. Keats might still have gone with George and Tom when they left at the end of the month. But an opportunity had since arisen of spending September with a bookish friend—a new friend quite different from Hunt, Haydon, or Reynolds—at Magdalen Hall, Oxford. He knew that if he went with George and Tom to Paris he was unlikely to continue writing as rapidly as he had been doing. He may well have been afraid lest he lose whatever momentum he had acquired. The decision to visit Oxford proved to be fortunate in every way.

3

In March or April, before he had left for the Isle of Wight, Keats had met two friends of John Reynolds', Benjamin Bailey and James Rice, both of whom were to become close friends of his own. Reynolds also introduced Keats to Charles Dilke and his kindly wife, Maria, who were living in Hampstead. Then, when Keats returned to Hampstead in June, he met another friend, Charles Brown. Rice and the Dilkes enter the Keats picture more prominently in the winter of 1817–18, and Brown very prominently indeed from the late spring of 1818 until the end. But during the summer of 1817 Keats saw Bailey frequently. Moreover, the impact on Keats of this earnest Oxford undergraduate was of a different sort from that of Rice, Dilke, or even Brown.

Benjamin Bailey was perhaps the last of Keats's close personal friends to affect his intellectual development in an essential, formative way. Yet he has been the least noticed of them, and in some respects the least charitably viewed. This is partly because less is known of him. His intimacy with Keats was very brief. By the summer of 1818 he had gone north to Carlisle, and in time he emigrated to Ceylon. Those who remained of Keats's friends by the 1840's had largely forgotten him; and Keats's first biographer,

Milnes, assumed that Bailey had died shortly after Keats.[4] If we try to piece together what can be known of him, we must rely heavily on letters only recently published in full or else on manuscripts preserved in a handwriting that usually puts those who try to decipher it in an irritable mood. Finally, there was a sanctimonious side to this industrious man. But when the interest is merely in a friend of Keats who was important at a particular time, and when no claim is made for anything exceptional, one is puzzled at the captious attitude toward Bailey and the tendency to apply to him merely pejorative adjectives—"pompous," "hypocritical," and the like.

As with no other friend of Keats, incongruities distract us in thinking of Bailey, from the time we first know much about him (in 1814, when he was twenty-three) to the time (1848) when, in far-off Ceylon, he insisted to Keats's first biographer that he had not died twenty-five years before, and then wrote for him an account (published in full only after World War II) that is easily one of the three or four most valuable left by any of Keats's friends. Though an admirer of Milton and Wordsworth, he himself wrote verse that was admittedly light—in fact very close to valentine verse. He had hoped as a young man to write moral discourses: yet any claim he may have to remembrance, aside from his friendship with Keats, is only for a dictionary of the Malayan language and some translations from the Malayan. Admired in his early twenties—especially by the Reynolds girls and their mother —as a man of Catolike rectitude, he was in his own way extraordinarily susceptible to women. His manner may have left something to be desired: he used to woo Reynolds's sister, as Keats later put it, "with the Bible and Jeremy Taylor under his arm." But if success did not result, he was ready enough to change the object of his wooing if not his tactics. Again, though far from being himself what is generally meant by "lovable," Bailey could use the word perceptively and with more vivid response than many less constricted souls. However rigid he himself might seem, for example, he could write to Milnes in 1848 that Keats "was the most *loveable* creature, in the proper sense of that word, as distinguished from

4 In a review of Milnes (*Athenaeum*, August 19, 1848), Dilke corrected Milnes, stating "The Rev. Benjamin Bailey is yet living—or was so not long since . . . at Ceylon." After reading this in Ceylon, Bailey got hold of the book, which had just arrived at the Public Library in Colombo, and began his correspondence with Milnes.

amiable, I think I ever knew as a man." Moreover, Keats "had abundantly more of the *poetical character,* a hundred times fold, than I ever knew in any individual." [5] Though he was concerned primarily with the larger moral uses of poetry, he has left the only valuable account we have of one of Keats's purely stylistic principles—a method of interrelating close and open vowels. Inclined to be somewhat censorious, he could speak feelingly of Keats's tolerance and sympathetic understanding: "he was uniformly the apologist for poor, frail human nature, & allowed for people's faults more than any man I ever knew, (except one, my dear & excellent old friend, Sir William Rough, late Chief Justice of Ceylon) & especially for the faults of his friends." More than Keats's other acquaintances, he believed in the necessity of formal education, felt that the lack of it was Keats's greatest handicap, and tended himself to be rather fixed in character. Yet no one saw better Keats's self-corrective capacity for growth: "like the Thames waters, when taken out to sea, he had the rare quality of purifying himself."

4

When Bailey entered Oxford in October 1816, he was already twenty-five—considerably older than the average undergraduate and more than four years older than Keats. During the winter of 1816, said Bailey,

> my friend, Mr. Reynolds, wrote to me at Oxford respecting Keats, with whom he & his family had just become acquainted. He conveyed to me the same impressions, which the poet made upon the minds of almost all persons who had the happiness of knowing him, & subsequently upon myself.

Bailey secured a copy of the *Poems* when they appeared in early March. On a visit to London shortly afterwards, he was introduced to Keats by John Reynolds and his sisters. "I was delighted with the naturalness & simplicity of his character, & was at once drawn to him by his winning & indeed affectionate manner towards those with whom he was himself pleased."

Bailey had some thought of writing poetry himself, though only

[5] Remarks of Bailey's quoted or mentioned in this chapter are from the two accounts he sent to Milnes, printed in *KC,* II.259–297.

as an avocation. He could jot down light verse with extraordinary speed—verse, as we have mentioned, as remote as possible from the moral and contemplative poetry he most admired, especially that of Dante, Milton, and Wordsworth. However self-confident he was in other ways, his fluency disappeared when he tried to do anything serious. A stiff sonnet of his "To Milton" had been published in the *Champion* (June 30, 1816), and he doubtless felt that when he had finished the heavy course of reading he had started at Oxford he would have the leisure to do this sort of thing better. He had written scores of trifling, sentimental lyrics that still remain unpublished. For three years, Bailey, Reynolds, and Rice had been flirting with the daughters of the late William Leigh—Mary, Sarah, and Thomasine—who lived in Slade House, near Sidmouth, though Bailey had recently begun to court Reynolds' sister Mariane. During this time, the three youths contributed poems to the commonplace books kept by the Leigh girls.[6] Rice managed to write nine poems, but Bailey and Reynolds together composed over a hundred. Elated with their fluency, Bailey and Reynolds in later 1816 decided to combine on a new manuscript—"Poems by Two Friends"—which they presented to Thomasine Leigh in December. Bailey was the more industrious: he wrote thirty-two and Reynolds twenty-five. The same diligence appears in his clerklike eagerness to copy out his poems on different occasions, to copy selections from other writers, and to index them carefully. But the years began to slip away. During an illness while serving as a clergyman in the north in 1824 he tried his hand at a verse tale that he hoped John Taylor would publish. Taylor thought it poor. Bailey painfully admitted it was not "poetry, for I agree entirely with you in the rareness of this spiritual essence," though he had hoped that at least as verse the tale might be tolerable. Years later (1849), when he was fifty-eight and far from well, the old habit of light verse reappeared somewhat pathetically in the little quatrain—labored in its humor and rhymes, short-winded when one thinks of his fluency thirty-five years before—

---

6 Typical titles of Bailey's verses are "To Poesy: Written at Night," "Sympathy a Sonnet," "Childhood," "Sensibility," "On Parting with my Sister." His ease of writing grew as the subject approached more closely to nonexistence, as when, according to Thomasine Leigh's diary (March 14, 1815), the assembled company walked along the seaside cliff near Slade House and "named the Rocks." A rock was named for each person, and Bailey then made up a series of poems, one for each. The twenty ms. commonplace books containing the poems of Bailey, Reynolds, and Rice are in the Leigh-Browne-Lockyer Collection in the Keats Museum, Hampstead.

that he enclosed in a letter to Milnes: "Verses on Benjamin Bailey's Alleged Death." [7]

5

During the summer vacation of 1817 Bailey again visited London. He now "saw much of Keats," usually at the home of the Reynolds family. He could hardly help being impressed by the fact that Keats, with a fraction of the advantages Bailey himself enjoyed, had already published a volume of verse and had almost finished half of a long poem. For whatever else may be said of the earnest, systematic Bailey, he seems to have been free of envy —partly, it is true, because of the strength of his own self-confidence. Keats's empathy and humor—neither of which qualities Bailey possessed even moderately—delighted him. They made the time pass more vividly, and helped to release him from his own rigidities. Keats's equable, kindly temper was also a relief. "His brother George says of him that to his brothers his temper was uncertain; [8] & [Keats] himself confirms this judgment of him" (Bailey refers to a contrite remark Keats wrote him when George was preparing to sail to America—"I have been ill temper'd with them, I have vex'd them") :

> This might have been so with his brothers. But with his friends, a sweeter tempered man I never knew, than was John Keats. Gentleness was indeed his proper characteristic, without one particle of dullness, or insipidity, or want of spirit. Quite the contrary. "He was gentle but not fearful," in the chivalric & moral sense of the term "gentle." He was pleased with everything that occurred in the ordinary mode of life, & a cloud never passed over his face, except of indignation at the wrongs of others.
>
> His conversation was very engaging. He had a sweet-toned voice, "an excellent thing" in *man,* as well as "in woman." A favorite expression of tranquil pleasure & delight at a fine passage of any au-

---

[7] "Dicky Milnes—Dicky Milnes! why what the deuce could ail ye
When you wrote the life of Keats—to write the death of Bailey—
The poet sleeps—oh! let him sleep—within the silent tomb-o
But Parson Bailey lives, and kicks—Archdeacon of Colombo."

[8] See George's statement in a letter to Dilke (April 20, 1825) : "From the time we were Boys at school where we loved, jangled, and fought alternately until we separated in 1818 I in a great measure relieved him by continual sympathy, explanation, and inexhaustible spirits, and good humour, from many a bitter fit of hypochondriasm, he avoided teazing any one with his miseries but Tom and myself and often asked our forgiveness; venting, and discussing them gave him releif" (*KC,* I.284–285) .

thor, particularly an old poet, was "that it was *nice*," which he pronounced in a gentle undertone.

The firmer qualities of Keats also impressed Bailey: "He had a
soul of noble integrity: & his common sense was a conspicuous part
of his character. Indeed his character was, in the best sense, manly."

Bailey, who was returning early in order to study, invited Keats
to come with him "to Oxford, & spend as much time as he could
afford with me in the silence & solitude of that beautiful place
during the absence of the numerous members & students of the
University." Keats eagerly accepted, and his five weeks there were
not only enjoyable but surprisingly productive. For at least the
first year or so of their friendship, he admired Bailey as much as
anyone he had known. He had met no one like this angular, industrious man—the only one of his friends who was going or had
gone to one of the great universities and who was openly committed to both a scholarly and clerical career. He thinks of the rigor
and sophistication with which Bailey devours books, and writes to
him:

> I should not like to be Pages in your way when in a tolerable
> hungry mood—you have no Mercy—your teeth are the Rock tarpeian
> down which you capsise Epic Poems like Mad—I would not for 40
> shillings be Coleridge's Lays [*Lay Sermons*] in your way.

To this idealization of Bailey the scholar was added an idealization
of Bailey as a man of calm moral vision. The serious philosophical
discussion of moral principles opened a new door to Keats; and
the word "philosopher" was henceforth to become a meaningful
—at times ambiguously used—part of his habitual vocabulary.
Shortly after he had arrived at Oxford, he wrote to the Reynolds
girls (September 14) that to them and their brother

> I shall ever feel grateful for having made known to me so real a fel-
> low as Bailey. He delights me in the Selfish and (please God) the
> disinterested part of my disposition. If the old Poets have any pleas-
> ure in looking down at the Enjoyers of their Works, their eyes must
> bend with double satisfaction upon him—I sit as at a feast when he
> is over them and pray that if after my death any of my Labours
> should be worth saving, they may have as "honest a Chronicler" as
> Bailey. Out of this his Enthusiasm in his own pursuit and for all
> good things is of an exalted kind.

The word "disinterestedness," which was also to become an essential part of his vocabulary, was probably acquired from Bailey

himself or through Hazlitt's *Principles of Human Action* (1805) and other reading that Bailey may have recommended. Within the next year the word and all it represented were to become something of a polar star. Now, quite naturally, he associated the word especially with Bailey himself. Disturbed by the personal quarrels, the self-absorbed moods, of some of his friends, particularly Hunt and Haydon, he writes to his brothers after he has been back at Hampstead for three months or so (January 13):

> I am quite perplexed in a world of doubts & fancies—there is nothing stable in the world . . . I do not mean to include Bailey in this . . . he is one of the noblest men alive at the present day. . . . That sort of probity & disinterestedness which such men as Bailey possess, does hold & grasp the tip top of any spiritual honours, that can be paid to any thing in this world.

6

Nothing shows better the impact that the high-principled and thoughtful Bailey made on his friends, Keats included, than the shock they all felt a year and a half later when he dropped Mariane Reynolds, whom he had been courting ardently but without success, and became engaged to another woman. So excessive was the reaction—out of all proportion to what Bailey did—that the incident is still brought up whenever Bailey is mentioned, usually with the unfair implication that he must have proved himself a hypocrite.

When Mariane declined Bailey's proposal, he apparently asked her to give it some more thought.[9] He left Oxford in April 1818, went north, and by August obtained a curacy in Carlisle. Already a little piqued at having been turned down by Thomasine Leigh the year before, he became impatient as the months passed. He then met Miss Hamilton Gleig, the daughter of Bishop George Gleig, proposed, and was accepted. Keats, writing to George in America (February 19, 1819), tries to entertain George and his wife by a "long story . . . about Bailey":

---

[9] So at least Charles Dilke said (in a note printed by H. B. Forman, III.383): "Bailey made an offer to Marianne Reynolds which was declined. He instructed her to take time and think over his proposal. Meanwhile he went to Scotland, fell in love with Gleig's sister, and married; much to the surprise of the Reynolds family, who thought he had behaved ill, and it led to a discussion and a quarrel."

> You know that Bailey was very much cut up about a little Jilt in the country somewhere [presumably Thomasine Leigh]; I thought he was in a dying state about it when at Oxford with him: little supposing as I have since heard, that he was at that very time making impatient Love to Marian Reynolds—and guess my astonishment at hearing after this that he had been trying at Miss Martin . . . So matters stood—when he got ordained and went to a Curacy near Carlisle where the family of the Gleigs reside—There his susceptible heart was conquered by Miss Gleig . . . He showed his correspondence with Marian to Gleig—returnd all her Letters and asked for his own—he also wrote very abrupt Letters to Mrs. Reynolds.

The response of the Reynolds family was understandable, partly because Bailey "showed his correspondence with Marian" to Miss Gleig's brother—though Bailey may have naively thought this the straightforward thing to do, and Gleig may even have expected it —and partly because of the "abrupt letters to Mrs. Reynolds" expressing resentment at having been misled by the flattering attentions she and the girls had showered on him. But Keats found himself swayed more by the high moral stand that the gentle James Rice now took: "Rice would not make an immature resolve: he was ardent in his friendship for Bailey; he examined the whole for and against minutely; and he has abandoned Bailey entirely." Rice was much closer to Reynolds—his future law partner—than to Bailey. Bailey was far from London, probably for good, and Rice could afford to make a strong expression of sympathy to the Reynoldses and assert that he had "abandoned" Bailey. Keats himself, in trying to understand the situation, gropes a bit and then suddenly puts his finger on the explanation. Bailey had been for so long viewed as the embodiment of moral righteousness that his brusque conduct not only startled the others but actually angered them by shaking their faith in their own perception of human nature. Moreover, Bailey had delighted all the Reynolds women— however Mariane felt about his proposal—by expressing on every occasion the most approved romantic sentiments about women: his manner was earnestly, even heavily chivalric. In speaking of the exuberant idealization of Bailey, based on a "literal" interpretation of certain aspects of a man, Keats is explaining to himself his own reaction as much as that of the Reynoldses; this little episode disturbed him only because it seemed so incongruous:

> No doubt his conduct has been verry bad. The great thing to be considered is—whether it is want of delicacy and principle or want

of Knowledge and polite experience—And again Weakness—yes that is it—and the want of a Wife—yes that is it—and then Marian made great Bones of him . . . Her conduct has been very upright throughout the whole affair—She liked Bailey as a Brother—but not as a Husband—especially as he used to woo her with the Bible and Jeremy Taylor under his arm . . . Marian's obstinacy is some excuse—but his so quickly taking to miss Gleig can have no excuse—except that of a Ploughman who wants a wife . . . It will be a good Lesson to the Mother and Daughters—nothing would serve but Bailey—If you mentioned the word Tea pot—some one of them came out with an a propos about Bailey—noble fellow—fine fellow! was always in their mouths—this may teach them that the man who rediculus romance is the most romantic of Men—that he who abuses women and slights them—loves them the most—that he who talks of roasting a Man alive would not do it when it came to the push—and above all that they are very shallow people who can take every thing literal

His discussion suddenly ends with one of the most suggestive passages in the letters:

A Man's life of any worth is a continual allegory—and very few eyes can see the Mystery of his life—a life like the scriptures, figurative—which such people can no more make out than they can the hebrew Bible. Lord Byron cuts a figure—but he is not figurative—Shakespeare led a life of Allegory; his works are the comments on it.

After his marriage (April 20, 1819), Bailey served as a country or village parson in various places. His wife became ill. He thought a sunnier climate would help, and took charge of a tiny English church in Marseilles—the number attending rarely exceeded twelve. After a year, finding the climate of no help, Bailey returned to England, and became vicar at Minster, in Kent. In another two years, Bailey and his wife decided to leave for Ceylon, where he was given the position of senior colonial chaplain. Mrs. Bailey died shortly after they arrived at Colombo. Despite his own poor health, he continued to write and publish—including his translations and his dictionary of Malay. In spare moments he kept a scrapbook, now at Harvard, in which he pasted letters and poems. He became Archdeacon in 1846, and re-entered the Keats story in 1848 when, having read in Milnes' biography that he had died shortly after Keats, he began his correspondence with Milnes. He at last returned to London in the autumn of 1852, hoping to

14. SHANKLIN DOWN, ISLE OF WIGHT, IN KEATS'S TIME

Not far from here Keats began to write Endymion.

15. THE MITRE INN, OXFORD

*Before the Mitre is the Defiance, the coach that
Keats and Bailey took to Oxford.*

16. MAGDALEN HALL, OXFORD

Here Keats stayed with Bailey in September 1817.

17. COVENT GARDEN IN KEATS'S TIME

18. WILLIAM HAZLITT

19. THE SURREY INSTITUTION

Here Keats heard Hazlitt lecture.

resume some friendships and to do some writing, but died eight months later, on June 25, 1853.

7

Bailey and Keats left for Oxford the morning of September 3. Their coach, colorfully named the "Defiance," arrived at the Mitre Inn in midafternoon, after a seven-hour trip.

The novelty and beauty of the surroundings, the confidence that he was about to make rapid headway, the reassuring companionship with Bailey, put him in the highest spirits. From the start everything about the visit contrasted with the lonely trip to the Isle of Wight the previous April, and the desperate second trip to "treeless Margate," which had proved to be so barren of results. The obsession with trees that the Margate trip had given him is now satisfied—there are "plenty of Trees thank God." The letter he wrote to Jane and Mariane Reynolds the day after he arrived shows how elated he was, for it consists of nothing except the rapid whimsy, the sustained playfulness, he would pour out when a correspondent delighted in it and he himself was happy. The first half of the letter is typical:

> There you are [at Little Hampton, Sussex] among Sands Stocks Stones Pebbles Beaches Cliffs Rocks Deeps Shallows Weeds ships Boats (at a distance) Carrots—turnips Sun Moon and Stars and all those sort of things—here am I among Colleges, Halls Stalls plenty of Trees thank God—plenty of Water thank heaven—plenty of Books thank the Muses—plenty of Snuff—thank Sir Walter Raleigh—plenty of Sagars, ditto—plenty of flat Country—thank Tellus's roling pin. I'm on the Sofa—Buonapa[r]te is on the Snuff Box—but you are by the [sea] side—argal you bathe—you walk—you say how beautiful— find out resemb[lan]ces between waves and Camels—rocks and dancing Masters—fireshovels and telescopes—Dolphins and Madonas— which word by the way I must acquaint you was derived from the Syriac and came down in a way which neither of you I am sorry to say are at all capable of comprehending: but as a time may come when by your occasional converse with me you may arrive at "something like prophetic strain" I will unbar the Gates of my Pride and let my Condecension stalk forth like a Ghost at the Circus—The Word Madon a my dear Ladies or—the Word—Mad-o-na—So I say! I am not mad—Howsumever When that aged Tamer Kewthon sold a Certain Camel Called Peter to the Overseer of the Babel Skyworks, he thus spake, adjusting his Cravat round the tip of his Chin

—My dear Ten Storyupinair—this here Beast though I say it as shouldn't say't not only has the Power of subsisting 40 day[s] and 40 Nights without fire and Candle but he can sing—here I have in my Pocket a Certificate from Signor Nicolini of the King's Theatre a Certificate to this effect . . .

His feeling of effervescence continued. Ten days later he wrote the girls a letter in the same vein, even longer, and concluded it by making up a little address—in prose—that Endymion will make to them after "my friend Keats" will have ceased "hawling me through the Earth and Sea with unrelenting Perseverance." Meanwhile to John Reynolds he wrote a parody of a poem of Wordsworth ("The Cock is crowing, / The stream is flowing,")—"sentences," says Keats, "in the Style of School exercises." [10]

Keats quickly fell into a regular pattern of work. The quiet of Bailey's lodgings at Magdalen Hall was a relief. Only a few students had remained during the long vacation or returned early in order to study; and this allowed Keats to feel much less like an outsider than he might otherwise have done. Above all there was the contagion of diligence: Bailey himself was capable of working for hours without interruption. On the wall was a picture of Bailey's hero, Jeremy Taylor, "who always looks"—wrote Keats to Jane Reynolds—"as though he were going to give me a rap with a Book he holds in a very threatening position." [11]

On September 5 he wrote the first fifty-one lines of Book III, jubilantly recording the date and place on the manuscript. "He wrote, and I read," said Bailey,

> sometimes at the same table, & sometimes at separate desks or tables, from breakfast to the time of our going out for exercise,—generally two or three o'clock. He sat down to his task,—which was about 50 lines a day,—with his paper before him, & wrote with as much regularity, & apparently with as much ease, as he wrote his letters. . . . Sometimes he fell short of his allotted task,—but not often: & he would make it up another day. But he never forced himself. When

[10] The Gothic looks solemn,—
   The plain Doric column
Supports an old Bishop & crosier;
   The mouldering arch,
   Shaded o'er by a larch,
Lives next door to Wilson the hosier.

   Vicè—that is, by turns—
   O'er pale visages mourns
The black-tassel trencher, or common-hat:

[11] I.156–157.

The Chauntry boy sings,
   The steeple bell rings,
And as for the Chancellor—dominat.

   There are plenty of trees,
   And plenty of ease,
And plenty of fat deer for parsons;
   And when it is venison,
   Short is the benison,—
Then each on a leg or thigh fastens.

he had finished his writing for the day, he usually read it over to me; & he read or wrote letters until we went out for a walk. This was our habit day by day. The rough manuscript was written off daily, & with few erasures.

That Bailey should have recalled the rate of Keats's writing so exactly after thirty-one years suggests how much of a point Keats had made of it as a goal. So regularly did Keats maintain it that within three weeks he had written half as much as during the previous four months. A brief spell of fatigue struck him after the first four days. He told his sister Fanny (September 10) : "I have been writing very hard lately even till an utter incapacity came on, and I feel it now about my head." But he is thinking very precisely of a deadline—October 1—and says that he will remain at Oxford "till I have finished the 3rd Book of my Story; which I hope will be accomplish'd in at most three Weeks from to day." On September 21, he wrote happily to John Reynolds: "I am getting on famous with my third Book—have written 800 lines thereof, and hope to finish it next week." He did; he completed it on September 26, triumphantly writing the date at the end of the draft.

8

In the late afternoon and early evening—at least during the first week—Keats and Bailey walked about the city and the adjoining countryside. If Bailey was not well, Keats went alone. He writes to Fanny:

> This Oxford I have no doubt is the finest City in the world—it is full of old Gothic buildings—Spires—towers—Quadrangles—Cloisters Groves & is surrounded with more Clear streams than ever I saw together—I take a Walk by the Side of one of them every Evening and thank God, we have not had a drop of rain these many days.

He intended this letter (September 10) to Fanny, now fourteen, as a deliberate beginning of a correspondence. If he had written her before, it had been only briefly. On his return to Hampstead, he had found how difficult it was to see her at Abbey's house in Walthamstow. Abbey did not welcome his visits. Keats "often spoke to me," said Bailey, "of his sister, who was somehow witholden from him, with great delicacy & tenderness of affection." Before leaving for Oxford, he bought her a present—Jane Taylor's *Essays in Rhyme, or Morals and Manners* (1816) , inscribing it "John Keats to his Dear Sister."

Her vacation over, Fanny was now back at the school of the Misses Tuckey, 12 Marsh Street, Walthamstow, living at the house of Miss Caley (no. 21), across the road, which lodged the overflow of the Tuckey school. Keats absent-mindedly addresses her "Miss Keats, Miss Kaley's School, Walthamstow." (When he next addresses her at school—in August of the following year—he remembers it as "Miss Tucker's.") His letter begins a little stiffly, even condescendingly:

> Let us now begin a regular question and answer—a little pro and con; letting it interfere as a pleasant method of my coming at your favourite little wants and enjoyments, that I may meet them in a way befitting a brother.
> We have been so little together since you have been able to reflect on things that I know not whether you prefer the History of King Pepin to Bunyan's Pilgrims Progress—or Cinderella and her glass slipper to Moor's Almanack. However in a few Letters I hope I shall be able to come at that and adapt my Scribblings to your Pleasure—You must tell me about all you read if it be only six Pages in a Week—and this transmitted to me every now and then will procu[r]e you full sheets of Writing from me pretty frequently—This I feel as a necessity: for we ought to become intimately acquainted, in order that I may not only, as you grow up love you as my only Sister, but confide in you as my dearest friend. When I saw you last I told you of my intention of going to Oxford and 't is now a Week since I disembark'd from his Whipship's Coach the Defiance in this place. I am living in Magdalen Hall on a visit to a young Man with whom I have not been long acquainted, but whom I like very much—we lead very industrious lives he in general Studies and I in proceeding at a pretty good rate with a Poem which I hope you will see early in the next year—Perhaps you might like to know what I am writing about—I will tell you—

He then summarizes in a few sentences the fable of Endymion—not his own version. Possibly she has read the fable and "the other beautiful Tales which have come down from the ancient times of that beautiful Greece. If you have not let me know and I will tell you more at large of others quite as delightful." Then the well-meaning condescension to the girl of fourteen suddenly disappears; nor does it ever return in the letters, however gently and clearly he tries to explain things. He plunges into his description of Oxford, and tells her of George and Tom, now on their visit to France:

I had a long and interesting Letter from George, cross lines by a short one from Tom yesterday dated Paris [12]—They both send their loves to you—Like most Englishmen they feel a mighty preference for every thing English—the french Meadows the trees the People the Towns the Churches, the Books the every thing—although they may be in themselves good; yet when put in comparison with our green Island they all vanish like Swallows in October. They have seen Cathedrals Manuscripts. Fountains, Pictures, Tragedy Comedy,—with other things you may by chance meet with in this Country such a[s] Washerwomen, Lamplighters, Turnpikemen Fish kettles, Dancing Masters, kettle drums, Sentry Boxes, Rocking Horses &c and, now they have taken them over a set of boxing gloves—I have written to George and requested him, as you wish I shou[ld,] to write to you.

He ends:

Now Fanny you must write soon—and write all you think about, never mind what—only let me have a good deal of your writing—You need not do it all at once—be two or three or four days about it, and let it be a diary of your little life. You will preserve all my Letters [13] and I will secure yours—and thus in the course of time we shall each of us have a good Bundle—which, hereafter, when things may have strangely altered and God knows what happened, we may read over together and look with pleasure on times past.

9

After his first week at Oxford, Keats and Bailey began to use the later afternoons for boating:

For these last five or six days [he writes Reynolds on September 21], we have had regularly a Boat on the Isis, and explored all the streams about, which are more in number than your eyelashes. We sometimes skim into a Bed of rushes, and there become naturalized riverfolks,—there is one particularly nice nest which we have christened "Reynolds's Cove"—in which we have read Wordsworth and talked as may be.

12 Tom may possibly have gone south to Lyons at this time. Nothing is known of the trip except what one can gather from a remark George made to Dilke (October 18, 1826; *KC*, I.301) discussing finances: Abbey "advanced some when Tom went to Lyons and subsequently to John & myself on account of the assistance we gave him." Miss Lowell (I.172) assumed that this took place in the winter of 1815–16; but it would have been a rather formidable excursion for a youth of sixteen to make alone.

13 She did preserve them, and in her old age said that they had been out of her possession only once.

He has also, he says, been browsing among Bailey's books. He was pleasantly surprised by the poems of Katherine Philips—"a friend of Jeremy Taylor's, and called 'the matchless Orinda'—you must have heard of her"; and he copies out the stanzas of one of her poems, "To Mrs. M. A. at Parting"; she has "a most delicate fancy of the Fletcher kind."

One is puzzled by his strong language about women with intellectual and literary pretensions before he mentions "the matchless Orinda," whom he finds refreshing by contrast.[14] The nearest approach to a bluestocking that he had ever met was Mrs. Reynolds herself, though Mrs. Hunt and especially her sister had some aspirations that went beyond their "manufacture" of laurel crowns. The general assumption that he is here discussing poor Mary Tighe, whose poem *Psyche* he had once admired, hardly explains this strong, personal feeling. A possible clue exists in one of the statements that preceded this sudden outburst:

> I think I see you and Hunt meeting in the Pit.—What a very pleasant fellow he is, if he would give up the sovereignty of a Room pro bono—What Evenings we might pass with him, could we have him from Mrs. H.

Two and a half weeks later, when he is back at Hampstead (October 8), Keats describes to Bailey the quarrels in which Hunt, Haydon, and Horace Smith are engaged; and only at the end of the account does he bring in something that has obviously been rankling:

> Haydon says to me Keats dont show your Lines to Hunt on any account or he will have done half for you—so it appears Hunt wishes it to be thought. When he met Reynolds in the Theatre John told him that I was getting on to the completion of 4000 Lines. Ah! says Hunt, had it not been for me [i.e., my excisions] they would have been 7000! If he will say this to Reynolds what would he to other People? Haydon received a Letter a little while back on this subject

---

14 "The world, and especially our England, has within the last thirty years been vexed and teased by a set of Devils, whom I detest so much that I almost hunger after an acherontic promotion to a Torturer, purposely for their accommodation; These Devils are a set of Women, who having taken a snack or Luncheon of Literary scraps, set themselves up for towers of Babel in Languages Sapphos in Poetry—Euclids in Geometry—and everything in nothing. Among such the Name of Montague [Elizabeth Montagu] has been preeminent. The thing has made a very uncomfortable impression on me.—I had longed for some real feminine Modesty in these things, and was therefore gladdened in the extreme on opening the other day" the poems of Katherine Philips (I.163).

from some Lady—which contains a caution to me through him on this subject—Now is not all this a most paltry thing to think about?

This is plainly the encounter with Hunt that Reynolds must have described in a letter to Keats at Oxford, and to which Keats refers in his reply to Reynolds: "I think I see you and Hunt meeting in the Pit." That Keats kept the incident to himself when he heard of it at Oxford, and is only now mentioning it to Bailey after he returns to Hampstead, suggests how much it hurt him. In all probability Hunt was accompanied to the theater by his wife and his omnipresent sister-in-law, whom Haydon later describes in a letter to Keats as "that horrid creature Miss Kent, looking like a fury & an old maid, mixed." One is tempted to think that Hunt's remarks about *Endymion* were followed by some sharp opinions from either Mrs. Hunt or, far more probably, her sister; and that if they were repeated in Reynolds' letter as coming from one of the Hunt women, Keats leapt to the conclusion that it was Mrs. Hunt. Trying unsuccessfully in his reply to avoid saying anything too unpleasant about Hunt himself, he falls into a mild irony for only a moment: Hunt he says, "agrees with the Northern Poet [Wordsworth] in this, 'He is not one of those who much delight to season their fireside with personal talk'—I must confess however having a little itch that way and at this present I have a few neighbourly remarks to make." Then follows the passage on the "set of Devils" whom he would like, he says, to torture.

Meanwhile Haydon, in a momentary mood of generosity, had written to Keats (September 17) asking him to find out what he could about a young artist, Charles Cripps. Haydon had noticed him earlier at Oxford copying an altarpiece, and thought "the copy promised something." If Keats can find Cripps, says Haydon,

> ascertain what his wishes in Art *are*—if he has *ambition*, if he seems to possess *power*—if he wishes to *be great*—all of which you can soon see—In these cases should any friend be disposed to assist him up to London & to support him for a Year I'll train him in the Art, with no o[ther] remuneration but the pleasure of seeing him advance . . . do oblige me by exerting Yourself perhaps Mr. Bailey will also feel an interest.[15]

Keats and Bailey, caught by Haydon's enthusiasm, did "exert" themselves. Keats found Cripps, read to him Haydon's letter,

15 I.161.

thought he might have talent, and was in any case moved at the opportunity suddenly open to the youth—"the finest thing," as he says to Haydon, "that will befal him this many a year." Cripps had no money. But Bailey, says Keats, is trying to think how to raise enough for his support, and Keats will try to help. What happened to deflate Haydon's interest is not clear. Bailey and Keats did not succeed in raising enough money for Cripps's support for more than a year, and this may not have satisfied Haydon; or Haydon may have decided to exact some apprenticeship fee after all. But the whole matter of Cripps keeps recurring in Keats's letters throughout the autumn and winter. Bailey, taking the initiative, apparently wrote in October to Haydon in order to present the situation; he received no answer. Keats, in a letter to Bailey (November 3), has the remark: "I hope you will receive an answer from Haydon soon—if not Pride! Pride! Pride! I have received no more subscriptions—but shall soon have full health [he has been unwell for two weeks or more] Liberty and leisure to give a good part of my time to [Cripps]." By mid-November Haydon wrote a rude reply to Bailey. "To a Man of your nature," said Keats, "such a Letter as Haydon's must have been extremely cutting . . . As soon as I had known Haydon three days I had got enough of his character not to have been surp[r]ised at such a Letter as he has hurt you with." But by January the matter appeared to be settling peaceably, at least for a while: Haydon was more amenable; and money was slowly being raised.[16]

10

Keats's reading during the weeks at Oxford—at least his approach to it—already begins to suggest the next level or plateau of his development. The momentum that came in writing so rapidly acted as a general stimulus. The confidence that *Endymion* would be finished after all, the freedom to think at times of the next step —which he hoped would indeed take him to a different level— the constant talks with Bailey, the books in Bailey's library, all encouraged (to use his own later vocabulary) a more "philosophical" openness. Bailey's poetic idols were Dante, Milton, and Wordsworth. He could justly say that he "was a great student of Milton when a young man," and in his copy, heavily underscored

16 I.183–184, 194, 201–203, 206, 210, 226.

and annotated, Keats browsed while at Oxford. "But, like Reynolds, [Keats] was then"—said Bailey,—"far more enamoured of
the beauties of Spenser & the Faery Queen. The subsequent study
of Milton gave his mind a mighty addition of energy & manly vigour, which stand out so nobly in Hyperion." There was indeed a
lag of a few months before Keats began to read Milton seriously.
But the impression had been made. So with Dante. Keats at least
dipped into Henry Cary's translation; he quotes from it, in fact,
three months later when he writes for the *Champion* a short article on Edmund Kean's acting. But the important thing again was
the impression. For after the crowded months ahead were over,
and he set off in June on his walking tour of Scotland, he took
Cary's three-volume translation with him.

There was no such lag in his reading—or rereading—of Wordsworth. For at least a year Keats had regarded him as on an entirely different plane from his other contemporaries. One thinks
back to Keats's remark the previous November when he had written the sonnet "Great spirits now on earth are sojourning," which
Haydon said he would forward to Wordsworth: "The Idea of your
sending it" to him "put me out of breath—you know with what
Reverence—I would send my Wellwishes to him." He was now altogether receptive to Bailey's enthusiasm; and throughout the next
half year or more, his thinking is permeated by Wordsworth. The
special, idealistic way in which he is viewing Wordsworth is shown
by a remark three days after he returned to Hampstead from Oxford. Writing to Bailey about the bickering of Hunt, Haydon,
Horace Smith, and others, he says, "I am quite disgusted with literary Men and will never know another except Wordsworth." In
December he was finally to meet Wordsworth.

"At this time," said Bailey, Keats most valued Wordsworth "in
particular passages." This was natural enough. It would even have
been understandable had he not gone much beyond it. Perhaps it
is in "particular passages" that Wordsworth, more than most of the
greater poets, captures us now. What we might call the flower-
pieces, admired or at least quoted in the nineteenth century, have
their place; and, paradoxically, mid-twentieth-century formalism,
with its neoclassic hunger for obvious unity and its dislike of the
embarrassments of amplitude, is also drawn to them, at least as
texts to explicate. And the numerous poems noted for starkness—
and occasionally awkward starkness—of statement have a genuine

psychological, and to some extent stylistic, interest as experiments illustrating the dilemmas of uncompromising sincerity in poetry. Still, it is in those haunting lines where Wordsworth's brooding meditation on life is so powerfully phrased—where he brings to bear so much "more of life," as Arnold rightly says, and becomes "inevitable, as inevitable as Nature itself"—that the profundity of Wordsworth is felt, and so much other poetry becomes, by contrast, a tinkling of cymbals.

"Our conversation," said Bailey, "rarely or never flagged, during our walks, or boatings, or in the Evening." Loving as he did to make notes, he jotted down "a few of [Keats's] opinions on Literature & criticism." At least half of them have to do with Wordsworth:

> The following passage from Wordsworth's ode on Immortality was deeply felt by Keats, who however at this time seemed to me to value this great Poet rather in particular passages than in the full length portrait, as it were, of the great imaginative & philosophic Christian Poet, which he really is, & which Keats obviously, not long afterwards, felt him to be.

> > "Not for these I raise
> > The song of thanks & praise;
> > But for those obstinate questionings
> > Of sense & outward things,
> > Fallings from us, vanishings;
> > Blank misgivings of a creature
> > Moving about in worlds not realized,
> > *High instincts, before which our mortal nature*
> > *Did tremble like a guilty thing surprized.*"

> The last lines he thought were quite awful in their application to a guilty finite creature, like man, in the appalling nature of the feeling which they suggested to a thoughtful mind.
>   Again, we often talked of that noble passage in the Lines on Tintern Abbey:—
> > > "That blessed mood,
> > In which *the burthen of the mystery,*
> > In which the heavy & the weary weight
> > Of all this unintelligible world
> > Is lightened."

> And his references to this passage are frequent in his letters.—But in those exquisite stanzas:—
> > > "She dwelt among the untrodden ways,
> > > Beside the springs of Dove—"
> ending,—

"She lived unknown & few could know
When Lucy ceased to be;
But she is in her grave, & oh,
The difference to me"—

The simplicity of the last line he declared to be the most perfect pathos.[17]

As an index to this growing interest in poetry with a direct applicability to human life, it is typical that the youth who six months before would spend a full evening with Haydon "spouting Shakespeare," and had been reading Shakespeare since he began *Endymion,* now especially "admired & was fond of reciting," said Bailey, the great speech of Ulysses, in *Troilus and Cressida* (III.iii) , beginning:

Time hath, my lord, a wallet at his back
Wherein he puts alms for oblivion.

"It was, he thought, pregnant with practical wisdom, such as Shakespeare alone could produce."

11

In the whole tenor of the reading, the approach, the citations dwelt on, we have to do with what Keats himself so graphically describes in a few months to Reynolds as the passage from the "infant or thoughtless Chamber" of life into a "Chamber of Maiden-Thought": an "awakening of the thinking principle," an awakening to the larger humane uses of poetry. We are dealing with an essential, though rapid, moral deepening—moral in the broadest sense of the word.

There were other moments at Oxford when Keats's interest anticipated the more purely formal or stylistic advances he was to

[17] "Among the qualities of high poetic promise in Keats was, even at this time, his correct taste. I remember to have been struck with this by his remarks on that well known & often quoted passage of the Excursion upon the Greek Mythology,— where it is said that
'Fancy fetched
Even from the blazing Chariot of the Sun
A beardless youth who touched a golden lute,
And filled the illumined groves with ravishment.'
Keats said this description of Apollo should have ended at the 'golden lute,' & have left it to the imagination to complete the picture,—*how* he 'filled the illumined groves.' I think every man of taste will feel the justice of the remark."

make during the year after *Endymion* was completed. Bailey speaks of Keats's fondness for the poetry of Thomas Chatterton:

> Methinks I now hear him recite, or *chant,* in his peculiar manner, the following stanza of the "Roundelay sung by the minstrels of Ella":
>> *"Come with acorn cup & thorn,*
>> Drain my hertys blood away;
>> Life & all its goods I scorn;
>> Dance by night or feast by day."
>
> The first line to his ear possessed the great charm. Indeed his sense of melody was quite exquisite, as is apparent in his own verses; & in none more than in numerous passages of his Endymion.

Bailey then goes on to say that one of Keats's "favorite topics . . . was the principle of melody in Verse, upon which he had his own notions, particularly in the management of open & close vowels." Keats's theory, as far as we can make it out, is more helpfully discussed when we reach verse of his own that exemplifies it.[18] He was writing *Endymion* far too quickly to do much about this "principle of melody in Verse" at the moment. Some starts were made in the following spring. But it is in the poetry from *Hyperion,* in the autumn of 1818, to the great odes of May 1819 that we find a rich, elaborate use of vowel interplay.

More than any of Keats's other contemporaries, William Hazlitt had been writing perceptively about some of the moral and most of the stylistic values toward which Keats himself was rapidly moving. Though Keats had met him a few times at Haydon's or Hunt's during the previous month, he seems to have known little about Hazlitt's work until his visit with Bailey. But now he was struck that a man who could write the *Principles of Human Action*—a rather impressive attempt to prove the "disinterestedness" of the human mind—should also be an unequaled practical critic of the drama. Keats wrote to Reynolds (September 21): "How is Hazlitt? We were reading his Table last night [the recently published essays, *The Round Table*]—I know he thinks himself not estimated by ten people in the world—I wishe he knew he is."

18 See below, Chapter XVI, section 10.

12

Keats also appears to have been reading the Bible during some of the hours he sat in Bailey's rooms. Bailey "as a Clergyman, & his friend when my own mind was fully & gravely determined to my sacred profession," naturally wished to say something about Keats's religious attitudes at this time. For he had "much earnest conversation with him on this subject" while they were together at Oxford. Bailey thirty years later, and with the advantage that time gave him, gently and perceptively puts his finger on the real explanation of Keats's religious attitudes—or lack of them—at this time, and the doubts that "the honesty of his character" led him to express if the subject came up:

> His confession of his sceptical nature in all things, "so as some-times to think poetry a Jack O Lanthorn" to amuse the idle, is indeed a dark view of his own mind, & of the moods of mind *some-times* in all thoughtful men. "At *sometime* (says the pious & judi-cious Hooker) who doubteth not? . . ."
>
> If so profound a Divine, & so devout a man as Hooker lays down this proneness to doubt as one of the inheritances of our fallen na-ture, we cannot, or we should not, be surprised that a mind so left to itself—an orphan mind—from his earliest years, & so full of thought, which is the very seed-plot of doubt, should be thus af-fected: & it is like the honesty of his character which made him thus speak out.—In one word his religious education seems to have been greatly or wholly neglected; and he was early thrown among men, such as his friend Mr. Hunt, (who I have heard, & *hope,* has amended this fatal error) and of others of the literary Society of that day. Yet he was no scoffer, & in no sense was he an infidel. When he visited me at Oxford, I had much earnest conversation with him on this subject. He well knew, & always respected my feel-ings & principles. He promised me, & I believe he kept his promise, that he would never scoff at religion. And when he returned to Lon-don,—it was remarked to me afterwards by one of his most intimate friends,—there was a decided change in his manner regarding reli-gion.

Bailey goes on to say that these are the "worst features of the case" that could be mentioned, and to express confidence in whatever later letters or statements might show. He is certain that, no mat-ter what else might be said, further statements can be taken at face value: "for his character of mind is perfectly transparent; he had no trick to hide his defects."

Bailey does not mention Keats's reading of the Bible. But the letters Keats wrote from Oxford are suddenly filled with allusions to the Old Testament. There are five allusions to Genesis (including three to the Tower of Babel, which seems to have caught his imagination) , and references also to I Samuel and to the Psalms. Bailey himself was meanwhile writing a moral essay he hoped to have published, and certainly read it to Keats.[19]

13

The thousand lines written between September 5 and 26, together with the general excitement, had left him exhausted. The elation he had felt when he completed them subsided within a couple of days. The poem begun five months ago was really not at all what he wanted to do now, though he tried to reassure himself that "Rome was not built in a day." "My Ideas with respect to" *Endymion,* he tells Haydon (September 28) ,

> I assure you are very low—and I would write the subject thoroughly again. but I am tired of it and think the time would be better spent in writing a new Romance which I have in my eye for next summer —Rome was not built in a Day. and all the good I expect from my employment this summer is the fruit of Experience which I hope to gather in my next Poem.

He spent another week with Bailey, too tired to think of making a start on Book IV. The two of them made an excursion to Stratford, and "went of course," said Bailey, "to the house visited by so many thousands of all nations of Europe, & inscribed our names in addition to the 'numbers numberless' of those which literally blackened the walls; and if those walls have not been washed, or our names wiped out to find place for some others, they will still remain together upon that truly honored wall of a small low attic apartment." They also went to the church, and signed the visitors' book (October 2) .[20] Keats "was struck, I remember, with the simple statue there." His enjoyment at Stratford "was of that genuine, quiet kind which was a part of his gentle nature; deeply feeling what he truly enjoyed, but saying little."

On Sunday, the fifth, he took the coach back to London, and

---

19 When it was not published, he still kept it. It survives in Bailey's scrapbook now at Harvard.
20 Colvin, p. 150. The book has since disappeared.

then another to Hampstead, where George and Tom, just returned from Paris, were waiting for him. Probably while still at Oxford he had caught the bad cold that troubled him all through October (by the twenty-eighth he had still "not been well enough to stand the chance of a Wet night"), and that the Reynolds girls feared might be related to Tom's illness. For his remark to Bailey (October 8), "The little Mercury I have taken" has "improved my Health," suggests that Bailey was already aware of it.[21]

As if to touch base again, he saw most of his friends as soon as he could. For "the next Morning finding myself tolerably well," he called on the Reynolds family with a parcel Bailey had asked him to deliver. From there he went over to Paddington, and dropped in on both Hunt and Haydon, who were once again neighbors though far from neighborly in spirit. Shelley was staying at Hunt's.

> Every Body seems at Loggerheads. There's Hunt infatuated [with Shelley]—there's Haydon's Picture in statu quo. There's Hunt walks up and down his painting room criticising every head most unmercifully—There's Horace Smith tired of Hunt. "The web of our Life is of mingled Yarn."

It was a relief the next day to visit his new friend at Hampstead, the burly, unaffected Charles Brown; and while he was there Reynolds also came. The three men passed a pleasant day, though Reynolds was a little unwell. But the bickering and dissatisfaction he had encountered the day before weighed on him. It seemed such a contrast with the happy atmosphere—at least as he had felt it—

---

21 Mercury was recklessly prescribed in the early 1800's for a large number of diseases as varied as croup, rheumatism, and tuberculosis. Unaware of this, W. M. Rossetti argued that Keats had acquired syphilis at Oxford—mercury, by Rossetti's time, being still used for syphilis but less for other diseases. Rossetti supported his argument by another remark of Keats's (letter to Bailey, November 22): "I think Jane or Marianne has a better opinion of me than I deserve—for really and truly I do not think my Brothers illness connected with mine—you know more of the real Cause than they do—nor have I any chance of being rack'd as you have been." Had there been even the slightest chance that syphilis would be regarded as the disease, Archdeacon Bailey, as Miss Hewlett says (p. 121), would have been very unwilling to allow Milnes to print or use this letter. The remark is readily explained by the context, as Amy Lowell, who discusses the whole matter in some detail (I.512–515), points out. Keats is saying that though "the world is full of troubles," he has "not much reason to think myself pestered with many." The fear of the Reynolds girls that his illness suggested consumption, and their belief that he was simply being brave in disregarding this, was too favorable an opinion of his courage. He "really and truly" believed Tom's illness was not connected with his own. Nor had he any chance of being "rack'd" as Bailey was—who was often ill ("Poor Bailey," Keats wrote to the Reynolds girls on September 14, "scar[c]ely ever well has gone to bed very so so").

only a year before when he had first met Hunt, Haydon, and Reynolds. It contrasted too with the quiet, productive weeks at Oxford. In addition to everything else he had been brooding a little about Hunt's bantering statement to Reynolds when they had met in the theater that, had it not been for him, Keats's 4,000 lines would be 7,000. After disclosing this to Bailey, Keats copies out for him the long extract from his letter to George the previous spring in which he defines this "test" or "trial," [22] and adds:

> You see Bailey how independant my writing has been—Hunts dissuasion was of no avail—I refused to visit Shelley, that I might have my own unfetterd scope—and after all I shall have the Reputation of Hunt's elevé—His corrections and amputations will by the knowing ones be trased in the Poem.

The writing of Book IV in October seemed dishearteningly slow. Within three weeks and a half after his return (October 30) , however, he had completed three hundred lines. This had been something of a struggle. He was too unwell even to go out of doors for two of these weeks; and the Bentley children downstairs were noisy. Their "horrid row" was one of the reasons, as he told Bailey, that "I regret I cannot be transported to your Room." Yet the three hundred lines were less than a third of what he had written in a shorter time at Oxford. "There is no altering a Man's nature and mine must be radically wrong for it will lie dormant a whole Month." But he hopes to "come to a conclusion in at least three Weeks." When that happens, he will be glad enough to "dismount for a Month or two—although I'll keep as tight a reign as possible till then nor suffer myself to sleep." The following day, October 31, was his twenty-second birthday.

14

By October, six reviews of Keats's first volume had appeared. The number was respectable, especially considering how small a sale the *Poems* had; and they were by no means unfavorable. On the other hand, three of them were written by friends—by Reynolds, G. F. Mathew, and Hunt. These came out early—Reynolds' in the *Champion* (March 9) , Mathew's in the *European Magazine* (May) , and Hunt's in three issues of the *Examiner* (June 1, July 6, July 13) .

22 See above, Chapter VIII, section 10.

Reynolds' review, like that of Mathew, is now readily available.[23] This friendly young man could hardly be expected to put his finger on anything very essential. His review was rushed through so that it would appear immediately after the *Poems* themselves were published. Looking for means of praise, Reynolds has only some of the more elementary catchwords at hand, particularly "nature"; and in so far as his review has a general theme it is that the author of the *Poems* "comes fresh from nature,—and the originals of his images are to be found in her keeping." Keats, of course, was altogether grateful, and wrote the same day it appeared (March 9) :

> Your kindness affects me so sensibly that I can merely put down a few mono-sentences—Your Criticism only makes me extremely anxious that I sho[d] not deceive you.
> It's the finest thing by God—as Hazlitt wo[d] say[.] However I hope I may not deceive you.

A very brief but appreciative notice of the *Poems* was printed in the *Monthly Magazine* (April 1).[24] Then, in the May issue of the *European Magazine,* Keats's old friend, George Felton Mathew, reappears. He had felt piqued since the early autumn of 1816 when Keats had become friends with Hunt, Haydon, and Reynolds; and the pique now emerges through the clouds of his Chadbandlike rhetoric. The review is admittedly of interest only if one is interested in Mathew. Reynolds, in his review, had stated that some of the poems smuggled into the center of the volume were "very inferior" to the others; "but Mr. Keats informs us that they were written at an earlier period than the rest." Mathew, of course, resented this remark. His own review is largely an answer to Reynolds, and could be partly described as Reynolds' review turned upside down. With delightful orotundity, Mathew picks for special praise only those poems written in 1815 and early 1816, when Keats had seen him frequently and followed the languid leadership of Mathew's taste. These, says Mathew, are "of superior versifica-

23 Both are reprinted by J. M. Murry, *Studies in Keats* (2nd ed., 1939), pp. 146–160. Reynolds' review is that erroneously assigned by Murry to Haydon.

24 "A small volume of poems, by Mr. Keats, has appeared; and it well deserves the notice it has attracted, by the sweetness and beauty of the compositions. For the model of his style, the author has had recourse to the age of Elizabeth; and if he has not wholly avoided the quaintness that characterizes the writings of that period, it must be allowed by every candid reader that the fertile fancy and beautiful diction of our old poets, is not unfrequently rivaled by Mr. Keats. There is in his poems a rapturous glow and intoxication of the fancy—an air of careless and profuse magnificence in his diction—a revelry of the imagination and tenderness of feeling, that forcibly impress themselves on the reader."

tion" to the rest, though the author seems to be "partly ashamed" of them "from a declaration that they were written earlier than the rest." He singles out the following lines as especially "spirited and powerful":

> Ah! who can e'er forget so fair a being?
> Who can forget her half retiring sweets?
> God! she is like a milk-white lamb that bleats
> For man's protection. Surely the All-seeing,
> Who joys to see us with his gifts agreeing,
> Will never give him pinions, who intreats
> Such innocence to ruin; who vilely cheats
> A dove-like bosom . . .

Mathew's exuberant praise of the worst poem in the book is followed by some strictures on the sonnet on Chapman's Homer, which is "absurd in its application" and falls into "unseemly hyperbole" in its line "Till I heard Chapman speak out loud and bold."

Mathew is really at a loss how to proceed. Fundamentally (aside from his personal resentments) his charge is that Hunt's style—and of course Keats's—is not sentimental enough. The energy and dispatch of the Hunt style are obtrusive. Far worse are the political principles that Hunt and Keats espouse. Most of what Mathew dislikes is paradoxically thrown under the heading of "Imagination." With this Keats's poems are only too plentifully supplied.[25]

The first part of Hunt's review (June 1) was devoted mainly to summarizing once again the premises and goals he had been championing. He knew that any active support he gave Keats could harm more than help—as indeed proved to be the case within the next year. One senses that he was sparring for time in order to find some possible way of being helpful. The first part of his review had ended with the remark that it would be "concluded next week."

[25] "While we blame the slovenly independence of his versification, we must allow that thought, sentiment, and feeling, particularly in the active use and poetical display of them, belong more to the maturity of summer fruits than to the infancy of vernal blossoms . . . We might transcribe the whole volume were we to point out every instance of the luxuriance of his imagination, and the puerility of his sentiments. With these distinguishing features, it cannot be but many passages will appear abstracted and obscure. Feeble and false thoughts are easily lost sight of in the redundance of poetical decoration. . . . We consider that the specimens here presented to our readers, will establish our opinion of Mr. Keats's poetical imagination; but the mere luxuries of the imagination, more especially in the possession of the proud egotist of diseased feelings and perverted principles, may become the ruin of a people . . ."

But the weeks passed. Finally, when he returned to London near the end of June, he decided to go ahead. The remainder of the review (July 6 and 13) includes a few gentle reservations in order to give the appearance of impartiality, and then, by a generous selection of the happier passages, tries to allow the merits of the book to present themselves.

Keats had naturally hoped that some of the established critical reviews would notice the *Poems*. Reynolds' review could be taken for granted as a friendly act. Hunt's, however tactful, could also be viewed as partial; and the prestige of the *Examiner* was limited. Mathew's confused remarks meant little. It could be expected that some time would have to elapse before any of the established journals printed a review of the book. Finally, in September and October, two appeared. They were on the whole judicious and fair. If they caused Keats some embarrassment, it was because he inwardly agreed with much that they censured. The *Eclectic Review,* the principal journal of the Nonconformists, always tended to be preachy in manner. But its editor, Josiah Conder, who wrote the review of Keats in the September issue, was deservedly respected for his good sense. A quick survey of the directions in which the poetry of the day was moving is followed by a frank recognition of the influence of Hunt on this volume. Conder, who thought well of the sonnets, found Hunt's influence most excessive and least pleasant in the longer poems. "Sleep and Poetry" is particularly condemned for its jaunty confusions; and, in a comment that may well have touched home, he says:

Mr. Keats has satirized certain pseudo poets, who,

> With a puling infant's force
> Sway'd about upon a rocking horse
> And thought it Pegasus.

Satire is a two-edged weapon: the lines brought irresistibly to our imagination the Authour of these poems in the very attitude he describes.

Yet the writer, he says, is a "young man of vivid imagination," and "a few years hence he will be glad to escape the remembrance" of some of the verses he has published here. Conder ends by stressing that there are "brilliant exceptions" to all he has said—that he may very well be wrong in his estimate.

Constable's *Scots Magazine* for October was more favorable—in fact, considering that it was reviewing a first volume, quite favorable. Some space is devoted to Hunt and his liabilities as a model. But the reviewer notes how frequently Keats transcends this influence by reverting "to a model more pure" than some of the Italian poets, particularly Pulci and Ariosto, whom Hunt was trying at times to follow—that is, Spenser. Many of the sonnets are warmly praised. The review ends with surprising generosity:

> Wc are sorry that we can quote no more of these sweet verses which have in them so deep a tone of moral energy, and such a zest of the pathos of genius. We are loth to part with this poet of promise, and are vexed that critical justice requires us to mention some passages of considerable affectation . . . "Leafy luxury," "jaunty streams," "lawny slope," "the moon-beamy air," "a sun-beamy tale."

15

Though no justifiable complaint could be made of the reviews of the *Poems,* a cloud was beginning to form. In the October issue of the new *Blackwood's Edinburgh Magazine* appeared the first of the notorious series of articles "On the Cockney School of Poetry" with the help of which *Blackwood's* hoped to build a reputation as an energetic, formidable journal. The magazine had been established in April by William Blackwood, a Tory bookseller in Edinburgh. From the beginning it set itself in opposition to the Whig publisher, Archibald Constable, and his *Scots Magazine* and *Edinburgh Review.* After a few months, not making the progress he expected, Blackwood reorganized the magazine, dismissed the editors, and, with John Wilson and John Gibson Lockhart as helpers, took personal charge. The attacks on the "Cockney School" were to be one of the features. Lockhart and Wilson collaborated on them, signing the articles with the letter "Z." For their motto they were able to dig up some unfortunate lines by a minor disciple of Hunt, Cornelius Webb. They used capital letters for the names of Hunt and Keats, thus suggesting that Keats would in time be given special attention:

> Our talk shall be (a theme we never tire on)
> Of Chaucer, Spenser, Shakespeare, Milton, Byron,
> (Our England's Dante)—Wordsworth—HUNT, and KEATS,
> The Muses' son of promise; and of what feats
> He yet may do.

Not even Hunt, for all his experience, was prepared for anything like the motiveless venom of the attack.[26] To Keats, abuse of this sort was entirely new. He was almost incredulous as he wrote to Bailey (November 3) about "the flaming attack upon Hunt" in the new magazine:

> I never read any thing so virulent—accusing him of the greatest Crimes—dep[r]eciating his Wife his Poetry—his Habits—his company, his Conversation—These Philipics are to come out in Numbers—calld 'the Cockney School of Poetry'   There has been but one Number published—that on Hunt to which they have prefixed a Motto from one Cornelius Webb Poetaster—who unfortunately was of our Party occasionally at Hampstead and took it into his head to write the following—something about—"we'll talk on Wordsworth Byron—a theme we never tire on" and so forth till he comes to Hunt and Keats. In the Motto they have put Hunt and Keats in large Letters—I have no doubt that the second Number was intended for me: but have hopes of its non appearance from the following advertisement in last Sunday's Examiner. "To Z. The writer of the Article signed Z in Blackwood's Ed[i]nburgh magazine for October 1817 is invited to send his address to the printer of the Examiner, in order that Justice may be executed of the proper person" [27] I dont mind the thing much—but if he should go to such lengths with me as he has done with Hunt I mu[s]t infalibly call him to an account—if he be a human being and appears in Squares and Theatres where we might possibly meet—I dont relish his abuse.

Though Lockhart did not actually get to Keats until the following August, the attack could be expected at any time. Keats's angry surprise at the injustice, the pointless malice of the whole thing,

26 A few sentences will illustrate the tone: "Mr. Hunt cannot utter a dedication, or even a note, without betraying the *Shibboleth* of low birth and low habits. He is the ideal of the Cockney Poet. He raves perpetually about 'green fields,' 'jaunty streams,' and 'o'er-arching leafiness,' exactly as a Cheapside shop-keeper does about the beauties of his box on the Camberwell road. . . . He would fain be always tripping and waltzing, and is sorry that he cannot be allowed to walk about in the morning with yellow breeches and flesh-coloured silk-stockings. . . . His poetry is that of a man who has kept company with kept-mistresses. He talks indelicately like a tea-sipping milliner girl. Some excuse for him there might have been, had he been hurried away by imagination or passion. But with him indecency is a disease, as he speaks unclean things from perfect inanition. The very concubine of so impure a wretch as Leigh Hunt would be to be pitied, but alas! for the wife of such a husband! For him there is no charm in simple seduction; and he glories over it only when accompanied with adultery and incest."

27 Neither this advertisement nor others inserted in the *Examiner* could persuade "Z" to disclose his identity. "Z" took a high moral tone, stressing his role as an avenging angel on behalf of the public. Meanwhile, in private, he wrote a letter to Hunt stating that he was John Graham Dalyell of Edinburgh. Hunt wrote to Dalyell and discovered he was a Whig whom "Z" thought it would be pleasant to embarrass.

became gradually absorbed into a more general bewilderment and sadness. Ever since he had returned and found Hunt, Haydon, and Horace Smith quarreling among themselves and with others, he had been thinking of the ease and unpredictability with which human nature—ostensibly in self-defense, but usually through envy, self-dissatisfaction, or boredom—could flare into hostility. A great deal of life appeared to consist of little more than "teasing and snubbing and vexation." One more instance was the absurd misunderstanding about poor Charles Cripps. Haydon, after a generous show of interest in him as a pupil he would take without charge, was now apparently dropping him at the very time Keats and Bailey were trying to raise money to help him study under Haydon. "The thought that we are mortal makes us groan," he writes Bailey. "I hope you will receive an answer from Haydon soon—if not Pride! Pride! Pride!" At the very time he writes this he is thinking about the *Blackwood's* attack. But he does not mention it yet. He is trying to keep his anxiety and surprise at arm's length. In doing so he devotes the first part of his letter partly to the matter of Cripps and Haydon, but especially to Bailey's bad news that his hope for a curacy has been held up by the Bishop of Lincoln. On this Keats suddenly allows himself to express a violence he cannot let himself feel—cannot think it generous or manly to feel—about the vitriolic series begun by *Blackwood's,* simply because he himself is marked as a future victim of its attack. He begins by describing Bailey's disappointment as "an unlook'd for piece of villainy"; and his way of putting it could also apply to the *Blackwood's* review, with its high moral stance:

> The Stations and Grandeurs of the World have taken it into their heads that they cannot commit themselves towards an inferior in rank—but is not the impertinence from one above to one below more wretchedly mean than from the low to the high? There is something so nauseous in self-willed yawning impudence in the shape of conscience—it sinks the Bishop of Lincoln into a smashed frog putrefying.

But after this, and the mention of Cripps and Haydon, he draws a strong line across the entire width of the page, as if to separate these, at least in his own mind, from what follows. Only then come the remarks about the "flaming" attack begun by *Blackwood's.*

Within the next several weeks we see Keats making a deliberate attempt to take these things in his stride: an attempt not to be "surprised" by them, but rather to expect them, to take them for granted without bitterness, and to preoccupy himself with other matters. When he leaves London in order to try to finish *Endymion,* and learns (November 22) that Bailey has at last received a reply from Haydon—but a very "cutting" one—his remarks are addressed as much to himself as to Bailey: "What occasions the greater part of the World's Quarrels? simply this, two Minds meet and do not understand each other time enough to p[r]event any shock or surprise at the conduct of either party—As soon as I had known Haydon three days I had got enough of his character not to have been surp[r]ised at such a Letter as he has hurt you with." And the statement introduces the first of his profound remarks on the poetic imagination—its humility, its absorption in what is outside—the remarks that begin with the famous statement, "I must say of one thing that has pressed upon me lately and encreased my Humility and capability of submission and that is the truth—Men of Genius are great as certain ethereal Chemicals operating on the Mass of neutral intellect—b[u]t they have not any individuality, any determined Character." [28] And the same day he writes Reynolds, "Why dont you—Now I was going to ask a very silly Question," but then, after a few words, he goes ahead anyway, "Why dont you, as I do, look unconcerned at what may be called more particularly Heart-vexations?"—coldness, hurt feelings, misunderstandings—"They never surprise me—lord! a man should have the fine point of his soul taken off to become fit for this world."

This firm assertion, "They never surprise me," may not be quite true at the moment. During the years at Edmonton and Guy's Hospital, his rapt idealization of the literary life—of everyone who had anything to do with it—had had some time in which to root itself; and just as laurel crowns could then be looked forward to as a fitting climax to "converse high," even someone like Lockhart, had he been encountered at that time, could have been expected to share some qualities with Shakespeare. Moreover, the fortunate year from October 1816 (when he met Hunt and Haydon) through the September at Oxford had been relatively free of disillusions—so free that only surprise could have explained the impatient remark to Bailey, as soon as Keats returned to Hampstead from Oxford, "I am quite disgusted with literary Men and will never know another except Wordsworth." Still, within two months

[28] See Chapter X.

after he tried to tell Reynolds that the "Heart-vexations" that people (even sophisticated people) create for each other "never surprise me," something has really happened or begun to happen. The ideal of "disinterestedness" that had caught him at Oxford was becoming less of a mere abstraction. His own ready empathy and instinctive capacity to get outside himself, challenged by unexpected experiences, were giving body and personal meaning to that ideal.

16

He had been approaching the final thousand lines of *Endymion* without much heart. The rate at which he was writing it was getting progressively slower: more than a thousand lines in the three weeks at Oxford; then, beginning Book IV, three hundred during the three weeks or so after his return; and now, during the first three weeks of November, only two hundred. Winter was fast approaching; and the hope—mentioned at the start of the poem—had been that "no wintry season" would

> See it half finished; but let Autumn bold,
> With universal tinge of sober gold,
> Be all about me when I make an end.

The loose couplet, which he had been using for all his longer poems since he began writing, was becoming vapid to his ear. After *Endymion* he was hardly ever to use it again; and the couplet of *Lamia,* more than a year and a half later, is in deliberate opposition to it. Josiah Conder's remark may well have recurred to him more than once throughout November: that the lines in "Sleep and Poetry" about poets "with a puling infant's force" sawing about "upon a rocking horse" were applicable to him. Of the five hundred lines he had thus far written of Book IV, over a quarter consisted of lyrical, or quasi-lyrical, insertions, written partly as a reaction to the monotony of the form. At the same time he had written two little songs, probably to please Jane and Mariane Reynolds.[29] But they provided no relief; their very triviality shows how preoccupied he was, if not with *Endymion* itself, at least with the need to get it done.

The only answer was to go away again for a few days in order—

---

[29] The song "Think not of it, sweet one," which Woodhouse dated "abt. 11 Nov. 1817," and possibly "Unfelt, unheard, unseen."

as he wrote to Bailey—"to change the Scene—change the Air and give me a spur to wind up my Poem, of which there are wanting 500 Lines." When this was done, there would be a chance to think of the readjustments that had to be made in the months ahead. Though Keats told others, and though he himself liked to think, that Tom was "much improved," he and George could no longer really doubt that Tom had consumption. There had been some thought that Tom might go to Lisbon for a while; but this was abandoned, probably because of the expense. It was decided instead that George and Tom would leave for Teignmouth, in Devonshire, in the middle of December. It might be of some help to Tom to get away from London. Later, when *Endymion* was finished, Keats could join them. Meanwhile George was getting restive. He had not been working. He did not see any possibility of getting ahead in business without some money of his own. The whole matter—as Keats wrote Bailey the following spring—"has weighed very much upon [George], and driven him to scheme and turn over things in his Mind" until he made his decision to emigrate. George was also thinking seriously of marriage.

The valley of Mickleham, a few miles south of London between the villages of Dorking and Leatherhead, was a spot where many attractions converged. It was well known to Hazlitt; and it was probably from Hazlitt's praise, either directly or through Reynolds, that Keats heard of it, and of the inn at Burford Bridge, the Fox and Hounds. Nearby is the little river Mole; and about fifty feet behind the Fox and Hounds (since enlarged and called the Burford Bridge Hotel), Box Hill—named for the box trees that grow on it—rises steeply to a height of almost five hundred feet. Lord Nelson had spent his last night in England there when he was on his way to Portsmouth to board the "Victory" and leave for what proved to be the Battle of Trafalgar. On either Friday, November 21, or more probably the next day, Keats boarded the Portsmouth coach, got off at Burford Bridge, and took a small room at the back of the inn. "I like this place very much," he wrote Reynolds on Saturday evening: "There is Hill & Dale and a little River—I went up Box Hill this Evening after the Moon—you a' seen the Moon—came down—and wrote some lines." [30]

Back in April he had taken his newly bought set of Shakespeare

[30] Possibly, as Miss Lowell argues (I.445–449) the passage on the moon in IV.496–502.

with him when he set off to begin his "test" or "trial." Now, in trying to "wind up" the effort, he instinctively carried at least part of the same amulet. "One of the three Books I have with me," he wrote Reynolds (November 22) , "is Shakespear's Poems: I ne[v]er found so many beauties in the sonnets—they seem to be full of fine things said unintentionally." Most of the letter to Reynolds, in fact, surprisingly duplicates the tone of the one he had written Reynolds (April 17–18) just after arriving at the Isle of Wight. Then, with a sort of breathless exuberance, he had jotted down quotations ("How can I help bringing to your mind the Line— *In the dark backward and abysm of time?*") . The same delight of phrase returns now: "Is this to be borne? Hark ye!"; and he quotes the quatrain from the sonnet beginning "When lofty trees I see barren of leaves." "He has left nothing to be said about nothing or anything: for look at Snails, you know what he says about Snails, you know where he talks about 'cockled snails'—well . . . this is in the Venus and Adonis"; and he quotes the fine stanza beginning: "As the snail, whose tender horns being hit, / Shrinks back into his shelly cave with pain":

> He overwhelms a genuine Lover of Poesy with all manner of abuse, talking about—
> > "a poets rage
> > And stretchèd metre of an antique song"—
>
> Which by the by will be a capital Motto for my Poem—won't it? He speaks too of "Time's antique pen"—and "aprils first born flowers" —and "deaths eternal cold."

To Bailey, either the same evening or earlier in the day, he wrote the long, considered letter we have noticed—speculating about "What occasions the greater part of the World's Quarrels," and applying the ideal of "disinterestedness" to genius and the imagination.[31] His own hope is to avoid self-centeredness at all costs, and to turn with interest and courage to what is outside himself rather than sit back and expect or count on "such a thing as Worldly Happiness to be arrived at, at certain periods of time marked out":

> I scarcely remember counting upon any Happiness—I look not for it if it be not in the present hour—nothing startles me beyond the Moment. The setting sun will always set me to rights—or if a

31 Above, section 15; see also Chapter X.

Sparrow come before my Window I take part in its existince and pick about the Gravel. The first thing that strikes me on hea[r]ing a Misfortune having befalle[n] another is this. "Well it cannot be helped.—he will have the pleasure of trying the resources of his spirit," and I beg now my dear Bailey that hereafter should you observe any thing cold in me not to [p]ut it to the account of heartlessness but abstraction.

So preoccupied were the "resources of his spirit" with the determination to finish *Endymion* that, in the state of "abstraction" that resulted, he wondered whether it was altogether for the good: "I sometimes feel not the influence of a Passion or Affection during a whole week—and so long [as] this continues I begin to suspect myself and the genuiness of my feelings at other times—thinking them a few barren Tragedy-tears."

17

The letters stop. Confining himself most of each day to his small room at the Fox and Hounds, he wrote an average of eighty to eighty-five lines a day. In six days—on Friday, November 28—the five hundred lines and, with them, *Endymion* itself were finished. He did not return at once. He spent another week at Burford Bridge. If he wrote any letters, they have not survived. But he did write a little song of three stanzas. The trees were now bare near the inn where he was staying. The thought of trees had been in his mind since the start of *Endymion* ("trees . . . sprouting a shady boon"), through his obsession with "treeless Margate," to the fertile month at Oxford, where there were "plenty of Trees thank God." Among the lines that kept recurring to him when he came to Burford Bridge were those of Shakespeare's sonnet:

> When lofty trees I see barren of leaves
> Which erst from heat did canopy the herd,
> And Summer's green all girded up in sheaves,
> Borne on the bier with white and bristly beard.

The song he wrote during these otherwise vacant days has an Elizabethan tone, though he took the form of the stanza from Dryden: the sense of regret, of anticlimax, is given a light, tripping meter. But the main interest is in the anticipation of those "happy, happy boughs" on the Grecian urn that "cannot shed" their

leaves—though the imperviousness of the inanimate to the pain
of regret and memory is here treated very differently:

> In drear-nighted December,[32]
> 　Too happy, happy tree,
> Thy branches ne'er remember
> 　Their green felicity:
> The north cannot undo them
> With a sleety whistle through them;
> Nor frozen thawings glue them
> 　From budding at the prime.

So with the brook, the diminutive river Mole, that can be content
with its "crystal fretting" of ice. But the human heart, by contrast,
"writhes"—and the word stands out from the conscious lightness of
the measure—at the irrevocability of the past:

> Ah! would 'twere so with many
> 　A gentle girl and boy!
> But were there ever any
> 　Writhed not at passèd joy?
> The feel of not to feel it,
> When there is none to heal it,
> Nor numbèd sense to steal it,
> 　Was never said in rhyme.

Around December 5 he returned to Hampstead. George and
Tom were getting ready to leave for Devonshire in a few days. He
would himself stay at Hampstead for a while, revising some lines
and making a clean copy of *Endymion* to send to Taylor and
Hessey.

[32] Difficulties in the text, discussed by Colvin (pp. 159–160) and Amy Lowell
(I.531–535) are now resolved by Alvin Whitley (*Harvard Library Bulletin*, V [1951],
116–122).

Negative Capability

FROM THE TIME he set out in April to begin his long poem, Keats had thought of the year's effort as one of plowing and sowing a field from which he hoped to reap a harvest before autumn closed. Though the slow start of the first few weeks had shaken him badly, the summer had been propitious and September bountiful. Yet from September on he had been feeling that the only good he could expect from all this labor was the "fruit of Experience."

By winter some of the gains were becoming apparent, and the next half year was to reveal more. One enormous gain was that any tendency toward paralysis before the empty page was permanently removed. From here until the end he was to compose with a speed few major poets have matched, at least since the time of Dryden. Even the most condensed of his great lyrics a year or so hence were written rapidly; and though they were extensively revised, the revision itself was done with dispatch—often immediately after a line or passage was written and before he began the next.

While learning the value of momentum, he was also learning what not to do—and by an active self-criticism that would have been impossible had he "been nervous about [*Endymion's*] being a perfect piece . . . & trembled over every page," in which case the poem "would not have been written" at all. "The Genius of Poetry must work out its own salvation in a man: It cannot be matured by law & precept, but by sensation and watchfulness—That which is creative must create itself." By this leap "headlong into the Sea," he had learned at first hand "the Soundings, the quicksands, & the rocks," and knew them in a way he could never have done if he had "stayed upon the green shore, and piped a silly pipe, and took tca & comfortable advice." [1]

One of the first results of this active self-criticism and self-

---

1 *Letters*, I.374.

redirection is to be seen in the way in which he swings back from
the dilution of style that the practice of writing verse epistles and
the influence of Hunt's idiom had encouraged and that *Endymion*
greatly increased; and the distinguishing quality of his writing
within less than a year is its massive condensation. Another reaction was his strong dislike henceforth of forcing himself to write
for the mere sake of writing. He could now indulge this, to be
sure, only because *Endymion* was behind him. The helpful habits
gained from that gymnastic exercise were already secured. For the
same reason he was henceforth to feel freer, if a longer poem was
not developing the way he hoped, to leave it unfinished and turn
to something else; and his eagerness to publish subsided until, by
contrast, it almost approached indifference. While copying *Endymion* for the press, he was developing some new "Axioms" for
the writing of poetry, which he describes in a famous letter to his
publisher (February 27), and with a candid admission "how far I
am from their Centre":

> 1st I think Poetry should surprise by a fine excess and not by Sin-
> gularity—it should strike the Reader as a wording of his own highest
> thoughts, and appear almost a Remembrance—2nd Its touches of
> Beauty should never be half way therby making the reader breath-
> less instead of content: the rise, the progress, the setting of imagery
> should like the Sun come natural to him—shine over him and set so-
> berly although in magnificence leaving him in the Luxury of twi-
> light—but it is easier to think what Poetry should be than to write
> it—and this leads me on to another axiom. That if Poetry comes
> not as naturally as the Leaves to a tree it had better not come at all.[2]

[2] The admiring Richard Woodhouse in an undated note (probably late 1819
or 1820) left an account of Keats's method of writing that confirms the last of the
remarks to John Taylor above: "He has repeatedly said in conversn that he never
sits down to write, unless he is full of ideas—and then thoughts come about him in
troops, as tho' soliciting to be accd & he selects—one of his Maxims is that if P[oetry]
does not come naturally, it had better not come at all. the moment he feels any
dearth he discontinues writing & waits for a happier moment. he is generally more
troubled by redundancy than by a poverty of images, & he culls what appears to
him at the time the best.—He never corrects [Woodhouse is not referring to alterations made in the actual process of writing the first draft], unless perhaps a word
here or there shd occur to him as preferable to an expression he has already used—
He is impatient of correcting, & says he would rather burn the piece in question &
write anor or something else—'My judgment, (he says,), is as active while I am actually writing as my imaginn In fact all my faculties are strongly excited, & in their
full play—And shall I afterwards, when my imagination is idle, & the heat in which
I wrote, has gone off, sit down coldly to criticise when in Posson of only one faculty,
what I have written, when almost inspired.'—This fact explains the reason of the
Perfectness, fullness, richness & completion of most that comes from him." (*KC*,
I.128–129.)

He even began to think, within a month or so after finishing *Endymion,* of the desirability of slow development. He was not being sardonic about poor Charles Cripps, the artist he and Bailey were trying to help, when he told Bailey "I have the greater hopes of him because he is so slow in development." The same day (January 23) he wrote his brothers:

> Nothing is finer for the purposes of great productions, than a very gradual ripening of the intellectual powers—As an instance of this—observe—I sat down to read King Lear once again the thing appeared to demand the prologue of a sonnet.

The implication here and in the sonnet, "On Sitting Down to Read King Lear Once Again," [3] is that something has been happening that could actually be called a development, "a very gradual ripening," but not at all what he had been thinking about when he had first outlined his year's project back in the spring. It seemed gradual because it had been so undeliberate; and what began it, as he now looked back, must have been operating subterraneously. He had bought the copy of Shakespeare in order to steel himself for the "test" of *Endymion.* But that constant recourse to Shakespeare—beginning with the trustful commitment, the gift of the engraving of Shakespeare, the "daring" hope that he might view Shakespeare as "Presider" over this adventure—had been proving formative in another development with which *Endymion* itself appeared to have little in common except in what it showed of personal courage and of occasional power of phrase.

Within another two months he himself was beginning to feel that this more general development, rather than *Endymion* itself, had been the primary gain. If the four thousand lines of *Endymion* could serve simply as a "Pioneer"—and he uses it in its older sense of a foot soldier, a digger of trenches—"I ought to be content. I have great reason to be content, for thank God I can read and perhaps understand Shakespeare to his depths." As for his long poem, which he is "anxious" to have "printed that I may forget it and proceed," he feels that he has moved only "into the Go-cart from the leading strings."

[3] See below, Chapter XI, section 9.

2

A few days after Keats returned to Hampstead, George and Tom left for Devonshire in the hope that Tom might profit from the change. Tom was becoming very frail; he was spitting blood; the symptoms were far from reassuring to his brothers. George, despite his restiveness and his feeling that he must get started on a career, was willing once again to take charge of things for a while. Keats himself was by no means eager to leave, though he was expected to join them in time. Some changes certainly had to be made in *Endymion,* and a clean copy prepared.

At the same time, John Reynolds, who had been writing the dramatic reviews for the *Champion,* wanted to go to Exeter just after Christmas for a holiday. He was courting Eliza Drewe, who lived there and whom he eventually married. He was also intending to leave the *Champion* anyway in January. With the encouragement of his friend James Rice, he had begun to study law in November. Rice was getting him a position in the law office of Francis Fladgate, had paid for him the fee of £110, and was later to arrange to take Reynolds into partnership in the law firm of himself and his father. Keats, thought Reynolds, could take his place on the *Champion,* and write a review. Although Keats's knowledge of the theater was limited, he had delighted in what he had the chance to see of it. He had been reading the dramatic criticism of Reynolds' own model, William Hazlitt. Edmund Kean, whose gusto Keats admired, would probably be returning to the stage after an illness of a few weeks. Before Reynolds left for Exeter, Keats, as a trial experiment, brought out a review, "Mr. Kean," in the *Champion* (December 21, 1817), written with the rapid verve, the darting impressionism, of Hazlitt's manner. Then, for the January 4 issue of the *Champion,* after Reynolds had left for Exeter, Keats wrote reviews of the play "Retribution" and a pantomime, "Harlequin's Vision." [4]

George and Tom had been gone about a week when Keats, alone in the upstairs lodgings in Hampstead shortly before Christmas, wrote them one of the most quoted, yet one of the most puz-

4 A review entitled "Richard, Duke of York" (in the December 28 issue of the *Champion*) is commonly ascribed to Keats; but as Leonidas Jones has argued (*Keats-Shelley Journal,* III [1954], 55-65), it was almost certainly written by Reynolds.

zling, of all his letters: quoted—and puzzling—because of the cryp-
tic references to "Beauty" and to "Truth," because of the curious
phrase, "Negative Capability," and because it is felt that Keats is
now at a level of speculation from which he is beginning to
touch on some of the highest functions of poetry.[5]

3

The letter distills the reactions of three months to the dimension of thinking that had opened to him in September. A background that helps to clarify these rapid, condensed remarks is provided by the long letter written to Bailey only a month before,[6]
just after Keats had arrived at Burford Bridge determined to
"wind up" the last five hundred lines of *Endymion*.

For weeks the ideal of "disinterestedness" about which they had
talked at Oxford had eluded his impulsive efforts to apply it to
his own personal experience. Given the complexities, the unpredictable problems even in one month of one life, no simple formula could serve. But perhaps that realization was itself a further
argument for the need of "disinterestedness" and a further indication of the futility, in a universe of uncertainties, of the brief, assertive postures we assume. The result, as he told Bailey, was a
healthful increase in "Humility and the capability of submission."
The significant word is "capability," not "submission." "Negative"
was to be the next word he would apply to the "capability" he had
in mind—"submission" could have very different connotations—
though even "negative" would still be far from adequate. Meanwhile he goes on:

> I am certain of nothing but of the holiness of the Heart's affec-
> tions and the truth of Imagination—What the imagination seizes as
> Beauty must be truth—whether it existed before or not—for I have
> the same Idea of all our Passions as of Love they are all, in their
> sublime, creative of essential Beauty . . . The Imagination may be

[5] Further difficulties are added by the inadequate text (the original is not
known). George took the letter together with others when he left for America.
After his death, when Milnes was seeking materials for his biography, the second
husband of George's wife, John Jeffrey, copied the letter for Milnes, making at least
one deletion. We also know that Jeffrey—quite understandably—was a hasty and
indifferent transcriber: he had no reason to be otherwise, and was gracious in
copying as much as he did for Milnes. The text we have is Jeffrey's transcript. On
the probable date, see I.191, 193.

[6] See above, Chapter IX, sections 15–16.

compared to Adam's dream [*Paradise Lost,* VIII.452–490]—he awoke and found it truth. I am the more zealous in this affair, because I have never yet been able to perceive how any thing can be known for truth by consequitive reasoning—and yet it must be—Can it be that even the greatest Philosopher ever arrived at his goal without putting aside numerous objections—However it may be, O for a Life of Sensations rather than of Thoughts!

Two general premises interweave here. Though they were common enough in the more thoughtful writing of the period, Keats has acquired them partly through self-discovery. Hence, far from being what Whitehead calls "inert ideas," they are invested with possibilities. The first is the premise of all objective idealism: what the human mind itself contributes to what it assumes are direct perceptions of the material world—supplementing, channeling, even helping to create them—is not, as the subjective idealist argues, something imposed completely *ab extra,* something invented or read into nature that is not really there. Instead, this cooperating creativity of the mind has, to use a phrase of Coleridge's, "the same ground with nature": its insights are to this extent a valid and necessary supplement in attaining the reconciliation or union of man and nature that constitutes knowledge. Keats, of course, knew nothing of contemporary German idealism, objective or subjective. He had dipped into a little of Coleridge: Bailey had been reading the *Lay Sermons,* and Keats in early November borrowed the *Sybilline Leaves* from Charles Dilke. But he seems to have caught very little from Coleridge at this point, and associated him a month later with an "irritable reaching after fact and reason" that contrasts with the ideal he is naively but brilliantly evolving throughout the next half year.

It is primarily from Wordsworth that Keats has picked up enough hints to enable him to go ahead with this "favorite Speculation," as he calls it. He was naturally unaware of the massive treatment of man's relation to nature in the *Prelude,* into which Wordsworth was putting so much that he was never satisfied that it was ready for publication. But what Keats had read of Wordsworth he had recently approached in a very different spirit from the way he had been reading poetry the year before. He was quicker to note what he was beginning to call the "philosophical" implications of poetry. By now this speculation about the mind's creativity has become peculiarly his own, and to such an extent that he has begun to toy with the possible antecedence or foreshadowing, through imaginative insight, "of reality to come." The mention of this and of "Adam's dream" introduces

> another favorite Speculation of mine, that we shall enjoy ourselves here after by having what we called happiness on Earth repeated in a finer tone and so repeated—And yet such a fate can only befall those who delight in sensation rather than hunger as you do after Truth—Adam's dream will do here and seems to be a conviction that Imagination and its empyreal reflection is the same as human Life and its spiritual repetition. But as I was saying—the simple imaginative Mind may have its rewards in the repeti[ti]on of its own silent Working coming continually on the spirit with a fine suddenness.

4

The second general premise involves the familiar romantic protest on behalf of concreteness and the conviction that the analytic and logical procedures of what Keats calls "consequitive reasoning" violate the organic process of nature. They abstract from the full concreteness, reduce the living process to static concepts, and substitute an artificial order.

Here again the immediate suggestions have come to Keats from Wordsworth but are further substantiated by what he has been reading of Hazlitt. More than any other literary critic of his day, Hazlitt continued the brilliant psychological tradition of eighteenth-century British empiricism, rephrasing and supplementing a descriptive study of the imagination that had been developing for at least sixty years, and applying it even more suggestively to genius in the arts, especially poetry. The great contribution of English psychological criticism throughout the later eighteenth century had been to describe and justify confidence in the imaginative act—an act whereby sensations, intuitions, and judgments are not necessarily retained in the memory as separate particles of knowledge to be consulted one by one, but can be coalesced and transformed into a readiness of response that is objectively receptive to the concrete process of nature and indeed actively participates in it. This entire approach to the imagination naturally involved a corollary protest against the sort of thing implied in Wordsworth's famous phrase, the "meddling intellect." The protest anticipates Whitehead's remarks on the "fallacy of misplaced concreteness":

abstraction by its very nature fails to conceive the full concreteness; it draws out particular elements for special purposes of thought; and the "misplaced concreteness" comes when these necessary "short-cuts" in thinking—as Hazlitt calls them—are regarded as equivalent to the concrete reality.

Keats had just begun to catch some of the implications of these ideas during his Oxford visit. Hazlitt's *Essay on the Principles of Human Action* had lit up a large zone of possibilities. Its persuasive argument on the possible "disinterestedness" of the mind, and its brilliant treatment of the sympathetic potentialities of the imagination, had especially won him. But it is enough for the moment to point out how quickly it led him to read other works of Hazlitt. Within a few weeks after he wrote this letter to Bailey, he was telling both Haydon and his brothers that "the three things to rejoice at in this Age" were Wordsworth's *Excursion,* Haydon's pictures, and "Hazlitt's depth of Taste." Hazlitt, by now, had completely replaced Hunt in the triumvirate of the year before.

Finally, Hazlitt's constant use of the word "sensations" in the traditional empirical sense—as virtually equivalent to concrete experience—added a new term to Keats's own habitual vocabulary (hence the remark at the moment about the "Life of Sensations": the bookish Bailey, inclining more toward philosophical analysis, "would exist"—says Keats—"partly on sensation partly on thought") . "Consequitive reasoning" applies to the piecemeal, step-by-step procedures of the analytic and selective intelligence.[7] But though Keats himself cannot perceive how truth can be known by this reductive means, and wonders whether the most astute reasoner "ever arrived at his goal without putting aside numerous objections," he is far from pushing the matter, and grants that it "must be" possible.

5

This letter to Bailey, written at Burford Bridge as he begins his determined seven-day effort to complete *Endymion,* has a sequel of its own. For Bailey seems to have been a little disturbed by portions of it—at least by the speculation about an afterlife in which

[7] The word "consequitive" remains in his mind. He soon tells John Taylor, his publisher, and with no derogatory implication, that Taylor, being a "consequitive Man," may think the change in the passage on happiness in *Endymion* a matter "of mere words," rather than "a regular stepping of the Imagination towards a Truth" (I.218) .

the "old Wine of Heaven" may consist of "the redigestion of our most ethereal Musings on Earth," and "what we called happiness on Earth repeated in a finer tone and so repeated." Bailey saw Keats in London in January and may have talked with him about the letter. If not, he certainly wrote to him in some detail, and may have taken some time to do so.

At all events, the matter is picked up again in a letter Keats wrote to him on March 13. This letter gives every indication that Keats has been trying to think over some of the remarks he had made before. What he is most eager to state is that he is not a dogmatist in his skepticism—that he is not, as he thinks, a complete skeptic at all. He wishes he could "enter into" all of Bailey's feelings on the matter, and write something Bailey would like (Keats was too "transparent," said Bailey, ever to be able to hide anything); and if he had appeared to be substituting the poetic imagination for religion as a means of arriving at truth, he is now beginning to have moments of doubt about poetry itself.

Then he turns to what he had been trying to express about the validity of the imagination's own contribution to its perception. Some things, certainly "real," may not require this "greeting of the Spirit" from the human mind or heart. But others—at least "things semireal"—do require that greeting, that contribution, for their fulfillment; and this union of the perceiving mind and the perceived object should not be confused with mere "Nothings" that are solely the product of human desires. He begins:

> You know my ideas about Religion—I do not think myself more in the right than other people and that nothing in this world is proveable. I wish I could enter into all your feelings on the subject merely for one short 10 Minutes and give you a Page or two to your liking. I am sometimes so very sceptical as to think Poetry itself a mere Jack a lanthern to amuse whoever may chance to be struck with its brilliance—As Tradesmen say every thing is worth what it will fetch, so probably every mental pursuit takes its reality and worth from the ardour of the pursuer—being in itself a nothing—Ethereal thing[s] may at least be thus real, divided under three heads—Things real—things semireal—and no things—Things real—such as existences of Sun Moon & Stars and passages of Shakspeare—Things semireal such as Love, the Clouds &c which require a greeting of the Spirit to make them wholly exist—and Nothings which are made Great and dignified by an ardent pursuit—Which by the by stamps the burgundy mark on the bottles of our Minds, insomuch as they are able to "consec[r]ate what'er they look upon."

The theme of much of the greater poetry to come—certainly of the "Ode on a Grecian Urn" and the "Ode to a Nightingale"—may be described as the drama of the human spirit's "greeting" of objects in order "to make them wholly exist"—a drama in which the resolutions are precarious, as in life itself, and the preciousness of the attainment ultimately crossed by tragedy. But for the moment he is unable to go further, and least of all to go further theoretically. In his remarks to Bailey, particularly about the "semi-real" as distinct from "Nothings," he is trying to grope toward a distinction that Locke could not make and that Hume thought it impossible to make. He can end only with a plea for openness, and by recurring to a thought that has been growing on him for some time: that the heart's hunger for settlement, for finality, cannot be answered unless we shut ourselves off from the amplitude of experience, with all its contradictory diversity. All he can do is to proceed honestly and empirically in this adventure of speculation, of openness, and (as he later phrased it) of "straining at particles of light in the midst of a great darkness."

Quite plainly he will "never be a Reasoner"; every point of thought quickly opens some further unexpected vista; and how could he be confident therefore of "the truth of any of my speculations"? His comic sense is suddenly aroused by the ineffectiveness of his discourse, which he burlesques for a moment; and he ends with a characteristic pun.[8]

6

The "Negative Capability" letter is best understood as another phrasing of these thoughts, with at least three further extensions. First, the problem of form or style in art enters more specifically. Second, the ideal toward which he is groping is contrasted more

---

[8] The speculation about "ethereal things"—the division into real, semireal and nothings—"may be carried—but what am I talking of—it is an old maxim of mine and of course must be well known that eve[r]y point of thought is the centre of an intellectual world—the two uppermost thoughts in a Man's mind are the two poles of his World he revolves on them and every thing is southward or northward to him through their means—We take but three steps from feathers to iron. Now my dear fellow I must once for all tell you I have not one Idea of the truth of any of my speculations—I shall never be a Reasoner because I care not to be in the right, when retired from bickering and in a proper philosophical temper—So you must not stare if in any future letter I endeavour to prove that Appollo as he had a cat gut string to his Lyre used a cats' paw as a Pecten—and further from said Pecten's reiterated and continual teasing came the term Hen peck'd."

strongly with the egoistic assertion of one's own identity. Third, the door is further opened to the perception—which he was to develop within the next few months—of the sympathetic potentialities of the imagination.

He begins by telling his brothers that he has gone to see Edmund Kean, has written his review, and is enclosing it for them. Then on Saturday, December 20, he went to see an exhibition of the American painter, Benjamin West, particularly his picture, "Death on the Pale Horse." Keats was altogether receptive to any effort to attain the "sublime," and West's painting had been praised for succeeding. Yet it struck Keats as flat—"there is nothing to be intense upon; no women one feels mad to kiss; no face swelling into reality." Then the first crucial statement appears:

> The excellence of every Art is its intensity, capable of making all disagreeables evaporate, from their being in close relationship with Beauty & Truth—Examine King Lear & you will find this exemplified throughout; but in this picture we have unpleasantness without any momentous depth of speculation excited, in which to bury its repulsiveness.

In the active cooperation or full "greeting" of the experiencing imagination and its object, the nature or "identity" of the object is grasped so vividly that only those associations and qualities that are strictly relevant to the central conception remain. The irrelevant and discordant (the "disagreeables") "evaporate" from this fusion of object and mind. Hence "Truth" and "Beauty" spring simultaneously into being, and also begin to approximate each other. For, on the one hand, the external reality—otherwise overlooked, or at most only sleepily acknowledged, or dissected so that a particular aspect of it may be abstracted for special purposes of argument or thought—has now, as it were, awakened into "Truth": it has been met by that human recognition, fulfilled and extended by that human agreement with reality, which we call "truth." And at the same time, with the irrelevant "evaporated," this dawning into unity is felt as "Beauty." Nor is it a unity solely of the object itself, emerging untrammeled and in its full significance, but a unity also of the human spirit, both within itself and with what was at first outside it. For in this "intensity"—the "excellence," he now feels, "of every Art"—we attain, if only for a while, a harmony of the inner life with truth. It is in this harmony that "Beauty" and "Truth" come together. The "pleasant," in the ordinary sense of the word, has nothing to do with the point being discussed; and to introduce it is only to trivialize the conception of "Beauty." Hence Keats's reference to *Lear*. The reality disclosed may be distressing and even cruel to human nature. But the harmony with truth will remain, and even deepen, to the extent that the emerging reality is being constantly matched at every stage by the "depth of speculation excited"—by the corresponding release and extension, in other words, of human insight. "Examine King Lear and you will find this exemplified throughout."

Hazlitt's short essay "On Gusto" had aroused his thinking about style when he read it at Oxford in the *Round Table;* and what he is saying now is partly the result of what he has assimilated from Hazlitt.[9] By "gusto," Hazlitt means an excitement of the imagination in which the perceptive identification with the object is almost complete, and the living character of the object is caught and shared in its full diversity and given vital expression in art. It is "power or passion defining any object." But the result need not be subjective. By grasping sympathetically the over-all significance of the object, the "power or passion" is able to cooperate, so to speak, with that significance—to go the full distance with its potentialities, omitting the irrelevant (which Keats calls the "disagreeables"), and conceiving the object with its various qualities coalescing into the vital unity that is the object itself. One result is that the attributes or qualities that we glean through our different senses of sight, hearing, touch, and the rest are not presented separately or piecemeal, but "the impression made on one sense excites by affinity those of another." Thus Claude Lorrain's landscapes, though "perfect abstractions of the visible images of things," lack "gusto": "They do not interpret one sense by another . . . That is, his eye wanted imagination; it did not strongly sympathise with his other faculties. He saw the atmosphere, but he did not feel it." Chaucer's descriptions of natural scenery have gusto: they give "the very feeling of the air, the coolness or moisture of the ground." "There is gusto in the colouring of Titian. Not only do his heads seem to think—his bodies seem to feel."

[9] Keats had also read Hazlitt's own essay on Benjamin West in the December issue of the *Edinburgh Review* (*Works,* XVIII [1933], 135–140), where West is censored for lack of "gusto."

7

This interplay and coalescence of impressions was to become a conscious aim in Keats's own poetry within the next six months, and, by the following autumn, to be fulfilled as richly as by any English poet of the last three centuries. Meanwhile, only a few days before he wrote the "Negative Capability" letter to his brothers, he had followed Hazlitt's use of the word "gusto" in his own review "On Edmund Kean as a Shakespearian Actor" (though he later returns to the word "intensity"—"gusto" perhaps suggesting a briskness or bounce of spirit he does not have in mind). He had been trying in this review to describe how "a melodious passage in poetry" may attain a fusion of "both sensual and spiritual," where each extends and declares itself by means of the other:

> The spiritual is felt when the very letters and points of charactered language show like the hieroglyphics of beauty;—the mysterious signs of an immortal free-masonry! . . . To one learned in Shakespearian hieroglyphics,—learned in the spiritual portion of those lines to which Kean adds a sensual grandeur: his tongue must seem to have robbed "the Hybla bees, and left them honeyless."

Hence "there is an indescribable gusto in his voice, by which we feel that the utterer is thinking of the past and future, while speaking of the present." [10]

Keats is here extending the notion of "gusto" in a way that applies prophetically to his own maturer style—to an imaginative "intensity" of conception, that is, in which process, though slowed to an insistent present, is carried in active solution. So with the lines he had quoted a month before to Reynolds as an example of Shakespeare's "intensity of working out conceits":

> When lofty trees I see barren of leaves
> Which erst from heat did canopy the herd,
> And Summer's green all girded up in sheaves,
> Borne on the bier with white and bristly beard.

Previous functions, and the mere fact of loss itself, are a part of the truth of a thing as it now is. The nature of the "lofty trees" in this season, now "barren of leaves," includes the fact that they formerly "from heat did canopy the herd"; nor is it only the dry, completed grain of the autumn that is "girded up in sheaves," but the "Sum-

---

10 Hampstead Keats, V.229–230.

mer's green" that it once was. This entire way of thinking about style is proving congenial to Keats in the highest degree; for though it has independent developments, it has also touched and is giving content to the ideal briefly suggested a year before in "Sleep and Poetry"—even before he saw the Elgin Marbles for the first time: an ideal of poetry as "might half slumb'ring on its own right arm." The delight in energy caught in momentary repose goes back to the idea he had "when a Schoolboy . . . of an heroic painting": "I saw it somewhat sideways," he tells Haydon, "large prominent round and colour'd with magnificence—somewhat like the feel I have of Anthony and Cleopatra. Or of Alcibiades, leaning on his Crimson Couch in his Galley, his broad shoulders imperceptibly heaving with the Sea." So with the line in *Henry VI,* "See how the surly Warwick mans the Wall." [11] One of the comments he wrote in his copy of Milton during the next year gives another illustration:

> Milton in every instance pursues his imagination to the utmost—he is "sagacious of his Quarry," he sees Beauty on the wing, pounces upon it and gorges it to the producing his essential verse. . . . But in no instance is this sort of perseverance more exemplified than in what may be called his *stationing or statu[a]ry.* He is not content with simple description, he must station,—thus here, we not only see how the Birds *"with clang despised the ground,"* but we see them "under *a cloud in prospect."* So we see Adam *"Fair indeed and tall— under a plantane"*—and so we see Satan *"disfigured—on the Assyrian Mount."* [12]

The union of the ideal of dynamic poise, of power kept in reserve, with the ideal of range of implication suggests one principal development in his own style throughout the next year and a half. The very triumph of this union—as triumphs often tend to do— could have proved an embarrassment to later ideals and interests had it become an exclusive stylistic aim. However magnificent the result in the great odes, in portions of *Hyperion,* or in what Keats called the "colouring" and "drapery" of the *Eve of St. Agnes,* it carried liabilities in both pace and variety that would have to be

[11] I.265.
[12] Hampstead Keats, V.303–304. The comment is written next to the passage in *Paradise Lost,* VI.420–423:

> but feather'd soon and fledge
> They summ'd their pens, and, soaring the air sublime,
> With clang despised the ground, under a cloud
> In prospect.

circumvented for successful narrative and, above all, dramatic poetry. But even at the moment, and throughout the next year, what he calls "intensity"—the "greeting of the Spirit" and its object—is by no means completely wedded to a massive centering of image through poise and "stationing." If his instinctive delight in fullness was strengthened in one direction by the Elgin Marbles—which he still made visits to see [13]—other, more varied appeals to his ready empathy were being opened and reinforced by his reading of Shakespeare.

8

The second and longer of the crucial parts of the "Negative Capability" letter is preceded by some more remarks about what he has been doing since his brothers left, and the remarks provide a significant preface. He had dinner—"I have been out too much lately"—with "Horace Smith & met his two Brothers with [Thomas] Hill & [John] Kingston & one [Edward] Du Bois."

Partly because he himself was so direct and—as Bailey said—"transparent," he was ordinarily tolerant of the more innocent affectations by which people hope to establish superiority. Moreover, such affectations appealed to his enormous relish for the idiosyncratic. As the next year passed, the very futility of such brief postures—the pointless intricacy of these doomed stratagems—against the vast backdrop of a universe of constantly unfolding "uncertainties, Mysteries, doubts," was also to take on a pathos for him. In fact, only a month after he tells his brothers about this dinner with Horace Smith and his literary friends, he was to write Bailey, speaking of "Reynolds and Haydon retorting and recriminating—and parting for ever—the same thing has happened between Haydon and Hunt":

> Men should bear with each other—there lives not the Man who may not be cut up, aye hashed to pieces on his weakest side. The best of Men have but a portion of good in them—a kind of spiritual yeast in their frames which creates the ferment of existence—by which a Man is propell'd to act and strive and buffet with Circumstance.[14]

[13] "He went again and again to see the Elgin Marbles," said Severn, "and would sit for an hour or more at a time beside them rapt in revery." One afternoon, as he delighted to tell Severn, a man who apparently knew Keats strolled by and viewed the sculptures "condescendingly through an eye-glass," and at last said, "Yes, I believe, Mr. Keats, we may admire these works safely" (Sharp, p. 32).

[14] I.210.

Even so, during these important transitional months he is entering, moments inevitably occur when the familiar comic sense and the deepening charity are suspended. Affectations particularly bother him at such moments. It is a great pity, as he tells Haydon (March 21), that "people should by associating themselves with the fine[st] things, spoil them—Hunt has damned Hampstead [and] Masks and Sonnets and [I]talian tales—Wordsworth ha[s] damned the lakes," and so on. Hazlitt is "your only good damner," because he damns in a different spirit. And Keats was enormously—almost amusingly—disturbed when Reynolds told him that his self-defensive Preface to *Endymion* savored of "affectation" in its own way. Keats kept protesting that, whatever else it showed, it certainly did not show "affectation," though he at once began anxiously to rewrite it.

So at Horace Smith's dinner, which he describes to George and Tom, where he met five other men of literary interests. Their entire way of talking about literature fatigued him for the moment. The possible uses of literature seemed frozen into posture, into mannerism. Given his attempts to approach his new ideal of "disinterestedness," and the thoughts of "Humility" and of openness to amplitude that had become more specific, even more convinced, within the last few months, the gathering typified the exact opposite of what was wanted:

> They only served to convince me, how superior humour is to wit in respect to enjoyment—These men say things which make one start, without making one feel, they are all alike; their manners are alike; they all know fashionables; they have a mannerism in their very eating & drinking, in their mere handling a Decanter—They talked of Kean & his low company—Would I were with that company instead of yours said I to myself! I know such like acquaintance will never do for me.

But his humor was to return when he found himself again in Kingston's company at Haydon's a week and a half afterwards. The "mannerism" in the "mere handling a Decanter" had caught his fancy as a symbol of the entire evening. At Haydon's, as he gleefully told George and Tom, "I astonished Kingston at supper . . . keeping my two glasses at work in a knowing way."

Shortly after Smith's literary party, he went to the Christmas pantomime at Drury Lane with Charles Brown and Charles Dilke. Walking with them back to Hampstead, he found himself having not a dispute but a disquisition with Dilke, on various subjects; several things dovetailed in my mind, & at once it struck me, what quality went to form a Man of Achievement especially in Literature & which Shakespeare possessed so enormously—I mean *Negative Capability*, that is when man is capable of being in uncertainties, Mysteries, doubts, without any irritable reaching after fact & reason—Coleridge, for instance, would let go by a fine isolated verisimilitude caught from the Penetralium of mystery, from being incapable of remaining content with half knowledge. This pursuèd through Volumes would perhaps take us no further than this, that with a great poet the sense of Beauty overcomes every other consideration, or rather obliterates all consideration.

Using what we know of the background, we could paraphrase these famous sentences as follows. In our life of uncertainties, where no one system or formula can explain everything—where even a word is at best, in Bacon's phrase, a "wager of thought"—what is needed is an imaginative openness of mind and heightened receptivity to reality in its full and diverse concreteness. This, however, involves negating one's own ego. Keats's friend Dilke, as he said later, "was a Man who cannot feel he has a personal identity unless he has made up his Mind about every thing. The only means of strengthening one's intellect is to make up ones mind about nothing—to let the mind be a thoroughfare for all thoughts. . . . Dilke will never come at a truth as long as he lives; because he is always trying at it." [15] To be dissatisfied with such insights as one may attain through this openness, to reject them unless they can be wrenched into a part of a systematic structure of one's own making, is an egoistic assertion of one's own identity. The remark, "without any irritable reaching after fact and reason," is often cited as though the pejorative words are "fact and reason," and as though uncertainties were being preferred for their own sake. But the significant word, of course, is "irritable." We should also stress "capable"—"capable of being in uncertainties, Mysteries, doubts" without the "irritable" need to extend our identities and rationalize our "half knowledge." [16] For a "great poet" especially, a sympathetic absorption in the essential significance of his object (caught and relished in that active cooperation of the mind in

[15] II.213.

[16] The mention of Coleridge's allowing "a fine isolated verisimilitude" to "go by" seems ludicrously inept, though forgivable considering how little Keats had read of him. However much Coleridge yearned for system, he could never attain it simply because he was able to let so little "go by"; and the glory of his critical writing consists in its numerous "isolated verisimilitudes."

which the emerging "Truth" is felt as "Beauty," and in which the harmony of the human imagination and its object is attained) "overcomes every other consideration" (considerations that an "irritable reaching after fact and reason" might otherwise itch to pursue) . Indeed, it goes beyond and "obliterates" the act of "consideration"—of deliberating, analyzing, and piecing experience together through "consequitive reasoning."

9

Such speculations could hardly be called more than a beginning. Taken by themselves they could lead almost anywhere. That, of course, was one of their principal assets. Even so, the need for at least some specific and positive procedures, helpful at any period of life, is particularly pressing at twenty-two. Keats understandably wavered throughout the next few months in trying to interpret whatever premises he had attained thus far—premises that were hardly more than the penumbra of the idea of "disinterestedness" as it touched his concrete experience. Such shadows at least involved extensions of a sort; and the thought of this was to give him some consolation as time passed.

But meanwhile he had moments when something close to mere passivity appealed strongly; and the image of the receptive flower, visited and fertilized by the bee, caught his fancy. The relentless labor of writing *Endymion* was producing a natural reaction. Insights, reconsiderations, "speculations" (to use his own word) overlooked during that huge scurry, were now presenting themselves more abundantly than ever before. Because the gains in having written the poem were becoming assimilated, they were at times almost forgotten. Slow development, maturity, rooted strength, leisure for growth, took on a further attraction. But in the very act of urging eloquently—and justly—the virtues of something not far from Wordsworth's "wise passiveness" the limitations would suddenly disclose themselves to him. He would begin to feel that this was not what he meant, or wanted, at all. At least it was not enough by itself. A letter to John Reynolds (February 19) finely illustrates the course of one "speculation." He starts with a now-favorite thought of his that any one point may serve as a fruitful beginning. A man could "pass a very pleasant life" if he sat down each day and read a certain Page of full Poesy or distilled Prose and let him wander with it, and muse upon it, and reflect from it, and bring home to it, and prophesy upon it, and dream upon it—untill it becomes stale—but when will it do so? Never—When Man has arrived at a certain ripeness in intellect any one grand and spiritual passage serves him as a starting post towards all "the two-and-thirty Pallaces."

The result would be a genuine "voyage of conception." A doze on the sofa, a child's prattle, a strain of music, even "a nap upon Clover," could all engender "ethereal finger-pointings." It would have the impetus, the strength, of being self-directive. "Many have original Minds who do not think it—they are led away by Custom." This insight, substantiated by his own experience, leads him next to turn upside down the old fable of the spider and the bee, especially as Swift used it. The appeal of the spider as a symbol is that the points of leaves and twigs on which it begins its work can be very few, and yet it is able to fill the air with a "circuiting." "Now it appears to me that almost any Man may like the Spider spin from his own inwards his own airy Citadel," which will then be creatively meaningful—it will be "full of Symbols for his spiritual eye." Of course his starting-points, his "circuiting," and the achieved "space for his wandering," would all differ from that of others. If we wish to be militant, complications would result. Here Keats comes to the heart of his thought:

> The Minds of Mortals are so different and bent on such diverse Journeys that it may at first appear impossible for any common taste and fellowship to exist between two or three under these suppositions—It is however quite the contrary—Minds would leave each other in contrary directions, traverse each other in Numberless points, and all [at] last greet each other at the Journeys end—A old Man and a child would talk together and the old Man be led on his Path, and the child left thinking—Man should not dispute or assert but whisper results to his neighbour, and thus by every germ of Spirit sucking the Sap from mould ethereal every human might become great, and Humanity instead of being a wide heath of Furse and Briars with here and there a remote Oak or Pine, would become a grand democracy of Forest Trees.

At no later time would he have disagreed with what he has just said. But he carries the ideal of receptivity further in sentences that are sometimes separated from context and interpreted as a new, fundamental credo:

> It has been an old Comparison for our urging on—the Bee hive—however it seems to me that we should rather be the flower than the

Bee . . . Now it is more noble to sit like Jove tha[n] to fly like Mercury—let us not therefore go hurrying about and collecting honey-bee like, buzzing here and there impatiently from a knowledge of what is to be arrived at: but let us open our leaves like a flower and be passive and receptive—budding patiently under the eye of Apollo and taking hints from every noble insect that favors us with a visit.

In this spirit he has just written the fine unrhymed sonnet, "What the Thrush Said," with its refrain "O fret not after knowledge." He had been "led into these thoughts . . . by the beauty of the morning operating on a sense of Idleness—I have not read any Books—the Morning said I was right—I had no Idea but of the Morning and the Thrush said I was right." [17]

But as soon as he copies the poem for Reynolds, he becomes "sensible all this is a mere sophistication, however it may neighbour to any truths, to excuse my own indolence." There is not much chance of rivaling Jove anyway, and one can consider oneself "very well off as a sort of scullion-Mercury or even a humble Bee." Two days later he also tells his brothers that "The Thrushes are singing"; but he himself is now "reading Voltaire and Gibbon, although I wrote to Reynolds the other day to prove reading was of no use."

10

Wherever the more general implications might lead, he was clearer and more certain in his growing interest in the impersonality of genius, "especially in Literature." For here the ideal of "disinterestedness" directly touched an internal fund both of native gift and (considering his age) accumulated experience.

[17] O thou whose face hath felt the Winter's wind;
Whose eye has seen the Snow clouds hung in Mist
And the black-elm tops 'mong the freezing Stars,
To thee the Spring will be a harvest-time—
O thou whose only book has been the light
Of supreme darkness which thou feddest on
Night after night, when Phoebus was away:
To thee the Spring shall be a triple morn—
O fret not after knowledge—I have none
And yet my song comes native with the warmth.
O fret not after knowledge—I have none
And yet the Evening listens—He who saddens
At thought of Idleness cannot be idle,
And he's awake who thinks himself asleep.

What strikes us most in his capacity for sympathetic identification, starting with the schooldays at Enfield, is its inclusiveness. This is not the volatile empathic range of even the rare actor. For the range is vertical as well as horizontal, and is distinguished more by an adhesive purchase of mind than by volubility. He might, in describing the bearbaiting to Clarke, instinctively begin to imitate not only the spectators but the bear, "dabbing his fore paws hither and thither," and, in diagnosing Clarke's stomach complaint and comparing the stomach to a brood of baby-birds "gaping for sustenance," automatically open his own "capacious mouth." But empathic expressions of this sort were mere side-effects—like the self-forgetful fights at Enfield—of an habitual capacity for identification that went deeper. When he picked up styles in the writing of poetry, it was not as a mimic or copyist but as a fellow participator identified even more with the other's aim and ideal than with the individual himself. If, when still a student at Guy's Hospital, he caught elements of Felton Mathew's style, he dignified them; and the result, poor as it is, transcends anything Mathew wrote. So later with Hunt. Except at the very start, and except for a few isolated passages afterwards, we have nothing of the routine mechanism of a copy. If anything, he brings Hunt more to life. Still later, in *Hyperion,* he was to write within little more than two or three months the only poem among all the Miltonic imitations in English that Milton himself might not have been ashamed to write.

Discussion of these larger manifestations would lead to a summary of his entire development as illustration. We can, however, linger for a moment on his delight in empathic imagery itself. For here, quickly and vividly, his ready sympathy appears long before anyone could have called his attention to such a thing or given him a vocabulary with which to describe it. We think back to Clarke's account of the lines and images that most caught Keats's imagination when they first read together at Enfield. Doubtless feeling the weight of the parting billows on his own shoulders, he *"hoisted himself up, and looked burly and dominant, as he said, 'what an image that is—sea-shouldering whales.'"* Much later there was the memorable introduction to Chapman's Homer, and the passage in the shipwreck of Ulysses that brought "one of his delighted stares": "Down he sank to death. / The sea had soak'd his heart through." His reading of Shakespeare, now that he was about to write with

less sense of hurry, was beginning to encourage his gift for empathic concentration of image; and within two years this was to
develop to a degree hardly rivaled since Shakespeare himself.
Among the passages he excitedly copied out for Reynolds, a month
before the "Negative Capability" letter, is the description of the
trembling withdrawal of a snail into its shell:

> He has left nothing to say about nothing or any thing: for look
> at Snails, you know what he says about Snails, you know where he
> talks about "cockled snails"—well . . . this is in the Venus and
> Adonis: the Simile brought it to my Mind.

> > Audi—As the snail, whose tender horns being hit,
> > Shrinks back into his shelly cave with pain,
> > And there all smothered up in shade doth sit,
> > Long after fearing to put forth again.[18]

So with the comment he later wrote in his copy of *Paradise Lost*
(IX.179–191):

> Satan having entered the Serpent, and inform'd his brutal sense—
> might seem sufficient—but Milton goes on *"but his sleep disturb'd
> not."* Whose spirit does not ache at the smothering and confinement
> —the unwilling stillness—the *"waiting close"?* Whose head is not
> dizzy at the possible speculations of satan in his serpent prison—no
> passage of poetry ever can give a greater pain of suffocation.[19]

Finally, before turning to the impact of Hazlitt, we may glance
back a few months to Severn's account of his walks with Keats on
Hampstead Heath during the preceding summer, while Keats was
still working on Book II of *Endymion*. Nothing could bring him
so quickly out of "one of his fits of seeming gloomful reverie" as
his vivid identification with organic motion in what he called "the
inland sea"—the movement of the wind across a field of grain. He
"would stand, leaning forward," watching with a "serene look in
his eyes and sometimes with a slight smile." At other times, "when
'a wave was billowing through a tree,' as he described the uplifting

---

[18] In a letter to Bailey written the same day is the often-quoted remark, "If a
Sparrow come before my Window I take part in its existence and pick about the
Gravel"—later echoed in the little poem, "Where's the Poet?":

> 'Tis the man who with a bird,
> Wren or eagle, finds his way to
> All its instincts; he hath heard
> The Lion's roaring, and can tell
> What his horny throat expresseth . . .

[19] Hampstead Keats, V.305.

surge of air among swaying masses of chestnut or oak foliage," or when he would hear in the distance "the wind coming across woodlands,"

"The tide! the tide!" he would cry delightedly, and spring on to some stile, or upon the low bough of a wayside tree, and watch the passage of the wind upon the meadow-grasses or young corn, not stirring till the flow of air was all around him.

Severn, who tended rather toward revery and vagueness, was repeatedly "astonished" at the closeness with which Keats would notice details, until Severn himself began to catch a little of it:

Nothing seemed to escape him, the song of a bird and the undernote of response from covert or hedge, the rustle of some animal, the changing of the green and brown lights and furtive shadows, the motions of the wind—just how it took certain tall flowers and plants —and the wayfaring of the clouds: even the features and gestures of passing tramps, the colour of one woman's hair, the smile on one child's face, the furtive animalism below the deceptive humanity in many of the vagrants, even the hats, clothes, shoes, wherever these conveyed the remotest hint as to the real self of the wearer.[20]

Severn's notice of Keats's delight in whatever conveyed "the remotest hint as to the real self of the wearer" carries us forward to the Chaucerian relish of character that we find increasingly in the longer letters and even in the mere underlinings and marginal notes of Keats's reading. "Scenery is fine," he writes to Bailey (March 13, 1818), "but human nature is finer—The Sward is richer for the tread of a real, nervous [E]nglish foot." Reading a month or so later in an old copy (1634) of Mateo Aleman's *The Rogue: or, the Life of Guzman de Alfarache*, which James Rice had just given him, he underlines the words, "his voice lowd and shrill but not very cleere," and writes in the margin: "This puts me in mind of Fielding's Fanny 'whose teeth were white but uneven'; it is the same sort of personality. The great Man in this way is Chaucer."

11

A fairly large internal fund was thus available to be tapped when Keats read, undoubtedly at Bailey's suggestion, Hazlitt's *Essay on*

20 Sharp, p. 20.

the Principles of Human Action, and bought a copy that was still in his library at his death.

Hazlitt's aim in this short book—his first published work—was to refute the contention of Thomas Hobbes and his eighteenth-century followers that self-love, in one way or another, is the mainspring of all human action, and to prove instead, as the subtitle states, "the Natural Disinterestedness of the Human Mind." Since British philosophy for a century had devoted more speculation to this problem than to any other, Hazlitt's youthful aim was quite ambitious (he began the book in his early twenties, and was twenty-seven when it appeared). His procedure was ingenious, and to some extent original. Moralists trying to disprove Hobbes had for fifty years or more been stressing the sympathetic potentialities of the imagination. Adam Smith's influential *Theory of Moral Sentiments* (1759) is the best-known example. The interest spread to the critical theory of the arts; and well over a century before German psychology developed the theory of *Einfühlung*—for which the word "empathy" was later coined as a translation—English critical theory had anticipated many of the insights involved.[21] It was the peculiar fate of many psychological discoveries of the English eighteenth century to be forgotten from the 1830's until the hungry theorization of the German universities in the late nineteenth century led to a rediscovery and a more systematized and subjective interpretation.

In his *Principles of Human Action,* Hazlitt went much further than Adam Smith's *Theory of Moral Sentiments.* His hope was to show that imaginative sympathy was not a mere escape hatch from the prison of egocentricity, but something thoroughgoing, something indigenous and inseparable from all activities of the mind. Sympathetic identification takes place constantly—even if only with ourselves and our own desired future. Hazlitt's psychology, in

[21] A brief discussion of the subject as it applies to eighteenth-century literary criticism may be found in *From Classic to Romantic* (1946) by the present writer, pp. 131–147, 153–156. The theory of *Einfühlung*, developed by Lotze and later the school of Wundt, and treated most fully in the *Ästhetik* (1903–1906) of Theodor Lipps, was more subjective in its premise: it signified less an actual participation in the object—less of an objective coloring of the mind by the object—than the attribution to it of qualities and responses peculiar to the imagination itself. The insight, in other words, though accompanied by the merging of the perceiving mind and the perceived object, is largely the by-product of the working of the imagination, projected upon the object. This restriction of *Einfühlung* is extended even more in the strict interpretation of "empathy"—the English equivalent popularized by Vernon Lee in 1912, and first supplied in 1909 by E. B. Titchener, a pupil of Wundt.

effect, is a more dynamic version of Locke's. Instead of the image of the mind as a *tabula rasa* on which experience writes, we have an image of it as something more actively adhesive and projective: equally dependent on what is outside itself for its own coloration, so to speak, but actively uniting with its objects, growing, dwindling, even becoming poisoned, by what it assimilates. Hazlitt's argument turns on the nature of "identity." Suppose that I love myself in the thoroughgoing way that the Hobbists claim—that everything I do, or plan, or hope, is in order to help myself or avoid pain in the future: that even what we call generous acts are done solely (as the Hobbists maintained) because I wish to be praised, or because I wish to get along with others, or because I wish—at least—to be able to live with myself. But how can I know, how especially can I "love," this "identity" that I consider myself? If we look at the problem with empirical honesty, we have to admit that any feeling we have that we are one person, the same person, from one moment to the next (that we have, in short, an "identity") comes directly through two means only—"sensation" and "memory." A child who has burned his finger knows only through "sensation" that it is he and not someone else who has done so. In a similar way, he knows only through "memory" that it was he and not someone else who had this experience in the past. If our identities until now depend on sensation and memory, what can give me an interest in my future sensations? Sensation and memory are not enough. I can picture my future identity only through my *imagination*. The child who has been burned will dread the prospect of future pain from the fire because, through his imagination, he "projects himself forward into the future, and identifies himself with his future being." His imagination "creates" his own future to him.

In short, I can "abstract myself from my present being and take an interest in my future being [only] in the same sense and manner, in which I can go out of myself entirely and enter into the minds and feelings of others." The capacity for imaginative identification, in other words, is not instinctively or mechanically obliged to turn in one direction rather than another: the sole means by which "I can anticipate future objects, or be interested in them," throwing "me forward as it were into my future being" and anticipating events that do not yet exist, is equally able to "carry me out of myself into the feelings of others by one and the same process . . . I could not love myself, if I were not capable of loving others." If stronger ideas than those of one's own identity are present to the mind, the imagination can turn more easily to them. Hazlitt here develops the belief of the associationist psychologists of the time, in whom he was widely read, that the mind instinctively follows and "imitates" what is before it. He expands the attitude of his old college tutor, Joseph Priestley, though Hazlitt is less of a mechanist than Priestley, and stresses the creative activity of the mind in its sympathetic and projective functions. Following Locke, Priestley had argued that, since the mind, as a *tabula rasa,* is conscious only of "the ideas that are present to it, it must, as it were, *conform* itself to them." In other words, since the mind receives everything from experience alone, it adapts itself to the character of what it receives, and does it

> so instantaneously and mechanically, that no person whatever hath reflection . . . to be upon his guard against some of the most useless and ridiculous effects of it. What person, if he saw another upon a precipice and in danger of falling, could help starting back, . . . as he would do if he himself were going to fall? At least he would have a strong propensity to do it. And what is more common than to see persons in playing at bowls, lean their own bodies, and writhe them into every possible attitude, according to the course they would have their bowl to take? . . . The more vivid are a man's ideas, and the greater is his general sensibility, the more intirely, and with the greater facility, doth he adapt himself to the situations he is viewing.[22]

The argument for "the natural disinterestedness of the mind" is not, of course, that most people are really disinterested, but that there is no mechanical determinism, such as Hobbes and his followers assumed, toward self-love. The disinterestedness exists as far as the *potential* development of the mind is concerned. Knowledge can direct and habituate the imagination to ideas other than that of our own identity. We commonly see that long acquaintance with another increases our sympathy, provided undesirable qualities in the other person, or sheer monotony, do not work against it. If the child is unsympathetic to others, it is not from automatic self-love but because of lack of knowledge—a lack that also prevents him from identifying himself very successfully with his own future interests. Greatness in art, philosophy, moral action—the

[22] *Course of Lectures on Oratory and Criticism* (1777), pp. 126–127.

"heroic" in any sense—involves losing the sense of "our personal identity in some object dearer to us than ourselves."

Hazlitt never developed the psychological implications of his theory much further. A practicing journalist forced to dash off articles and reviews in order to make ends meet, he looked back nostalgically on his *Principles of Human Action* as typical of work he hoped to resume. But the years passed; and the habit of more rapid, less analytic writing became ingrained. His concept of the sympathetic character of the imagination, however, serves as a general premise to much of his literary criticism, especially his writing on Shakespeare. It underlies his conception of the drama as the most objective and therefore the highest form of poetry. It is much in his mind when he turns to the poetry of his own day. Sensing more clairvoyantly than any other English critic of the time the large subjective movement taking place in the arts, of which romanticism constituted the first stage, he feared a growing split between artist and society through the narrowing (even though partly in self-defense) of the artist's sympathies. His harsher criticism of his own contemporaries—including poets as diverse as Wordsworth and Byron—turns on what he feels to be an obtrusion of the poet's personal feelings, interests, defenses, and the danger of losing that "high and permanent interest beyond ourselves" to which art should aim.

12

Less than three weeks after Keats wrote the "Negative Capability" letter to his brothers around Christmastime, Hazlitt began a course of lectures at the Surrey Institution, just south of Blackfriars Bridge, every Tuesday evening at seven o'clock. These were the famous *Lectures on the English Poets,* the first of which was on January 13 and the last on March 3. Keats looked forward to hearing them all, and, as far as we know, missed only one ("On Chaucer and Spenser," January 20), when he arrived too late. A few sentences at the start of the third lecture, "On Shakespeare and Milton" (January 27), which Keats told Bailey he definitely planned to attend, may have especially struck him. Shakespeare, said Hazlitt,

was the least of an egotist that it was possible to be. He was nothing in himself; but he was all that others were, or that they could become. He not only had in himself the germs of every faculty and feeling, but he could follow them by anticipation, intuitively, into all their conceivable ramifications, through every change of fortune, or conflict of passion, or turn of thought. . . . He had only to think of anything in order to become that thing, with all the circumstances belonging to it.

By contrast, much modern poetry seems to have become engaged in a competition to "reduce" itself "to a mere effusion of natural sensibility," surrounding "the meanest objects with the morbid feelings and devouring egotism of the writers' own minds."

The immediate effect of Hazlitt's lectures was to open Keats's eyes much sooner than would otherwise have happened to the limitations of the prevailing modes of poetry—limitations that were far from obvious to most writers until a full century had run its course.[23] But the ideal of the "characterless" poet, touching as it did qualities and habits of response intrinsic to himself, gradually took a secure hold of his imagination throughout the months ahead, though still later it was to appear to him as something of an oversimplification. The extent to which it became domesticated in his habitual thinking is shown by a letter the following autumn, at the beginning of the astonishing year (October 1818 to October 1819) when his greatest poetry was written. He is writing to Richard Woodhouse (October 27):

As to the poetical Character itself, (I mean that sort of which, if I am anything, I am a Member; that sort distinguished from the wordsworthian or egotistical sublime; which is a thing per se and stands alone) it is not itself—it has no self—it is everything and nothing—It has no character—it enjoys light and shade; it lives in gusto, be it foul or fair, high or low, rich or poor, mean or elevated—It has as much delight in conceiving an Iago as an Imogen. What shocks the virtuous philosop[h]er, delights the camelion Poet. It does no harm from its relish of the dark side of things any more than from its taste for the bright one; because they both end in speculation. A Poet is the most unpoetical of any thing in existence; because he has no Identity—he is continually in for—and filling some other Body— The Sun, the Moon, the Sea and Men and Women who are creatures of impulse are poetical and have about them an unchangeable attribute—the poet has none; no identity—he is certainly the most unpoetical of all God's Creatures. . . . When I am in a room with People if I ever am free from speculating on creations of my own brain, then not myself goes home to myself: but the identity of every

23 See below, Chapter XIII, section 16.

one in the room begins to press upon me [so] that I am in a very little time annihilated—not only among Men; it would be the same in
a Nursery of children.

Woodhouse, who by now had acquired a close knowledge of Keats,
found these remarks a good description of Keats's own bent of
mind, and wrote to John Taylor,

> I believe him to be right with regard to his own Poetical Charac-
> ter—And I perceive clearly the distinction between himself & those
> of the Wordsworth School. . . . The highest order of Poet will not
> only possess all the above powers but will have [so] high an imag^n
> that he will be able to throw his own soul into any object he sees or
> imagines, so as to see feel be sensible of, & express, all that the ob-
> ject itself wo^d see feel be sensible of or express—& he will speak out
> of that object—so that his own self will with the Exception of the
> Mechanical part be "annihilated."—and it is [of] the excess of this
> power that I suppose Keats to speak, when he says he has no iden-
> tity—As a poet, and when the fit is upon him, this is true. . . .
> Shakesp^r was a poet of the kind above ment^d—and he was perhaps
> the only one besides Keats who possessed this power in an extr^y
> degree.

Keats had talked with Woodhouse about the subject before, and
had thrown himself into it with the fanciful exuberance he found
irresistible when he was among serious people. For Woodhouse
adds the comment noticed earlier: "He has affirmed that he can
conceive of a billiard Ball that it may have a sense of delight from
its own roundness, smoothness volubility & the rapidity of its
motion." [24]

13

We have been anticipating, of course: the implications of the
"Negative Capability" letter have encouraged us to look ahead a
few months. Back in December, as he felt himself emerging onto
this new plateau of thinking, the memory of *King Lear* kept recurring. When he had begun *Endymion* at the Isle of Wight, it was
the sea—remembered from the cliff near Margate the summer before (1816) —that had led him to return to the play on this second
venture: "the passage . . . 'Do you not hear the Sea?' has haunted
me intensely." Now that *Endymion* was finished, and a third ven-

---

[24] *KC*, I.57–60. When he was preparing to leave Margate for Canterbury, after
beginning *Endymion*, he hoped "the Remembrance of Chaucer will set me forward
like a Billiard-Ball" (I.147) .

ture or transition lay ahead, he was remembering the play somewhat differently. It was probably in December, certainly by early
January, that he bought a copy of Hazlitt's *Characters of Shakespear's Plays* (published late in 1817). With only one exception,
all his underscorings and marginal comments are concentrated in
the chapter on *Lear*.[25] They provide in their own way a further
gloss to that "intensity" of conception—that identification and
"greeting of the Spirit"—of which he had been thinking when he
wrote to George and Tom ("Examine King Lear & you will find
this exemplified throughout"): an identification especially prized
when—as Hazlitt said in a passage Keats underlines—"the extrem-
est resources of the imagination are called in to lay open the deepest movements of the heart." "The greatest strength of genius,"
said Hazlitt, "is shown in describing the strongest passions: for the
power of the imagination, in works of invention, must be in proportion to the force of the natural impressions, which are the subject of them." Double-scoring this in the margin, Keats writes:

> If we compare the Passions to different tuns and hogsheads of
> wine in a vast cellar—thus it is—the poet by one cup should know
> the scope of any particular wine without getting intoxicated—this is
> the highest exertion of Power, and the next step is to paint from
> memory of gone self storms.

And beside another passage he draws a line, underscoring the itali-
cized words, and writes "This passage has to a great degree hiero-
glyphic visioning":

> We see the ebb and flow of the feeling, its pauses and feverish
> starts, its impatience of opposition, its accumulating force when it
> has time to recollect itself, *the manner in which it avails itself of
> every passing word or gesture, its haste to repel insinuation, the al-
> ternate contraction and dilatation of the soul.*

Endymion, which he began to copy and correct for the press during the first week of January, seemed remote indeed from the
thoughts that now preoccupied him. So in fact did romances generally, though he was to write two more (*Isabella* and the *Eve of
St. Agnes*). On Thursday, January 22, he finished copying the first
book of *Endymion;* and then, as he told his brothers the next day,
"I sat down . . . to read King Lear once again the thing appeared

---

[25] Harvard Keats Collection. Marked passages and comments are printed in
Lowell, II.587–590, and Hampstead Keats, V.280–286.

to demand the prologue of a Sonnet, I wrote it & began to read."
It is hardly one of his best sonnets—he never even bothered to publish it—but the occasion meant something to him. For he was approaching the play with a new understanding of how much lay beyond the "old oak Forest" of "Romance." [26]

It was only another beginning, and it would have to proceed
much more slowly than the other beginnings. But he was prepared, he thought, for "a very gradual ripening of the intellectual
powers"; and all he can say now is that "I think a little change has
taken place in my intellect lately." Then he turns to the sonnet,
copies it out for George and Tom, and adds: "So you see I am getting at it, with a sort of determination & strength, though verily I
do not feel it at this moment—this is my fourth letter this morning
& I feel rather tired & my head rather swimming."

[26] See below, Chapter XI, section 9.

Another Beginning

→☺→→☺→*→☺→*→☺→*→☺→*→☺→*→☺→*→☺→*→☺→*→☺→*→☺→*→☺

December and January, 1817–18

IN EARLY DECEMBER Wordsworth was in town for a visit of several weeks. He was staying with his brother Christopher at the rectory in Lambeth, and spending a few days now and then at the home of his wife's cousin, Thomas Monkhouse, in Cavendish Square.

Haydon, eager to introduce Keats to the man they both regarded as the greatest poet of the day, relayed the news to Keats, himself just returned (on December 5) from the inn at Burford Bridge where he had gone to "wind up" *Endymion*. The "reverence" Keats felt for Wordsworth the year before (when the thought of Haydon's sending along the sonnet, "Great spirits now on earth," had put him "out of breath") had deepened. He could even become excited when he "met a friend," as he wrote Haydon in August, "who had seen Wordsworth's House the other Week." In September, at Oxford, he would quote to Bailey from the great Immortality ode, and the two would talk frequently of Wordsworth, of whom Bailey thought more highly than any other poet since Milton. Wordsworth's high-mindedness had always made him seem a being apart. Now that Keats was seeing more of the literary world, the contrast appeared greater. Distressed after his return from Oxford by the quarreling and petty jealousies he encountered, he had told Bailey, in a moment of fatigue, that he was "disgusted with literary Men and will never know another except Wordsworth." Now the opportunity to know Wordsworth had come. Haydon sent a note to Thomas Monkhouse:

> Will Mr. Wordsworth be at home tomorrow morning at Lambeth as Keats is down and very anxious to see him—or will he do you think be so occupied with business as not to be able for a few minutes to see us.[1]

---

[1] The undated note (printed by T. O. Mabbott, *Notes and Queries*, CLXXX [1941], 328) may well have been sent and the visit itself made before George and

2

Wordsworth, who was now forty-seven, was never in the best of moods when he came to London: crowds and cities sapped his optimism about human nature. This month he was particularly grumpy, to judge from the diary of Crabb Robinson, who saw much of him. He was chafing, thought Robinson (December 4), at Coleridge's criticism of him in the *Biographia Literaria*: the criticism was generous, but some of it touched Wordsworth where he was least certain of himself. By December 27, at a dinner at Charles Lamb's, the admiring Robinson finally admitted that he was "for the first time in my life not pleased with Wordsworth, and Coleridge appeared to advantage in his presence. Coleridge spoke of painting in that style of mysticism which is now his habit of feeling. Wordsworth met this by dry, unfeeling contradition."

Monkhouse gladly arranged a visit at his own house. As they walked toward Cavendish Square, Keats kept expressing, said Haydon, "the greatest, the purest, the most unalloyed pleasure at the prospect." When they arrived,

> Wordsworth received him kindly, & after a few minutes, Wordsworth asked him what he had been lately doing, I said he has just finished an exquisite ode to Pan—and as he had not a copy I begged Keats to repeat it—which he did in his usual half chant, (most touching) walking up & down the room—when he had done I felt really, as if I had heard a young Apollo—Wordsworth drily said
>
> > "a Very pretty piece of Paganism"—
>
> This was unfeeling, & unworthy of his high Genius to a young Worshipper like Keats—& Keats felt it *deeply*.[2]

Wordsworth's scorn of disguising anything and his obstinacy in stating exactly what he thought, even if it showed his own egocentricity, were as well known to Haydon as to his other friends. But Haydon was unprepared for this remark. He had doubtless thought that the "Hymn to Pan" in *Endymion* would please Wordsworth since its use of myth derived largely from Wordsworth himself.

Tom left for Devonshire. For in the detailed account he gives them of all his actions and of the people he sees after they leave, he makes no mention of the first interview with Wordsworth. There is the possibility that he felt too much hurt or embarrassed by what happened to feel like mentioning it, at least at the time. But his intimacy with his brothers was without inhibition; and he did not feel too chagrined to talk to Clarke about the incident.

2 *KC*, II.143–145.

Haydon's account, though written twenty-eight years later, is still sharp. As devoutly orthodox as Wordsworth, he still felt it to have been

> nonsense of Wordsworth to take it as a bit of Paganism for the Time, the Poet ought to have been a Pagan for the time—and if Wordsworth's puling Christian feelings were annoyed—it was rather ill-bred to hurt a youth, at such a moment when he actually trembled, like the String of a Lyre, when it has been touched.

Hunt, Clarke, and Joseph Severn, none of whom was present, all gave their own accounts. It was Hunt's version in his *Lord Byron and Some of His Contemporaries* (1828)—stating that the incident took place at Haydon's famous dinner party on December 28—that provoked Haydon to write the account just quoted.[3] Clarke, often confused about dates but otherwise reliable, remembered Keats's telling him of two other incidents, which Clarke associated with this first meeting but which probably took place later:

> Someone having observed that the next Waverley novel was to be "Rob Roy," Wordsworth took down his volume of Ballads, and read to the company "Rob Roy's Grave;" then, returning it to the shelf, observed, "I do not know what more Mr. Scott can have to say upon the subject." [4]
>
> [Wordsworth] was dilating upon some question in poetry, when, upon Keats's insinuating a confirmatory suggestion to his argument, Mrs. Wordsworth put her hand upon his arm, saying—"Mr. Wordsworth is never interrupted." [5]

Severn, with no one to contradict him, gave an elaborate account, pretending he himself was present at the time. He may indeed have met Wordsworth in Keats's and Haydon's company, and Words-worth's attempt at a joke, which is beyond Severn's gift for invention, may actually have been made at the time (or Severn may have heard it from someone else, possibly even from Keats). But Hunt, whom he brings into the story, was not present, and in fact, after Haydon had introduced him to Wordsworth in 1815, did not meet Wordsworth again for thirty years. It was in Haydon's house, said Severn that,

---

[3] Haydon sent it to Edward Moxon, Milnes's publisher, for Milnes to use in his biography. But the letter was mislaid; Haydon was dead within another seven months; and Milnes followed Hunt's version.

[4] *Recollections,* pp. 149–150.

[5] "Recollections of Keats," *Atlantic Monthly,* January 1861.

in the company of Keats, I first met the famous poet Wordsworth; when, also, were present Leigh Hunt and Reynolds. The burden of conversation was the fashion of a vegetable diet, which was then pursued by many, led on by the poet Shelley—enthusiasts who had persevered for some time, to the injury of their constitutions . . . Leigh Hunt most eloquently discussed the charms and advantages of these vegetable banquets, depicting in glowing words the cauliflowers swimming in melted butter, and the peas and beans never profaned with animal gravy. In the midst of this rhapsody he was interrupted by the venerable Wordsworth . . . "If," he said, "by chance of good luck they ever met with a caterpillar, they thanked their stars for the delicious morsel of animal food" . . . It was on this occasion that Keats was requested by Haydon to recite his classical Ode to Pan from his unfinished poem "Endymion;" which he forthwith gave with natural eloquence and great pathos. When he had finished, we all looked in silence to Wordsworth for praise of the young poet. After a moment's pause, he coolly remarked, "A very pretty piece of Paganism," and with this cold water thrown upon us we all broke up.[6]

3

If Keats was wounded, as Haydon says he was, he kept it to himself. He may have been more surprised than hurt. The remark could hardly be considered a crushing blow; and it could have been pronounced in different ways—Wordsworth may have stressed "very," or "pretty," or both, rather than "paganism." Moreover, when Keats arrived, Wordsworth "received him kindly," and we can be confident, despite Severn, that the interview did not end immediately after Wordsworth's comment. Expressions of outrage would otherwise have appeared in Haydon's *Diary;* and the meetings that followed, which seem to have been congenial enough, would have been difficult if not impossible.

Keats in retrospect may even have found the remark an amusing revelation of character, without personal application to himself. The two other incidents he mentioned to Clarke ("I do not know what more Mr. Scott can have to say upon the subject" and "Mr. Wordsworth is never interrupted") suggest the amused relish in the idiosyncratic that we find increasingly in the letters. We may dismiss the belief that Keats's admiration for Wordsworth's poetry was altered. He does express reservations about it, of course, but mainly in contrast with Shakespearean impersonality and "dis-

[6] Sharp, p. 33.

interestedness." If there is an edge to his remarks that would have been absent had he not known Wordsworth personally, his brilliant perception of Wordsworth's profundity and of the fundamental advance Wordsworth had given to poetry amply compensate. The halo may have slipped from Wordsworth as an individual (and not because of this one episode but rather because of the cumulative impression left by several meetings) ; yet Keats was rapidly becoming mature enough to take this in his stride. The letters throughout the following month or two—letters that continue to explore the vein opened by the remarks on "Negative Capability"—are filled with the recognition that, though "the Minds of Mortals are so different and bent on such diverse Journeys," they can still "traverse each other in Numberless points, and at last greet each other at the Journey's end"; that "Man should not dispute or assert but whisper results to his neighbour." If such observations could have been partly prompted by the contrast of Wordsworth's example, they could also be applied to one's own reactions, including reactions to Wordsworth. "Men should bear with each other," he said to Bailey (January 23) ; "there lives not the man who may not be cut up, aye hashed to pieces on his weakest side. The best of men have but a portion of good in them—a kind of spiritual yeast in their frames which creates the ferment of existence."

4

Haydon, back in 1815, had taken a life mask of Wordsworth to guide him in the portrait he planned to include in "Christ's Entry into Jerusalem." He now used the chance to go ahead with the portrait, since Wordsworth's visits to London were rare. During one of the days spent at Haydon's studio (December 22) , Wordsworth read the whole of Book IV of the *Excursion* "in his finest manner" while Haydon worked on the painting. That evening, in his *Diary*, Haydon speculated at some length on Wordsworth as a moral and psychological poet, and contrasted him with Shakespeare. The beginning of what he says parallels remarks Keats himself was to make in the coming months:

> Wordsworth's great power is an intense perception of human feel-
> ings regarding the mystery of things by analyzing his own, Shake-

speare's an intense power of laying open the heart & mind of man by analyzing the feelings of others acting on themselves.[7]

Haydon was meanwhile planning a dinner party, also to take place in his studio, on Sunday, December 28. There would be five guests: Wordsworth, Thomas Monkhouse, Charles Lamb, Keats, and Reynolds (who, however, could not come). Hunt was deliberately omitted. Others were to drop in afterwards: John Landseer, the painter, whose three sons (one of them Edwin Landseer) Haydon had taken as pupils; a young surgeon, Joseph Ritchie, who was planning to leave soon for Africa; and John Kingston—the Kingston who had been present at Horace Smith's "literary" dinner, where everyone talked of "fashionables." Kingston, who was Deputy Comptroller of Stamps, had called on Haydon the same morning: "He said he knew my friends, had an enthusiasm for Wordsworth, and begged I would procure him the happiness of an introduction." Wordsworth since 1813 had held the lucrative position of Distributor of Stamps for Westmorland: a clerk looked after the accounts, and incidentally helped Wordsworth with his gardening. Kingston, as Deputy Comptroller, had corresponded with Wordsworth on business, but would now like to see Wordsworth in his other role. Haydon "thought it a liberty," but told him of the party that evening and asked him to come. Keats, in mentioning the dinner to his brothers, speaks of Joseph Ritchie, the young surgeon turned African explorer, whom Tom had met in Paris in September: "he is going to Fezan in Africa there to proceed if possible like Mungo Park—he was very polite to me and enquired very particularly after you." Ritchie, who was being sent by the government to find a new route to the Niger but died in Fezzan (November 1819) before achieving his object, had read some of Keats's poetry, was impressed by him now, and during the following year wrote to a friend that he thought Keats might well prove to be "the great poetical luminary of the age to come." Besides Ritchie, said Keats, "there was Wordsworth, Lamb, Monkhouse, Landseer, Kingston and your humble Sarvant. Lamb got tipsey and blew up Kingston—proceeding so far as to take the Candle across the Room hold it to his face and show us wh-a-at-sort-fellow he waas."

Haydon's vivid account of the "immortal dinner," however well known, can only be quoted again:

[7] *Diary*, II.171.

On 28th December, the immortal dinner came off in my painting-room, with "Jerusalem" towering up behind us as a background. Wordsworth was in fine cue, and we had a glorious set-to—on Homer, Shakespeare, Milton, and Virgil. Lamb got exceedingly merry, and exquisitely witty; and his fun in the midst of Wordsworth's solemn intonations of oratory was like the sarcasm and wit of the fool in the intervals of Lear's passion. Lamb soon got delightfully merry. He made a speech and voted me absent, and made them drink my health. "Now," said Lamb, "you old lake poet, you rascally poet, why do you call Voltaire dull?" We all defended Wordsworth, and affirmed there was a state of mind when Voltaire would be dull. "Well," said Lamb, "here's Voltaire—the Messiah of the French nation, and a very proper one too."

He then, in a strain of humour beyond description, abused me for putting Newton's head into my picture—"a fellow," said he, "who believed nothing unless it was as clear as the three sides of a triangle." And then he and Keats agreed he had destroyed all the poetry of the rainbow, by reducing it to the prismatic colours. It was impossible to resist him, and we all drank "Newton's health, and confusion to mathematics." It was delightful to see the good-humour of Wordsworth in giving in to all our frolics without affectation, and laughing as heartily as the best of us.

Then Ritchie appeared, and Haydon introduced him as "a gentleman going to Africa." Lamb, now lost in his thoughts, took no notice for a while, and then suddenly "roared out, 'Which is the gentleman we are going to lose?' We then drank the victim's health, in which Ritchie joined." As they now moved out to the other room, they found Kingston waiting in dignity for his introduction. Lamb quickly took a dislike to him ("I had an instinct," he said later, "that he was the head of an office. I hate all such people"). Finding the company far more spirited than he had expected, Kingston began to address the quieter Wordsworth, who was not, however, an easy person to draw out; and seeking something uncontroversial, said to him, after a while,

"Don't you think, sir, Milton was a great genius?" Keats looked at me, Wordsworth looked at the comptroller. Lamb, who was dozing by the fire, turned round and said, "Pray, sir, did you say Milton was a great genius?" "No, sir, I asked Mr. Wordsworth if he were not." "Oh," said Lamb, "then you are a silly fellow." "Charles, my dear Charles," said Wordsworth; but Lamb, perfectly innocent of the confusion he had created, was off again by the fire.

After an awful pause the comptroller said, "Don't you think Newton a great genius?" I could not stand it any longer. Keats put his head into my books. Ritchie squeezed in a laugh. Wordsworth seemed asking himself, "Who is this?" Lamb got up, and, taking a candle, said, "Sir, will you allow me to look at your phrenological development?" He then turned his back on the poor man, and at every question of the comptroller he chaunted:

> "Diddle diddle dumpling, my son John
> Went to bed with his breeches on."

The man in office, finding Wordsworth did not know who he was, said in a spasmodic and half-chuckling anticipation of assured victory, "I have had the honour of some correspondence with you, Mr. Wordsworth." "With me, sir?" said Wordsworth. "Not that I remember." "Don't you, sir? I am a comptroller of stamps." There was a dead silence; the comptroller evidently thinking that was enough. While we were waiting for Wordsworth's reply, Lamb sung out:

> "Hey diddle diddle,
> The cat and the fiddle."

"My dear Charles," said Wordsworth.

> "Diddle diddle dumpling, my son John,"

chaunted Lamb; and then rising, exclaimed, "Do let me have another look at that gentleman's organs." Keats and I hurried Lamb into the painting-room, shut the door, and gave way to inextinguishable laughter. Monkhouse followed, and tried to get Lamb away. We went back, but the comptroller was irreconcilable.

Throughout the whole performance, Haydon said in his *Diary*, Landseer—who was very deaf—sat astonished, "& with his hand to his ear & his eye was trying to catch the meaning of the gestures he saw." Kingston, despite his pomposity, was by no means as bad a person as Keats thought. The gathering of wits at Horace Smith's party had so disturbed and fatigued Keats that his reaction extended indiscriminately to everyone there except Smith, whom he had known and liked for some time. Kingston's affectations were mainly social, not literary, and he appears to have been empty rather than malicious. Most of the company tried now to soothe him, while sounds of Lamb's struggles kept coming from the painting room. Haydon asked Kingston to remain for supper. "He stayed, though his dignity was sorely affected. However, being a good-natured man, we parted all in good humour, and no ill-effects followed."

Wordsworth's fine intonation as he quoted Milton and Virgil, Keats' eager inspired look, Lamb's quaint sparkle of lambent humour, so speeded the stream of conversation, that in my life I never passed a more delightful time. All our fun was within bounds. Not a word passed that an apostle might not have listened to. It was a night worthy of the Elizabethan age, and my solemn "Jerusalem" flashing up by the flame of the fire, with Christ hanging over us like a vision, all made up a picture which will long glow upon

> that inward eye
> Which is the bliss of solitude.

Keats made Ritchie promise he would carry his "Endymion" to the great desert of Sahara, and fling it in the midst.

Poor Ritchie went to Africa, and died, as Lamb foresaw, in 1819. Keats died in 1821, at Rome. C. Lamb is gone, joking to the last. Monkhouse is dead, and Wordsworth and I are the only two now living (1841) of that glorious party.[8]

Haydon's dinner party broke the ice, if any ice needed to be broken. Three days later Keats met Wordsworth walking on Hampstead Heath. Either then or shortly afterwards, Wordsworth asked him to dinner on Monday, January 5, at the home of Thomas Monkhouse, where he was now staying. Kingston meanwhile extended an invitation to both Wordsworth and Keats for January 3. Keats turned it down. But Wordsworth paid his respects to officialdom not only by going but by dressing up for the occasion. Keats called on him "before he went to Kingston's and was surp[r]ised to find him with a stiff Collar. I saw his Spouse and I think his daughter" (probably his sister-in-law, Sara Hutchinson, since Wordsworth's daughter had remained home). This may have been the occasion when Mrs. Wordsworth told Keats that "Mr. Wordsworth is never interrupted." At some point he also met Dorothy Wordsworth; for he later refers to Wordsworth's "beautiful wife and his enchanting Sister." By January 10, he had "seen Wordsworth frequently." Afterwards the visits declined. In fact no one seemed to see much of Wordsworth during the remaining week and a half that he spent in London. Keats later told Haydon that it has "been a mystery to me how and when Wordsworth went." Apparently he "went rather huff'd out of Town—I am sorry for it. He cannot expect but that every Man of worth is as proud as himself." Certainly the disappointed impression left on many people—as Keats justifiably told his brothers—was one of "egotism" and "vanity" ("yet he is a great Poet," and his *Excursion* is one of the "three things to rejoice at in this Age"). But Words-

---

8 *Autobiography*, pp. 231–233; *Diary*, II.173–176.

worth was unaware of such impressions, and was far from "huff'd." He was preoccupied with his own affairs. For one thing, since he held the position of Distributor of Stamps, his accounts were due early in January; and they were not ready. Keats might think it beneath Wordsworth to dine at Kingston's, "stiff Collar" and all. But the new acquaintance with Kingston had its advantages. Wordsworth shortly afterwards dropped around to the stamp office to explain that it was inconvenient for him to leave London at once, and he was told by Kingston's clerk that the accounts could be submitted by January 31. He then returned in time to prepare them. By sheer ill luck, the parcel containing them was then mislaid by the proprietor of the Kendal coach and lost for several days. A letter came from the Stamp Office rapping Wordsworth's knuckles for the inconvenience he was causing the department. Grateful now for the accident of having met Kingston, Wordsworth wrote directly to him (February 2), asking him to explain the situation "to the Board, so that I may stand free of any charge of negligence or inattention."

5

While seeing Wordsworth, Keats was also leading a more active social life than he had ever done before. Exhausted from the eight months of writing *Endymion,* he was hardly prepared to begin anything new at the moment. Moreover, with George and Tom away, the upstairs lodgings at Bentley's seemed bleak and lonely.

From December 17, when he attended Horace Smith's dinner party, until January 22, when he wrote his sonnet on rereading *King Lear,* after which he started to write again, twenty-six of the thirty-seven days (to judge merely by what we can piece together from his letters) were filled with social engagements. He spent evenings with Charles Wells and James Rice and Charles Dilke. He attended the theater at least four times. At Drury Lane he met Lamb and William Godwin; and at Covent Garden he went back into the sidings and "had a good deal of curious chat" about actors and acting with "Bob" Harris (presumably the elderly manager, Thomas Harris). He went to a ball given by a man named Redhall on January 3, and to two other dances, one at the London Coffee House and one given by the Dilkes. He describes Redhall graphically to George a year later. A tiny man, with an "innocent, powdered upright head; he lisps with a protruded under lip—he has two Neices each one would weigh three of him." Redhall at his gatherings supplied inexhaustible wine. Even for a mere supper, bottles were ranged "all up the kitchen and cellar stairs." Keats, on this first visit, found himself drinking rather heavily. Between dinner and the dance, while the ladies were absent, the talk turned to bawdy puns, though there were present "two parsons" and also Benjamin Bailey, who was in town for the holidays and who "seemed to enjoy the evening." The day after Redhall's dance, Charles Wells and Joseph Severn dined with Keats, and he

> pitched upon another bottle of claret—Port—we enjoyed ourselves very much were all very witty and full of Rhyme—we played a Concert [in which each took the part of an instrument, with Keats as the bassoon] . . . I said on that day the only good thing I was ever guilty of . . . I wondered that careful folks would go [to the one-shilling gallery] for although it was but a Shilling still you had to pay through the Nose.

The next day, January 5, was again typically crowded. Though the weather was so bad that he was tempted to stay indoors, and though this active social life was beginning to wear on his health, he went to town in the morning and called on the surgeon, Solomon Sawrey, in order to talk about Tom, who had been spitting blood. Sawrey reassured Keats and asked that Tom send him a careful account of the symptoms. Keats then walked over to the Featherstone Buildings in Holborn and called on Charles Wells. While there he began a long letter to his brothers, then went off to have dinner with Wordsworth and Monkhouse in Mortimer Street, and afterwards returned to Holborn to have supper with Wells. He also tells George and Tom about a card-playing club that gathered every Saturday evening in James Rice's place at 50 Poland Street. The youthful club had "a little Cant" all of its own constructed of Regency slang and Shakespearean allusions ("they call dr[i]nking deep dying scarlet . . . they call good Wine a pretty tipple, and call getting a Child knocking out an apple, stopping at a tave[r]n they call hanging out," and so on).

By January 10 he could justly say that he had "been racketing too much, & do not feel over well." But he still continued to go out frequently. He was seeing at least something of Hazlitt. Haydon on January 11 invited Keats to start coming to dinner every Sunday at three ("accept this engagement as long as we live," said

Haydon) ; and when Keats went to Haydon's on the eighteenth he found Hazlitt and the artist Thomas Bewick there. Hazlitt's "Lectures on the English Poets," at the Surrey Institution every Tuesday at seven, had already begun. On the twentieth, forgetting the hour, Keats showed up at the second lecture "just as they were coming out, when all these pounced upon me. Hazlitt, John Hunt & son, Wells, Bewick, all the Landseers, Bob Harris, Rox of the Borough [9] Aye & more." Keats was meanwhile busy trying to raise money for Charles Cripps, the young artist from Oxford who hoped to study under Haydon. He even intended, as he told Haydon, to "ask Kingston and C° to cash up."

The fourteen-year-old Fanny was also in town during the holidays from her boarding school in Walthamstow, and Keats saw her as often as possible. She asked him to tell George and Tom to write her

> a Co-partnership Letter . . . I think she will be quick—Mrs. Abbey was saying that the Keatses were ever indolent—that they would ever be so and that it was born in them—Well whispered Fanny to me "If it is born with us how can we help it."

The visits were strained, with Abbey or his wife always present. But Keats continued to call until Fanny left around January 20. He tells his brothers that Abbey "appeared very glum, the last time I went [to] see her, & said in an indirect way, that I had no business there," and adds that he gathers Abbey "does not overstock you with Money—you must insist."

6

The bickering among his friends that had distressed him when he returned from Oxford, full of his ideal of "disinterestedness," was meanwhile proceeding merrily. It had struck him forcibly then because his eye had hitherto been elsewhere and he had simply not noticed it. When he first met Hunt, Haydon, and Reynolds, and wrote the sonnet on Chapman's Homer, he had been preoccupied with the excitement of discovery, of extended horizons. He had assumed—he still somewhat assumed—that there was a brotherhood in the arts, a brotherhood in all good endeavors. This was one reason why the motiveless, vitriolic attack by Lockhart,

[9] Possibly one of the men named Rokes mentioned by Rollins, *Letters,* I.214.

in the first article on the "Cockney School," had stunned him at first.

Since then he had been trying to understand the quick, unpredictable changes of the human heart—its temptations to censure rather than praise, its ready suspicion of possible or imaginary threats, its eagerness to establish a moment's or a day's superiority; and he had been trying to replace an open naiveté subject to sudden disillusion with a charity and tolerance no less open. He might be swept at moments by a strong and fatigued distaste (as when he told Bailey that he was "disgusted with literary Men," or came away from Horace Smith's dinner thinking how much he would prefer what the others thought of as "Kean & his low company"). But generally he was "perplexed." The word, or its equivalent, keeps recurring. "Things have happen'd lately," he tells Bailey (January 23), "of great Perplexity—You must have heard of them—Reynolds and Haydon retorting and recriminating—and parting for ever—the same thing has happened between Haydon and Hunt . . . Men should bear with each other." He tells George and Tom of the "sharp & high note to Reynolds" that Haydon sent when Reynolds forgot to tell him that he could not attend the "immortal dinner." Reynolds, quick to take offense, immediately replied with "one of the most cutting letters I ever read; exposing to [Haydon] all his own weaknesses"; for Haydon himself, of course, was habitually negligent of appointments. "I am quite perplexed in a world of doubts & fancies—there is nothing stable in the world." As for Hunt and Haydon, the last explosion began trivially enough. Mrs. Hunt

> was in the habit of borrowing silver of Haydon, the last time she did so, Haydon asked her to return it at a certain time—She did not—Haydon sent for it; Hunt went on to expostulate on the indelicacy &c. they got to words & parted for ever—All I hope is at some time to bring them all together again—Lawk! Molly there's been such doings.

The last phrase, echoing Smollett's *Humphry Clinker*, has an interest in this context. For Keats's instinctive comic sense was beginning to reassert itself. He was now reading Smollett and Fielding, both a healthful contrast to "Romance" (that ideal of "Romance" that he speaks of laying aside in the sonnet a few days later "On Sitting Down to Read *King Lear* Once Again"). His brothers, writing from Devonshire, ask him the difference between Scott's and Smollett's novels. Scott, he answers, tries to throw a romantic coloring on "common and low characters" in order to elevate them:

> Smollett on the contrary pulls down and levels what with other Men would continue Romance. The Grand parts of Scott are within the reach of more Minds tha[n] the finest humours in Humphrey Clinker—I forget whether that fine thing of the Sargeant is Fielding's or Smollets but it gives me more pleasure tha[n] the whole Novel of the Antiquary—you must remember what I mean. Some one says to the Sargeant "thats a non sequiter," if you come to that" replies the Sargeant "you're another." [10]

7

Meanwhile Keats was seeing much of two other friends, James Rice and Charles Wentworth Dilke, whom he had met the previous spring and had come to know well after he returned from Oxford in the autumn; and he was also becoming acquainted—or, if he had already met him, better acquainted—with Richard Woodhouse, the young legal adviser to the publishing firm of Taylor and Hessey.

Constantly ailing, the generous, witty Rice kept his own attention as well as that of others away from his health. Hearing Rice had suddenly taken a bad turn for the worse, Keats dropped around to visit him "and lo! Master Jemmy had been to the play the night before and was out at the time—he always comes on his Legs like a Cat." At Redhall's party, Rice threw himself into the dance, oblivious equally of the late hour and of musical time, "dancing," said Keats, "as if he was deaf." The guiding spirit of the "Saturday Club" that Keats describes to his brothers, snatching at convivial pleasures and given to off-color puns, Rice was respected by everyone not only for his integrity—which though gentle was uncompromising—but also for the perceptive detachment, the quiet good judgment that would come immediately to the fore if occasion needed it. He wore well. Much later (September 17, 1819) Keats, who had since lived with him for a full month at the Isle of Wight, told George he thought Rice "the most sensible, and even wise Man I know—he has a few John Bull prejudices; but they improve him." Three years older than Keats, he

---

10 I.200. The remark is from *Tom Jones* (IX.vi) .

had long been a friend of Reynolds and Bailey.[11] He was now a member of his father's law firm (James Rice and Son, 62 Marlborough Street), and had recently persuaded Reynolds, who needed to make a start in something and who hoped before long to marry, to study law. He paid for Reynolds' articles, and in time took him into partnership.[12] The chronic illness all through the time that Keats knew him (his life, said Dilke, "has been but a long lingering . . . although his good heart & good spirits kept him up") proved fatal in 1832.

The hard-working, methodical Dilke, six years older than Keats, worked for the Navy Pay Office at Somerset House, though he lived out in Hampstead. He is one of those extraordinary examples we encounter in the early nineteenth century of men who make their way up in the middle echelons of business or administration and yet manage to acquire, despite that concentrated, apparently single-minded effort, and without any help that a university might offer, a dedicated interest in the arts. Dilke had been judicious or lucky when he married, at an early age, the warm-hearted Maria Walker. In 1814, when he was only twenty-five, he began to publish his six-volume edition, *Old English Plays,* a supplement to Dodsley's famous *Collection,* and finished it two years later. Meanwhile he and Charles Brown, whom he had known at school, built their double house in Hampstead, Wentworth Place, into Brown's portion of which Keats moved after the death of Tom. In January 1817 Dilke took over from Reynolds the theatrical reviews for the *Champion.* Throughout the next two years, the Dilkes were to become very close to the Keats brothers, who would drop over, said Dilke, at least "three times a week, often three times a day."

On his son Charles (later Sir Charles Wentworth Dilke) the father gradually began to lavish an anxious attention that finally struck his friends as obsessive. The ambition of this "Godwin perfectibility Man"—as Keats called Dilke with affectionate disagreement about fundamental premises—became so locked to the ideal of the son's future (so unpredictable, so elusively unsusceptible to

11 Sent to Sidmouth for his health in 1814, he had quickly become acquainted with the three Leigh girls, to whom he introduced Reynolds and Bailey. Among the poems written by the three youths for the Leigh sisters, mentioned in Chapter IX, nine are by Rice.

12 Perhaps a year or two before his death he retired from the law firm, and went to live with his father in Putney. The firm, which then became Reynolds and Simmons, had been handling the affairs of George and Fanny Keats, who later complained of Reynolds' careless management.

the step-by-step procedures that the orderly Dilke could follow in his own person, in his own actions) that he knew no rest after the boy entered Westminster School two years later (June 1819). In his "parental mania," as Keats said, the otherwise clear-headed Dilke moved down to Great Smith Street in Westminster two months in advance in order to be near the school, renting his half of the Hampstead house to Mrs. Frances Brawne and her children. Friends would discover him sitting at the window waiting for his son:

> The boy [Keats tells George, April 15, 1819] has nothing in his ears all day but himself and the importance of his education—Dilke has continually in his mouth "My Boy" This is what spoils princes: it may have the same effect with Commoners. . . . But what a shameful thing it is that for that obstinate Boy Dilke should stifle himself in Town Lodgings and wear out his Life by his continual apprehension of his Boys fate in Westminster school, with the rest of the Boys and the Masters—Eve[r]y one has some wear and tear—One would think Dilke ought to be quiet and happy—but no—this one Boy—makes his face pale, his society silent and his vigilanc[e] jealous —He would I have no doubt quarrel with any one who snubb'd his Boy—With all this he has no notion how to manage him.

The sort of man "who cannot feel he has a personal identity unless he has made up his Mind about everything," Dilke had moments of "quiet fun" that, in their contrast with his usual behavior, delighted Keats as unpredictable expressions of character. Keats tells George of one such moment—in a little scene that had struck him as "dramatic" at the time, though he felt the "identity" of the thing was lost after he had described it.[13]

By January 1818, with George and Tom away, Dilke's lodgings in Wentworth Place were fast coming to seem like another home;

13 Mention of the Dilke house in Westminster near the school "puts me in mind of a circumsta[n]ce occurred lately at Dilkes—I think it very rich and dramatic and quite illustrative of the little quiet fun that he will enjoy . . . some of the windows look out into one Street, and the back windows into another round the corner— Dilke had some old people to dinner . . . two old ladies among them—Brown was there—they had known him from a Child." Brown behaved so winningly that "they became hand and glove together and a little complimentary. Brown was obliged to depart early. He bid them good bye and pass'd into the passage—no sooner was his back turn'd than the old women began lauding him. When Brown [who was almost completely bald] had reach'd the Street door and was just going, Dilke threw up the Window and call'd 'Brown! Brown! They say you look younger than ever you did!' Brown went on and had just turn'd the corner into the other street when Dilke appear'd at the back window crying 'Brown! Brown! My God, they say you're handsome.' You see what a many words it requires to give any identity to a thing I could have told you in half a minute" (II.190–191).

and when Dilke moved into town fifteen months later in order to be near his son at Westminster, the wrench—with Tom dead by then, and George in America—was greater than Keats cared to admit.[14] Dilke's systematic, unruffled temperament tended to steady Keats—as Bailey's methodical habits had steadied him at Oxford, and as those of Charles Brown were to do later. When he finally took up *Endymion* again, he got "in the habit," as he told his brothers (January 24), "of taking my papers to Dilkes and copying there; so I chat and proceed at the same time." Illuminating the whole household were the quick sympathy, the unfailing generosity and good sense, of "the merry Mrs. Dilke," as George called her. Though little older than Keats himself, Maria Dilke was almost motherly to him and his brothers, and later, as far as Abbey would allow, she did what she could to help their sister. Typically, when Keats and Brown took a trip to Chichester a year later, they felt free to write jointly a pretended love-letter to their "charming dear Mrs. Dilke," enclosing it in a letter to Dilke himself. Her quick comic sense used to delight Keats and would immediately release his own. Once, in the midst of a letter to George (January 3, 1819; he was by then living with Brown on the other side of Wentworth Place), he heard Mrs. Dilke "knocking at the wall for Tea is ready—I will tell you what sort of tea it is and then bid you—good bye." He ran over; and when the tray was brought in, the two found themselves suddenly pretending they were fencers and "had a battle with celery stalks." Nothing could shake her confidence in Keats's poetry. Eagerly awaiting the reception of Keats's 1820 volume, she wrote her father-in-law: "If the public cry him up as a great poet, I will henceforth be their humble servant; if not, the devil take the public."

Richard Woodhouse, now just twenty-nine, had been legal (and later a general literary) adviser to Taylor and Hessey for about

---

[14] Keats's relations with the Dilkes remained close until Keats's last few months in England, and were then somewhat strained by the Dilkes' disapproval of his engagement to Fanny Brawne. In 1830, nine years after Keats's death, Dilke took over the editorship of the *Athenaeum;* he managed it until 1846, and then turned to the studies of eighteenth-century writers by which he is still remembered. After the death of his wife (1850) and his daughter-in-law (1853), he and his son lived together, the elder Dilke dying in 1864 and the younger five years later. Sir Charles Wentworth Dilke, the second baronet (1843–1911), shared his grandfather's lifelong interest in Keats and his family, and left to the Hampstead Public Library the notable Dilke collection of Keats.

five years. With the precise, clerklike habits of the lawyer, he combined a good practical knowledge of several languages, including Spanish, Portuguese, and Italian, and a sensitive, inquiring interest in literature.[15] Like Bailey, Dilke, and Charles Brown, he contrasted strongly with Hunt and Haydon. All were men of steady perseverance. Woodhouse reminds us particularly of Bailey. These two most bookish of Keats's friends had a painstaking, even pedantic cast of mind. Each seems to have been incapable of boredom with detail, and neither (Woodhouse less than Bailey) had much sense of humor. Here the similarity stopped. Bailey was more absorbed in general ideas, and Woodhouse in people and concrete problems. Bailey, in studying for the ministry, felt freer to professionalize his instinctive moralism. In argument as in much else, his procedure was rectilinear. Woodhouse (an equally religious man), was more generous, open, and flexible in his judgments, and was virtually free from self-righteousness. His constant tact (a quality Bailey's warmest admirers never found in him) sprang not only from general kindliness—though he was kindly enough—but from a perceptive sympathetic grasp of others. An example would be his delicacy when Keats later needed money desperately: Woodhouse scraped together what he could find and then had it given Keats as an advance from the publishing house of Taylor and Hessey. There was a chance that Keats might simply lend it to others; but Woodhouse would have thought it niggling to hesitate on that account. He wanted to make it a steady and "Rational principle" to try to do for Keats what people say they would have done for Shakespeare and Chatterton. He understood very well what Keats meant by saying that the poetic character "has no self . . . It has no character." Significantly, it was to Woodhouse that Keats wrote his famous comment on the subject; and Woodhouse's ample notes

15 The eldest of fifteen children, Woodhouse came from Bath (b. December 11, 1788), where his father was owner or part owner of the flourishing White Hart Inn. After being sent to Eton, he spent two years in Spain and Portugal, with which relatives engaged in wine importing had business relations. (He later brought out [1815] a *Grammar of the Spanish, Portuguese, and Italian Languages*.) When he returned to England, he studied law, and, as a conveyancer, met Taylor and Hessey (1811). Becoming afflicted with tuberculosis himself, while in his mid-thirties, he spent a year or two in Madeira (1829–1830), eventually went to Italy (1832), and felt improved enough to return to London. But he became rapidly worse and died on September 3, 1834. The most complete account of his life is given by Rollins (KC, I.cxliv–cl). For further information on his family, see Joanna Richardson, *KSMB*, No. 5 (1953), 39–44.

on Keats's letter show to what an extent he already appreciated the empathic nature of Keats's own imagination.[16]

Woodhouse may have met Keats in 1817; but it was not until he was reading parts of *Endymion* for Taylor and Hessey, early in 1818, that he also took up Keats's first volume and read it.[17] From here on he made a special effort to collect whatever he could find about Keats's poems—their dates, backgrounds, and various drafts, expressing his confidence in posterity's interest. Four large volumes of transcripts and other information survive. A fifth was probably lost in 1883 in a fire. In the autumn of 1818, after the attacks on *Endymion* appeared, he wrote to his cousin, Mary Frogley, who wished he had been present to "defend Keats" among some people she had seen: "Such a genius, I verily believe, has not appeared since Shakespeare & Milton." If *Endymion* is compared with Shakespeare's *Venus and Adonis,* it stands up very well. Keats "has great faults—enough to sink another writer": the interesting thing is the extent to which they spring from "luxuriance" of talent. In any case, while Keats is unknown, or despised, Woodhouse is ready to "prophesy" that

> during his life (if it please God to spare him to the usual age of man . . .), [Keats] will rank on a level with the best of the last or of the present generation: and after his death will take his place at their head.[18]

8

Throughout these crowded weeks of mid-December and early January the thought of *Endymion,* raw and unrevised, continued to nag at Keats. Because of the effort of writing it, above all of completing the last book, and also because of the disparity between it and the sort of thing to which he hoped to turn next, the desire to forget it was overwhelming. Moreover, he knew the value of putting it aside until he could return to it freshly and with more perspective. To put it aside for too long, however, involved a risk. The need for drastic revision might become too clear, too clamorous to be denied. But to revise the poem thoroughly, to spend the next few months on it—perhaps longer—was one of the last things he wished to do. He had gone beyond the poem. It was not the way he now wanted to write. It was necessary, as he said later, that "this

---

[16] *KC,* I.57–60.   [17] See Finney, I.344–345.
[18] I.383–384.

youngster should die away." All this, of course, provided a fair argument for not publishing it at all. But this was out of the question. Too much had been invested in it—too much hope, too much self-demand: this was the "long Poem" (more than that, a completed long poem) that had been the challenge when, still at the Hospital, he had begun "Calidore" and the "Specimen of an Induction," and had to give them up. It had been the challenge when he set off to Margate in the summer of 1816, and then ended only with verse letters. Moreover, a finished poem was promised the firm of Taylor and Hessey; and his publishers had been generous in their advances.

Finally, on January 5, 1818, he announced to his brothers, "I have not beg[u]n my corrections yet: tomorrow I set out." He made some headway the first three or four days, though he soon found that even his favorite passages sounded "vapid." He wrote Taylor on Saturday, January 10, in such a way as to suggest that he was back on a timetable once again, and a very short one indeed: "I have made a vow not to call again without my first book: so you may expect to see me in four days." Then, for whatever reason, he appears to have spent the next two days in town. While there on other business, he may have decided impulsively to drop in to see Taylor and talk about the poem, and Taylor may then have come out to Hampstead to see what Keats had thus far revised.[19] Keats still continued to go out. For perhaps the first time he was (by his previous standards) really negligent. In spare hours (usually at Dilke's house, where, as he said, "I chat & proceed at the same time"), he quickly finished his revision of Book I by January 19, and "shall take it," he tells his brothers, "to Taylor's tomorrow—intend to persevere." The alterations—especially when compared with those in the next three books—were numerous but, with a few exceptions, of incidental importance. Taylor was far from dissatisfied, and proposed publishing the volume in quarto if Haydon would draw a scene from it as a frontispiece. Haydon agreed to do so if Keats insisted. Otherwise, since he was occupied,

---

19 This may have been the occasion of the undated note in Keats's handwriting (see Lowell, I.547, and *Letters*, I.195) of which Woodhouse remarked: "Keats Persuaded Mr Taylor to accompany him one afternoon to Hampstead & wrote for him the following note." The note reads: "To Any friend who may call Mr Taylor's Compts to any Ladies or gentlemen his friends who may call, and begs they will pardon him for being led away by an unavoidable engagement, which will detain him till eleven o'clock to night."

he would rather defer it for another edition. Then he would do not
a drawing but a real painting—something that would be "an honor
to both of us." Meanwhile, he would make an engraving of Keats
himself for the first edition. This, "from a Chalk drawing of
mine—done with all my might—to which I would put my name,
would answer Taylor's Idea more than the other . . . and as I
have not done it for any other human being—it will have an effect." Haydon forgot all about the engraving of Keats. As for the
painting of a scene from the poem itself in some later edition,
Keats proposed (January 23) that Haydon "wait for a choice out
of *Hyperion*"—the first suggestion of what he hopes to be his next
long poem, about which he already has some general idea; for he
goes on to say that

> when that Poem is done there will be a wide range for you—in En-
> dymion I think you may have many bits of the deep and sentimental
> cast—the nature of *Hyperion* will lead me to treat it in a more naked
> and grecian Manner—and the march of passion and endeavour will
> be undeviating.

9

During the two days before this first mention of *Hyperion,* something happened to turn his mind almost entirely to the future, and
to make him more impatient than ever to be rid of *Endymion.* He
did indeed start to copy and revise Book II the same day he wrote
to Haydon, and hastily finished it on February 5. But even during
these mere thirteen days he by no means devoted his full time to
the revision.

What had happened is that he had at last begun to write again,
and with an enormous sense of relief. Less than two months had
actually passed since he had returned to Hampstead with the last
part of his poem. But the time seemed very long to him. Then he
had suddenly found, as he told his brothers (January 23) , that he
could not "bear to be uninterested or unemployed, I, who for so
long a time, have been addicted to passiveness." He was not thinking of the revision he had been making of Book I of *Endymion,*
the dramatic reviews for the *Champion,* the numerous letters, the
scurrying to and fro—these all come under the heading of "passiveness." What was there otherwise? Only an impromptu, playful sonnet (January 16) for Mrs. Reynolds and her daughters—not really

very amusing—on their aging cat ("Cat! who hast past thy Grand Climacteric"). But he now rejoiced in this "long" lapse. It helped to convince him that "Nothing is finer for the purposes of great productions, than a very gradual ripening of the intellectual powers." For he felt he was making a new start. True, when he said this to his brothers, he had written only two new poems, neither of which he ever published and with the first of which he was certainly dissatisfied: "Lines on Seeing a Lock of Milton's Hair," and the sonnet "On Sitting Down to Read *King Lear* Once Again." But he felt that he was at least entering a vestibule. The subjects of both of these poems are curiously analogous. Each in its own way involves again the approach to greatness by what he had called, long ago, the "genius-loving heart"—though now, he thought, the approach was at a very different level and with a new understanding.

The sudden release that was to lead to the prolific output of the next three months had come when he called on Hunt on January 21. Keats had not been seeing much of him. Embarrassed that the months had passed without his showing Hunt at least a part of *Endymion,* Keats took with him the first book. Hunt went through it rather rapidly. He "allows it not much merit as a whole," Keats told his brothers:

> says it is unnatural & made ten objections to it in the mere skimming over. He says the conversation is unnatural & too high-flown for the Brother & Sister. Says it should be simple forgetting do ye mind, that they are both overshadowed by a Supernatural Power, & of force could not speak like Franchesca in the Rimini. He must first prove that Caliban's poetry is unnatural,—This with me completely overturns his objections—the fact is he & Shelley are hurt & perhaps justly, at my not having showed them the affair officiously & from several hints I have had they appear much disposed to dissect & anatomize, any trip or slip I may have made.

Whatever Hunt thought of the new poem, he was elated because he had just acquired a lock of Milton's hair for his collection. Playful as ever, and eager to convert any occasion to capital (he himself had already managed to compose three sonnets on his new acquisition), he urged Keats to write some lines. Keats was neither so naively excited nor so paralyzed as a year before when he was expected to write a sonnet on receiving a laurel crown. He does not seem to have been overeager to take up the challenge. But Hunt, without second thought, thrust before him a notebook, in which he himself had been writing a poem of his own ("Hero and Leander"), opened to some blank pages. Keats, after a few minutes, good-naturedly began, while Hunt presumably continued to look through the first book of *Endymion*. Weary of the heroic couplet he had been using so constantly—probably weary of the five-foot line itself—he resisted the temptation to jot down a sonnet, which, as he knew, was what Hunt doubtless expected. He began instead an irregular ode. He was far from feeling involved; the circumstances were artificial and inhibiting. He fumbled at first with the unfamiliar short lines, and completed a stanza understandably a little hollow and declamatory.[20] Using the notebook in which Hunt was writing his "Hero and Leander" was not somehow very satisfactory. Keats finished another seven lines in the vein of the first stanza; and then—though there are many other blank pages he could have used—he, or Hunt, found a separate sheet.[21] The character of the poem then quickly changes as he turns not only from Hunt's notebook but from the particular occasion itself; and we suddenly have a direct statement of the uncertainties, the self-questionings, that this new evolution in thought and expectation has been carrying with it:

> When every childish fashion
>   Has vanish'd from my rhyme,
> Will I, grey-gone in passion,
>   Leave to an after-time
>   Hymning and harmony
> Of thee, and of thy works, and of thy life;
> But vain is now the burning and the strife.
> Pangs are in vain, until I grow high-rife
>   With old Philosophy,
> And mad with glimpses of futurity!

[20]   Chief of organic Numbers!
       Old Scholar of the spheres!
     Thy spirit never slumbers,
       But rolls about our ears
     For ever and for ever!
     O what a mad endeavour
         Worketh he
     Who, to thy sacred and ennobled hearse
     Would offer a burnt sacrifice of verse
         And melody!

[21] The notebook and separate sheet on which Keats continued are in the Harvard Keats Collection.

For many years my offerings must be hush'd;
  When I do speak, I'll think upon this hour,
Because I feel my forehead hot and flush'd,
  Even at the simplest vassal of thy power,—
    A lock of thy bright hair,—
    Sudden it came,
And I was startled, when I caught thy name
    Coupled so unaware;
Yet at the moment, temperate was my blood.
I thought I had beheld it from the flood.

"Perhaps I should have done something better alone and at home," he told Bailey. But the habit of writing verse had returned, and the occasion proved catalytic. For he was at once provoked to rephrase what these verses had begun to disclose: to rewrite them (and to do so twice again) in another context, without Hunt and his lock of Milton's hair, and to put more closely what he was now discovering that he wanted to say. He did not discard the "Lines on Seeing a Lock of Milton's Hair," however. With an association we can hardly help finding suggestive, he copied them into his folio Shakespeare.

The very next day, reassured by the renewed fluency, he turned to something very different from Hunt and Hunt's writing contests. He had been thinking about *King Lear* again for at least two months. As the horizon of poetry kept moving before his own advance, the play became increasingly a symbol of what he hoped ultimately to reach. His decision to reread it seemed to him invested with significance, and "appeared to demand the prologue of a Sonnet." [22] But the preoccupation of the lines he had just written is very much present ("When every childish fashion / Has vanish'd from my rhyme / Will I . . . Give to an after-time?"). He returns

22 O golden-tongued Romance with serene lute!
    Fair plumèd Syren! Queen of far away!·
  Leave melodizing on this wintry day,
Shut up thine olden pages, and be mute:
Adieu! for once again the fierce dispute
    Betwixt damnation and impassion'd clay
  Must I burn through; once more humbly assay
The bitter-sweet of this Shakespearian fruit.
Chief Poet! and ye clouds of Albion,
    Begetters of our deep eternal theme,
When through the old oak forest I am gone,
    Let me not wander in a barren dream,
But when I am consumèd in the fire,
Give me new Phoenix wings to fly at my desire.

to it now. When he has gone through the "old oak forest" of romance, will he, in effect, have died as a poet, or is another stage possible to him? (The questionings are to recur more urgently until they culminate in the powerful fragment, the *Fall of Hyperion,* at the end of his poetic career.) Can there be "new Phoenix wings" to lift him from those ashes? He was more satisfied with the sonnet than with the lines he wrote the day before; it was at least more condensed; he had "done something better alone and at home." "You see I am getting at it," as he told George and Tom after copying it for them. A few days later, he writes the celebrated letter to his publisher (January 30) slightly changing the passage from *Endymion,* "Wherein lies happiness," in order to make it read as a general hope of development—his "first Step towards the chief Attempt in the Drama—the playing of different Natures with Joy and Sorrow." Moreover, he has either just written—or within a few hours is about to write—the first of his new sonnets, "When I have fears that I may cease to be."

10

The feeling that he is at last getting started encourages a momentum and produces an exhilaration he wants to share with someone. The next morning (January 31) he begins an effervescent letter to Reynolds that turns almost entirely into verse. He makes up a song of five stanzas as he writes (the somewhat off-color "O blush not so"), and then stops, saying, "I proposed to write you a serious poetical Letter." But a reference to Milton's "Il Penseroso" ("Hence vain deluding joys") sets him off again:

> I cannot write in prose, It is a sun-shiny day and I cannot so here goes,
>> Hence Burgundy, Claret & port
>> Away with old Hock and Madeira
>> Too couthly ye are for my sport
>> There's a Beverage brighter and clearer.

He jots down another twelve lines. But once again the mere activity of impromptu writing begins to touch essential preoccupations. The lighthearted doggerel, as it turns to both poetry and the sunny day outside, finally leads to the mention of Apollo—always the most symbolically weighted of mythological names for Keats. One of his very earliest poems had been the youthful "Ode to Apollo,"

written at Hammond's surgery almost exactly three years earlier
(February 1815), with its roll call of great poets—Homer, Virgil,
Shakespeare, Milton, Spenser, Tasso: those "bards" who, as he said
later in the sonnet on Chapman's Homer, stood "in fealty to
Apollo." After the laurel-crown episode that had left him feeling
like a fool, there had been the mock-penitent but genuinely uneasy "Hymn to Apollo" ("where slept thine ire, / When like a
blank idiot I put on thy wreath?"). And of course the planned
epic of *Hyperion* was, as he had already implied to Haydon, to
take Apollo as one of its principal characters.

Suddenly, at the mention of Apollo in the doggerel he has just
been jotting down, he draws a line. Then, in emphatic, three-
foot verse he starts writing what turns into a very different poem
indeed—far more serious, though still extemporaneous:

> God of the Meridian
>   And of the East and West
> To thee my soul is flown
>   And my body is earthward press'd.

What follows becomes another version or rephrasing of the misgivings that had broken out in the poem he had written at Hunt's
("vain is now the burning and the strife" until he becomes far
more of a philosopher; "For many years my offerings must be
hush'd"). But the attempt to reconcile himself to slow preparation is now almost forgotten in the urgent desire to proceed directly. The short lines fall into couplets, becoming something of
a chant:

> Aye, when the Soul is fled
> To[o] high above our head
> Affrighted do we gaze
>
> .   .   .   .   .
>
>   God of Song
> Thou bearest me along
> Through sights I scarce can bear
> O let me, let me share
> With the hot Lyre and thee
> The staid Philosophy.
> Temper my lonely hours
> And let me see thy bow'rs
> More unalarm'd!—

With the dash after "unalarm'd" he stops. For he is also beginning to rewrite (more nakedly, with far less detachment) the new

sonnet he has wanted to show Reynolds. He concludes his letter quickly:

> My dear Reynolds, you must forgive all this ranting—but the fact is I cannot write sense this Morning—however you shall have some—I will copy my last Sonnet.

> When I have fears that I may cease to be
>   Before my pen has glean'd my teeming brain,
> Before high pilèd Books in charactery
>   Hold like full garners the full ripen'd grain—
> When I behold upon the night's starr'd face
>   Huge cloudy symbols of a high romance
> And feel that I may never live to trace
>   Their shadows with the magic hand of Chance:
> And when I feel, fair creature of an hour,
>   That I shall never look upon thee more
> Never have relish in the faery power
>   Of unreflecting Love: then on the Shore
>   Of the wide world I stand alone and think
>   Till Love and Fame to Nothingness do sink.

> I must take a turn, and then write to Teignmouth [to George and Tom].

Exactly a year before when he was waiting (as he is now) for an almost finished volume to appear, and the next uncertain venture lay ahead, his sonnet, "After dark vapours" had jumped from that bleak, anxious January not only to the thought of spring but of "fruit ripening in stillness—autumn suns . . . quiet sheaves"; and the thought and imagery of harvest continue to recur before each large step until the final great poem, "To Autumn." So in this January he thinks, with both uncertainty and hope, of a future that might "glean" his "teeming brain," and of books that might "Hold like rich garners the full-ripen'd grain." There is also the thought, however cloudy, of other "romances," far beyond *Endymion*. The romance form might not be an ultimate goal, but he certainly intended to write a few more. When Taylor wished to change the subtitle of *Endymion*, "A Poetic Romance," Keats defended the romance as "a fine thing notwithstanding the circulating Libraries." Curiosity about the possible identity of the "fair creature of an hour" is inevitable (he is probably thinking of the woman he had once seen at Vauxhall) ; but the allusion is very incidental. The lines, always felt to be something of a drop, are plainly there to help fill out the sonnet. The thought of love still remains general and abstract, and subsidiary to what is put at the start. The close of the sonnet ("then on the shore / Of the wide world . . .") picks up something of the youthful ideal of "disinterestedness" and the thought of "staid Philosophy" with which he hopes to share his commitment to "the hot lyre." He also, of course, partly echoes Shakespeare's famous sonnet:

> Not mine own fears, nor the prophetic soul
> Of the wide world dreaming on things to come.

Keats's own sonnet, in fact, is the first of a series in the Shakespearean form in which he breaks deliberately not only with those he has written before but also with the sonnet as conventionally used in this period—a break that was at least a small by-product of the attempt to make an entirely fresh start. Though his heart was never much in the form, and, within a year or so, he was to tire of it and indeed of sonnets generally, his new sonnets approximate the style of Shakespeare's more closely than any other sonnets of the century. This is especially true of his first attempt, "When I have fears," in which the recurring theme of Shakespeare's sonnets—the precarious lease of love and ambition, so quickly "forfeit to a confin'd doom"—actually shapes the poem.

Removed from context (a context that also includes the fact that it is a deliberate Shakespearean imitation), the poem has tempted readers to regard it, with biographical simplicity, as a sort of clairvoyant anticipation of early death. Naturally the death of so many close to Keats while he was young had long since left something of the sobering effect, the acute awareness of the transience of life, that becomes more pronounced in most of us (at least at the present day) only in middle age. Moreover, Tom's illness certainly weighed on him. But all this needs to be kept in perspective.[23] The thought of his own death is general rather than immediate: it could be twenty or forty years ahead, and the desire he has in mind could still be impossible of fulfillment. Put another way, the principal concern behind the sonnet is the need, and with it the attempt, to view in a way "More unalarm'd" a very general

---

[23] He had been accustomed to thinking of himself, with some justice, as having a robust physique; and he was certainly blessed with a robust mind. Miss Lowell (I.514–516) thought the severe cold Keats had in the autumn already a sign that consumption had begun. This is certainly doubtful. In any case he himself would probably never have made the association. Compared with his other friends (certainly Bailey, Rice, and Reynolds) he seems to have been remarkably free of illness until the latter part of the Scottish tour.

fear of unfulfillment—an anxiety that has mounted because he feels he is about to make another, more important beginning. Every strong desire breeds the fear that it may fail of accomplishment, if not in one way then in another; and both the desire and the fear provoke the temptation to put them at arm's length, as indeed this sonnet attempts to do at the end. The fear of failing through sheer incapacity ("when the soul is fled / Too high . . . Affrighted do we gaze") is what is alarming; and it is this of course that pervades the other poems we have been noticing. But this apprehension could not by itself admit the relatively simple aesthetic resolution that the sonnet, following Shakespearean convention and invoking the general thought of death, is able to attain: he could hardly, without empty and obvious bravado, deny everything in which he had most devoutly believed, and view both his aspiration and his incapacity as capable of sinking "to nothingness." Only by universalizing fear and employing this wider proscenium—and with it a further reduction of goals to the abstractions of "Love and Fame"—can he attain the disengagement; and through this generality the sonnet is able to make a detour around the more personal, immediate alarm. Though he did not publish the poem in his last volume, he was far from dissatisfied with it now. It was at least not "ranting," as the other lines he had just written—which are directly personal and which lack resolution—struck him as being; and it was not "ranting" partly because he could feel that, in its way, it was rather detached and impersonal.

11

What really sobered him, of course, was his new appreciation, increasing now with every week, of the distance he still had to go, a distance that would make ten years—over three times the number during which he had been doing any writing at all—seem too brief a preparation. Three years ago, sitting in the upstairs room at Hammond's surgery, he had written the timid, stiff sonnet on the death of his grandmother. But it was only a year and a half since he had first really tried to write poetry seriously, and, after taking his examination at Apothecaries' Hall, had gone off to Margate alone in order to see what he could do. Those eighteen months might now, at twenty-two, seem long to him; they certainly had been crowded. Yet any change, any improvement, not only seemed small compared with what was needed but also seemed confined to a development and refinement within particular grooves. That limitation had struck him as he was bringing *Endymion* to its close in the autumn. And by December he could realize that the writing of which he was then beginning to speak, as in the "Negative Capability" letter, was very different in kind; *King Lear,* for example, was not simply a higher rung on the same ladder. Since then, to be sure, he had done little: he had changed to the Shakespearean form in his sonnets, and had written rather "rantingly" in two or three poems after Hunt challenged him to compose something on the lock of Milton's hair. But at least the attitude was new, or partly new, as an active ideal. The next eight months were to provide very little poetry that would illustrate a striking, dramatic development. They were months of preparation. A part of the interest is that they were months, not years.

Devonshire and *Isabella*

✻ↄ֍ↄ✻ↄ֍ↄ✻ↄ֍ↄ✻ↄ֍ↄ✻ↄ֍ↄ✻ↄ֍ↄ✻ↄ֍ↄ✻ↄ֍ↄ✻ↄ֍ↄ✻ↄ֍ↄ✻ↄ֍ↄ✻ↄ֍ↄ✻ↄ֍ↄ

February to April, 1818

THE THOUGHT OF SLOW, deliberate preparation for this new beginning dominates the next few months. But the question, of course,
was what preparation. It became far more serious later in the
spring, after *Endymion* was out of the way. Until then he was always able to console himself that he lacked a free mind. But even
during the present weeks he still wanted to be "getting at it, with
a sort of determination & strength." While continuing to tell himself that he was in no hurry to turn to other writing, and that the
preparation, whatever it might be, would take years, he was racing
through his revision of *Endymion* at a speed that left him a fair
amount of free time. He was not going out nearly so much as he
had in December and early January. To be sure, he was now "writing at intervals many songs & Sonnets," as he told his brothers
(February 14); but though they provided exercise of a sort, they
were not seriously intended.[1]

He was beginning to read intensively, however, and had already
started the close study of Milton that he was to apply the following
autumn in *Hyperion*. Hazlitt's lectures incited him to turn to
writers whom he knew slightly or not at all. He was even plunging
into Voltaire and Gibbon, probably with the thought that they
were hard-headed realists; and within two months he was planning
to learn Greek and Italian. Of course books alone were hardly the
answer. He had moments when he even felt like arguing to "prove
reading of no use." When he started to do so, his sense of humor
would be caught, and he would see his argument as "mere sophisti-

---

[1] The "songs," which attempt to capture an Elizabethan or seventeenth-century
tone, doubtless include those published by Milnes (1848) as "Extracts from an
Opera"; probably the three songs "Shed no tear," "Ah, woe is me," and "Spirit here
that reignest"; the little song of opposites, "Welcome joy, and welcome sorrow";
and those enclosed in his January 31 letter to Reynolds ("O blush not so," and
"Hence Burgundy"). The "rondeaus" and most of the sonnets are briefly discussed
below.

cation . . . to excuse my own indolence," though still the thought "may neighbour" to some truths. Granted that other experience was necessary, the frustrating problem kept recurring: what experience in particular, and how did one go about acquiring it?

He was fortunate in being already experienced as a practicing writer—experienced, that is to say, in the more active habits of composition—before the temptations to self-consciousness became as strong as they did from the late spring through the following year. He was already becoming more aware of the increased self-consciousness of modern poetry as a whole, or at least of some of the by-products of it. While resolving not to be hypnotized or "rattlesnaked" into following that course—the opposite of his new ideal of Shakespearean "disinterestedness" and "Negative Capability"—he was uneasy.

As the spring passed, he was to think out for himself some of the gains (or at least challenges) as well as liabilities in the situation with which poetry was now confronted. But for the moment the directions in which it was moving were beginning to seem rather pinched, defensive, and egocentric. A sigh for the freedom and amplitude of earlier poetry appears in a letter (February 3) three days after he sent Reynolds the poems that included the sonnet, "When I have fears." Reynolds, in this little game by which the two friends were trying to amuse each other while occupied with other matters, sent along two sonnets he had written on Robin Hood.[2] Keats, who signs himself Reynolds' "Coscribbler," finds some good things to say about the two sonnets on Robin Hood, but gently chides him for a sentimental, Huntian phrase, "tender and true"—"the more because I have had so much reason to shun it as a quicksand . . . We must cut this, and not be rattlesnaked into more of the like." From the thought of Hunt, he turns to a very different writer, Wordsworth:

It may be said that we ought to read our Contemporaries. that Wordsworth &c should have their due from us. But for the sake of a few fine imaginative or domestic passages, are we to be bullied into a certain Philosophy engendered in the whims of an Egotist—Every man has his speculations, but every man does not brood and peacock over them till he makes a false coinage and deceives himself. Many a man can travel to the very bourne of Heaven, and yet want confidence to put down his halfseeing. Sancho will invent a Journey

2 "The trees in Sherwood Forest" and "With coat of Lincoln green," published in the *Yellow Dwarf* (February 21), and later in Reynolds' *Garden of Florence* (1821).

heavenward as well as any body. We hate poetry that has a palpable design upon us—and if we do not agree, seems to put its hand in its breeches pocket. Poetry should be great & unobtrusive, a thing which enters into one's soul, and does not startle it or amaze it with itself but with its subject. . . . Old Matthew spoke to [Wordsworth] some years ago on some nothing, & because he happens in an Evening Walk to imagine the figure of the old man—he must stamp it down in black & white, and it is henceforth sacred—I don't mean to deny Wordsworth's grandeur & Hunt's merit, but I mean to say we need not be teazed with grandeur & merit—when we can have them uncontaminated & unobtrusive. Let us have the old Poets, & Robin Hood   Your letter and its sonnets gave me more pleasure than will the 4th Book of Childe Harold.

He is beginning to feel that a common quality may underlie the cozy, sentimental corner-retreat of Hunt, the unshakable self-absorption of Wordsworth, and the flaring, obvious egocentricity of Byron—the poetry, as Keats says, "of anybody's life and opinions." At least they all, however diverse they might be in other ways, contribute to something that strikes him as a loss in poetry. The loss comes in what seems to him a general retreat from amplitude, a concentration on the small and specialized, a defensive primness which, "if we do not agree, seems to put its hand in its breeches pocket." A year or so before, he had been able to echo back, in happy confidence, the stock slogans of the day implying that it was the constricting effect of the eighteenth century that had driven poetry into smaller, less vital areas. But the whole situation was beginning to appear a little more complicated now. Even the new rebels against the eighteenth century had specialized preserves of their own on which they defensively concentrated. They were to the Elizabethans, it seemed to him, as a petty ruler, like the Elector of Hanover, to an emperor of vast provinces.

2

Keats's determination to be a free agent is certainly apparent: "I will cut all this—I will have no more of Wordsworth or Hunt in particular . . . Why should we be owls, when we can be Eagles?" But the problem still remained, how to be an eagle instead of an owl? This was something for the future, however. After all, "For many years my offerings must be hush'd," as he had said only ten days before. Meanwhile he wanted to thank Reynolds for what he called his "dish of filberts" from the greenwood. In return, said

Keats, "I have gathered a few Catkins, I hope they'll look pretty." And he encloses two poems in the light seven-syllable couplets of the seventeenth century: "Robin Hood" ("To J. H. R. In answer to his Robin Hood Sonnets") and "Lines on the Mermaid Tavern." The first comes close to mock-threnody: "No! those days are gone away . . . their minutes buried all . . . the bugle sounds no more . . . Never one, of all the clan . . . Gone, the merry morris din." Robin is in "his turfèd grave," his oaks long since fallen beneath the strokes of the dockyard axes and "rotted on the briny seas." With the rollicking meter transforming the dirgelike repetitions, the nostalgia is kept lighthearted. "I hope you will like [the verses]; they are at least written in the Spirit of Outlawry."

It was in something of a "Spirit of Outlawry" against the direction of modern poetry that the three months from February through April began—months that were to end with a very different conception of what next to do. The "Lines on the Mermaid Tavern," probably composed a few days before "Robin Hood," are even more spirited in their evocation of a healthful past ("Souls of Poets dead and gone"), and, by linking the close with the beginning, make up what Keats later called "a sort of rondeau which I think I shall become partial to." The form was at least a relief from the sonnet, which imposed a rather pretentious solemnity whether one wished it or not. Both poems continued, to his own mind, to wear well. When he came to assemble his next and final volume, he included, of all his poems between *Endymion* and *Hyperion*, only these two—"Robin Hood" and the "Lines on the Mermaid Tavern"—and the short romance he was soon to begin, *Isabella*. He included no sonnets at all. Yet he was continuing to write sonnets, though of a different sort. In turning to the Shakespearean pattern, beginning with "When I have fears," he was making at least a gesture both of independence and of his new start. For with the exception of the loose heroic couplet—which he also abandoned after *Endymion*—no form was so closely associated with his previous poetry as the Petrarchan sonnet. And the associational drag of the Petrarchan form was even less pleasant than that of the couplet. From the first primitive efforts back at the Edmonton surgery, through the sentimental sonnets of the Felton Mathew period at Guy's Hospital, and then through the year and a half of Hunt's influence, it represented both subjects and mannerisms of which he was ashamed, including sonnet contests, feminine "occasions" for poetry, and responses to gifts of roses or laurel crowns. By the end of January 1818 he had written at least forty-one sonnets, all in the Petrarchan form. But from now until the end he was to write little more than half that number—a total of twenty-five. Of these a fifth—dashed down on the spur of the moment when he reverted to old habit—are Petrarchan. Of two others, one is unrhymed ("What the Thrush Said") and the second is deliberately experimental ("If by dull rhymes"). The remaining eighteen are either basically or entirely Shakespearean.[3]

He was not so deluded as to think that, by merely switching from the conventional tepid Petrarchan form to the now less common Shakespearean (and generally Elizabethan) pattern, he was recapturing the spirit of an earlier, more healthful poetry. In fact, the sonnet as a whole may already have begun to seem stale (the adjective he uses for both rhyme schemes a year later is "dull"); and in any case his ambitions were directed to a "long Poem." But everything in his experience had taught him the value of beginning to make some effort at once—however much the immediate course of action fell short of the ideal—rather than remaining in a state of paralysis: through the mere activity one's faculties became sharper at detecting unexpected openings. (That confidence was to be richly justified a year later when he developed his new ode stanza from the *disjecta membra* of the two sonnet forms.) At the same time there were some attractions. He had begun to reread Shakespeare's sonnets in the autumn, and the structure, cadence, and rhetorical devices were in his mind. If more than mere rhyme scheme were followed, the form would be a fresh if minor challenge; it would at least help to work against the particular version of the Petrarchan pattern that he had taken over from Hunt and,

---

3 The five Petrarchan sonnets include "To the Nile," written in Hunt's sonnet contest; three sonnets from the Scottish Tour ("On Visiting the Tomb of Burns," "To Ailsa Rock," "On Hearing the Bag-Pipe"); and the purposely trivial "The House of Mourning." Of the eighteen Shakespearean sonnets, seven were written between late January and the end of April ("When I have fears," "Time's Sea," "To Spenser," "Blue! 'tis the life of heaven," "The Human Seasons," "To J.R.," and probably "To Homer"), and these are the most Shakespearean in prosodic and other stylistic ways. After two from the Scottish tour ("This mortal body" and "Read me a lesson, Muse") and "Translation from a Sonnet of Ronsard" (which lacks the couplet), only eight more were written: six are Shakespearean in rhyme scheme, though less so in other ways ("Why did I laugh tonight," "On a Dream," "Fame, like a wayward Girl," "The day is gone," "I cry your mercy," and the disputably dated "Bright star"); and two use a basically Shakespearean structure with variations ("To Sleep" and "How fever'd is the man").

with sympathetic tenacity, absorbed into habit. Hunt, in fact, disliked the Shakespearean form; to the end of his days he maintained the superiority of "the Sonnet Called the Legitimate" (to quote from the title of one of his essays; the terms "Petrarchan" and "legitimate" were interchangeable in the early nineteenth century). Keats was much in the mood, as *Isabella* very soon illustrated, to use devices not only of versification but of phrasing (such as parallelism, repetition, and antithesis) on which Hunt frowned. Finally, the form was by no means hackneyed at the present moment. There had been a brief surge of sonnets in the Shakespearean form back in the 1790's. But these had been largely forgotten, and the few flaccid sonneteers who still used the form missed everything Shakespearean except the rhyme scheme. Hunt's opinion, on this issue if on little else, was an accurate barometer of the conventional attitude. The Shakespearean form was, to Keats, temptingly unpopular.

The sonnets Keats now began to write at odd moments—at least the first eight or ten—still remain the most truly Shakespearean sonnets of the nineteenth (or, for that matter, twentieth) century, whether in metrical variation, pause, quatrain division, or even rhetorical devices. Of special interest, since he is seeking a cleanliness of phrase that we also find him trying to attain in *Isabella,* are the various forms of balance within the line that Shakespeare used so prodigally. Thus Shakespeare would balance the line with simple repetition: *"Music to hear,* why *hear'st* thou *music* sadly"; "Against that *time,* if ever that *time* come." So in Keats: "That one poor *year* a thousand *years* would be"; "At thought of *idleness* cannot be *idle."* Ordinary balance by parallelism in Shakespeare ("Give not a windy night a rainy morrow"; "In praise of ladies dead and lovely knights") is duplicated by Keats ("Will for thine honour and his pleasure try"; "Of thee I hear and of the Cyclades"). Extremely common in Shakespeare is the use of alliteration for balance: "And *b*urn the long-lived phoenix in her *b*lood" "When *l*ofty trees I see barren of *l*eaves, / Which erst from *h*eat did canopy the *h*erd"; and Keats follows Shakespeare with gusto: "The *t*ent of Hesperus, and all his *t*rain"; "Read me a *l*esson, Muse, and speak it *l*oud." Finally, though he could have had any number of other models in mind, he follows Shakespeare's abundant use of antithetical balance ("Most worthy *comfort,* now my greatest *grief"; "Love* is my *sin,* and thy dear *virtue hate"*) : "Aye, on the shores of *darkness* there is *light*," writes Keats in "To Homer": "There is a *triple sight* in *blindness* keen." Or again: "And *grief* unto my darling *joys* dost bring"; "Felt *parting* and warm *meeting* every week."

3

Keats had told his brothers in early December that he would soon join them in Devon. But by now it was the middle of February. His ostensible reason for delaying in London—to revise *Endymion* and proofread the books as they came from the press—was not the real one; the work did not actually demand his presence. But the weeks that followed the new beginning in later January were haunted with hope. "To thee the Spring will be a harvest-time," the thrush had seemed to keep saying: "To thee the Spring shall be a triple morn."

He conscientiously kept his social engagements to a minimum. It was not hard to do so. He did not want to go out much now, but preferred to read. He went to Hazlitt's lectures on Tuesday evenings. There were a few visits with Reynolds, a dinner at Hunt's with the Shelleys, Peacock, and James Hogg; and he went once to the British Gallery. One evening (February 4) he dropped in on Hunt after attending an informal concert. Shelley was also present. Hunt proposed another of his sonnet contests: each of them was to write "a Sonnet on the River Nile" in fifteen minutes. Keats and Shelley finished theirs in time. Neither was much aroused by the occasion; and their sonnets showed it. Hunt, who may have already had the subject in mind, kept working at his until two o'clock in the morning, and turned out one of the best sonnets he ever wrote.[4]

The truth is that Keats did not want to go down to Devon. He felt that he was just on the verge of something; and though he would never have been able to admit it consciously to himself, he was almost afraid of the psychological effect, at this crucial moment, of living daily with the distress of Tom's illness. So preoccupied was he that it did not occur to him that George was getting very restless. Least of all did it occur to him that, during the past year of unemployment and of serving as Tom's nurse, George

---

[4] Keats's sonnet ("Son of the old moon-mountains") is notable for its lack of Egyptian imagery, and Shelley's ("Month after month the gather'd rains descend") for its abstractions ("Frost," "Heat," "Tempest"). Hunt alone was confident enough to print his poem ("It flows through old hush'd Egypt").

might be developing some radical plans of his own. His conscience
was jolted when, on February 21, a letter arrived for George at
the Hampstead address from Georgiana Wylie. He encloses it in a
letter to his brothers: "does she expect you in town George? I have
been abominably id[l]e since you left—but have just turned over a
new leaf." Within another six days, by February 27, he had finished his revision of Book III of *Endymion*, started on Book IV,
and begun reading proof on the first two books. He wrote John
Taylor that day his well-known letter containing his new "axioms"
in poetry: that poetry should "surprise by a fine excess"; that if it
comes "not as naturally as the Leaves to a tree it had better not
come at all"; that though in *Endymion* he has moved only into
"the Go-cart from the leading strings," he "cannot help looking
into new countries with an 'O for a Muse of fire to ascend!'—If
Endymion serves me as a Pioneer perhaps I ought to be content."

Then, sometime between February 28 and March 4, George suddenly appeared.[5] On February 28 he was twenty-one. He was determined to do something about his prospects. He may have mentioned his thought of emigrating if their guardian, Richard Abbey,
would advance enough money. More probably he referred to it
as only one of several possibilities. At the same time, Tom sent
John a letter saying that he was better and would probably come
back to London himself. It was plain that Tom did not want to
stay down in Devon alone. Nor indeed should Tom be alone, as
Keats very well knew.

4

On Wednesday evening, March 4, Keats took the 7:30 coach for
Exeter (a trip of about twenty-seven hours); and from Exeter he
would then take a provincial coach the remaining fifteen miles to
Teignmouth. Though it was already beginning to rain, he sat on
the outside of the coach in order to save money. As the night went
on, one of the worst storms to strike England in several years arose:

[5] George dropped into the shop of Taylor and Hessey on March 6 (*KC*, I.12),
bearing a message from John ("his Brother the Poet is gone into Devonshire & has
left the third Book with him," Hessey writes Taylor). He also informed Hessey that
his brother had left the night of the great storm (March 4) "on the *outside* of the
Coach." He would not have known this, nor could Keats have left the message he
did with George, unless they had been together in London. Keats would naturally
have been unable to talk with George in Teignmouth: he did not arrive there until
March 6, the day George called on Hessey. On the storm of March 4, see Rollins'
note in *KC*, I.12–13.

trees kept crashing across the roads, houses were toppled, and the wind blew over many coaches, killing some of the passengers. The Exeter coach avoided any serious accident, though it was certainly late: Keats probably did not arrive at Teignmouth before the after-noon of March 6. Meanwhile the rain continued heavily for six more days. His whole impression of Devon, with George gone, Tom ill, and the constant rain, was far from pleasant; and his let-ters begin to nag at the place in a way that contrasts with his cus-tomary eagerness to be pleased. He plunged at once into his revi-sion of the last book of *Endymion,* and finished it in eight days (March 14) .

At some time during that rainy week he went to the local theater. While there, he tells Reynolds, he "got insulted, which I ought to remember to forget to tell anybody; for I did not fight." The day before he finished the revision of *Endymion,* which he was so eager to have "printed that I may forget it and proceed," the omnipres-ent thought of the seasons, of the harvest this spring was to create, grew sharper; and he took off a short time to write the sonnet "The Human Seasons." But just after he had copied it out in a letter to Benjamin Bailey (March 13) , Tom suddenly had a hemorrhage. The experience shook Keats. Writing the next day to Reynolds— who had himself been ill for a month with rheumatic fever—he tries to manage his anxiety through attempted lightness:

> I intend to cut all sick people if they do not make up their minds to cut sickness—a fellow to whom I have a complete aversion, and who strange to say is harboured and countenanced in several houses where I visit—he is sitting now quite impudent between me and Tom—He insults me at poor Jem Rice's . . . I shall say, once for all, to my friends generally and severally, cut that fellow, or I cut you.

He delayed sending the fourth book of *Endymion* to his pub-lisher until he could enclose with it a preface. There were so many things that he wanted to say, while at the same time he knew it should be brief, that he was uncertain how to begin; and the days passed. He wrote a couple of light lyrics that he sent off to Hay-don.[6] He was getting to know some people. "Atkins the Coach-man," he tells Reynolds (March 14) , "Bartlet the Surgeon, Sim-

---

[6] "For there's Bishop's Teign" and "Where be ye going, you Devon Maid?" A few days later (March 24) he wrote another in a letter to James Rice ("Over the hill and over the dale") . The fragment "The Castle Builder" was probably written be-tween January and May of this year.

mons the Barber, and the Girls over at the Bonnet Shop say we shall now have a Month of seasonable Weather." [7] George and Tom had already become good friends with the Jeffrey family: a widow, Margaret Jeffrey, and her daughters, Marian, Sarah, and Fanny. George flirted a little with them and, when he went back to London, sent the two elder girls a long, exuberant letter. "I would send you kisses by way of John and Tom, but I can't say I should relish your acknowledgement of them, so I'll e'en entreat you Marianne to kiss Sarah and she must fancy it is from me. She must do the same and you must use your imagination in like manner." He is curious to know what they think of John. "Is he not very original? he does not look by any means so handsome as four months ago, but is he not handsome? I am sure you must both like him very much, but don't forget *me*." [8] Tom seems to have been petted by all of them, especially by Marian, a quiet, steady girl who later in life published a book of poems. A legend persisted in the family that Marian fell in love with Keats. If so, Keats showed no response; but he became friendly with all three of these kindly girls. A later reference to one of them (probably Fanny, the youngest) —"long-haired" with a "great brown hard fist"—suggests some playful scuffling. When he and Tom left Teignmouth, Sarah apparently accompanied them on the coach as far as Honiton. Throughout the next year he received some letters from the elder girls, but apparently neglected to answer them until he wrote a year later to ask their help in finding a place in Devon to live during the summer.

After a week of hesitation he managed to finish a preface to *Endymion,* and then sent it off at once to John Taylor with the fourth book and a dedication (to Chatterton). The preface, twice the length of that which he later substituted for it, bristles with defensiveness. In any great nation, he begins, the work of a single individual is of "so little importance," his "pleadings and excuses are so uninteresting," that a preface is an impertinent bow to strangers who care nothing about the writer. At the very least it should al-

---

[7] The Keats brothers apparently had rooms at No. 20, the Strand (now Northumberland Place). The bonnet shop was probably at No. 35, nearly opposite No. 20 (I.79). "Bartlet" was apparently Jacob Bartlett, the surgeon, of Regent's Place (I.246n). He may have been consulted by Tom; but Tom's physician at Teignmouth was William Turton (1762–1835), a well-known authority on consumption. He was also a conchologist; his collection is now at the Smithsonian Institution in Washington (I.274n). For an account of the Jeffrey family, see Rollins' introduction (I.78–80).

[8] *KC,* I.13–16.

low the reader to "catch an idea of an Author's modesty and non opinion of himself—which I sincerely hope may be seen, in the few lines I have to write." Then, with affected lightness, he reveals his "modesty," or at least a debonair unconcern:

> About a twelve month since, I published a little book of verses; it was read by some dozen of my friends who lik'd it; and some dozen who I was unacquainted with, who did not. Now when a dozen human beings, are at words with another dozen, it becomes a matter of anxiety to side with one's friends;—more especially when excited thereto by a great love of Poetry.

He goes on to speak about the writing of *Endymion* itself. He had been far from sure at the start where it might lead: "as I proceeded my steps were all uncertain." Hence the poem

> must rather be considered as an endeavour than a thing accomplish'd: a poor prologue to what, if I live, I humbly hope to do. In duty to the Public I should have kept it back for a year or two, knowing it to be so faulty: but I really cannot do so:—by repetition my favourite Passages sound vapid in my ears, and I would rather redeem myself with a new Poem—should this one be found of any interest. . . .
>
> It has been too much the fashion of late to consider men bigotted and addicted to every word that may chance to escape their lips: now I here declare that I have not any particular affection for any particular phrase, word, or letter in the whole affair. I have written to please myself and in hopes to please others, and for a love of fame; if I neither please myself, nor others, nor get fame, of what consequence is Phraseology?
>
> I would fain escape the bickerings that all works, not exactly in chime, bring upon their begetters:—but this is not fair to expect, there must be conversation of some sort and to object shows a man's consequence. In case of a London drizzle or a Scotch mist, the following quotation from Marston may perhaps 'stead me as an umbrella for an hour or so: 'let it be the Curtesy of my peruser rather to pity my self-hindering labours than to malice me.'

Neither Reynolds nor Taylor, nor anyone else who saw the preface, felt that it would do. Reynolds, in his reply, apparently said two things that cut Keats to the quick: that the manner and tone were "affected" and that the attempted flippancy savored of Leigh Hunt. For Keats, in response, sends one of the two or three most defensive letters he was ever to write:

> Since you all agree that the thing is bad, it must be so—though I am not aware there is any thing like Hunt in it, (and if there is, it

is my natural way, and I have something in common with Hunt)
. . . I have not the slightest feel of humility towards the Public—or
to any thing in existence,—but the eternal Being, the Principle of
Beauty,—and the Memory of great Men.

Why should he therefore assume a false modesty now before the
"public"? "I never wrote one single Line of Poetry with the least
Shadow of public thought." This feeling he is expressing—this refusal to truckle—has nothing to do with lack of love for humanity.
"I could not live without the love of my friends—I would jump
down Ætna for any great Public Good—but I hate a Mawkish
Popularity." Then what he is talking about becomes plainer; and
the feeling he is expressing anticipates the bitter attack he wrote
and then wisely deleted in the *Fall of Hyperion* and the strange involved letter he wrote about that time (August 23, 1819) to John
Taylor. By the "public" he does not really mean the large, often
good-humored group of readers that the word usually suggests. He
means the "thousand jabberers about Pictures and Books," with
their affectations of disdain, and the envious readiness to raise
their quills, like "porcupines," to pierce whatever they approach.
He would like to turn on these porcupines "with a torch." The affected mannerisms of men like Kingston, whom he had met at
Horace Smith's dinner party in December (who had made him
think by contrast of Shakespeare's "Negative Capability" and the
capacity to lose one's ego in what is greater than oneself), rush
back into his mind. He wants now, he says, to be free of "Kingston
criticism"—to "escape" and forget it.

Reynolds' justifiable charge that the preface was "affected"
therefore cut all the more cruelly. Keats protests wistfully: "if
there is any fault in the preface it is not affectation but an under-
song of disrespect to the Public." He was really more unsettled by
Reynolds' reaction than he admitted. He would take a few days to
think over a possible revision of that preface. If one did not come
in the mail, Reynolds could tell Taylor to publish *Endymion*
without a preface. But Keats began to work at it immediately, and
overnight wrote the very short, manly preface that was published
with the poem.[9] The next day (April 10) he sent it off to Reyn-

---

9 "Knowing within myself the manner in which this Poem has been produced, it
is not without a feeling of regret that I make it public.
"What manner I mean, will be quite clear to the reader, who must soon perceive
great inexperience, immaturity, and every error denoting a feverish attempt, rather

olds: "I am anxious you sho^d find this Preface tolerable. If there is an affectation in it 'tis natural to me." He is almost timid. He is also weary of the self-questionings of the past night: "I had an idea of giving no Preface; however, don't you think this had better go? —O, let it—one should not be too timid—of committing faults."

5

Most of what had been happening since he came to Devon on March 4—most of what was to happen until he left with Tom on May 4, exactly two months later—was altogether inward. He was continuing to study Milton intensively, puzzling, as he did so, over the contrasts between the poetry of Milton's era and that of his own day. This was only one aspect of the general "labyrinth" into which he seemed to have come. It never occurred to him to consider the larger questions of poetry (what it had done, what it might yet do) apart from those of life itself. Tom's situation pressed on his imagination daily, and with it a deepening sense of the precariousness of life, its brevity and unpredictability, and the refusal of events to fit not merely the clean categories of man's "imperious" will but apparently even the heart's simplest standards of justice. When the weather was good, he tried to see something of the surrounding country. But the weather did not much improve. In three weeks, he said, there had been only six good days. He went to Dawlish Fair on Easter Monday (March 23). But except for visits with the Jeffreys, little occurred to interrupt this rather

---

than a deed accomplished. The two first books, and indeed the two last, I feel sensible are not of such completion as to warrant their passing the press; nor should they if I thought a year's castigation would do them any good;—it will not: the foundations are too sandy. It is just that this youngster should die away: a sad thought for me, if I had not some hope that while it is dwindling I may be plotting, and fitting myself for verses fit to live.

"This may be speaking too presumptuously, and may deserve a punishment: but no feeling man will be forward to inflict it: he will leave me alone, with the conviction that there is not a fiercer hell than the failure in a great object. This is not written with the least atom of purpose to forestall criticisms of course, but from the desire I have to conciliate men who are competent to look, and who do look with a zealous eye, to the honour of English literature.

"The imagination of a boy is healthy, and the mature imagination of a man is healthy; but there is a space of life between, in which the soul is in a ferment, the character undecided, the way of life uncertain, the ambition thick-sighted: thence proceeds mawkishness, and all the thousand bitters which those men I speak of must necessarily taste in going over the following pages.

"I hope I have not in too late a day touched the beautiful mythology of Greece, and dulled its brightness: for I wish to try once more, before I bid it farewel."

brooding life he was leading until James Rice came down to Teignmouth for a short visit (April 18–20), a pleasant interlude that led Keats to write the sonnet "To J. R." On April 24 he received an advance copy of *Endymion,* which was to be published in another three or four weeks. Meanwhile the rain still continued. "I lay awake last night," he tells Reynolds (April 27), near the end of his stay,

> listening to the Rain with a sense of being drown'd and rotted like a grain of wheat—There is a continual courtesy between the Heavens and the Earth—the heavens rain down their unwelcomeness, and the Earth sends it up again to be returned to morrow.

Even the letters, with two notable exceptions, tell relatively little of this inner life until late April, when he is finishing up *Isabella.* One of these exceptions [10] is a letter in verse with which he hoped to amuse John Reynolds (March 25), who had been ill now for over a month. Though Keats was utterly weary of the couplet after *Endymion,* he naturally used it now, for it came to him almost as easily as prose. The more than hundred lines of the verse letter were written in one evening. The thought was only to give Reynolds something of a change. It would have disturbed rather than flattered Keats that, long after his death, these lines, like so much of his impromptu verse, were salvaged, printed as "poetry," and then approached with formal expectations that are wildly irrelevant. He starts out by chatting about pictures that came to him as he lay in bed the previous night. Our century is perhaps over-eager to interpret dreams and near-dreams. But knowing how intense Keats's thinking had been about the relation of different periods of poetry and philosophy (especially the relation of classical Greece and of the Elizabethans to the eighteenth and nineteenth centuries),[11] we cannot but yield to the temptation to notice the juxtaposition of periods in this half-awake dreaming. Alexander the Great appeared in a modern nightcap, Socrates was attempting to tie a modern cravat, Voltaire strode by with medieval armor. Hazlitt, who so admired the "masculine boldness and creative vigor" of the English writers of the sixteenth and seventeenth centuries, and who constantly attacked the "mediocrity" of the pres-

---

10 The other is the noteworthy letter to Bailey (March 13) about the "greeting of the Spirit" and its object, to which the whole conception of the odes a year later owes so much (below, Chapter XIX).
11 See below, Chapter XIII.

ent, was playing with one of the many cats owned by the eminent "blue-stocking," Maria Edgeworth. The repeated attacks on the bluestocking in Keats's letters would suggest that it had become another stock symbol of the forces that were emasculating poetry and distracting it from its pristine vigor and variety.[12] Junius Brutus Booth, who rendered so thunderously for the present time the great passages of Shakespeare, was seen meandering tipsily toward Soho for further solace through drink. But Keats could never write satirically with much gusto. Other pictures that passed before him, more innocently descriptive, begin to take over. In one of them the opening three lines anticipate images that return a year later in the "Ode on a Grecian Urn":

> The sacrifice goes on; the pontif knife
> Gleams in the sun, the milk-white heifer lows,
> The pipes go shrilly, the libation flows:
> A white sail shews above the green-head cliff
> Moves round the point, and throws her anchor stiff.

Then, in the last third of the letter, the tone suddenly changes:

> O that our dreamings all, of sleep or wake,
> Would all their colours from the sunset take:
> From something of material sublime.

He is thinking, of course, of the famous lines in Wordsworth's "Tintern Abbey" ("A sense sublime / Of something far more deeply interfused, / Whose dwelling is the light of setting suns"). But too often our dreams are simply the "shadow" of our own hearts, of our daily preoccupations and anxieties in a world where we all "jostle." He then breaks off: the subject is hopelessly complex; and

> to philosophise
> I dare not yet! Oh, never will the prize,
> High reason, and the lore of good and ill,
> Be my award! Things cannot to the will
> Be settled, but they tease us out of thought.

The immense blurring complexity of life eludes the imperious "will" of the mind in its craving for clear-cut meaning. Is it that

---

12 Four days before the present letter to Reynolds, Keats praises Hazlitt as the "only good damner" he knows: "Hazlitt has damned the bigotted and the blue-stockin[g]ed how durst the Man?" One of Keats's ambitions, he says later to Bailey (August 14, 1819), is to "upset the drawling of the blue stocking literary world." (Cf. Herschel Baker, *William Hazlitt* [1962], p. 225.)

the imagination, as soon as we cease merely to accept concreteness and begin to probe for a further significance, suddenly finds itself lost in a "Purgatory" where no "standard law" of either heaven or earth applies?

> is it that imagination brought
> Beyond its proper bound, yet still confin'd,
> Lost in a sort of Purgatory blind,
> Cannot refer to any standard law
> Of either earth or heaven? It is a flaw
> In happiness, to see beyond our bourn,—
> It forces us in summer skies to mourn,
> It spoils the singing of the nightingale.
>
> Dear Reynolds! I have a mysterious tale,
> And cannot speak it.

The "mystery," which he lacks the resources to understand or express, is the "eternal fierce destruction," the huge hungry diversity of life, for which the heart, with its simple presuppositions, is so unprepared. He could walk to the sea, delight in its calm wideness, the foam, the flat brown sand:

> but I saw
> Too far into the sea, where every maw
> The greater on the less feeds evermore.—
> But I saw too distinct into the core
> Of an eternal fierce destruction.

The quiet garden, with the young spring leaves and the wild strawberry, teems with that same "fierce destruction":

> the hawk at pounce,—
> The gentle robin, like a pard or ounce,
> Ravening a worm.

This innocent verse letter, designed only to amuse an invalid, was plainly turning into something different from the intention. He tries to end it by mimicking the title ("Moods of my own Mind") that Wordsworth gave to some of his poems: "Away . . . Moods of one's mind!" Let Reynolds—and Tom—hurry to "get health." He himself will meanwhile take "refuge" from these "detested moods in new romance."

6

The "new romance" was *Isabella; or, the Pot of Basil;* and any
"refuge" it offered was limited. Back in the winter, Reynolds and
Keats had talked about bringing out a book of short narrative poems based on stories in Boccaccio. Reynolds may already have begun one or two [13] before he dropped his literary ambitions in mid-
February and turned to the law. Keats, for his part, had begun a
few stanzas in early February on the story of the Pot of Basil (probably following up a suggestion he had heard in one of Hazlitt's
lectures). Had he worked at it throughout any period of time
while he was in Devonshire, he would probably have mentioned it
in his letters. He always assumes that his friends are interested in
what he is doing; and we can follow the progress of *Endymion,
Hyperion, Lamia,* and the *Fall of Hyperion* fairly well. Except for
the general remark on March 25 that he will "Take refuge" from
the moodiness of his thoughts in a "new romance," his only mention of *Isabella* during these weeks is to tell Reynolds (April 27)
that he has just finished it. We can infer that most of it was written between March 25 and April 27; and knowing something
about his speed of composition, especially when the plot of a narrative poem was already prepared, we are at liberty to doubt
whether the actual writing filled more than a fraction of this
month.

Isabella has traditionally defied general criticism, as distinct
from the technical criticism of style. The reasons interlock. One is,
of course, the nature of the genre. Since it is a verse adaptation of
a prose tale, any offense or pleasure given by the narrative as such
must be principally attributed to Boccaccio rather than Keats.
Strictly relevant in the criticism of Keats himself are only his judgment in selecting the tale in the first place, any essential change he
makes in the story, and, finally, whatever is attained through the
idiom and the verse. The matter of judgment in the choice of the
tale is in this case a very minor consideration. The Italian romance
was being revived in England; for the reading public generally
there was an air of novelty about it; "The Pot of Basil" was one of
Boccaccio's better stories, and even the admired Hazlitt thought
it a good choice. As for the plot, Keats makes no real changes,

---

[13] Those he published after Keats's death in *The Garden of Florence* (1821),
pp. 1–28, 153–175.

though it should be noted that he used an English translation of 1620 in which the original starkness of tone is somewhat modified. Isabella, living in the house of her merchant brothers in Florence (Boccaccio lays the story in Messina; he gives Isabella three brothers, and Keats reduces the number to two), loves secretly their young clerk, Lorenzo, who is equally devoted to her. When the brothers discover this, they take Lorenzo to a forest and kill and bury him. Lorenzo's ghost appears to Isabella, tells her what happened and where he is buried. She finds the body, digs it up, removes the head, and puts it in a pot of basil. The basil tree, growing from his brain and watered by Isabella's tears, is taken from her by her brothers, and she dies of grief. Though the actual plot is closely followed, two changes in the general treatment of it may be noticed. The first in no way alters the course of the narrative. Only too conscious that this is a genre which, in English, goes back to Chaucer, Keats inserts occasional brief digressions and invocations in the Chaucerian vein: he stops to protest against shedding tears too effusively for the tragedies of lovers; he stops to rebuke (quite successfully—the stanzas are among the best in the poem) the mercantile hardness and avarice of Isabella's brothers; a third digression invokes and praises Boccaccio; and a fourth, half ironically and half sentimentally, stops to implore Melancholy to "linger here awhile" before the poem proceeds to its conclusion. These conventions of the medieval romance may leave us a little cold, especially in a nineteenth-century poem. But they are not long enough to obtrude. A second change, however, does affect the poem as a whole. Boccaccio had allowed the events to speak entirely for themselves. Keats tries to make the later events more convincing by stressing the strength of the passion Isabella and Lorenzo feel for each other. In doing so, he comes near to defeating his own purpose. For, to begin with, the reader, who would otherwise have taken the love affair for granted, is prompted to look at it more closely. And at the same time the tone and diction of the poem are colored by the further emphasis that Keats is placing on sentiment.

We find ourselves turning, therefore, to the language and the verse. Though he had declared war on sentimentality some months ago (such phrases as "tender and true" he was trying to shun as though they were "quicksand"), Keats unquestionably falls back, throughout much of *Isabella,* on some of the stock phrasing he had picked up in 1816 and 1817 from Hunt, if for no other reason than that he has no ready vocabulary yet for this kind of longer poem (another vocabulary was easier to find for "short pieces"). Of course it can be said that one way to avoid these older habits would be to attempt a very different kind of longer poem. That was exactly what Keats intended to do. And, all things considered, the time he took before he made that attempt was very short. It was, indeed, surprisingly short. For the way to another sort of poem—or at least the sort that he had in mind—was as difficult as any he could have selected: it was one in which the presiding geniuses were to be Milton and ultimately Shakespeare. And if there was a third example, it was Wordsworth; yet Wordsworth, even at his best, seemed to conflict with that other, larger ideal represented by Shakespeare and Milton, and this added a further complication. A little time had to pass first; at least a few months, though Keats kept telling himself that it would have to be a period of "many years."

Meanwhile he went on with this poem. "Life," as he told Bailey, "must be undergone," and something has to be done to fill out the vacuities of it. He was only too aware that the vocabulary, the phrasing, of Hunt was helping to fill out the interstices of this poem (which, within another year, he was to dislike more than any of his other long poems). And, already in reaction to Hunt in so many ways, he swung impetuously against Hunt in many of the stylistic features of the poem. This demanded a deliberate wrestle when writing in a genre so closely associated with Hunt; and a brusque impatience bursts out for a moment in a letter to Haydon (March 21): "It is a great Pity that People should by associating themselves with the fine[st] things, spoil them—Hunt has damned Hampstead [and] Masks and Sonnets and italian tales." If in occasional phrasing, especially of tender passages, Keats goes back to a Huntian vocabulary that he had said he would "cut," he tries in other ways to do everything that Hunt advised against in prosodic and rhetorical devices. The verse form he selected was *ottava rima* (*a b a b a b c c*), and he used as a model Edward Fairfax's translation of Tasso (1600), of which he had a copy. Fairfax abounded in mannerisms caught from his own Italian models; and of many of these Hunt, fond as he was of the Italians in other ways, disapproved. They struck him as "artificial," formal, stylized. His *Critique on Fairfax's Tasso* attacks Fairfax's—and Marino's—frequent use of antithesis. Keats, already making a point of using antithesis in the Shakespearean sonnets he was writing, does so now with zest ("The *little sweet* doth kill *much bitterness"*; "She *weeps* alone for *pleasures* not to be"). Hunt disliked Fairfax's Italianate tendency to "heap a line with descriptive nouns and adjectives." Keats follows Fairfax ("He might not in house, field, or garden stir"). Hunt disliked repetitions generally. *Isabella* uses them more than anything else Keats ever wrote, beginning with the first line, "Fair Isabel, poor simple Isabel." Hunt, in his *Critique,* sighs that Pulci carries repetition so far as to begin "a whole stanza with the same word." Keats begins line after line in the same stanza with the same words:

> And she forgot the stars, the moon, the sun,
>   And she forgot the blue above the trees,
> And she forgot the dells where waters run,
>   And she forgot the chilly autumn breeze.

Keats's deliberate attempt to keep this up in defiance of Hunt sometimes comes close to the comic. He begins a stanza on the two brothers:

> Why were they proud? Because their marble founts
>   Gush'd with more pride than do a wretch's tears?—
> Why were they proud? Because fair orange-mounts
>   Were of more soft ascent than lazar stairs?—
> Why were they proud? Because red-lin'd accounts
>   Were richer than the songs of Grecian years?—

He has already pushed the phrase to the point of exhaustion. But he is resolved to hammer it in further, and ends lamely:

> Why were they proud? again we ask aloud,
> Why in the name of Glory were they proud?

Meanwhile he has completely dropped most of what he had taken over from Hunt's versification two years before. Feminine endings, so abundant in the 1817 volume (about 25 per cent), have now been cut to about 3 per cent; Hunt's limp use of feminine caesuras late in the line—one of the distinguishing features, as we have noticed in Keats's earlier verse—has drastically waned. The soft polysyllabic diction of Hunt and the early Keats is beginning to give way to shorter words of stronger consonantal body; adjectives generally decrease, and the proportion of verbs rises.

The result is not wholly a hodge-podge. There is a certain cleanliness about the quick walk of *Isabella* that partly succeeds in modifying the sentimentality. Yet, even so, we come back to the poem's continued defiance of general criticism. Keats himself, a year later, indicated the reason. It relies too heavily on the reader's predisposition; one either brings a readiness to enter into the direct pathos of a poem like this (in which case specific criticism is irrelevant; for it is then a moving, a "sincere" poem, which, as Lamb said, "should disarm criticism") ; or else, if one cannot come prepared with that predisposition, the poem seems absurd and embarrassing. The nineteenth century delighted in it: Woodhouse, Taylor, Reynolds, and Lamb [14] thought highly of it, among Keats's own friends; and the poem continued to be praised throughout the Victorian era. Sir Sidney Colvin (1917) still felt that in *Isabella* Keats "reaches his high-water mark in human feeling, and in felicity both imaginative and executive." In another seven years, Amy Lowell, speaking perhaps a little abruptly for a very different generation, found the poem a deplorable, unexplained retrogression in Keats's writing. When Keats argues with Woodhouse about *Isabella* (September 1819)—which, said Woodhouse, Keats could no longer "bear"; he thought it hopelessly "mawkish"—he seems to waver for a moment. Perhaps he is being too personally embarrassed by its "simplicity of knowledge," which "might do very well after one's death, but not while one is alive." He himself, having to live with the poem if it were published (and he did not want to have it published), would rather "use more finesse with the Public"; he would rather write things that "cannot be laugh'd at in any way." "Were I a reviewer"—and this is now equivalent, to Keats, to saying if one were deliberately trying to find weak spots— *Isabella* "is what I should call . . . 'A weak-sided Poem' with an amusing sober-sadness about it." Then he hesitates: "Not that I do not think Reynolds and you are quite right about it." If one really accepts its approach, and enters into it dramatically, the poem may satisfy. "If I may say so, in my dramatic capacity I enter fully into the feeling; but in Propria Persona I should be apt to quiz it my-

[14] Lamb's famous review of the 1820 volume (*The New Times,* July 19, 1820) describes *Isabella* as "the finest thing in the volume." He contrasts it with *Lamia:* "To *us* an ounce of feeling is worth a pound of fancy." Of the stanzas (46–53) on Isabella's arriving and digging the grave, he writes: "There is nothing more awfully simple in diction, more nakedly grand and moving in sentiment, in Dante, in Chaucer, in Spenser" (an opinion echoed by Colvin: "Is any scene in poetry written with more piercing, more unerring vision" than that in the first two of these stanzas?) .

self." Quickly changing the subject, with obvious relief, to his latest narrative poem, he goes on: "There is no objection of this kind to Lamia—A good deal to St. Agnes eve—only not so glaring." [15]

Keats's own reaction to the poem, a year after writing it, is closer to that of the twentieth century than that of the nineteenth; and his feeling about it even now was divided (he already hints, when he tells Reynolds that he has finished it, that publication of this joint enterprise of theirs is not an important consideration: "The Compliment is paid to Boccacce, whether we publish or no; so there is content in this world"). In any case his mind was very much on other matters, some of them directly personal. As for the writing of poetry itself, the great problem was how to proceed; and *Isabella,* whatever may be said for or against it, had little to do with the large choice he must soon make. With it, as with the other poems he had been writing since the new beginning three months ago, he was only marking time.

[15] II.162, 174–175.

The Burden of the Mystery: The Emergence
of a Modern Poet

Spring 1818

BACK IN JANUARY George Keats had begun to think seriously of emigrating to America; and by April, if not before, he decided to leave as soon as he could, preferably by midsummer.

No stable or attractive work had appeared since George had left Abbey's countinghouse in the winter of 1816–17. We put it more accurately—but in a way that no one wished to put it—if we say that he was no longer personally free to make the most of what opportunities he might find in England. For he had ended by becoming, in effect, Tom's nurse. During the spring of the year before he had been glad enough to face the domestic difficulties this involved: Tom's illness could be thought of as temporary, and John, he felt, should have the chance to go away and start on *Endymion* without distractions. But the summer of 1817 had begun to pass with John still preoccupied with *Endymion*. His brothers had kept deferring the trip to France that they had all agreed to take together. Finally, in August, John—whose struggle with *Endymion* had been getting a little desperate—had made it plain that he would be much happier if he could accept Benjamin Bailey's invitation to spend September in Oxford; and the two younger brothers had then gone off to France alone. George seems to have enjoyed the visit. But his self-respect was disturbed. He should be starting at some sort of work; he had been idle for the better part of a year. When they returned from France, and John returned from Oxford, nothing had changed: Tom was no better, and John still had a quarter of his long poem to write. As November passed, Tom became worse. Everyone had seemed to agree that the winter climate in Devonshire would be, if not a help, at least less harmful. The brothers would go there as a group, John remaining for only a short while in London in order to put the finishing touches on *Endymion* and get it to the press.

But down in Teignmouth the pattern had again repeated itself.

The weeks passed. John, spurred by conscience, raced through his revision of *Endymion*. Yet distractions had kept arising during this short, hurried time. He had the chance to write his dramatic reviews for the *Champion*. He met Wordsworth. He was attending Hazlitt's lectures. More important, he felt a large, general change taking place in his whole conception of poetry; and if he made a point of keeping his brothers posted on his struggles with *Endymion,* he also, with his usual transparency, conveyed to them some sense of the larger demands and challenges that he now felt opening. This understandable clutch at time, this reluctance to leave, could seem to Keats himself to involve only a short delay. But as the weeks of January and then February passed, they seemed long to George. He began impatiently to think of the time when he himself, as well as John, could make a start. On March 1 he became of age. (He was actually born on February 28, but he and the family thought it was a day later.) Though all the children assumed that they had to wait until the youngest was twenty-one before their grandmother's estate was distributed, George could at least feel that he was now justified in asking for an advance from Abbey in order to help him begin.

Viewed with stark frankness—a frankness, in this one case, that neither John nor George could have faced—their eighteen-year-old brother was a heavy encumbrance. They both knew by now that Tom's illness was serious, however much they tried to deny it. George could hardly help reflecting that he would be unable even to marry under the present circumstances. Tom himself was only too aware of the complications he was innocently creating: but what were the alternatives? The only hope for any of the brothers was that time might bring some answer. It would be difficult to find three youths, orphaned so early, who could have continued to bring more good will to each other and more idealism about fraternal affection and loyalty. But this was proving to be one of those instances where the situation was simply too much for idealism and good will, however strong. Quite humanly, George, now that he was thinking of leaving, began to persuade himself that Tom was really much better—in fact, George found himself (once he had left Tom's company) habitually thinking of Tom as in "nearly good health"; [1] and, in thinking about John, he could assume—as

---

[1] After returning to London, George was surprised to hear that Tom was worse, and wrote John (March 18) : "Whenever he has occured to my thoughts he has ap-

people who do not write usually assume about those who do—that, in contrast to himself, John could work just as well at home, in Tom's company, as anywhere else. John and Tom, for their part, once they learned of George's decision, were loyally prepared to see every reason why George should go. They were as confident in George's ability as he was, probably more so, and resented his apparent lack of opportunity in England. In any case he would be wishing to get married within a year or two. Since they had moved into 76 Cheapside a year and a half before, and John had written the happy sonnet on Tom's seventeenth birthday celebrating the reunion of "fraternal souls," their home together had always had an atmosphere of impermanence about it. Each would in time have to go his own way. But because until this spring only John had been of age, and because Tom's illness had become progressively worse the past year, any practical thinking about their future together—except possibly in George's own mind—had thus far been postponed, and was repressed instead into general uneasiness.

2

George's departure, Keats realized as soon as he knew about it, would mean a radical change in his own way of living. Of the Keats family there would now be left only a brother of eighteen, who was probably dying, and a sister, not yet fifteen, of whom Abbey allowed him to see very little. Nor was it simply a matter of their makeshift home coming to an abrupt end. "My Brother George," as Keats told Sarah Jeffrey a year after George left, "always stood between me and any dealings with the world—Now I find I must buffet it." And there was also the matter of the freedom to write, to move about with the restless hope of prodding himself further, to visit Bailey at Oxford (which proved so valuable), to linger for a while in London (which had also proved valuable)—a freedom, as we have repeatedly noticed, that existed only because George was there to look after Tom. Simply because of these personal advantages, Keats could hardly have thought it

---

peared nearly in good health, every answer I have given to enquiring Friends, has been 'much better' and 'improving every day' I can hardly believe this melancholy news, Having so long accustomed myself to think altogether otherwise . . . Tom must never again presume on his strength, at all events untill he has *completely* recover'd" (I.247) .

manly or just to try to dissuade George (nor could George have been so confident about his decision, not only now but later, had there been any personal pressure). Just as understandably, Keats would have avoided any remark that would have made Tom feel, any more acutely than he already did, the extent to which he was complicating the already uncertain lives of his two brothers.

Keats may have had a general sense of what was afoot when he left for Teignmouth on March 4. George would certainly have had to give some explanation for appearing in London so precipitously, but he could have mentioned the thought of emigration as one of several prospects—as something he wished to look into, though perhaps with no immediate timetable in mind. Before being more specific, he would have wanted to talk with Abbey, who of course held the purse strings. He would need funds not only to get across the Atlantic but to travel to the interior and make a start at something when he arrived. He would also have wished to come to some understanding with Georgiana Wylie, whom he had been courting for at least a year. Probably by mid-April George wrote to his brother in more detail.[2] Whatever the embarrassments of discussing it, he would hardly have waited until John reached London (about May 10) to tell him that within another two and a half weeks he was marrying Georgiana Wylie and preparing to leave. Indeed, Tom, in a letter to Marian Jeffrey after they returned to London, refers to George's departure as though the Jeffrey sisters already knew of it (very soon, he says, "John will have set out on his Northern Expedition, George on his Western"); and it was doubtless Tom rather than John who had first told them about it in Teignmouth.

It is typical that Keats could not bring himself to mention the matter in any of his own letters until he finally did so to Bailey (May 21) shortly before George's wedding, adding "I feel no spur at my Brothers going to America and am almost stony-hearted about his wedding." However "transparent" (to use Bailey's word)

---

2 The single letter that survives from George (March 18) makes no mention of the subject. On the other hand, we know that George had written several times by April 27 (I.273). That these letters were not kept may suggest that Keats did not wish Tom to read them (not in order to keep Tom in ignorance of George's plans—he plainly knew about them—but because the problem of looking after Tom would naturally have been a subject of correspondence between John and George). George apparently addressed his letters to John in care of the post office at Teignmouth rather than to the house where his brothers were living.

he was in other ways, yet, when confronted with personal loss or calamity, Keats's instinctive tendency was always to dig in, to try to get his bearings, and to come to some sort of inner settlement. The heavy feeling of depression in the letters of late April is always expressed indirectly, or given a momentary relief through caustic remarks on the Devonshire climate. It was not until almost two weeks after his brother's wedding that he could express himself very specifically (June 10). He has been speaking to Bailey of the dark unpredictabilities of life; and then goes on to say that perhaps

> if my affairs were in a different state I should not have written the above—you shall judge—I have two Brothers one is driven by the "burden of Society" to America the other, with an exquisite love of Life, is in a lingering state—My love for my Brothers from the early loss of our parents and even for earlier Misfortunes has grown into a[n] affection "passing the Love of Women"—I have been ill temper'd with them, I have vex'd them—but the thought of them has always stifled the impression that any woman might otherwise have made upon me—I have a Sister too [whom of course he cannot leave] and may not follow them, either to America or to the Grave—Life must be undergone.

Probably he is being subjective: "I am not old enough or magnanimous enough to annihilate self." But of course it was not merely of himself, in the narrow sense of the word "self," that he was thinking in brooding over this final violent dislocation of what was left of his family—one brother leaving permanently for a place five thousand miles away, and another, with his "exquisite love of Life," so unaccountably and helplessly dying. It was only the "self" in so far as that term can be stretched to include any interest or concern one can have, however altruistic. And of course we naturally have to use the "self," even in order to get beyond the self. The question is whether the self is an end or a means. The greater poetry of the next year (the odes, much of the *Fall of Hyperion*) was to return to that distinction, so difficult to draw in any honest, clear-cut way and yet so obviously called for. Attempting to tread toward, and to feel out, the boundary between self and object, the poetry of the year following discloses a new possibility of drama.

In any case, when he thinks back on that embarrassing episode of the laurel crown, it now seems more hopelessly naive than ever. Without explaining anything of the background of what his allusion really means to him, he suddenly bursts out, in this same letter to Bailey (June 10), that "were it in my choice I would reject a petrarchal coronation—on accou[n]t of my dying day, and because women have Cancers." The protest is by no means one of despair (true enough, he is now "never alone without rejoicing that there is such a thing as death"; but at the same time he can still honestly say that he will place his "ultimate" hope in "dying for a great human purpose"). The reaction is against smugness, withdrawal, and infidelity to the enormous complexity of open experience. It is also a protest on behalf of sincerity.

3

Certainly the eight and a half weeks that he stayed in Devon were a time of profound transition for Keats. Though the results did not show themselves in his poetry for a few more months, his letters take on a new tone or mood. One can say that (in addition to everything else we find in these letters) he now begins to merge into the main stream of the nineteenth and twentieth centuries, and to participate in a development of poetry that took the course it did partly because of Keats himself.

Up to this time, despite brief phases of dejection, inevitable for one of mercurial temperament and much tossed about in the world, nothing had diminished the general spirit of trust that we have been noting. There were infinite new horizons—he always loved a wide prospect—that seemed to beckon man's enterprise. "Great Spirits now on earth are sojourning"; nor did the great spirits of the past seem impossibly remote and alien. A poet could still hope to write with the inclusive, impartial sympathy of Shakespeare or with the epic sweep of Milton. He could hope to range beyond narrow boundaries of personal experience, dominating and ordering vast tracts of knowledge. But then the experiences that we have been noticing began to qualify this valuable innocence of hope, though they did not succeed in destroying it. During these weeks down in Teignmouth, with the rain pelting, and with Tom fretful and coughing, Keats was left alone with his thoughts. To some extent we have been able to notice from the letters what those thoughts were. "Young Men for some time have an idea that such a thing as happiness is to be had," he wrote John

Taylor (April 24), but gradually, instead of striving to avoid "un-easiness," they learn to expect it "as an habitual sensation, a pannier that is to weigh upon them through life." Moreover, the need to seek knowledge was pressing on Keats's mind as never before; and by knowledge he meant both wide experience and the systematized understanding of experience that he hopefully credited to formal philosophy. Without this, poetry itself may be only a "Jack a lanthern to amuse whoever may chance to be struck with its brilliance."

With every further step in knowledge, to be sure, the inscrutable mystery of things seems only to deepen, and the uncertainty of human judgments to become more obvious. Yet if, at the moment, "We see not the ballance of good and evil," and "are in a mist," that only means that the life of a thinking man must be a search, and, perhaps, that poetry should take the path not of Shakespeare and Milton—at least in any obvious, direct way—but rather of Wordsworth, who "can make discoveries" in the "dark Passages." Finally, Keats was beginning to share—largely through his own perception—an idea of history that was relatively new in the nineteenth century. Or perhaps it was not so much the idea that was new as its sophistication and influence; it gradually pervaded and transformed almost every field of thought. Gibbon, after all, did not suppose that a Roman in the age of the Antonines was essentially different from himself. This assumption could lead to blind lapses in sympathy and understanding, but it could certainly encourage the hope of learning directly from the past and even imitating it. But now Keats began to think of history as a process in which the changes that take place are fundamental. Men and their achievements must be seen in relation to the age in which they live. Though Milton, "as a Philosopher, had surely as great powers as Wordsworth," his philosophy can no longer be completely adopted. At the same time, it was inevitable that Milton should accept the "seeming sure points of Reasoning" newly reached in his time. If this means that "a mighty providence subdues the mightiest Minds to the service of the time being," it also means that the past is, in a very real way, somewhat closed to us. One cannot go back and write exactly as Milton or Shakespeare did. Out of all this comes a new realization of crucial importance. Keats saw, in effect, that he was and could only be a modern poet: that he could hardly escape a poetry that was turned more to the inner life.

4

This new self-clarification, indispensable to the poetry of his final year and a half, did not come easily. In fact, it was very much against the grain; and though it began with unexpected suddenness this spring, it was still in the process of working itself out when his career ended. For it would ultimately involve, if not the surrender, at least the thorough modification of something very precious to him: his consuming ideal of the great poets of the past that had proved so formative in his own development. That confident approach, however inadequate he might feel his own performance as an individual might be, had never really been shaken before. In his first serious effort to write, it is true, he had shown that even the gifted, relatively untutored poet is to some extent affected by the time in which he is living—a time, in this case, already self-conscious and acutely aware of past achievement. For when he left Guy's Hospital in the summer of 1816, and—not yet twenty-one—tried to see whether he could really write poetry, his inspiration was almost purely literary. And in turning, during those desperate weeks, to writing poetry about his desire and personal struggle to write poetry, and about his hope and need to find subjects, he was exemplifying what the more sophisticated critical intelligence of his own generation and the generation before had shrewdly taken for granted as the probable lot of the poet of the future (and for decades there had been a serious question whether the result would not be thin). But of this Keats had known little or nothing.

It was only during the winter of 1817, as he was finishing *Endymion,* that he may have begun to feel consciously that this poetry of the past, to which he was attaching so much of his idealism, might be different—in a more fundamental way than he had suspected—not only from what he himself was writing at the moment (that could be taken for granted) but from what his contemporaries, even Wordsworth, were doing. The thought was sobering. For Wordsworth was easily the greatest of his contemporaries—at least to Keats's own mind. Those haunting passages he had read and quoted at Oxford had something in common with Shakespeare—power of image, concurrence with the human heart, meditative depth, inevitability of phrase. But when Keats's own empathic gifts, his year-long absorption in Shakespeare, and his new reading of Hazlitt all led him to clarify his ideal of the poet as a "Man of great *Negative Capability*," he had himself posed a fundamental distinction. That ideal was altogether dramatic; and whatever else could be said of Wordsworth, he was no dramatist.

Keats's new beginning, therefore—his rededication after the "Negative Capability" letter—was quickly crossed by the uneasy feeling that, in the years of preparation ahead, he might be swimming upstream against more than one current. Hazlitt's lectures, which he had started attending in January, kept underlining the difference between the poetry of even the best of his contemporaries and that of the older poets whom Keats had been approaching so trustfully and, at the beginning, even jauntily—a difference not simply in degree but in kind. The thought was to continue to lurk behind in the shadows—occasionally coming forward—throughout the final year and a half of his writing. It fortunately remained free of the complete historical determinism with which the more sophisticated discourage themselves as well as others, and it never occurred to him to abandon the salutary near-truth that most paths are open to us always. But he was somewhat shaken. The situation would involve an additional loneliness that he had not anticipated, and it certainly emphasized the distance still to be traveled. If he failed, as he told Taylor (February 27), he hoped that at least his friends would attribute "any change in my Life and Temper to Humbleness rather than to Pride—to a cowering under the wings of great Poets rather than to a Bitterness that I am not appreciated." A month before he said this to Taylor, he had spoken caustically—very caustically for Keats—of the extent to which poetry now seemed saturated with autobiography, and confined in its subjects to whatever could be wrung out of one's own personal, subjective experience. Poets who had hitherto struck him as radically different—Wordsworth, Hunt, Byron—could, from this point of view, seem all of a piece, representing a poetry of one's "life & opinions." Hence the sigh for amplitude, when he wrote the poem on "Robin Hood" in response to Reynolds' sonnets on Robin Hood. The desire for that freer, more bracing air was in his mind when he spoke of the subjectivity of Wordsworth as well as Hunt. I will "cut all this," he said; and he had good reasons.[3] Milton, whom he was now reading carefully, kept illustrating the contrast. Shakespeare's "disinterestedness," his compre-

---

[3] See above, Chapter XII, section 1.

hensive sympathy and grasp of human character, might be an impossibly demanding ideal by which to judge other poetry. But Milton, so different from Shakespeare in other ways, also had scope. They and their contemporaries not only were "uncontaminated" by the modern egocentricity but, in their purview, were "Emperors" who drew tribute from whole provinces:

> Modern poets differ from the Elizabethans in this. Each of the moderns like an Elector of Hanover governs his petty state, & knows how many straws are swept daily from the Causeways in all his dominions & has a continual itching that all the housewives should have their coppers well scoured: the antients were Emperors of vast Provinces, they had only heard of the remote ones and scarcely cared to visit them.

5

He was now facing directly what he had thus far met only in the most indirect way—the problem with which the sophisticated mind of the English eighteenth century had so often wrestled. Did the waning of the "greater genres," such as the epic and the tragic drama, really mean that the poetry of western Europe, after the Renaissance and the seventeenth century, was moving into a less vital era? Were polish, refinement, nuance, and the corners of art all that were left? Was the obsession with originality, which the later eighteenth century had foisted on the modern world, the cause of the difficulty? And even if the mania for originality, and the mistaken confusion of mere originality with integrity and sincerity, were kept in bounds, were not the larger functions of poetry being constantly reduced by the fact that the imagination of the modern poet is nourished primarily by literature itself, his experience coming to him second-hand; and can great literature be written on a diet that consists principally of literature? Hazlitt was later to raise that question very seriously, and with no foolish thought of advising that we therefore put on blinkers and disregard what past literature has done. Could we not be getting into a situation where, as John Wilson felt in more reflective moments, the cultivation of the imagination through art alone would inevitably result in a poetry different from the objective poetry—dramatic or epic—produced by writers whose imaginations were daily exercised by concrete experience? [4] Wilson, and many others, were

4 Wilson, speaking of the decline of the poetic drama after the mid-seventeenth century, felt that the imagination was no longer "submitted to life, and dwelling in the midst of it," as was the case with "the tragic poets of England, in the age of

developing the point so unwillingly admitted by Johnson in *Rasselas:* "The first writers took possession of the most striking objects . . . and the most probable occurrences . . . Whatever be the reason, it is commonly observed that the early writers are in possession of Nature, and their followers of art"—that "strength and invention" seem more common in the former, and various kinds of "refinement" in the latter. And even if a certain amount of free will could be brought to bear by the poet himself in his use of his own experience and in his refusal to be cornered, what of his increasingly sophisticated and articulate public, and the limitations of what that public itself would allow him to do? Throughout the remarkable half century before Keats was born, and throughout his own lifetime, the question of decline, in one form or another, kept recurring: was modern England, in the future that its critical intelligence began to consider so shrewdly after 1750, becoming a new Rome to the Greece of the late Renaissance (the late sixteenth and early seventeenth centuries)? Had a Silver Age followed a Golden Age, and was an Age of Brass ahead?

Loathing any thought of decline as a reflection on man's free will, Johnson had repeatedly swung against any temptation to shut art off from the amplitude of experience, and, above all, to retreat only because of fear and self-consciousness. Johnson's cleansing remarks on those who felt they could write only at certain times ("imagination operating on luxury," he called it; and while such an idea "has possession of the head, it produces the inability which it supposes") would equally express his attitude toward those who felt that growing refinement and self-consciousness, increased and enriched by our knowledge of past effort, intimidate us into lowering our sights. Reynolds, in his last discourse before the Royal Academy, disowned his previous caution and said that, if he had his life to live over, he would at least try to follow the kind of thing Michelangelo exemplified, however inadequate might be the result. But the fact remains that Johnson did not himself turn to poetry, though all who knew him felt that in fertility of metaphor and image he would have succeeded had he brought a fraction of his brilliant, indolence-caught imagination to bear on it. Reynolds,

---

our dramatic literature." "The whole character of our life and literature seems to us to show in our cultivated classes a disposition of imagination to separate itself from real life, and to go over into works of art." The lyric nature of "the great overflow of poetry in this age may be in part from this cause." ("A Few Words on Shakespeare" [1819], *Works* [Edinburgh, 1847], VII.430.)

moreover, was giving his advice only after his own career was over. Both men would have admitted their failure to exemplify their own counsel. And in the gifted generation that followed, however brave the intention and effort, the situation of poetry was not encouraging. Already by 1818—in fact more than a decade before— Coleridge had virtually ceased to write poetry; and it was becoming increasingly plain, in the critical prose to which Coleridge was now devoting himself, that the only poet who could possibly fulfill all the requirements was Shakespeare. Wordsworth, Byron, Shelley, had each been bold in his way (and so, of course, had Blake, though Keats knew little if anything of him). But there had been a sacrifice in every case. If the word "sacrifice" was too commendatory for Byron, as Keats was now beginning to view Byron, there had at least been a loss. Shelley's pure pursuit of abstract ideal was not for Keats: whatever else could be said for it, this brave continued song in the face of all circumstances was that of a radically different being. The one modern poet who had steadied him throughout those crucial months of the autumn and winter had been Wordsworth himself—Wordsworth whom he had increasingly found so self-absorbed, so restricted in sympathy.

Keats might say in early February "I will cut all this," and be willing to face both a long preparation and even a sense of isolation from the work of his contemporaries. But the question continued to nag: what preparation, what experience? How did he begin, however slowly, to prepare to write a *Paradise Lost* or a *King Lear?* Take the first poems to mark his new beginning, his rededication, back in January—"Lines on Seeing a Lock of Milton's Hair," the sonnet "On Sitting Down to Read *King Lear* Once Again" ("you see I am getting at it"), the suddenly serious lines to Apollo about the "terrible division," the "gulph austere," the need to face the prospect "More unalarm'd." What were they but mere personal expressions of aim, of redirection? They were just as much a poetry "of any body's life & opinions" as that of the other moderns who, like the Elector of Hanover, rule a petty state and see that the coppers are kept scoured in each kitchen: who, even if they have wings (to shift to Keats's other metaphor), are like owls, guarding their own neighborhoods from their perch: "Why should we be owls, when we can be Eagles?" Of course those poems he had written in January were never intended to be more than impromptu verse. For that matter, even the new sonnets, written frankly in imitation of Shakespeare, were viewed as little more than exercises, however much improvement they showed over the earlier sonnets.

But by the end of April, three months after the new resolve and beginning had been made, Keats seemed as far as ever from understanding what path to take, what exercise or experience was necessary. He was hardly yet in a position to be caustic about Wordsworth. In any case he found his thoughts recurring (as if to a touchstone for understanding the present day better) to the greatest poet among his own contemporaries—a poet who, with all his lacks, had an obstinate integrity, and who was at least completely loyal to his experience, though his experience was admittedly limited. Perhaps, after all, epic sweep and grandeur, however desirable, were not the sole answer—were not even the principal answer.

6

His attempt to "branch out" from the state of perplexity in which he found himself is put in one of the three or four most remarkable letters he was ever to write: a long letter to Reynolds, on May 3, which begins by saying that he has been in so "uneasy a state of Mind as not to be fit to write to an invalid. I cannot write to any length under a dis-guised feeling." In the several pages that follow—pages that sum up the solitary reflections of the weeks in Devon and serve as a preface to his effort of the next year and a half—he is frankly reverting to his own experience thus far, and trying honestly and slowly to work from that.

The thinking in this letter spreads far beyond Milton and Wordsworth. But the whole character of his experience is colored by the very special concern so understandably important to him now (and it also has its universality, its relevance to every generation of writers of the past two centuries)—a concern that could partly be expressed by the question: if we look honestly into our hearts, can we subscribe completely to beliefs and premises that seem to us to underlie the poetry of the past that we most admire? Of course once we ask such a question, other questions are in order. We could ask, for example, whether we really need to subscribe wholly to those premises in order to write poetry of comparable value. After all, the greater poets of the past had, in their own way, often been explorers. Were they really "certain" about those assumptions with which (we say) they were blessed and we are not? Could we not be merely searching for excuses? The contrast between the Renaissance and his own day, between Milton (an "Emperor of vast Provinces") and Wordsworth, continued to "tease" Keats's mind—to use one of his own favorite words. He had told Bailey (March 13) that "eve[r]y point of thought is the centre of an intellectual world—the uppermost thoughts in a Man's mind are the two poles of his World he revolves on them and every thing is southward or northward to him through their means." In his desire to reground himself, these "two uppermost thoughts" of Wordsworth and Milton were becoming polar: the attempt to distinguish and yet, if possible, to reconcile them seemed one way out of the "painful . . . labyrinth" in which he now found himself. From this "labyrinth" (he goes on, in this letter to Reynolds of May 3) :

> My Branchings out . . . have been numerous: one of them is the consideration of Wordsworth's genius and as a help, in the manner of gold being the meridian Line of worldly wealth,—how he differs from Milton.—And here I have nothing but surmises, from an uncertainty whether Miltons apparently less anxiety for Humanity proceeds from his seeing further or no than Wordsworth: And whether Wordsworth has in truth epic passion, and martyrs himself to the human heart, the main region of his song—In regard to his genius alone—we find what he says true as far as we have experienced and we can judge no further but by larger experience—for axioms in philosophy are not axioms until they are proved upon our pulses: We read fine—things but never feel them to the full until we have gone the same steps as the Author.—I know this is not plain; you will know exactly my meaning when I say, that now I shall relish Hamlet more than I ever have done—Or, better—You are sensible no man can set down Venery as a bestial or joyless thing until he is sick of it and therefore all philosophizing on it would be mere wording. Until we are sick, we understand not;—in fine, as Byron says, "Knowledge is Sorrow"; and I go on to say that "Sorrow is Wisdom"—and further for aught we can know for certainty! "Wisdom is folly"—So you see how I have run away from Wordsworth, and Milton; and shall still run away from what was in my head, to observe, that some kind of letters are good squares others handsome ovals, and others some orbicular, others spheroid—and why should there not be another species with two rough edges like a Rat-trap?

A page in which he tries to get his bearings then follows: he speaks of his thoughts' playing at leapfrog of association. Seven weeks before, he had begun to think seriously, in a letter to James

Rice (March 24) , of this same general idea. He was then wondering whether an "advance" had taken place in the modern intellect as a whole. He was thinking how pleasant it would be if only we had "a sort of Philosophical Back Garden . . . but Alas! this never can be: for as the material Cottager knows there are such places as france and Italy and the Andes and the Burning Mountains—so the spiritual Cottager has knowledge of the terra semi incognita of things unearthly; and cannot for his Life, keep in the check rein." And turning to Milton, who has been so much in his mind, he playfully speculates to Rice whether Milton had not usurped the available intelligence of his time, and sucked it into his head to the impoverishment of others.[5]

In writing thus to Rice back in March, he could only give up before the complexities of the whole problem: that problem being whether there had been a general "advance" or not (and the pressing question that follows, of course, is whether such an "advance" —assuming it has taken place—has really changed the character of what can be honestly written at the present day) . But now, by early May, some inner settlement has taken place, at least for the time being. If Keats runs away from the subject on this occasion, he returns to it, despite his feeling that this letter is now taking the shape of a "Rat-trap" (with perhaps some suggestion that present-day poetry is the hapless rat) . Instead of assuming the stable reassuring form of a "good Square" or the graceful shape of a "handsome oval," his letter has "two rough edges," just as his situation generally has two roughly understood (and roughly pressing) opposites on each side: on the one hand, the epic achievement of Milton and the character of his and Shakespeare's era, and, on the other hand, Wordsworth and all that Wordsworth suggested of an-

[5] "My dear fellow I must let you know that as there is ever the same quantity of matter constituting this habitable globe—as the ocean notwithstanding the enormous changes and revolutions taking place in some or other of its demesnes—notwithstanding Waterspouts whirpools and mighty Rivers emptying themselves into it, it still is made up of the same bulk—nor ever varies the number of its Atoms—And as a certain bulk of Water was instituted at the Creation—so very likely a certain portion of intellect was spun forth into the thin Air for the Brains of Man to prey upon it—You will see my drift without any unnecessary parenthesis. That which is contained in the Pacific and lie in the hollow of the Caspian—that which was in Miltons head could not find Room in Charles the seconds—he like a Moon attracted Intellect to its flow—it has not ebbd yet—but has left the shore pebble all bare—I mean all Bucks Authors of Hengist [a poor play that had appeared in 1816] and Castlereaghs of the present day—who without Miltons gormandizing might have been all wise Men."

other kind of poetry. The image of a "Rat-trap," as soon as he mentions it, taps his ready sense of humor, and he wonders whether "by merely touching the spring delicately and etherially, the rough edged will fly immediately into a proper compactness." That hope was never to leave him, at least while he was still able to write.

7

For the moment, he wonders whether the age of Milton ("I hope it is not too presuming") was more direct and confident because it was simply more innocent. Emerging from the Middle Ages, the men of the Renaissance "got hold of certain points and resting places in reasoning which were too newly born to be doubted." [6]

During these weeks in Devon, he has been reflecting on his own experience, and on the complexity that each addition of knowledge seems to bring; and he is simply speculating that there may be an analogous effect on societies generally. In doing so he anticipates questions and speculations that were to become endemic in the sophisticated literary world from the later and middle nineteenth century to the present day, especially after the first World War, when discussions of modern art and literature often begin with the premise Keats only suggests: our life and thinking, when we contrast our own situation with that of the Renaissance, inevitably suffer from the embarrassments of complexity; and since modern life is difficult, complex, involved, then modern art must naturally and perhaps morally ought to be difficult, complex, and involved. If Keats remains healthily free from a passive or self-

[6] "From the Paradise Lost and the other Works of Milton, I hope it is not too presuming, even between ourselves to say, his Philosophy, human and divine, may be tolerably understood by one not much advanced in years. In his time englishmen were just emancipated from a great superstition—and Men had got hold of certain points and resting places in reasoning which were too newly born to be doubted, and too much opposed by the Mass of Europe not to be thought etherial and authentically divine—who could gainsay his ideas on virtue, vice, and Chastity in Comus, just at the time of the dismissal of Cod-pieces and a hundred other disgraces? who would not rest satisfied with his hintings at good and evil in the Paradise Lost, when just free from the inquisition and burning in Smithfield? The Reformation produced such immediate and great benefits, that Protestantism was considered under the immediate eye of heaven, and its own remaining Dogmas and superstitions, then, as it were, regenerated, constituted those resting places and seeming sure points of Reasoning—from that I have mentioned, Milton, whatever he may have thought in the sequel, appears to have been content with these by his writings—He did not think into the human heart, as Wordsworth has done."

excusing determinism, it is partly because he is not taking over the notion from someone else as a stock or inert idea. Instead he is opening the door to this speculation by himself, with the surprising clairvoyance he was to show in so many other ways. He is doing so by consulting his own experience as honestly as he can, and then applying it to this large problem of literary history, which means so much to him personally. Whatever the complexities that our increase in awareness brings, we shall get nowhere by shutting our eyes. Moreover, knowledge can bring reassurance as well as fears.

> An extensive knowledge is needful to thinking people—it takes away the heat and fever; and helps, by widening speculation, to ease the Burden of the Mystery: a thing I begin to understand a little, and which weighed upon you in the most gloomy and true sentence in your Letter. The difference of high Sensations with and without knowledge appears to me this—in the latter case we are falling continually ten thousand fathoms deep and being blown up again without wings and with all [the] horror of a bare shoulderd Creature—in the former case, our shoulders are fledge, and we go thro' the same air and space without fear.

And more than mere reassurance is involved. He is also thinking of the ways in which knowledge—when actively used by the honest and adventurous mind—is always moving from its starting point into other areas, disclosing, as it crosses other knowledge, unexpected solutions or at least unexpected paths of approach:

> Were I to study physic or rather Medicine again,—I feel it would not make the least difference in my Poetry; when the Mind is in its infancy a Bias is in reality a Bias, but when we have acquired more strength, a Bias becomes no Bias. Every department of knowledge we see excellent and calculated towards a great whole. I am so convinced of this, that I am glad at not having given away my medical Books, which I shall again look over to keep alive the little I know thitherwards.

A little more than a week before (April 24) he had told John Taylor:

> I was purposing to travel over the north this Summer—there is but one thing to prevent me—I know nothing I have read nothing and I mean to follow Solomon's directions of "get Wisdom—get understanding"—I find cavalier days are gone by. . . . There is but one way for me—the road lies through application study and thought. I will pursue it and to that end purpose retiring for some

years. I have been hovering for some time between an exquisite sense of the luxurious and a love for Philosophy—were I calculated for the former I should be glad—but as I am not I shall turn all my soul to the latter.

8

In this context of modesty, hesitation, and independent experience, he now returns to the large question whether Wordsworth has "circumscribed grandeur"—an admitted grandeur of moral utterance and yet limited, by contrast, to the small Hanoverlike province to which the modern poet seemed to be retreating—or whether Wordsworth has indeed a potential epic sweep, and has thus "martyred himself to the human heart"—martyred the freer, older uses of poetry to the inevitably pressing needs of the modern age. And the verb "martyr" puts the case as Keats vividly feels it. For should he himself be forced to surrender or modify drastically that direct ideal of the great poets of the past with which he had been living for so long, it would indeed be a martyrdom.

> I will return to Wordsworth—whether or no he has an extended vision or a circumscribed grandeur—whether he is an eagle in his nest, or on the wing—And to be more explicit and to show you how tall I stand by the giant, I will put down a simile of human life as far as I now perceive it; that is, to the point to which I say we both have arrived at.

Then follows the notable passage:

> I compare human life to a large Mansion of Many Apartments, two of which I can only describe, the doors of the rest being as yet shut upon me—The first we step into we call the infant or thoughtless Chamber, in which we remain as long as we do not think—We remain there a long while, and nothwithstanding the doors of the second Chamber remain wide open, showing a bright appearance, we care not to hasten to it; but are at length imperceptibly impelled by the awakening of the thinking principle—within us—we no sooner get into the second Chamber, which I shall call the Chamber of Maiden-Thought, than we become intoxicated with the light and the atmosphere, we see nothing but pleasant wonders, and think of delaying there for ever in delight: However among the effects this breathing is father of is that tremendous one of sharpening one's vision into the heart and nature of Man—of convincing ones nerves that the World is full of Misery and Heartbreak, Pain, Sickness and oppression—whereby This Chamber of Maiden Thought becomes gradually darken'd and at the same time on all sides of it many

doors are set open—but all dark—all leading to dark passages—We
see not the ballance of good and evil. We are in a Mist—*We* are now
in that state—We feel the "burden of the Mystery," To this point
was Wordsworth come, as far as I can conceive when he wrote "Tintern Abbey" and it seems to me that his Genius is explorative of
those dark Passages. Now if we live, and go on thinking, we too shall
explore them.

Here, in one essential way, it could be said that "Wordsworth is
deeper than Milton." If so, it is by no means because of any individual superiority of genius. Any difference would depend "more
upon the general and gregarious advance of intellect, than individual greatness of mind." The consideration of this was to give
Keats during the next autumn a theme for his new "epic," an epic
paradoxically written in a somewhat Miltonic idiom.

His whole concept of *gradus ad Parnassum,* in short, was changing; the impact of experience was making the picture less simple
and clean-cut. Of course it had never been completely simple. By
any standard, he had a long way to go. But the general sense he
now had was of a "labyrinth" rather than of steps. He was far from
confident of the validity of the distinction he had been making
between Milton and Wordsworth. Moreover, his way of posing the
problem was one that could lead to a fundamental dilemma. When
he speculates whether Wordsworth has "martyred" himself to the
human heart, he touches on a further unforeseen complication
that romanticism was to bequeath to later poetry—the ideal of direct, even naked sincerity. If poetry is to be written only when we
are confident that we are completely sincere, something is going
to happen both to our subject matter and to our general fluency.
Wordsworth was already both articulating and typifying this large
self-demand; and the next century and a half could avoid it only
by moving (often with an uneasy conscience) in an opposite direction, as the art-for-art's sake group did, or else by trying to
channel or pinpoint the overriding concern with sincerity into special, compartmentalized concerns of style. The difficulties, in fact,
sprouted richly as soon as one began to think honestly about the
demand of complete sincerity to the heart's aspirations and experience. Retrenching scrupulously to our own most honest feelings,
where are we to stop in this "journey homeward to habitual self"?

The possible liabilities had been in Keats's mind for months. "I
will cut all this," he had said in February. He would have the

purity, amplitude, cleanliness of the "old poetry." And with every week that had passed he had been divided. Even as late as his letter to that devoted Wordsworthian, Benjamin Bailey (May 25), he again repeats jokingly the echo of Wordsworth's title of a section of his poems ("Moods of My Own Mind") at which he had already half jested in his uneasy letter to Reynolds (March 25): "I am troubling you," he tells Bailey, "with Moods of my own Mind or rather body—for Mind there is none."

Without any real hesitation—except for a few weeks—Keats's habit of meeting circumstance directly had reasserted itself. If the "dark Passages" are there, then "if we live, and go on thinking, we too shall explore them." The decision was a turning point, and the greater poetry that follows could not have been written without the recognition it implied.

9

Keats's long letter to Reynolds, written as these crucial, self-examining weeks in Teignmouth were drawing to a close, has a further interest. For it also contains some lines of poetry he had written just two days before (May 1): a fourteen-line fragment of an "Ode to Maia" or "Ode to May." Over the years, between April and November the recurring deaths in the family had been mercifully suspended. Those months had always seemed in the nature of a reprieve, and a year and a quarter later—when his active career was almost over—he was to speak of that moment

> When in mid-May the sickening east wind
> Shifts sudden to the south, the small warm rain
> Melts out the frozen incense from all flowers,
> And fills the air with so much pleasant health
> That even the dying man forgets his shroud.

Two winters (1816–17, and then 1817–18)—challenging and also, in their way, reassuring—had not modified the strong symbolic poignance that the seasons held for Keats, a poignance that was to increase during the next year, when all the great odes but one were written near May Day (the one exception was to be frankly entitled "To Autumn").

The same length as a sonnet—in some ways rather like a sonnet —this fragmentary "Ode to Maia" serves as a trial or threshold step to the odes of May 1819, when he was finally to abandon the sonnet (the lyric form that had become habitual to him since he wrote those first sonnets back at the Edmonton surgery) , and then to take elements from both the Petrarchan and the Shakespearean sonnet forms and coalesce them into a stanza at once richer and yet more flexible. The richness is already suggested in the "Ode to Maia." The flexibility came when the new stanza was seen not as a self-contained unit but as susceptible of dramatic development: the drama being the trialogue of the heart with its ideal and with actual experience.

The unfinished "Ode to Maia," with its quiet reserve of power, is little more than a question followed by a wish or hope. In a sense, the question (or questions) followed by a hope shapes the frame of poem after poem he had written, from the epistles to George Keats and to Cowden Clarke, through "Sleep and Poetry," to the "Lines on Seeing a Lock of Milton's Hair." And the pattern continues, in one form or another, to the end. Time after time, he is pulling himself up to—and also by means of—his Longinian ideal of greatness; and the greatness and the hope deepen as the first *Hyperion* and then the second *Hyperion* are written. But there are also moments when the effort brings immediate returns: when the view is suddenly enlarged, and the growing debate of the heart's wish with actuality is successfully universalized. It is so now, though in a small way, with these unfinished lines of an "Ode to Maia," so much richer than that sonnet of less than a year and a half before (the dedication sonnet to Leigh Hunt, written for the 1817 volume) , where Keats had asked whether, if the "Glory and loveliness" of the imaginative, direct-hearted poetry of an earlier world has indeed "passed away," that poetry and all that sustained it could not still be approached.

"Mother of Hermes," he begins—mother of the messenger, of the communicator between men and gods, between brief-living man and the ideal: can the poet still attain the large simplicity, the "old vigour," of the poetry addressed to her so long ago? Can he write with the same confidence and "content" as they did, even if only to a "little clan"? For weeks he has had the thought that the modern poet either has to retreat, or else thinks he has to retreat, from that purity and freedom. Keats might say in this same letter to Reynolds that earlier ages did not know enough; and he might speak honestly and perceptively of Wordsworth's opening new paths. Yet the question returns, as it always had in other contexts, and was to return until the end: can the poet still leave "great verse"?

> Mother of Hermes! and still youthful Maia!
> > May I sing to thee
> As thou wast hymnèd on the shores of Baiae?
> > Or may I woo thee
> In earlier Sicilian? or thy smiles
> Seek as they once were sought, in Grecian isles,
> By Bards who died content on pleasant sward,
> > Leaving great verse unto a little clan?
> O give me their old vigour, and unheard,
> > Save of the quiet Primrose, and the span
> > Of Heaven, and few ears,
> Rounded by thee, my song should die away
> > Content as theirs,
> Rich in the simple worship of a day.

10

Most of Keats's fragments, from now until the end, are really complete. He says as much as he really wants to say; after *Endymion* he never again tried to pad out a poem.[7] So now with the fragment of the "Ode to Maia." "I wrote [the lines] on May-day," he told Reynolds, "and intend to finish the ode all in good time." It was indeed "all in good time" before he returned to it; it was not, in fact, until the next May Day was approaching. Then he started freshly from the beginning, writing with far more care than he had given any poem before. That new version was to bear the title "Ode to Psyche"; and, in addressing it to Psyche (Psyche, who came "too late," he said for the classical hierarchy: "never worshipped or sacrificed to with any of the ancient fervour—and perhaps never thought of in the old religion") , Keats was returning, after a year of personal difficulty and fertile experiment, to a still more candid admission—altogether self-won—that the principal use of poetry now was to sharpen "one's vision into the heart and nature of Man." The challenge, the aim, the procedure, were all "late-born" when contrasted with those of the great epic poets of the past.

---

[7] At least until *Otho the Great* and the *Cap and Bells*, both of which were written in the hope of making money.

The new version, the "Ode to Psyche," was still far from being a solution: it was only one way of meeting a problem. But in trying to meet it, in the "Ode to Psyche," he was not only to write the first of his great odes but to create something of a prototype for the greater lyric of the past century and a half.

The Departure of George Keats
and the Scottish Tour

✳◈✳◈✳◈✳◈✳◈✳◈✳◈✳◈✳◈✳◈✳◈✳◈✳◈

Summer 1818

PLANNING for the next few months, even if new complications had not arisen, would have been a problem. On the one hand there would soon be a pressing need to earn money, though Keats was trying to live so economically. Abbey, mysterious and coy about their grandmother's estate (and completely silent about their grandfather's bequest), might be willing to advance enough to carry Keats through one more year; but he still had the brothers well habituated to the thought that no final settlement could be expected until Fanny became twenty-one (June 1824). Hence Keats's practical need to establish himself as a poet within a year or two, and his hope (so effectively destroyed the next autumn) that *Endymion*—even if it should not itself make much money— might at least be favorably received. Keats was optimistic. He wanted desperately to travel, for example, and saw no reason why, after another few books, he could not "take all Europe in turn." Nor was his optimism altogether unreasonable. If a poem ever happened to catch on, it brought large returns.[1]

But the financial pressure to hurry had for months conflicted with the preparation he knew was necessary for the kind of poetry he really wanted to write. "I know nothing," as he told John Taylor, "I have read nothing and I mean to follow Solomon's directions of 'get wisdom—get understanding.' " In addition to improving his Latin and French, he was going to learn Greek and Italian (of course he would have to teach himself; but there was no alternative, and he bought dictionaries and a Greek grammar) ; and he

---

[1] For example, Longman (though he offered Wordsworth and Coleridge only £80 for the second edition of *Lyrical Ballads*) paid Tom Moore 3,000 guineas for *Lalla Rookh*. When John Murray offered Byron 1,500 guineas for a single canto of *Childe Harold* (No. IV), Byron cited the amount Longman paid Moore and asked for 2,500. Joseph Johnson made £10,000 from the continued sale of Cowper's *Task*.

also hoped to prepare himself "to ask Hazlitt in about a years time the best metaphysical road I can take." There seemed no way to do all this except to "retire from the World" and try to live on next to nothing for a while. Yet at the same time he knew only too well that "there is something else wanting to one who passes his life among Books and thoughts on Books."

Back in February, before Keats had come down to Devonshire, Charles Brown, who was in the habit of taking long vigorous walking trips each summer, had suggested that Keats join him this summer in a tour of the Lake Country and Scotland. They could do it very cheaply: most of it would be done on foot; and lodging, if one kept one's standard low enough, cost little. The prospect was tempting. The trip would be far more challenging than the little visits he had made here and there: it could in its way be another "prologue," as *Endymion* (and for that matter whatever else he was writing now) was "a poor prologue to what, if I live, I humbly hope to do." Finding Tom "greatly better" by the first of April, and with George's plans not yet completely settled (at least as far as Keats yet knew), he had begun seriously to think of setting off on this trip in early May, if Brown could leave that early; and he told Haydon (April 8):

> I purpose within a Month to put my knapsack at my back and make a pedestrian tour through the North of England, and part of Scotland—to make a sort of Prologue to the Life I intend to pursue —that is to write, to study and to see all Europe at the lowest expence.

But by mid-April George had made his decision to leave in the early summer; Tom's health, after a short improvement, became very uneven; and Keats, after hesitating about the walking trip (April 24), seems to have dropped the thought of it. He began to toy with the idea of staying in Devon for a few more months (April 27) and devoting himself wholly to study; for it was obvious that Tom, who had become a great pet of the Jeffrey sisters, preferred Teignmouth to Hampstead. But Tom was also vividly aware of his brother's despondence and need for change (no one, said George years later, understood John's "character perfectly but poor Tom"); and he began to pretend that he really wanted to get back. In any case they both wished to see something of George, who was to be married at the end of May. Rather than hesitate further, they decided suddenly to leave for London, and took the coach on May 4 or 5.

2

When the coach arrived at Bridport, in Dorsetshire, Tom had another hemorrhage, and lost so much blood that they stayed in the inn for two or three days. Back once again in Hampstead (May 8 or 9), Tom made so much of an effort to appear better (talking confidently of his intention to take a trip of his own to southern Europe) that Keats began to think once again about the walking trip to Scotland. He now half persuaded himself—as George had persuaded himself in the spring—that Tom was at last on the road to recovery; and Tom continued to try to reinforce that impression, laughing and joking so much that, as Keats wrote to the Jeffrey sisters, "Tom is taken for a Madman." They both decided that Keats should still go ahead with the walking trip. Keats ran about for a week or two and called on most of his friends, as he always did whenever he returned to London after an absence. Haydon describes a small dinner of his, which Keats attended, as typical of the "anticks of people of real Genius" when relaxing from effort.[2] But Keats, because of George's departure, was feeling more heavy-hearted each day; and when *Endymion* appeared (May 19), he showed—probably felt—little of the excitement that the publication of his first volume had aroused. Throughout the next month, two friendly if uninfluential reviews appeared, each inspired with the knowledge that the poem would probably be attacked in the quarterlies.[3] One, by Bailey, appeared in an Oxford paper. Keats thanked Bailey, of course, but was at the same time "hurt": hurt because Bailey had written with such simple kindness, while "the world is malignant enough to chuckle at the most

[2] "May 11. The excessive mad anticks of people of real Genius when they meet after hard thinking is perfectly unintelligible to people who having no minds to exert are never in need of relaxation. Keats, Bewick, & I dined together, Keats brought some friend of his, a noodle. After dinner to his horror when he expected we should all be discussing Milton & Raphael &c., we burst into the most boisterous merriment. . . . I proposed to strike up a concert. Keats was the bassoon, Bewick the flagellet, & I was the organ & so on. We went on . . . till we were ready to burst with laughing. Then I took a pianoforte & they something else, and so on we went, while the Wise acre sat by without saying a word, blushing & sipping his wine as if we meant to insult him." (*Diary*, II.198–199.)

[3] Bailey's review appeared in the *Oxford University and City Herald* (May 30 and June 6, 1818); the second review, in the *Champion* (June 7 and 14), was probably by John Scott.

honorable simplicity—and that Idea makes me sick of it." He had recently found himself in moments of despair when he not only expected the worst in everything but "suspected every Body"—a remark on which Bailey commented long afterwards: "On the contrary, he was uniformly the apologist for poor, frail human nature."

He had not yet been able to digest the thought of George's permanent absence. Telling Bailey about George's plans (May 21), and about his own intention to come north and also visit Bailey during the course of his trip, he suddenly breaks off: "I am so depressed that I have not an Idea to put to paper—my hand feels like lead—and yet it is an unpleasant numbness it does not take away the pain of existence—I don't know what to write." Four days later (three days before George's wedding) he tries to begin the letter again:

> You see how I have delayed—and even now I have but a confused idea of what I should be about . . . I am in that temper that if I were under Water I would scarcely kick to come to the top—I know very well 'tis all nonsense.

But he may have felt ashamed when he thought of the courage with which George himself was facing his own problems, and he kept being impressed by the "disinterestedness" and lack of self-centeredness that the young Georgiana showed in being willing to face the trials ahead. This adaptability to fact in the best women, he tells Bailey, "puzzles" him, and their lack of the brooding anxiety and guilt that afflict so many men. Perhaps "Women must want Imagination and they may thank God for it."

George was hesitating between two alternatives, according to either of which he would go "to the back settlements of America," said Keats, and "become farmer and work with his own hands." George of course knew nothing about farming. Still less could he or John envisage the labor of cutting down even a mere hundred acres of the great hardwood trees that covered most of the Midwest and of slowly pulling out the stumps, one by one, with oxen teams before the ground could be tilled. But they knew that George and his young wife would be lonely, that the work would be new to them as well as heavy, and that they would possibly have to build their own house. One of George's alternatives was to buy, for a nominal sum from the American government, 1400 acres of uncleared land in the southern part of the old Northwest Territory (Ohio, Indiana, or Illinois). Another was, at somewhat greater cost, to join a particular settlement there about which he had been reading in a book just brought out by Taylor and Hessey —Morris Birkbeck's *Letters from Illinois*. Birkbeck had bought up 16,000 acres, and was selling the land—some of which was fairly clear of forest—in lots of 640 acres.

George finally decided to try the Birkbeck settlement, though most of the better land was now taken and none at all remained with buildings already on it. Returning Birkbeck's book to John Taylor, George says that, although "there will be no house to receive us,"

> the disappointment is not immense; when I thought these things might be [already] done the advantage seemed great, but when I consider the having to do them myself, I only feel an addition of pride to undertake and accomplish the task myself.[4]

Keats applauded his brother's courage and shared his pride. George, he tells Bailey, "is of too independent and liberal Mind to get on in trade in this Country." Keats would "sooner he should till the ground than bow to a Customer." But Keats still had some very dispiriting moments. Then, in early June, he caught what seems to have been a bad cold. He half hesitated again about the walking trip, telling Bailey (June 10), "I am not certain whether I shall be able to go [on] my Journey on account of my Brother Tom and a little indisposition of my own." But Tom continued to encourage him. The final decision to go was made. Abbey reluctantly put down £500 to Keats's credit, possibly with the understanding that no more money was available to him until Fanny, six years hence, would be twenty-one, by which time Abbey may have hoped to recoup on the personal investments for which he was unquestionably using the trust fund. In any case Abbey seems never to have allowed Keats any money thereafter, except for a few pounds. The £500 lasted Keats for only about a year, principally because of his incorrigible habit of lending money to his friends.

3

The boat on which George booked passage was expected to leave Liverpool on June 24, or within a few days afterwards; transatlan-

4 *KC*, I.29–30.

tic ships did not operate then on a strict schedule. Keats was eager to accompany George and his wife to Liverpool, from which he and Brown could then set off on their own trip north; and Brown good-naturedly agreed. In case the boat should leave promptly on June 24, George decided to take the Monday morning coach (June 22) from London: the trip lasted thirty-two hours, and they would thus arrive at Liverpool in the late afternoon of June 23.

On the coach, which left Cheapside at nine, all of them except Brown were uneasy at the parting to come. Keats might talk—and continue to talk in the weeks ahead—about coming to America to visit George within another two or three years. But the enormous distance—especially the eleven or twelve hundred arduous miles from the East Coast to the interior—staggered one's thought. The coach stopped for dinner at Redbourne, near St. Albans. Henry Stephens, who had been one of Keats's roommates when they were students at Guy's Hospital, was now in practice at Redbourne as a surgeon. Keats sent him a message from the inn; and Stephens hurried over to talk with them for a few minutes before the coach left.[5]

When they arrived at the Crown, in Liverpool, it seemed pointless to the Keats brothers to drag out the farewell. It was impossible to talk easily; the event was too serious. They spent the evening together, and then said good-bye; Keats and Brown would leave the next day before George arose. Except for a few hurried days in January 1820, when George returned to try to collect his share of Tom's estate, Keats never saw him again; and Georgiana did not return to visit England until several years after Keats's death.

The long trip ahead of George, still only twenty-one, was to bring him and his wife of twenty some surprises and discouragements. When they landed at Philadelphia, George, who had little

---

[5] Stephens' account of Keats, written almost thirty years later, mentions the incident. "Our interview was brief, he enquired a little into my prospects and I into his. I found he had no intention of practising in the Medical profession, but was still devoted to Poetry. His brother George's wife was rather short, not what might be strictly called handsome, but looked like a being whom any man of moderate Sensibility might easily love. She had the imaginative poetical cast.—Somewhat singular & girlish in her attire, whether from her own taste, or whether she had accommodated herself to the taste of her husband, or to that of the Poet, the presiding Genius of the family, I know not; but there was something original about her, & John seemed to regard her as a being whom he was delighted to honour, & introduced her to me with an evident satisfaction. As I before said, our Interview was short—they departed by the Coach, & I to my home, & this was the last I ever saw of John Keats." (*KC*, II.212.)

notion of what it meant to cross the Allegheny Mountains, bought a carriage and horses for the trip West. He and his wife then set out across the mountains to Pittsburgh—a winding, hazardous journey of over five hundred miles. Arriving at Pittsburgh somewhat shaken, they then went down the Ohio River by keelboat for still another six hundred miles, proceeded to the Illinois territory, found that most of the remaining land consisted of virgin forest that had yet to be cleared, and then despondently turned south to the frontier settlement of Henderson, in western Kentucky.

There, barely ten years after Lincoln was born in a Kentucky cabin, George was to have a bad year and to lose much of the money he had brought with him. He moved up the river to Louisville, and started over again. By the early 1830's, he was prospering, with a large lumber mill and also a flour mill; and his large house in Louisville, built in 1835, served as something of a center for people with literary interests. He died of tuberculosis at the age of forty-four (December 24, 1841), almost twenty-one years after the death of John Keats. Of the seven children who survived him (five daughters and two sons), the one named for the poet—a civil engineer in Missouri—died at the age of ninety (1827–1917).[6]

4

Very early the next morning (June 24), Keats and Brown took the coach to Lancaster, from which their walking trip was to begin.

Brown, so prominent in the Keats story from here until the end, was now a man of thirty-one. Like almost all of Keats's friends except for those he had made before the spring of 1817 (such as Hunt, Haydon, and Reynolds), this tall, bald-headed, vigorous man was distinguished by qualities of practical prudence, steadiness, and a tireless capacity for detail. Of these four friends—Bailey, Dilke, Woodhouse, and Brown—only Woodhouse could be thought of as unusually sensitive. With the exception of Bailey, all were closely connected with the mercantile world, and possessed an interest in the arts and a readiness to admire imagination

---

[6] A list of the descendants still living in 1941 is given in the August issue for that year of the *Southern Literary Messenger*, IV.356. Two years after the death of George Keats, his widow (d. 1879) married John Jeffrey, a civil engineer of Scottish extraction. It was Jeffrey who made copies for Milnes of many of the papers George Keats left, including autograph poems and of course the valuable letters Keats sent after his brother's emigration.

typical of many such men in the nineteenth century (Richard Abbey was not of this type). George Keats, on whom his brother depended so much, was himself this sort of man.

Of partly Welsh and Scottish extraction, Brown (the sixth of seven sons) [7] had started work in a London merchant's office at the age of fourteen, and then, at eighteen, had gone to St. Petersburg in partnership with his brother John. Returning to London when the business failed, he had joined his brother James—a merchant who was rapidly making money in the East India Company—and in his spare time he wrote a comic opera (*Narensky, or the Road to Yaroslaf*), which was produced at Drury Lane in 1814. From James he had recently inherited enough income (about £300 a year) to lead a life of what he intended to be literary leisure. With his old schoolfellow Charles Dilke he had built the now famous two-family house in Hampstead, Wentworth Place, in Brown's portion of which Keats was to live after Tom's death. Brown first met Keats in the summer of 1817, and doubtless saw him frequently that autumn and winter, when Keats was a constant visitor at the Dilkes' in the other side of the house. But their close friendship begins with the walking tour in the summer of 1818.

There were other friends who influenced Keats's thinking in a way that Brown never did or could—Hunt, Haydon, and Benjamin Bailey; and there were others—certainly Reynolds—to whom he probably felt closer. But the rugged, undemanding Brown was a relief in his own way; and he was later able not only to help Keats to an extent that no one else seemed willing or able to do but also to treat the matter so much in the spirit of routine business that Keats felt relieved of the discomfort of continued obligation. "Methodical, hospitable, kind hearted, and very cool in the presence of danger"—as Brown's son described him in a memoir long after his death—Brown had a quick, tough, and curious mind; he was an inveterate traveler; and, as his drawing of Keats shows, he was not an unskillful artist. At thirty-one, he was already set in his ways. Brown—wrote Keats to Bailey when they reached the Isle of Mull—

[7] In 1838 he assumed a middle name, Armitage (a family name on his mother's side), "bearing in mind," his son writes, "what Trelawney said to him, 'Brown, your name is that of a tribe, not of a family.'"

keeps on writing volumes of adventures to Dilke—when we get in of an evening and I have perhaps taken my rest on a couple of Chairs he affronts my indolence and Luxury by pulling out of his knapsack 1st his paper—2ndy his pens and last his ink—Now I would not care if he would change about a little—I say now, why not Bailey take out his pens first sometimes—But I might as well tell a hen to hold up her head before she drinks instead of afterwards.

The methodical habits, the neat handwriting, the careful financial accounts, were by-products of the self-control of an energetic, hotly suspicious, and often roughly ebullient nature rather than of a mild or mechanical temperament free from inner struggle. His humor reveals a certain coarseness of fiber. We can see its effect in the *Cap and Bells*—the wearisome satiric poem that (with the best intentions) he prodded Keats to write after he became ill, thinking it would help to keep his mind occupied; and the history of his relations with his maid, Abigail O'Donaghue, by whom he had a son, suggests a lack of delicacy. Moreover, with all his shrewdness and methodical coolness, he was given to quick prejudices (Keats mentions later how Brown, meeting Woodhouse, took one of his "funny odd dislikes"). His grudges, if he felt injured, could be as strong as his loyalties. In St. Petersburg, according to his son, Brown had been engaged to a Miss Kennedy, who jilted him for an English merchant with more money. Though the merchant became bankrupt and died a year or so later, Brown "had suffered too keenly to forget or forgive the injury; and it was his intention to gibbet the lady in a novel he had commenced, but which was not completed." [8] Quarreling years later with Dilke, whom he thought guilty of "infamous treachery" to him, Brown tells his son (1839) : "If he should accidentally meet with you, and civilly accost you—spit in his face." The quarrel had been about George Keats, who, according to Brown, had taken money from his brother at a time (1820) when it was desperately needed. The fierceness of Brown's reaction was partly the result of his unswerving loyalty to a friend who he felt, after a meticulous study of the accounts, had been callously treated by his brother; and Dilke, disregarding Brown's evidence, supported George. Dilke's own comment on Brown, six years after Brown died (1842) in New Zealand, is often cited (he is referring to the bill that Brown sent George for all he

8 *KC*, I.lv.

himself had lent John Keats with interest added). Brown, said Dilke,

> was the most scrupulously honest man I ever knew—but wanted no-bleness to lift this honesty out of the commercial kennel—He would have forgiven John what he owed him with all his heart—but had John been able & offered to pay, he would have charged interest, as he did George. He could do generous things too—but not after the fashion of the world. His sense of justice led him at times to do acts of generosity—at others of meanness—the latter was always noticed the former overlooked—therefore amongst his early companions he had a character for any thing rather than liberality—but he was liberal.[9]

5

At Lancaster (June 24) the inns were full. A parliamentary election was approaching. Because of industrial troubles, the election was unusually controversial; the city was noisy as well as crowded, and drink flowed plentifully. After waiting two hours, Keats and Brown were at last able to get dinner, and then found lodging in a private house.

They arose and were ready to start at four in the morning. Breakfast was not to be had in the house; and it was raining too heavily for them to start walking. Brown had brought with him a copy of Milton, and Keats a three-volume miniature set of Cary's translation of Dante. These were their only books. Otherwise in their knapsacks they carried only pens, paper, ink, and a few clothes. For three hours they sat waiting for the rain to stop. They spent the time, said Brown (who kept a detailed journal), in talking about Milton, and he himself "preached patience out of *Samson Agonistes*." At seven the rain turned to a drizzle, and they walked four miles to the town of Bolton, where they ate breakfast. Later in the day, the rain returned. They spent the night at End-moor; and Keats began the first of the series of journal letters that he was writing for Tom. Then, the next day (June 26), they at last entered the beautiful country Keats had always associated with Wordsworth. "I cannot forget the joy, the rapture of my friend," said Brown, "when he suddenly, and for the first time, became sensible to the full effect of mountain scenery."[10] It was just before

---

[9] In his annotations to Milnes's biography (Morgan Library); *KC,* I.lxix.

[10] Brown wrote the following account in his journal: "The country was wild and romantic, the weather fine, though not sunny, while the fresh mountain air, and many larks about us, gave us unbounded delight. As we approached the lake, the

they entered the village of Bowness; and they suddenly saw, as Keats wrote Tom that night,

> the Lake and Mountains of Winander—I cannot describe them— they surpass my expectation—beautiful water—shores and islands green to the marge—mountains all round up to the clouds. . . . The two views we have had of it are of the most noble tenderness— they can never fade away—they make one forget the divisions of life; age, youth, poverty and riches; and refine one's sensual vision into a sort of north star which can never cease to be open lidded and sted-fast over the wonders of the great Power.

When they stopped in Bowness at the White Lion Inn for din-ner, Keats excitedly asked the waiter if he had ever met Words-worth. "He said he knew him, and that he had been here a few days ago, canvassing for the Lowthers." (William Lowther, the Tory candidate for Parliament, was campaigning against the Whig, Henry Brougham.) "What think you of that," Keats con-tinues to Tom: "Sad—sad—sad—and yet the [Lowther] family has been his friend always. What can we say?" In any case, they hope to call on Wordsworth the next day: "You shall hear all about our visit."

After spending the night in Ambleside, "We arose this morning at six"—an hour or two later than they had been arising since they started—"because we call it a day of rest, having to call on Wordsworth who lives only two miles hence." Before breakfast they hurried to see the waterfall at Ambleside—"the first waterfall I ever saw." And this new sight of motion within form (or, put an-other way, of a form existing only through motion) gave him the same empathic delight as the "inland sea" of grain had always done when the wind would pass through it in billows and he would leap

---

scenery became more and more grand and beautiful; and from time to time we stayed our steps, gazing intently on it. Hitherto, Keats had witnessed nothing su-perior to Devonshire; but, beautiful as that is, he was now tempted to speak of it with indifference. At the first turn from the road, before descending to the hamlet of Bowness, we both simultaneously came to a full stop. The lake lay before us. His bright eyes darted on a mountain-peak, beneath which was gently floating on a silver cloud; thence to a very small island, adorned with the foliage of trees, that lay beneath us, and surrounded by water of a glorious hue, when he exclaimed: 'How can I believe in that?—surely it cannot be!' He warmly asserted that no view in the world could equal this—that it must beat all Italy—yet, having moved onward but a hundred yards—catching the further extremity of the lake, he thought it 'more and more wonderfully beautiful!' The trees far and near, the grass immediately around us, the fern and the furze in their most luxuriant growth, all added to the charm." (Printed as "Walks in the North," *Plymouth and Devonport Weekly*, October 1–22, 1840; reprinted by Rollins, *Letters*, I.421–442.)

on a stile and exclaim, "the tide!" In his letters to both George and Tom he speaks about the "tone and intellect" of this novel sight. He tries to put it more specifically to Tom, though he feels that "descriptions are bad at all times":

> What astonishes me more than any thing is the tone, the coloring, the slate, the stone, the moss, the rock-weed; or, if I may so say, the intellect, the countenance of such places. The space, the magnitude of mountains and waterfalls are well imagined before one sees them; but this countenance or intellectual tone must surpass every imagination and defy any remembrance.

Their first days of the trip were indeed moving him in a way that he continued to remember; and with excited resolve he immediately goes on to tell Tom:

> I shall learn poetry here and shall henceforth write more than ever, for the abstract endeavor of being able to add a mite to that mass of beauty which is harvested from these grand materials, by the finest spirits, and put into etherial existence for the relish of one's fellows. I cannot think with Hazlitt that these scenes make man appear little. I never forgot my stature so completely—I live in the eye; and my imagination, surpassed, is at rest

In the late morning they walked over to Rydal in order to call on Wordsworth. But neither Wordsworth nor anyone else in the family was at home. "I was much disappointed. I wrote a note for him and stuck it over what I knew must be Miss Wordsworth's Portrait." Wordsworth had gone off to Lowther Hall with his family, and was actively helping Lowther in the campaign. Brown, in the manuscript of his memoir of Keats, adds a sentence that he later crossed out: "The young poet looked thoughtfull at this exposure of his elder." The word exposure would have been far too strong for Keats himself. The Lowthers, as he had told Tom, were personal friends of Wordsworth; and "What can we say?"

Throughout the rest of the day they walked on through Grasmere to Wythburn, near the foot of Helvellyn, which was too thick in mist to climb, and stayed at the Nag's Head (June 27) : "many fleas," said Brown, "were in the beds." Keats there began a letter to George, and wrote an acrostic for Georgiana. The next day they walked eight miles before having breakfast at Keswick, strolled around Derwent Water, and saw the waterfall of Lodore, famous later because of Southey's poem and because, to the visitor who expects to find anything, it has usually diminished to a trickle by the end of June. Going north again, they saw the "Druid Circle," two miles east of Keswick, and the next day rose at four to climb Skiddaw before breakfast. This was an arduous climb and descent of ten miles. Keats describes it simply as being like a "cold bath" before breakfast: "I felt as if I were going to a Tournament." But from here on we begin to notice moments of fatigue.

6

By June 30, the next day, they were in Carlisle. Keats tells Tom of a country dancing school for children that they saw in the market town of Ireby, on the way:

> It was indeed "no new cotillon fresh from France" [he says, thinking of the line of Burns in "Tam o' Shanter"]. No they kickit & jumpit with mettle extraordinary, & whiskit, & fleckit, & toe'd it, & go'd it & twirld it, & wheel'd it, & stampt it, & sweated it, tattooing the floor like mad; The differenc[e] between our country dances & these Scotch figures, is about the same as leisurely stirring a cup o' Tea & beating up a batter pudding. I was extremely gratified to think, that if I had pleasures they knew nothing of, they had also some into which I could not possibly enter   I hope I shall not return without having got the Highland fling, there was as fine a row of boys & girls as you ever saw, some beautiful faces, & one exquisite mouth. I never felt so near the glory of Patriotism, the glory of making by any means a country happier. This is what I like better than scenery.

To walk for the next thirty or forty miles, thought Brown, "would be toil without remuneration"; and Keats seems to have been quite willing to follow Brown's suggestion that they take the coach across the Scottish border to Dumfries, where they went before dinner to visit the tomb of Burns in the churchyard.

Keats was still somewhat fatigued from the hard climb to the top of Skiddaw. To one from southern England, it was a little chilly for July; the light and the landscape seemed almost primeval, something completely distinct from the long warm summers he associated with classical Europe or the southern medieval Europe of chivalry: "I know not how it is, the Clouds, the sky, the Houses, all seem anti Grecian & anti Charlemagnish—I will endeavour to get rid of my prejudices, & tell you fairly about the Scotch." The sonnet he encloses for Tom, "On Visiting the Tomb of Burns," was "written in a strange mood, half asleep." "All is cold Beauty." This pale summer is won only for an hour from an almost omnipresent winter; and the realization of this brevity in any summer, any life, returns like the memory of a dream. The later lines anticipate the "Ode on Melancholy": "pain is never done"; for what human mind is able, as though it were a judging Minos, to separate beauty objectively from the knowledge of brevity and death that suffuses our experience of beauty? But in responding as he has, he "sins" against these "native skies" of Burns.[11]

Keats tried to throw himself into this new part of their trip with more gusto as they turned west from Dumfries to the coast. "We have now begun upon whiskey—called here *whuskey* very smart stuff it is—Mixed like our liquors with sugar & water tis called toddy, very pretty drink, & much praised by Burns." As they entered the country associated with Scott near Kirkcudbright, Brown told him about *Guy Mannering,* which Keats had not yet read. The character of Meg Merrilies caught Keats's fancy, said Brown, and he suddenly pointed to a place near the path: "There, in that very spot, without a shadow of doubt," mused Keats, "has old Meg Merrilies often boiled her kettle"; and when they stopped for breakfast, he began a letter to Fanny in which he tried to amuse her by writing the ballad "Meg Merrilies" ("Old Meg she was a gipsy, / And liv'd upon the moors"). If Fanny likes ballads of this sort, "I will now and then scribble one for you." The next night (July 3) he took up the letter again. They were at Kirkcudbright, "at which place I will write you a song about myself":

11 The town, the churchyard, and the setting sun,
    The clouds, the trees, the rounded hills all seem,
    Though beautiful, cold—strange—as in a dream,
I dreamed long ago, now new begun.
The short-liv'd, paly Summer is but won
    From Winter's ague, for one hour's gleam;
    Though sapphire-warm, their stars do never beam:
All is cold Beauty; pain is never done:
For who has mind to relish, Minos-wise,
    The Real of Beauty, free from that dead hue
        Sickly imagination and sick pride
        Cast wan upon it? Burns! with honour due
            I oft have honour'd thee. Great shadow, hide
    Thy face; I sin against thy native skies.

The punctuation is sufficiently debatable (the only copy is a transcript of the letter by John Jeffrey) to affect the sense of the middle lines. For discussion, see esp. J. C. Maxwell, *Keats-Shelley Journal,* IV (1955); J. M. Murry, *Keats* (rev. ed., 1955), pp. 199–201; and G. Yost, *Journal of English and Germanic Philosophy,* LVII (1958), 220–229.

There was a naughty Boy
A naughty boy was he
He would not stop at home
He could not quiet be—
    He took
    In his knapsack
    A Book
    Full of vowels
    And a shirt
    With some towels—
    A slight cap
    For night cap—
    A hair brush
    Comb ditto
    New Stockings
    For old ones
    Would split O!
    This knapsack
    Tight at's back
    He rivetted close
And follow'd his Nose
    To the North
    To the North
And follow'd his nose
    To the North.

And so he continues, for another ninety-three lines of doggerel, recalling, in some that we have already noticed, the time when they
lived with their grandmother at Edmonton, and ending with the
discovery that in travel at least some things are found to be much
the same as at home—

        So he stood in
        His shoes
        And he wonderd
        He wonderd
        He stood in his
        Shoes and he wonder'd—

My dear Fanny I am ashamed of writing you such stuff, nor would I
if it were not for being tired after my day's walking, and ready to
tumble into bed so fatigued that when I am asleep you might sew
my nose to my great toe and trundle me round the town like a
Hoop without waking me.

7

They were averaging about twenty miles a day, and had fallen into a routine of sorts. They were generally up about five and, probably at Brown's urging, would invariably walk five to ten miles before breakfast. They ate dinner in the middle of the afternoon, by which time they usually hoped to have completed twenty miles. Then, unless they had to go farther, they read or wrote. Brown kept his journal meticulously. Keats would often write fully to Tom; but the length of what he wrote was becoming more uneven. He was of course reading carefully in the translation of Dante that he had brought with him. By eight or nine they would have tea or a light supper. The diet was becoming less attractive, and both Keats and Brown were soon to have something of an obsession about oatcakes. Once they had left the Lake District, they had found that tourists on foot were an unfamiliar sight. Their knapsacks and Brown's spectacles attracted attention. "We have been taken for Spectacle venders," said Keats, "Razor sellers, Jewellers, travelling linen drapers, Spies, Excisemen . . . When I asked for letters at the Post Office, Port Patrick; the man asked what Regiment." Keats wore a battered fur cap. Brown describes himself in a letter to Dilke's father: "Imagine me with a thick stick in my hand, the knapsack on my back, 'with spectacles on nose,' a white hat, a tartan coat and trowsers, and a Highland plaid thrown over my shoulders . . . Keats calls me the Red Cross Knight, and declares my shadow is ready to split its sides as it follows me." [12]

They had hoped to cross the North Channel, spend at least a few days in Ireland, and see the Giant's Causeway while there. Reaching Portpatrick (July 6), they took a mail boat to Donaghadee, and walked the next day to Belfast. But the unexpected expenses worried them: everything cost about triple what it did in Scotland. They walked back to Donaghadee the next day and took the return boat. The short visit, however, struck Keats, whose attention, after the novelty of the first week, had been gradually turning from scenery to people. He was astonished at the difference once they got out of the domain of the Scottish Kirk. All through Scotland he had felt the repression of the Kirk: the children "will scarcely laugh." Is this a gain or not? It helps to form the growing youth into a "thrifty army." And given the poverty of

[12] I.362.

so many of the people in both Scotland and what little he had seen of Ireland, it was hard to say which was better off: Ireland, where the chambermaid at the inn is "fair, kind and ready to laugh," or Scotland, where everyone from the aged down to the infant is "careful," and where "they have banished puns and laughing and kissing (except in cases where the very danger and crime must make it very fine and gustful) ."

He starts to think of Burns (July 9) :

> Poor unfortunate fellow—his disposition was southern—how sad it is when a luxurious imagination is obliged in self defence to deaden its delicacy in vulgarity, and riot in thing[s] attainable that it may not have leisure to go mad after thing[s] which are not.

Since he lacks "sufficient reasoning faculty to settle the doctrine of thrift—as it is consistent with the dignity of human society," he can only deplore the poverty, the wretched lot of the cottage-weavers, the dirt and hunger that result unless one practices the most pinching thrift:

> The present state of society demands this and this convinces me that the world is very young and in a very ignorant state—We live in a barbarous age . . . What a tremendous difficulty is the improvement of the condition of such people—I cannot conceive how a mind "with child" of Philanthropy could gra[s]p at possibility—with me it is absolute despair.

Though his reflections were becoming more somber, there were still some marvelous, picturesque moments—one of which "I can never forget": an old woman carried along in a parody of a sedan chair:

> The Duchess of Dunghill—It is no laughing matter tho—Imagine the worst dog kennel you ever saw placed upon two poles from a mouldy fencing—In such a wretched thing sat a squalid old Woman squat like an ape half starved from a scarcity of Buiscuit in its passage from Madagascar to the cape,—with a pipe in her mouth and looking out with a round-eyed skinny lidded inanity—with a sort of horizontal idiotic movement of her head—squab and lean she sat and puff'd out the smoke while two ragged tattered Girls carried her along—What a thing would be a history of her Life and sensations.

Back in Scotland, they started north to Ballantrae, Ayr, and Glasgow. Since Charles Dilke considered himself something of an antiquarian, Brown wanted to fool him by getting Keats to compose a ballad in Scotch dialect that Dilke would think was genuine.

Keats tried to oblige, and wrote "A Galloway Song" ("Ah! ken ye what"), taking the subject from a wedding party they saw on the road; but, as Keats remarked simply, "it won't do"—no Scot would think it genuine after the first two lines. They passed Ailsa Rock, which, looming up over a thousand feet from the sea, "struck me very suddenly—really I was a little alarmed"; and in the inn at Girvan (July 10), Keats tried a sonnet "To Ailsa Rock," less interesting than that "On Visiting the Tomb of Burns" but less uneven.

The thought of Burns kept recurring, and Keats began to look forward to seeing the cottage in Ayr where he was born. Nine miles away from it, as they stopped to eat, his excitement grew, and he took off a few minutes to start a letter to Reynolds (July 11) "because I am approaching Burns's Cottage very fast":

> One of the pleasantest means of annulling self is approaching such a shrine as the Cottage of Burns—we need not think of his misery—that is all gone—bad luck to it—I shall look upon it hereafter with unmixed pleasure as I do upon my Stratford on Avon day with Bailey.

But his eagerness to "annul self" received a jolt, and he felt the common irritation of the informed at the mechanical and imperceptive remarks of custodians. Moreover, the place was partly used as a whiskey shop, presided over by "a mahogany faced old Jackass who knew Burns":

> We went to the Cottage and took some Whiskey—I wrote a sonnet for the mere sake of writing some lines under the roof—they are so bad I cannot transcribe them [13]—The Man at the Cottage was a great Bore with his Anecdotes . . . O the flummery of a birth place! Cant! Cant! Cant! It is enough to give a spirit the guts-ache—Many a true word they say is spoken in jest . . . I cannot write about scenery and visitings . . . One song of Burns's is of more worth to you than all I could think for a whole year in his native country— His Misery is a dead weight upon the nimbleness of one's quill—I tried to forget it—to drink Toddy without any Care—to write a merry Sonnet—it wont do—he talked with Bitches—he drank with Blackguards, he was miserable—We can see horribly clear in the works of such a man his whole life, as if we were God's spies.

Throughout the next ten days, the account Keats wrote for Tom becomes more perfunctory. The novelty of travel, of course, was

---

[13] Brown, however, made a copy; and the sonnet ("Written in the Cottage Where Burns was Born") was printed in the remains by Milnes (1848).

beginning to wear off; other interests or anxieties were beginning to return; the weather and countryside had some depressing aspects for a non-Scot; and he was becoming more easily tired. During this time (July 12–21), they continued north through Glasgow and Inverary to Oban. Throughout the last fifteen miles it rained heavily. Despite his dislike of peevishness, he begins to complain of the food (usually eggs and oatcake), and in such a way as to suggest that he is physically as well as mentally a little uneasy:

> July 20th. For these two days past we have been so badly accomodated more particularly in coarse food that I have not been at all in cue to write. . . . [July 21] All together the fare is too coarse—I feel it a little . . . I fell upon a bit of white bread to day like a Sparrow—it was very fine—I cannot manage the cursed Oatcake.

The tone of the occasional verses he jots down also changes. Of the three that he wrote during these ten days, two are wearily comic expressions of irritation,[14] and a third, despite its beginning ("There is a charm in footing slow"), becomes somberly reflective.

Already soaked with the rain, they crossed over to Mull, and walked thirty-seven miles across the island "over bog and rock and river with our Breeches tucked up and our Stockings in hand." On the way, Keats caught a bad cold, though he did not mention it at the time. Iona interested him: "Who would expect to find the ruins of a fine Cathedral Church, of Cloisters, Colleges, Mona[s]teries and Nunneries in so remote an Island"? He wrote Tom a little sketch of the history of its settlement, and picked up some pebbles to take to Fanny. Staffa caught his imagination, especially Fingal's Cave, which looked as though "the Giants who rebelled against Jove had taken a whole Mass of black Columns and bound them together like bunches of matches—and then with immense Axes had made a cavern in the body of these columns."

The northern trip was expected to last four months. It was now (July 26) a month and three days since they had said good-bye to George and Georgiana at Liverpool.

8

One of Keats's hopes from this walking trip, as he told Bailey, was that it would help him to "identify finer scenes load me with

---

14 His complaint of the summer affliction of northern countries ("The Gadfly"), and the satiric sonnet "On Hearing the Bag-Pipe."

grander Mountains, and strengthen more my reach in Poetry." It is interesting to note the number of spontaneous phrases and images in his letters now that are later echoed in the poetry, especially in the odes, though in all candor we must admit that the number is not substantially greater than can be gleaned from one or two other comparable periods of time.[15] Anticipating the "Ode to Psyche" is the line in the poem posted to Tom Keats (July 1), "Though *sapphire*-warm, their *stars*," and his description to Tom of the rocks "all *fledged* with ash and other beautiful trees." A description of another scene anticipates the images in the "Grecian Urn" of the heifer "lowing," the "green" altar, the little town "by river or sea shore, / Or mountain-built." Our road, Keats now writes Tom after they left Cairn, "lay half way up the sides of a *green mountainous shore*," after which he and Brown turned into a glen "with a *Mountainous Stream* winding down . . . the effect of *cattle lowing* I never had so finely." In the "Ode to a Nightingale," the "magic casements opening on the foam" are anticipated frequently throughout his writing; and his occasional glimpses of Windermere, as he and Brown walked along the lake, were one of the memories that, as he said when he saw the lake, "can never fade away." Thus, in October, listing some of the images that occurred to his imagination as attractive, he speaks of a "Window opening on Winandermere." The morning after he and Brown first saw Windermere, they hurried before breakfast to see the waterfall at Ambleside; and the phrases in the letter to Tom remind us again of the "Ode to a Nightingale" a year later—the close of it where the nightingale flies

> over the still stream,
> Up the hill-side; and now 'tis buried deep
> In the next valley-glades.

Looking for the Ambleside stream, they found it by the noise; for "it is *buried in trees,* in the bottom of the *valley*—the *stream* itself is interesting"; and he and Brown watched it "half way down the first fall, *buried deep* in trees." Other poems besides the odes echo phrases or images. The reappearance of the "Druid Circle" in *Hyperion* has been often noticed; and in the description of the climb up Ben Nevis, some of the images (the "large dome curtains" and

---

15 See, for example, the list given by David Perkins, *Keats-Shelley Journal,* II (1953), 52–60.

"cloud-veils") may remind us of Hyperion's palace with its "domes" and "curtains of Aurorean clouds." Describing his first two views of Windermere, he says that they not only "can never fade away" but will "refine one's sensual vision into a sort of north star which can never cease to be open lidded and steadfast over the wonders of the great Power." And later, in the "Bright Star" sonnet, are the phrases "would I were *steadfast* as thou art," and "watching, with eternal *lids* apart." [16]

The memory of Fingal's Cave recurs a year later in the description of the vast sanctuary in the *Fall of Hyperion,* with its "roof august" and the "massy range" of its huge columns, surpassing all that he had seen "Of gray cathedrals," "The superannuations of sunk realms, / Or Nature's rocks toil'd hard in waves and winds." Describing Fingal's Cave to Tom—"For solemnity and grandeur it far surpasses the finest Cathedrall"—Keats tries to picture for him the "whole Mass of black Columns," the high roof "arched somewhat gothic wise," the length of the cave of which "the Sea has done the work of excavations and is continually dashing there." "But it is impossible to describe it," he ends, and starts jotting down some verses for Tom:

> Not Aladin magian
> Ever such a work began,
>
> .   .   .   .   .
>
> Not St. John in Patmos isle
> In the passion of his toil
> When he saw the churches seven
> Golden aisled built up in heaven
> Gazed at such a rugged wonder.

He imagines the figure of Lycidas, sleeping on the cold marble pavement in this vast "Cathedral of the Sea" (an image that re-

---

[16] Mr. Gittings (pp. 25–26), struck by the echo in the "Bright Star" sonnet, questions the date traditionally assigned to the sonnet on the authority of Brown (1819), and argues that it must have been written in October 1818 (and hence addressed to Mrs. Isabella Jones). For Keats at that time sent on to George the first three letters he had written Tom during the walking tour; he would not later have had the letters around to help him compose; and "It can only be while he had this passage [the words quoted above] actually before his eyes that he wrote the first eight lines of the sonnet; the likeness is so close that there is no question of memory." Mr. Gittings is the more convinced that the sonnet had to be written while Keats still had these letters before him because "Such quotations," as he calls these echoes, "never occur again"—never occur, that is, after October 31, 1818. Not only do phrasal anticipations of poems much later than October 1818 appear in these particular letters but, as we have repeatedly seen, the recurrence of images and phrases from the letters generally, from 1817 on, is commonplace.

minds us of the icy marble pavement in the *Fall of Hyperion,* on which the poet is condemned to suffer) ; and the verses then turn to the tourists who, like himself, are intruding into the primitive majesty of the place with their "fashion boats," their "cravats and . . . Petticoats."

He breaks off the verses: "I am sorry I am so indolent as to write such stuff as this." The whole trip had increasingly driven into him how futile the attempt at mere literal description is. "A first rate drawing" is far preferable to a faithful verbal description of a scene. "Let any of my friends see my letters," he had told Tom a month before (June 27). Of course "they may not be interested in descriptions—descriptions are bad at all times." He made the effort he did to describe scenes for Tom only because he knew how little else Tom now had to amuse him. He felt free to avoid this sort of detail in writing to Reynolds, and begins his only letter to him of the trip by saying "I'll not run over the Ground we have passed"; this is as "bad as telling a dream—unless perhaps I do it in the manner of the Laputan printing press" (he refers to the elaborate computing machine in the third voyage of *Gulliver*—a machine to "give the world a complete body of all arts and sciences," into which nouns, adjectives, and verbs are fed by several young students working under a member of the Academy of Lagado) :—

> That is I put down Mountains, Rivers Lakes, dells, glens, Rocks, and Clouds, With beautiful enchanting, gothic picturesque fine . . . Grand, sublime—a few Blisters &c—and now you have our journey thus far.

9

In breaking off the little poem on Staffa and Fingal's Cave, Keats also confided to Tom: "I have a slight sore throat and think it best to stay a day or two at Oban. Then we shall proceed to Fort William and Inverness." The cold and sore throat, which he had caught in walking through thirty-seven miles across the wet bogs of Mull, had bothered him now (July 26) for four days.

The weather became worse as Keats and Brown made their way to Fort William and to Ben Nevis, which, because it was the highest mountain in Great Britain (4406 feet), they felt they had to climb; and after doing so (August 2) Keats told Tom, "I will never ascend another in this empire . . . I am heartily glad it is done—it is almost like a fly crawling up a wainscot." They had started the climb at five in the morning; and Keats, describing it next day to Tom in a letter headed "Ah mio Ben," tries to do justice to the vast crags and the large curtains of mist and cloud. But Ben Nevis was a fearful trial. He begins, in the fatigue that followed ("Twas a most vile descent"), to recount, with quick comic imitation, their scramble over the loose stones during their climb:

> Sometimes on two sometimes on three, sometimes four legs—sometimes two and stick, sometimes three and stick, then four again, then two, then a jump, so that we kept on ringing changes on foot, hand, Stick, jump, boggle, s[t]umble, foot, hand, foot, (very gingerly) stick again, and then again a game at all fours.

After all, only a few years before, a Mrs. Cameron, fifty years old—"the fattest woman in all inverness shire"—got up this mountain. Of course she had servants. "She ought to have hired Sisyphus—'Up the high hill he heaves a huge round—Mrs. Cameron.' 'Tis said a little conversation took place between the mountain and the Lady." And he stops to write some verses in which the mountainous Mrs. Cameron, solacing herself with whiskey, debates with her fellow mountain. Keats tried, at the top, to write a sonnet. It was of course only a gesture; and the situation itself was not helpful to considered composition (he was later to speak of the advantage of having a blank wall as one's view while writing). He sat perched, said Brown, "on the stones, a few feet away from the edge of that fearful precipice, fifteen hundred feet perpendicular from the valley below, and wrote this sonnet." The principal interest of the sonnet is in what it shows of the preoccupations in his own mind even at such a moment ("We are in a Mist," as he had said to Reynolds in the letter on the "Chamber of Maiden-Thought": "We see not the ballance of good and evil"). At "the top of Nevis blind in Mist," he begins this sonnet: "Read me a lesson, Muse." He looks overhead, "And there is sullen mist"; and this seems to be all that mankind can tell of heaven. Looking down he also sees mist: this is all man can know of hell. Moreover,

> mist is spread
> Before the earth, beneath me,—even such,
> Even so vague is man's sight of himself!
>   Here are the craggy stones beneath my feet,—
> Thus much I know that, a poor witless elf,
>   I tread on them,—that all my eye doth meet

Is mist and crag, not only on this height,
But in the world of thought and mental might!

He was becoming too ill to go much farther. He himself had characteristically said nothing except for the casual remarks to Tom about his sore throat and the unpleasant descent from Ben Nevis, which "shook me all to pieces." In another three days, he and Brown walked into Inverness (August 6). He tried to write a pleasant letter that day to Georgiana's mother, Mrs. James Wylie, and, probably at Brown's urging, saw a physician, who, said Brown, thought Keats "too thin and fevered to proceed on our journey." They had already walked, Brown computed, 642 miles, over difficult country, crossing bogs and climbing mountains in wet, cold weather. They had eaten poor food and slept in huts. The vigorous Brown was in no mood to turn back; he was quite prepared to put Keats on a boat for home and continue the tour alone. Their original intention had been to walk down the eastern coast from Inverness to Edinburgh, then go to Carlisle to visit Bailey, and afterwards return to London.

Keats was unquestionably making as light of his illness as he could. When they took the coach to the port of Cromarty, they stopped to visit Beauly Abbey, where they saw some piles of skulls that they took to be those of long-dead monks. Brown, doubtless thinking it would help to keep Keats's mind occupied, proposed that they together write a humorous poem on the skulls and bones. The weary Keats could contribute only a few scattered lines; but Brown was able to grind out ninety. The boat that Keats took left Cromarty for London on August 8, probably late in the evening. He arrived at London on the eighteenth and made his way to Hampstead that night.

Reviews, the Writing of *Hyperion*,
the Death of Tom Keats

❋⟶❂⟶❋⟶❂⟶❋⟶❂⟶❋⟶❂⟶❋⟶❂⟶❋⟶❂⟶❋⟶❂⟶❋⟶❂⟶❋⟶❂⟶❋⟶❂

Autumn 1818

SOME DISTURBING NEWS was waiting for him as he stopped at the
Dilkes' the night of August 18 on his way home to Well Walk,
looking, said Mrs. Dilke, "as brown and as shabby as you can imagine, scarcely any shoes left, his jacket all torn at the back, a fur
cap, a great plaid, and his knapsack." He quickly guessed that further trouble had arisen. But he sat back in the unaccustomed comfort of the cushioned chair (as Joseph Severn later heard), looked
up with a tired smile, and quoted from *A Midsummer Night's
Dream,* "Bless thee, Bottom! bless thee! thou art translated."

Tom Keats had been persistently cheerful since his brother left.
A brief note still survives that he sent as soon as he heard Dilke
himself was a little unwell. The eighteen-year-old Tom was confined to the house much of the time, and Dilke's ailment was minor in comparison. Tom, however, had walked slowly down to
the small fruit-stall in Hampstead and bought some cherries to
send Dilke:

> I am really concerned that you should be so ill as Mrs. Bentley re-
> ports this morning. Could you and Mrs. Dilke come out again, you
> would be sure to find me out of bed—sick people are supposed to
> have delicate stomachs, for my part I should like a slice of under-
> done surloin. I have sent you a trifle of fruit—the cherries are not so
> fine as I could wish.[1]

But at almost the very time that Keats himself cut short his trip
to London, Tom had such a serious hemorrhage and became so
gravely ill that Dr. Sawrey (as Mrs. Dilke wrote her father-in-law
two days before Keats unexpectedly arrived),

> begged that his brother might be sent for. Dilke accordingly wrote
> off to him, which was a very unpleasant task. However, from the
> journal received from Brown last Friday, he says Keats has been so

[1] Keats Museum, Hampstead.

long ill with his sore throat, that he is obliged to give up. I am rather glad of it, as he will not receive the letter, which might have frightened him very much.[2]

Keats, of course, immediately went back to the rooms that he and Tom shared at the Bentleys'. We can only speculate about his feelings, or whether Tom had been receiving any nursing help other than that which Mrs. Bentley, the landlady, had been able to give. A few friends, of course, had dropped by, among them William Haslam, whose kindness to Tom moved Keats enormously. Without question he condemned himself bitterly for having allowed himself in June to believe that Tom was getting better. The next day he wrote a short note to his sister explaining why he was back (he had also acquired a violent toothache) and telling her that he would immediately see Abbey in order to get permission for her to visit Tom. The tone of the letter suggests that she had not yet heard about Tom's relapse. Of course there was no one really to tell her: most of Keats's more intimate friends were away except for the Dilkes; and they knew little about Fanny except that she was kept under strict watch out in Walthamstow by Abbey and his wife. Of the troubled week that now passed we know nothing. Keats was too preoccupied to write anyone. He seems to have continued to be unwell himself, and Abbey was apparently unwilling to let Fanny leave Walthamstow. For Keats, a week after he returned, wrote her again about Tom, and added that he himself could not get out to see her because of "a little Indisposition of my own."

Abbey's almost pathological desire to keep Fanny from seeing Keats may be interpreted in various ways. One possible interpretation, offered as a mere speculation, is that it stemmed from the chronic suspicion of a guilty man that her brothers, older and shrewder than Fanny, might begin to think more curiously about the inheritance of which they had received only a part—a relatively small part—and an anxiety lest, young though she was, Fanny be prompted to spy. He at length allowed her to make a visit. When she did come, however, Keats introduced her to some of his friends, Fanny babbled about the visit, and Abbey used this as an excuse to forbid further visits. Keats's negotiations with the man, in order to allow her to see Tom again, continued for weeks. At length, trying to muffle his rising anger, he writes to rebuke

2 Dilke, *Papers of a Critic* (1875), I.5.

her gently (October 26) for ever having told Abbey that she saw anyone except Tom:

> I called on Mr Abbey in the beginning of last Week: when he seemed averse to letting you come again from having heard that you had been to other places besides Well Walk—I do not mean to say you did wrongly in speaking of it, for there should rightly be no objection to such things: but you know with what People we are obliged in the course of Childhood to associate; whose conduct forces us into duplicity and fa[l]shood to them. To the worst of People we should be openhearted: but it is as well as things are to be prudent in making any communication to any one, that may throw an impediment in the way of any of the little pleasures you may have. I do not recommend duplicity but prudence with such people.

2

The unpredictability of things, which he long before thought he was taking for granted as an adult, began to strike home even more. The "spring," he had thought back in February, would bring a "harvest-time." The harvest appeared to be a series of blows, and the year was far from finished. There had been the trying weeks in Devon, and, during them, the struggle to think out honestly the nature of the challenge and needs of poetry now—a challenge and needs that seemed at times to cut across the most vivid ideals of poetry that he had. Coming with this was the departure—quite obviously permanent—of George Keats, and all this meant to Keats's own personal freedom and well-being as well as to the family life the three of them had preserved. The walking trip, which he had approached with so much hope—this Spartanly economical excursion, which was to get him out of his parochial groove, and serve as a "prologue" to a life where he would see all Europe and America—was cut short, after a few weeks, because of illness (and an illness that he may have begun to fear went further than a sore throat, however distracting that might be by itself; for his susceptibility to fatigue now was very new). Then, on his return, he had found Tom in this appalling state. He did not really want to get started writing anything serious yet. The whole year had been filled with the thought of the need for long preparation.

Throughout the rest of August and much of September, he went out relatively little. Tom needed almost constant attention, and Keats himself continued unwell. Meanwhile, in the course of a month, appeared the three famous attacks on *Endymion* in the Tory journals: the August issue of *Blackwood's* was published on September 1; the *Quarterly Review*, almost always late, brought out its April number on September 27; and the June issue of the *British Critic* also appeared at some time during September.

Ever since *Blackwood's* the year before had begun its series on the "Cockney School" with what he described as a "flaming attack" on Hunt, Keats had assumed that he was marked out for similar treatment. Sheltered by the anonymity which was then almost universal in reviews, Lockhart and Wilson had enjoyed the frustrated attempts of Hunt and others to discover the identity of "Z," their pen name, and to call him to account. Lockhart (for it was probably he that wrote most if not all of the review of *Endymion*) was less scurrilously personal about Keats than he had been about Hunt: he knew fewer details of Keats's life that he could turn to use. It was, ironically, through the good intentions of Benjamin Bailey that Lockhart picked up as much as he did.[3] In late July, on a visit to Scotland, Bailey had met Lockhart, who was known to be a contributor to *Blackwood's*. Lockhart "abused poor Keats in a way that, although it was at the Bishop's table [that of Bishop Gleig, Bailey's future father-in-law], I could hardly keep my tongue":

> I said that I supposed he would be attacked in Blackwood's. He replied "not by *me;*" which would convey the insinuation he would by someone *else.* The objections, he stated, were frivolous, in the extreme. They chiefly respected the *rhymes.*

Bailey then tried to tell him something about Keats, and to dissociate Keats from Hunt and Hunt's politics (of which Bailey himself disapproved) :

> I took occasion, therefore, seriously to expostulate with this Gentleman regarding Keats; that he was a young man, to whom Mr. Hunt had shown kindness which called forth gratitude in so young & warm a bosom,—but that he himself mingled in no party politics, & as I could confidently say, from his own lips, saw the weakness of his friend, & the impolicy of having his name mixed up with so decidedly a party-man as Mr. Hunt. I gave him an outline of Keats' history—that he had been brought up as a surgeon and apothecary; & though not highly, that he was respectably educated. Insisted, if I rightly remember, on the injustice & cruelty of thus condemning & crushing a young man who, from feelings most honorable to hu-

3 For Bailey's three detailed accounts, see *KC*, I.34–35, 245–247, II.286–288.

man nature, adhered personally to the man who had befriended him when he was friendless, & needed a kindly eye & a helping hand. But I distinctly remember saying something to this effect, "Now do not avail yourself of my information, which I give you in this friendly manner, to attack him in your next number of Blackwood." His answer, too, I well remember, was to the effect *that he certainly should not do so.*

Lockhart, his eagerness whetted by Bailey's information, begins his review with a sorrow flecked by joy:

> Of all the manias of this mad age, the most incurable, as well as the most common, seems to be no other than the *Metromanie.* The just celebrity of Robert Burns and Miss Baillie has had the melancholy effect of turning the heads of we know not how many farm-servants and unmarried ladies; our very footmen compose tragedies, and there is scarcely a superannuated governess in the island that does not leave a roll of lyrics behind her in her bandbox.

To witness "disease" of mind, even among those who are already endowed with only a feeble intelligence, is distressing to "Z." But his melancholy deepens when a person has talents that would enable him, if rightly used, to become a "respectable if not an eminent citizen." Such is the case with Keats:

> His friends, we understand, destined him to the career of medicine, and he was bound apprentice some years ago to a worthy apothecary in town. But all has been undone by a sudden attack of the malady to which we have alluded. Whether Mr. John has been sent home with a diuretic or composing draught to some patient far gone in the poetical mania, we have not heard. This much is certain, that he has caught the infection, and that thoroughly.

Except for some remarks about "Cockney rhymes," "Z" has relatively little to say about his style. He allows quotations to speak for themselves, and of course selects those that strike him as the worst. He looks back into Keats's first volume, and plucks out for ridicule Keats's statements of his high poetic ideals. "We venture to make one small prophecy, that his bookseller will not a second time venture £50 upon any thing he can write":

> It is a better and a wiser thing to be a starved apothecary than a starved poet; so back to the shop, Mr. John, back to the "plasters, pills, and ointment boxes," &c. But, for Heaven's sake, young Sangrado, be a little more sparing of extenuatives and soporifics in your practice than you have been in your poetry.

Long afterwards, when he had married Sir Walter Scott's daughter and had settled into a calmer, less defensive self-approbation, Lockhart was to plead the excuse of extreme youth: his early reviews, he said, were the mere "jibes and jokes" of a "raw boy." The "raw boy" was a year and three months older than Keats.

Blackwood's had hitherto been afraid of tackling Hazlitt, who was quite capable of taking care of himself and whose capacity for invective—once he was aroused—far excelled the thin and strident petulance of Lockhart and Wilson. But the courage of the two reviewers was now mounting; and in the same issue that attacked *Endymion,* "Z" contributed a vitriolic article, "Hazlitt Cross-Questioned." The tone was again one of jejune but savage snobbishness (Hazlitt was a London "quack," insufficiently educated, who hung around third-rate bookshops and lived a morally loose life) .

An old hand at battles, Hazlitt was doubtless spoiling for a fight. As a matter of course he started legal action. This, as he knew only too well, was an involved and expensive procedure; but it was an effective beginning in his endeavor to frighten *Blackwood's* and force it to pay something out of court. He got Francis Jeffrey and others prepared to help him, and then sat down to write with gusto an attack ("A Reply to Z") which he sent off to Archibald Constable for later use. Getting wind of Hazlitt's "Reply to Z," and then on October 6 receiving a summons to answer Hazlitt's suit for damages, William Blackwood was more worried than he pretended to be, and privately paid Hazlitt £100 and expenses. Feeling this was sufficient payment for the insult and relieved by the enjoyment of writing his "Reply to Z," Hazlitt—who had other business to attend to—then let the matter go.[4]

3

The attack by *Blackwood's,* however unpleasant, was not dangerous. It was far too personal. It was beginning to be taken for granted that *Blackwood's* had become blithely irresponsible (in fact, the noted publisher, John Murray, who was Blackwood's agent in London, withdrew after Hazlitt started his suit) . More influential was the stand taken by the *Quarterly Review,* though the

[4] Herschel Baker gives a detailed account in his *William Hazlitt* (1962) , pp. 370–376.

character of its editor—the cold and saturnine William Gifford, certainly one of the least attractive figures of the day—was before much longer to tarnish the magazine's prestige. John Taylor had been afraid that Gifford (who in an early poetic satire had boasted that he was born "To brand obtrusive ignorance with scorn") would enjoy the chance of attack, and had called on him to express his hope that *Endymion* would at least not be automatically condemned because of politics. Gifford announced that the review was already written, and was as unmoved as he was later, when Mrs. Hoppner, the wife of the artist, dropped in on him indignantly, according to Haydon, and found Gifford "writing with his green shade before his eyes, totally insensible to all reproach or entreaty. 'How can you, Gifford, dish up in this dreadful manner a youth who has never offended you?' 'It has done him good,' replied Gifford."

It was to John Wilson Croker, whom Hazlitt called "the talking potato," that Gifford assigned the job of disposing of Keats. Macaulay was not quite fair when he said that Croker would go "a hundred miles through sleet and snow, on the top of a coach, in a December night, to search a parish register, for the sake of showing that a man is illegitimate, or a woman older than she says she is." Croker had the coldness and self-righteousness of Gifford; but, unlike Gifford, he was imperceptive and ill-tempered rather than malicious. Fulfilling his name with an aptness that reminds us of the characters of Dickens, Croker—a man capable of enormous industry—constantly complained of suffering from tedium whenever he encountered anything different from the dullness he himself so plentifully exuded. He begins his review of *Endymion* with a heavy weariness. He has "made efforts almost as superhuman as the story appears to be, to get through it." But "we have not been able to struggle beyond the first of the four books" of this poem by "Mr. Keats (if that be his real name, for we almost doubt that any man in his senses would put his real name to such a rhapsody)." The poet has surrendered or abused whatever talent he may have by becoming a

> disciple of the new school of what has been somewhere called Cockney poetry; which may be defined to consist of the most incongruous ideas in the most uncouth language . . . This author is a copyist of Mr. Hunt; but he is more unintelligible, almost as rugged, twice as diffuse, and ten times more tiresome and absurd than his prototype.

Warming to his subject, Croker then ridicules the preface to *Endymion,* and Keats's humble admission of inexperience and immaturity, "every error denoting a feverish attempt, rather than a deed accomplished." "Of the story we have been able to make out but little; it seems to be mythological." Unable to get further than Book I, the reviewer is forced to concentrate on the language and versification of that Book. Croker then presents a collection of "the new words with which, in imitation of Mr. Leigh Hunt, he adorns our language." He pounces heavily on the versification. Keats has "been amusing himself and wearying his readers with an immeasurable game at *bouts-rimés;* but, if we recollect rightly, it is an indispensable condition at this play, that the rhymes when filled up shall have meaning." Croker cannot find any meaning; Keats, a "simple neopyhte," has thought he was writing a poem if only he could find rhymes. Croker advises against buying the poem.

Finally the *British Critic* brought out in September its June issue. The attack united Lockhart's gift of personal ridicule with Croker's incapacity to mention any phrase or line except what could be censured. One rather long sentence is typical of the remarks on style:

> It seems that one evening when the sun had done driving "his snorting four," "there blossom'd suddenly a magic bed of sacred ditamy," (Qu. dimity?) and he looked up to the "lidless-eyed train of planets," where he saw "a completed form of all completeness," "with gordian'd locks and pearl round ears," and kissed all these till he fell into a "stupid sleep," from which he was roused by "a gentle creep," (N.B. Mr. Tiffin is the ablest bug-destroyer of our days,) to look at some "upturn'd gills of dying fish."

With the aggressive prudery of the sexually obsessed, the reviewer pounces on the "immoral images" that lie beneath "the flimsy veil of words":

> We will not disgust our readers by retailing to them the artifices of vicious refinement, by which, under the semblance of "slippery blisses, twinkling eyes, soft completion of faces, and smooth excess of hands," he would palm upon the unsuspicious and the innocent, imaginations better adapted to the stews.

The review ends:

> We do most solemnly assure our readers that this poem, containing 4074 lines, is printed on a very nice hot-pressed paper, and sold

for 9/— by a very respectable London bookseller. Moreover, as the Author has put his name on the title page, and told us, that though he is something between man and boy, he means by and by to be "plotting and fitting himself for verses fit to live." We think it necessary to add that it is all written in rhyme, and for the most part, (when there are syllables enough) in the heroic couplet.

4

These three attacks, all appearing within a single month, and at a time when Keats was feeling rather helpless—with George gone, Tom fatally ill, and himself still unwell—naturally struck home, if for no other reason than that they expressed some of the misgivings he himself had. But they probably worried his friends more than they did him. "Real grievances," as he later said, "are displacers of passion. The imaginary nail a man down for a sufferer, as on a cross; the real spur him up into an agent." And he was beset with far too many "Real grievances" (and, in his own writing, he was far too concerned with the immense problems of the next step) to dwell on these attacks with the refined anguish of those less mentally occupied and more habituated to the comforts and supporting approval of others.

Bailey tried to persuade *Blackwood's* to allow him to publish a reply to their review. When his request was turned down, he sent his article to Constable's. It was returned without comment. Reynolds, down in Devonshire, wrote a defense that was little noticed.[5] A protest against the injustice of the *Quarterly's* attack was also published in the *Morning Chronicle* (October 3), signed by "J.S." —probably John Scott (who was later killed in a duel with J. H. Christie, who wrote for *Blackwood's*), or possibly James Smith, the brother of Horace Smith; and a second protest was published in the *Morning Chronicle* a few days later from a correspondent signed "R.B." Hoping to cheer Keats, James Hessey sent him a copy of the first of these; and Keats wrote back (October 8):

> I cannot but feel indebted to those Gentlemen who have taken my part—As for the rest, I begin to get a little acquainted with my own strength and weakness.—Praise or blame has but a momentary effect on the man whose love of beauty in the abstract makes him a severe critic of his own Works. My own domestic criticism has given me pain without comparison beyond what Blackwood or the Quarterly

---

[5] It appeared in the *Alfred, West of England Journal* (October 6); and Hunt then reprinted it, somewhat abridged, in the *Examiner* (October 11).

could possibly inflict. and also when I feel I am right, no external praise can give me such a glow as my own solitary reperception & ratification of what is fine. J. S. is perfectly right in regard to the slip-shod Endymion.

Then follows the fine passage cited before in another context.

Had I been nervous about its being a perfect piece, & with that view asked advice, & trembled over every page, it would not have been written; for it is not in my nature to fumble—I will write independantly—I have written independently *without Judgment.*—I may write independently & *with judgment* hereafter.—The Genius of Poetry must work out its own salvation in a man: It cannot be matured by law & precept, but by sensation & watchfulness in itself—That which is creative must create itself—In Endymion, I leaped headlong into the Sea, and thereby have become better acquainted with the Soundings, the quicksands, & the rocks, than if I had stayed upon the green shore, and piped a silly pipe, and took tea & comfortable advice.

Keats meant what he told Hessey. His instinctive common sense was able to absorb these blows as far as they applied to any real judgment on his work.[6] But he was naturally anxious lest these obstacles completely kill not only the sale of *Endymion*—that could be taken for granted—but also the future sale of any poetry he wrote throughout the next year or two. His hope of future leisure to write poetry at all depended on his ability to earn his living as a writer. But he never allowed himself to refer to the reviews in a whining spirit. The effect appeared only indirectly, and then very much later. Beginning his final three months of effort (July 1819), he tells his young sister not to worry: he has enough knowledge of his "gallipots" to be able to go back to them (as Lockhart advised) and make a living in that way. And, in the spring of 1819, there is the obvious *katharsis* he feels when he reads Hazlitt's attack on Gifford (who Keats and others assumed had written the review in the *Quarterly*).

[6] Cf. his remark to George (October 14), after mentioning the attacks of *Blackwood's* and the *Quarterly:* "This is a mere matter of the moment—I think I shall be among the English Poets after my death. Even as a Matter of present interest the attempt to crush me in the Quarterly has only brought me more into notice and it is a common expression among book men, 'I wonder the Quarterly should cut its own throat.' It does me not the least harm in Society to make me appear little and ridiculous: I know when a Man is superior to me and give him all due respect—he will be the last to laugh at me and as for the rest I feel that I make an impression upon them which insures me personal respect while I am in sight whatever they may say when my back is turned."

Just as Hazlitt had entered indirectly as an avenger after the attack by *Blackwood's*, he appeared again, far more vigorously, soon after the review in the *Quarterly*. For the *Quarterly* also selected this year to launch an attack on Hazlitt, using for the occasion a review of his *Lectures on the English Poets*. Bounding into the fray, Hazlitt sat down and wrote one of the half dozen most sustained pieces of invective in English, the notable *Letter to William Gifford*. From the opening sentence ("You have an ugly trick of saying what is not true of any one you do not like; and it will be the object of this letter to cure you of it"), Hazlitt's *Letter*—as Keats said to George with admiring relief—"yeasts and works itself up." Step by step, throughout forty pages, Hazlitt undercuts this "literary toadeater" to social position and "taster to the court," whose thick vanity is still ready to "pander" to cold interest and whose chronic malice is ready to pause and "truckle" when it conflicts with the "love of power"—this "invisible link" between "literature and the police," grown dirty and gray "in the service of corruption." From these pages, Keats, understandably delighting in Hazlitt's Swiftian indignation, copies out two or three for George (March 12–13),[7] and then—suddenly fatigued by the whole thought of quarrel, and of the amount of energy that people spend in attempting to pull each other down during their tragically brief lives—he drops the subject and turns to other things.

As for Gifford, he became warier after Hazlitt's whirlwind response. Wanting the last word, he personally wrote the *Quarterly*'s attack on Hazlitt's *Political Essays* the following year; but Gifford's tone was flat, and he afterwards let Hazlitt alone. Hazlitt, however, was only beginning, and the brilliant essay on Gifford in the *Spirit of the Age* (1824–25), more condensed and thus more effective than the *Letter*, has a further interest to readers of Keats, for there Hazlitt devastatingly contrasts passages of Keats (dead now for four years) with some of Gifford's own poetic effusions.

5

For a while in September the sore throat disappeared. Tom did not seem to require constant attention, and Keats occasionally went out during the day. On September 14 he attended a dinner

7 See below, Chapter XVIII, section 4.

party given by James Hessey, to which Hazlitt, Woodhouse, and a few others were also invited. Probably little was said about the reviews. That in the *Quarterly* had not yet appeared; and the kindly Hessey wished this to be a pleasant occasion.

But we know of one subject that was discussed; and Keats's own remarks reflect the uncertainties and frustration with which he began *Hyperion*. This subject was the new, almost uniquely modern self-consciousness about originality in the arts, and the extent to which this forces the poet to retreat to increasingly minor and subjective interests. The thought, and with it the whole problem of our relation to the past, had of course been much in Keats's mind for months.[8] But it was becoming more urgent now as he debated within himself whether to plunge at once into a major poem: a poem in which, however much he would try to follow out what he felt to be the great modern challenge to poetry, he also naturally wanted to catch what he could of the amplitude and vigor that we honor in earlier works while fearing to do other than imitate our contemporaries. "Give me their old vigour," he had written in the little credo on May Day, the fragment of an "Ode to Maia," and he would be content, however few would be those who noticed or cared. But how to acquire their "old vigour"—what Keats's admired Hazlitt, who was present this evening, called their "venturous magnanimity"—if one of our principal emotions is the anxiety to be different? One of the first fruits of such an anxiety, as Hazlitt often noted, is that the eye of the writer begins to turn from other subjects to himself; or else he retreats in self-defense to a specialized preserve where, as Keats had said, he becomes "like an Elector of Hanover" concentrating on his "petty state." Able in the past to joke occasionally about the whole situation, Keats was now very articulate in his pessimism. To live up to the demand for originality was impossible, or led one only to small corners. He for his part was ready to give up the writing of poetry and to spend his free time in reading. We know about this particular evening because Woodhouse—who was on the point of leaving London to visit his family for a while—brooded anxiously over Keats's remarks for the next month. While Woodhouse was gone, Croker's review in the *Quarterly* appeared. If Keats had felt as he did at Hessey's, thought Woodhouse, what must he feel now? On his return he prepared a long, thoughtful letter to Keats (Oc-

8 See Chapter XIII above.

tober 21). After speaking of the *Quarterly*'s attack, Woodhouse turns to the point of his letter [9]—that is,

> to address you on the subject of our late conversation at Hessey's, on which I have often since reflected, and never without a degree of pain—I may have misconceived you,—but I understood you to say, you thought there was now nothing original to be written in poetry; that its riches were already exhausted,—& all its beauties forestalled —& That you should, consequently, write no more.—I cannot assent to your premises, and I most earnestly deprecate your conclusion.— For my part I believe most sincerely, that the wealth of poetry is unexhausted & inexhaustible—The ideas derivable to us from our senses singly & in their various combin[ns] with each other store the mind with endless images of natural beauty & perfection—the Passions add life and motion—& reflection & the moral Sense give order relief unity & harmony to this mighty world of inanimate matter.

But within a week after the evening at Hessey's, Keats had already begun *Hyperion*. He was only too convinced that this was not yet the time to start the poem: he simply did not know enough. But, he tells Dilke (September 21), "my throat has become worse after getting well, and I am determined to stop at home till I am quite well." And with Tom so ill, so uncomplaining—"His identity presses upon me so all day"—he would have to go out occasionally; and on returning he was "obliged to write, and plunge into abstract images."

By the time he received Woodhouse's letter, he may already have finished the first book of *Hyperion;* for a month had now passed, and the total time he appears to have spent on the first two books occupied a little more than two months—from about September 20 to the end of November. In any case, he was feeling confident for the moment about his own writing, if about very little else. In his considered—and grateful—reply to Woodhouse (October 27), he tries to "make some observations on two principle points." In taking up the first, he elaborates his whole thought of the sympathetic nature of the poetic imagination—its lack of any assertive "identity" of its own.[10] Rather puckishly he now uses this argument to pacify Woodhouse: he finds himself sympathetically caught up in certain concepts as well as people: he lacks a sufficiently fixed and stable "identity" to be able to give a hard-and-fast opinion on

---

[9] Printed in full, I.378–382; cf. I.383–385, 388–390.
[10] For discussion of Keats's remarks and Woodhouse's later comment on it, see Chapter X, "Negative Capability."

most things. Woodhouse should not have taken him too seriously
that night.

> In the second place I will speak of my views, and of the life I pur-
> pose to myself—I am ambitious of doing the world some good: if I
> should be spared that may be the work of maturer years—in the in-
> terval I will assay to reach to as high a summit in Poetry as the nerve
> bestowed upon me will suffer. The faint conceptions I have of Po-
> ems to come brings the blood frequently into my forehead.

He will go on writing, he assures Woodhouse, "even if my night's
labours should be burnt every morning."

                                  6

Within a few days after he began *Hyperion,* Keats dropped in
on the Reynolds sisters and their mother. He was not particularly
eager to see them. Much as he liked John Reynolds, Keats increasingly found him "very dull at home"; they would both sit glumly
amid the constant chattering and gossip of the four girls and their
mother. It was even worse when Reynolds was away; and he was
away now. He had become engaged to Eliza Drewe, and had
snatched an opportunity to go to Exeter to visit her and the Drewe
family.

Now except for Mrs. Dilke, of whom he was understandably
fond, Keats had not become really well acquainted with any
women since he first got to know the Hunts and the Reynoldses
two years before. He had grown quickly fond of Georgiana Wylie,
but he had seen little of her before the month that she married
George. The Jeffrey girls, down in Teignmouth, hardly counted.
They were very young; and Keats was altogether preoccupied during those troubled weeks. Without his quite knowing it at first,
Mrs. Reynolds and her four daughters had been subtly affecting
his more routine, offhand impression of women. Undoubtedly his
strong language and almost amusingly mechanical reaction to anything that savored of the "blue-stocking" derived as much from his
contact with the Reynoldses as it did from the opinions of Hazlitt,
to whom the bluestocking was one more symbol of what was happening to literature, one more symbol of the difference between
the modern era and the bold art of the earlier periods. This reaction was to remain with Keats to the end, and is by no means irrele-

vant to the attraction he came to feel for the very different Fanny Brawne. But as far as his more general attitude toward women was concerned, Keats needed only a little prompting and a few moments of honest reflection to become aware that he had developed an "obstinate prejudice" and to resolve to "find the root" of it and "so cure it." The occasion had to do with that inveterate wooer, Benjamin Bailey.

Back in June, Keats had suddenly blurted out to Bailey his distress at the crumbling of what remained of his family life—one brother "driven by the 'burden of Society' to America; the other, with an exquisite love of life, in a lingering state"; and he went on to tell how close their affection had grown because of the early loss of their parents. "The thought of them has always stifled the impression that any woman might otherwise have made upon me." [11] The whole tone of the letter made Bailey worry about the loneliness that Keats would soon face. Bailey had not yet given up his own hopeless courtship of Mariane Reynolds; and he doubtless thought Keats would be wise to look to the Reynolds family, as he himself was doing, for a future wife. But he had gathered, and probably through some rather sharp remarks from the Reynoldses, that Keats had virtually stopped visiting their house; and this "grieved" him. Keats in his answer (July 18) begins a little sharply. He has, after all, "Books to read and subjects to think upon." Perhaps realizing that this may seem to be a reflection on Bailey, who did visit them persistently, he adds: "Moreover I have been too often in a state of health that made me think it prudent not to hazard the night air." But then his conscience plainly bothers him. He was willing to hazard the night air for that riotous party at Haydon's last May, busy (and depressed) as he was. The truth is that he just "cannot enjoy Society small or numerous" because of the kind of thing that is done and talked about there. He prefers to be with a few friends. And women, at social gatherings, probably appreciate having him stay away. Then, after this preliminary shuffle, he suddenly admits: "I am certain I have not a right feeling toward Women—at this moment I am striving to be just to them but I cannot—Is it because they fall so far beneath my Boyish imagination?" (Bailey later told Milnes that he had been struck by the "poetic feeling" with which Keats approached women; and he was speaking of Keats when he knew him best, when he was seeing him, in fact, daily—a year before the present time.)

Writing rapidly, Keats begins to think out the matter. He had often been infatuated even when a schoolboy: "My mind was a soft nest in which some one of them slept though she knew it not." This may not have been the best approach: "I have no right to expect more than their reality." Discovering women to be by no means "above Men," he finds them "perhaps equal." Months later (December 31), in a letter to George and Georgiana, he elaborates the idea: "The more we know the more inadequacy we discover in the world to satisfy us—this is an old observation; but I have made up my Mind never to take any thing for granted—but even to examine the truth of the commonest proverbs." For example,

> Mrs. Tighe and Beattie once delighted me—now I see through them and can find nothing in them—or weakness—and yet how many they still delight! Perhaps a superior being may look upon Shakspeare in the same light—is it possible? No—This same inadequacy is discovered (forgive me little George [Georgiana]—you know I don't mean to put you in the mess) in Women with few exceptions—the Dress Maker, the blue Stocking and the most charming sentimentalist differ but in a Slight degree and are equally smokeable—But I'll go no further—I may be speaking sacrilegiously.

To go back to the letter in which he tries to think out the matter to Bailey: he believes that, on the whole, he is fairly free from "spleen" and from the desire to puncture affectations, and in fact views that sort of thing as "malice"—as something of a "crime" or "insult" to another human being. Yet he has it when among women (meaning specifically, of course, the Reynoldses):

> When I am among Men I have no evil thoughts, no malice, no spleen—I feel free to speak or to be silent—I can listen and from every one I can learn—my hands are in my pockets   I am free from all suspicion and comfortable. When I am among Women I have evil thoughts, malice spleen—I cannot speak or be silent—I am full of Suspicions and therefore listen to no thing—I am in a hurry to be gone.

The language of this letter reminds us that we are dealing with a mind that, in habits of perception, in the use of models, in style, in ultimate growth and assimilation, and in almost every other way, is strongly empathic or sympathetic—a mind so habituated to identifying itself with what it conceives that, if such an identifica-

tion is lacking, it becomes ill at ease, quickly exaggerating its unaccustomed reaction and using words ("malice," "spleen") that
less sympathetic natures reserve for more aggressive feelings.

In any case, as he tells Bailey, "I must absolutely get over this—
but how? The only way is to find the root of evil, and so cure it."
This is not easy. "An obstinate Prejudice can seldom be produced
but from a gordian complication of feelings, which must take
time to unravel and care to keep it unravelled." But when he returned to Hampstead after the Scottish tour, he did not drop in
to see the Reynoldses. Far too much had been happening the past
month for him to keep that particular resolution in the forefront
of his mind. When Jane Reynolds suggested that she herself might
come out to Hampstead to see him and Tom, he put her off (September 1). In his long October letter to George and Georgiana,
he tells them (October 14) about the visit he finally did make.
"The Miss Reynoldses are very kind to me—but they have lately
displeased me in this way." They were "in a sort of taking or bustle
about a Cousin of theirs"—Jane Cox, the daughter of a brother of
Mrs. Reynolds, who had gone out to India:

> At the time I called M^rs. R. was in conference with her up stairs
> and the young Ladies were warm in her praises down stairs, calling
> her genteel, interesting and a thousand other pretty things to which
> I gave no heed, not being partial to 9 days wonders—Now all is com-
> pletely changed—they hate her; and from what I hear she is not
> without faults—of a real kind: but she has othe[r]s which are more
> apt to make women of inferior charms hate her. She is not a Cleo-
> patra; but she is at least a Charmian. She has a rich eastern look; she
> has fine eyes and fine manners. When she comes into a room she
> makes an impression the same as the Beauty of a Leopardess. She is
> too fine and too conscious of her Self to repulse any Man who may
> address her—from habit she thinks that nothing *particular*. [Being
> "particular," in Regency slang, meant flirting.] I always find myself
> more at ease with such a woman; the picture before me always gives
> me a life and animation which I cannot possibly feel with anything
> inferiour—I am at such times too much occupied in admiring to be
> awkward or on a tremble. I forget myself entirely because I live in
> her. You will by this time think I am in love with her; so before I go
> any further I will tell you I am not—she kept me awake one Night
> as a tune of Mozart's might do.

The contrast with the Reynolds sisters was immense. Jane Cox
was beautiful, and in an unusual way (the comparison with a
"leopardess" reminds us a little of "La belle dame" and *Lamia*).

Moreover, she completely lacked the awkward imitations of the masculine that bothered him in the bluestocking; she also seemed free of envy and spite; she spoke with confident and quiet directness. At the same time he liked her practical and sophisticated good sense.[12] An undated letter to John Reynolds about this time also mentions the incident. Speaking of Reynolds' engagement, he says:

> I never was in love—Yet the voice and shape of a woman has haunted me these two days—at such a time when the relief, the feverous relief of Poetry seems a much less crime [less of a crime considering Tom's perilous state]—This morning Poetry has conquered —I have relapsed into those abstractions [in writing *Hyperion*] which are my only life—I feel escaped from a new strange and threatening sorrow.—And I am thankful for it—There is an awful warmth about my heart like a load of Immortality.

7

The same poise and sophisticated good sense had struck him in the experienced Mrs. Isabella Jones, the woman he had met in Hastings over a year ago (May or June, 1817), flirted timidly with, and kissed.[13]

Two or three weeks after he had met Jane Cox, he ran into Mrs. Jones again while walking from Bedford Row to Lamb's Conduit Street; and he tells George and Georgiana about it (October 24). George may recall that when he and Keats had gone to the Lyceum Theatre in May, they had seen her briefly. Well, "I have met with that same Lady again." He passed her on the street, and then turned back to say hello. "She seemed glad of it." She was walking to Islington to see a friend of hers who kept a boarding school, a Mrs. Green. Keats strolled along with her. "She has always been an enigma to me—she has been in a Room with you and Reynolds and wished we should be acquainted without any of our common acquaintances knowing it." Keats's curiosity could hardly

---

12 "You will suppose I have by this had much talk with her—no such thing— there are the Miss Reynoldses on the look out. They think I dont admire her because I did not stare at her—They call her a flirt to me—What a want of knowledge! She walks across a room in such a manner that a Man is drawn towards her with a magnetic Power. This they call flirting! they do not know things. They do not know what a Woman is."

13 Detailed information on Mrs. Jones is given by Gittings, pp. 30–33, 57–63, and *passim,* and in his *Mask of Keats* (1956), pp. 45–53. The details about her here are summarized from Mr. Gittings.

but sharpen at her request of secrecy. He may not yet have known that Mrs. Jones (the identity of Mr. Jones is a mystery) was a good acquaintance of two of his bachelor friends, John Taylor and Richard Woodhouse (though the strict and scrupulous Woodhouse probably knew her solely because of her friendship with Taylor). But he must certainly have been aware that she had what we may call a patron—an elderly, rich Irishman named Donat (or Donal) O'Callaghan, who spent the summers in or near Hastings.

"As we went along," said Keats, in his disarmingly impetuous account, "some times through shabby, sometimes through decent Street[s] I had my guessing at work, not knowing what it would be and prepared to meet any surprise." But all they did was stop and visit Mrs. Green at the boarding school. In all of what Keats is writing immediately after this meeting, one detects a combination of feelings. There is a great deal of sheer, youthful curiosity. There is also just a suggestion of humor—humor about the whole incident, at Mrs. Jones's "enigmatic" situation, and at his own prying curiosity. Moreover he is obviously attracted by this mysterious woman, at once so shrewd and kindly. The kindliness was genuine. She could hardly be expected to be strongly interested in this raw, far from affluent young man. The men to whom she was accustomed moved in a different world; and she was also perceptive enough to note how much of his interest consisted of sheer curiosity. Yet her conduct with Keats shows not only a grave courtesy but a gentle tact. Returning from Islington, says Keats—delighting in this opportunity to give George and Georgiana an interesting circumstantial story of an incident full of novelty to Keats himself—"I pressed to attend her home":

She consented and then again my thoughts were at work what it might lead to, tho' now they had received a sort of genteel hint from the Boarding School. Our walk ended in 34 Gloucester Street [now Old Gloucester Street] Queen Square—not exactly so for we went up stairs into her sitting room—a very tasty sort of place with Books, Pictures a bronze statue of Buonaparte. Music, aeolian Harp; a Parrot a Linnet—A Case of choice Liqueurs &c, &c. &c. she behaved in the kindest manner—made me take home a Grouse for Tom's dinner—Asked for my address for the purpose of sending more game—As I had warmed with her before and kissed her—I though[t] it would be living backwards not to do so again—she had a better taste: she perceived how much a thing of course it was and shrunk from it—not in a prudish way but in as I say a good taste: she cont[r]ived to disappoint me in a way which made me feel more pleasure than a simple kiss could do—she said I should please her much more if I would only press her hand and go away. Whether she was in a different disposition when I saw her before—or whether I have in fancy wrong'd her I cannot tell—I expect to pass some pleasant hours with her now and then: in which I feel I shall be of service to her in matters of knowledge and taste: if I can I will.

I have no libidinous thought about her—she and your George are the only women à peu près de mon age whom I could be content to know for their mind and friendship alone.

Keats's account covers most of what we know of his relations with Mrs. Jones. He saw her at least occasionally throughout the next four months. She indeed abided by her promise to send some game for Tom; the gifts continued for a while even after Tom's death. It was she who, according to Woodhouse, suggested the legend of the Eve of St. Agnes as a subject for a romance. A short lyric or song that Keats wrote sometime later in the year may refer to her relation with the elderly Mr. O'Callaghan.[14] She continued to remember him with kindness; and doubtless John Taylor, after finding they were acquainted, talked with her occasionally about this young poet from whom he expected so much. After Keats's death, Taylor showed her some of Severn's letters about Keats's last weeks. The response of Mrs. Jones, so quickly perceptive in her estimate of men, comes as a refreshing contrast to the Victorian sentimentalization of Severn. She saw at once how much of what Severn wrote betrayed the self-centeredness of that weak, if kindly, man.[15]

[14] The song beginning "Hush, hush! tread softly," which Charlotte Reynolds said Keats composed to a Spanish air she was playing on the piano, and which Brown dated 1818. Despite J. M. Murry's counterargument, Mr. Gittings is persuasive (pp. 54–63) in pointing out the relevance to Mrs. Jones and old Mr. O'Callaghan of some of the lines ("All the house is asleep, but we know very well / That the jealous, the jealous old bald-pate may hear, / Tho' you padded his night-cap— O sweet Isabel"). It is difficult to agree with him, however, in dismissing the date given it by the meticulous Brown, and viewing the song as an indication of an active liaison between Keats and Mrs. Jones. The poem could have actually been written in December 1818 to a song that Charlotte Reynolds was playing, while Keats puckishly used the occasion (he was full of "spleen" around the Reynolds girls) to bring in a subject of which they were ignorant. Mr. Gittings' argument that there was an affair between Mrs. Jones and Keats rests heavily on the assumption that the "Bright Star" sonnet was written not to Fanny Brawne, later on, but to Mrs. Jones. But this is only an assumption. It relies, in turn, on verbal parallels in a letter written during the Scottish tour. Such parallels, as we have noted, can be found with many of Keats's poems, including the odes and the *Fall of Hyperion*, the date of which we know.
[15] The letter is printed by Gittings, pp. 231–233.

Keats's meetings with Jane Cox and Isabella Jones, and his reactions to them, naturally interest us when we glance ahead to Fanny Brawne. A few thoughts may occur to us at once. To begin with, these three women—however dissimilar in other ways—were all very different from the Reynolds sisters. Secondly, this new sensitivity and interest coincide with the disintegration and disappearance of the precarious family life that had begun when he and his brothers, kept apart for so long, moved into 76 Cheapside (November 1816) and he wrote the gentle, touchingly hopeful sonnet about their new home together ("To My Brothers"). A third—less obvious and more puzzling—reflection turns on the differences between Fanny Brawne and these two other women. One feels that the quiet, perceptive grace of the first two women struck Keats immediately and strongly (he tells George and Georgiana half playfully about Jane Cox, who had "the Beauty of a Leopardess," "I should like her to ruin me, and I should like you to save me"), and that the uncertain, almost adolescent liveliness of Fanny Brawne, with her interest in clothes and dances, created a more divided impression (however intense) that still persists when the famous love letters begin in the summer of 1819.

Meanwhile he has no intention of being tied down. The idea of marriage is much on his mind, particularly when he thinks of George and Georgiana. They were now expecting a child; and Keats tells them how happy he would be if "one of your Children should become the first American Poet"; and he stops to compose for them a lullaby with this refrain:

> Bard art thou completely
> Little Child
> O' the western wild.

But as for himself, too many demands and interests "form a barrier against Matrimony which I rejoice in." And immediately after his account of meeting Mrs. Jones, he tells his brother and sister-in-law:

> I shall in a short time write you as far as I know how I intend to pass my Life—I cannot think of those things now Tom is so unwell and weak. Notwithstand^{g} your Happiness and your recommendation I hope I shall never marry. Though the most beautiful Creature were waiting for me at the end of a Journey or a Walk; though the carpet were of Silk, and Curtains of the morning Clouds; the chairs and Sofa stuffed with Cygnet's down; the food Manna, the

Wine beyond Claret, the Window opening on Winander mere, I should not feel—or rather my Happiness would not be so fine, as my Solitude is sublime. Then instead of what I have described there is a Sublimity to welcome me home. The roaring of the wind is my wife and the Stars through the window pane are my Children. The mighty abstract Idea I have of Beauty in all things stifles the more divided and minute domestic happiness—an amiable wife and sweet Children I contemplate as a part of that Bea[u]ty, but I must have a thousand of those beautiful particles to fill up my heart. I feel more and more every day, as my imagination strengthens, that I do not live in this world alone but in a thousand worlds—No sooner am I alone than shapes of epic greatness are stationed around me . . . According to my state of mind I am with Achilles shouting in the Trenches or with Theocritus in the Vales of Sicily. Or I throw my whole being into Troilus, and repeating those lines, "I wander like a lost soul upon the stygian Banks staying for waftage," I melt into the air with a voluptuousness so delicate that I am content to be alone. . . .

I have written this that you might see I have my share of the highest pleasures and that though I may choose to pass my days alone I shall be no Solitary. You see there is nothing spleenical in all this . . . I am as happy as a Man can be—that is in myself I should be happy if Tom was well, and I knew you were passing pleasant days —Then I should be most enviable—with the yearning Passion I have for the beautiful, connected and made one with the ambition of my intellect.

8

By mid-October, his sore throat seems to have disappeared for a while; and throughout the next two weeks he went out frequently, though usually only during the daytime.[16] He was nearing the end of the first book of *Hyperion,* and had led a confined life for weeks. He was naturally eager for a change. Tom, after a few bad days (October 9–15), seemed a little better. One evening Georgiana's two brothers, Charles and Henry, came out to Hampstead and ate dinner with him and Tom (October 18). We can assume that the dinner brought up by Mrs. Bentley was unpretentious.

Except for visits to Abbey's countinghouse to ask that Fanny be

---

[16] He called on Georgiana's aunt, Mrs. Millar (October 15), and on the Dilkes the next day. About this time he saw Haydon, the Hunts, and James Rice. On October 22 he met Hazlitt in town and walked with him as far as Covent Garden ("he was going to play Rackets"), dined with the Wylies at Mrs. Millar's, and saw Hessey later in the evening. He called on Hunt the next day, ran into Charles Ollier, and, on October 24, met Mrs. Jones. Reynolds paid him and Tom a visit (October 25), and Haslam dropped by on Keats's birthday (October 31).

allowed to come and visit Tom, Keats now rarely left the house. "I have seen Mr. Abbey three times about you," he tells Fanny on November 5, "and have not been able to get his consent—He says that once more between this and the Holydays will be sufficient. What can I do? I should have been at Walthamstow several times [in order to visit her], but I am not able to leave Tom for so long a time." That the anxieties of Abbey should have blocked his permission to Fanny to visit Tom at such a time further confirms the suspicion that is constantly suggesting itself: the suspicion that the prim and panicky tea broker was already deeply involved in his speculation with the money that belonged to the Keats children; that his principal emotion, overriding every other consideration, was the dread of any possibility of the children's putting their heads together.

Meanwhile Keats went ahead with *Hyperion*, trying single-mindedly to keep away other thoughts. A pleasant moment intervened in early November. A man (or woman) using the signature "P. Fenbank" sent him a sonnet and a £25 note from Teignmouth. This may have been Woodhouse, or more probably someone else whom Woodhouse put up to it. Keats brooded over it for weeks. However bad the sonnet,[17] the compliment touched him. It was sent, and he received it, in the aftermath of the *Blackwood's* and *Quarterly* attacks.[18] Keats at once told all of his friends about it. His pleasure and wry embarrassment appear in his account of it to George weeks later (December 29). He had mentioned it earlier.

[17] Star of high promise!—not to this dark age
    Do thy mild light and loveliness belong;—
    For it is blind intolerant and wrong;
  Dead to empyreal soarings, and the rage
  Of scoffing spirits bitter war doth wage
    With all that hold integrity of song.
    Yet thy clear beam shall shine through ages strong
  To ripest times a light and heritage.
  And there breathe now who dote upon thy fame,
    Whom thy wild numbers wrap beyond their being,
  Who love the freedom of thy Lays—their aim
    Above the scope of a dull tribe unseeing—
  And there is one whose hand will never scant
  From his poor store of fruits all *thou* canst want.
[18] Keats at least thought he could tell the difference between the handwriting of a man and a woman (see II.90); and he assumes that the present and the sonnet came from a man. But the Jeffrey girls, as Mr. Gittings suggests (p. 39), may have been the donor, and Marian may have written the sonnet. The strongest argument against the Jeffrey sisters is that, living in Teignmouth, they would naturally have been the first people to occur to Keats, and he appears to have dismissed them as a possibility.

"I will now copy out the Letter and Sonnet I have spoken of." He describes the way it was addressed, and then copies out the sonnet complete with its date (November 1818), though "I would not copy [it] for any in the world but you—who know that I scout 'mild light and loveliness' [one of the phrases] or any such nonsense in myself." Then he tells about the £25 note. "Now this appears to me all very proper—if I had refused it—I should have behaved in a very bragadochio dunderheaded manner—and yet the present galls me a little." He wonders whether he ought not to return it if he ever discovers the identity of the donor, "after whom to no purpose I have written."

9

Tom was now sinking daily. During November Keats not only stayed with him almost constantly but, except for three or four perfunctory notes, could not even bring himself to write letters.

With the frail Tom coughing and tossing, Keats, when unable to help Tom directly, sat near him continuing to work on *Hyperion*. He was concentrating every capacity for "judgement" on this work. Only by the most complete absorption of all his faculties could it give him any kind of relief, any kind of satisfaction to weigh against this daily, pressing grief. In this condensed verse, he went slowly now—slowly, at least, compared with his earlier practice. He averaged about ten lines in a day. Tom's birthday passed on November 18 without remark. He then became nineteen. On the night of November 30 he was obviously dying.

The next morning, at eight o'clock, the gentle, cheerful invalid, who had felt himself such a burden to his brothers, quietly died. Nothing now was left of Keats's small family life. He was altogether adrift. He left the body and walked over to Wentworth Place. He perhaps did not want to disturb the Dilkes. He was not looking for sympathy. Too much was now facing him. His instinctive tendency was to turn to one who was cool, detached, and roughly independent (for it was exactly this that he felt he must learn to become). Instead of knocking on the door of the Dilkes, he entered the side of the house used by his old companion of the Scottish tour. Brown was still asleep. "I was awakened in my bed," as he later wrote, "by a pressure on my hand. It was Keats, who came to tell me that his brother was no more." Brown arose, and wrote brief notes to what friends the Keats brothers had. One survives from Brown to Woodhouse (December 1) : "Mr. Keats requests me to inform you his brother Thomas died this morning at eight o'clock quietly & without pain. Mr. Keats is pretty well & desires to be remembered to you."

Hyperion and a New Level of Writing

Hyperion stands at the beginning of the final year of Keats's writing, and most of the poetry by which he is remembered follows in the comet's tail of this brilliant effort. The year that it ushers in (starting about mid-September, 1818) may be soberly described as the most productive in the life of any poet of the past three centuries. The mere variety in style is difficult to parallel within the same limit of time.

The poem was begun, as he said, in a virtual "siege of contraries." For this was to have been the work written with such careful thought and preparation—the work to which everything thus far was only a "poor prologue." To "leap headlong into the Sea" had its advantages; and he had learned a good deal from this in the past. But now he was almost twenty-three, and other things were necessary—had been eagerly insisted on as necessary for three-quarters of a year: he had begun reading history, was seriously preparing to study philosophy, and was about to begin Greek and Italian. (Even in this distressing autumn, James Hessey wrote to Taylor, "He is studying closely, recovering his Latin"; and the very week he began *Hyperion,* he borrowed the remaining volumes of Gibbon from Dilke, and, while starting to brush up on his French in spare hours, wrote a translation of a sonnet by Ronsard.) Meanwhile, for a year and a half, he had been saturating himself in Shakespeare, and more lately Milton, convinced that if we mean what we say when we praise their achievement, we should not remain cozily on a perch in our small territory, asleep to the day and awake only in the protective dark of our subjectivity ("Why should we be owls, when we can be Eagles?"). And then, throughout the late spring, had come his searching reconsideration of the nature of the whole modern demand and challenge.

Divided before several ideals—the intensity and range of the classical and Miltonic epic (he had also been reading Dante), the Wordsworthian and modern exploration of the human mind, and, as an ultimate ideal, the Shakespearean drama—he could not focus solely on one and shut his eyes to the others. He could proceed confidently only through assimilation, not exclusion. But assimilation took time—at least a little time. He did not even have a workable subject clearly in mind, only a very general idea; and the moments were growing when he felt that "there was now nothing original to be written in poetry"—that the carpet had been pulled from under us by ampler creative eras.

Hence to "plunge" prematurely now "seems a crime to me," as he told Dilke the very week he began the poem; and the expression of despair was so strong for him that he felt he ought to burn the letter. He does not, of course, mention his own health, George's departure, the hostile reviews, the anxiety about money. But Tom's "identity presses upon me so all day . . . his countenance his voice and feebleness";

> and although I intended to have given some time to study alone I am obliged to write . . . it seems a crime to me, and yet I must do so or suffer—I am sorry to give you pain—I am almost resolv'd to burn this—but I really have not self-possession and magnanimity enough to manage the thing othe[r]wise.

To try to fill time by writing another romance or two, or to keep tossing off short verses, offered no solution to anything. He had to do something that he really cared about.

2

But one immense problem faced him before he could begin even the first line: the idiom and verse form. Other matters could be deferred, other problems solved along the way. Moreover, once the general choice of style was made, he would have to remain with it, whatever else developed as he went ahead; and it could well become a limiting factor.

In the early weeks of September, trying to meet each day as it came, hesitating whether or not to begin the poem, he settled, perhaps with no complete conviction, on a norm. At the very least he needed something as different as possible from the prettiness and lush fluency of his first models—qualities that so painfully embarrassed him now. A severely majestic idiom had strong attractions.

By means of it he might shed, once and for all, everything that made him most cringe when he remembered his earlier writing. Throughout the spring he had been reading Milton with vivid empathy; and the strength and sweep of the greatest of English epics (however different Keats felt that his own ultimate purpose must be from Milton's) provided an immensely challenging stair by which to rise permanently from the cozy and the pretty. Perhaps his choice of the idiom and versification of *Paradise Lost* as a suggestive model would have come in any case, even if *Hyperion* had been deferred another year. It is difficult to say. Milton, of course, had been one of the presiding geniuses of the new beginning back in January; and the very next day (January 22), after writing his lines on Milton as a preface to a new start, he had immediately turned to Shakespeare as a necessary supplement and, in a kind of ritual, read *King Lear* once again (as he had back in April 1817, when he began *Endymion*). So now, as this most gifted of Milton's apprentices prepared to sit at his feet for a time, he instinctively found himself turning again to Shakespeare in free hours, and especially to *Lear*. In his copy of the folio edition he underlined the words "Poor Tom" and next to them wrote "Sunday evening, Oct. 4, 1818."

The subject of the new effort had come to him, however vaguely, almost a year before. As he had begun to revise *Endymion*, another mythological theme—or basis for a theme—had suggested itself: the displacement of the Titans, in classical mythology, by the Olympian gods. The subject, if imaginatively approached, seemed to have several diverse possibilities; an exploration of the development of consciousness, epic grandeur, and possibly even something of drama were all potentially there in solution. For, to begin with, each group could be used to represent a different stage of consciousness. That theme of unfolding awareness (so vividly ratified by his own experience, and in turn reinforcing his conviction of the formative effect of knowledge) had become more keenly felt and yet, in its "branchings out," less clear and simple. Moreover, the Titans, as contrasted with the figures of Endymion's world, could be given epic stature (something that, despite his willingness to surrender it if absolutely necessary, he wanted at least to try to attain). Keats's love of the statuesque was stirred as well—the power held in repose suggested by the Elgin Marbles, the ideal of "might half slumb'ring on its own right arm." The cleanliness of structure in the first two books is also notable. In January, as he copied and hastily revised *Endymion,* he had fretted at the loose, episodic structure. Hence he was determined that the pace of the new poem would be brisker—even (by contrast with *Endymion*) "undeviating": he will write it, he tells Haydon (January 23, 1818), "in a more naked and grecian Manner—and the march of passion and endeavour will be undeviating."

Finally, this was to be no solitary search for self-discovery in the manner of *Alastor* or *Endymion.* A more capacious and objective scale was demanded. The number of active characters, as contrasted with *Endymion,* was large and fairly diverse. We become a little short-sighted when we concentrate on just a few of what we think Keats's preoccupations were, and (forgetting the strong interests in form and style that any major artist has) leap forward with mechanical regularity to the third book of the poem and focus on the figure of Apollo. Naturally Apollo—so closely associated with poetry itself, and a powerful symbol to Keats from the beginning—was to be crucial; and, just as naturally, Apollo's painful evolution into growing consciousness would tap, perhaps closely parallel, personal experiences of his own. But the development of the poetic imagination involves more than absorption in one's own predicament. (Nothing could illustrate this better than the extraordinary technical effort that now begins to show itself in diction, imagery, and versification.) For over a year he had been thinking concretely of the drama; and we recall his excitement when, in revising *Endymion,* he suddenly saw that Endymion's speech about the development of consciousness and the "gradations of Happiness" was also potentially dramatic, that this aspiration was one way of looking at things, one voice in the interplay of feeling, the interplay of human beings with each other—"my first Step towards the chief Attempt in the Drama—the playing of different Natures with Joy and Sorrow." More than one voice was to be heard, therefore, in this further "Step," in which "different Natures" are confronted with the overwhelming knowledge—the joy and tragic loss—of inevitable change. Despite the epic framework Keats had chosen, and the tendency of the style to encourage his gift for "stationing" and the statuesque, the "identities" of these "different Natures" were thought of distinctly and at least quasi-dramatically; and a full 58 per cent of the lines of the first two books consist of dialogue. Writing to Woodhouse in the early stages of the poem, after stating that the poet has no "identity" of his own but is always entering sympathetically "some other Body," he says, "Might I not at that very instant"—when he had made the remark that so troubled Woodhouse (the remark that all the subjects of poetry had been exhausted, and that he might give up the writing of poetry)—"Might I not at that very instant [have] been cogitating on the Characters of saturn and Ops?"—and have been himself identified with their sense of defeat and futility? More important would be Hyperion himself. For if the central Olympian god in the new poem was to be Apollo, then—since this epic-drama was to include conflict, tragedy, and fall—he would settle, for his title (and possibly for the principal character in the action), on Hyperion, Apollo's counterpart among the Titans.

3

The imposing fragment that resulted (written mainly in the two months between late September and the death of Tom on December 1) drew more praise from Keats's own contemporaries than anything else he ever wrote. And despite changes in taste, it continues to fascinate writers as well as readers.

Like his contemporaries, we wonder how he ever managed to do it. The Miltonic blank-verse epic may not now seem to us the ideal form for a modern poet. *Hyperion,* moreover, is only a fragment; and twentieth-century formalism, with its hunger for intricate neatness, is automatically impatient before the incomplete. But Keats's richly diverse achievement throughout his final year washes aside such prejudices, freeing not only a more considered honesty but also our natural human curiosity. We find ourselves admitting that the style Keats now chose as a working base is, after all, one of the most demanding of all formal styles; and that the gymnastics involved in attaining that style—and within only a few months—are quite as formidable as any we set for ourselves. Whatever our stock responses, we may even begin to wonder whether the exercise was not more therapeutic than those we preach. Perhaps our obsessive fear of "imitation" (in which we never seem to include imitation of our own contemporaries, or of minor, relatively unnoticed artists of the past) is not the most fruitful state of mind in which we can begin; and the brave innocence that storms the main gate, less thoughtful of itself and of each step it takes than of what it seeks to enter, may—as Longinus said—be able to reach and carry away more. As we sober from prejudice into honesty before this fragment, our curiosity is prompted further. For the particular time of Keats's life during which it was written would, by most criteria, be thought of as anything but propitious.

No English poem of any length since Milton—complete or fragmentary—begins with more majesty and sureness of phrase than *Hyperion*. Though *Endymion* had been published and *Isabella* written less than half a year before, we are at once on an altogether different plane of writing:

> Deep in the shady sadness of a vale
> Far sunken from the healthy breath of morn,
> Far from the fiery noon, and eve's one star,
> Sat gray-hair'd Saturn, quiet as a stone,
> Still as the silence round about his lair;
> Forest on forest hung above his head
> Like cloud on cloud. No stir of air was there,
> Not so much life as on a summer's day
> Robs not one light seed from the feather'd grass,
> But where the dead leaf fell, there did it rest.
> A stream went voiceless by, still deadened more
> By reason of his fallen divinity
> Spreading a shade: the Naiad 'mid her reeds
> Press'd her cold finger closer to her lips.

The inevitability of phrase, the richness and control of versification (so like and yet unlike Milton) continue without lapse throughout the entire first two books. The stylistic advance in so brief a time, sustained at such length (a total of 748 lines), is unparalleled. Nor was *Hyperion* an isolated tour de force in style. Formidable even as a unique stylistic achievement, it merely ushers in the varied technical mastery of Keats's final year.

In considering any fragment, a certain amount of summary may be helpful. When the course that the poem might have taken is so unclear and debatable, and we can speculate about it honestly only after a careful scrutiny of what we do have, analyses that are purely categorical or topical are apt to become a subjective mirror of the critic's special interests. Categorical criticism, except when it focuses on restricted aspects of style, needs the underpinning of fact that only a finished work, with an acknowledged conclusion, can give. *Hyperion* (probably because it was written with such conflicting intentions) has especially been pulled in one way or another through strictly categorical approaches. A glance is given at the Miltonic (or partly Miltonic) style, and it is inferred that Keats was here taking the wrong tack—he was himself "Shakespearean," not "Miltonic." Or the speech of Oceanus is stressed: here is a discussion of human development and progress, and one can find remarks in the letters that coincide. Obviously this is the heart of the poem. This was what he wanted to say; and having said it, his poem was substantially finished. Or, mindful of the drama of Keats's own poetic development, we forget the first two books (or dismiss them as "setting") and pounce upon the figure of Apollo near the end of the fragment. Did not Keats identify himself with Apollo, always an important symbol to him? Naturally, we say, this was to be Apollo's poem.

4

To this quiet retreat with which Keats begins, Saturn, the king of the Titans, has come—a fallen, more epic Lear:

> Upon the sodden ground
> His old right hand lay nerveless, listless, dead,
> Unsceptred; and his realmless eyes were closed.

Thea, Hyperion's spouse, approaches him, a "listening fear" in her face, "As if calamity had but begun." She speaks to the silent form of Saturn. Her words (ostensibly to ease herself—for she can offer him no comfort) give background and stress the finality of what has happened. This first speech is prudently kept short, as though Keats distrusted his ability to begin the dialogue ("O how frail," he prefaces it, "To that large utterance of the early Gods!"). And as soon as it is over, he at once reinforces it with one of the finest descriptive passages in English blank verse:

> As when, upon a trancèd summer-night,
> Those green-rob'd senators of mighty woods,
> Tall oaks, branch-charmèd by the earnest stars,
> Dream, and so dream all night without a stir,
> Save from one gradual solitary gust
> Which comes upon the silence, and dies off,
> As if the ebbing air had but one wave;
> So came these words and went; the while in tears
> She touch'd her fair large forehead to the ground,
> Just where her falling hair might be outspread

A soft and silken mat for Saturn's feet.
One moon, with alteration slow, had shed
Her silver seasons four upon the night,
And still these two were postured motionless,
Like natural sculpture in cathedral cavern;
The frozen God still couchant on the earth,
And the sad Goddess weeping at his feet:
Until at length old Saturn lifted up
His faded eyes, and saw his kingdom gone.

But if there was some timidity in allowing Thea to speak at length, there is none in Saturn's reply. Here, for a full fifty lines, Keats is able to tread the (almost impossible) line between the severely epic, statuesque form to which he is now committed and the dramatic instinct to lay bare the psychology of this fallen king. The question that continues to beat at Saturn's imperious mind is "Who?"—

Who had power
To make me desolate? Whence came the strength?
How was it nurtured to such bursting forth,
While Fate seem'd strangled in my nervous grasp?

As a king, habitually accustomed to identify order with himself, he is personal in his puzzlement. It is the frustration of this imperious habit of sway that has swept away his sense of "identity," and left him an alien:

I am gone
Away from my own bosom: I have left
My strong identity, my real self,
Somewhere between the throne, and where I sit
Here in this spot of earth.

The questions "Who?" and "Why?" from this Lear whose sense of justice is so outraged lead him to rise in protest (though in a protest that is only fitful) :

cannot I create?
Cannot I form? Cannot I fashion forth
Another world, another universe,
To overbear and crumble this to nought?
Where is another Chaos? Where?

Meanwhile the other Titans remain frozen with fear, loss, or anger, waiting for Saturn's guidance. One of the mammoth brood, however, still retains his sovereignty—"Blazing Hyperion on his orbèd fire"—though omens and fears, "portion'd to a giant nerve,'' assail him. Imaginatively full of the Miltonic idiom, Keats turns with pleasure and confidence to the setting:

> His palace bright
> Bastion'd with pyramids of glowing gold,
> And touch'd with shade of bronzèd obelisks,
> Glar'd a blood-red through all its thousand courts,
> Arches, and domes, and fiery galleries;
> And all its curtains of Aurorian clouds
> Flush'd angerly: while sometimes eagle's wings,
> Unseen before by Gods or wondering men,
> Darken'd the place; and neighing steeds were heard,
> Not heard before by Gods or wondering men.
> Also, when he would taste the spicy wreaths
> Of incense, breath'd aloft from sacred hills,
> Instead of sweets, his ample palate took
> Savour of poisonous brass and metal sick.

The uneasy, still unfallen Titan nightly paces the halls of his vast palace, restless until day permits him to ride the sun across the sky. Now, as he strides from nave to nave, from vault to vault, he comes to the large main cupola, and, stamping, speaks out his uncertainty and determination in lines that echo those of Satan in *Paradise Lost:*

> Saturn is fallen, am I too to fall?
> Am I to leave this haven of my rest,
> This cradle of my glory, this soft clime?
> .   .   .   .
> Fall!—No, by Tellus and her briny robes!
> Over the fiery frontier of my realms
> I will advance a terrible right arm
> Shall scare that infant thunderer, rebel Jove,
> And bid old Saturn take his throne again.

Compelled to act in order to break the intolerable uncertainty, Hyperion suddenly turns to the eastern gates, a full six hours before the sun should mount the sky. He bursts wide the gates to the orb of fire he drives; and the sun, obedient and ready to his coming, expands its wings. But Hyperion's gesture is futile: the sun cannot, in the scheme of things, rise before its ordained time. Here Keats understandably wavers for a moment, uncertain how to present an inevitability before which even the god of the sun is powerless. He simply asserts it, and then turns to Hyperion, who,

> Unus'd to bend, by hard compulsion bent
> His spirit to the sorrow of the time.

Humbled in this impetuous attempt to assert himself against the cosmos, Hyperion lies back; and in a low whisper the voice of Coelus (Uranus, the sky, father of the Titans) comes to him. Coelus is powerless. He himself can only wonder before the limitless mystery of the universe. But of one thing he is confident: the "sky-engendered" but "earth-born" Titans are losing their godhood partly by their own surrender to fear, wrath, and frustration; and is Hyperion, the "brightest of my children," to do the same?

> I have seen my sons most unlike Gods.
> Divine ye were created, and divine
> In sad demeanour, solemn, undisturb'd,
> Unruffled, like high Gods, ye liv'd and ruled:
> Now I behold in you fear, hope, and wrath;
> Actions of rage and passion; even as
> I see them, on the mortal world beneath,
> In men who die.

Hyperion is at least partly free to act, while Coelus is

> but a voice;
> My life is but the life of winds and tides,
> No more than winds and tides can I avail:—
> But thou canst. Be thou therefore in the van
> Of Circumstance.

Urged to seek out Saturn, Hyperion, after meditating, plunges earthward through the night.

5

Meanwhile, as Book II opens, Saturn and Thea have reached the vast rocky den of the Titans. Both the situation and the debate were suggested by the council of the fallen angels in *Paradise Lost*. The principal difference lies in the character of the Titans themselves, especially as Keats is portraying them. For they are on the whole a rather innocent group: their rule was far from evil; and if they now lack perspective and charity, they at least have cause. Whether intentionally or not, Keats sympathetically begins to humanize these large epic figures, despite the formal structure and idiom with which he is working: in this "sad" place the "bruisèd Titans" are hiding; they have instinctively withdrawn to a cavern "where no insulting light" can betray their tears of anger or puzzled disbelief. Here, in this retreat, are "big hearts / Heaving in pain"; the large dreaming Asia ("More thought than woe was in her dusky face") ; and Enceladus, who—however "tiger-passion'd" he may now be, as he lies meditating, reliving the past, plotting for the future—was "once tame and mild," as calm as the grazing ox in the meadow.

The problem the Titans face is how to meet circumstance as it waters and brings unpredictable sproutings from the "wide arable land of events." (Be ever "in the van / Of circumstance," Coelus whispered to Hyperion.) How indeed does one confront the hurt of loss? The question had been familiar to Keats since the age of eight. The immediate temptation, of course, is to swing impotently against the injustice of circumstance. Those unpredictable sproutings of a "poison fruit which we must pluck" are only too often undeserved. So with these large Titans, conceived by Keats as almost Egyptian colossi, yet quickly qualified toward humanity. Their era, in that "infant world," had been a golden age. Is there something fundamentally wrong—altogether unjust, disregarding of hearts created in and through its own processes—about the universe itself? Yet this altogether human protest is as futile as that of the Titan Iäpetus, who held in his grasp a serpent:

> its barbèd tongue
> Squeez'd from the gorge, and all its uncurl'd length
> Dead; and because the creature could not spit
> Its poison in the eyes of conquering Jove.

Though other Titans express this outrage against injustice, Saturn —until the brooding Enceladus rises to answer the calm wisdom of Oceanus—is its principal voice: a natural response indeed, as Oceanus says, for a King "blind from sheer supremacy" and unused to stoop. Before the council of Titans, Saturn (alternately imperious and shaken, like Lear) repeats his bewilderment before the injustice of this great change:

> Not in my own sad breast,
> Which is its own great judge and searcher out;

nor, look as he may for "sign, symbol, or portent," can he in other ways "unriddle" an explanation. He has been astonished at the "severe content" in the face of the wise Oceanus, the fallen god of the sea. He turns to this sage among the Titans: "give us help!"

The long reply of Oceanus, certainly one of the crucial parts of the poem, was something of a triumph for Keats. In these seventy lines he was able, for the first time in his poetry, to present at some length the ideal of "disinterestedness" that had been in his mind since his reading at Magdalen Hall, Oxford, the year before. Equally important, he was able to adapt it dramatically as a vehicle for the character of Oceanus himself. And that dramatic function should be kept in mind when we are tempted to focus too exclusively on the speech as Keats's own final argument. The speech is a significant part of that argument—perhaps even the apex—but it is not the whole. The Titans, Oceanus begins, have disintegrated before their loss by lapsing into self-absorption, "nursing" their defeat, snatching futilely at thought of revenge. With something of the Stoic's pride, he tells them they "must be content to stoop" before the truth. The essence of this truth is that

> We fall by course of Nature's law, not force
> Of thunder, or of Jove.
>
> .   .   .   .
>
> as thou wast not the first of powers,
> So art thou not the last; it cannot be:
> Thou art not the beginning nor the end.

Keats almost echoes the play that above all others caught his imagination: Edgar's remark in *Lear* that

> men must endure
> Their going hence, even as their coming hither:
> Ripeness is all.

In the beginning, "the sullen ferment" of "Chaos and parental darkness"

> for wondrous ends
> Was ripening in itself. The ripe hour came,
> And with it Light.

And from Light "engendering / Upon its own producer" came another fulfillment—"we the giant-race," now passing—transcending its parentage in awareness, capacity to act, and friendship:

> In form and shape compact and beautiful,
> In will, in action free, companionship,
> And thousand other signs of purer life;
> So on our heels a fresh perfection treads,
> A power more strong in beauty, born of us
> And fated to excel us, as we pass

In glory that old Darkness: nor are we
Thereby more conquer'd, than by us the rule
Of shapeless Chaos.

Should the soil quarrel with the "proud forests it hath fed," or the tree resent the freely moving bird its branches shelter? Like the forest trees, the Titans have "bred forth . . . eagles golden-feather'd":

'tis the eternal law
That first in beauty should be first in might:
Yea, by that law, another race may drive
Our conquerors to mourn as we do know.

Oceanus himself has seen the young god of the sea, his "dispossessor," and been forced to acknowledge that his own empire is ended. But "sovereignty" of another kind is still possible—that of saluting the inevitable with full and dispassionate understanding:

for to bear all naked truths,
And to envisage circumstance, all calm,
That is the top of sovereignty.

The premise of this long admonition from the Ulysseslike, prudent Oceanus is hard-won: knowledge (philosophy, or knowledge acted upon by wisdom) is not only a good in itself, but it also, as Keats had written to Reynolds the previous May, "takes away the heat and fever; and helps, by widening speculation, to ease the Burden of the Mystery: a thing I begin to understand a little." It is this "widening of speculation" that Oceanus enjoins: a transferring of attention from personal loss to the larger process of which one is only a part. But on the other hand—as Keats immediately added in the same letter to Reynolds—the trust in knowledge and understanding to modify personal pain and bewilderment is like "running one's rigs on the score of abstracted benefit"; and in speaking as though the heart could at once begin to follow or "parallel" the head, he has plainly been "treading out [of] my depth . . . as school-boys tread the water." Knowledge can act formatively—"a thing I begin to understand a little"—but it is impossible to draw a close "parallel of breast and head . . . it is impossible to know how far knowledge will console us for the death of a friend and the ill 'that flesh is heir to.' " Later (April 1819), at the time he gives up *Hyperion,* he is even less certain: "Let the fish philosophise the ice away from the Rivers in wintertime and they shall be

at continual play in the tepid delight of the summer." "Receive
the truth," says Oceanus at the close of his discourse, "and let it be
your balm." His speech to the Titans gives a legitimate, even a
needed, answer; but, whatever else may be said of it, it is hardly
Shakespearean in fellow feeling. In fact, it is in some ways a little
self-righteous. The Titans, it is true, were not originally conceived
as human beings; and the protests of the fitful, defensive human
heart against fact, against the knowledge it needs, are theoretically
irrelevant. But these Titans have fallen; they have become very
much like mortals; and, in any case, Keats's habitual empathy was
beginning to humanize them further.

The "balm" that Oceanus, with his "severe" contentment, offers
to his fellow Titans appears to provide very little solace, even
though the gentle Titaness, Clymene, is moved to add her own experience in confirmation: she has heard the young Apollo sing,
and became sick with "joy and grief at once." The large Enceladus,
leaning on his arm, dismisses with contempt both Oceanus ("Sham
Monarch of the Waves") and Clymene—the first "over-wise," the
latter "over-foolish." He taunts the assembled Titans with coward-
ice. Rising with pleasure at their response ("What, have I rous'd /
Your spleens with so few simple words as these?"), he reminds
them that more is involved "than loss of realms": those days that
have passed were "days of peace," innocent of war; and this clean
innocence has been shattered by the new, obtruding generation.
Finally, Hyperion, "Our brightest brother, still is undisgraced"—
Hyperion who is even now arriving; and the faces of the Titans
shine with reflected light as "a granite peak / His bright feet
touch'd" (Keats is here using what he calls the Miltonic "stationing") :

> Golden his hair of short Numidian curl,
> Regal his shape majestic, a vast shade
> In midst of his own brightness like the bulk
> Of Memnon's image at the set of sun
> To one who travels from the dusking East.

But the very brilliance of his light betrays the condition of the
Titans to themselves. Hyperion for his part stands motionless,
looking down upon the scene with troubled contemplation. Before that ominous brooding, the fallen Titans again shrink into
despondence, many of them seeking to hide their faces from the
searching light of Hyperion. Enceladus and three others, however,

stride boldly forward, shouting the royal salute of "Saturn." The response of the remaining Titans comes from hollow throats; but that of Hyperion, on his granite peak, is spoken firmly.

6

The stage was now set for the development of what Leigh Hunt, in a suggestive phrase, called "the transcendental cosmopolitics" of *Hyperion*. But this striking background of the first two books had been an exhausting effort. Moreover, if Keats should try to make the narrative more supple and the dialogue more dramatic, the very success of the style with which he had already begun would create technical problems of form and idiom. Above all, the distressing autumn and winter during which he worked on *Hyperion,* far from ideal for any composition, were especially unfavorable for a poem so optimistically premised as this new, more considered "trial of Invention": a poem in which, as he had hopefully said months before, "the march of passion and endeavour will be undeviating."

Nursing Tom daily, he might try, while hoping to steady his mind, to "plunge into abstract images to ease myself of his countenance his voice and feebleness." But after Tom's death, on December 1, the thread was snapped. To go back to the poem was almost insuperably difficult. Two and a half weeks (December 19) after Tom's death, he writes to George in America: "I feel I must again begin with my poetry." Going out to visit people, or to attend parties, "smothers" him now: he is

> never relieved except when composing—so I will write away. Friday [the next day]. I think you knew before you left England that my next subject would be "the fall of Hyperion" I went on a little with it last night—but it will take some time to get into the vein again.

Then on December 22 (three days later) : "Just now I took out my poem to go on with it—but the thought of my writing so little to you came upon me and I could not get on." He is also confined to his rooms because of a sore throat. Other activities intervene. On February 14 he writes: "I have not gone on with Hyperion— for to tell the truth I have not been in great cue for writing lately —I must wait for the sp[r]ing to rouse me up a little." Off and on he may have worked a little at *Hyperion*. Finally, by April 20, he has given up this effort that was now proving to be so much against the grain.

If we search the poem itself for the point where the thread of composition snapped around December 1, we are certainly justified in placing it after the two relatively firm books that introduce the poem and before the fragmentary third book, with its strangely altered style. To begin with, action almost evaporates in the third book. The evolution of Apollo into godhood, so crucial to this new poetic exploration of the passages that open from the "Chamber of Maiden-Thought," is suddenly condensed into a few lines, as if to provide at least a partial, half-hearted hint of what might have followed. It can be argued, of course, that Keats had simply outrun his experience by the time he approached the challenging theme of the third book—a theme for which he had no obvious guide from his reading in classical mythology. Certainly, in facing this challenge, he would have been more on his own than in the earlier books. But his reading had not been confined to classical mythology; and the imaginative, thoughtful letters of 1818 suggest that he was by no means without resources. In any case, there is a second, more puzzling shift in style that accompanies this fatigued but brisk dispatch through summary. The imagery, frequently the idiom, even the conception of Apollo himself, begin to remind us disturbingly of *Endymion*. Trying to force himself to continue the poem after the death of Tom, he fell back numbly—as we all do before calamity—upon familiar stances and habitual idiom; and the early stock phrasing, so deliberately discarded in the new beginning that followed *Endymion*, begins to reappear: "soft warble from the Dorian flute"; clouds that "float in voluptuous fleeces." Apollo comes perilously close to Endymion himself. At the start he leaves "his mother fair / And his twin-sister sleeping in the bower" in order to wander musingly "Full ankle-deep in lilies of the vale." The resurrected images from *Endymion* continue to move ghostlike through the forced lines that now follow: examples are Apollo's "white melodious throat," his quickly "suffused eyes," his petulant tendency to "moan" or to "Spurn the green turf as hateful to my feet" when he feels stirring within him an ideal beyond the small, quiet isle in which he lives.

Searching for a transition from the magnificent first two books, Keats begins, almost mechanically, by briefly invoking the muse for the first time. That invocation, surely the weakest in any poem of remotely comparable quality, suggests how numb his usually perceptive faculties were as he continued to force himself. Three times within five lines he repeats his request to leave the Titans and turn elsewhere ("O leave them, Muse! O leave them to their woes . . . Leave them, O Muse!"). The theme now—and the phrases are nakedly subjective, far from fulfilled by the lines that follow—is a "solitary sorrow," a "lonely grief." And he pictures Apollo, in the early dawn, wandering through a vale, his bright tears "trickling down the golden bow he held." The Titaness, Mnemosyne (Memory, mother of the muses), steps forward from beneath the boughs. Apollo knows that he has either seen or dreamt of that face before. He has indeed dreamt clairvoyantly of her, she says. Leaving the Titans because of "prophecies of thee, and for the sake / Of loveliness newborn"—for Apollo is to become "the Father of all verse"—she has watched over him since his infancy; and it is she who left by his side the golden lyre that he discovered when he woke from his dream of her. But why is he afflicted now with this vague grief? As Apollo begins to reply, her name suddenly returns to him: "Mnemosyne!" The cause of this sorrow, he goes on, is unknown to him, though surely it is already known to her. He spurns the present moment through hunger for "some unknown thing": "Are there not other regions than this isle?" What are the stars and the other celestial bodies? And there is the mystery of thunder: what hand, what divinity makes that alarm among the elements while he himself sits idle on the shores, listening "In fearless yet in aching ignorance"? Will not Mnemosyne dispel this "aching ignorance"? She remains silent. But the moment indeed has come for Apollo; and as he questions the mute figure, he begins to read

> A wondrous lesson in thy silent face:
> Knowledge enormous makes a god of me.
> Names, deeds, gray legends, dire events, rebellions,
> Majesties, sovran voices, agonies,
> Creations and destroyings, all at once
> Pour into the wide hollows of my brain,
> And deify me, as if some blithe wine
> Or bright elixir peerless I had drunk,
> And so become immortal.

The episode sways dangerously on the brink of the grotesque. The all-important evolution from "aching ignorance" to knowledge is being attained by something close to hypnotism, with Apollo, before the eyes of the mute goddess, "trembling" (his own eyes becoming "enkindled") and hurrying to catalogue the experiences that "pour" into him ("Names, deeds, gray legends, dire events, rebellions") , until finally

> wild commotions shook him, and made flush
> All the immortal fairness of his limbs;
> Most like the struggle at the gate of death;
> Or liker still to one who should take leave
> Of pale immortal death, and with a pang
> As hot as death's is chill, with fierce convulse
> Die into life: so young Apollo anguish'd.

Throughout this conclusive struggle,

> Mnemosyne upheld
> Her arms as one who prophesied.—At length
> Apollo shriek'd;—and lo! from all his limbs
> Celestial   *   *   *   *   *   *   *

There the fragment of *Hyperion* ends.

7

We are naturally tempted to speculate about what would have happened if Keats had continued. According to Richard Woodhouse, the original plan had been quite elaborate. The poem

> would have treated the dethronement of Hyperion, the former god of the Sun, by Apollo—and incidentally of those of Oceanus by Neptune, of Saturn by Jupiter, etc., and of the war of the Giants for Saturn's re-establishment—with other events, of which we have but very dark hints in the mythological poets of Greece and Rome. In fact, the incidents would have been pure creation of the poet's brain.[1]

But this extensive plan, as Ernest de Selincourt long ago pointed out, was already being modified in the first two books. The Titans, except for Hyperion, are already fallen; the real "war" is over. Enceladus indeed calls for a new conflict, and Hyperion seems to agree. But it would have had to be confined to a few individuals. Support from the other Titans, half-hearted and bewildered, would hardly have been more than token.

Yet in doubting whether the original plan would have been car-

---

1 *The Poems of John Keats,* ed. Ernest de Selincourt, 5th ed. (1926) , p. 486.

ried out, we need not swing to the opposite extreme and assume that the poem was inevitably over at the point where the fragment itself stops. This is frequently said to be the case; and the principal argument is that Apollo's development into godhood was— or had at least now become—the primary concern of the poem, and that, as soon as this was attained, little more remained for Keats to say. But is it the sole or even primary concern? The first two books suggest a larger pattern of action of which Apollo's evolution was to be only a part, however important. In any case, is that evolution really made, or do we have merely an abrupt, not very inventive summary for possible development? It was perhaps necessary, after Clymene's speech about him (II.252–299), to present Apollo on his island. But it was by no means necessary, or even advisable, to look forward to his development into godhood this early in the poem, or, least of all, to telescope it into a few lines. We are tempted to believe that these lines were written only after Keats had decided not to go on with the poem (at least for a while), and that they were jotted down to get the section off his chest and to provide, to any eye that looked at the poem in its present state, some hint of what lay ahead.

By the time the fragment breaks off, three characters of particular importance have emerged: Hyperion himself; the calm, clairvoyant Oceanus, already established as a Chorus; and, of course, Apollo. Whatever might have been done with Apollo—in whatever way his development might have been portrayed (and this may have been a far more taxing problem to Keats than what to do with the Titans)—Hyperion was certainly ready to be used both dramatically and epically. The poem, after all, was named for him; and Keats, when he named a poem after a character, was invariably direct: from "Calidore" through *Endymion* and *Isabella* to *Lamia*, the personal names in his titles apply to the main character or to at least one of two.

Moreover, the ground had been carefully prepared for Hyperion as a tragic figure. He has his counterpart among the Olympians who is to replace him, and a Chorus (Oceanus) to stress the inevitable. He alone among the Titans is portrayed in a manner that will permit an impressive further development. He is shown in a situation full of alarm and tension, and with the menace yet to come. There is every suggestion that he feels the danger but does not understand it. Significantly, Keats allows him to join the Titans in their lair only after the long, admonitory speech of Oceanus: Hyperion is therefore not forced prematurely to enter a debate; whatever he learns will have to come to him from experience. Hyperion, in fact, is the only character who could possibly be the subject of a tragic narrative; and for at least a year the tragic drama had haunted Keats's imagination as a poetic ideal, sometimes conflicting and sometimes coalescing with his thought of the epic. Not only is Hyperion the only character in the poem capable of tragic development. We could go further and say that —within the limits of the mythological epic framework that Keats chose—Hyperion is an ideal figure for tragedy. He has magnificence and stature, and is menaced by a danger that we know (from Oceanus) is inevitable. But he himself does not understand, though his previous bewildered alarm is supplemented by a new pondering as he stands ("a granite peak / His bright feet touch'd"), looking down upon the Titans when he arrives. And because he does not understand—as Oceanus does—Hyperion will struggle, though the tragic struggle might not—indeed could not—take the form of prolonged war, and though it might end in a harried conflict of conscience.

But here already was an almost insuperable difficulty for Keats, joining with technical and formal difficulties that were closely— even organically—related. These Titans were not only becoming humanized, despite their grandeur; they, and the whole tone of the poem, were also becoming quite civilized. That ideal of joining the old and the new, of combining epic grandeur (and also dramatic tragedy) with the Wordsworthian exploration of conscience, ran headlong against one wall after another. For if you want the sublimity of primitive grandeur, can you then afford all the complication of issues, embarrassments of choice, that attend upon the refinements of conscience? He had already expressed a doubt the previous spring, and now the actual experience seemed to be confirming that doubt. For example, warfare, in the simple-minded sense, was hardly the framework for the more individual and inward struggle shaping up; and this certainly modified the possibilities of direct action if that action continued to be construed in conventionally epic terms. For the real antagonist was not personal but, as Oceanus said, time itself. If there was a "march of Intellect" (which, even so, involved painful experience and the fact of loss), there was also, as a part of the scheme of things, the mysterious process that had shaken Keats when he wrote his verse letter to Reynolds (March 1818), and

> saw
> Too far into the sea, where every maw
> The greater on the less feeds evermore.—
> . . . saw too distinct into the core
> Of an eternal fierce destruction.

Apollo, it is true, is ultimately to become a "fore-seeing God" who will be able to "shape his actions like one." But he too will have to face "that law" whereby, as Oceanus says, still

> another race may drive
> Our conquerors to mourn as we do now.

Moreover, as a "fore-seeing God," his development will by definition include a poignant sympathy for the tragic figure of Hyperion, whom he is destined to replace.

8

At the same time there were the formal problems that unpredictably sprouted as he tried to combine so much. The whole attempt of *Hyperion* was contrary to the development of romantic poetry: the romantic effort is personal, and *Hyperion* starts with epic objectivity; the romantic ideal of style prizes spontaneity, and *Hyperion* is highly wrought. To have been told this would hardly have distressed Keats at the start. The poem was to be a protest on behalf of the possibilities of union between the old and the new. The truth is that, though he could speak equally well on both sides of the debate, he was hardly yet able to achieve both simultaneously. A short poem could counterpoint these disparate ideals (something like this for a short poem was to suggest itself to him soon after he put *Hyperion* aside); and in the poetic drama, of course, diversity of idiom and versification was not only permissible but welcome. But *Hyperion* was not a play, however much Keats aspired to incorporate some dramatic elements; and its stylistic norm was the most elevated (and, to use his own later word, "artful") in English—that of *Paradise Lost*. The embarrassment arose through the very success with which Keats attained a similar elevation. The success had little or nothing to do with the rhetorical devices so often mentioned, such as the inversion of noun and adjective ("omens drear" "palace bright"). This last convention, in fact, reminds one again of Johnson's sigh about those who believe that "not to write prose is certainly to write poetry," and of his little parody of Thomas Warton ending, "Wearing out life's evening gray" ("*Gray evening,*" said Johnson, "is common enough; but *evening gray* he'd think fine"). Mannerisms of this sort appear in moderation when *Hyperion* is compared not only with eighteenth-century "Miltonic" imitations but even with the run-of-the-mill blank verse of Keats's own period.

Where Keats really begins to approach Milton is in far more difficult and essential ways—that is, in rhythm and pausing.[2] One of the fascinations of Keats to both the poet and the prosodist is his unerring ability to catch the use of the caesura or pause in any poet he uses as a suggestive model. Management of pause was still considered one of the primary tests for the poet. (The modern student of style is far less aware of such matters than were the earlier writers he discusses; with all his Alexandrian hunger for analysis, he is eye-minded, and focuses on image or metaphor.) Keats alone, among the dozens of writers who have tried to catch the Miltonic line, apportions his pauses, in *Hyperion*, almost exactly as Milton does, using as the most frequent the grave sixth-syllable caesura that was equally common in Milton and that Johnson thought the noblest in the pentameter line:

> But where the dead leaf fell, (x) there did it rest.
> A stream went voiceless by, (x) still deaden'd more . . .
>
> Had stood a pigmy's height; (x) she would have ta'en
> Achilles by the hair, (x) and bent his neck . . .

One enormous liability of beginning with the most elevated style possible is that any later change, whatever else is gained, also involves descent. The power of the Miltonic stride and grasp had so successfully aroused Keats's empathy with the sublime that he had now created something he could neither live with nor live without in this poem. Even Byron, otherwise so vitriolic about Keats, admitted that the fragment of *Hyperion* "seems actually inspired by the Titans, and is as sublime as Aeschylus"; and the unpleasant stanza in *Don Juan* about Keats's being "snuffed out by an article" grants that Keats here

> Contrived to talk about the Gods of late,
> Much as they might have been supposed to speak.

2 *Stylistic Development,* pp. 66–91, and, on the close approximation to Milton's caesura-placing, pp. 74–76.

As Keats approached the next stage after the first two books—the transition to Apollo, and all that this involved—descent seemed inevitable, and this created a particularly unhappy problem at this time. He had indeed climbed beyond the pretty, the sentimental; he had completely mastered his stride on this new and difficult plateau. But he had not yet created a ready style for the middle reaches. To descend meant to return almost all the way to the Hunt valley or to a valley very much like Hunt. When we admit that, in these two months, he had not yet created a ready idiom and prosody for a mean between that valley and this particular plateau, the word "ready" should be stressed; and we should remind ourselves that we are dealing with a chronology involving months, not years. The strength that can directly scale a cliff is probably capable of clearing paths; and, apart even from the unrivaled exercise, much had been acquired along the way. A few months, however, were needed.

Meanwhile it cost him heavily to give up *Hyperion*. It cost him heavily for the very reason that we (forgetting the other difficulties, and how little time there was) are so ready to conclude that it was impossible—namely that he was trying to combine so many different things.

9

It is during the writing of *Hyperion* that Keats develops many of the qualities that we associate with his poetry from now until the end, and especially with that of the eight months that take us through the great odes, after which still further developments begin. Because of the richness and variety of these styles, any introductory summary, however condensed, seems a little silly. Yet we may dwell for a moment on one general quality, mentioning a few of the particular forms it takes—the union of intensity and restraint that has continued to attract every generation of readers from the Victorian era to the present day.

The essence of this appeal lies partly in the number of different ways in which it is made: if one form of it is not prized in a given generation, another form of it is. But some of them cut across changes in taste throughout the last century and a half. One is the empathic imagery, the Shakespearean in-feeling, that since the time of Landor and Arnold has always evoked comparisons of the styles of Shakespeare and Keats. We have noticed Keats's own sympathetic response to such phrasing and imagery. And of course examples in his earlier poetry are numerous (minnows "staying their wavy bodies 'gainst the stream"; the organic image of "Ere a lean bat could plump its wintry skin") . But now the in-feeling becomes habitual, even while Keats is walking with the Miltonic stride in *Hyperion:*

> Also, when he would taste the spicy wreaths
> Of incense, breath'd aloft from sacred hills,
> Instead of sweets, his ample palate took
> Savour of poisonous brass and metal sick.
>
> . . . .
>
> . . . through all his bulk an agony
> Crept gradual, from the feet unto the crown,
> Like a lithe serpent vast and muscular
> Making slow way, with head and neck convuls'd
> From over-strainèd might.

One thinks back to Keats's immediate organic sharing in the phrase in Spenser he had so liked as a schoolboy, "sea-shouldering whales," or in the lines in Shakespeare,

> As the snail, whose tender horns being hit,
> Shrinks back into his shelly cave with pain.

The same kinesthetic gift of image, felt organically and distilled, appears in the interplay of sense impressions that far exceeds anything that was done (with success or even mere ingenuity) until over a half century after Keats's death. Typically, in being so much a pioneer, he did not confine himself to one specialized aspect of it. What we later learned to call "synesthesia"—the use of one sense to replace another—appears far more often in Keats than in his contemporaries, English, French, or German, and almost as much as in writers seventy years later, except for a few who concentrated very specifically on it ("fragrant . . . light," "the touch of scent," "scarlet pain," and the like) . But—what the later nineteenth century never so well attained—this imagery is less concerned with replacing one sense with another than it is with substantiating one sense by another, to give further dimension and depth. Here again Keats reminds us of Shakespeare: "the *moist* scent of flowers"; incense is made tangible, even visible and "hanging" in the growing dark:

> I cannot see what flowers are at my feet,
> Nor what soft incense hangs upon the boughs.

As in imagery, so in peculiarities of mere diction. From Shakespeare and Milton he caught (and exploited, for a few months, far more than they ever did) the use of the past participle as adjective: the energy of the verb could here be imprisoned, concentrated; and the effect was the reverse of the fleeting *y*-ending adjectives of Hunt and his Elizabethan models ("sphery," "streamy," "towery," "spangly") . Instead, as in a line like "Tall oaks, *branch-charmèd* by the earnest stars," the oak branches receive the energy: the spell cast by the earnest stars becomes concentrated within them. He changes a line in the *Eve of St. Agnes* to read "Unclasps her *warmèd jewels,* one by one": warmth is now more than a mere attribute; it has been caught and concentrated within the object. In *Hyperion,* in the *Eve of St. Agnes* especially (where, because of the thinness of the challenge in other ways, he became the more concerned about these aspects of style) , and even in the odes ("Cooling an age," used of the wine in the "Ode to a Nightingale," is changed to "Cool'd a long age in the deep-delvèd earth") , he works toward this sort of condensation of epithet in his revisions. One result is that the *y*-ending adjectives drop from about 30 per cent to only 7 per cent in *Hyperion* and the *Eve of St. Agnes,* whereas the past-participle adjective ("branch-charmèd") jumps to a fifth of all epithets in *Hyperion* and to a quarter in the *Eve of St. Agnes.*

Metrically, in his craving for the most concentrated expression, he moves toward the weighted line. This appears in any number of ways. For example, much as he followed Milton's versification in *Hyperion,* he avoided his extreme enjambment and kept to a norm half as frequent. He had already had enough of the run-on line in his own *Endymion* (even though the model and aim there were far different) . Among the metrical means by which he was simultaneously working toward concentration, we may mention the use of the masculine caesura (the pause after an accented foot) instead of the feminine caesura he had earlier caught from Hunt, and his growing fondness for the spondee, the doubly accented foot—

> *Tall oaks,* | *branch charm*|èd by the earnest stars
> Dream, and | *so dream* | *all night* | without a stir.

Some students of Keats, more interested in the date of a trivial impromptu poem than in his art, have dismissed such considera-

tions as the height of pedantry. But, impatient as we may be before all forms of dullness other than our own, we should pause (as
Sainte-Beuve tells us) to consider how the writer we are considering would regard *us* and what we are saying, and the extent to
which we are noticing at least a few of his own interests as a
craftsman. This predilection for the weighted foot (as for the
weighted line, the weighted stanza) took hold of Keats now in his
reaction to what he called the "slip-shod" *Endymion,* to the "dif-
fuseness" that soon began to bother him even in Spenser. In his
own early verse he would vary the iambic foot with the unstressed
pyrrhic—

> A thing of beau|*ty is* | a joy forever:
> Its love|*liness* | increas|*es; it* | will never . . .

When frequently used, stress-failure lent itself to the debonair and
rapid briskness (and occasional simper) that Hunt affected.
Spondees in Keats's early verse, as in Hunt, are relatively rare. We
could, in fact, make a striking graph of his use of the spondee:
it mounts through the odes, reaching an apex in the richest of
them. In the weakest of the odes (the "Ode on Indolence") they
are five times as frequent as in the early sonnets, and in "Melancholy" and the "Grecian Urn," between six and seven times. The
fact is mentioned as only one interesting metrical accompaniment
of the desire now to concentrate (not in one but in every possible
way) and, to use the phrase in the famous letter to Shelley, "load
every rift . . . with ore." Within a few months he was to feel that
he had gone too far in attaining this weighty and choked-in richness. *Lamia* and the *Fall of Hyperion* begin new styles. Copying
out the opening Induction of the latter poem to send it to George
(September 21, 1819), he muses: "My Poetry will never be fit for
anything it doesn't cover its ground well—You see she is off her
guard and doesn't move a peg . . . Now a blow in the spondee
will finish her."

10

Beginning with *Hyperion,* and continuing through the odes of
the following May, we also find Keats putting into practice a
theory of assonance and of other forms of vowel interplay about
which he had been thinking for a year or more. The essential
principles—as far as we can understand them—are by no means

unique. But what is unusual, first of all, is the degree to which they are now exemplified. Saintsbury was right when he said that the deliberate and constant use of assonance in English poetry begins with Keats. What is still more unusual is that this surprising technical experimentation usurped less of Keats's attention and interest than did other aspects of style. Unlike such poets as Poe or Swinburne, he was far from being interested solely or even primarily in the musical potentialities of verse. Even if we restrict ourselves to style in the narrow sense of the word (and this is a formidable restriction for so eventful a year), he had much else on his mind besides vowel music.

Benjamin Bailey, remembering Keats's stay at Oxford during September 1818 (though he may also be recalling later conversations), states:

> One of his favorite topics of discourse was the principle of melody in Verse, upon which he had his own notions, particularly in the management of open & close vowels. I think I have seen a somewhat similar theory attributed to Mr Wordsworth. But I do not remember his laying it down in writing. Be this as it may, Keats's theory was worked out by himself. He was himself, as already observed, a master of melody, which may be illustrated by almost numberless passages of his poems. As an instance of this, I may cite a few lines of that most perfect passage of *Hyperion,* which has been quoted by more than one of your Reviewers—the picture of dethroned Satan in his melancholy solitude. Keats's theory was, that the vowels should be so managed as not to clash one with another so as to mar the melody,—& yet that they should be interchanged, like differing notes of music to prevent monotony.[3]

We can draw at least two inferences from what Bailey says. First, by "open" and "close" vowels he refers not at all to what the modern linguist means but to what were traditionally and loosely called "long" and "short" vowels. As soon as we use this criterion, we find that, beginning with *Hyperion* and continuing through the *Eve of St. Agnes* to the odes of April and May 1819, line after line falls into pattern or near-pattern.[4] Thus, if we allow *a* to represent traditionally "long vowels" and diphthongs, and *b* to indicate what were traditionally called "short" vowels, we might get simple alternation:

[3] *KC,* II.277.
[4] A more detailed discussion of the whole problem and also of assonance is offered in *Stylistic Development,* pp. 50–65.

And purple-stainèd mouth
(*b a b a b a*)

Away! away! for I will fly to thee
(*b a b a b a b a b a*)

A scurry of "short" vowels may precede this kind of alternation:

Sudden from heaven like a weeping cloud
(*b b b b b | a b a b a*)

A progressive use of "short" vowels may appear in a quiet, somber line:

As are the tiger-moth's deep-damask'd wings
(*b | a b | a b b | a b b b*)

These are admittedly clean-cut examples, though the admission can be supplemented by three relevant points: the frequency of such examples far exceeds that in any other major poet; it far exceeds that in Keats's verse written before *Hyperion* or after the odes (except for the ode "To Autumn"); if only a slightly less regular interplay is expected, then the frequency even more exceeds what we can find in Keats's other verse or in the writing of other major poets.

A second inference from Bailey's account is that he is also referring to assonance. (His examples, " 'Sãt grey-haired Sãturn'— and 'fõrest on fõrest,' " indicate as much.) The elaborate assonance in Keats's poetry from *Hyperion* on, and especially from *Hyperion* through the odes, is one of the most intriguing things in the history of English versification. It is intriguing because this sort of thing is not found in the same degree in poets like Poe, Lanier, and Swinburne, whom we associate with experiment in sound (their use of assonance is far simpler—"Pale beyond porch and portal"). It is found far more (though to a less extent than in Keats's poetry of 1818–19) in poets whom we should assume to have other pressing concerns in mind: Shakespeare, especially in the sonnets (though also in a few of the set speeches), and Milton. Other poets who come closest to Shakespeare and Milton in this one way include Coleridge and Shelley (brilliantly but occasionally), Tennyson (more constantly but more simply), and, once in a while, Chatterton. In fact, Bailey, talking about Keats's ear for "melody" in verse, wrote "Methinks I now hear him recite or chant" the poem of Chatterton beginning,

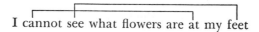

Come with acorn cup and thorn

This sort of vowel interplay, in Keats's poems from *Hyperion* through the odes, is commonplace. There will be the simple alternation that we have just noted in Chatterton:

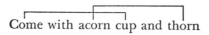

I cannot see what flowers are at my feet

Triple repetition is almost as common:

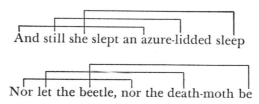

And still she slept an azure-lidded sleep

Nor let the beetle, nor the death-moth be

But this is only a beginning. Consecutive assonance may interlace with it:

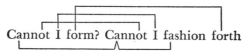

Cannot I form? Cannot I fashion forth

And, after writing a line in *Hyperion* ("And bid old Saturn *seize* his throne again"), Keats alters "seize" to "take" in order to give

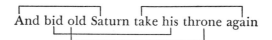

And bid old Saturn take his throne again

By the time one reaches the *Eve of St. Agnes,* this sort of interplay becomes even richer. It frequently continues beyond the limits of a single line. A few examples will illustrate:

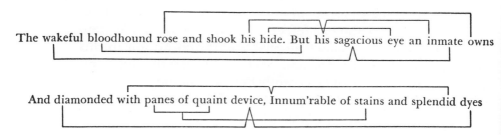

The wakeful bloodhound rose and shook his hide. But his sagacious eye an inmate owns

And diamonded with panes of quaint device, Innum'rable of stains and splendid dyes

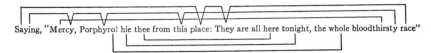

Saying, "Mercy, Porphyro! hie thee from this place: They are all here tonight, the whole bloodthirsty race"

Though Bailey reports that Keats thought that vowels can be used in interplay "like differing notes in music," one can only too easily overstress the conscious art involved. Conscious art is strongest at the start, as learning to play a musical instrument illustrates. It is probable that most of this deliberate effort was made in *Hyperion*, during the last eight weeks of Tom Keats's life. At that time, working slowly (for Keats) at an average of ten lines a day, and determinedly compressing into this poetry all the resources he could tap, he tried to meet the challenge into which, as he felt, he had prematurely "plunged": the challenge of preserving the greatest of the past while pushing forward into the exploration of the "dark Passages" ahead. It was through what he learned in the process of making this attempt that he became the poet he did.

chapter xvii

Fanny Brawne; *The Eve of St. Agnes*

✻⟲✻⟲✻⟲✻⟲✻⟲✻⟲✻⟲✻⟲✻⟲✻⟲✻⟲✻⟲✻⟲✻⟲✻

Winter 1818–19

CHARLES BROWN, when Keats woke him to say that his brother had just died, realized how lonely Keats would now be in the rooms so much associated with George and Tom. "Have nothing more to do with those lodgings,—and alone too. Had you not better live with me?" Keats, after a moment, said, "I think it would be better." [1]

Within another two weeks or so he had moved to Wentworth Place. He had a small sitting room of his own across the hall from Brown's parlor—his was in the back and Brown's in the front of the house—and upstairs his bedroom was immediately above his sitting room. As was common in houses of the period, the kitchen and a simple dining room (damp much of the year) were in the basement. Keats contributed £5 a month. This was a good sum for room and board at the time: probably he and Tom together had not paid much more than £7 or £8 a month to Mrs. Bentley. Years later Dilke, who by then had quarreled with Brown, sniped at the arrangement. Talking about Brown's memoir of Keats, Dilke cites with irritation "the 'come live with me' scene—why Brown, from the first hour that he kept house to the last before he left England for New Zealand . . . was accustomed to have people live with him—it helped him to eke out a small income." [2] But the businesslike arrangement was one of the principal attractions to Keats, and it was doubtless he who insisted on the sum of £5 a month. Here, except for trips away from London, he lived for a year and a half, until May 1820; and it is these rooms, combined with those in Dilke's half of the house, that are preserved as the Keats Museum in Hampstead.

Keats's friends busied themselves to entertain him and occupy his mind. Weary, long before this last numbing calamity, of the

---

[1] Brown, p. 53.   [2] *KC*, II.105.

trivialities and forced merriment of social life, he now found himself for the next month or two caught up in a round of engagements, some of them arranged with laborious tact. He was led off to the famous prize fight at Crawley Hunt, Sussex, on December 5 (the fight between Jack Randall and Ned Turner). Tom was buried at St. Stephen's, Coleman Street, on December 7, and two or three days later Mrs. Dilke went with Keats out to Walthamstow to call on Fanny. He was distressed to find that Abbey was about to remove Fanny from school (she was only fifteen). Meanwhile the active social life continued. He went to a play, called on the Wylies, saw Haydon and others. "Within the last Week," he tells George (December 16), "I have been everywhere." He had stopped all writing. "My pen seems to have grown too gouty for verse."

Quite understandably, the thought of separation is constantly on his mind:

> The last days of poor Tom were of the most distressing nature; but his last moments were not so painful, and his very last was without a pang—I will not enter into any parsonic comments on death— yet the common observations of the commonest people on death are as true as their proverbs. I have scarce a doubt of immortality of some nature o[r] other—neither had Tom . . . Sometimes I fancy an immense separation, and sometimes, as at present, a direct communication of spirit with you. That will be one of the grandeurs of immortality—there will be no space and consequently the only commerce between spirits will be by their intelligence of each other— when they will completely understand each other—while we in this world merely comp[r]ehend each other in different degrees.

But whether others are physically near or distant, if one's mind is actually catching and sharing in their "Ways and Manners and actions"—their "manner of thinking," and the "shape" their joy or their sorrow would take—does this sharing not constitute a genuine extension of one's own "identity"? Desperately lonely, he goes on at length ("I have been so little used to writing lately that I am afraid you will not smoke my meaning"). He knows— feels the impress—of the "shape" of the joy and sorrow George and Georgiana themselves feel—"I know the manner of you[r] walking, standing, sauntering, sitting down, laughing, punning, and eve[r]y action so truly that you seem near to me." Perhaps they remember him in the same way.

He suddenly has a thought: "I shall read a passage of Shakespeare every Sunday at ten o Clock—you read one at the same time and we shall be as near each other as blind bodies can be in the same room."

2

Mrs. Frances Brawne, a widow now for eight years, had rented Brown's half of the house when he and Keats had left in June to accompany George to Liverpool and then set off on their walking tour. With her were her three children: Fanny, who became eighteen in August; a boy, Samuel, of fourteen; and Margaret, who was only eleven.[3] Her husband (whose father was a cousin of the celebrated Beau Brummell) had died of consumption when Fanny was ten. But Mrs. Brawne had an independent income that took care of them comfortably. Indeed, some members of her own family (the Ricketts family), which included men who had served as administrators in the West Indies (Jamaica, Tobago, and Barbados), could be described as well-to-do. The Brawnes had lived in or near Hampstead for years. Fanny herself was born in the adjacent hamlet of West End.

The Brawnes, of course, were still in the other side of Wentworth Place when Keats, the night of his return from Scotland (August 18), dropped by at the Dilkes' on his way home to Well Walk. But throughout the next seven weeks he was hardly aware of them except in the most casual way. He was confined to Well Walk much of the time; he was somewhat ill himself; he was nursing Tom; and he had begun *Hyperion* in late September. When he finally had a few free days in mid-October, he ran into town when he could. If any woman was in his mind during these weeks, it was Jane Cox or, later, Isabella Jones. By then the Brawnes had moved to Elm Cottage on Devonshire Hill, though they still visited the Dilkes. When Tom became so much worse in Novem-

[3] Samuel died of consumption before the age of twenty-four (1828). The following year Mrs. Brawne had a fatal accident. As she took a candle to light a guest across the garden, her dress caught fire and she burned to death. In 1833 both Fanny and Margaret married. Fanny's husband was Louis Lindo (later Lindon), who came from a well-known Sephardic Jewish family. They had three children, Edmund, Herbert Valentine, and Margaret, and lived on the Continent much of the time until 1859. They then returned to England, where Fanny died in 1865 and her husband (twelve years younger than she) in 1872. Margaret Brawne married a Brazilian nobleman, and also lived much of the time on the Continent, dying at the age of seventy-eight in Lausanne (1887). For detailed information on the Brawne, Ricketts, and Lindo families, see Joanna Richardson, *Fanny Brawne* (1952)

ber, and Keats all but stopped going into the city, he himself had no place to which he could go briefly except the Dilkes'. It was probably on one of these visits that he met Fanny Brawne around the middle of November.

3

Few women have had their memory more harshly treated without justification than Fanny Brawne for the first century after Keats's death. The hardy Victorian legend was that of a dying poet consumed with unsatisfied love for a heartless flirt. So strong a hold did it take that we still find it lingering on as a general impression despite the frequent efforts made to correct it. Three circumstances in particular seem to have contributed to the growth of that legend.

In the first place, Monckton Milnes, collecting information for the first biography of Keats (1848), considered it indelicate to inquire into the past affairs of a woman now married. He scrupulously avoided any mention of her name, therefore, and simply referred in a general way to a woman to whom Keats had been devoted. A vacuum was thus created into which almost anything could move.

Second, it was quite human of Keats's friends to look askance, after his death, at a woman they had known only slightly and who had consequently treated them in a casual and independent spirit. All of them, and George as well, felt a little guilty after Keats's death. Even if they could not have saved his life, they could always have the uneasy sense that they might have done a little more. Hence it was a relief to have something of a scapegoat in Fanny Brawne: they could convince themselves that nothing more could really have been done to help him in those last months in England when his mind was so hopelessly preoccupied with her. There may also have been a little pique on their part that they had been relatively unaware of this relationship until those last few months. The envious hostility of the Reynolds sisters had already begun to infect their brother by the time it became apparent that Keats was seriously unwell. Keats himself felt this, deplored it, and finally resented it. Writing to Taylor (September 1820) of Keats's trip to Italy, Reynolds says: "Absence from the poor idle Thing of woman-kind, to whom he has so unaccountably attached himself, will not be an ill thing." George (after he met her on his return to England), the Dilkes, and even Brown joined in the general shaking of heads over the attachment. Much of what they said among themselves over the next few years was unknown to the public until the last generation or two. But the effect was to harden prejudice within the Dilke family over the years; and it was they who served as the Victorian storehouse of information about Keats. By the time Sir Charles Dilke was publishing his grandfather's papers (1875), he was persuaded by old William Dilke, his great-uncle, that Fanny Brawne was "not a lady with whom a Poet so sensitive as John Keats would be likely to fall in love. Your grandfather would probably say she made the advances without really caring much for him." [4] Sir Charles, himself ready to believe the worst, gave quasi-official support to this notion of Fanny Brawne, and quoted out of context a statement by her that henceforth became current: "When the first memoir was proposed [a memoir of Keats by Charles Brown], the woman he loved had so little belief in his poetic reputation, that she wrote to Mr. Dilke, 'The kindest act would be to let him rest for ever in the obscurity to which circumstances have condemned him!' " The real story is that Brown, preparing his memoir in Italy, wrote to ask if, without mentioning her name, he could include a letter Keats had written to him about her from Rome and also some of the poems he had addressed to her. His letter arrived (December 1829) at a time of new calamity for her. Her brother had died of consumption; and her mother, only a month before, had been burned to death when her dress caught fire. With typical self-control, Fanny Brawne makes no mention of this. She gives Brown the permission he asks, though in doing so she despondently makes the remark Sir Charles Dilke cites and attributes to a letter to his grandfather.[5]

Third, to minds already prepared to bend in this direction, the publication in 1878 of Keats's letters to her seemed to provide a further indictment of Fanny Brawne, when, if the actual context had been known, the bitter implications that appear in some of them could have been seen as an expression of conflicts within Keats himself—conflicts, moreover, at a time when he felt that

---

[4] *KC*, II.338. For a condensed summary of the nineteenth-century reputation of Fanny Brawne, see *KC*, I.l–lii.

[5] See the discussion in J. M. Murry, "Fanny Brawne," *Keats* (4th ed., 1955), pp. 69–76.

everything for which he had most hoped was slipping from him.

Extremes, of course, beget their opposites, and an anti-Victorian reaction in favor of Fanny Brawne gathered force in the 1920's and 1930's. A strange Boston collector, F. Holland Day, had years before secured from the family of Keats's sister, in Spain, thirty-one letters that Fanny Brawne had written her between September 1820, when Keats left for Italy, and June 1824. Day, a man not far from insanity, played an elaborate cat-and-mouse game with Amy Lowell, allowing her to read and use a few passages.[6] Though the letters did not really reveal very much, they at least showed Fanny Brawne in a pleasant light. But so ingrained was the prejudice against Fanny Brawne that even the mild passages quoted by Miss Lowell were heavily attacked as spurious. When Day gave the letters to the Keats Museum at Hampstead, they were published; and throughout the next twenty years they were used as a basis for rescuing Fanny Brawne from the Victorian legend. So warm and eager was the rescue that she was either transformed into a pillar of strength or else sentimentalized in a way she would have been the first to scorn: as a clinging, gently naive girl, ready to surrender herself with passive simplicity. After the second World War another counterreaction began.

The result has been a general clouding of the picture of Keats's life from October or November, 1818, until the summer of 1819. The brute truth is that of no important aspect of Keats's life do we know less than of his relations with Fanny Brawne before the summer of 1819. It can be very seriously argued that those relations were not especially important until that time—that too much else was going on. But we cannot defer taking up Fanny Brawne until then. We need not anticipate what we know of Keats's own later reactions: this is too much a part of his own story as an individual. But we may legitimately jump ahead in getting some notion of Fanny Brawne herself. For of this vivacious girl of eighteen, at the time Keats met her, what little we know can be pieced together only from what we can find out about her later on: from the letters Keats wrote to her, which do not begin until seven months from now; from remarks made long afterwards by Keats's friends and acquaintances; from the letters that

---

[6] For the bizarre story of Day and the letters, see H. E. Rollins and Stephen Parrish, *Keats and the Bostonians* (1951).

she herself wrote to Keats's sister, Fanny; from the scrapbooks and other memorabilia that survive in the Keats House at Hampstead, most of which apply to a later period; and, last, from what we know of her family life after she married Louis Lindo until her death at sixty-five (1865).

4

Keats's first mention of Fanny Brawne is in his journal letter to George on December 16, 1818:

> Mrs. Brawne who took Brown's house for the Summer, still resides in Hampstead—she is a very nice woman—and her daughter senior is I think beautiful and elegant, graceful, silly, fashionable and strange —we have a little tiff now and then—and she behaves a little better, or I must have sheered off.

Fanny, twenty years later, gave her own first impression of Keats: "His conversation was in the highest degree interesting, and his spirits good, excepting at moments when anxiety regarding his brother's health dejected them." Two days after his first mention of her, Keats added a little more in the detailed letter he was writing for George and Georgiana. The discussion seems relatively casual in tone. In this letter he was listing almost everything that was happening to him day by day. He had stopped writing *Hyperion* after Tom's death on December 1; he was swept up in the social life with which his friends tried to occupy him; and, unable to compose poetry, he was turning with relief to this long, chatty letter. After speaking about Redhall, the small, energetic man who loved to give parties, and after getting off on the machinery and bustle of social gatherings generally, Keats returns to Fanny (December 18):

> Shall I give you Miss Brawn? She is about my height—with a fine style of countenance of the lengthen'd sort—she wants sentiment in every feature—she manages to make her hair look well—her nostrils are fine—though a little painful—he[r] mouth is bad and good—he[r] Profil is better than her full-face which indeed is not full but pale and thin without showing any bone—Her shape is very graceful and so are her movements—her Arms are good, her hands badish—her feet tolerable—she is not seventeen [actually she was eighteen and three months]—but she is ignorant—monstrous in her behaviour flying out in all directions, calling people such names—that I was forced lately to make use of the term *Minx*—this I think no[t] from any innate vice but from a penchant she has for acting stylishly.

In the light of later accounts by other people, this brief sketch seems quite objective. Her face, for example, really was aquiline and thin. Two portraits exist: a miniature, and also a silhouette by Augustin Edouart, whom many people thought the best silhouette-cutter in England. That silhouette, which shows her at the age of twenty-nine, was thought by her children to have caught her in a very characteristic pose. Keats's remark that her nostrils were "a little painful" would fit the observations of others that she sometimes looked rather haughty. Yet every account also stresses her quick liveliness of manner and movement. We get a somewhat birdlike impression as we read the remarks of her contemporaries as well as the letters she later wrote to Keats's sister; and we feel something sharp and direct in her observations. She herself told Fanny Keats she was "not at all bashful and hardly modest," but lost her poise and became awkward if she tried to pay compliments. Keats's word "Minx" was not solely an attempt, as Amy Lowell sentimentally divined, to disguise to George his feelings about Fanny Brawne. George himself had a somewhat similar impression when he met her in January 1820, and mentions it in a letter to his sister a few years afterwards (April 1824):

> Knowing John's affection for that young Lady I feel very much disposed to like her [;] altho' I was informed by persons I very much respect [probably the Reynoldses] that she was an artful bad hearted Girl, all I saw to object to in her was an appearance of want of affection for her Sister and respect for her Mother.[7]

Moreover, her sharp tongue in later years was an acknowledged fact, though we also know that in her maturity she was a woman of considerable self-control. In time she acquired something of a reputation for her wit. Gerald Griffin, possibly expecting a simple-minded and sentimentally pining woman, was surprised in 1825 to find her "most animated, lively, and even witty in conversation." An old Hampstead neighbor, Mrs. Rosa Perrins, told Harry Buxton Forman that she remembered how people in Hampstead (she is referring to the years after Keats's death) "used to repeat her latest *bon mots*." We can assume that this general vivacity and quick directness of manner may, when she was eighteen, have been relatively unschooled; that it may at moments have seemed to be "flying out in all directions."

7 *More Letters and Poems of the Keats Circle*, p. 20.

Some of the businesslike energy that we have noticed in several of Keats's friends (friends made after the Hunt and Haydon period) is apparent, though in a very special feminine version, in Fanny Brawne. If she was relatively untroubled by the larger sorrows of humanity, she was also free from anything that could be called sloppiness. She was not even very sentimental at a time when the cult of sensibility was as extreme as it has ever been. Keats, indeed, was quick to sense this at the very start: "she wants sentiment in every feature." Since Keats himself was obsessed now with the ideal of effort, of concentration, she by no means displeased him with her capacity to concentrate on detailed work (whether in reading French, learning German, doing fine needlework, or keeping scrapbooks of her hobby—fashion plates and historical costume).

She had, in her own way, what we can only call a certain self-contained efficiency. True, it was efficiency in a small way—it was analogous to Charles Brown's painstaking concentration on accounts (or his concentration on any number of "problems"—he had a somewhat problem-loving mind), or to that almost finicky and pedantic relish for detail that we see in men like Dilke, Woodhouse, or Bailey. Such capacities to focus energy, if relatively unempathic in themselves, had something of the self-contained "assertiveness" of identity that the poet, as Keats later said, delights in contemplating ("the creature hath a purpose and its eyes are bright with it"). They would inevitably appeal to a richly sympathetic imagination that enjoyed the self-sufficiency of others. Moreover, from September 1818 on, Keats was working against a fearful timetable, and against the inevitable cloggings of conscience that openness of empathy brings—against the conflicts of nuance, the embarrassments and hesitations, that arise from fairness to multiplicity of insight and to the existence of "contraries." He increasingly found relief, during these two years of 1818 and 1819, in the companionship of persons who were clear-cut, direct, and uncomplicated.

Though Fanny Brawne could hardly be called a linguist, she had already learned French well enough to read and speak it easily. She had also at least begun German—a rare thing in the England of this time. She wanted to learn languages; but no more than most people who do so was she consumed with a desire to read the poetry and literature written in them. That, indeed, was a refreshing difference, to Keats, between her and the Reynolds sisters, who were always deluding themselves about their motives. Languages were associated with a part of the larger world in which she naturally hoped to move. At an early age our motives can be even more mixed than they are later. No doubt a part of this effort was sustained (as it is for so many of us) by what Keats calls her "penchant . . . for acting stylishly." And life allowed her a chance to fulfill that particular interest. After she married Louis Lindo in 1833, she, her husband, and her children spent many years on the Continent. She not only spoke French and German habitually by then but also learned Italian, which she typically began to study in a brisk, businesslike way. She even translated some German stories for publication, the manuscript of one of which still remains (the story of a German robber, "Nickel List and his Merry Men"). Yet she had no literary pretensions. She liked Gothic horror stories; and as for novels generally, she preferred those with energy and quickness of action, however lacking they might be in other ways. More than once she admitted that she would argue on behalf of her tastes if she were talking with people she did not respect: it would be a way of making the time pass briskly. But before those that she did respect she at once dropped this aggressiveness, not because she was ashamed of her opinions but simply because she took it for granted her tastes were different and more confined, and because she frankly cared more about other things. Before she knew Keats, she admired Byron; she liked his energy. Keats, of course, cared little for Byron; and Fanny later told Keats's sister that, because he thought so little of Byron's serious poems, she herself had gradually "taken a sort of dislike to [Byron] when serious and only adore him for his wit and humour." Keats cared nothing for light novels, but Fanny later admitted (November 15, 1821), "I go on as usual, reading every trumpery novel that comes in my way spoiling my taste and understanding." She also confessed to Fanny Keats: "I am by no means a great poetry reader—and like few things *not* comic out of Shakespeare. Comedy of all sorts pleases me."

She was not betraying mere coyness or indirect design but simply speaking the truth when she told Fanny Keats (December 1821) that she would never "open my lips about books before men at all clever, and stupid men I treat too ill to talk to at all. Women generally talk of very different things." Keats later wrote her that he found it delightful that she should "have liked me for my own sake and for nothing else—I have met with women whom I really think would like to be married to a Poem and to be given away by a Novel." What interested her did not exclude books. It simply did not center in them.

5

Already at eighteen, the energetic girl who was to become adroit in languages and to live much of the time on the Continent had begun her lifelong and in its way almost pedantic interest in everything relating to clothes, perhaps encouraged by the knowledge that her father was a cousin of Beau Brummell. Blue-eyed, she would select ribbons for her brown hair that would match her eyes; and she carefully curled her hair every day. She not only studied the colors and textures of cloth and every change in design of dress, but also had begun to pride herself on her knowledge of historical costume. She may already have started to put together her neat scrapbooks of dress compiled from French magazines and costume cards (those that still survive at Hampstead appear to date from a later period). And when she began to write Keats's sister after Keats left for Italy, her letters then and for the next few years go into the greatest detail about clothes. She draws careful sketches of gowns, sleeves, and hats in order to help the naive Fanny Keats, so long sequestered at Abbey's house in Walthamstow. A few months before Fanny Keats's twenty-first birthday, Fanny Brawne gave her helpful advice on carriage and manner that also tells us a little about herself:

> Don't alarm yourself about Miss Lancasters appearance, I trust you could cut a better figure than she did. You might feel shy at first (which is not that I know of her failing) but any person of sense who goes out a little can soon get over all that—dress, manner and carriage are just what she wants, a person must be a great beauty to look well without them, but they are certainly within the reach of any body of understanding.[8]

Enough has already been suggested about this alert, direct, and on the whole relatively self-controlled girl to give some background to those first remarks of Keats himself: that she has a "penchant . . . for acting stylishly"; that, in addition to every-

8 Brawne, p. 92.

thing else, she is "fashionable." For at least a year—since that highly mannered dinner party at Horace Smith's after which he thought by contrast of Shakespeare and "Negative Capability"—the word "fashionable" had suggested the opposite of all that he had put before himself as an ideal in poetry. But what he encountered in Fanny was at least not the "fashionable" in literature that made him ready to echo Hazlitt's remarks about blue-stockings as one of his indirect ways of speaking about what he felt to be the real enemy—that is, the abuse and trivialization of literature and art for the purposes of disdain or vanity: the sort of thing typified by the sterile young Lockharts of the world, by the endless elbow-jostle and snatches at modishness among "the thousand jabberers about Pictures and Books," with their "bustle and hateful literary chitchat," distracting the human spirit from the simplicities of greatness and preventing man's effort to touch honestly and proceed directly from the rich past. This was the real "wolfsbane of fashion and foppery and tattle." Innocent social affectations seemed nothing in comparison. True enough, he had months before spoofed the "fashionable" in other areas than literature when at a dinner he "astonished Kingston"—one of those who at Horace Smith's party had "talked of fashionables" and were full of "mannerism in their very eating & drinking, in their mere handling a Decanter"—by "keeping my two glasses at work in a knowing way." But these things were by now quite unimportant.

6

Keats's impression was obviously somewhat divided, and we can assume that it continued to be rather divided throughout the next six or seven months, though the attraction was unquestionably growing. For when the famous love letters begin in July 1819, we find a response that is far indeed from simple, and that can hardly be said to settle toward a more single-minded acceptance until autumn. But all this lies ahead. For the moment we know only that Keats met Fanny Brawne before the end of November 1818, and that he had the reactions he mentioned to George and Georgiana. Then, in addition, we are at liberty to draw whatever inferences we can from two other remarks—one by Keats and one by Fanny—each of which has been repeatedly strained at or dismissed in a variety of ways. One is a remark Keats made in a letter to Fanny months later (July 25). We have no reason not to take it more or less literally despite the defensive context. He is apparently answering a complaint by Fanny that he has been "an age" in coming to an understanding. "I have, believe me, not been an age in letting you take possession of me; the very first week I knew you I wrote myself your vassal; but burnt the Letter as the very next time I saw you I thought you manifested some dislike to me." The second remark occurs in a letter of Fanny Brawne to Keats's sister (December 13, 1821), in which she is speaking of the Christmas ahead, when the Brawnes will go to dine with the Dilkes. The occasion, she says, will probably be

> like most people's Christmas days melancholy enough. What must yours be? [Fanny Keats is still at Abbey's.] I ask that question in no exultation. I cannot think it will be much worse than mine for I have to remember that three years ago was the happiest day I had ever then spent, but I will not think of such subjects for there are much better times and ways to remember them.[9]

We are tempted to assume that there was something like a declaration of love, though the remarks might mean no more than that this was the first time that she really came to know Keats, the first time that they talked together alone and in a mutually receptive way. It in no case refers to an engagement. That, as we know from Fanny Brawne herself, did not take place until the autumn of 1819.[10] Beyond these remarks, we have nothing on which to pro-

---

[9] Brawne, p. 55.

[10] Miss Lowell, the first biographer to know of the letters to Fanny Keats, was understandably eager to erase the unfavorable impression of Fanny Brawne that had been built up during the Victorian period. In the process of doing so, she tended to push back the date of the love affair, and even argued that the above remark of Fanny Brawne's suggested that Fanny and Keats became engaged at Christmas 1818 (Lowell, II.148–149). After Miss Lowell, this became a widespread notion. But students of Keats have long assumed otherwise. Fanny Brawne makes it unmistakably clear that the engagement took place at some time after September 1819. In a letter to Fanny Keats (May 23, 1821; Brawne, p. 33), she is speaking of George ("He is no favorite of mine and he never liked me"), and of John's offer to send him "any assistance of money in his power." This was in September 1819. "At that time," she continues, "he was not engaged to me." George probably "had no thought of accepting his offers" until he returned to England (January 1820). "By that time your brother wished to marry himself, but he could not refuse the money." The engagement, in short, was made between October 1819, when Keats returned to Hampstead, and January 1820. This would also fit the remark Fanny wrote in a draft of a letter to Charles Brown (December 26, 1829)—a remark often quoted against her: "I was more generous ten years ago [December 1819]: I should not now like the odium of being connected with one who was working his way against poverty and every sort of abuse" (see J. M. Murry, Keats, p. 73, and below, Chapter XXII, section 8).

ceed with any confidence until we come to the first of the love letters, in July 1819.

7

As Keats continued to be swept up in social engagements, he was rapidly becoming surfeited, and a note of exasperation as well as fatigue creeps into the letter he is gradually compiling in December for George and Georgiana. He is particularly dissatisfied with himself because he cannot seem to get back to *Hyperion*. He calls on Mrs. Millar, Georgiana's aunt ("Miss Millar gave me one of her confounded pinches. N.B. did not like it."). "Hunt keeps on in his old way—I am completely tired of it all—He has lately publish'd a Pocket-Book called the literary pocket-Book—full of the most sickening stuff you can imagine." This was a small diary for 1819 containing, besides the blank pages, short essays by Hunt on each of the months ahead, information on matters of literary interest, a little anthology of poems, and the like. (Two of Keats's own sonnets were included—"Four seasons" and "To Ailsa Rock.") Hunt took Keats and Brown with him to a party at the home of Vincent Novello, the organist and composer (whose daughter Charles Cowden Clarke married in 1828):

> There was a complete set to of Mozart and punning—I was so completely tired of it that if I were to follow my own inclinations I should never meet any one of that set again . . . [Hunt] understands many a beautiful thing; but then, instead of giving other minds credit for the same degree of perception as he himself possesses—he begins an explanation in such a curious manner that our taste and self-love is offended continually. Hunt does one harm by making fine things petty and beautiful things hateful—Through him I am indifferent to Mozart, I care not for white Busts—and many a glorious thing when associated with him becomes a nothing —This distorts one's mind.

The whole thing has to stop:

> I feel I must again begin with my poetry—for if I am not in action mind or Body I am in pain—and from that I suffer greatly by going into parties where from the rules of society and a natural pride I am obliged to smother my Spirit and look like an Idiot—because I feel my impulses given way to would too much amaze them—I live under an everlasting restraint—Never relieved except when I am composing—so I will write away.

The next day he takes up the letter again. He "went on a little" with *Hyperion* the night before, he says, "but it will take some time to get into the vein again." It is now that he gives his second, more complete account of Fanny Brawne.[11]

The thought of the evening at Novello's suddenly returns to him as he ends by telling George and Georgiana about Fanny Brawne's "penchant . . . for acting stylishly," and about her friend, Caroline Robinson, whom Fanny considers

> a Paragon of fashion, and says she is the only woman she would change places with—What a Stupe—she is superio[r] as a Rose to a Dandelion. When we went to bed Brown observed as he put out the taper what an ugly old woman that Miss Robinson would make—at which I must have groan'd aloud for I'm sure ten minutes.

From Miss Robinson, he turns to Kingston, so knowledgeable in the art of "handling a Decanter," and then, inserting Hazlitt for contrast—so refreshingly surly and out of place in such company— he begins to jot down a little comic scene (somewhat easier to grasp if we follow the suggestion of Robert Gittings and quote it as an excerpt from a play rather than in the form in which Keats hurriedly crowds it into his letter) :

> I shall insinuate these Creatures into a Comedy some day—and perhaps have Hunt among them—
>
> Scene, a little Parlour—Enter Hunt, Gattie [Ollier's brother-in-law], Hazlitt, Mrs. Novello, Ollier.

Gattie: Ha! Hunt! got into you[r] new house? Ha! Mrs. Novello, seen *Altam and his Wife?* [A new tale by Charles Ollier.]

Mrs. N: Yes *(with a grin)* . It's Mr. Hunt's, isn't it?

Gattie: Hunt's: no, ha! Mr. Ollier, I congratulate you upon the highest compliment I ever heard paid to the Book. Mr. Haslit, I hope you are well.

Hazlitt: Yes, sir—no, sir.

[Hunt goes to the piano.]

Mr. Hunt (at the Music) : La Biondina &c. [singing]. Mr. Hazlitt, did you ever hear this?—La Biondina &c. [resuming his singing].

Hazlitt: O no Sir—I never—

Ollier: Do, Hunt, give it us over again—*divino!*

Gattie: Divino!—Hunt, when does your *Pocket Book* come out? [His *Literary Pocket Book* for 1819.]

Hunt: "What is this that absorbs me quite?" [Quoting from Pope's "Dying Christian to His Soul."] O, we are sp[i]nning on a little [referring to the *Literary Pocket Book*], we shall floridize

11 See section 4 above.

[flower into publication] soon I hope—Such a thing was very much wanting—people think of nothing but money-getting—now for me I am very much inclined to the liberal side of things—but I am reckon'd lax in my Christian principles—& & & &c.

Meanwhile Woodhouse, who was already worried about Keats's morale back in September and was the more anxious now that Tom had died, wrote to encourage him, and also told him that two authoresses who admired his poetry would like to meet him. These were the kindly Jane Porter, who wrote *Thaddeus of Warsaw* and *The Scottish Chiefs,* and her sister Anna. But Keats had a chance now to work. Brown was taking his nephews off to see the sights of London. Bentley the postman had just brought over a clothesbasket full of Keats's books from his old lodgings at Well Walk. Keats wrote back to Woodhouse (December 18) that he was flattered; but his temper was also a little worn. He would be glad to see the Porter sisters "if they alone and not Men were to judge" of the kind of poetry he wants to write. The time is passing. He must turn to his writing:

I should like very much to know those Ladies—tho' look here Woodhouse—I have a new leaf to turn over—I must work—I must read—I must write—I am unable to afford time for new acquaintances—I am scarcely able to do my duty to those I have—Leave the matter to chance.

8

The Dilkes thought it would be pleasant for Keats to go off to Chichester with Brown and spend a few weeks with Dilke's parents there, and also with Dilke's sister, Laetitia Snook, and her husband, in Bedhampton. Keats was not eager to go. "They say," he had told George (December 18), that "I shall be very much amused—But I dont know—I think I am in too huge a Mind for study—I must do it—I must wait at home, and let those who wish come to see me. I cannot always be (how do you spell it?) trapsing." Then a few days later (December 22) he got a touch of the sore throat again. Severn, who saw Keats a little in November and December, recalled that he often seemed "distraught and without that look of falcon-like alertness which was so characteristic of him." He was determined not to go out, and Brown prepared to set off to Chichester alone; Keats would join him later. There was no reason, thought Keats, why he could not now get to work. That very day he again sat down to make a start, despite the sore throat. But after a short while, making no progress, he put *Hyperion* aside, and, welcoming the distraction that his long letter to George and Georgiana provided him, tells them:

> Just now I took out my poem to go on with it—but the thought of my writing so little to you came upon me and I could not get on—so I have begun at random—and I have not a word to say—and yet my thoughts are so full of you that I can do nothing else. I shall be confined at Hampstead a few days on account of a sore throat.

And so the letter continues as he looks back for news, telling them some of the details of the past month that we have already noticed.

Meanwhile another irritation had arisen. It was trifling enough. But it had to do with money, and even worse, with the need for it to help a friend. Haydon was often troubled with his poor eyesight. He was especially troubled with it now. Something was necessary to tide him over until he could continue his interminable work on "Christ's Entry into Jerusalem." He turned, as might be expected, to the most generous of his acquaintances. Keats was torn with sympathy: though he had become only too aware of Haydon's limitations throughout the past year, his loyalty remained, and a large distress was beginning to take the place of his more simple-minded admiration of two years before. Of course he would do what he could to help Haydon. But could not Haydon "Try the long purses"—"ask the rich lovers of art first"? (This is the day, December 22, when the depressing sore throat has returned.) He goes on: "I'll tell you why—I have a little money which may enable me to study and to travel three or four years— I never expect to get anything by my Books: and moreover I wish to avoid publishing." But Haydon did not get the hint. He wrote back enthusiastically: "Keats! Upon my Soul I could have wept at your letter; to find one of real heart & feeling . . ." He will try others first, but he is gratefully ready to accept Keats's offer to help. Keats, harassed in every way, then made trips into town to see Abbey, first in a vain effort to try to ask that his sister be allowed to stay in school and second to secure money for Haydon. Abbey was adamant in turning down the request that Fanny remain at school. He seems to have hedged, for the moment, about the second, and Keats was put off for the time being.

9

Another week passed. His sore throat began to disappear. But his inability to do anything with *Hyperion* really worried him. A major transition was necessary at the start of Book III, and unless he could make that transition the poem had no place to go.

He had long since discovered that he could jolt himself back into continuing work if, for a short while, he wrote something very different. This did not mean simply a short lyric or two (he had already in the past month written a couple of extemporaneous songs).[12] At some time between mid-December and January 18 or 19, Isabella Jones suggested that he try a short romance again, and take as a subject the legend of the Eve of St. Agnes. This, to be sure, would be a very different poem from *Hyperion*. But the change might also appear to be a step backward. He was as tired of the sentimental as he was of "fashion." Hence Hunt's rather innocent *Literary Pocket Book* seemed "sickening," and the thought of his own *Isabella* made him cringe.

Instead of turning at once to another romance, therefore, he found himself going back to the light, tripping meter and seventeenth-century spirit of those poems he had sent Reynolds back in February ("Robin Hood" and "Lines on the Mermaid Tavern") when, in hoping to make a new start, he had also protested against both the sentimentality and the self-involved solemnity of so much modern poetry. At some time between mid-December and January 2, he wrote another brace of poems, also in heptasyllabic couplets and closely similar in other ways to the first two, though on a more advanced plane. As in "Robin Hood," a potentially serious theme interplays with the jaunty meter in the lines "Ever let the Fancy roam, / Pleasure never is at home": so much so that the premise of the poem is best understood in the light of later and better poems that develop it further, especially the odes. For the moment it may be enough to point out that the theme, however merry-hearted the rhythm, is somber: the transitoriness of things is matched by the mind's own incapacity to remain content. The "enjoying of the spring" fades just as much as does the actual "blossoming"; the rich fulfillment of autumn, even if it remained stationary, would "cloy"; and "Where's the cheek that doth not

[12] "I had a dove" ("a little thing I wrote off to some Music as it was playing") and "Hush, hush! tread softly."

fade, / Too much gazed at," or the eye that does not ultimately
"weary"? Only through the constant rearrangement and recombi-
nation of things by the imagination can the heart's desire appear
to be fulfilled. But here the liabilities, so much the concern of the
later poetry, are only gently implied. Keats sighs a bit after he
copies out for George the 112 lines (he later omitted some) : "I
did not think this had been so long a Poem." "Bards of Passion
and of Mirth" carries on from the "Lines on the Mermaid Tavern" ("Souls of Poets dead and gone"), except that the theme
now, as he tells George, is "the double immortality of Poets." In
addition to their own Elysium, they have also left their "souls on
earth" to "Teach us, here, the way to find you"—still continuing
to "speak / To mortals of their little week." One thinks ahead to
Keats's remark about Milton's still remaining, long after his
death, "an active friend to man"—as the Grecian Urn itself is "a
friend to man."

Whatever else could be said of the two poems, they were at
least a change not only from *Hyperion* but also from what now
seemed to him the cloying familiarity, the monotonous slow walk
within so short a room, of the fourteen lines of the sonnet. And the
meter was too brisk to allow sentimental lingering. The two
poems, he tells George, "are specimens of a sort of rondeau which
I think I shall become partial to—because you have one idea am-
plified with greater ease and more delight than in the sonnet." Of
course they are simple things, these occasional short pieces. He will
see how they accumulate over the years and then select a few: "It is
my intention to wait a few years before I publish any minor poems—and then I hope to have a volume of some worth."

10

It was early January now. *Hyperion* still was not going ahead.
The two "rondeaus" had not seemed to help. What writing he has
done over the past few weeks, as he tells Haydon (January 10), is
"nothing to speak of." He feels as though he were "moulting,"
and is chronically discontented with himself in the process. Meanwhile Haydon is prepared for Keats's loan—"I now frankly tell
you," Haydon has just written, "I will accept your friendly offer."
Haydon's only hopes of surmounting "the concluding difficulties

of my Picture lie in *you*." Keats, in reply, declares that he will do what he can, and "do not let there be any mention of interest."

On January 18 or 19 he went to Chichester, joining Brown at the home of Dilke's parents. These gentle, elderly people knew all about Tom's lingering illness and death and about George's departure, and were prepared to exert themselves to make the time as pleasant as possible. Brown, who liked elderly people when they were themselves kindly, had already brought gusto and what he considered to be humor into the household. Hoping to distract Keats, he tried even harder after his friend's arrival. He was constantly clowning. Miss Sarah Mullins—a pleasant woman in her seventies with whom Brown pretended to be flirting—had persuaded him to shave off his whiskers. They all laughed at the change, and told Brown that he looked like a woman. Eager to oblige, the burly Brown appeared at breakfast wearing old Mrs. Dilke's hood and talking in a high feminine voice. Thus these four or five days passed, and on two evenings they all went out together, said Keats, "to old Dowager card parties," which would last until ten o'clock.

But throughout the visit he was brooding on the need to start writing something, and, as if in a gesture of determination, had brought with him the paper (several thin sheets that William Haslam had given him) on which he had been jotting down his long letter to George and Georgiana. Within a day or so he began to think more seriously of the suggestion of Isabella Jones that he write on the legend of St. Agnes' Eve (the Eve itself was January 20); and he may even have made a start on the poem. He and Brown then walked the thirteen miles to Bedhampton (January 23) in order to stay with John Snook and his wife, Dilke's brother-in-law and sister, at their house, which still stands (the Old Mill House).[13] Here, during the next nine or ten days, Keats wrote the *Eve of St. Agnes*, averaging about thirty-five to forty lines a day. He scarcely left the house except when they all went (January 25) to see the dedication of a chapel built by Lewis Way, a wealthy man who had just bought Stansted Park (a huge estate of 5,500 acres near Bedhampton) and had decided to turn it into a

[13] For discussion, see Guy Murchie, *The Spirit of Place in Keats* (1955), pp. 141–151.

sort of college for the conversion of the Jews to Christianity.[14] The day afterwards, Brown returned to Hampstead. Keats stayed on for another five days (until February 1 or 2), having caught another sore throat in the meantime. Probably by the time he returned, the *Eve of St. Agnes* was finished.

11

Prolonged work at any serious poem—particularly if, like *Hyperion,* it was not developing as he had hoped—frequently produced another result for Keats, as it has for so many other writers. If he turned temporarily to a less ambitious poem in a different form, the gate would quickly open and he would find himself not only writing with remarkable fluency but also incorporating, with rapid and effortless abundance, features of idiom and versification that had been part of the conception of the earlier, more demanding work. The *Eve of St. Agnes* was in every way a relief from *Hyperion.* The plot was simple. He was able to relax the autumn's brave effort to follow Shakespeare, Milton, and Wordsworth simultaneously—to combine epic power and, if possible, dramatic variety with an exploration of the modern consciousness, of the dimly descried "march of Intellect." He could indulge his gift for descriptive setting, and allow the momentum of creating it to suggest incident—and perhaps even some development of character—as he wrote; and in this temporary respite from the "naked and grecian Manner" of *Hyperion*—a manner already creating serious problems for him—he now chose the Spenserian stanza with its opportunities for separate pictorial units. It is still frequently

---

[14] A full account of Way and of the dedication of the chapel is given by Gittings, pp. 75–82, who persuasively points out (pp. 87–89) the connection of images in lines 30–38 of the *Eve of St. Mark* with the Stansted Chapel. An interesting possibility is a connection between some of the detail in the windows and that in the casement stanza of the *Eve of St. Agnes* (pp. 79–81). But here the shapes and colors, however sumptuously Keats describes them, are conventional. If we stress particular sources, an equally good possibility would be the parish church at Enfield which Keats had seen so frequently at an impressionable age. Not only the large central window over the altar (a source of some local pride at the time) but the ten large side windows were "triple-arched." At that time, beneath the central rose window, were also two large diamond-shaped windows, each of them subdivided into four smaller diamonds. Knights were shown on one side and "ladies praying" on another; "shielded scutcheons" and "heraldries" were in all of the windows. For an engraving and descriptions, see William Robinson, *History and Antiquities of Enfield* (1823), II.5, 25–30. For various figures on tombs, some now removed, cf. II.32, 41–56.

said that, in turning from *Hyperion* to the *Eve of St. Agnes*, Keats was changing to a theme and mode of poetry more "congenial" to his talent. In this case we are either assuming that the more "congenial" is that which demands less, and are therefore stooping with a condescension grotesquely out of place, or else (if the remark is meant as a compliment to the *Eve of St. Agnes*) we reveal the gentle bias of our own poetic interests.

If he had not felt that he was a maturer artist than when he wrote *Isabella*—though less than a year had passed—he would probably have been less willing to commit himself to another romance, even if only as a respite and in a desire to re-exercise himself in a familiar mode. But the autumn's effort with *Hyperion* had brought an enormous change. We return to a path with far more dispatch, with far less anxiety about what lies beyond the turns ahead of us there, when we have already walked successfully on higher, more difficult ground. The uncertainties so obvious in *Isabella* are now completely absent; and the richness of epithet, phrase, and sound pattern begun in *Hyperion* spread without interruption or hesitation through the new romance. So hypnotic and sustained is the effect that we sometimes overlook another large difference between it and the earlier romances, *Endymion* and *Isabella,* and forget what actually takes place in the poem. Hence a prose statement in one sentence, like the following, seems more unfairly reductive—appears more to violate our total impression—than does an equally stark summary of the action of most other narrative poems. An ardent lover, Porphyro, uses the opportunity of St. Agnes' Eve to have access, through "stratagem," to the bedchamber of the unsuspecting Madeline; and there he is able in effect to seduce her while she is still half asleep. To keep this honestly in mind—and Keats later said he wished to emphasize it even more clearly—embarrasses our present-day eagerness to transcendentalize the poem into something at least quasi-philosophic. But it still has more than one interest. To begin with, Keats's own partial identification with the lover is obvious enough. Madeline, it is true, is no Fanny Brawne. In fact she is significantly different: Madeline timid and subdued, Fanny "flying in all directions"; Madeline serious and devout, Fanny with her delight in clothes, her concern for fashion, and her quick tongue—"calling people such names." In entering into the character of Porphyro,

Keats is able to take some vicarious pleasure in the lover's "stratagem"; and when Woodhouse later objected to the seduction scene,
Keats waywardly replied (as the distressed Woodhouse went on to
tell John Taylor) that he would "despise a man who would be
such an eunuch in sentiment as to leave a maid, with that Character about her, in such a situation: & shoᵈ despise himself to write
about it &c &c &c—and all this sort of Keats-like rhodomontade."
But the identification with Porphyro can take us only so far, and
other factors enter into the course the plot takes.

Quite as relevant to the central episode was Keats's growing
exasperation with the insipidities that sugared the romances of the
period; and his exasperation had its own personal edge. It had
been his luck, or lack of it, as a beginning poet to have such romances among his own first models; and their tone and mannerisms had been so early assimilated into his own habits of composition that he seemed to be unable to get completely clear of them
as long as he wrote in one of the romance forms. At least *Isabella*
had suggested as much. One thinks ahead to his embarrassed remarks to Woodhouse about the "mawkish" *Isabella* ("He said he
could not bear it") , and his intention to "write fine things that
cannot be laugh'd at in any way"—laughed at because of their "inexperience of li[f]e, and simplicity of knowledge." Of course one
way to avoid the pitfall was to stay clear of the romance itself, as
he had in *Hyperion;* and after the *Eve of St. Agnes* he did just that
during the short time that remained. For the next and final attempt that could be thought of as comparable to a romance—
Lamia, written six months later—turns the narrative into an exploration of illusion in which illusion is frankly punctured; and it
also deliberately employs a verse form reminiscent of Dryden and
Pope and somewhat at odds with the conventional romances of
Keats's own day. That later impulse to turn romance almost in-
side-out, if only to shake off the insipidities associated with it, is
already present in embryo as he writes the *Eve of St. Agnes.* This
is not to say it is an overriding consideration in a poem that, when
once begun, answered temporarily so many other needs or interests, including the need, in the face of loss and difficulty, to retreat
in some way to the familiar—to what he knew beforehand he
could do without much effort—though it was also necessary that
the familiar be modified in order to fit the far more exacting standards he now had.

12

The poem takes the special (but still relatively simple) form that it does partly because of the ways in which Keats's growing uneasiness with the romance as a genre and his intention of writing something different from the "mawkish" *Isabella* continue to operate against—and yet are constantly being modified by—the descriptive and musical richness of setting. And in speaking of the setting (so frankly—and so successfully—important an element in the poem), the peculiar opportunities and limitations of the Spenserian stanza itself should be kept in mind. "Mrs. Tighe and Beattie," he wrote George shortly before he began the poem, "once delighted me—now I see through them and can find nothing in them—or weakness." And, as if in a spirit of open challenge, he selected the same verse form they themselves had used, the Spenserian stanza, though he was altogether unpracticed in it and in fact had hardly used it except in his first poem (the four-stanza "Imitation of Spenser"), written back in the Edmonton surgery. But of course there were also good formal arguments for using the stanza; and the mere fact that it was chosen, and that he began to exploit its opportunities so quickly, contributes in turn to the character of the poem. To begin with, the stanza is capacious enough not to pinch the writer into the affectations of compression that *ottava rima* so frequently does, as Keats himself had found in *Isabella*. Yet at the same time it is very much of a unit. The result is that it tempts poetic narrative toward tableau, ample and yet self-contained. The musical potentiality of the stanza's structure is analogous in its effect, permitting massiveness while it also compels unity (unity, that is, within each individual stanza). For the central recurring rhyme (the *b*-rhyme of *a b a b b c b c c*) can sustain as well as interlock, continuing to act as a kind of sounding board until the reverberation is lost in the long wave of the concluding six-foot line. There were opportunities, then—however specialized because of the nature of the verse form—for the coalescence of economy and richness that distinguishes his style generally from *Hyperion* through the odes. And this characteristic, from the first stanza, further helps to set the *Eve of St. Agnes* (whatever it lacks otherwise) apart from every other romance in English.

Within this context of musical and pictorial setting appear char-

acters by no means idealized (at least one of the two principal
ones being somewhat deluded about his own motives). But they—
like the seduction itself—are either elevated or else protectively
muffled as one haunting stanza majestically concludes and makes
way for another. The situation was in every way fertile for what,
if he had not thought of it very explicitly before he started, quickly
became a distinguishing quality once the poem began, that is, the
ebb and flow of emerging contrasts and partial resolutions, such as
the advanced age and frailty of the two minor characters and the
youth of the lovers; the temporary inner warmth and the all-
enveloping cold; music and silence; the interplay of the religious
and the erotic, which Keats caught from *Romeo and Juliet;* and
even the divided reactions within the characters themselves (no-
tably Porphyro, who is touched to tears at the thought of Madeline's innocent trust in the legend of St. Agnes' Eve and yet at the
same time evolves his ruse to take advantage of it). The apex is
reached when the central episode builds on Keats's familiar theme
of dreaming and waking.

The aged Beadsman is the first—and he returns to be the last—
of the characters that move both with and against the "coloring"
and "drapery" that Keats felt to be the principal merit of the
poem if it had any:

> St. Agnes' Eve—Ah, bitter chill it was!
> The owl, for all his feathers, was a-cold;
> The hare limp'd trembling through the frozen grass,
> And silent was the flock in woolly fold:
> Numb were the Beadsman's fingers, while he told
> His rosary, and while his frosted breath,
> Like pious incense from a censer old,
> Seem'd taking flight for heaven, without a death,
> Past the sweet Virgin's picture, while his prayer he saith.

"Meagre, barefoot, wan," he rises from his knees and walks down
the freezing chapel aisle past the "sculptur'd dead." One thinks of
the phrase Keats so liked in Shakespeare's sonnets: "death's eternal
cold." As the Beadsman passes those long-dead knights and ladies
forever "Emprison'd in black, purgatorial rails," the "weak spirit"
of this frail man is touched with sharp sympathy "To think how
they may ache in icy hoods and mails." The poignance is put
briefly as the soft prelude of the music comes to him from the hall:

> Northward he turneth through a little door,
> And scarce three steps, ere Music's golden tongue
> Flatter'd to tears this aged man and poor.

But with the habits of a lifetime he turns from the music:

> His was harsh penance on St. Agnes' Eve:
> Another way he went, and soon among
> Rough ashes sat he for his soul's reprieve,
> And all night kept awake, for sinners' sake to grieve.

Like his counterpart, the aged nurse Angela, he will shortly die; and the implication at the end of the poem—gentle, not labored—is that his death is nothing to be admired but only the inevitable falling of a leaf before the winter of fact.[15] Meanwhile, in the hall, the soft prelude fades, and the "silver, snarling trumpets" begin to "chide" as if in response to the throng of guests who now burst in, their brains "stuff'd" with expectations of romance. Above the chiding trumpets and fluctuating life,

> The carvèd angels, ever eager-ey'd
> Star'd, where upon their heads the cornice rests,
> With hair blown back, and wings put cross-wise on
>   their breasts.

Another contrast begins to emerge. The innocent Madeline, her own brain "stuff'd" with the legends she has "heard old dames" tell her about St. Agnes' Eve, is preparing to keep it with literal fidelity: by following certain rituals and going supperless to bed, she will see in dream her future husband. "Full of this whim," she fails to notice the suitors who approach; "The music, yearning like a God in pain, / She scarcely heard." She is "Hoodwink'd with faery fancy; all amort, / Save to St. Agnes and her lambs unshorn." But an atmosphere of hatred permeates the castle and threatens this stir of love. Like Juliet or Isabella, she is surrounded by a family at mortal feud with that of the man she hopes to wed.

15 Nothing shows more graphically Keats's later reaction to the poem (September) than his impetuously harsh and flippant revision of the last three lines of the poem:

> Angela went off
> Twitch'd by the palsy—and with face deform
> The Beadsman stiffen'd—twixt a sigh and laugh
> Ta'en sudden from his beads by one weak little cough.

Woodhouse said that he wanted the poem to "leave off with this Change of Sentiment—it was what he aimed at, & was glad to find from my objections to it that he had succeeded" (II.163)

Meanwhile, eager to catch some glimpse of Madeline, the young Porphyro has ridden across the wintry moors, and, like Romeo, enters a festive hall fraught with danger. His only possible help is Angela, Madeline's aged nurse—considerably less staunch than Juliet's nurse. Her palsied frailty is made almost ludicrous: she has not only a "dizzy head" but "agues in her brain" (at the close of the poem she dies "palsy-twitch'd"). But, like the Beadsman, she is always being assimilated by the atmosphere against which she begins to move in contrast. The potentially grotesque gestures are softened, as when she cackles at Madeline's gullible trust in the dream to come ("Feebly she laugheth in the languid moon") or falls into senile mutter as she leads Porphyro to a place where his enemies will not find him:

> He follow'd through a lowly archèd way,
> Brushing the cobwebs with his lofty plume,
> And as she mutter'd "Well-a-well-a-day!"
> He found him in a little moonlight room,
> Pale, lattic'd, chill, and silent as a tomb.

As Angela tells him of Madeline's hope for a vision, Porphyro is both touched and also inspired with a plan: Angela is to take him secretly to Madeline's chamber, hide him in a closet from which he can look out, and bring fruits for a feast he will spread. He will then sing and awaken Madeline, and she will see the future husband of whom she has been dreaming. Angela is understandably shocked at the proposal (he is "wicked" and "impious," not at all the same person that he had seemed). But Porphyro swears his intentions are good, and is indeed himself convinced that they are ("Good Angela, believe me by these tears"); and he then impulsively threatens that he otherwise will shout until his enemies in the castle discover him. The threat further unnerves the palsied Angela. The mercurial Porphyro seems a little ashamed; and he begins to speak with "such deep sorrowing" that Angela agrees and leads him to Madeline's chamber.

His spirits again raised, the ardent lover takes "covert" before Madeline (a "ring-dove") enters:

> Now prepare,
> Young Porphyro, for gazing on that bed.

Keats is recalling the famous scene in *Cymbeline* where the evil Iachimo conceals himself in order to look on Imogen while she

20. MANUSCRIPT OF STANZAS 24-26 OF "THE EVE OF ST. AGNES"

sleeps; even some of the phrasing is echoed. Keats's young impulsive lover is by no means a Iachimo. But his actions are far from
those of the heroes in the romances Keats and Felton Mathew
("the valiant Eric") had once read, and far from what we should
have expected from the decorous Lorenzo in *Isabella*.[16] In any case
the atmosphere once again pervades and modifies; and at this crucial moment it does so dramatically—through the effect, that is,
on Porphyro himself. For immediately after Madeline enters the
room, the magnificent stanza (xxiv) on the triple-arched casement
follows. The rich interplay of color into which the protecting
casement turns the cold moonlight not only shelters the undressing
of Madeline but, as she kneels to pray, also serves to shake once
again Porphyro's single-mindedness:

> Rose-bloom fell on her hands, together prest,
> And on her silver cross soft amethyst,
> And on her hair a glory . . .
>   . . . Porphyro grew faint:
> She knelt, so pure a thing, so free from mortal taint.

Now and in the next few stanzas Porphyro is feeling that he is
in something very like a "paradise." But the word has been over-
stressed in discussions of the poem. For the quasi-religious imagery
that follows the casement stanza significantly subsides, and, with
one minor exception, is confined throughout the remaining 150
lines of the poem to only two remarks by Porphyro himself (one
of which, that he is a "famish'd pilgrim,—saved by miracle," by no
means describes honestly to Madeline the calculated "stratagem"
by which he has arrived). We go too far, in other words, when we
equate the religious and the erotic in this poem. A remark that
Keats wrote in his copy of the *Anatomy of Melancholy* is relevant:
"nothing disgraces me in my own eyes so much as being one of a
race of eyes nose and mouth beings" who "have always mingled
goatish winnyish lustful love with the abstract adoration of the
deity." The "paradise," in other words, is altogether subjective,
within Porphyro himself. Nor is it a paradise to him solely because
the erotic is frankly reinforcing itself—as any passion tends to
do—by incorporating other feelings. Rather he has been genuinely
struck by a diversity of impressions, all of them strong (and they
also include fear and guilt: he has "stol'n" here; he "creeps" from

16 For a perceptive discussion of Porphyro's character, and indeed the entire
poem, see J. C. Stillinger, *Studies in Philology*, LVIII (1961), 533–555.

the closet) . This very diversity of impression, in effect, numbs him. In a specialized way, and applied to a particular character, we have an anticipation of the "numbness" (the "being too happy") that later provides a beginning to the "Ode to a Nightingale": the "yearning" or "aching" that fills the mind comes not in the satisfaction of a single emotion ("Where's the cheek that doth not fade, / Too much gaz'd at?" he had written in the lines on "Fancy") but in the active interplay of diverse feelings still in the process of working toward resolution and "winning near the goal." Creeping from the closet and dreading discovery, Porphyro, "half-anguish'd," lays the table for a feast, and then beseeches Madeline to awake, "Or I shall drowse beside thee, so my soul doth ache." But in his faintness he is really only "whispering." His arm goes about her; she does not awaken. Finally he pulls himself away, takes his lute, and sings the ballad "La belle dame sans mercy" close to her ear. Her eyes open.

But Madeline's partial awakening from the dream is far from reassuring. In this almost deliberate variation of Adam's dream ("he awoke and found it truth") , she finds the sight of Porphyro a "painful change": the dream has proved to be more attractive than the reality. These are "sad eyes" that now look at her, while those in her vision had been "spiritual and clear." The figure next to her is, in comparison, "pallid, chill": where are those "looks immortal"? The play of dream and reality is thus built into the plot. But we strain at the poem when we assume that, because of Keats's more serious use of it elsewhere, it carries an equally heavy symbolic weight at all times. It is natural for a writer to be attracted to similar situations, and especially to have recourse to them when the action is slight, when the poem is written swiftly, and when his attention (as is very much the case in this poem) is particularly concentrated on idiom and versification. But the context at least allows us to note one relatively simple but recurring thought of Keats which is to become more prominent in the poetry of 1819: a dream—like innocence—cannot be lived in the world without being violated; and yet, whatever is lost, actual happiness is impossible without an awakening from dream to reality. At all events, the dream again completely absorbs the half-asleep Madeline. The first version—and also the one finally printed—then moves with quick delicacy. "Beyond a mortal man impassion'd far," the lover rises from his knees:

> Into her dream he melted, as the rose
> Blendeth its odour with the violet,—
> Solution sweet.[17]

But the finality of what has happened is plain. "St. Agnes' moon hath set," and the storm outside immediately rises. Completely awakening, Madeline realizes her situation. ("No dream, alas!"; she is "a deceivèd thing"; a "traitor" has brought Porphyro here; what if he now forsakes her?) Protesting the integrity of his love, assuring her that they will wed, he instinctively capitalizes on her desire for the continuation of the magic of St. Agnes' Eve and on his own half-conviction that he has been "sav'd by miracle": this rising storm outside, he says, is elf-inspired for their escape; ("an elfin-storm from faery land / Of haggard seeming, but a boon indeed"). And the poem ends with no warm, confident response from Madeline. "She hurried at his words, beset with fears." The apprehensive lovers "glide, like phantoms, into the wide hall," through the castle, quietly slipping the bolts, one by one. Nor is there any assurance that they survived:

> And they are gone: ay, ages long ago
> These lovers fled away into the storm.

That night the Baron and his warrior guests were plagued with troubled dreams; Angela died; and

> The Beadsman, after thousand aves told,
> For aye unsought for slept among his ashes cold.

[17] It is here that Keats made the revision to which Woodhouse especially objected, adding that, if in the previous version "there was an opening for doubt what took place, it was [Keats's own] fault for not writing clearly." Woodhouse told Taylor that "This alteration is of about 3 stanzas." The surviving copy involves only part of two stanzas. The close of stanza xxxv (where Madeline says simply "Oh leave me not in this eternal woe, / For if thou diest, my Love, I know not where to go") was temporarily changed to "See while she speaks his arms encroaching slow / Have zon'd her, heart to heart—loud, loud the dark winds blow." Then stanza xxxvi (which in the published version was printed as above) emphasizes more specifically that Madeline is asleep, describes her dream as "wild," omits the saccharine phrase "solution sweet," and stresses the sudden rise of the storm:

> and still the spell
> Unbroken guards her in her repose
> With her wild dream he mingled as a rose
> Marryeth its odour to a violet.
> Still, still she dreams.—Louder the frost wind blows.

13

The result is a poem begun with mixed and even negative feelings (including fatigue and grief, the need to keep his mind occupied in this trying time, thoughts of Fanny Brawne, acute anxiety about his inability to continue *Hyperion,* and the determination not to revert to another *Isabella*) , and yet a poem that at the same time turns into a feat of craftsmanship—a triumph of idiom and versification over the limitations of the subject—because the new artistry he had gained through *Hyperion* was freshly and yet very simply challenged. It is no accident that the most complete worksheet we have of any of Keats's poems is the first draft of the *Eve of St. Agnes.* Because he was working rapidly, he used the same copy instead of making successive drafts; and he made his changes line by line as he was writing his first draft, sometimes fumbling and sometimes leaping toward more effective expression. Rarely in any poem after *Endymion* has he ever written a phrase that can be compared in flatness and banality to those that frequently begin a stanza, a line, or a sentence, as he writes the *Eve of St. Agnes.* The poem as such is by no means absorbing him. Yet immediately, as soon as the phrase is jotted down, his judgment is piqued, and he alters and then, with quick exasperation, alters again.[18] Some are amusing. At least one is also a little poignant. "Have you some warm furs?" he had asked George and Georgiana in December. And the following year, when he becomes so ill, the constant chilliness turns into an obsession: in letter after letter he tells both his sister and Fanny Brawne: "Be very careful to wear warm cloathing in a thaw"; "Be very careful of open doors and windows and going without your duffle grey"; "Remember to be very careful of your cloathing." Now, as Porphyro rouses Madeline at the close of the poem to prepare to flee into the storm ("the morning is at hand, / The bloated wassailers will never heed, / Let us away . . ."), Keats finds himself, at first, impulsively writing "Put on warm cloathing sweet, and fearless be." The most involved of all his struggles, and one accompanied by abysmal plunges, is with the stanza on Madeline's preparation for bed (xxvi) . The near-comedy of the struggle and Keats's growing exasperation can be followed

---

18 A full discussion of the manuscript revisions is given in M. R. Ridley, *Keats' Craftsmanship* (1933) , pp. 112–190. I merely summarize a few examples from Mr. Ridley's detailed and perceptive analysis.

only when the writing of the whole of the stanza is followed step by step in Mr. Ridley's account.[19] From it we may select just a few moments. In the final version, the stanza begins:

> Anon his heart revives: her vespers done,
> Of all its wreathèd pearls her hair she frees;
> Unclasps her warmèd jewels one by one;
> Loosens her fragrant boddice; by degrees
> Her rich attire creeps rustling to her knees.

But Keats, when he first started it, got himself into various troubles, one of which is an unwanted intrusion of abrupt motion—Madeline virtually pulls her headdress from her hair:

> But soon his heart revives—her prayers said
> She ⟨lays aside her veil⟩   pearled
>   Stript her hair of all its ∧ wreathed ⟨pearl⟩
> Unclasps her bosom jewels

He is far from satisfied as he writes this, and least of all with the line he next jots down in trying to get a rhyme for "said": "And twists it in one knot upon her head." Beginning all over, and gradually improving those lines, he enters the next part of the stanza with uncertainty, "Loosens her boddice from her . . . ," crosses it out, and goes through the following changes, "Loosens her Boddice lace string," "Loosens her Boddice and her bosom bare," and (something hard to explain except that he is probably rather flurried with exasperation) "Loosens her bursting boddice." Clearing this up, he goes on and pictures her "Half hidden like a Syren of the Sea." Recalling that the association with "sirens" has an unpleasant side, he finally replaces it with:

> by degrees
> Her rich attire creeps rustling to her knees:
> Half-hidden like a mermaid in sea-weed.

To follow out an entire stanza briefly, we can take that on the casement (xxiv). Keats begins, "A casement ach'd" (as usual, when writing rapidly, he is forgetting his *r*'s), crosses out "a[r]ch'd," and elaborates:

> A Casement ⟨ach'd⟩ tripple arch'd and diamonded
>   With many coloured glass fronted the Moon
> In midst ⟨of which⟩ wereof a shilded scutcheon shed
>   High blushing gules, upon

---

[19] Pages 153–156.

The light is to fall on Madeline. But in the previous stanza she has only just entered the door, full of excitement. Needing first to have things calmed and stationed a bit, he crosses out "upon," and writes:

> 　　　　　　　　　　　a shilded scutcheon shed
> High blushing gules: she kneeled saintly down
> And inly prayed for grace and heavenly boon;
> The blood red gules fell on her silver cross
> And her white hands devout.

The last half line is especially bald; and, while hesitating generally about the whole stanza, he crosses out "her," altering the phrase to "And whitest hands devout."

　Here, hastily put together, is some raw material. And Keats, as Mr. Ridley says, "takes it all to pieces," and "begins to put the fragments together in a different design," postponing Madeline until later and focusing more on the casement itself. He crosses out all that he has written and starts afresh (forgetting his *r*'s again in "triple"), inserts "There was" at the beginning, and goes on:

> There was a Casement tipple archd and high
> All garlanded with carven imageries
> Of fruits & trailing flowers and sunny corn.

But the third line lacks rhyme. He crosses out "trailing," and makes the line read "Of fruits & flowers and sunny corn ears parch'd" (the final two words are far from satisfactory; but the problem of rhyme is on his mind for the moment; and he is thinking of changing the first line to end "high and triple-arch'd"). Then suddenly, after this tinkering, he feels that a breakthrough is coming. He again crosses out everything he has done, and writes so rapidly that his word "garlanded" is momentarily lost in this garden of flowers and fruits, and he puts down "gardneded":

> A Casement high and tripple archd there was
> 　All gardneded with carven imageries
> Of fruits and flowers and bunches of knot grass;
> 　And diamonded with panes of quaint device
> 　Innumerable of stains and splendid dies
> 　As is the wing of evening tiger moths;
> 　And in the midst 'mong ⟨man⟩ thousand heraldries
> 　And dim twilight

Separating "dim" and "twilight" he ends the stanza:

And twilight saints and dim emblazonings
A shielded scutcheon blushd with Blood of Queens and Kings.

To get a rhyme for "Kings" and "emblazonings" he must now
change the final word in the line "As is the wing of evening tiger
moths." He writes above it, "As is the tiger moths rich," crosses
out "rich" and writes "deep damasked wings," hesitates about
"damasked," and writes "sunset" above it ("deep sunset wings"),
and so leaves it, though returning in the final version to "As are
the tiger-moth's deep-damask'd wings":

> A casement high and triple-arch'd there was,
> All garlanded with carven imag'ries
> Of fruits, and flowers, and bunches of knot-grass,
> And diamonded with panes of quaint device,
> Innumerable of stains and splendid dyes,
> As are the tiger-moth's deep-damask'd wings;
> And in the midst, 'mong thousand heraldries,
> And twilight saints, and dim emblazonings,
> A shielded scutcheon blush'd with blood of queens and kings.

To sum up, nothing else that he wrote shows so much the un-
leashed freedom with which the technique of composition can
itself become a dominant emotion. Keats was enough of a disciple
of Hazlitt not to take seriously any thought that concern with
technique alone can lift the artist above apprentice writing. (Was
Titian, said Hazlitt, "when he painted a landscape, . . . pluming
himself on being thought the finest colourist in the world, or making himself so by looking at nature"?) In fact one rarely creates
or discovers technique—a means to an end—except by trying to
do something besides employ technique for its own sake. But
larger challenges were not what Keats required at the moment. Because of the daily distress of nursing Tom, he had hurried himself
prematurely into beginning *Hyperion*. Yet much that he had
learned through *Hyperion* remained, as it were, in suspension—
all the readier for use because the original hope was frustrated, at
least for the time being. He later spoke slightingly of the "colouring" and "drapery" of the *Eve of St. Agnes*. Of course he would
have ideally preferred "a Poem in which Character and Sentiment
would be the figures to such drapery." But in this altogether necessary respite, everything worked temporarily toward "drapery" or
tapestry, including the mere existence of a new ability in weaving
it and a welcome brief freedom from subjects he felt to be more
substantial and demanding.

chapter xviii

A Period of Uncertainty

February to April, 1819

BACK IN HAMPSTEAD, still plagued by the sore throat that had flared up again, Keats resolved to shake the thing once and for all and to remain indoors for as long as necessary. The only medical help he could get was the advice to do just that, and he had been disregarding it.[1] The sore throat was becoming not only exasperatingly monotonous but a cause of some worry. It had now bothered him, off and on, since he had caught the bad cold in the Isle of Mull seven months ago. He could not afford to have this continue: there was too much ahead to do.

For about ten days in early February he forced himself to stay in, reading much of the time. Unable to get started again on *Hyperion,* he was becoming daily more dissatisfied; and the thought of beginning something else as mere exercise, after already doing this in the *Eve of St. Agnes,* was unappealing. He had also been having trouble with Abbey. Just before Keats had left for Chichester he had seen Abbey again, still hoping to get something to lend the insistent Haydon. The matter of Tom's estate came up. Abbey talked darkly about the provisions in the will that probably necessitated waiting until Fanny was twenty-one—five and a half years hence.[2] Uneasy at Keats's probing, and constantly suspicious of the letters passing between Keats and his sister, Abbey then told Fanny that he strongly disapproved of their writing so much to each other. Fanny, somewhat frightened at Abbey's sternness,

---

[1] On the relation of the sore throat to his later illness, see below, Chapter XXII, section 4.

[2] He does not appear to have said flatly that this was the case, probably for fear lest Keats get ideas of trying to fight it legally. Instead Abbey seems to have tried to give the impression that he was uncertain but was looking into it. Hence Keats's own uncertainty when he tells Haydon: "What I should have lent you . . . was belonging to poor Tom—and the difficulty is whether I am to inherit it before my Sister is of age." But he is certainly beginning to suspect Abbey—"I am nearly confident 'tis all a Bam"—that is, a hoax (II.40) .

wrote her brother about this while he was still at Bedhampton; and Keats, puzzled and distressed about the matter, far from guessing what lay behind it, wrote back to her while confined to his rooms at Hampstead (February 11): "Your letter to me at Bedhampton hurt me very much,—what objection can the[r]e be to your receiving a Letter from me?" He feels himself "the only Protector" she has. He does not tell her that he is going to write or see Abbey about this, though he is determined to do so. He simply says "I am in hopes Mr. Abbey will not object any more to your receiving a letter now and then from me—How unreasonable!" He then, as he told George later, sent Abbey a strong letter. "I expect from this to see more of Fanny—who has been quite shut out from me." The tone in which he is writing to George and Georgiana—he is now beginning the long journal letter he had promised them—is one of fatigue: he is seeing

> very few Persons—being almost tired of Men and things—Brown and Dilke are very kind and considerate towards me—The Miss Reynoldses have been stoppi[n]g next door lately—but all very dull—Miss Brawne and I have every now and then a chat and a tiff—Brown and Dilke are walking round their Garden hands in Pockets making observations. The Literary world I know nothing about.

He was certainly not in the most pleasant of moods. Meanwhile Valentine's Day was approaching. Brown, who always had plenty of time, was writing some of his tediously comic verses for the occasion. One of the women for whom he composed a valentine was Fanny Brawne, who, he thought, had snubbed him. This showed no particular interest on Brown's part, and he was yet unaware of Keats's own feelings about her. But her amusement and pleasure in receiving the valentine (the poem remained fixed enough in her mind so that she could still repeat it to her children)[3] annoyed

---

3 It was far from distinguished. Her daughter recollected four stanzas, and wrote them out for Buxton Forman (printed in *Some Letters and Miscellanea of Charles Brown*, ed. M. B. Forman [1937], pp. xiii–xiv):

Whene'er we chance to meet
    You know the reason why
You pass me in the street
    And toss your head on high—
	Because you think my coat
	    Too often has been worn,
	And the tie about my throat
	    Is at the corners torn.

Because my walking stick
    Is not a dandy twig,
Because my boots are thick,
    Because I wear a wig.
	To see me thus equipped
	    What folly to be haughty!
	Pray were you never whipped
	    At school for being naughty?

Keats, though he said nothing at the time. Meanwhile, in an impulsive gesture of indifference, he himself presented her with his copy of Hunt's *Literary Pocket Book,* which had become a kind of symbol of the union of affectation and sentimentality that so repelled him now.[4] Within a few weeks, if not before, she probably discovered Keats's low opinion of it, though she still continued to use it a little for memoranda.

2

On Saturday, February 13, having remained indoors eleven days, he went into town. He saw Abbey, and ran into a few people, including Woodhouse, whom he found looking into the window of a bookshop in Newgate Street.

The mere stimulus of getting out of the house and going into town may have prompted him to decide to try to write something, no matter what. For that evening he began another short narrative poem, the *Eve of St. Mark,* of which in three or four days he wrote about a hundred lines, and then put it aside. He spoke of it to George as "a little thing," and, referring to its title and that of the *Eve of St. Agnes,* added: "You see what fine mother Radcliff names I have." He will send it to George if he finishes it. But he never did finish it, and it was not until months later that he finally sent it along with the comment that he had begun it "in the spirit of Town quietude. I th[i]nk it will give you the sensation of walking about an old country Town in a coolish evening. I know not yet whether I will ever finish it." It is little more than the setting of a poem. He pictures a cathedral town on a Sunday evening in spring—the Eve of St. Mark (April 24) ; he is obviously thinking of Chichester:

> Upon a Sabbath-day it fell;
> Twice holy was the Sabbath-bell,
> That call'd the folk to evening prayer;
> The city streets were clean and fair

---

4 In it she copied out the song in which Keats seems to refer to Isabella Jones and her old patron, Donat O'Callaghan ("Hush, hush! tread softly"). She may simply have seen the verses and asked to copy them. But Mr. Gittings argues persuasively (pp. 83–85) that Keats actually gave them to her either in pique or in a general attempt to convince himself that his own feelings were not too serious.

From wholesome drench of April rains;
And, on the western window-panes,
The chilly sunset faintly told
Of unmatur'd green vallies cold.

Dwelling in the old Minster Square is a young woman, Bertha (a name he probably took from Chatterton), who in the growing dusk begins to read from an illustrated manuscript-book about St. Mark. Some lines (which Keats may have started to add later) then follow, in a Middle English that reminds us of Chatterton's imitations but appears to be a little closer to Chaucer and especially Gower. It is possible that, whatever might have become of the poem, Bertha was merely reading the story of the martyrdom of St. Mark. It is more probable that Rossetti's guess was right: Keats's story would have used the legend that, on St. Mark's Eve, anyone standing near the church porch at twilight would see entering the church the apparitions of those who would become ill during the year ahead, and who, if their apparitions did not leave the church again, would die. Certainly the legend might have interested Keats. It was at least potentially freer from sentimentality than the *Eve of St. Agnes*.

There are several points of interest in the fragment, all of them, in a general way, stylistic. To begin with, these mere four or five days of writing produced a hundred lines or so that delighted (and anticipated) the Pre-Raphaelites a half century later. To some of them, especially Rossetti, the poem ranked with Keats's "La belle dame sans merci" as the finest prototype of their own ideals of poetic style; chaste, fresh, simple, it had an April-like cleanliness that reminded them of late medieval painting and tapestry and Chaucer's octosyllabic couplets. (Paradoxically the actual setting is not medieval at all: the story—at least the opening part—is laid in Keats's own time.) For much the same qualities (though not for the medieval suggestions), the fragment also attracted the Imagists of the early twentieth century.

These later appeals of the poem are relevant when we return to Keats himself, beginning the "little thing," as he called it, while confined to his room attempting to get rid of his sore throat, and hoping to spur himself, by a radically different meter and theme, to a momentum with which he could return to the really important work. For in these three to five days he exemplified in miniature what the next seven months were to illustrate very graphically: he had reached the point, which we find as a rule only in the very greatest poets, where he could not begin a serious poem of any length without creating for it a new style of its own. This was to happen throughout the great odes (each of them in some respects different) , then *Lamia,* then the *Fall of Hyperion.* The particular style, as in the *Eve of St. Mark,* might be a relatively small concern to Keats himself; but it could still serve as a starting point and even an ideal for the more specialized (and leisurely) work of later writers. In this prodigal richness of creativity, the *Eve of St. Mark* was written (or rather begun; for it was only begun) as merely another interim effort. In the weeks ahead, there would have been ample time in which to finish it, if he had written it with only a fraction of his usual speed. But legends no longer interested him.

3

After he broke off the *Eve of St. Mark* on February 17, he wrote less poetry for the next two months than at any time since he had left Guy's Hospital. His attempts to jolt himself back into activity by trying temporarily to write something very different had, for the first time, not succeeded. Such a poem as the *Eve of St. Agnes,* or even the fragment of the *Eve of St. Mark,* could be regarded as itself quite sufficient by even the strictest taskmaster. But to Keats they hardly counted. It had been, after all, a full year since that rededication of his that had followed the "Negative Capability" letter—a rededication in which the poetry of "romance," and all that it meant, were to be put aside in favor of the greater forms. Of course he had been assuming all through the spring—all through the summer, in fact—the need and value of a very "gradual ripening of the intellectual powers." And he had also been prepared, as he thought, for difficulties. But so many of the difficulties for which we steel ourselves are not the ones that actually descend on us; or, if they are, it is not in the expected way or at the expected time. The thought of this, and of the unpredictable strangeness of things, was to grow on him from now until the end—until he took that totally unexpected trip to Italy, and found himself at Rome at a time and under circumstances he would

never have envisaged even a year before. As for the long preparation, during which "for many years" he would be studying hard,
building foundations, and writing only occasionally: he had become too much in the habit of writing not to feel uneasy unless he
was keeping it up to some extent; and it would be pleasant to feel
that at least a little progress was being made. But where, from his
own point of view, was the progress? The real work, *Hyperion*,
was stalled. And, however difficult the time had been for writing,
basically the poem was stalled for the most disturbing of all reasons: that he had been losing faith in it. He had been able to keep
up *Endymion*, and at a rapid pace, even after he had lost faith in
its value. But that was fifteen months or so ago; he could feel then
that he was still learning the rudiments—learning to progress, as
he said, into the "Go-cart" from the "leading strings."

The need for a fallow period of two months, indeed of two
years, could be taken for granted while Keats tried to get his
bearings, even had nothing else been happening to him during the
past eight or ten months. Yet of the many who continue to be
caught up in the drama of his development, few seem to stop
to make that allowance. Even those most closely familiar with the
strain of writing, who know at first hand how necessary fallow periods are, seem to forget their own experience when they turn to
this short period in Keats's life. Health, the death of Tom, the effect of the reviews catching up with him, anxiety about money,
even the proximity of Fanny Brawne, are all blamed separately or
in various combinations for this interruption. It is not that we are
unsympathetic when we act as though we expected his development to proceed briskly and assume that only sharp personal difficulties could have interfered. It is rather that we become too eager
(and, in that eagerness, too specialized) in our sympathy. Caught
up in a development so steady and self-corrective, we find ourselves
experiencing something of the *katharsis* that we usually receive
only in fiction: years become melted down into moments, and, in
the fillip this gives to the mind, our own impatient aspirations, released in this gratifying identification, outrun our recollection of
our own experiences. We become in more of a hurry than we
should otherwise be to see this development proceed without hindrance. What could be stopping him now? Our approach to these
months is shaken back to a saner perspective if we put that ques-

tion with an honest acknowledgment of what is really in our minds—an acknowledgment that at once shows the foolishness of the question: we know that the great odes are to come in late April and early May, and, after them, the enormous productivity of the summer that follows; and, since this is so, what is preventing that writing, or something of comparable quality, from appearing now?

Of course Keats himself felt that this period into which he was moving was sterile: it is hard to regard a time in our own lives as innocently fallow until after it is over and we have the warm assurance that something was really produced later. And all through these painful weeks a feeling of genuine apprehension is obvious. What is more, it is relatively new. When he had left Guy's Hospital for Margate, he was naturally afraid lest he really have nothing to say. But at that time he had nothing much to lose. There had also been the painful, frightened weeks when he was trying to start *Endymion,* and was rushing around from place to place. But even then he could still accept the fact that he was really a novice. Now, however, he did have something to lose. It was not reputation or money (had he known them, he would doubtless have enjoyed Johnson's remarks about those who suffer misery in being "condemned" to live up to what they consider to be their reputation). What he now stood to lose was the toehold he had at last felt he was getting on the greater uses of poetry. "I see by little and little," he told Haydon, "more of what is to be done, and how it is to be done, should I ever be able to do it." He could fear he was losing that hold; for what had he done since *Hyperion* was interrupted about the time Tom died? He had tried to turn down the social engagements that were smothering him ("look here Woodhouse—I have a new leaf to turn over—I must work—I must read—I must write"). Bentley had brought over his books. He was ready for serious work, and this did not mean taking time off in Chichester or Bedhampton to write another short romance.

The door was slammed shut on romance when he decided to stop work on the *Eve of St. Mark* on February 17, and to stop it not because he lacked a possible story. These side excursions had gone on long enough. He simply did not care that much about them. Short poems especially hardly entered his head during the next two months.[5] He had to get back to the main work, and to

5 Two poems to Fanny Brawne were thought by Colvin to have been written during this time (pp. 334–336) : "Physician Nature" and "Bright Star." An equally

try to make something of it. Yet with every attempt he made to return to it, *Hyperion* seemed increasingly to be on the wrong track, or rather a series of different tracks. The inclusive optimism of its premise perhaps struck him now as simply jaunty or (to use a term he was employing now) "smokeable"; and the style was unquestionably beginning to seem too inflexibly formal for that growing concern with the human with which (either dramatically or meditatively) he also hoped to enrich the poem.

Hyperion, in short, had turned into something that he could live neither with nor without at this point. His own critical faculty had outraced it. With *Hyperion,* however prematurely, he was to have made at least a start toward the greater poetry. But was it really much closer to *King Lear* or to Milton or to Dante than what he had written before? In some aspects of style, of course, there had been an advance. "It is true," he told Haydon (March 8), "that in the height of enthusiasm I have been cheated into some fine passages, but that is nothing." Of course it was nothing, given his own standards; for his standards, like the horizon, kept flying before him as he moved toward them. Yet until he had something to take its place, he could not simply put *Hyperion* away and forget it; and there was nothing in sight to supplant it—no conceivable way of taking up in poetry any of the ideas about which he was feeling most seriously, for which *Hyperion* itself, as it was now constituted, had no place. Remarks that reflect his frustration keep recurring during these weeks:

[March 8 (to Haydon)] I am mostly at Hampstead, and about nothing . . . not exactly on the road to an epic poem . . . I have come to the resolution never to write for the sake of writing, or making a poem, but from running over with any little knowledge and experience which many years of reflection may perhaps give me—otherwise I will be dumb.

[March 13 (to George)] I know not why Poetry and I have been so distant lately. I must make some advances soon or she will cut me entirely.

[March 17 (to George)] On Sunday . . . I dined—and had a nap. I cannot bare a day an[ni]hilated in that manner—there is a great difference between an easy and an uneasy indolence.

[April 12 (to Fanny Keats)] I have thought also of writing to you often, and I am sorry to confess that my neglect of it has been but a

possible if not more probable date is, for the first, the autumn of 1819, and, for the second, the late autumn or early winter of 1819 (on "Bright Star," see below, Chapter XXII, section 5).

small instance of my idleness of late—which has been growing upon me, so that it will require a great shake to get rid of it. I have written nothing, and almost read nothing—but I must turn over a new leaf.

[April 13 (to Haydon)] I dread as much as a Plague the idle fever of two months more without any fruit.

[April 15 (to George)] I am still at a stand in versifying—I cannot do it yet with any pleasure—I mean however to look round at my resources and means—and see what I can do without poetry.

4

At the same time, of course, he was digesting the past year. Above all, the impact of Tom's illness—especially during those hopeless, impotent last three months of Tom's life when Keats was with him daily—was probably only now beginning to be felt completely. Compared with that, and compared with his anxiety about his work, most of the present irritations of a more personal sort were minor. By late February, his sore throat began to get better, and he was to stay relatively free of it for three months or more. Any uncertainty he felt about Fanny Brawne was no greater than most love affairs show at the start. His unpleasant relations with Abbey hardly added to his peace of mind; but he was not yet seriously in need of money, and he was able to feel that he had scored a triumph over Abbey in one matter at least—that of being free to see and write to his sister.

On the other hand, he was certainly disturbed by the fact that his second volume had by now as effectively died as the first (he had recently heard that John Murray had just sold four thousand copies of the last canto of Byron's *Childe Harold*). He tries to convey the news to George with detachment and fortitude (February 19):

> I have not said in any Letter yet a word about my affairs—in a word I am in no despair about them—my poem has not at all succeeded—in the course of a year or so I think I shall try the public again—in a selfish point of view I should suffer my pride and my contempt of public opinion to hold me silent—but for your's and Fanny's sake I will pluck up a spirit, and try again—I have no doubt of success in a course of years if I persevere—but it must be patience.

Now, for the first time, he begins to speak of the reviews with a little bitterness, though the remarks are kept general and he does not refer specifically to the attacks on himself. It will be a long struggle to achieve any success, he tells George, simply because of the increasing power of the critical reviews. Too many among the reading public seem afraid to "think for themselves," or even to look at a work that does not come to them with the escort of approving reviews. He changes the subject, and tries to turn to lighter things. Brown is writing a satiric poem, and making painfully slow progress. He is "walking up and down the room a breeding—now at this moment he is being delivered of a couplet—and I dare say will be as well as can be expected—Gracious—he has twins!" But when he visited John Taylor a few days later, the sight of the unsold copies of the poem shook him again. He tells George (March 3):

> I have been at different times turning it in my head whether I should go to Edinburgh & study for a physician; I am afraid I should not take kindly to it, I am sure I could not take fees—& yet I should like to do so; it is not worse than writing poems, and hanging them up to be flyblown on the Reviewshambles—Every body is in his own mess.

Throughout the next week he continued to brood over the matter, becoming more exasperated with things generally as his own self-dissatisfaction increased. In a letter to Haydon (March 8), he suddenly breaks out:

> What a set of little people we live amongst. I went the other day into an ironmonger's shop, without any change in my sensations—men and tin kettles are much the same in these days. . . . Conversation is not a search after knowledge, but an endeavour at effect. In this respect two most opposite men, Wordsworth and Hunt, are the same . . . With respect to my livelihood I will not write for it, for I will not mix with that most vulgar of all crowds the literary.

Returning after nine days (March 12) to the journal letter he was writing for George, he tells him that he has been reading that near-masterpiece of invective, Hazlitt's *Letter to William Gifford,* which has just appeared. With a vicarious pleasure that is only too obvious, Keats says "perhaps you would like an extract or two from the highly seasoned parts," and proceeds to copy them out ("the force and innate power with which it yeasts and works up itself—the feeling for the costume of society; is in a style of genius—[Hazlitt] hath a demon as he himself says of Lord Byron"). It gives Keats some relief. His mind then turning to George and Georgiana, he wonders just what they are doing at this moment. He wants to try to picture them. He will give them a picture of himself right now of the sort he would like them to send him. The candles are burned down, and "the fire is at its last click":

> I am sitting with my back to it with one foot rather askew upon the rug and the other with the heel a little elevated from the carpet —I am writing this on the Maid's tragedy which I have read since tea with Great pleasure. Besides this volume of Beaumont & Fletcher— there are on the tabl[e] two volumes of chaucer and a new work of Tom Moores called "Tom Cribb's memorial to Congress"—nothing in it. These are trifles—but I require nothing so much of you as that you will give me a like description of yourselves, however it may be when you are writing to me—Could I see the same thing done of any great Man long since dead it would be a great delight: as to know in what position Shakspeare sat when he began "To be or not to be"— such thing[s] become interesting from distance of time or place. I hope you are both now in that sweet sleep which no two beings deserve more tha[n] you do—I must fancy you so—and please myself in the fancy of speaking a prayer and a blessing over you and your lives —God bless you—I whisper good night in your ears and you will dream of me.

5

Something obviously had to be done to get out of this rut. If he could not start writing a poem that he cared about, he would at least see people. Even while his throat was still bothering him, he had attended a dance given by Georgiana's cousin Mary Millar (February 19). But he had found it an empty thing; and it is the last dance, he tells his sister, that he will "go to for twelve months again." [6] Since February 24 he had been going into town frequently: he had spent two days with Taylor, and had visited the British Museum with Severn. He was also seeing Abbey every few days. Abbey did not welcome these visits, and had thought up a new gambit in order to distract Keats's attention from Tom's estate—a suggestion that Keats become a hatter; and Keats would

---

[6] It is often thought that Keats could not dance, because in a letter to Fanny Keats (February 27, 1819), he says he would like her "to teach me a few common dancing steps." But he had been going to dances ever since those held by the Mathew girls and their cousin Felton. (See also Rollins' note, II.42.) He may not have danced well and may have thought Fanny could help him brush up on it; and he may also have wished to give her the pleasure of instructing him in something she had learned at the school of the Misses Tuckey, from which Abbey had now removed her.

go away speculating about the nature of Abbey's mind and curious interests.[7]

Some remarks of Haydon's, apparently applying to this time, have been repeatedly cited, dismissed, brought back, and dismissed again. Always hyperbolic, Haydon, who loved to conceive of people as at the extreme of either desperation or joy, wrote long afterwards that Keats, crushed by the reviews and

> not having strength of mind enough to buckle himself together like a porcupine and present nothing but prickles to his enemies . . . began to despond, and flew to dissipation as a relief, which after a temporary elevation of spirits plunged him into deeper despondency than ever. For six weeks he was scarcely sober, and—to show what a man does to gratify his appetites when once they get the better of him—once covered his tongue and throat as far as he could reach with cayenne pepper in order to appreciate the "delicious coldness of claret in all its glory"—his own expression.
>
> The death of his brother wounded him deeply, and it appeared to me that he began to droop from that hour. I was much attached to Keats, and he had a fellow-feeling for me. I was angry because he would not bend his great powers to some definite object, and always told him so. Latterly he grew irritated because I would shake my head at his irregularities and tell him that he would destroy himself.[8]

The passage, when Haydon's *Autobiography* was published (1853), drew an indignant attack on "that ill-ordered being, Haydon," from Cowden Clarke, who had seen Keats around this time: Keats, said Clarke, could not have afforded the expense of this long debauch; it was utterly unlike him anyway; and as for the cayenne pepper, "if the stupid trick ever was played, I have not the slightest belief in its serious sincerity." The pepper episode, as Clarke implies, need not be taken too solemnly. Haydon almost certainly never witnessed it himself; and whatever actually happened, the furnace of Haydon's imagination had twenty-five years in which to transmute it.[9] As for his statement that Keats was "scarcely

---

[7] Abbey had money invested in a hatmaking concern; Keats did not know this, although he was beginning to suspect it. Abbey "began again," Keats tells George (March 17), about "that hat-making concern"—"he has don[e] it frequently lately"—saying that George himself had been intrigued by the idea. "He wants to make me a Hat-maker—I really believe 'tis all interested: for from the manner he spoke withal and the card he gave me I think he is concerned in Hat-making himself."

[8] *Autobiography,* ed. Penrose (1927), pp. 259–260.

[9] For Clarke's account, see *KC,* II.319–321. It was exactly the kind of thing Keats might have been tempted to say he had done (or more probably was thinking of doing) when the humorless and teasable Haydon, whose own irregularities were

sober" for six weeks, it would certainly add dramatic variety if we could say that Keats went through a period of distressing dissipation before starting his greatest work. But any drinking half so prolonged as Haydon describes would have worried Brown, have been noticed with shock by the Dilkes, and have been impossible to hide from others in the small neighborhood of Hampstead. The more prosaic fact, though in its own way rather interesting, is that a very little wine went a good way with Keats. He was enormously fond of the taste of claret, a far from intoxicating wine (claret, said Johnson, is "for boys"—"a man would be drowned by it before it made him drunk") ; and Keats thought he was indulging exuberantly when he drank half a bottle of it. "I never drink now above three glasses of wine," he tells George (February 19) , "and never any spirits and water." But he mentions a delightful exception: while he was in town, "Woodhouse took me to his coffee house— and ordered a Bottle of claret—now I like Claret whenever I can have Claret I must drink it"; and he goes on to extol it in ways altogether associative and imaginative, echoing Falstaff's eulogy of sack. He thinks of it as "cool and feverless," associates it with "summer evenings in an arbour," thinks of Bacchus, and dismisses other wines as too heavy and strong. Two months later (April 16) he tells George of another "claret feast," where "We all got a little tipsy—but pleasantly so." A "little" is probably the right description; and the others present consisted of a relatively self-controlled group, including Dilke and Brown. In other words, the grain of truth in Haydon's story may be only that Keats occasionally drank a half bottle or more of claret; and this could seem something of an excess to Keats, however amusing the notion might seem to men of the Regency who could take five or six bottles of port in an evening.

　　Yet the despondency Haydon speaks of was real enough. Around the middle of March, after a rather hollow evening in which he had been trying to get away from himself, he wrote a sonnet, the latter part of which reminds us of the sonnet written a year before at a time when he was also trying to get his bearings ("When I have fears that I may cease to be") :

---

more of the mind, was shaking his head. Had Haydon actually seen it, he would almost certainly have told Keats's other friends, and the story would have become widely known. At the very least he would have mentioned it in his *Diary*.

Why did I laugh tonight? No voice will tell:
　　No God, no Deamon of severe response
Deigns to reply from heaven or from Hell.—
　　Then to my human heart I turn at once—
Heart! thou and I are here sad and alone;
　　Say, wherefore did I laugh? O mortal pain!
O Darkness! Darkness! ever must I moan
　　To question Heaven and Hell and Heart in vain!
Why did I laugh? I know this being's lease
　　My fancy to its utmost blisses spreads:
Yet could I on this very midnight cease,
　　And the world's gaudy ensigns see in shreds.
Verse, fame and Beauty are intense indeed
But Death intenser—Death is Life's high mead.[10]

He was immediately ashamed of it, and put it aside. Whatever his self-doubts and his sense of hollowness and fatigue, his chronic dislike of whining and self-pity was far stronger. He would never have enclosed the poem in his letter to George had not his self-confidence, two or three days later, begun to return:

> I did not intend to have sent you the following sonnet—but look over the two last pages and ask yourselves whether I have not that in me which will well bear the buffets of the world. It will be the best comment on my sonnet; it will show you that it was written with no Agony but that of ignorance; with no thirst of anything but knowledge when pushed to the point though the first steps to it were throug[h] my human passions—they went away, and I wrote with my Mind—and perhaps I must confess a little bit of my heart.

The "last two pages," to which he refers, contain the first really serious and extended speculations to appear in his letters for months.

6

What had happened was that he felt he had begun to think with a little more "disinterestedness." There is no way of accounting for it. On March 18, deciding to try to do something active, he had gone out and played cricket. A ball struck his eye. "This is the second black eye I have had since leaving school." Brown had a little opium, and gave him some of it that evening as a palliative. The next day his feelings, as he tells George (March 19),

---

10 Printed as Keats copied it for his brother (March 19).

were "all asleep from my having slumbered till nearly eleven." His old humor returns as he describes this state of indolence: "if I had teeth of pearl and the breath of lillies I should call it languor— but as I am I must call it Laziness." Perhaps thinking of a dream he had, he goes on:

> Neither Poetry, nor Ambition, nor Love have any alertness of countenance as they pass by me: they seem rather like three figures on a greek vase—a Man and two women—whom no one but myself could distinguish in their disguisement. This is the only happiness; and is a rare instance of advantage in the body overpowering the Mind.

At this moment he stopped. For there was someone at the door with a message from that generous friend of his, William Haslam, who had been so kind to Tom while Keats was on the Scottish tour ("His behaviour to Tom during my absence," Keats had told George, "and since my return has endeared him to me for ever") :

> I have this moment received a note from Haslam in which he expects the death of his Father who has been for some time in a state of insensibility—his mother bears up he says very well—I shall go to town tomorrow to see him. This is the world—. . . Circumstances are like Clouds continually gathering and bursting—While we are laughing the seed of some trouble is put into the wide arable land of events—while we are laughing it sprouts i[t] grows and suddenly bears a poison fruit which we must pluck—Even so we have leisure to reason on the misfortunes of our friends; our own touch us too nearly for words. Very few men have ever arrived at a complete disinterestedness of Mind: very few have been influenced by a pure desire of the benefit of others—in the greater part of the Benefactors [of] & to Humanity some meretricious motive has sullied their greatness—some melodramatic scenery has fa[s]cinated them—From the manner in which I feel Haslam's misfortune I perceive how far I am from any humble standard of disinterestedness.

Speculating for the next few pages about his own remoteness from even a "humble standard of disinterestedness," he touches upon questions that, within only a month, he is to pursue with a new profundity. We can discuss them best in that later context.

For the moment this new activity of thinking, which was soon to prove so therapeutic, at least helped him to regard his own problems as less pressing, and he began to feel more confident than he had for weeks. He went back to *Hyperion* for one final try, wrote most of the fragment that begins Book III, and then decided firmly to give up the whole thing. It had hung over his head long enough. If he could find nothing else to write for which he cared as much, there were other and more certain ways of earning a living. His journal letter to George and Georgiana stops during this time, and we know little of what he was doing except that he made some visits to friends in town. Severn wanted to hang his miniature of Keats at an exhibit in the Royal Academy. Keats tried unsuccessfully to dissuade him: "Will it not hurt you? . . . Even a large picture is lost in that canting place—what a drop of water in the ocean is a Miniature?" If any who happened to notice it "had ever heard of either of us" and knew "what we were and of what years [he] would laugh at the puff of the one and the vanity of the other." Dilke was meanwhile preparing to leave Wentworth Place and move to Westminster in order to be near his boy, who was to attend Westminster school as a day scholar. The Dilkes had been immensely valuable as friends. Their departure would have distressed Keats more than it did (as it was, he himself began to toy with the idea of moving to Westminster) were it not that he knew the Dilkes were renting their place to Mrs. Brawne. The Brawnes may very well have leased their present house until June, at which time many Hampstead houses were rented each year to summer residents; and they were certainly in Wentworth Place by June. But they had probably moved by early May if not before.

On Sunday, April 11, Keats took a walk across Hampstead Heath in the direction of Highgate, where Coleridge was now living. When he came to the lane, he tells George,

> that winds by the side of Lord Mansfield's park I met Mr. Green [Joseph Green] our Demonstrator at Guy's [Hospital] in conversation with Coleridge—I joined them, after enquiring by a look whether it would be agreeable—I walked with him a[t] his alderman-after dinner pace for near two miles I suppose   In those two Miles he broached a thousand things—let me see if I can give you a list— Nightingales, Poetry—on Poetical sensation—Metaphysics—Different genera and species of Dreams—Nightmare—a dream accompanied by a sense of touch—single and double touch—A dream related—First and second consciousness—the difference explained between will and Volition—so m[an]y metaphysicians from a want of smoking the second consciousness—Monsters—the Kraken—Mermaids—southey believes in them—southeys belief too much diluted—A Ghost story— Good morning—I heard his voice as he came toward me—I heard it as he moved away—I had heard it all the interval—if it may be called so. He was civil enough to ask me to call on him at Highgate.

Coleridge himself recalled the meeting long afterward; but, since he himself had done most of the talking, he remembered this slow, two-mile walk, which probably lasted three-quarters of an hour, as lasting only "a minute or so," and his imagination also added a dramatic touch:

> A loose, slack, not well-dressed youth met Mr. —— and myself in a lane near Highgate. —— knew him, and spoke. It was Keats. He was introduced to me, and stayed a minute or so. After he had left us a little way, he came back and said: "Let me carry away the memory, Coleridge, of having pressed your hand!"—"There is death in that hand," I said to ——, when Keats was gone; yet this was, I believe, before the consumption showed itself distinctly.[11]

The meeting with Coleridge probably interested Keats more than his casual tone suggests. We need not go so far as to see in this moment, as so many have been eager to do, a virtual program for the next stage of Keats's writing. Little that Coleridge men-

[11] *Table Talk*, August 14, 1832. Another account is given in a conversation recorded in 1830 by John Frere (printed by E. M. Green, *Cornhill Magazine*, April, 1917; see Lowell, II.210–212). But here also Coleridge, who had as usual been absorbed in his own ideas, had the impression that their meeting had lasted only a few moments. Frere's conversation with him was as follows:

F. You have not read much of Keats, Sir, I think?

C. No, I have not. I have seen two Sonnets which I think showed marks of a great genius had he lived. I have also read a poem with a classical name—I forget what. Poor Keats, I saw him once. Mr. Green, whom you have heard me mention, and I were walking out in these parts, and we were overtaken by a young man of a very striking countenance whom Mr. Green recognized and shook hands with, mentioning my name; I wish Mr. Green had introduced me, for I did not know who it was. He passed on, but in a few moments sprung back and said, "Mr. Coleridge, allow me the honour of shaking your hand."

I was struck by the energy of his manner, and gave him my hand.

He passed on and we stood still looking after him, when Mr. Green said, "Do you know who that is? That is Keats, the poet."

"Heavens!" said I, "when I shook him by the hand there was death!" This was about two years before he died.

F. But what was it?

C. I cannot describe it. There was a heat and a dampness in the hand. To say that his death was caused by the Review is absurd, but at the same time it is impossible adequately to conceive the effect which it must have had on his mind.

It is very well for those who have a place in the world and are independent to talk of these things, they can bear such a blow, so can those who have a strong religious principle; but all men are not born Philosophers, and all men have not those advantages of birth and education.

Poor Keats had not, and it is impossible I say to conceive the effect which such a Review must have had upon him, knowing as he did that he had his way to make in the world by his own exertions, and conscious of the genius within him.

tioned—at least in Keats's summary—had not long been the subject of some of Keats's own speculation (except doubtless those very Coleridgean distinctions between "first and second consciousness" and between "will and volition"). But the talk of a man so eminent, though already widely viewed as a ruin, was bound to impress him in some of its details, and much more in a general, less definable way. Here, after all, was a poet whom he knew to be speculating, whether with success or not, on some of the ultimate problems of philosophy. But Keats had little leisure for the moment to digest this brief meeting. The very next day Haydon, by now almost paranoid from his inability to raise money and his trouble with his eyes, wrote Keats a sharp, heady complaint at never receiving the loan that Keats had been weakly and good-naturedly promising to raise: "Why," said Haydon, "did you hold out such delusive hopes [in] every letter on such slight foundations?—you have led me on step by step, day by day; never telling the exact circumstances; you paralized my exertions in other quarters . . . you should have told me so at once." Shaken, Keats tried to reply calmly the next day:

> When I offered you assistance I thought I had it in my hand; I thought I had nothing to do, but to do. The difficulties I met with arose from the alertness and suspicion of Abbey: especially from the affairs being still in a Lawyer's hand—who has been draining our Property for the last six years of eve[r]y charge he could make. I cannot do two things at once, and thus this affair has stopped my pursuits in every way.

But this jostle with Haydon had touched a precarious equilibrium he was now trying to maintain. As he goes on, he suddenly blurts out what he had thus far been keeping to himself, that he had already lent almost £200 to various friends, and then, in his altogether untypical remark that he is "maim'd again," he reveals how painful these weeks have been in other ways: "I have more than once done with[out] little sums which might have gradually formed a library to my taste—These sums amount together to nearly 200, which I have but a chance of ever being repaid or paid at a very distant period." Why should Haydon be writing so sharply?

> It must be some other disappointment; you seem'd so sure of some important help when I last saw you—now you have maim'd me again; I was whole I had began reading again—when your note

came I was engaged in a Book—I dread as much as a Plague the idle fever of two months more without any fruit. I will walk over the first fine day: then see what aspect you[r] affairs have taken, and if they should continue gloomy walk into the City to Abbey.

That evening he went to a party given by their old family doctor, Solomon Sawrey. Much as he liked Sawrey, he had dreaded the thought of another large social occasion, and had spoken of it as "a rout—a thing I am not at all in love with." But "it was made pleasant by Reynolds being there, and our getting into conversation with one of the most beautiful Girls I ever saw," a statement suggesting (like his thought of moving to Westminster and being near the Dilkes) that he is not exclusively absorbed in Fanny Brawne at this time.

Two days later he went over to the lodgings he and Tom had shared at Bentley's and collected the old letters still there belonging to the three brothers. As he looked through them, he came upon those love letters to Tom of two and a half years before, sent by the fictitious "Amena" and actually written as a prank by Charles Wells. Keats brooded over them angrily, as they brought the dead Tom so vividly to mind. He tells George he will try to write him about them later, meanwhile adding heavily: "I wonder how people exist with all their worries." Brown's nephews were visiting at Wentworth Place now. "They make a bit of a racket—I shall not be sorry when they go" (the next day he was to add that "they have been a toothache to me . . . Their little voices are like wasps stings") . As he goes on, trying to fill his letter with gossip, he suddenly stops: "Shall I treat you with a little extempore?" And he begins to make up some strange lines, which, however else they may arouse interest, do so in at least two ways especially. There is a nightmarish, gruesomely comic effect if he is indeed writing about himself and his brothers (he has just this day been looking over all their old letters, as well as the "Amena" letters to Tom in which Wells had burlesqued Keats's early style) . In the second place, the lines could be found somewhat pertinent to the situation in the strangely beautiful ballad, "La belle dame," that he was to write five days later. They also have, very unexpectedly, something of the ring of Dryden's couplets. Keats was probably already beginning to read Dryden, whom less than three months later he was to use as a tentative model in *Lamia*. These extemporaneous lines are ostensibly an excerpt from a comic nar-

rative poem ("When they were come unto the Faery's Court").
A "fretful princess" travels to this court with an ape, a dwarf, and
a fool. Finding no one at home, she flies into a rage: the dwarf
trembles, the ape stares, the fool does nothing. The princess takes
her whip in order to turn on her three attendants, and "The dwarf
with piteous face began to rhyme" in order to distract her. It has
been suggested that Keats, in these verses, was thinking of Wordsworth as the ape, Coleridge as the fool, and himself as the dwarf.
More probably, as Gittings says, these lines have a family relevance
that George would understand at once: George himself, with his
long jaw, is the ape; the dead Tom is the fool (Tom Fool) who
has fallen asleep; and Keats is the rhyming dwarf. In his rhyme,
the dwarf tells the princess that each of the three had been born
a prince, but each has committed a "crime." He, the dwarf, spent
his early youth in a never-never land, and thoughtlessly used his
wand as a "whipstock" for playing at tops there. As a result, his
"top"—and, in the pun, he also means his head—"has henceforth
slept in faery land." The ape has "Picklock'd a faery's boudoir"—
a possible reference to George's marriage; and the fool "fell a
snoring at a faery's ball" (and if the fool is indeed "Tom Fool,"
he also fell asleep when he thought these fanciful love letters from
"Amena" genuine).

Since he stayed in the next day because of the rain, deferring the
trip to town he was planning to take, he tells George about a dream
he recently had:

> The fifth canto of Dante pleases me more and more—it is the one
> in which he meets with Paulo and Francesca—I had passed many
> days in rather a low state of mind, and in the midst of them I
> dreamt of being in that region of Hell. The dream was one of the
> most delightful enjoyments I ever had in my life—I floated about
> the whirling atmosphere as it is described with a beautiful figure to
> whose lips mine were joined a[s] it seemed for an age—and in the
> midst of all this cold and darkness I was warm—even flowery tree
> tops sprung up and we rested on them sometimes with the lightness
> of a cloud till the wind blew us away again.

He had even tried a sonnet on the dream ("As Hermes once took
to his feathers light").[12] The next day, the rain being over, he

[12] In the dream he is carried

> Not to pure Ida with its snow-cold skies,
>   Nor unto Tempe, where Jove griev'd a day;

went into town, and while there dropped in at one of Henry Aston Baker's new shilling-panoramas in Leicester Square—a panorama with which he was "very much pleased . . . of the ships at the north Pole—with the icebergs, the Mountains, the Bears the Walrus—the seals the Penguins—and a large whale floating back above water." He then went with Rice and Reynolds to Covent Garden and saw the new musical drama, *The Heart of Midlothian* ("dull"). He was also in town during the next two days, visiting Taylor, Mrs. Wylie, and others, hurrying back the afternoon of Monday, April 19, since Taylor, Woodhouse, and Reynolds were coming for dinner with him and Brown. Reynolds had written a parody of Wordsworth's *Peter Bell,* and he now persuaded Keats to write a review for next Sunday's *Examiner.* That evening a heavy storm arose, and the guests could not think of returning to town. They therefore began to play cards around nine o'clock and continued until daylight. Woodhouse, who was unenthusiastic about cards, used the opportunity that night to look through Keats's manuscripts, and the next morning took with him *Hyperion,* the *Eve of St. Agnes,* and the *Eve of St. Mark,* all of which he intended to copy.

There was a certain finality now in having the poems out of the house. The slate was wiped clean. From the all-night session, Keats was naturally fatigued the next day, and "not worth a sixpence." But the morning after that he sat down and wrote the review of Reynolds's parody. Then sometime during the afternoon (Wednesday, April 21), he started the ballad "La belle dame sans merci." Early in the evening he returned to the journal letter to George, jotting down the stanzas he had already written and finishing the poem then and there.[13] He followed it that same night with the remarkable pages on the "Vale of Soul-Making." With

But to that second circle of sad Hell,
  Where in the gust, the whirlwind, and the flaw
Of rain and hail-stones, lovers need not tell
  Their sorrows—pale were the sweet lips I saw,
Pale were the lips I kiss'd, and fair the form
I floated with, about that melancholy storm.

The same day (April 16) Keats also wrote three Spenserian stanzas, as part of his letter, describing Brown as a "melancholy Carle"; for Brown, he says, "is writing some spenserian stanzas against Mrs. [and] Miss Brawne and me; so I shall amuse myself with him a little."

[13] That the latter part of the poem was composed while he was writing this draft in the letter is suggested by the revisions there, especially that in the next-to-last stanza necessary to attain a rhyme (II.96).

this evening begins the extraordinary productivity of Keats's final five months of writing.

7

Like most ideals, that of "disinterestedness" had seemed far easier to attain when it had first caught his imagination than it did as time went on. This thought of the shedding or purification of the self through identification appealed as much as ever to his own empathic nature. But the picture here, as in other ways, was beginning to appear less simple and clear-cut: circumstances generally were proving to be so much more varied and unpredictable, and the human heart so much more capricious and obdurate, than he had suspected. He himself, despite all his talk the year before, had been for months immersed in his own problems, trying every *ad hoc* method he could think of to pull himself into activity; and yet meanwhile (as he was suddenly reminded by the news on March 19 that Haslam's father was dying) in the "wide arable land of events" difficulties for everyone and everything were constantly sprouting and coming to harvest, of all of which he himself had been oblivious. "I perceive how far I am from any humble standard of disinterestedness."

Moreover, only a year before, that "eternal fierce destruction" whereby one thing feeds on another, which shocks the heart when we look "too far into the sea," could seem somewhat more alien to the nature of life and separable from it in our thinking. But the moments were now increasing when much of what we include in the word "evil" seemed inextricably knit into the very nature of that same finitude which also permits a finite creature to exist at all: death, the transitoriness in other ways of what we love, the sheer fact that we cannot proceed in one direction without giving up the opportunity to proceed in others, and that the capacity to enjoy the present moment is as limited and elusive as the present itself. So also with the sharp eager concentration of the living creature as, in its brief finitude, it hurries instinctively to its purposes, enmeshed in activity from the moment of its birth: inevitably its focus is limited and distorted. In such a compelling, instinctive context, we certainly need have no fear that moral ideals of complete selflessness will neutralize humanity. The danger is all the other way. The heart's inability to reach such a point is so patent that any ideal of "disinterestedness," as he goes on to say (March 19), ought to be

> carried to its highest pitch, as there is no fear of its ever injuring society—which it would do I fear pushed to an extremity—For in wild nature the Hawk would loose his Breakfast of Robins and the Robin his of Worms The Lion must starve as well as the swallow— The greater part of Men make their way with the same instinctiveness, the same unwandering eye from their purposes, the same animal eagerness as the Hawk—The Hawk wants a Mate, so does the Man —look at them both they set about it and procure on[e] in the same manner—They want both a nest and they both set about one in the same manner—they get their food in the same manner—The noble animal Man for his amusement smokes his pipe—the Hawk balances about the Clouds—that is the only difference of their leisures. This it is that makes the Amusement of Life—to a speculative Mind. I go among the F[ie]lds and catch a glimpse of a stoat or a fieldmouse peeping out of the withered grass—the creature hath a purpose and its eyes are bright with it.

Yet in the midst of this charged welter of instinctive life (which it is very much the province of poetry to grasp and portray) we do find instances of the strange and precious human capacity to grow toward "disinterestedness"—the self-corrective, self-purifying capacity to extend one's purpose and identity:

> I go amongst the buildings of a city and I see a Man hurrying along—to what? The Creature has a purpose and his eyes are bright with it. But then as Wordsworth says, "we have all one human heart"—there is an ellectric fire in human nature tending to purify —so that among these human creature[s] there is continu[a]lly some birth of new heroism—The pity is that we must wonder at it: as we should at finding a pearl in rubbish.

No doubt "thousands of people never heard of have had hearts complete[l]y disinterested." He himself thinks at once of "Socrates and Jesus—their Histories evince it." Whatever may have been done by those who have "revised" the spirit of Jesus into system (two weeks before, Keats had told George that he hoped soon to study church history, and had thought of starting on the five-volume *History of the Church of Christ,* by Joseph and Isaac Milner), "yet through all this I see his splendour." Keats, for his own part, is remote indeed from those disinterested "thousands" (a distinction movingly developed four or five months later in the

Fall of Hyperion, I.154ff) .[14] In his own efforts to understand, in
this world of "uncertainties, Mysteries, doubts,"

> I myself am pursueing the same instinctive course as the veriest hu-
> man animal you can think of—I am however young writing at ran-
> dom—straining at particles of light in the midst of a great darkness—
> without knowing the bearing of any one assertion of any one opin-
> ion. Yet may I not in this be free from sin?

As he speculates, he finds himself adding a further nuance to two
"contraries" counterpointed with each other ever since those
weeks at Oxford, a year and a half ago, when he had first come
upon the ideal of "disinterestedness": one, the sympathetic grasp
of the instinctive "energies" of life in ourselves and every sort of
creature about us (whether those energies and purposes are "erro-
neous" or not), the dramatic or expressive rendering of which is
the obvious first aim of poetry; and the other, that freedom of "disinterestedness" which he associates with philosophy:

> May there not be superior beings amused with any graceful,
> though instinctive attitude my mind m[a]y fall into, as I am enter-
> tained with the alertness of a Stoat or the anxiety of a Deer? Though
> a quarrel in the Streets is a thing to be hated, the energies displayed
> in it are fine; the commonest Man shows a grace in his quarrel—By a
> superior being our reasoning[s] may take the same tone—though
> erroneous they may be fine—This is the very thing in which consists
> poetry; and if so it is not so fine a thing as philosophy—For the same
> reason that an eagle is not so fine a thing as a truth—Give me this
> credit—Do you not think I strive—to know myself? Give me this
> credit, and you will not think that on my own accou[n]t I repeat
> Milton's lines
>
>> "How charming is divine Philosophy
>> Not harsh and crabbed as dull fools suppose
>> But musical as is Apollo's lute."

The last passage especially is crucial. The speculation that "poetry
is not so fine a thing as philosophy" is an intrinsic part of the next
development of Keats's thought. It reflects the growing conviction
of one of the most consummate stylists in the history of poetry that
the impassioned expression of concrete reality, however necessary
in poetry, is not by itself enough—that poetry must justify itself
on still broader grounds.

For the moment, after quoting Milton's lines about philosophy,
he goes on to emphasize that he has not cited them because they

14 See below, Chapter XXI, section 10.

apply to himself—he is still too far from being a philosopher:
"No—no[t] for myself—feeling grateful as I do to have got into a
state of mind to relish them properly." Given his own empirical
nature, working as he does by "straining at particles of light," for
him "nothing ever becomes real till it is experienced—Even a
Proverb is no proverb to you till your Life has illustrated it."

8

Now, a month later (April 21), he takes up the thought again.
Lonely, and wondering rather helplessly what George and Georgiana are doing (he still has not heard from them and is beginning
to worry more with every week), he has started on William Robertson's four-volume *History of America,* parts of which he had
already read at Enfield. At the same time he has also been reading
Voltaire's five-volume *Siècle de Louis XIV.* "It is like walking
arm and arm between Pizarro and the great-little Monarch." And
comparing the court of Louis XIV with what had been eulogized
for a half century as a simple and more healthful life—that of the
Indians in Central and South America, "where men might seem
to inherit quiet of Mind from unsophisticated senses"—Keats feels
that in each case the disappointments, difficulties, frustrations, appear at first glance to balance themselves out. If the amenities of
civilization relieve us in some ways, we also encounter "a fresh set
of annoyances" that prove quite as much a hurdle to happiness.
There is, to begin with, the inescapable fact of our finitude:

> The whole appears to resolve into this—that Man is originally "a
> poor forked creature" subject to the same mischances as the beasts of
> the forest, destined to hardships and disquietude of some kind or
> other. If he improves by degrees his bodily accomodations and com-
> forts—at each stage, at each a[s]cent there are waiting for him a fresh
> set of annoyances—he is mortal and there is still a heaven with its
> Stars abov[e] his head.

Then there were also the implications of that commonplace on
which, as he had told George back in December, he was beginning
to reflect once again:

> My thoughts have turned lately this way—The more we know the
> more inadequacy we discover in the world to satisfy us—this is an
> old observation; but I have made up my Mind never to take any
> thing for granted—but even to examine the truth of the commonest
> proverbs.

One immediate result of his thoughts' having "turned lately this way" had been that rondeau he had written a day or two later on "Fancy" ("Pleasure never is at home"). Despite the dancing rhythm, the implied theme was nothing less than that described by Johnson as "the hunger of imagination which prays incessantly upon life"—a hunger that, in search of "supplemental satisfactions" to fatten or give meaning to the present, is always jumping ahead to the future or back to the past or over to other absent elements, images, or abstractions (equally ductile to the heart's wish simply because they are absent and thus screened from the more pressing and undeniable pains of what is empirically and sharply present).

Of course those recombinations or redistillations that we call "ideals," as contrasted with the consecutive step-by-step sequence of brute sensory experience, can turn into complete escape from fact. Yet at the same time the very process of selection and re-ordering of thought into ideals is by definition the means by which we fulfill our nature as human beings—the means by which we can try to understand reality, try to come to terms with it, and bring to it any possible "greeting of the Spirit." To be sure, everything, it can be said, depends on what is being selected, and how, and in what combination. We all agree abstractly on the premise and on the end. The real problem comes in the practical, *ad hoc* selections that are being made in our feelings every hour; the area of debatability there is as wide as life itself; and we are thus back again to the "Burden of the mystery," to the dark passages, where "we see not the ballance of good and evil."

In any case, in whatever way the capacity for idealization is used, the very act of idealizing heightens our sense of "inadequacy" when the inevitable "journey homeward" to fact begins—above all to the facts inherent in our finite nature. The thought naturally intrigues Keats most as it applies to art (the whole tantalizing, elusively shifting problem of which becomes so important a concern in all his writing during the four or five months to come). Art exercises and feeds capacities that can be used in so many different directions (hence the remark he had made a month before: poetry, if all that he had been saying about it at that moment was true, "is not so fine a thing as philosophy"). Considering all this, the most open question possible is that of the enormously varying uses of the human imagination, and the balance of the gains and limitations in its various functions. The odes were to explore both the opportunities and the limitations with a new profundity and delicacy; *Lamia,* immediately afterwards, was to concentrate more on the limitations with briskness and even some humor; and the *Fall of Hyperion* was again to consider both, and in a way that opened still further questions.

9

It was at this very moment, when the next stage of Keats's development was about to start, that he wrote the ballad "La belle dame sans merci" on April 21. It was only a single afternoon's or an early evening's episode, though the stanzas have haunted readers and poets for a century and a half. Of course the poem is altogether remote from anything like a program, even in miniature, of his thinking now, in the sense that so many of his earlier poems had been. Instead it is a lyrical distillation of diverse feelings, and at a troubled though richly thoughtful moment. It is, in short, a by-product, as far greater art than this timeless short ballad often tends to be: a by-product that could not have existed without a large reservoir of concern and preoccupation, though at the same time it also necessitated an effective disengagement from that concern. The disengagement comes partly through the use of still another new meter (new, that is, for Keats, habituated as he himself was to the richer potentialities of the pentameter line), and partly through the typical romantic association of the Middle Ages with clean simplicity and brevity. Any number of things from the life of Keats, as also from his reading, may be summoned up as a means of helping, embarrassing, or replacing our receptivity to the poem itself. For a good poem by definition distills a great deal.[15]

Whatever else can be said of the ballad, one essential element in it is the crucial if silent fact of hesitation or pause of judgment. The meeting of the knight-at-arms—now so "woe-begone"—with "la belle dame" puts in another setting one of those symbolic pair-

---

15 Literary sources of the more tangential sort, phrasal and otherwise, range all the way from the title of the medieval French poem, by Alain Chartier, which Keats takes for his title, through Spenser, William Browne (whose refrain "Let no birds sing" is echoed in Keats's "And no birds sing") and Burton's *Anatomy of Melancholy,* to Keats's own contemporaries Wordsworth, Coleridge, and Peacock. The principal source is Spenser: the seduction of the Red Cross Knight by Duessa in the *Faerie Queene* and Arthur's vision (I.ii and I.ix), combined with details from the story of Cymochles and Phaedria (II.vi) and that of the false Florimel (III–IV).

ings of mortal and immortal that are so familiar in Keats after
Endymion, and that soon begin to take diverse forms in Psyche, the
Grecian urn, Lamia, and Moneta in the *Fall of Hyperion.* (Even
the "Ode to a Nightingale"—in one of its many aspects—makes
use of such a pairing, through the apostrophe to the bird near the
end; and so, for that matter, does the "Ode on Melancholy," with
its "sovran shrine" hung with trophies from the mortal world.)
But in this ballad all clues to ready judgment are withheld, though
perhaps unintended clues can be detected if we look ahead to his
other writing, especially *Lamia* and the revised *Hyperion.* True
enough, this knight-at-arms is now forlorn in an autumnal world,
and the implications of this are increased by the most jarring of
the needless changes that Keats later made (apparently at the suggestion of Hunt), where the "knight-at-arms" is called "wretched
wight": [16]

> O what can ail thee, knight-at-arms,
>   Alone and palely loitering?
> The sedge has wither'd from the lake,
>   And no birds sing.
>
> O what can ail thee, knight-at-arms,
>   So haggard, and so woe-begone?
> The squirrel's granary is full,
>   And the harvest's done.
>
> I see a lily on thy brow,
>   With anguish moist and fever dew,
> And on thy cheeks a fading rose
>   Fast withereth too.

But despite the forlorn situation of the knight, the real question is
left altogether open. Was it indeed a Circelike figure that deliberately seduced the knight-at-arms into a moment of delusive happiness; or was it not that the knight fell in love with her at once,
and then persisted in trying to establish complete contact with
something not wholly human? She herself would merely look
"sidelong" after he had put her next to him on his steed, and sing

[16] The revisions were made when Keats was far too ill to have any confidence at
all in his own judgment (early May, 1820); and then the revised poem was printed
by Hunt in the *Indicator* (May 10, 1820). One can only suppose that Hunt—possibly Woodhouse—thought, with myopic good-will, that the magic, dreamlike quality
of the poem would be considered "sentimental" and wished him to take a less am-
biguous stand.

"A faery's song" that he could not understand. Even as far as the reciprocation of his love is concerned, it was he himself who interpreted her as responding, though in a language far from definite. ("And sure in language strange she said / I love thee true.") The food she finds for him—roots, "honey wild and manna dew"—is meant neither to delude him nor to starve him by preventing him from taking other food. However inadequate it is for him, it is appropriate enough to her, and the only food she is able to provide. There is another complicating touch in the mention of this mysterious figure (about which we think again when we come to *Lamia*, and, just before it, that strange, tired "Ode on Indolence," where Keats, of all the figures that pass before him that he cannot reach, speaks of that which he loves most, "my demon Poesy"). After the knight has come to her grot, she weeps:

> She took me to her elfin grot
>   And there she wept and sigh'd full sore,
> And there I shut her wild wild eyes
>   With kisses four.

Keats's only comment on the poem, written after he had finished it as a part of his letter to George, is deliberately whimsical, and refers to this stanza (where actually he simply follows ballad convention in naming a specific number of kisses) :

> Why four kisses—you will say—why four because I wish to restrain the headlong impetuosity of my Muse—she would have fain said "score" without hurting the rhyme—but we must temper the Imagination as the Critics say with Judgment. I was obliged to choose an even number that both eyes might have fair play: and to speak truly I think two a piece quite sufficient—Suppose I had said seven; there would have been three and a half a piece—a very awkward affair.

Finally, though the ultimate impossibility of contact between the human and this elusive, only half-human figure is premised throughout, no suggestion that she is sinister is made except through the subjective response of the knight's own imagination. He himself does not actually witness the "horrid warning" of starvation that this attempted union may bring. That anticipation, which may be genuine or primarily the expression of his own uneasiness, has come to him only in a dream—a dream that has also banished "la belle dame." And if the dream is now proving to be prophetic, it is again through his own divided nature, his own act, his persistence in continuing to loiter on the cold hillside even though the autumn is about to become winter:

> I saw pale Kings, and Princes too,
>   Pale warriors, death pale were they all;
> They cried, La belle dame sans merci
>   Hath thee in thrall.
>
> I saw their starv'd lips in the gloam
>   With horrid warning gapèd wide,
> And I awoke and found me here
>   On the cold hill's side.
>
> And this is why I sojourn here
>   Alone and palely loitering;
> Though the sedge is withered from the Lake
>   And no birds sing.

The ballad was to take another form when Keats wrote *Lamia*. But if we apply our reading of *Lamia* to the ballad, our hindsight can oversimplify. For *Lamia* was written three months later with needs in mind that further specialize only some of those needs that apply now to "La belle dame." In comparison, "La belle dame" is less urgent and more open.

10

Keats returns in his letter, the same evening that he wrote "La belle dame," to the "fresh set of annoyances" that touch home to us as we feel further the "inadequacy" of things in the light of any ideal. The thought strikes him parenthetically: if the heart ever did receive its wish completely and at the same time were changed so that it could adjust to that fulfillment, and relish it intensely for long periods, what a fearful thing death would be:

> But in truth I do not at all believe in this sort of perfectibility—the nature of the world will not admit of it—the inhabitants of the world will correspond to itself—Let the fish philosophise the ice away from the Rivers in winter time and they shall be at continual play in the tepid delight of summer. Look at the Poles and at the sands of Africa, Whirlpools and volcanoes. Let men exterminate them and I will say that they may arrive at earthly Happiness—The point at which Man may arrive is as far as the paralel state inanimate nature and no further—For instance suppose a rose to have sen-

sation, it blooms on a beautiful morning it enjoys itself—but there comes a cold wind, a hot sun—it cannot escape it, it cannot destroy its annoyances—they are as native to the world as itself; no more can man be happy in spite, the world[l]y elements will prey upon his nature.

The phrase that catches us most, when we look back to these weeks from the vantage point of the poetry that is yet to be written, is that the "annoyances," to use Keats's gentle word here, anything encounters "are as native to the world as itself"—are as native to the process of things as the object or person that itself is coming into existence or passing through it, working through as well as against the finitude that permits it to become concrete if transitory.

The thought of the complexities, the repeated obstacles to any continued happiness, the uncertainties, the limitations, throws us back to the "common cognomen of this world" as a "vale of tears." From this "vale" it is assumed by the more hopeful that "we are to be redeemed by a certain arbitrary interposition of God and taken to Heaven." But surely this is a "circumscribed" notion. This consolation, Keats feels, not only disregards but also contradicts the nature of that process through which we hourly acquire our experience. Could we not rephrase it?—

> Call the world if you Please "The vale of Soul-making" Then you will find out the use of the world (I am speaking now in the highest terms for human nature admitting it to be immortal which I will here take for granted for the purpose of showing a thought which has struck me concerning it) I say *"Soul making"* Soul as distinguished from an Intelligence—There may be intelligences or sparks of the divinity in millions—but they are not Souls till they acquire identities, till each one is personally itself. I[n]telligences are atoms of perception—they know and they see and they are pure, in short they are God—How then are Souls to be made? How then are these sparks which are God to have identity given them—so as ever to possess a bliss peculiar to each ones individual existence? How, but by the medium of a world like this? This point I sincerely wish to consider because I think it a grander system of salvation than the [Christian] religion—or rather it is a system of Spirit-creation—This is effected by three grand materials acting the one upon the other for a series of years—There three Materials are the *Intelligence*—the *human heart* (as distinguished from intelligence or Mind) and the *World* or *Elemental space* suited for the proper action of *Mind and*

Heart on each other for the purpose of forming the *Soul* or *Intelligence destined to possess the sense of Identity.*

He then starts all over. He is not expressing very well "what I but dimly perceive":

yet I think I perceive it—that you may judge the more clearly I will put it in the most homely form possible—I will call the *world* a School instituted for the purpose of teaching little children to read —I will call the *human heart* the *horn Book* used in that School— and I will call the *Child able to read, the Soul* made from that *school* and its *hornbook*. Do you not see how necessary a World of Pains and troubles is to school an Intelligence and make it a soul? A place where the heart must feel and suffer in a thousand diverse ways! Not merely is the Heart a Hornbook, It is the Minds Bible, it is the Minds experience, it is the teat from which the Mind or intelligence sucks its identity—As various as the Lives of Men are—so various become their souls, and thus does God make individual beings, Souls, Identical Souls of the sparks of his own essence—This appears to me a faint sketch of a system of Salvation which does not affront our reason and humanity.

He is altogether uncertain as he writes this. He is trying to clear his way to truth in a manner that is admittedly that of "the veriest human animal you can think of . . . Straining at particles in the midst of a wide darkness." The phrase "Spirit-creation" catches his mind. He wonders whether much that the Zoroastrians and Hindus, as well as the Christians, have evolved does not include premises analogous to a "System of Soul-making."

The evening of Wednesday, April 21, is becoming very late. "La belle dame" and all that he is trying to say now have been crowded into it. He wonders whether he has been writing too impulsively. He wants to get his bearings. He will try to put George and Georgiana, he says,

in the place where I began in this series of thoughts—I mean, I began by seeing how man was formed by circumstances—and what are circumstances?—but touchstones of his heart—? and what are touchstones?—but proovings of his heart? and what are proovings of his heart but fortifiers or alterers of his nature? and what is his altered nature but his soul?—and what was his soul before it came into the world and had these proovings and alterations and perfectionings?— An intelligence—without Identity—and how is this Identity to be made? Through the medium of the Heart. And how is the heart to become this Medium but in a world of Circumstances?

He has really nothing more to say at the moment. "There now I think what with Poetry and Theology you may thank your Stars that my pen is not very long winded."

11

Within another nine days, in addition to some shorter poems,[17] he has finished the first of the great odes, the "Ode to Psyche," and then, in another day or two, the "Ode to a Nightingale." By the middle of May he has completed two other odes, the "Grecian Urn" and "Melancholy." The productivity of the three and a half weeks that begin on April 21 is difficult to parallel in the career of any modern writer. Yet to Keats it was not even a new beginning. It was rather a matter of becoming more alive in preparation for the next beginning.

Almost at once he began feeling better than he had for months. His young sister had been hoping that he might pick up some plants at the Tottenham nursery so that she could start a little garden at Walthamstow. He had been neglecting to do it. But on May 1 he writes her in high spirits that he will get her some "seasonable plants" at once. The warm weather was returning. "O there is nothing like fine weather, and health, and Books, and a fine country, and a contented Mind, and Diligent habit of reading and thinking, and an amulet against the ennui." As he writes (he has just finished the "Ode to Psyche," and he has probably written the "Ode to a Nightingale") , he falls into exuberant doggerel:

> Two or three Posies
> With two or three simples
> Two or three Noses
> With two or th[r]ee pimples—
> Two or three wise men
> And two or three ninny's
> Two or three purses
> And two or three guineas
> Two or three raps
> At two or three doors
> Two or three naps
> Of two or three hours—

[17] "To Sleep," the two sonnets "on Fame," and "If by dull rhymes," one or two of which may have been written before. He also on April 21 enclosed, or more probably wrote extemporaneously in the letter to George, the short-lined "Chorus of Fairies," a series of near-nonsense verses composed between "La belle dame" and the thoughtful speculations that follow.

So the doggerel continues for another sixteen lines; and he ends, on this threshold of what the next four months were to bring:

Good bye I've an appoantment—can't stop pon word—good bye —now dont get up—open the door myself—go-o-od bye—see ye Monday.

The Odes of April and May, 1819

✻╼⊛╼✻╼⊛╼✻╼⊛╼✻╼⊛╼✻╼⊛╼✻╼⊛╼✻╼⊛╼✻╼⊛╼✻╼⊛╼✻╼⊛╼✻╼⊛╼✻╼⊛╼✻╼⊛

No SINGLE interpretation of any of the odes—still less of the odes as a group—satisfies anyone except the interpreter. Too many different elements converge. This, of course, is one explanation for their success, as it is for the success of any great work of art. That commonplace is one of those truths of which, as Johnson said, though we may not need to be informed, we need to be reminded. For, while few of us deny it in principle, most of us tend to betray it in practice. To seek relief in particular details is inevitable to a finite being. In reading a poem, in contemplating any work of art, we may genuinely feel the active coalescence of the diverse. But when we come to speak about it, we have to proceed consecutively: one thing has to be mentioned before another; in the process of noticing them individually, we find some considerations striking us more than others, if only because in our own phrasing of them we begin to tap essential concerns within ourselves; and we are led by the momentum of our own cooperating eloquence to narrow our interpretation. (A great work, of course, not only permits but invites that eager subjective response to different parts of it.) Moreover, the existence of previous commentary further specializes our attitude if we feel called upon to contribute our mite. For in the heat of debate, or even in the honest desire to return to the amplitude of the work of art, our recoil from what we consider to be partial, single-minded interpretations encourages us to champion those details that we feel were overlooked, and to contradict or minimize considerations that we might otherwise have wished only to supplement.

Whatever else we may say of the odes of late April and May, 1819, we do them little justice unless we also see them—not wholly, but partly—in the mainstream of Keats's thought as it had begun to clarify itself in the letter to Reynolds (May 3, 1818) about the "Chamber of Maiden-Thought." He was now, after a difficult but fertile year, going back to that sonnet-length "Ode to Maia" which he had written on the previous May Day—the fragment that he had said he would finish "all in good time." In his long journal letter to George and Georgiana in America, begun back in February, he wrote (April 30), as this new May Day, the final one of his active career, approached:

> The following Poem—the last I have written is the first and the only one with which I have taken even moderate pains—I have for the most part dash'd of[f] my lines in a hurry—This I have done leisurely—I think it reads the more richly for it and will I hope encourage me to write other thing[s] in even a more peaceable and healthy spirit.

2

The sixty-seven lines of the new poem, an "Ode to Psyche," have always puzzled readers. It is justly felt that the ode may be something of a prototype for the others that follow it within the next month—that Keats was trying to do something in this first ode that he develops or redirects in the later ones. But, finding the poem so elusive, we return to it only after we know the others far better. If we had hoped to use them as keys, we discover they do not quite fit the lock. Meanwhile they have given us a standard hard to equal. Hence we either feel a disappointment about the "Ode to Psyche" or else, remembering the care Keats supposedly gave it, we once more put the poem aside for future consideration.

Our puzzlement extends to technical details, partly again because we know that he worked on the poem in a more "leisurely" way than on most of his earlier poetry. The later odes were probably written much more rapidly (at least the first draft of the "Ode to a Nightingale" was completed in one morning); but the structure of the "Ode to Psyche" seems much less firm. Moreover, from *Hyperion* on, sureness of phrase had become habitual to him, even in his most rapid writing. Yet in the opening stanzas of this new ode (and to some extent in the third book of *Hyperion*, on which he had been recently working) we encounter banalities of diction that carry us back to *Endymion:* "Fainting with surprise"; "tender eye-dawn of aurorean love"; or, until it was later changed, "O Bloomiest." A few of them come from Mary Tighe's *Psyche* (1805), which he had read as a youth, and only four months ago he mentioned to George: "Mrs. Tighe and Beattie once delighted me—now I see through them and can find nothing in them—or weakness." That he was relatively uncritical, as such phrases came back to his mind, suggests how preoccupied he was, in these first stanzas, with something else.

On what part or aspect of the poem, then, were the new "pains" and "leisure" bestowed? He probably refers to the general effort (which is partly technical) to find some way shorter than narrative, or dramatic tragedy, of capturing the drama of that "greeting of the Spirit" and its object about which he had once written to Benjamin Bailey. The "march of intellect" since the age of Milton had disclosed or created new complexities and doubts that embarrassed the confidence and completeness of this "greeting." Whether one liked it or not, poetry—if it was to retain its honesty—would have to become more inward. This at least had been his feeling exactly a year before. For on the one hand was the majestic confidence of classical and Renaissance poetry—poetry that rested on "seeming sure" points of reasoning; and on the other hand were the growing uncertainties, the impact of further knowledge, that he had suggested in his image of the darkening "Chamber of Maiden-Thought," the doors of which are gradually opening but all leading to dark passages ("We see not the ballance of good and evil. . . . *We* are now in that state"). Here Wordsworth, though he may have "martyred" himself in the process and been forced to surrender epic grandeur by circumscribing his effort, had been honest before this demand; "and it seems to me that his Genius is explorative of those dark Passages. Now if we live, and go on thinking, we too shall explore them."

The challenge ahead included the further exploration of the human psyche as it tries to come to terms with life, and especially with increasing knowledge. Reading again about the goddess Psyche in Lemprière, and then turning directly from Lemprière to Apuleius and finding that Psyche was made a goddess only after the Augustan age—only after the era of "Olympus' [now] faded hierarchy" was already coming to an end—he was struck by the relevance of this "late" deity to what seemed to him now the proper object of poetry and of his own efforts. He goes on, in his letter to George, before copying the new ode:

> You must recollect that Psyche was not embodied as a goddess before the time of Apulieus the Platonist who lived afteir the A[u]gus-

tan age, and consequently the Goddess was never worshipped or sacrificed to with any of the ancient fervour—and perhaps never
thought of in the old religion—I am more orthodox tha[n] to let a
he[a]then Goddess be so neglected.

The story of Psyche and Cupid, which Keats read in William
Adlington's translation (1566) of Apuleius (chapter 22), also had
a potential moral that caught his imagination and, to some extent,
merged with the general thought of the poem. Psyche, the youngest and most beautiful of three princesses, arouses the jealousy of
Venus, who then commands her son Cupid—or Eros—to force
Psyche to fall in love with the "most poore, most crooked, and the
most vile" creature he can find. Meanwhile, all of Psyche's admirers, owing to the intervention of Venus, withdraw. Her bewildered
father consults the oracle of Apollo, and is told to clothe her in
mourning and leave her on a barren rock: she will in time be wed
by a serpent. Seeing no alternative, the unhappy Psyche assents.
"Then they brought her to the appointed rocks of the high hill
. . . and so departed. The Torches and lights were put out." At
length, however, the gentle Zephyrus carries the weeping Psyche
"downe into a deepe valley," where she lies "sweetly couched . . .
as in a bed of sweet and fragrant flowers" (some of Adlington's
phrases and images reappear in the poem). Rested, she wanders for
a while and then comes to a palace. A voice tells her it is the palace
of her husband. She is waited on by invisible servants. At night
her unknown husband comes; and so the days pass.

What has happened, of course, is that Love—hitherto mischie-
vous and vagrant—has been won over to the mind or soul: Eros or
Cupid, sent to make Psyche infatuated with the vilest and "most
crooked" of objects, has himself fallen in love with her. But he
can meet her only secretly and in the dark. Never seeing her husband, the curious Psyche pines with uncertainty. Her sisters, whom
she is allowed to visit, persuade her that her husband is indeed the
serpent predicted by Apollo's oracle. Following their advice, she
hides a burning oil lamp, then brings it out as soon as her husband
is asleep, and prepares to cut off his head with a razor. But seeing
the form of Cupid, she falls trembling to her knees and hides her
razor. A drop of burning oil falls from the lamp onto the shoulder
of the god; he awakens, wounded with the burn, and flees. She tries
to follow. Her wanderings are many and painful (one of them
takes her to the precarious "ridge" of a "mountain"—echoed in

Keats's phrase, "the wild-ridgèd mountains"). In time Cupid himself, healed of his wound, escapes through "a window of the chamber where hee was inclosed" and joins Psyche. Jupiter, at Cupid's petition, sanctions the marriage and makes Psyche immortal; and Love may thus be said to have rescued the mind.

3

A "greeting of the Spirit" and its object was still possible, in other words—and a greeting by the spirit of something not fully known or explored in that earlier age of what Keats now calls "happy pieties." With a sort of credo in mind—and so many of his poems had consisted of credos—he tried to face the subject directly: he addressed the poem to Psyche herself.

The latter, climactic part of the new poem was to be one more assertion of intention, like "Sleep and Poetry," the sonnet "On Sitting Down to Read *King Lear* Once Again," or the "Lines on Seeing a Lock of Milton's Hair." But the ode, he plainly hoped, would consist of more than the credo, the statement of intention: it was to have a more objective and if possible a more nearly dramatic structure. The new leisure and "pains" may well have included his effort to follow up the story of Psyche and Cupid in Apuleius, and then to think over its possible use. But the care was also technical in the strict sense. Reverting to the lyric after the narrative—or quasi-epic—*Hyperion,* which had not succeeded, he was attempting, as we have seen, to circumvent the sonnet (now so habitual to him) and to develop a longer, more flexible form.

With an uncertainty that extends for almost half the poem, he begins. Love (Eros or Cupid) could approach Psyche—as the myth went—only in darkness. But the poet (though it may have been merely a dream) now sees the two together in daylight. Could the sight have been genuine, and have come to him through a new understanding and through "awaken'd eyes"? The question, familiar in the earlier poems, is now basic in almost all the odes, especially the "Nightingale," "Indolence," and, in another way, the "Grecian Urn":

> O Goddess! hear these tuneless numbers, wrung
>   By sweet enforcement and remembrance dear,
> And pardon that thy secrets should be sung
>   Even into thine own soft-conchèd ear:

> Surely I dreamt to-day, or did I see
>   The wingèd Psyche with awaken'd eyes?
> I wander'd in a forest thoughtlessly,
>   And, on the sudden, fainting with surprise,
> Saw two fair creatures, couchèd side by side.

The figures, like those on the Grecian urn, are somewhat apart: "Their lips touch'd not, but had not bade adieu." The poet could hardly help recognizing Cupid. His own situation is analogous (however far he is from being a god) : he himself has been vagrant, if only through ignorance; he has been won over to the mind; he is ready to build a palace for this new subject, this new demand of conscience, as Cupid (in the tale by Apuleius) built one for Psyche. But he is so eager to get on to that resolve that the quick, feigned hesitation about the other figure is expressed in the banal phrasing of his early poems ("O happy, happy dove"), and the rapid transition, the acknowledgment, is effected in three words of mere exclamation:

> The wingèd boy I knew;
> But who wast thou, O happy, happy dove?
> His Psyche true!

The twenty-three lines thus far consist of little more than filler: they are there to provide a setting. Three years before, in his primitive attempt at Guy's Hospital to write the "Specimen of an Induction," he had found descriptive setting inevitably usurping his attention; and after the setting, the poem then dwindled. Trying to overcome this temptation in his youthful second attempt at narrative, "Calidore," he had made his hero—after the descriptive opening—dart ludicrously across the lake to a castle and then "leap along" the halls. The present quick recognition and bow, "His Psyche true!" derives from that effort. The "pains" bestowed on the "Ode to Psyche" affect the first third of it only in so far as they helped to keep down the sheer length of the preface, the setting. Such prefaces are dropped in the next three odes: setting is dispensed with, or merely implied. The modern, respectful attitude toward this ode is deserved. But the itch for novelty has encouraged a few critics to suggest that the poem, in some dark but fundamental way, has more to it as a whole than do the later odes. Among the many interests of the ode, the principal one is that, through writing it, Keats learned better how to proceed.

With the setting condensed to twenty-three lines, he is now able to turn to what he wants to say. The real preface to the long, expanded sentence that makes up the close of the ode is put in the two next stanzas. Those two stanzas are parallel in form and wording, but somewhat antithetic in emphasis. The first stresses the nonacknowledgment thus far of this "latest born" yet "loveliest" among all "Olympus' faded hierarchy." This personification of the mind, of human understanding, far exceeds those simpler conceptions in the Olympian hierarchy, Diana and Venus:

> Fairer than these, though temple thou hast none,
>   Nor altar heap'd with flowers;
> Nor virgin-choir to make delicious moan
>   Upon the midnight hours;
> No voice, no lute, no pipe, no incense sweet
>   From chain-swung censer teeming;
> No shrine, no grove, no oracle, no heat
>   Of pale-mouth'd prophet dreaming.

The catalogue, however lyrically chanted, is deprecatory, by its very excess, and is put with mock nostalgia. It is only the externals, the ceremonial trappings, that have been denied Psyche because she came too late. (Perhaps unconsciously he remembers and echoes the phrases about the pagan deities in Milton's "On the Morning of Christ's Nativity.") Used in this way, the list permits the rhetoric of the following stanza: the catalogue of apparatus—which would have seemed sentimental and hyperbolic had it appeared there for the first time—can now be repeated as an answering assertion. Writing hastily—not even noticing when he copied out the poem for George that he begins the stanza "O Bloomiest! though too late for antique vows"—he continues, in what is the finished draft:

> O brightest! though too late for antique vows,
>   Too, too late for the fond believing lyre,
> When holy were the haunted forest boughs,
>   Holy the air, the water, and the fire.

The regret, though genuine, is not complete. The "pieties" by which the elements were regarded as holy were indeed "happy pieties"; and we think ahead to the "happiness" of the nightingale and the "happy" boughs and figures on the Grecian urn. But the word "fond," in "fond believing lyre," also includes the older meaning of "foolish." However far removed the present may be from that era of simple, happy belief, he can now see ("by my own

eyes inspired"—the insight has to be self-won), among the faint
shadows of the Olympians, the living, fluttering movement of the
wings of Psyche, who was traditionally represented by the butter-
fly:

> Yet even in these days so far retir'd
>   From happy pieties, thy lucent fans,
>   Fluttering among the faint Olympians,
> I see, and sing, by my own eyes inspired.
> So let me be thy choir, and make a moan
>   Upon the midnight hours;
> Thy voice, thy lute, thy pipe, thy incense sweet
>   From swingèd censer teeming;
> Thy shrine, thy grove, thy oracle, thy heat
>   Of pale-mouth'd prophet dreaming.

4

The essential part now follows—the reassertion of aim that was
in his mind when he began the poem, the commitment to explore
the "dark Passages," the "untrodden region"; and if phrases from
Mary Tighe's *Psyche* ("untrodden forests," "paths untrodden")
return to him, he is also echoing his own sonnet "To Homer":

> Aye, on the shores of darkness there is light,
> And precipices show untrodden green.

For the "untrodden region" of the mind, in this closing credo of
the "Ode to Psyche," is also associated with precipices and steep
mountainsides. Back in "Sleep and Poetry" he had spoken of his
hope and anxiety, his "ardent prayer" and sense of inadequacy, in
approaching the "very fane . . . of Poesy." But both the fear and
the hope had been simply conceived. The "fane," in this new region he now hopes to explore, is not there to be discovered. It has
to be built. And he now promises to do just that in this place
where "branchèd thoughts" reach upward and fledge the surrounding hills (we recall the "labyrinth" of speculation he had described
to Reynolds in the letter about the "Chamber of Maiden-
Thought"—"My branchings out therefrom have been numerous"). The growth in awareness will bring new pain as well as
pleasure, or rather unforeseen combinations of both.

> Yes, I will be thy priest, and build a fane
> In some untrodden region of my mind,

> Where branchèd thoughts, new grown with pleasant pain,
>   Instead of pines shall murmur in the wind:
> Far, far around shall those dark-cluster'd trees
>   Fledge the wild-ridgèd mountains steep by steep.

In this protective labyrinth, still to be explored, there will be a "sanctuary" with all that a "working brain" may find or construct. And Fancy, seen as a "gardener," will, as Woodhouse had tried to assure Keats six months before, grow plants completely unknown and "without a name." "I understood you to say," Woodhouse had written (October 21, 1818), "that there was now nothing original to be written in poetry; that its riches were already exhausted." And Woodhouse went on to stress that the combination of ideas possible is almost infinite; that the development of "reflection & the moral sense" can, in an active mind, open new doors; that the complaint that there is nothing left to write is a rationalization of one's subjective fears and of one's "own dull brain" (a phrase that Keats within two weeks was to use in his "Ode to a Nightingale"). The ode continues:

> And in the midst of this wide quietness
> A rosy sanctuary will I dress
> With the wreath'd trellis of a working brain,
>   With buds, and bells, and stars without a name,
> With all the gardener Fancy e'er could feign,
>   Who breeding flowers, will never breed the same.

Naturally there will be uncertainty. The word "feign" is double-edged: there is the possibility of mere illusion as well as creativity. And he also thinks back to the lines from "The Recluse" that Wordsworth had printed as a "Prospectus" to his great endeavor, and from which Keats had quoted in the letter on the "Chamber of Maiden-Thought" ("the Mind of Man— / My haunt, and the main region of my song"). Wordsworth, for the task ahead, had invoked the aid of "a greater Muse" than Milton's: "For I must tread on shadowy ground." In Keats's own prospect, thought will inevitably be "shadowy" ("We see not the ballance of good and evil. We are in a Mist"). Nor can there be promise of the epic passion Wordsworth himself had to sacrifice, nor of dramatic intensity. The "delight" may be only "soft." But there will at least be whatever "shadowy thought can *win*." The spirit, in short, will include a devotion and commitment that can only be called Love. And from the tale by Apuleius, he perhaps recalls the passage where poor Psyche was left abandoned on the rocks of a high hill; and as the people departed "The Torches . . . were put out." He may even have thought of that window by which Cupid, near the end of the story, escaped from the chamber in which he was enclosed, though the open window had long since become an habitual image to Keats. In any case, a torch will now be burning brightly, and the window will be altogether open:

> And there shall be for thee all soft delight
>   That shadowy thought can win,
> A bright torch, and a casement ope at night,
>   To let the warm Love in!

And, as he finishes copying out the new poem for George, he writes, with a playfulness released by satisfaction and sudden confidence: "Here endethe yᵉ Ode to Psyche."

5

At least some attention may be given to the verse form of the poem, which serves as a transition from Keats's earlier lyrics to the form of the great odes that follow. Returning to the lyric after the ampler exercise of *Hyperion,* the *Eve of St. Agnes,* and the fragment of the *Eve of St. Mark,* he encountered an increased frustration. For as always when he went back to the lyric, the sonnet stood in his way. It had become habitual to him at an impressionable time—in the year at Guy's Hospital and in the first few months after he met Leigh Hunt. The shift to Shakespearean sonnets in the spring of 1818 brought only a temporary satisfaction. He had made fitful attempts to get away from the sonnet entirely the past year—in occasional songs, the "rondeaus" (like "Bards of Passion") to which he said he was getting "partial," the ballad "La belle dame." But he was never completely happy with short lines. The far richer potentialities of the five-foot line were constantly drawing him back to it. The "Ode to Psyche" was written partly in the context of this growing frustration with the sonnet, especially after eight or nine months of writing in longer forms.[1] But this time he did not try to avoid the sonnet (as he had in what he called his

---

[1] Garrod (*Keats* [1926], pp. 85–90) first pointed out the connection of the ode stanza with Keats's desire to "discover a better sonnet stanza than we have." Garrod's point has been developed and qualified by Ridley (pp. 202–204) and by the present writer (*Stylistic Development,* pp. 125–133).

"rondeaus"). Instead he simply broke up the fourteen-line sonnet that had become habitual to him, and then—still retaining the five-foot line as a norm—took over the *disjecta membra* of the two sonnet forms (especially the Shakespearean) and used them in a more extended lyric.

What happened is that two separate interests that had been developing now suddenly coalesced. There was his general hope of finding a more richly capacious form than the sonnet (or, for that matter, the song and the ballad). This meant, in effect, what had been called for a century "the greater ode" (as distinct from short-lined and Horatian odes). There were two available models. One was the irregular ode, developed a century before from the so-called "false Pindaric." A triumphant example was Wordsworth's "Intimations of Immortality," the powerful phrasing of which Keats so much admired. This was an altogether "open" form. But because of Keats's reaction to his own *Endymion,* he had been moving for a year toward greater compactness. The openness of the irregular ode had no appeal or challenge at the moment. An alternative, of course, was the "true Pindaric." But it was a weak alternative. The excessive complexity of the form irritated the English ear. Thomas Gray's Pindarics, for example, were considered mere curios. The effect was both antiquarian and involved.

At the same time Keats had been hoping to find a more satisfying form for the sonnet itself, provided he was to continue to write sonnets at all. When he copies out the new "Ode to Psyche" for his brother, he tells him that he has also been

> endeavouring to discover a better sonnet stanza than we have. The legitimate [i.e., the Petrarchan or Italian form] does not suit the language over-well from the pouncing rhymes—the other kind appears too elegaic—and the couplet at the end of it has seldom a pleasing effect.

To an ear still reacting against the two thousand couplets of *Endymion,* the three couplet-rhymes of the Petrarchan octave seemed obtrusive (*a b b a a b b a*), the second line of each couplet "pouncing" out, with mechanical regularity, to match the first. In the Shakespearean form, the three alternate-rhyming quatrains (the traditional "elegiac" quatrain of the eighteenth century) had an elegiac monotony from the regular pendulumlike swing of the lines, *a b a b, c d c d, e f e f;* and the final couplet (*g g*) came with such contrast that, even in Shakespeare, it often seemed a detachable tag. In three experimental sonnets ("To Sleep," "How fever'd is the man," and "If by dull rhymes"), he tried to avoid these effects.[2] The last of the three sonnets illustrates his conservative spirit—the aim is to conserve some elements of the sonnet forms, and to work organically from them:

> If by dull rhymes our English must be chain'd,
> And, like Andromeda, the Sonnet sweet
> Fetter'd, in spite of painèd loveliness;
> Let us find out, if we must be constrain'd,
> Sandals more interwoven and complete
> To fit the naked foot of poesy;
> Let us inspect the lyre, and weigh the stress
> Of every chord, and see what may be gain'd
> By ear industrious, and attention meet;
> Misers of sound and syllable, no less
> Than Midas of his coinage, let us be
> Jealous of dead leaves in the bay-wreath crown;
> So, if we may not let the Muse be free,
> She will be bound with garlands of her own.

While he was working on these experimental sonnets, an idea for a new lyric form, longer than the sonnet, occurred to him. Getting rid of some of the distinguishing features of the two sonnet types made the form malleable and capable of extension. The "Ode to Psyche" suddenly begins, in a fresh context, to incorporate what he had already done in these sonnets. The first fourteen lines are similar to "How fever'd is the man"; after a broken series (lines 15–23) the next twelve lines rhyme like a normal Shakespearean sonnet without the concluding couplet: the next fourteen are not far from the rhyme scheme of the sonnet "To Sleep." The last eighteen lines (the credo) consist of a Shakespearean sonnet, with the couplet after the octave (probably in order to break the flow of continued alternate rhyming) instead of at the close, and then a concluding Shakespearean quatrain (a b a b).

The result, of course, was complicated—perhaps needlessly so. Swinging back somewhat, he then developed the stanza that we associate with the great odes that come after "Psyche." This ten-line stanza starts with a single Shakespearean quatrain (a b a b) and,

---

[2] The first two are predominantly Shakespearean except in the following respects: (1) the pattern of three alternate-rhyming quatrains is modified, with the third quatrain interrupted by a couplet or moved to the end; and (2) the final couplet-tag is avoided. "If by dull rhymes" avoids both couplets and quatrains, and moves somewhat toward units of three lines (a b c a b d c a b c d e d e).

instead of continuing with the alternate rhymes of more quatrains, concludes with a Petrarchan sestet (*c d e c d e*): "pouncing rhymes," "elegiac" alternate rhyming, and concluding couplet tags are all avoided. This is the essential pattern of the four odes that follow—the "Nightingale," the "Grecian Urn," "Melancholy," and "Indolence." [3] He now had a form capable of extension for a poem many times the length of a sonnet, yet one that was also "interwoven and complete."

6

The "Ode to Psyche" proved catalytic in the most valuable way. For within two or three weeks—at most a month—all the five remaining odes except "To Autumn" were written. The exact order in which he wrote them is unknown. Conventional opinion has placed the "Ode to a Nightingale" first, in late April or early May, then the "Grecian Urn" and "Melancholy," and finally the "Ode on Indolence."

In this sudden release and fluency, coming after three months of uncertainty, the first incitements may have had more to do with form and technique than we tend to allow. The new odes, as one quickly followed another, were hardly thought of as by themselves a first step in the promised exploration of the "untrodden regions of the mind." That self-demand was considered in larger terms. In addition to whatever he might be able to do with *Hyperion*, it was another "long Poem"—or rather a series of them—that would represent the real beginning and—as he told Taylor the following November—eventually "nerve me up to the writing of a few fine Plays—my greatest ambition." But the new ode form could hardly have appealed to him so strongly—exciting him, in fact, to four further efforts in rapid succession (a total of 220 lines)—had not his use of it also begun to tap some of his other most urgent preoccupations: preoccupations, moreover, that for three months had been "dodging Conception" or stopping just short of expression.

With whatever ode he began—probably the "Nightingale"—he suddenly found himself developing an instrument with two very different voices, capable of two modes of lyric expression rarely dis-

---

[3] The "Grecian Urn" differs merely in changing the sestet in stanzas 1 and 5 to *c d e d c e* and in stanza 2 to *c d e c e d*. The second stanza of the "Nightingale" continues with the *a*-rhyme (*a b a b c a d c a d*); the last stanza of "Melancholy" has *a b a b c d e d c e*; and, in "Indolence," the fifth has *a b a b c d e d c e* and the sixth *a b a b c d e c e d*.

covered together. One was the odal hymn, of which the "Ode on Melancholy" and the later "To Autumn" are triumphant examples. The sustained "Hymn to Pan" excelled any other part of *Endymion,* but it had been written in couplets and was inseparably associated with *Endymion,* which he had quickly wanted to forget. Thereafter, the possibilities of the odal hymn seem never to have occurred to him again until his conscious attempt to find a "more interwoven and complete" sonnet structure led to, or coincided with, the transitional "Ode to Psyche." Of course there is no reason why the possibilities should have occurred to him. Since his hasty revision of *Endymion,* the year had been as crowded as any one year in the history of any writer's life; and, even more than before, his poetic ambition—and, until February, most of his poetic effort—had been dedicated to longer poems. Naturally, in writing mere impromptu verses, he would simply fall into mere octosyllabics, or an occasional song or sonnet; and when he began to feel in the spring that he ought to compromise his ambition a little and think at least temporarily of a more serious lyric form (the haunting ballad "La belle dame" was very much an exception), it was also natural that he should have begun his thinking by reconsidering the form most familiar and even habitual to him —the sonnet.

Even by itself, apart from such other uses of the ode as we find in the "Grecian Urn" or the "Nightingale," Keats's rapid discovery of the odal hymn created a new tone for the English lyric. For, to begin with, its capaciousness allowed at least some of his fertile thinking of the past three months to cross the threshold of poetry —thinking of the sort that his earliest poetic ideals and his strenuous self-education as a poet had taught him to associate with the long poem rather than with "short pieces." However felicitous he may have been in writing them, these short poems of one of the greatest of English lyrists are the by-product of other efforts; and those habits of both ideal and practice left him more dissatisfied than he would otherwise have been with the pressure of most lyric forms toward quick, neat solution. Not that he wished to go back to the open-ended poem, such as the verse epistles and "Sleep and Poetry." The new ode form appealed also because it was sufficiently confining to challenge his conscience as a craftsman. Finally, the union of amplitude and formal challenge offered unique opportunities as well for the concentrated intensity and concreteness of idiom that he had begun to master in *Hyperion*—qualities that had, significantly, been won in and through the writing of a long poem, had then been lavished effortlessly on the *Eve of St. Agnes,* and had since then been floating, so to speak, without any real anchorage.

But in the "Nightingale" and the "Grecian Urn" a second voice interplays with that of the odal hymn, questioning, reluctantly qualifying, and joining in a form of lyric debate that moves actively toward drama. For this is no simple dialogue of the divided heart with itself before two choices. Divisions of loyalty and sympathy are forced upon it by the inevitable nature of things, and only as the poem evolves; and the drama emerges through the actual experience that the "greeting of the Spirit" and its object— however eager the spirit—can never be complete or lasting. Nor are the limitations solely the result of our own finite nature. In each poem the dominant symbol—the urn, the song of the nightingale—is given the major voice and offered every resource of empathy and hymnal tribute that the poet can bring; and it is as much through its own limitations as through those of the finite spirit attempting to approach it that hesitation, question, even misgiving, begin to arise. Hence we also find the two odes creating the most striking single precedent, as David Perkins has brilliantly shown, for the modern poetic development of symbolic debate, al- • though at the same time "we are dealing with a talent, indeed an entire approach to poetry, in which symbol, however necessary, may possibly not satisfy as the principal concern of poetry, any more than it could with Shakespeare, but is rather an element in the poetry and drama of human reactions." [4] Because they are essentially dramatic, and concerned both with human reaction and its object, the odes are analogous to experience as a whole. We therefore continue to return to them as we could not if they betrayed experience by oversimplifying it. The challenge, the experience, remains alive, and thus perennially fertile as well as debatable.

7

It was probably in the actual process of writing the "Ode to a Nightingale" that the full possibilities of the new form at last dis-

[4] *The Quest for Permanence: The Symbolism of Wordsworth, Shelley, and Keats* (1959), pp. 228–257, 299–301.

closed themselves. Charles Brown implied that the poem was written very soon after the "Ode to Psyche." [5] If it was, then—as so often with Keats—the deliberate care bestowed on one poem laid a
foundation and permitted the rapid writing of another. For the
"Ode to a Nightingale" was composed in a single morning. Of no
other of the dozen—or score—of the greatest lyrics in English do
we know, as a fact, that it was written in so short a time. Moreover, this poem is no brief song but an ode of eighty lines in an in-
tricately regular stanza. We are free to doubt whether any poem in
English of comparable length and quality has been composed so
quickly. The four-thousand-line "test of Invention," so painfully
begun two years before in the Isle of Wight with the little sketch
of Shakespeare before him as a "Presider," was once again bringing results. (The picture was still usually near him when he wrote,
decorated with the silk tassels Georgiana had woven for him before
she and George left for America; "I am sitting opposite" the picture now, he had written in February.) Charles Brown described
the time of composition as lasting "two or three hours":

> In the spring of 1819 a nightingale had built her nest near my
> house. Keats felt a tranquil and continual joy in her song; and one
> morning he took his chair from the breakfast-table to the grass-plot
> under a plum-tree, where he sat for two or three hours. When he
> came into the house, I perceived he had some scraps of paper in his
> hand, and these he was quietly thrusting behind the books. On in-
> quiry, I found those scraps, four or five in number, contained his
> poetic feeling on the song of our nightingale.

Nothing illustrates better the release that has finally come than
the sudden reawakening in all the odes that follow "Psyche," and
especially in the "Nightingale," of phrases and images from Keats's
letters during the previous year, particularly the spring just passing.[6] Aside from images and phrasing, familiar devices appear, but

[5] This at least is the inference from Brown's remark, following his mention of the
poem, that "Immediately afterwards I searched for more of his (in reality) fugitive
pieces, in which task, at my request, he again assisted me" (*KC*, II.65). On April 30
Keats tells George that "Brown has been rummaging up some of my old sins—that
is to say sonnets." Hence the assumption that the "Nightingale" was written before
April 30. On the other hand Brown is writing almost twenty-two years after the
event; he could have copied some poems on April 30; the ode could have been
written a few days later; and Brown could afterwards have made an even more energetic effort to copy other poems. Moreover, Keats on April 30 refers to "Psyche" as
his "last" poem.
[6] See David Perkins, *Keats-Shelley Journal*, II (1953), 51–60. A few examples may
be cited. With the "draught of vintage . . . Cool'd . . . in the deep-delvèd earth,"

in altered form. There is a credo, for example, as there so often is; but this assertion significantly comes not at the end but in the stanza that precedes the final one; and in the old alternation of question and answer, the question appears last. The struggle with the two sonnet forms, Petrarchan and Shakespearean, is resolved (as most struggles of Keats with poetic form are resolved) by assimilation. The poetic uses of dream, sleep, and awakening, with which we have been familiar from the little elegy on the death of his grandmother ("Can death be sleep") through "Sleep and Poetry" to the *Eve of St. Agnes,* reappear, but now as a part of the dramatic interplay.

The form of the "Nightingale" and the "Grecian Urn," in some ways so much alike, naturally differs because of the radical diversity of the two symbols themselves. The urn is teasingly silent, whereas the essence of the nightingale's appeal is the song that it is "pouring forth . . . / In such an ecstasy." Yet the inanimate urn is the work of human imagination and hands, while the altogether vital bird eludes the human. The urn is viewed close up, while the nightingale is unseen and can be placed only in "some melodious plot" amid "shadows numberless." The nightingale finally flies away, and the poem ends with a question; the urn "will remain," and the ode ends with at least a qualified assertion. In short, whereas the steadiness of the symbol in the "Grecian Urn" permits a progressive development, the development of the "Nightingale," where the symbol is more vitally immediate and yet so elusive, takes the form of constant rise and ebb. It begins—as it also ends—with the heart, and with the heart so caught by hope of empathy with the song of the unseen bird that, for the moment, the restless, questioning intellect is paralyzed as if by drug:

---

the references to "Flora," "Bacchus," and "summer eves," compare the letters: "Claret to drink on summer evenings . . . cool and feverless . . . Bacchus . . . cellar of claret"; "claret-wine out of a cellar a mile deep . . . Flora." (II.56, 64.) With the passages on youth growing "pale, and spectre-thin," and on the flowers of the "seasonable month," cf. II.51–52, 56. With the famous close, where the song of the nightingale is "buried deep / In the next valley-glades," compare, among others, the remarks in the letter to Tom about the sound of the Ambleside stream "buried in trees, in the bottom of the valley," "buried deep in trees" (I.300). Among several anticipations of the open "casement" (in the rooms near Guy's Hospital Keats's favorite spot, said Henry Stephens, was by the window), two can be noted from the letters. The most beautiful objects he can imagine, he tells George and Georgiana, would include a "Window opening on Winander mere" (I.403); and in his playful letter to his sister in March, he tells her he would like to sit "before a handsome painted window . . . I should like the picture to open onto the Lake of Geneva—and there I'd sit and read all day like the picture of somebody reading" (II.46).

> My heart aches, and a drowsy numbness pains
>   My sense, as though of hemlock I had drunk,
> Or emptied some dull opiate to the drains
>   One minute past, and Lethe-wards had sunk.

The numbness of near-dream, as often in Keats, is associated with a diversity of strong impressions where one actively shades into another, and where, in "winning near the goal" rather than in reaching it, different possibilities still remain in suspension. Identification with the bird is not really complete; awareness of self is still partly present ("My heart aches"). We have, in short, a state in which self-consciousness is not yet lost but in the process of being lost, and the hope of identification is rising.

The ode falls into two almost equal portions, the break coming near the close of the fourth stanza. The first half of the poem continues to try to assert the precarious, almost-attained identification with the bird or with its song. The real premise of the poem is the heart's desire to slow the remorselessness of process: to possess the past and future in distillation while at the same time the present is fully experienced and retained. More than any of the other odes, the "Nightingale" picks up the theme of the impromptu lines a few months before, "Ever let the Fancy roam, / Pleasure never is at home": the hope to "Open wide the mind's cage-door," and to know "all together" the "April's lark," the hyacinth of "mid-May," the full "summer," the distant "harvest-carols" of autumn. With "mysterious stealth," the freed Fancy (which at the close of the "Nightingale" is admitted to be one that "cheats") can

> mix these pleasures up
> Like three fit wines in a cup.

The first half of the ode looks back not only to those quick, spirited lines but also to their companion rondeau ("Bards of Passion and of Mirth"), where, in a purely fancied Elysium, the daisies are given the scent of roses, and

> Where the nightingale doth sing
> Not a senseless, trancèd thing,
> But divine melodious truth.

But the blitheness of these two rondeaus has completely disappeared in the rich, troubled stanzas that begin the ode. For something not far from those jauntily phrased hopes has now been so poignantly experienced that honesty and caution are immediately stirred, complicating the conception from the first stanza. Because the heart is almost drugged with the music, the bird—near the beginning of May—can be felt to sing "of summer in full-throated ease," and later—even when the attempted union of the poet with the bird is relaxed—the still half-freed fancy can continue to "guess," in the growing darkness, not only the "fading violets" of April but also the "coming musk-rose" of "mid-May"—already in imagination serving as "The murmurous haunt of flies on summer eves." Yet at the very start there is a hesitation between reality and unreality. This "light-wingèd" creature, which cannot be definitely placed, is partly thought of as unreal—a "Dryad" from the world of Arcadia.

The brevity of the experience is also known and frankly implied at the start. As if to underline it further (for the nightingale will quickly "fade away into the forest"), the second stanza turns to the immediate wish for a supporting intoxication, though one hardly less transitory:

> O for a draught of vintage! that hath been
>   Cool'd a long age in the deep-delvèd earth,
> Tasting of Flora and the country green,
>   Dance, and Provençal song, and sunburnt mirth!
> O for a beaker full of the warm South,
>   Full of the true, the blushful Hippocrene,
>   With beaded bubbles winking at the brim,
>   And purple-stainèd mouth;
>   That I might drink and leave the world unseen,
>   And with thee fade away into the forest dim.

But the list of associations with wine—"the country green, Dance . . . sunburnt mirth . . . the warm South"—is already fading as the second stanza closes: "leave the world" and "with thee fade away" betray the inevitable return to self and introduce the third stanza, which can now continue the assertion only negatively:

> Fade far away, dissolve, and quite forget
>   What thou among the leaves hast never known,
> The weariness, the fever, and the fret
>   Here, where men sit and hear each other grown;
> Where palsy shakes a few, sad, last gray hairs,
>   Where youth grows pale, and spectre-thin, and dies.

To say that the attempted identification with the bird is flagging, and that the assertion is becoming negative (or, as in the next stanza, fitful and frantically willed), by no means implies a lapse or stagger in the poem, though the lines are sometimes described as such. Partly because of its bare phrasing, the third stanza, with its poignant reference to Tom's death, reinforces the two that precede it by rescuing them (as well as the stanza that follows) into the direct urgency of drama: those wishes to leave a world "Where but to think is to be full of sorrow," far from being idle, are seen both as massively justified and yet—in so compelling a context—as ultimately helpless.

8

It is this ultimate helplessness that underlies the troubled fourth stanza, near the close of which the poem makes its essential turn. After the stark directness of the preceding lines, little more than a straining assertion is possible ("Away! away! for I will fly to thee"; "Already with thee!"). Not wine but "Poesy" and the activity of writing may slow the growing division between the "greeting Spirit" and its elusive object:

> for I will fly to thee
> Not charioted by Bacchus and his pards,
> But on the viewless wings of Poesy,
> Though the dull brain perplexes and retards.

Then, in three words, the union is simply declared. But the short effort of "Poesy"—used solely in this way for escape or illusion—results only in two lines of futile ornament (the "Queen-Moon" attended by her "starry Fays"). This brief gesture of poetic supernaturalism reminds us of Endymion's illusion (II.184–195) before that "journey homeward to habitual self" which also applies so well to the close of the "Nightingale." Endymion believes he has joined the moon and "all the stars / That tend" her "bidding":

> I do think the bars
> That kept my spirit in are burst—that I
> Am sailing with thee through the dizzy sky!

His illusion is almost immediately shattered ("My spirit fails—/ Dear goddess, help! or the wide-gaping air / Will gulph me"); and he is saved by a return to a region neither "Dark, nor light, . . . But mingled up." So, in the ode, the unconvincing lines are followed by the admission that the poet is not really there, after all, but "here," in the deep twilight:

> Already with thee! tender is the night,
> And haply the Queen-Moon is on her throne,
>   Cluster'd around by all her starry Fays;
>   But here there is no light,
> Save what from heaven is with the breezes blown
>   Through verdurous glooms and winding mossy ways.

From now until the end of the ode the separateness of the poet and the bird is presupposed. Henceforth the poet sits and listens ("I cannot see what flowers . . . Darkling I listen"). And ironically, with this acceptance of reality, the appeal to poetry for liberation is answered, though not at all in the way originally asked —not as a means to "fly to" the bird on "viewless wings" and leave the actual world of process. (Since January Keats had hoped that he was "moulting," and, as he said again in July, "not for fresh feathers & wings: they are gone, and in their stead I hope to have a pair of patient sublunary legs.") For the first time in the ode we have a stanza in which all that the poet is trying to escape is completely absent. The liberation, as always, has come through a direct sympathetic response to concrete reality. The strain and exclamations ("O for . . . O for"; "Away! Away!") disappear; he is content to "guess"; and the thick cluster of classical associations used to reinforce the impossible imaginative leap ("Lethe," "Dryad," "Flora," "Hippocrene," "Bacchus") give way to naturalistic detail, firmly imagined despite the growing dark:

> I cannot see what flowers are at my feet,
>   Nor what soft incense hangs upon the boughs,
> But, in embalmèd darkness, guess each sweet
>   Wherewith the seasonable month endows
> The grass, the thicket, and the fruit-tree wild;
>   White hawthorn, and the pastoral eglantine;
>   Fast fading violets cover'd up in leaves;
>   And mid-May's eldest child,
>   The coming musk-rose, full of dewy wine,
>   The murmurous haunt of flies on summer eves.

The acceptance of process, of course, involves the acceptance of death, as the serene ode "To Autumn" especially illustrates; and while the hypnotic song of the bird continues, the thought of death, almost intolerable before ("Where youth grows pale, and spectre-thin, and dies"), now becomes "easeful":

> Now more than ever seems it rich to die,
>   To cease upon the midnight with no pain,

> While thou art pouring forth thy soul abroad
> In such an ecstasy!

The personal poignance is obvious enough: Keats's constant exposure to death since the age of eight; the accumulated fatigue of
the effort of the past four years; his uneasy feeling about his own
future since he returned from Scotland with the "haunting sore-
throat." Add to all this his attempts to manage this inevitable preoccupation with death. If a part of him tried to keep it out of his
mind, another part instinctively tried to muffle the sense of its cruelty and injustice, tending to reduce thoughts and symbols of
death to the two attractions that so often alternate in his emotional
life—"intensity" and "easefulness." And among other lines, the
sonnet "Why did I laugh tonight?" is usually cited:

> Why did I laugh? I know this Being's lease,
>   My fancy to its utmost blisses spreads;
> Yet would I on this very midnight cease,
>   And the world's gaudy ensigns see in shreds;
> Verse, Fame, and Beauty are intense indeed,
> But Death intenser—Death is Life's high meed.

But the "best comment" on that sonnet, as Keats said to George
immediately afterwards, is what he had been writing in his journal
letter, which will show, he hopes, that he has "that in me which
will well bear the buffets of the world." [7] So, in the sixth stanza of
the ode, the thought of "easeful death" turns into one more element in what is rapidly becoming a drama of symbolic debate.

To begin with, this is no undivided attraction to death; its counterpart has been the massive protest against mortality in stanza
three. It has emerged only after he has relinquished the struggle
to escape from the world of process, with which death is inevitably
connected. Even so, it is qualified: he has been, at such moments
before, only "half in love with easeful death"; and despite the
drugging effect of the music, the impulsive statement of the sonnet
—"yet would I on this very midnight cease"—is now modified into
what Keats calls "speculation" (*"seems* it rich to die"). At the
same time the image of departing breath opens another contrast:
"to take into the air my quiet breath," in a cessation "with no
pain," would be the reverse of the living breath and music of the
bird, "pouring forth [its] soul abroad, / In such an ecstasy." The
contrast continues: with death, however "easeful," he would then

[7] See above, Chapter XVIII, section 5.

become a "sod" to this vital song; the body's ears would exist "in vain" to what would now be a "high requiem" for the dead. In short, if the desire to "leave the world unseen" were granted in the only way that is possible, the result would be the reverse of union with the bird:

> Still wouldst thou sing, and I have ears in vain—
> To thy high requiem become a sod.

One thinks ahead to Keats's last letter before he left England, when he knew that everything was over. The boat from which he wrote to Charles Brown (September 30, 1820) lay off the Isle of Wight—painfully associated by then with his first ambitious effort, his "test of Invention":

> I wish for death every day and night . . . and then I wish death away, for death would destroy even those pains which are better than nothing. Land and Sea, weakness and decline, are great seperators, but death is the great divorcer for ever.

The contrast, in the thought of that possible "high requiem" above the mortal "sod," brings together the two major implications that have been developing throughout the poem, and prepares for the separate prominence given each in the two final stanzas: the reassurance and value of this object and experience, and also its limitations for man. At the same time the two voices that he is discovering in the new form—the interplay of odal hymn with question and debate—are somewhat separated in this two-stanza close, or coda, to the poem. The tribute to the bird in the first of the two stanzas is the distillation of the odal hymn, relatively unqualified by question until the final word, "forlorn":

> Thou wast not born for death, immortal Bird!
> No hungry generations tread thee down;
> The voice I hear this passing night was heard
> In ancient days by emperor and clown.

There is admittedly some strain in the leap to this apostrophe, as there is also in the parallel assertion in the "Grecian Urn" ("Beauty is truth . . ."). It is the first line that creates the strain, leading to the familiar quibbling about the mortality of birds as well as men. But the third line recovers by turning attention to the "voice" of the nightingale, which, by implication, is that of the species. As it suggests the range that this music can touch or haunt, the stanza moves gently from the actual past ("emperor and clown") , through the realm of possibility and Biblical story, to the remote world of fancy—or rather to the mere thought of it, imagined from a distant shore:

> Perhaps the self-same song that found a path
>   Through the sad heart of Ruth, when, sick for home,
>   She stood in tears amid the alien corn;
>   The same that oft-times hath
>   Charm'd magic casements, opening on the foam
>   Of perilous seas, in faery lands forlorn.

The closing word becomes the hinge to the final stanza:

>   Forlorn! the very word is like a bell
>   To toll me back from thee to my soul self!

Those impossible lands are "forlorn" because they are not at all for man. They are like the imagined "little town" in the "Grecian Urn," which is "desolate" because no one can ever return to it. "Scenery is fine," as Keats once wrote to Bailey, "but human nature is finer—The Sward is richer for the tread of a real, nervous, english foot—the eagles nest is finer for the Mountaineer has look'd into it." And if release from reality through fancy is impossible—if "the fancy cannot cheat so well / As she is fam'd to do, deceiving elf"—it is because of the limitations not only of ourselves but also of "Things semireal," however valuable, even necessary, they may be as a "friend to man." But the regret is strong; and as the bird leaves, the poet's own "journey homeward to habitual self" is completed. The song of the bird, if it was thought of before as a possible "high requiem," is now only "plaintive" as it fades.

The poem ends, as it began, with the heart, but with the heart now frankly questioning. Was this short "greeting of the Spirit" and its object a genuine heightening of experience, with something of "vision," and is he now returning to unawareness or "sleep"; or is he waking to reality from what was only subjective half-dream?

>   adieu! thy plaintive anthem fades
> Past the near meadows, over the still stream,
>   Up the hill-side; and now 'tis buried deep
>   In the next valley-glades:
> Was it a vision, or a waking dream?
>   Fled is that music:—Do I wake or sleep?

9

Brown's picture is unforgettable of Keats coming into the house from the grassplot after his morning's writing and quietly thrusting behind some books the loose scraps of paper that contained the ode—an action typical, Brown thought, of Keats's negligence about some of his shorter poems. But the further potentialities of the new form had plainly caught Keats's interest. For so consistently is the "Grecian Urn" given qualities the "Nightingale" lacked—though in the process it loses the personal urgency of the other ode—that whatever else entered into the writing of it, we find in it the concentration of a second attempt and of a conscious effort to learn from the first. The use of the song of the nightingale had been fortuitous. Some reflection may have preceded the choice of the steadier symbol of the urn—a symbol that would permit closer focus and a more craftsmanlike exploration of its potentialities and limitations. In contrast to the rapid shifts of pace in the "Nightingale," the "Grecian Urn," like the "Ode on Melancholy," reflects the leisurely and "peaceable" spirit in which he hoped to write these new poems. Finally, with a determined objectivity, the poet—so prominent in the other ode—is now kept as completely out of the poem as possible. It is in every way a more considered poem than the "Nightingale." This is not to say that it is superior. For it achieves its success partly because it is more limited in what it tries to say.

The lyric debate implied throughout the "Ode on a Grecian Urn" (it is significantly an ode *on,* and not, like the "Nightingale," an ode *to*) has grown in the most organic way from sympathies as selfless and committed as they are divided, though personal preoccupations are also obvious and inevitable. The most abbreviated catalogue is enough to remind us of the strength of one commitment: the sonnet on Chapman's Homer, and those on the Elgin Marbles; the general ideal of "intensity"; the relish in power caught momentarily in repose (the "Miltonic stationing"). He was still returning frequently to see the Elgin Marbles, and perhaps within recent months had made the tracing that still survives, in the Keats House in Rome, of the Sosibios Vase.[8] But another com-

---

8 From the *Musée Napoléon,* a four-volume collection of engravings of work of art pillaged by Napoleon. Keats probably saw it at Haydon's. Attempts continue to be made to determine a particular vase or urn that Keats may have had in mind

mitment, probably even stronger now, can be suggested by the phrase that so haunted him, "the Burden of the Mystery"; by remarks about Wordsworth's thinking more into the human heart than Milton; by the thought of the heart as a "hornbook" from which the mind, in a world of "uncertainties, Mysteries, doubts," tries to spell out experience. This commitment to remain honest to human reactions—to explore the heart with its questionings and doubts—sustains the second voice that interplays with that of the odal hymn; and it is one of the several considerations we forget when we concentrate on the two closing lines of the poem ("Beauty is truth . . .") as an unqualified credo either to embrace or attack.

But debate is by no means predicated at the start. The essence of the urn is its potentiality waiting to be fulfilled. Unlike the song of the nightingale, so independent of human needs, the very origin of the urn presupposed the hope that it would be rescued into full existence by some later "greeting of the Spirit." For the actual parentage of the urn was the forgotten artist working with marble. It was only afterwards left to be the "foster-child of silence and slow time," though it has taken on the character of its foster-parents: it has lasted so long, and depicts a world now dead. Throughout that long fostering it has become pledged as a "bride of quietness." But this virginal bride is "still unravish'd," either by the infidelity of speaking or by the marriage consummation with "quietness" itself.[9] Finally, it is already able within limits to "express" a "tale," all the "more sweetly" because, like those early Italian prints Keats had described to George in December, there is "left so much room for Imagination." Hence, in contrast to the "Nightingale," where questions appear only at the end, the pattern here is one in which they begin, from the first stanza, to interplay

when he wrote the ode. Especially with a poem so distinguished by its universality, one thinks of Keats's own remark, written not long before the "Grecian Urn," that "They are very shallow people who take everything literal." In all probability he was thinking principally of the Elgin Marbles. But a large collection would hardly have given him the focus he now wanted, however ready he may have been two years before to write his two general sonnets on the Marbles. Together with the Sosibios Vase, the Townley Vase in the British Museum and especially the engravings of the Borghese Vase in the Louvre (see Colvin, p. 416) may have suggested the idea of an urn.

9 "Still," as an adverb, intensifies the possibility that it may yet be "ravish'd." But the word may have been intended as an adjective and was first printed thus ("Thou still, unravish'd bride of quietness") in *Annals of the Fine Arts*, IV (1820), No. 15.

with direct address. Half playful, they still presuppose a partial confidence. They begin as a general musing about the possibility of an elusive story or meaning beyond the actual figures on the urn: "What leaf-fring'd legend haunts about thy shape / Of deities or mortals or of both . . . ?" But as the imagination becomes more closely caught, it begins irresistibly to particularize, both in its own contribution or "greeting" and in its hope for response:

> What men or gods are these? What maidens loth?
> What mad pursuit? What struggle to escape?
> What pipes and timbrels? What wild ecstasy?

The eager questions, beginning to accumulate in rising empathy, are dismissed. Any communication from the urn must come otherwise, "to the spirit." In this withdrawal from question, the fact of the urn's silence in ordinary human terms is not only accepted but affirmed and even, for the moment, preferred:

> Heard melodies are sweet, but those unheard
> Are sweeter; therefore, ye soft pipes, play on;
> Not to the sensual ear, but, more endear'd,
> Pipe to the spirit ditties of no tone.

If a legend or hoped-for meaning "haunts about" the urn, then the imagination must do the same—"content with half-knowledge" and without "irritable reaching" after certitude. The approach now, therefore, is meditative. The poet simply addresses the figures without seeking to identify them. He adopts, in other words, the conventional romantic form of the *ut pictura poesis* tradition, in which the poet contemplates the work of art, often while directly addressing it, and derives from it a subject for meditation; and the theme of this meditation—in a sense the theme of all Keats's odes except "Psyche"—is that of process, and either the acceptance of it, or the hope to escape from it, or both in dramatic interplay with each other:

> Fair youth, beneath the trees, thou canst not leave
> Thy song, nor ever can those trees be bare;
> Bold Lover, never, never canst thou kiss,
> Though winning near the goal—yet, do not grieve;
> She cannot fade, though thou hast not thy bliss,
> For ever wilt thou love, and she be fair!

Yet if the questions that close the first stanza have been dismissed, the claims and frustrations of human needs have begun gently to reappear in another guise, preparing to become more assertive. They reappear, ironically, in the very act of approaching the urn not with impossible questions but with a meditative justice and delight that will acknowledge its unique character, its freedom both from process and from the distresses of the directly personal. Nor is freedom from process confined solely to freedom from physical change. The "enjoying of the Spring," as Keats had written in the lines on "Fancy," fades just as inevitably as the actual "blossoming"; the ripeness of autumn ultimately "cloys"; the most beautiful eye will soon "weary"; nor is there any "voice, however soft," that "one would hear too oft."

But to acknowledge is partly to define or distinguish, and thus, by implication, to separate. At the very height of the acknowledgment (the beginning of the third or central stanza, in the latter part of which the ode makes its turn) we have the nostalgia of the outsider:

> Ah, happy, happy boughs! that cannot shed
>   Your leaves, nor ever bid the Spring adieu;
> And, happy melodist, unwearièd,
>   For ever piping songs for ever new.

In attempting to approach the urn in its own terms, the imagination has been led at the same time to separate itself—or the situation of man generally—still further from the urn. The result is the sudden release, in the middle of the third stanza, of diverse feelings shifting into each other but still fundamentally in opposition. Sympathy divides. In part it begins to desert the urn for the painful world of process, of which the urn is oblivious; and envy, incompatible with complete sympathy, follows. Yet the separation is not one-sided—there are at least two sides to any boundary—and no possible fulfillment exists for the figures on the urn apart from what the responsive mind can give them. As one sympathy withdraws from the urn, another seeks to redress the balance not merely by responding but by bestowing: love, in these frozen figures forever poised, is not only perennially young but "For ever warm" and even "For ever panting." Hence also the peculiar excess of exclamation in which a hastening reassurance and its opposite, nostalgic envy, equally join. As in the fourth stanza of the "Nightingale," where the poem made its turn, there is a sense of strain. The repetitions there ("Away! away! for I will fly to thee") are matched by repetitions here that are possibly as urgent and certainly as helpless: the five "for ever's," and "More happy love! more happy, happy love!" As the stanza closes, the wrestle of feelings subsides into what appears to be an oversimple contrast:

> All breathing human passion far above,
>   That leaves a heart high-sorrowful and cloy'd,
>   A burning forehead, and a parching tongue.

But more is being deprived the figures on the urn than is bestowed. They are now conceived negatively, through what they lack; and in only the weak final line does their lack suggest much advantage. "All breathing human passion" is a weighted phrase: "above," half ironic, loses its evaluative force and begins to connote unawareness. "Cloy'd" at least implies fulfillment. Finally a "heart high-sorrowful" is able to experience the mystery of sorrow for which Keats, in the revised *Hyperion*, was soon to find an image in the countenance of Moneta.

10

The second and especially the third stanzas have been a digression. We have only to apply the simple test of omitting them both, or else the third alone, and we find that what remains will still make a complete poem, though admittedly less rich. On the other hand, if we keep all the others and omit the fourth, or if we simply glance at the close of the third and the opening of the fifth, we can see that there would be no transition at all and that, in the third stanza, Keats has found himself moving away from the principal feelings that the urn at first suggested to him: a receptive delight in its permanence of form, its mystery and inscrutability.

Hence the primary function of the fourth stanza is to return more concretely to the Grecian urn and to some of the feelings that were present at the start. As it does so, we find a result similar to what happens in the fifth stanza of the "Nightingale." Each of these stanzas is preceded by an impasse: an overeager, subjective, and finally frustrated empathy has tried to make the symbol carry more than it can, and to use it in a massive protest against limitation or finitude, although that protest is itself divided. In each case the attempt to go beyond the possibilities of both symbol and imaginative identification is finally abandoned; the approach is resumed in a more subdued key; and then, paradoxically, a genuine empathy suddenly results. Freed from the strain of taking the figures on the urn as literally alive, the mind is able to develop if not to complete the suggestions offered by them. The "imagination projecting itself into certain situations . . . working up its imaginary feelings to the height of reality"—to use the remark Keats had enthusiastically quoted from Hazlitt—is gently transferred from the figures themselves to the world of which they remain an emblem or representative. The references to them become general: a "mysterious priest," a "heifer," "this folk." The "green altar" to which they are going is not even shown on the white urn, nor is the "little town," the location of which is unknown:

> Who are these coming to the sacrifice?
>   To what green altar, O mysterious priest,
> Lead'st thou that heifer lowing at the skies,
>   And all her silken flanks with garlands drest?
> What little town by river or sea-shore,
>   Or mountain-built with peaceful citadel,
>   Is emptied of this folk, this pious morn?
> And, little town, thy streets for evermore
>   Will silent be; and not a soul to tell
>   Why thou art desolate, can e'er return.

It is not simply because the figures are forever imprisoned on the urn that no one can ever return to the empty town but because the actual inhabitants disappeared in the remote past—a past from which no one remains except as figures on an urn or in other works of art.

As the mind has turned to the thought of the remote, forgotten life beyond the urn, the figures on it have become reduced to a stylized "brede" of "marble men and maidens"; and, as at the beginning of the poem, it is the urn as a whole that is now addressed. But in contrast to the beginning, where it had been approached as a possible "historian" that might reveal a "legend" of "deities or mortals," it is now acknowledged as only a "shape," or "form":

> O Attic shape! Fair attitude! with brede
>   Of marble men and maidens overwrought,
> With forest branches and the trodden weed;
>   Thou, silent form, dost tease us out of thought
> As doth eternity.

The perennially disputed close of the poem then follows. The focus of the dispute is the final two lines, discussion of which already fills a small book of critical essays. The principal difficulties have been three, one of which has been almost completely resolved and another of which is largely of our own making. First, the abstractions "beauty" and "truth" are forced to carry the heavy, subjective load of meaning that Keats habitually gives them in his rapidly written letters. In his poetry, however, he tends to use abstractions of this sort sparingly and far less subjectively. Second, he was probably too ill to oversee the publication of the 1820 volume, where the lines were printed:

> "Beauty is truth, truth beauty,"—that is all
> Ye know on earth, and all ye need to know.

Hence it was long assumed that the final remark is the poet's own personal comment on the aphorism, either as a consoling admonition to his fellow human beings (addressed as "ye" though he has been speaking in terms of "us" and "other woe / Than ours") or else as a congratulatory bow to the figures on the urn (though the whole burden of the stanza is what the urn, as a "friend," is offering to man). The texts of the transcripts make it plain that the entire two lines are meant as the message or reassurance to man from the urn, without intrusion by the poet.[10] Third, partly for these reasons, partly because of the aphoristic character of the final lines, they are constantly being separated not only from the context of the poem but even from the sentence in which they occur, and the efforts to put them back into their context only increase the concentrated focus on these innocent words. Perhaps the modern critical irritability with the phrasing would be less sharp if the Victorians themselves had not so frequently isolated the lines from their context and quoted them enthusiastically as what I. A. Richards calls a "pseudo-statement." Nothing so quickly arouses critical opposition as what we consider to be unthinking approval, though our irritabilities are in danger of becoming more concerned with replying to enthusiasms than with the full nature of the object in question. The spread of twentieth-century dissatisfaction may be

[10] Fully discussed by A. Whitley, *KSMB*, No. 5 (1954), 1–3, and J. C. Stillinger, *PMLA*, LXXII (1957), 447–448. All four transcripts (those of George Keats, Brown, Woodhouse, and Dilke) lack a full stop after "truth beauty," lack quotation marks, and by dashes break the final lines not into two parts but into three. That of Dilke is typical: "Beauty is truth,—truth beauty,—that is all . . ."

typified by writers as diverse as Sir Arthur Quiller-Couch and
T. S. Eliot. Quiller-Couch regards the lines as "a vague observation—to anyone whom life has taught to face facts . . . actually an
uneducated conclusion, albeit most pardonable in one so young
and ardent." Eliot, far more receptive, still finds the close a "blemish" or at least "grammatically meaningless." [11]

11

The full sentence of the close is as follows:

Cold Pastoral!
When old age shall this generation waste,
Thou shalt remain, in midst of other woe
Than ours, a friend to man, to whom thou say'st,
"Beauty is truth, truth beauty,—that is all
Ye know on earth, and all ye need to know."

The final two lines are in the vein of the inscriptions on Greek
monuments addressed to the passing stranger. The elusive message
is meant to be that of the urn, not of the poet speaking for himself. In even the most spontaneous letters of a year and a half before (and we are significantly forced to go back that far in order
to find remarks at all analogous), Keats never comes close to anything as bald as the simple equation of these two abstractions,
"beauty" and "truth," that he permits the urn to make here (least
of all does he advance anything seriously comparable to the words
that follow). Not that those earlier remarks of Keats are irrelevant,
as the purist would have it. They at least suggest something of the
general premise involved in the urn's message. This very general
premise, as far as Keats's own personal thinking is concerned, is
that the "greeting of the Spirit" is itself as much a part of nature,
or reality, as is its object. In the act of conception, with the result·

11 Eliot is taking issue with I. A. Richards, who, in discussing "pseudo-state-
ments," speaks of those who misread the close of the "Grecian Urn" and "swallow
'Beauty is Truth, truth beauty . . . ,' as the quintessence of an aesthetic philosophy,
not as the expression of a certain blend of feelings" (*Practical Criticism* [1929],
pp. 186–187). Eliot goes on: "I am at first inclined to agree with [Richards] . . .
But on re-reading the whole Ode, this line strikes me as a serious blemish on a
beautiful poem, and the reason must be either that I fail to understand it, or that
it is a statement which is untrue. And I suppose that Keats meant something by it,
however remote his truth and his beauty may have been from these words in ordinary use. And I am sure that he would have repudiated any explanation of the line
which called it a pseudo-statement. . . . The statement of Keats seems to me meaningless: or perhaps the fact that it is grammatically meaningless conceals another
meaning from me." "Dante," *Selected Essays* (1932), pp. 230–231.

ing harmony ("beauty," "intensity") of the greeting mind and its object, we have a fresh achievement altogether within nature: a "truth—whether it existed before or not" in which reality has awakened further into awareness.

More specifically, the poem is ending with the assumption (which may not be completely justified) that the expression has been prepared for: that the urn maintains decorum—to use the classical term—by an expression dramatically appropriate to the character it has itself exemplified, the character of a work of art of a particular kind. Persisting through time, it itself remains ready to come alive ("wholly exist") as music on the printed page becomes alive when the inked notes are scanned and interpreted by some later imagination. The "spiritual," as Keats had written in his dramatic review for the *Champion* after he went to see Edmund Kean, "is felt when the very letters and points of charactered language show like the hieroglyphics of beauty"; and while these "mysterious signs" rise into life and meaning, we ourselves, approaching them from another age, begin to participate with them in a kind of "immortal free-masonry." Something of this experience is offered by the urn as a possibility. As such it will "remain, in midst of other woe / Than ours, a friend to man." So Milton, as Keats wrote earlier, continues even "since his death" to serve as "an active friend to Man." The thought is similar to that in the rondeau Keats had written in December ("Bards of passion and of mirth"). In addition to any Elysium where they may now be, the great poets of the past have also left souls behind to "Teach us, here, the way to find" them. Never slumbering, "never cloying," they continue to "speak / To mortals, of their little week."

Even so, the special and restricted character of the urn is stressed before its inscriptional message is permitted. Qualification is gradually built into the last two stanzas and particularly the closing sentence. Very much a part of the "truth" of human experience is the fact that every generation that views the urn is in the process of wasting, and living "in the midst of other woe / Than ours." Aloof from the brevity and sharp claims of human life, the urn is not only freer but also more limited: freer to advance the message it does in a way that no human being could confidently do, and yet, as a work of art, limited to the realm in which its message applies. The message is like itself: "teasing," perpetually available for certain valuable human experiences, and altogether oblivious of others—a message strictly applicable only to its own confined nature, in which beauty is not "a truth" (and it is the phrase "a truth" that Keats so commonly uses) but simply "truth" and is all that it itself knows or needs to know. But it is not all that man knows or needs to know: "how then are Souls to be made . . . but by the medium of a world like this? . . . Do you not see how necessary a World of Pains and troubles is to school an Intelligence and make it a soul?" The inanimate character of the urn is emphasized at the start of the final sentence as at no other point in the poem—"Cold Pastoral!" The message is that of a "shape," a "form," above all an "attitude," with the inevitable restrictions that this involves. Nor do we even receive it until this "shape" is first able to "tease us out of thought."

The word "attitude" is indeed of the essence of the poem's conclusion, and helpful to recall when we are tempted to concentrate on the last two lines as a subjective intrusion on the part of the poet, either directly or as a form of ventriloquism. It is also salutary to bear in mind Keats's robust realism, his sense of proportion and ready humor that apply as much to himself as to anything else. Like the Victorians, we are tempted to approach the great odes of April and May with more solemnity (which we too often equate with sincerity) than their creator ever thought it desirable or found it possible to sustain. We are willing to grant abstractly that his humor was irrepressible on even the most serious occasions. Struggling to understand the differences between the great poetry of the past and the challenge of the future, and only too aware of his own inadequacy, he could write movingly of the "Burden of the Mystery" and the "Chamber of Maiden-Thought," and yet at the same time he could play with the picture of himself creating a "rat-trap," with these two large demands (and with them the figures of Milton and Wordsworth) looming on each side. Forced by illness to return from the hopeful walking trip through the north, encountering the dying Tom, the hostile reviews, the serious effort of the next large poem, he could squirm comfortably on a cushioned chair when he reached Hampstead, look up with a tired grin, and say: "Bless thee, Bottom: bless thee! thou are translated." But when we come to the impassioned odes, we feel that we are dealing with a very different Keats. Yet he could finish writing out the ambitious "Ode to Psyche" with a flourish impossible to imagine from Wordsworth or Shelley or from any number of other poets: "Here endethe yᵉ Ode to Psyche." And not long before he wrote the "Grecian Urn" he could tell his sister that he was going to buy her some paste gems and seals at Tassie's shop, like the one he used as a seal for his own letters, and then ask her whether she wanted "heads of great Men such as Shakespeare, Milton &c—or fancy pieces of Art; such as Fame, Adonis &c—those gentry you read of at the end of the English Dictionary." "Fancy pieces of Art," with figures on them: what is the Grecian Urn? And "those gentry" one finds at the end of the dictionary include the characters not only of the embarrassing *Endymion* but of the great new effort, *Hyperion*. So on April 30, when Keats is finishing his long letter to George, the previous part of which closes with the pages about the "Vale of Soul-Making" and the human heart as the primer or "hornbook" to the mind. He has a few minutes to kill while he waits for Brown to finish copying some of his recent sonnets so that he himself can include them and the "Ode to Psyche" in his letter. In this vacant moment Keats starts an extemporaneous sonnet "On Fame" ("How fever'd is the man") which, within a line or two, turns to something rather different from what the title implies. It turns to man's general inability to accept his mortal, finite condition "with temperate blood," and to the tendency of the heart, through this self-defeating protest and anxiety, to "spoil" the very experiences possible to us as living, conscious creatures. Keats was completely aware of his own state of mind. With self-amusement, he heads the sonnet with a motto—firmly underlined—that could apply not only to the odes, to which he now turned, but also to the strange, brisk *Lamia* that follows them:

> *You cannot eat your cake and have it too*
> Proverb.

12

Meanwhile the momentum gained in using the new stanza continued during the writing of the "Ode on Melancholy." This poem matches the "Nightingale" and the "Grecian Urn" in restrained intensity of language and versification. An important difference, however, is that it lacks a dominant symbol. Keats is therefore forced to storm the main gate of the subject directly. This was not a decisive handicap. He was used to it. Partly because of his lack of formal education and his early freedom from the self-consciousness it often creates, he had begun writing poetry in this way, reassured by the large directness of earlier poetry, and without thought of the "winding stair" which is often necessary, said Bacon, for rising. And alone among the major modern poets, Keats was able to get away with it. The ode "To Autumn" is a triumphant example. Yet, for over a year and a half, his ultimate ideal had been dramatic; and in the "Nightingale" and the "Grecian Urn" he had at last found himself developing a form of dramatic lyric that included symbolic debate. The burden of the "Ode on Melancholy" is carried by the massive last stanza in what again reminds us of Keats's direct credos: a richly complex credo now, distilling much that had been actively dramatized in the other odes, especially the "Nightingale." But a direct assertion of belief, whatever else may be said of it, can hardly be dramatic unless there is either some form of debate or else a developing discovery by the poet of what he really believes. Neither of these is present in the "Ode on Melancholy." Keats's own awareness of this may explain the unusual stance he decides to give the poem—unusual for him, however common otherwise: that in which the poet addresses an imaginary person with protest or exhortation. Wordsworth especially was fond of it, often turning it into what seems to be a form of hectoring ("Up! up! my Friend, and quit your books"); and it was doubtless one of the mannerisms of Wordsworth that Keats had in mind when he spoke of poetry that "bullies us" and, "if we do not agree, seems to put its hand in its breeches pocket." The mode was so alien to Keats's habitual thinking that no other poem he wrote uses the device in this direct way.

But he faced a practical problem. Given the feelings that were settling, with eloquence and strength, into the last two stanzas (for it is they that put what he really wishes to say), and lacking the obduracies of a dominant symbol that he can debate, how can the poem assume a length appropriate to the capacious stanza he is using and acquire movement and the presence of a living voice? The temptation was to introduce himself as if in debate with someone else: and in contrast with the opening of the other odes, the first stanza starts with abrupt protest:

No, no, go not to Lethe, neither twist
Wolf's-bane, tight-rooted, for its poisonous wine.[12]

The protest of the first stanza is against the conventional symbols of oblivion, death, and melancholy. In this indirect presentation of the absent voice he wishes to answer, the stanza fails to progress, though the language is no less condensed than later. Instead, images conventionally associated with melancholy—he had been lately reading Burton's *Anatomy of Melancholy*—are simply piled upon the same point:

Nor suffer thy pale forehead to be kiss'd
By nightshade, ruby grape of Proserpine;
Make not your rosary of yew-berries,
Nor let the beetle, nor the death-moth be
Your mournful Psyche, nor the downy owl
A partner in your sorrow's mysteries;
For shade to shade will come too drowsily,
And drown the wakeful anguish of the soul.

The passing of shade to deeper shade, of twilight into night, will bring only the deadening of awareness. It is wakefulness that is prized, the capacity to savor, even if it include "wakeful anguish" —a heart, as he wrote in the "Grecian Urn," "high-sorrowful and cloy'd."

Anticipating the ode "To Autumn" of four months later, the second stanza then turns directly to the vivid acceptance of process. In the very springing of the flowers and the new green of the hill, transience falls upon them like a "shroud" as they emerge into being. But the same process in which death is implicit is also leading things into existence and fostering them toward fulfillment. This is an "April shroud," promising existence as well as death:

---

[12] A still earlier stanza was rejected, partly in favor of the direct beginning of the present one and partly because, with a full two stanzas, too much space was being devoted to what melancholy was not. The grisly humor may also have struck Keats as excessive, and the final three lines show haste:

Though you should build a bark of dead men's bones,
And rear a phantom gibbet for a mast,
Stitch creeds together for a sail, with groans
To fill it out, blood-stainèd and aghast;
Although your rudder be a dragon's tail
Long sever'd, yet still hard with agony,
Your cordage large uprootings from the skull
Of bald Medusa, certes you would fail
To find the Melancholy—whether she
Dreameth in any isle of Lethe dull.

> But when the melancholy fit shall fall
>   Sudden from heaven like a weeping cloud,
> That fosters the droop-headed flowers all,
>   And hides the green hill in an April shroud;
> Then glut thy sorrow on a morning rose,
>   Or on the rainbow of the salt sand-wave,
>   Or on the wealth of globèd peonies;
> Or if thy mistress some rich anger shows,
>   Emprison her soft hand, and let her rave,
>   And feed deep, deep upon her peerless eyes.

Even if the objects at which we clutch were to remain as relatively impervious to process as the Grecian urn, we, in our own reactions, could not. "Where's the eye," as Keats wrote in the lines on "Fancy," that does not "weary"?

> Not a Mistress but doth cloy.
> Where's the cheek that doth not fade
> Too much gaz'd at?

Yet even if our feelings and their objects could continue to sustain each other, and we possessed an uninterrupted happiness—a "happiness carried to an extreme," as he wrote George in April,

> What must it end in?—Death—and who in such a case could bear with death . . . But in truth I do not believe in this sort of perfectibility—the nature of the world will not admit of it . . . The point at which Man may arrive is as far as the paralel state in inanimate nature and no further—For instance suppose a rose to have sensation, it blooms on a beautiful morning it enjoys itself—but there comes a cold wind, a hot sun—it cannot escape it, it cannot destroy its annoyances—they are as native to the world as itself; no more can man be happy in spite, the world[l]y elements will prey upon his nature.

The knowledge both of our own brevity and of the brevity of what we seek to hold awakens the drowsy, easily distracted attention, and fosters a heightened awareness that will match the transient process it salutes—an awareness that itself inevitably leads to the "sovran shrine" of melancholy. For it is not simply the knowledge of transience that brings sorrow or pain. In a response sufficiently intense—a response duplicating and identifying itself with the active process it acknowledges and shares—the full emotional resources of our nature are called into play. Pain and "aching pleasure" pass organically into each other as the nectar sipped by the bee passes into the poison sting within its body. Images of pleasure and pain are now coalesced in the final stanza. For the contrast now is not of one with the other but rather of both, in organic combination, with the dimly allegorical background (the "temple," "Veiled Melancholy" and her "sovran shrine," the "cloudy trophies")—allegorical images that Keats had once so warmly incorporated in narrative but that now (as later in the *Fall of Hyperion*) loom abstract and shadowlike, suggesting the permanence of the nonhuman:

> She dwells with Beauty—Beauty that must die;
>   And Joy, whose hand is ever at his lips
> Bidding adieu; and aching Pleasure nigh,
>   Turning to poison while the bee-mouth sips:
> Ay, in the very temple of Delight
>   Veil'd Melancholy has her sovran shrine,
>   Though seen of none save him whose strenuous tongue
>   Can burst Joy's grape against his palate fine;
> His soul shall taste the sadness of her might,
>   And be among her cloudy trophies hung.

13

Keats had now, within about three weeks, written four of the great lyric poems in English. Whatever he thought of them (while composing them he was too preoccupied to write letters, and immediately afterwards other matters suddenly became urgent), they were at least bringing back the habit of composition, and with it some of the confidence that had been so shaken during the previous months, though the rise in confidence was not apparent for a few weeks. Together these four odes came to two hundred and twenty-seven lines, well over half the length of one of the books of *Hyperion;* and of course it was to *Hyperion,* or to something like it, that he really wanted to turn. Yet the thought of having to "strain my ne[r]ves at some grand Poem" so soon after being forced to put aside *Hyperion* also intimidated him. He would need time. But by the middle of May, time—at least for a few years—did not seem available.

The Final Beginning: *Lamia*

✻⊹۞⊹✻⊹۞⊹✻⊹۞⊹✻⊹۞⊹✻⊹۞⊹✻⊹۞⊹✻⊹۞⊹✻⊹۞⊹✻⊹۞⊹✻⊹۞⊹✻⊹۞

May to July, 1819

WITHIN A FEW WEEKS he would once again have to find a place to
live. Charles Brown was as usual planning to rent his half of the
house for the summer; it never occurred to him to do otherwise.
The money it brought each summer was a help, and he enjoyed
the chance to get away from London. Nor did it occur to Keats to
make the slightest suggestion that Brown alter his plans. Especially
since he already owed Brown so much, Keats wished to be as small
a problem as possible. But the thought preyed on his mind. The
irritating sense of helplessness, the dependence on others, the lack
of a congenial place of his own in which to live and work, all symbolized his inability to get started successfully in any one thing.

The strain he was under is shown by his sudden flurry of alternating resolution, uncertainty, and guilt when, on May 12, the
long-awaited letter from George arrived, describing, among other
matters, his need for money. The Birkbeck Settlement in Illinois
had proved bitterly disappointing. The land still available was
heavily forested and had to be cleared before it was tilled. He was
prepared to build his own house; but meanwhile he and Georgiana were expecting a baby. He had turned south, and was now in
Kentucky, where he thought he had a good opportunity to get
started in business. He was writing to Abbey about his needs; but
the implication of his letter was that he would also welcome any
free money his brother might wish to lend him.

The extent to which Keats exaggerated George's need tells us
something about his own state of mind; and the jolt may have been
the more unsettling because, for two or three weeks, he had been
almost completely absorbed in writing the odes. Ironically, George
was, at this very moment, on the point of losing about half of the
money he took with him: but the news of this loss did not arrive
until September. Meanwhile Keats, with his ready sympathy, was

touched to the quick. George, who had so often helped him in the past, now depended on him. A large reservoir of guilt, accumulating since Keats had left Guy's Hospital, was also suddenly tapped. Though he himself was the oldest of the brothers, it was George who had so often performed the patient function of an older brother, looking after Tom and dealing with Abbey. As Keats wrote not long afterwards (May 31): "I have been always till now almost as careless of the world as a fly—my troubles' were all of the Imagination—My Brother George always stood between me and any dealings with the world—Now I find I must buffet it."

As soon as he received George's letter, Keats hurried to town to show it to Georgiana's mother, Mrs. Wylie, and left it with her so that her two sons might read it. He dashed off a note the same day to William Haslam, telling him that the Wylies would be forwarding the letter to him immediately and asking him, as soon as he had read it, to "Send it me like Lightning" so that he could take it at once to his sister. Meanwhile he posted a note to her: "I have a Letter from George at last—and it contains, considering all things, good news." He tells her he will walk over with it as soon as he receives it from Haslam. There was little else that he could do at the moment. Nothing would be gained and something might well be lost if he himself went to see Abbey, who disliked the sight of him and still continued to discourage his visits to Fanny. Abbey had always appeared friendly to George, however, and might be open to a direct appeal from George if Keats himself only kept out of the way.

But within another two weeks Keats had quietly formed a new resolution. He would do one of two things. He might devote himself to writing for just a few more months, if he could manage it financially. And in that case, he would try to put every other interest completely out of his mind. This would include Fanny Brawne, to whom he was almost certainly not yet engaged. It would also involve beginning, without further delay, another long poem, whether he felt prepared for it or not. The second choice was to turn to immediate practical use the one other skill he felt that he had learned—that of a surgeon. It was a measure of his own desperation that he thought of this choice only in the most drastic terms, and began to consider signing up as ship's surgeon on an Indiaman. Perhaps only by going to that extreme could he be sure of keeping himself to the decision once it had been made. To remain in London as a surgeon, in the midst of all its associations with literature and his effort of the last four years, would be too poignant a defeat. The only solution would be to put all this behind him. When Haslam belatedly returned George's letter—it had been accidentally torn in several pieces with some other papers and lost for a while—Keats wrote to Fanny (May 26) that he would come over the next day and tell her what the letter had contained; and he added gently: "I want also to speak to you concerning myself. Mind I do not purpose to quit England as George has done; but I am affraid that I shall be forced to take a voyage or two." He tried to reassure her for the moment by telling her that they need not think of the voyage "for some months." But actually, within three or four days, he thought he had almost made up his mind.

He began to grasp at gestures of resolution to steady himself. Two days after he walked over to Walthamstow to see his sister, he wrote to his publishers, Taylor and Hessey, "I am this morning making a general clearance of all lent Books—all." He did not explain what was on his mind. But a brief undated note to Charles Dilke survives, undoubtedly written at the same time:

> As Brown is not to be a fixture at Ham[p]stead I have at last made up my mind to send home all lent Books—I should have seen you before this—but my mind [h]as been at work all over the world to find out what to do—I have my choice of three things—or at least two—South America or Surgeon to an I[n]diaman—which last I think will be my fate—I shall resolve in a few days.

2

Poetry, it is plain, was beginning to recede as a possibility. And he tried to convince himself that he did not care. In a mood both of fatigue and self-defense he suddenly found himself writing one more ode, the sixty-line "Ode on Indolence," to which he prefixed the motto "They toil not, neither do they spin." For the general framework of it, he went back to the morning he had described to George on March 19 (the day after he received a black eye while playing cricket), when he had felt "indolent and supremely careless . . . from my having slumbered till nearly eleven," and had been relaxed to such a happy degree that pleasure has no show of enticement and pain no unbearable frown. Neither Poetry, nor Ambition, nor Love have any alertness of countenance as they pass by me: they seem rather like three figures on a greek vase—a Man and two women— whom no one but myself could distinguish in their disguisement.

Far below the standard of the other odes (a curious feature is the extent to which it languidly echoes phrases and images from them),[1] its value is primarily biographical. It was omitted from the volume in which the others appeared, and remained unprinted until twenty-seven years after Keats's death. So strong, however, was the pressure to get started at something that the poem pleased Keats for the moment. It was a gesture of at least mild defiance. "You will judge of my 1819 temper," he told Sarah Jeffrey (June 9), "when I tell you that the thing I have most enjoyed this year has been writing an ode to Indolence."

The six stanzas, unlike the other odes (except for the beginning of the "Ode to Psyche"), relax into first-person narrative:

> One morn before me were three figures seen,
>   With bowèd necks, and joinèd hands, side-faced;
> And one behind the other stepp'd serene,
>   In placid sandals, and in white robes graced;
> They pass'd, like figures on a marble urn,
>   When shifted round to see the other side;
>   They came again . . .

Twice the figures pass by him and then fade. The third and final time they turn their faces. He now recognizes them: Love, Ambition, and

> The last, whom I love more, the more of blame
>   Is heap'd upon her, maiden most unmeek,—
>   I knew to be my demon Poesy.

The interest of the poem lies in the unexpected confessions that emerge in the last two stanzas. What had started as a mere rendering of a mood of passivity begins to betray a divided attitude crossed by inconsistent attempts at self-persuasion. When he recognizes the figures, the poet really wishes to follow them. It is only because he cannot do so that he ends by dismissing them. To begin with, love—at least at this moment—is very much in third place.

[1] For example, echoing "Psyche": "My head cool-bedded in the flowery grass"; from the "Nightingale": "Benumb'd," "O for," "man's little heart's short fever-fit," "ach'd for wings" to "follow," and the "open casement" letting in the song of the throstle; and throughout, images that recall the "Grecian Urn."

A brief rhetorical flourish suffices: what is love, and where is it anyway? The attempt to condescend to "poor Ambition," and wave it aside, demands a more deliberate effort of phrase. Before Poesy ("whom I love more") he is really helpless: he is too committed to be able to find any effective reason at all for even pretending to dismiss it. He is certainly not prepared to reduce it, like ambition, to a mere "short fever-fit." He can only give it a general "no" (immediately followed by a qualification, "at least for me") :

> I wanted wings:
> O folly! What is Love! and where is it?
> And for that poor Ambition! it springs
> From a man's little heart's short fever-fit;
> For Poesy!—no,—she has not a joy,—
> At least for me,—so sweet as drowsy noons,
> And evenings steep'd in honied indolence;
> O, for an age so shelter'd from annoy,
> That I may never know how change the moons,
> Or hear the voice of busy common-sense!

That poetry is now proving to be such an effort is another implicit confession. The sense of effort, of working against the grain, had already been growing for at least two reasons, which strengthened each other through combination. Even before George's letter arrived, there had been the obvious need of some success within the next year or two merely in order to secure a livelihood. Throughout the autumn he had been able to take the reviews of *Endymion* in his stride, partly because of the daily anxiety about Tom and partly because he was so preoccupied with *Hyperion*, which was then going forward rapidly. But in the months that followed the death of Tom, moments of misgiving and self-uncertainty had multiplied. Prejudiced as the reviews might be, there was the fact that they represented a possible barometer of taste, and hence of likely sales; or at least they might affect sales. But it was not only the need to earn a livelihood, sharp as it was, that was creating such a hurdle of discouragement. What had the months brought otherwise since he had returned from the north? The odes had indeed reawakened some of his confidence, more than he knew at the time. But the really large effort of *Hyperion*—and it represented so much—had trailed off into nothing. It, or "some grand Poem," was the essential thing. When he said (June 9) that he had "been very idle lately, very averse to writing," partly because of "the overpowering idea of our dead poets," he was not speaking of the two or three weeks that had passed since the odes of early May. He was thinking of all the months that had passed since the bulk of *Hyperion* was written. Since December he had been able to write only the ineffective, fragmentary Book III. Neither a finished "grand Poem" nor even the semblance of a modest financial return seemed near.

Was he really surrendering very much, therefore, if he signed up as a ship's surgeon for a year or two? True, he had received praise and expectation aplenty from a small circle of kindly friends. But this was no assurance that he was not simply another poetaster who, like Hunt, was "deluding" himself. ("There is no greater Sin after the 7 deadly than to flatter oneself into an idea of being a great Poet.") No, these three figures in the ode whom he was preparing to dismiss were as unattainable, as fundamentally unreal, as those figures on that other Grecian urn that he had been unable to join. Let them be regarded as what they were—mere figures. He would not, for these three "Ghosts" or "Phantoms," raise his head from the grass. He would not be misled.

> For I would not be dieted with praise,
>   A pet-lamb in a sentimental farce!
> Fade softly from my eyes, and be once more
>   In masque-like figures on the dreamy urn.

> .   .   .   .

>   Vanish, ye Phantoms! from my idle spright,
> Into the clouds, and never more return!

3

While returning all the books he had borrowed over the last year or two, he also decided to make "a general conflagration of all old Letters and Memorandums." In the process of doing so, he came across some letters from the Jeffrey sisters, in Teignmouth, who had been so kind to George and Tom the year before, and with whom Keats too had become friends when he went down to Devon in order to look after Tom and allow George to return to London.

He suddenly found himself thinking of the small villages on or near the Devon coast. It might be possible to live there very cheaply. Moreover, he would be forced to be completely alone:

there would be no temptations to distract him. The thought of making one final try, and with a completely fresh start, grew on him; and the resolution to go off alone once again appealed to his need for decisiveness. He hesitated for another day or two, and then wrote to the eldest of the Jeffrey sisters, Sarah (May 31), asking her whether she would

> Enquire in the Villages round Teignmouth if there is any Lodging commodious for its cheapness; and let me know where it is and what price. I have the choice as it were of two Poisons (yet I ought not to call this a Poison) the one is voyaging to and from India for a few years; the other is leading a fevrous life alone with Poetry— This latter will suit me best—for I cannot resolve to give up my Studies It strikes me it would not be quite so proper for you to make such inquiries—so give my love to your Mother and ask her to do it. Yes, I would rather conquer my indolence and strain my ne[r]ves at some grand Poem—than be in a dunderheaded indiaman.

He is embarrassed about being in this dilemma; it must doubtless sound very strange. "Pray let no one in Teignmouth know any thing of this." He is only beginning to face up to responsibilities:

> I must take my Stand upon some vantage ground and begin to fight—I must choose between despair & Energy—I choose the latter— though the world has taken on a quakerish look with me, which I once thought was impossible—
>> 'Nothing can bring back the hour
>> Of splendour in the grass and glory in the flower'
> I once thought this a Melancholist's dream—
> But why do I speak to you in this manner? . . . I do not do so to strangers. I have not quite made up my mind.

Sarah Jeffrey suggested a place in the village of Bradley. But Keats was beginning to have second thoughts about the south of Devon. It would be continually reminding him of Tom. This was one reason why he had not wanted to go back to the old Hampstead lodgings that he and his brother had shared in the house of Bentley the postman, the other reasons being the noise of the Bentley children—"the young carrots"—and Keats's feeling that, if he were really to throw himself into writing without interruption, he had to get away from London entirely. In any case, a new claim on his generosity had just been made. James Rice, whose health was now even worse than usual, asked Keats on June 8 to come and spend a month with him in the Isle of Wight. Pleasant though

Rice's company generally was, his illness would be a trial: Keats had faced illness in those closest to him for so long; Tom's final autumn especially haunted him; and now he was not completely well himself. But he could hardly say no to Rice. At the same time the need to help someone else rescued him from further indecision. The alternative of signing up as a ship's surgeon was put out of mind for the time being. He wrote to Miss Jeffrey the next day that he would stay with Rice for a month, and then, in all probability, go to Bradley.

The thought of the whole blurring complexity of things kept striking him. He had been writing to George throughout the spring not only about the need of facing the unpredictability of circumstance but about the opportunities this very unpredictability brings. But how philosophically had he been applying that realization to his own life? As he wrote to Sarah Jeffrey on June 9, the thought of the self-defensive "Ode on Indolence," which he had so recently written, came to his mind. True enough, he had enjoyed writing it; and he had indeed been "very idle lately, very averse to writing; both from the overpowering idea of our dead poets and from abatement of my love of fame." But there were more effective ways of refusing to be a "pet-lamb in a sentimental farce" than by simply giving up the thought of writing: "I hope I am a little more of a Philosopher than I was, consequently a little less of a versifying Pet-lamb." Miss Jeffrey's advice to put aside the thought of joining an Indiaman "just suits me." Not that she is right in saying that it would sap the "energies of Mind." Such a challenge, he tells her, would "strengthen them":

> To be thrown among people who care not for you, with whom you have no sympathies forces the Mind upon its own resourses, and leaves it free to make its speculations of the differences of human character and to class them with the calmness of a Botanist. An Indiaman is a little world.

Has anything ever been intrinsically, formatively acquired except by directly facing challenge? He is naturally reassuring himself, but with insight partly won from his own experience:

> One of the great reasons that the english have produced the finest writers in the world; is, that the English world has ill-treated them during their lives and foster'd them after their deaths. They have in general been trampled aside into the bye paths of life and seen the festerings of Society. They have not been treated like the

Raphaels of Italy. And where is the Englishman and Poet who has given a magnif[i]cent Entertainment at the christening of one of his Hero's Horses as Boyardo did? He had a Castle in the Appenine. He was a noble Poet of Romance; not a miserable and mighty Poet of the human Heart. The middle age of Shakspeare was all c[l]ouded over . . . Ben Johnson was a common Soldier and in the Low countries, in the face of two armies, fought a single combat with a french Trooper and slew him.

Not that he would for this reason blindly rush on board an India-man, "nor for examples sake run my head into dark alleys: I dare say my discipline is to come, and plenty of it too."

He felt a sudden relief in having finally come to a decision. Dashing off a note the same day to his sister, and speaking of his last visit to her at Abbey's house ("They really surprised me with super civility—how did Mrs. A. manage it?"), he exuberantly closes with a little parody of the conversation there at lunch. How could Mrs. Abbey be so extravagant as to have offered him a glass of Lisbon wine?

had she drained the Gooseberry? Truly I cannot delay making another visit—asked to take Lunch, whether I will have ale, wine take sur g ar,—objection to green—like cream—thin bread and butter—another cup—agreeable—enough sugar—little more cream—too weak 12 shillin & &c &c lord I must come again.

9|6|1819

4

He would be having to steel himself to call at Abbey's office in a few days. Some money was needed not merely for the trip to the Isle of Wight but for the rest of the summer; and he had almost nothing left. James Elmes, the editor of the *Annals of the Fine Arts*, had heard from Haydon about the "Ode to a Nightingale," and negotiations had started for publishing it in the July issue. But this would bring very little. On Monday, June 14, he was unable to fulfill his promise to visit his sister. He could not afford to take the coach to Walthamstow, and meanwhile "I have my sore-throat coming again to prevent my walking."

Finally, on Wednesday the sixteenth, he forced himself to go to town and see Abbey. But Abbey had a surprise already prepared, effective because of the ignorance in which he deliberately kept the Keats children in all matters concerning their grandparents' estate. He pulled out a letter from the solicitor of Margaret Jennings, the widow of their uncle Midgley, containing, as Keats said, "the pleasant news that she was about to file a Bill in Chancery against us." Abbey told Keats that this would completely freeze his grandmother's estate. Actually it would do nothing of the sort. If the suit were ever begun—and it never was, although Abbey kept stating for months that it was about to begin—it would have touched only one small part of it: that half of Midgley's own share of his father's estate which, after his death, the court had transferred to his mother.[2] The bulk of what Alice Jennings left her grandchildren would have been completely unaffected. With deliberate falsehood, Abbey also capitalized on Keats's generosity. Even if Margaret Jennings were unsuccessful in this threatened suit, the expenses, he said, would be heavy; and they would have to be paid out of Abbey's own pocket. Hence, as Keats told Haydon the next day (June 17), "I could not ask him for any more money . . . till the affair is decided." And if the suit went against Abbey, Keats supposed "I must in conscience make over to him what little he may have remaining." Before Keats left the office, Abbey showed him a letter from George mentioning the birth of a daughter.

He was naturally shaken, and tried to think what next to do. He could not get over to tell his sister about the matter: the coach fare was now even more prohibitive than it had been three days before, and his throat was still too sore to allow him to walk that far. So he wrote to her of his interview with Abbey. He was preparing, he said, to go out and look "for a Situation with an Apothecary." But Charles Brown, who was able to lend him some money for current expenses, had persuaded him "to try the press once more; so I will with all my industry and ability." One of Brown's proposals was that they collaborate on a play in which they might be able to interest Edmund Kean. Brown would plan out the play, which he may have had in mind for some time, and jot down each scene in prose. Keats, even if busy with other writing, could then turn the scenes into verse. It could probably be done quickly.

Meanwhile Keats, rather too optimistically, wrote at once, as he tells his sister (June 17), "to several people to whom I have lent money, requesting repayment." He is full of ideas of reformation.

2 The total transferred, in the "Order of 26 July 1811 of the Lord High Chancellor," came to £1,690.12. See Appendix III.

"I shall shake off my indolent fits, and among other reformation be more diligent in writing to you." With some embarrassment, he wrote to Haydon, to whom, after considerable effort to find it, he had lent £30 a few weeks before:

> My purpose is now to make one more attempt in the Press if that fail, "ye hear no more of me" as Chaucer says—Brown has lent me some money for the present. Do borrow or beg some how what you can for me. Do not suppose that I am at all uncomfortable about the matter in any other way than as it forces me to apply to the needy.[3]

Haydon was unable to repay anything. "That was no wonder," Keats wrote George three months later (September 20) ; but Keats felt hurt because Haydon "did not seem to care much about it," though he "could have sold his drawings to supply me." Perhaps Keats's letters to the others who owed him money were too delicate. In any case they brought no result. For he finally (August 23) , with great reluctance, wrote to John Taylor:

> I have been rather unfortunate lately in money concerns—from a threatened chancery suit—I was deprived at once of all recourse to my Guardian I relied a little on some of my debts being paid—which are of a tolerable amount [actually they came to £230]—but I have not had one pound refunded.

So involved, indirect, and embarrassed does the letter become from here on—with talk of pride as both good and bad; of his confidence that he may become a "popular writer"; of his determination not to be a "popular writer"—that Taylor, in desperation, had to send the letter to Woodhouse in the hope of finding out what Keats was really trying to say.[4]

Looking back on these weeks, Keats later confided to George that, in the whole "see-saw game of Life," it was now that he felt "nearest to the ground." Before leaving he talked with Fanny Brawne about his prospects. If a formal engagement was discussed, it was almost certainly with the understanding that it could not take place at this time. Whatever we can guess of the conversation must be based on a single sentence in a letter he wrote to her shortly afterwards (July 1) : "As I told you a day or two before I left Hampstead, I will never return to London if my Fate does not turn up Pam [a high trump] or at least a Court-card."

[3] II.120.   [4] See below, Chapter XXI, section 4.

5

When he took the coach to Portsmouth on Sunday, June 27, he sat on top in order to save money. But the day turned cold, and a heavy rain fell so constantly that, as he wrote his sister, "I may say I went to Portsmouth by water." Before he reached the Isle of Wight, he had caught a bad cold, and as usual it flew to his throat. The sore throat was still nagging him three weeks later. Money, enough of a problem before, became more so within a week after he arrived. For on July 6 he received another letter from George, this time openly asking him whether he himself could lend any money. Keats immediately wrote Abbey (July 7), received no reply, and sent a second letter (July 16), which survives in so mutilated a condition that we are tempted to infer that Abbey himself tore it in irritation, and then decided to keep it.

He was now back, strangely enough, in the same place to which he had set off a little more than two years before in his desperate effort to begin the "test" of *Endymion*. Now, as then, he got out his books and paper. But there was no temptation to take off even a day to see the scenery, as he had so excitedly done on his first visit. Nor, with his sore throat, did he feel like doing so anyway. After talking briefly with Rice, he tried to plunge immediately into work. He had at least three sizable projects in mind. The first was a new narrative poem, *Lamia,* in a very different style from any he had attempted. The second was the five-act tragedy he was to put into blank verse for Charles Brown. It was to be called *Otho the Great;* and before Keats left, Brown had given him a prose version of the first act, which was to have three scenes. Lastly, there was *Hyperion* itself, about which Keats was now determined to do something. He was making enough progress after a week to be able to echo, with at least a semblance of lightness, Lockhart's savage review of the preceding autumn ("back to the shop Mr. John, back to the 'plasters, pills, and ointment boxes' "). Telling his sister again (July 6) of his determination "to try the fortune of my Pen once more," he assures her "I have some confidence in my success"; but if things do not work out, "I have enough knowledge of my gallipots to ensure me an employment & maintenance."

He began first on *Lamia,* devoting his spare and more fatigued hours to *Otho the Great.* Within twelve or thirteen days, he had

"proceeded pretty well with Lamia," he tells Reynolds (July 11),
"finishing the 1st part which consists of about 400 lines," and, in
the same time, he had completed the first act of *Otho*. More important, while writing *Lamia*, "I have great hopes of success because I make use of my Judgment more deliberately than I yet
have done; but in Case of failure with the world, I shall find my
content." Even leaving aside *Otho*, he was averaging, in short, almost forty lines a day, not much below the high average of fifty
lines a day that he had maintained for Book III of *Endymion*,
back in September 1817. Yet the difference in quality hardly permits comparison; his sore throat was bothering him constantly;
and at the same time the writing of the first act of *Otho* amounted
to another forty lines a day. One compensation in being "alone
at my task" was the freedom from "the bustle and hateful literary
chitchat" of London, the affectations of which had become increasingly unpleasant during the past year. He went out very little from
the cottage where he and Rice were staying at the southern end of
High Street in Shanklin. It was almost the height of the tourist
season at the Isle of Wight, and the place was filled with visitors
wandering about, with spyglasses, in search of picturesque scenery. Keats, after a while, thought he should take some walks. "Tomorrow," he tells Fanny Brawne (July 15), if his "health continues to improve during the night," he will try to "take a look
fa[r]ther about the country, and spy at the parties about here who
come hunting after the picturesque like beagles." But by the end
of the month, as he told Dilke, what little he had seen did not prod
him to continue the effort. He tried to give the place credit for the
"Surprise" he might have felt if he had not already lost his "cockney maidenhead" to scenery two or three years before. "But I may
call myself an old Stager in the picturesque, and unless it be something very large and overpowering I cannot receive any extraordinary relish."

Confined so much to the cottage, he and Rice inevitably wore
on each other's nerves. Summing up the month to Charles Dilke,
Keats later confessed (July 31) that

> Rice and I passed rather a dull time of it. I hope he will not re-
> pent coming with me. He was unwell and I was not in very good
> health: and I am affraid we made each other worse by acting upon
> each others spirits. We would grow as melancholy as need be. I con-

fess I cannot bear a sick person in a House especially alone—it weighs upon me day and night—and more so when perhaps the Case is irretrievable—Indeed I think Rice is in a dangerous state.

The situation was all the more painful because of the pathos of Rice's constant efforts to "conquer his feelings and hide them from me" with a joke or a "forc'd Pun."

6

The room in which Keats worked and slept began on the third day to remind him of a "Sepulchre," and later, as it seemed to get smaller, of a "little coffin." Throughout the day he could keep in focus his grim determination not to return to London without solid accomplishment. But the nights depressed him. It was with something close to resentment that he found his thoughts turning to Fanny Brawne; and the strange tone of the first of the famous love letters (for it is now that they begin) may well have disturbed her. He starts by telling her (the morning of July 1) that he had written her another letter the night before; but he has decided not to send it because it reads like something out of Rousseau's *La Nouvelle Héloïse*. This came of having written it at night, when, lonely and tired, he could so easily slip into those passionate "Rapsodies which I once thought it impossible that I should ever give way to, and which I have often laughed at in another." Then the critical passage follows:

> I have never known any unalloy'd Happiness for many days together: the death or sickness of some one has always spoilt my hours —and now when none such troubles oppress me, it is you must confess very hard that another sort of pain should haunt me. Ask yourself my love whether you are not very cruel to have so entrammelled me, so destroyed my freedom.

He tries to soften what he has just said by an element of playfulness. She must sit down and "confess" that this was an unfortunate thing for her to do, and put her confession

> in the Letter you must write immediately and do all you can to console me in it—make it rich as a draught of poppies to intoxicate me—write the softest words and kiss them that I may at least touch my lips where yours have been. For myself I know not how to express my devotion to so fair a form: I want a brighter word than bright, a fairer word than fair. I almost wish we were butterflies and

liv'd but three summer days—three such days with you I could fill with more delight than fifty common years could ever contain.

Of the three strands that recur almost constantly in the letters to Fanny Brawne until Keats returns to Hampstead in late October, two are thus present at the very start of the first one he sends her. One is the strong element of protest or resistance, put with surprising frankness or at least lack of inhibition. Balancing this is a devotion expressed with the passionate surrender that so embarrassed the Victorians. (A vivid example would be the often-quoted remarks from his fourth letter [July 25]: "All I can bring you is a swooning admiration of your Beauty . . . I hate the world . . . would I could take a sweet poison from your lips to send me out of it . . . I will imagine you Venus tonight and pray, pray, pray to your star like a He[a]then. Your's ever, fair Star.") [5] So closely do the two reactions interrelate that, with few exceptions, any very strong expression of either one begins to evoke the other. Occasionally they coalesce in a single sentence or two:

> I look not forward with any pleasure to what is call'd being settled in the world; I tremble at domestic cares—yet for you I would meet them, though if it would leave you the happier I would rather die than do so.   (July 25)

> It seems to me that a few more moments thought of you would unchrystallize and dissolve me—I must not give way to it—but turn

[5] None of Fanny Brawne's letters to Keats survives. But her uneasy reaction to this letter can be inferred from the opening sentence of Keats's next (August 5): "You say you must not have any more such Letters as the last: I'll try that you shall not . . ."

Because of parallels in phrasing, an argument can be advanced that the sonnet "Bright star" was composed at this time: see De Selincourt, ed., *Poems* (1926), p. 588, and A. Ward, *Studies in Philology*, LII (1955), 75–85. But, as we have seen, parallels in Keats's letters are never an effective argument for dating, and frequently anticipate phrases in the poems by several months (e.g., the echoes in the "Grecian Urn" and the "Nightingale" from the Scottish tour). The use of the star, moreover, is utterly different: Fanny is here associated with the evening star, Venus; in the sonnet Keats wishes to identify himself with the steadfastness of a star (a common image in Keats: cf., in *Hyperion*, "the earnest stars," "the same bright patient stars"). The one fact we know about the sonnet is that it was written in 1819 (Brown). The reference to the "new soft fallen mask / Of snow" is not determining, but, other things being equal, would sway us a little from July either to early 1819 (which is probably too early; the relationship does not seem to have been that intense at that time) or to the winter of 1819, when he was back at Hampstead and had virtually surrendered other ambitions. Finally, had Keats composed the sonnet in July, he would almost certainly have copied it in one of his letters to Fanny (all of which she kept). There would have been no reason to conceal it; it was hardly so outspoken as the letters he was sending.

to my writing again—if I fail I shall die hard—O my love, your lips are growing sweet again to my fancy—I must forget them.

(August 16)

After his absence of three and a half months, he finally sees her for a day (October 10). Writing to her another three days later, he lets slip an open admission that doubtless gave Fanny Brawne a further jolt. Throughout those long weeks, during which he was writing such passionate letters, he was trying to reason down his affection, and even started to do so again after seeing her:

> You have ravish'd me away by a Power I cannot resist; and yet I could resist till I saw you; and even since I have seen you I have endeavoured "to reason against the reasons of my Love." I can do that no more—the pain would be too great—My Love is selfish.

As his first letter to her closes, a third element appears that also continues. This is the strongly apprehensive jealousy (often accompanied by protests against his own "selfishness" and by resolutions to learn to be less selfish and possessive) that did so much to give Fanny Brawne a reputation for flippancy, creating as it did the impression that she was giving him constant provocation. But the context in the first letter is revealing. He is reminding Fanny of what he told her before he left: that he "will never return to London if my Fate does not turn up Pam or at least a Court-card." It is, in short, he who is really committed to other interests (though of course any success he attains can be rationalized as being as much for her sake as his own).[6] Yet, without transition, he immediately goes on, ending with a quotation from Massinger's *Duke of Milan* (which he had been reading probably in the hope of getting into the mood for *Otho the Great*):

> Though I could centre my Happiness in you, I cannot expect to engross your heart so entirely—indeed if I thought you felt as much for me as I do for you at this moment I do not think I could restrain myself from seeing you again tomorrow for the delight of one embrace. But no—I must live upon hope and Chance. In case of the worst that can happen, I shall still love you—but what hatred shall I have for another! Some lines I read the other day are continually ringing a peal in my ears:

---

6 From a sentence in his fourth letter (July 25) we can infer that it is he rather than Fanny Brawne who has been reluctant to come to any specific understanding. Protesting in answer to her, he states: "I have, believe me, not been an age in letting you take possession of me" (II.132).

To see those eyes I prize above mine own
Dart favors on another—
And those sweet lips (yielding immortal nectar)
Be gently press'd by any but myself—
Think, think Francesca, what a cursed thing
It were beyond expression!

As we continue to meet such expressions, two peculiarities be-gin to strike us, neither of them completely distinct from the other. The first—and the thought can be only speculative—is that the uncertainty so necessary to jealousy is often being reinforced by his own divided attitude toward Fanny: reinforced by an uneasy, half-guilty suspicion that, while he himself is struggling against his affection for her, she may possibly be devoting at least a fraction of the same effort to questioning her affection for him. We are the more tempted to assume the presence of this common corollary of passionate love—common, at least, when there is also a desperate effort to fulfill another aim within a very limited time—because of his tendency to project on her other aspects of his own situation. A touching example is health, after he becomes fatally ill the following winter: the poorer his own health becomes, the more he worries about hers; the more penetrating the cold he constantly feels, the more he urges her to wear warm clothing.

But whatever the extent to which the projection of his own mis-givings enters into the chemistry of this assertive jealousy, a more general and important consideration is undeniable: this floating anxiety lacks specific object and focus. No actual third person is involved, and he knows it. (The old belief that Fanny Brawne must have been an irrepressible flirt has no basis.) [7] What we find, in other words, is not so much jealousy in the ordinary sense as a readiness for jealousy, an expectant preparation for it to become specific. The anxiety is entirely ideal, leaping forward from the present to a possible future: "In case of the worst that can happen, I shall still love you—but what hatred shall I have for another"; "So let me speak of you[r] Beauty, though to my own endanger-ing; if you could be so cruel to me as to try elsewhere its Power"; "If you should ever feel for Man at the first sight what I did for you, I am lost." Without the letters to Fanny Brawne, we should

---

[7] If a third person were involved, we can be positive he would have been named in these letters that are so impulsively ready to vent any apprehension. It is signifi-cant that Keats was unable to find any candidate until he was about to have to leave for Italy. Then, lacking anyone else, he pounced on Charles Brown.

perhaps be less ready to acknowledge the extent to which, since he was eight, circumstances (including the reception of his poetry) had created in him a strong temptation to expect the worst in most things. For little hint of this appears in his other letters or ever showed itself in his conversation. The general impression, in fact, is very much otherwise. His sympathetic ability to become absorbed in interests outside himself had been an effective guard against self-pity. But resolution and effort had also been necessary: the circumstances, after all, had been rather extreme. The rare admissions of this temptation to expect the worst appear almost exclusively in the letters to Fanny Brawne:

> You must have found out by this time I am a little given to bode ill like the raven; it is my misfortune not my fault; it has proceeded from the general tenor of the circumstances of my life, and rendered every event suspicious. However I will no more trouble either you or myself with sad Prophecies. (July 15)

> The time is passed when I had power to advise and warn you again[s]t the unpromising morning of my Life—My love has made me selfish. (October 13)

Not only had there been an "unpromising morning." The moments were increasing when, quite understandably, it could be doubted whether there would be any future at all of any sort. But of this deeper anxiety Keats could not bring himself to speak. It was preferable to keep that uneasiness indirect: to focus it more toward Fanny and away from more general, less manageable ambitions, and, in doing so, to conceive of some future lover, some future husband, supplanting him while he was still alive. "In case of the worst that can happen," he will at least still be there: "I shall still love you."

Whatever conclusions we may draw from these letters, we should also keep in mind the age of both Keats and Fanny Brawne. Keats was now twenty-three, and Fanny Brawne was to become nineteen on August 9. Finally we should try to remember the actual context of these letters that caused such surprise (a surprise sometimes mixed with genuine distaste, and sometimes spiced with the gladness of gossip) when they were long afterwards discovered and published. Because of Keats's stature as a poet, things connected with him take on a timeless quality; and this includes the love letters. We begin to think and speak of them as though this correspondence had been going on throughout most of his active career. But actually there are only two groups of letters: the ten that he wrote from July 1819 until he returned to Hampstead in late October; and those that begin the following February. The first were written while, with almost everything against him, he was trying to make one last effort, an effort crossed by so many shadows of apprehension that it was demanding more courage, and taking a larger toll of his resources, than any he had yet made. Still another consideration is appropriate to the poignant letters from February until August 1820, when he could no longer bring himself to write directly to her. These were written after everything for which he had most hoped had begun rapidly to dissolve.

7

After finishing the first half of *Lamia* in twelve or thirteen days, Keats put it aside to simmer for a while (July 10 or 11). He was impatient to see whether he could make at least a start at the project that had continued most to elude him: a reconsideration—if necessary a total reconception and rewriting—of *Hyperion*. It was the beginning of this new *Hyperion* to which he referred when he told Fanny Brawne (July 25) that he had been "all day employ'd in a very abstr[a]ct Poem."

He would doubtless have returned to *Lamia* sooner than he did except that Charles Brown descended on the cottage at Shanklin (July 22), impatient for them both to get ahead with their verse-play, *Otho the Great*. Keats obligingly agreed, and in a few days, as he told Dilke, he and Brown were "pretty well harnessed again to our dog-cart." It was not until the play was finished (August 23) that Keats, in another burst of energy that lasted a week or so, completed *Lamia*. But the poem is justly identified with the early summer, when the first half of it was written. For the plot, which he had taken from an account in Burton's *Anatomy of Melancholy*, was at least roughly predetermined. It was to end in a general puncturing of illusion. Not only was the resolution of the plot ready at hand, the principal character developed, and the first half of the poem itself written by July 11; but he was also moving fluently within the verse form he had chosen—a form that was another new departure for him. A far smaller effort would ordinarily be required to bring the poem to a close. But aside from the commitment to work on *Otho* and his eagerness to make a trial start at a new *Hyperion,* there may have been some reluctance to dispatch *Lamia* too quickly. By the time he had finished the first half of it, he was becoming more closely identified with the characters and the story than with those of any poem he had written; and *Lamia* would have been a much thinner poem, would have tapped fewer urgent concerns, or none, had he not. The connection with his complex reactions to Fanny Brawne at this time is particularly obvious. (This does not mean that the relation is simple or controlling; and, as usual with any good poem, it throws far more light on the life and mind of the writer than details gleaned from the life can throw upon it.) The preordained end of *Lamia,* involving the death of one character and the possible death—or at least painful dissolution—of another, could have its unwelcome side: felt with too close an involvement, it could create temptations to protest or at least pathos. But neither protest nor pathos was what he wanted. This new use of myth was to be brisk, objective, detached, and to possess at least some elements of the comic.

Much of the appeal of the simple fable, as he read it in Burton's *Anatomy of Melancholy,* lay in the challenge of its novelty. It could indeed be turned into an *Endymion* in reverse, refreshingly free of the "amusing sober-sadness" of *Isabella* and the sentimentality of the *Eve of St. Agnes* (only a little "less glaring," as he thought, than that of *Isabella*). Aside from his craftsmanlike attraction to the general challenge of a new departure, and the hope of jolting himself into another try at *Hyperion,* at least two other interests were touched by this potential novelty. He was thinking of the poetry-reading public, and wanted a narrative poem that would "take hold of people in some way—give them either pleasant or unpleasant sensation. What they want is a sensation of some sort." [8] Then there was the interest of applying a clean-cut, rather drastic resolution to the poetic treatment of the problem that had intrigued him for months: that of living with illusion and then being forced to disengage oneself from it. Attempts to explore it throughout the past half year had been lyrical and restricted: the jaunty rondeau, "Fancy"; the single, if suggestive, episode of "La belle dame"; the impulsive, subjective sonnet, "Why did I laugh tonight?" Of course the twin odes, the "Nightingale" and the

8 II.189.

"Grecian Urn," had, in their luminous ways, played about the subject, though asking more than they settled. But as for longer poems, the *Eve of St. Agnes* had only a hint or two; and nothing at all had come of the *Eve of St. Mark*. A welcome aspect of the fable of *Lamia* was that two things about it forced his hand to a new, abrupt treatment, and appeared to work against temptations either to tenderness or to subtlety of qualification. The source of attraction, Lamia, is a serpent, or at least she is a serpent much of the time. Distance was gratifyingly imposed at the start. This was no mere "belle dame sans merci," liable to develop difficulties or trials of her own if she were brought onto the stage as an actual character. Again, the ardent victim who lives with her cannot remain afterward to pine and wander about like the knight-at-arms in "La belle dame." He dies. Burton's account, which Keats had printed at the close of the poem, is as follows:

> Philostratus, in his fourth book *de Vita Apollonii*, hath a memorable instance in this kind, which I may not omit, of one Menippus Lycius, a young man twenty-five years of age, that going betwixt Cenchreas and Corinth, met such a phantasm in the habit of a fair gentlewoman, which taking him by the hand, carried him home to her house, in the suburbs of Corinth, and told him she was a Phoenician by birth, and if he would tarry with her, he should hear her sing and play, and drink such wine as never any drank, and no man should molest him; but she, being fair and lovely, would live and die with him, that was fair and lovely to behold. The young man, a philosopher, otherwise staid and discreet, able to moderate his passions, though not this of love, tarried with her a while to his great content, and at last married her, to whose wedding, amongst other guests, came Apollonius; who, by some probable conjectures, found her out to be a serpent, a lamia; and that all her furniture was, like Tantalus' gold, described by Homer, no substance but mere illusions. When she saw herself descried, she wept, and desired Apollonius to be silent, but he would not be moved, and thereupon she, plate, house, and all that was in it, vanished in an instant: many thousands took notice of this fact, for it was done in the midst of Greece.

In preparation for the poem Keats had also been looking for a verse form as different from those of his earlier poetry as possible, and yet flexible enough for rapid narrative.[9] The form should not only help him to avoid the sentimental but, if possible, work

[9] A more detailed discussion than this paragraph can attempt may be found in my *Stylistic Development of Keats*, pp. 146–171.

against it. Nor was there any call for sublimity or grandeur. Such qualities would ludicrously conflict. He had begun a few months before to read Dryden; and his tact led him to consider taking as a model the crisp, worldly couplets of Dryden that, two or three years ago, would have typified to him the reverse of what poetry should be.

Before he began *Lamia,* according to Brown, Keats made a careful study of Dryden's versification. But his extraordinary mimetic gift for catching styles and then carrying them one step further had been balanced since he began *Hyperion* by his own maturing independence. He studied Dryden (and to some extent Pope) not to follow but to select. In his early couplets he had tried deliberately to do everything that the neoclassic couplet did not—to turn it, in effect, inside out. The temptation to swing now to the other extreme was qualified by definite aims. The couplet is closed much of the time, but less frequently than in Dryden. Keats takes over, but with some restraint, the balance and antithesis common in Dryden and Pope: balance of adjectival phrase ("Strip'd like a zebra, freckled like a pard, / Eyed like a peacock, and all crimson-barr'd") ; and antithesis of verb ("Pearls, while on land they wither'd and adored") and of adjective ("Wither'd at dew so sweet and virulent") . Always sensitive to devices of metrical pause and variation, he comes closest to Dryden in his use of the masculine fourth-syllable caesura ("Fast by the springs (x) where she to bathe was wont, / And in those meads (x) where sometime she might haunt") , and in varying the pentameter couplet with alexandrines and triplets. Of more general interest is his ability to catch the colloquial idiom of Dryden without the neoclassic periphrasis, often counterpointing the normal word order of prose against the formality of the couplet ("I was a woman, let me have once more / A woman's shape, and charming as before. / I love a youth of Corinth . . .") . A final interest is the sudden modification in *Lamia* of stylistic means by which, since *Hyperion,* Keats had been working toward condensed richness of expression. So habitual had these become in the months from *Hyperion* through the odes, even in his most rapid writing, that their relative absence now can only be construed as deliberate. One example is the adjectival past participle ("unclasps her warmèd jewels," "Tall oaks, branch-charmèd by the earnest stars") , in which energy is concentrated into a potentially dynamic repose: when it appears now it is conventional ("wingèd heels," "crimson barr'd") or relatively unhindered by nuance ("wreathèd tomb"). Another example is the virtual disappearance, except in casual or simple form, of the vowel interplay that had become so elaborate in the poems from *Hyperion* to the odes, reaching its apex in the *Eve of St. Agnes*.

8

As distinguished from most of his earlier poems, *Lamia* thus promised a comparative single-mindedness as well as spareness— sacrificing the richness for freedom from the cloggings and complications of empathy, and hedged for distance or detachment in everything from plot to the character of Lamia and the consciously neoclassic verse form. Any good poem, he thought, should be a "search after truth." But there was a deliberate limit to what he was trying to do at the moment. His primary hope was to handle poetic narrative with pace and verve—something that he rightly felt he had not yet learned.

Lamia was not to be the principal effort of the summer, still less of the half year or so ahead. He himself spoke of it as a "short poem"; and the phrase, as usual, suggested only a preparation for something more serious afterwards. But the poem was still too capacious—as distinct from even a lengthy lyric like the odes—not to lead him to put into it many of the things that were pressing on his mind, some of which were highly conflicting. This alone would have been enough to prevent a simple interpretation of the poem. He perhaps felt the more at liberty because of the formal safeguards with which he began; and this feeling was justified. The extraordinary formal interest of the poem for the modern reader lies in the success with which those safeguards continue to function actively until the end, permitting as rapidly shifting an interplay of ambiguity as can be found in any narrative poem in the language. Yet we are still often tempted by the original simplicity of the fable into trying to pin down the poem to an exclusive interpretation. The Victorians, preoccupied with the struggle they themselves dramatized between science and poetry, saw *Lamia* as an allegorical attack, the theme of which was the blighting effect of science and analytic philosophy on the poetry of either the sensuous or the visionary imagination. Turning this upside down, we often assume that the indictment is the other way: Lamia, after all, is a serpent; what she offers is only illusion; Lycius is a weak sort; a poetry that cannot withstand the confrontation of philosophic analysis is itself ultimately illusory.

Meanwhile biographical interpretations continue to dart at the relation with Fanny Brawne to the exclusion of other considerations: (1) The innocent Fanny is identified with the half-serpent Lamia (as she is also with "La belle dame sans merci") ; she and love are a threat to Keats's independence, and offer nothing but an illusion from which a bitter awakening will come. (2) So much in love is Keats that, after taking over the fable of *Lamia* from Burton, he is irresistibly led to humanize his main character in the most attractive way—to give her, in short, qualities that have won him in Fanny (qualities that he would presumably have been unable to imagine or see elsewhere had he not found them in Fanny) . The threat to their happy love is the threat generally of the cold, hostile world (analogous to the cold storm outside the castle in the *Eve of St. Agnes*) . The philosopher Apollonius is occasionally equated with the hostile reviewers of *Endymion*. (3) The fragile palace of love in which Lycius and Lamia live is altogether a retreat; and Keats himself wished desperately to retreat—he was both ill and unsuccessful. The death of Lycius illustrates Keats's own death wish. The sonnet "Bright star, would I were steadfast as thou art," states in its original version that he wishes to die upon his love's breast "Half-passionless, and so swoon on to death." (4) Keats was indeed identified with Lycius, and wished genuinely to retreat: the whole story up to, but not including, the climax is complete wish fulfillment. But Keats realized that he had to be up and doing. Lycius, to be sure, dies; but Keats's identification with Lycius stops before that point is reached.

Finally, in reaction to the various allegorical and biographical interpretations, the poem is sometimes regarded as a formal, almost dialectical play of opposites. This approach, though it can easily be carried too far, has at least the great merit of bringing us back to some of the maturities of poetry: it presupposes the fact that Keats has developed somewhat since *Endymion,* that indeed, however rapidly the poem was written and however trying the circumstances, we are dealing with a writer who is becoming one of the supreme craftsmen in English poetry.

9

Almost from the start of the poem, the treatment of illusion and reality became richer, more diversely faceted, than he had perhaps consciously planned. For the story touched an interest that had deepened immensely since he had written "Sleep and Poetry" two and a half years before. It was an "old maxim" of his—as he had once said—that in an original mind any interest or idea quickly becomes a "starting post" to a universe of others, an active beginning and "centre of an intellectual world." So with the whole subject of reality and illusion. He had long since found that it could lead to the consideration of everything else.

In fact, "illusion" ceases to be a very meaningful concept when we pass from a simple notion of it to the thought of the vast range of human reactions that are constantly playing against—or interpenetrating—the human experience of reality: the ambitions, fears, and interests that take possession of the head; the "disquietude" and "fresh set of annoyances" that, as man improves his "bodily accommodations and comforts," are still "waiting for him" at each stage; the extent to which we live vicariously in the past, the future, or in conjecture of what is occupying the minds of others. If most of the happiness and misery of life—indeed all of it except that determined by direct sensation, and possibly a good deal of this too—is within the imagination, then where and how do we draw the line between the "real" in our experience and the virtual omnipresence of what we call the illusory? "This it is that makes the Amusement of Life—to a speculative Mind." We walk among the fields and see a stoat or fieldmouse "peeping out of the withered grass—the creature hath a purpose and its eyes are bright with it." Among the buildings of a city we see "a Man hurrying along—to what? The Creature has a purpose and his eyes are bright with it." [10] The question continues to recur to the speculative mind : "hurrying along—to what?" We are of imagination all compact. The events that make up human tragedy, whether in actual life or in literature, would plainly cease to be tragic if only the people involved could be brought not to care. If there would have been no tragedy at all in *King Lear* provided Lear had suddenly ceased to care—ceased to protest—then how much of Lear's passionate concern, how much that underlay the "fierce dispute"

10 See above, Chapter XVIII, section 7.

of this "impassioned clay," was "illusion"? The thought continued
to tease him in the weeks after he wrote the sonnet "On Sitting
Down to Read *King Lear* Once Again." As he said to Bailey
(March 13, 1818):

> I am sometimes so very sceptical as to think Poetry itself a mere
> Jack a lanthern to amuse whoever may chance to be struck with its
> brilliance—As Tradesmen say every thing is worth what it will fetch,
> so probably every mental pursuit takes its reality and worth from the
> ardour of the pursuer—being in itself a nothing.

This, of course, was too reductionistic a way of putting it; and he
immediately went on to qualify it with his distinctions of "real,"
"semireal," and mere "Nothings which are made Great and dignified by an ardent pursuit." The difficult problem, of course, lay
with "Things semireal" (like the Grecian urn or the song of the
nightingale); and within the past two or three months, as we have
been noticing, this *terra incognita* or "untrodden region," where
the greeting spirit and the semireal occasionally meet (or more often only partly meet, or just miss touching), had begun to seem
the most challenging province of poetry and art: a province, moreover, that nothing else (certainly not "consequitive reasoning")
could hope to reach so well. For art was itself turned Januslike
in both directions—toward illusion, and all that the word may
suggest, and also toward reality.

Certainly his own experience was constantly bringing him back
to a fresh consideration of the subject. The same adhesive sympathy of imagination that gave him so firm a purchase on concrete
reality had also been turned for years with equal identification and
self-forgetfulness to poetry. If this twofold experience was always
in the process of dawning into moments of union, it was just as
constantly redividing. Art, to be sure, was—or could be—an extension of reality: an unparalleled nuancer and developer of our
experience of reality, as Hazlitt was always asserting in the passages that so delighted Keats. Yet it was also something different.
This was not merely because so much art was deliberately conceived in a spirit remote from experience. That could be taken for
granted. But even the works of those poets most tenaciously rooted
in the empirical world were not—simply because they were works
of art—the same thing as direct, personal experience, though we
are better able to see their closeness to it when "we have gone the
same steps as the Author." In the very process of supplementing or

ramifying our concrete experience, they tap in us uses of the mind
—projection, vicariousness, the potentiality for dream—that can
actively work against reality while at the same time bringing us
closer to it. Perhaps it was not so much the degree of projection
and vicariousness involved in art—other aspects of life evoke (or
demand) as much—as it was the restricted nature of some of the
materials art necessarily employs and the inevitable absence of
others. This had been one of the implications dramatized by the
"Ode on a Grecian Urn."

With every new encounter, the subject was becoming more complicated, less easily reducible to pat formula. The odes, opening
and exemplifying other considerations, had carried him one step
further. We take it for granted that illusion, by definition, is eva-
sive; but what of the evasiveness of reality (including the reality
or truth about illusion and about the whole fluctuating body of
aspiration and purpose, of "shadowy thought" and emotion, that
the human psyche is always bringing to life)? Phrases from the
time of the "Negative Capability" letter and the months that follow keep recurring to the mind: the need to accept "half-knowledge" lest, in our rigid or "irritable" clutch at one exclusive or
systematic chain of reasoning, we lose a "fine isolated verisimilitude" that does not fit the pattern. One especially thinks back to
the "Epistle to Reynolds" (March 1818) : "Things cannot to the
will" of imperious reasoning "Be settled, but they tease us out of
thought"; the sincere imagination—"Lost in a sort of Purgatory
blind"—apparently lacks "any standard law / Of either heaven or
earth" to which to refer. Not that he was embracing an easy skepticism. It was simply that "to philosophise / I dare not yet." Nor
was he ready to do so now.

10

It began to seem that, in trying to come to terms with any large
problem (and this would include the elusiveness of reality as a
general concept) , we have little choice except to start out by articulating it through contrasted terms—using one contrasting
thought or expression to supplement, or bring out what is disregarded by, another. Always a tendency of his mind (and gradually
of his poetic style, once he got beyond the juvenile poems) , his
habit of using contraries had developed genuinely and organically,
in part because of the instinctive range of his own sympathies and

in part because he was forced to work so independently, without opportunities to have much of his thinking predigested for him. The whole of the discussion of the "Chamber of Maiden-Thought" and the consideration of Wordsworth ("and as a help . . . how he differs from Milton") provides a graphic example from the letters. By the time he wrote the *Eve of St. Agnes,* the use of contrarieties had become one of the distinguishing qualities of his idiom and imagery, and, within another three months, it had become dramatically incorporated into the thematic and structural conception of three major odes: the "Nightingale," the "Grecian Urn," and "Melancholy." This indeed has been one of the many fascinations of Keats to the twentieth-century reader and poet. It may be doubted whether there has been any writer of the past century and a half who has employed contrasts in more essential and intrinsic ways and who at the same time has been by temperament, and in ultimate aim, so unsympathetic to the love of paradox or the juggling of disparates for their own sake. As in no other poem that Keats wrote, contrasts are built into *Lamia.* There are, at least, more of them, and of more different kinds; and in comparison with the concentrated and progressive development of the odes, the impression now is of rapidly shifting interplay (an impression increased by Keats's use of the opportunities for antithesis offered by the neoclassic couplet) .

Several of the contrasting (but not always opposing) terms that run through Keats's expression at this time apply, in one way or another, to *Lamia.* Poetry and philosophy, the immortal and the human, permanence and change, pleasure and "its neighbour pain," loom prominently. Intermingling with them are dream and reality, love and ambition, pursuit and satiety, passion and thought, retreat from the world and active participation. In kaleidoscopic variety, the pairs of contrasting terms create still another level of contrast simply by opposing or supplementing each other as pairs. Thus the happy (possibly clairvoyant) dream versus a reality that is both harsh and unknowable is matched by its counterpart—the delusive dream versus the healthful recognition of reality. More explicit by far than in the *Eve of St. Agnes* is the contrast, on the one hand, of seclusion or retreat (and with it love) and, on the other, the hostile world. But equally emphatic, if not more, is the reverse opposition that was completely absent in the *Eve of St. Agnes:* seclusion or retreat, and to some extent love, in contrast to the salutary challenge and enterprise of the public world. If passion is opposed to the consecutive plod and restricted view of the "dull brain," it is also contrasted by implication with "disinterested" thought—by implication since the philosopher Apollonius is also remote from that ideal. Hovering in between is the opposition of passion and the mere act of reflection, whether the reflection be limited and partial, or disinterestedly comprehensive, or even the momentary straying of attention. So when Lycius, in their palace retreat, begins to think restively of the "noisy world," the "ever-watchful" Lamia is struck with fear, "knowing well / That but a moment's thought is passion's passing bell."

It is around this body of contrasts that the poem is built. To emphasize their inevitability to human nature is one function of the little episode with which Keats decided to introduce the poem: a miniature love idyl of the god Hermes and a wood nymph, the conclusion of which is in direct opposition to that of the main story. The implication is that the happy union to which Lycius later aspires is possible only to immortals. This is equivalent to saying that it is impossible altogether. For there is not the slightest hint of the serious emotion Keats so often brought to myth before —of his nostalgic hope to recapture those "happy pieties." This is mere myth; and the treatment of it is half mocking, offhand, even flippant. Not only is the realm unreal, but myth mirrors the restless human hearts that invent it, and this is no transcendental love between Hermes and the nymph. What happens is that a virgin is taken by Hermes with dispatch, assurance, and complete freedom from self-question. (Keats may have hoped that his brisk treatment would also have a ring of the worldly and experienced, like that which he found in his model, Dryden: he wanted the poem, after all, to give a "sensation of some sort.") This is simply one more conquest, then, for the roving, "ever-smitten Hermes"; and the frankness of his desire is not only stressed but almost laughed at as its blush rises in "celestial heat," and burns "from his wingèd heels to either ear." The subjectivity of his single-minded intentness is also hinted: "Ah, what a world of love was at her feet! / So Hermes thought." And when the nymph appears to him, it may possibly have been a dream. But this would not matter. In the realm of myth, as distinct from our own, contrarieties are no problem. Dream and reality can change place with no loss: "Real are the dreams of gods."

A second function of the episode is to lift Lamia from the mere story of Lycius, and to highlight the mysterious complexity that Keats has decided to give her: a complexity altogether absent from Burton's simple account of a "phantasm in the habit of a fair gentlewoman" who meets Lycius and takes him "home to her house." Even a god, it turns out, is dependent on the kind of thing Lamia is uniquely able to do. This compassionate serpent has made the wood nymph invisible in order to protect her from the threat of the pursuing satyrs. She can bring the nymph back to Hermes' sight simply by breathing upon his eyes. Being amoral as well as compassionate, she is ready to do so provided he in turn assists her to regain a woman's shape—something that, with all her arts, she is unable to do by herself.

11

From her first appearance, Lamia is deliberately conceived as an enigma: virtually every quality has its opposite, real or potential. To begin with, we are never sure whether she is essentially a woman or a serpent. She herself says only that she "was a woman once"; but that does not mean she was so originally. At least four transformations are assumed by the poem: "a woman once," she is now a serpent; she becomes a woman again; and at the end, when she vanishes, she presumably becomes a serpent again, unless she is dead. Nor do we know whether she is a mortal or an immortal, or something that falls between, or, more probably, something essentially different from either category though capable of participating in both. The astronomical imagery associated with the gods (Hermes is addressed as "Bright planet" or referred to as "star of Lethe") is applied to her, but as something evanescent or in constant, elusive motion. On this bright "palpitating snake" are

> silver moons, that, as she breath'd,
> Dissolv'd, or brighter shone, or interwreathed
> Their lustres with the gloomier tapestries.

On her head is something like a tiara. Yet it is not solid: it is "a wannish fire / Sprinkled with stars." Like the immense capacity for diverse kinds of illusion that she—at least in part—symbolizes, the contradictions are so extreme as to be grotesque. While the moons of a divinity alternately shine and fade on her moving skin, the colors and patterns on her "rainbow-sided" body also suggest those of other animals:

> Striped like a zebra, freckled like a pard,
> Eyed like a peacock, and all crimson barr'd.

At the same time a "complete" set of teeth, of the sort often described in pastoral love imagery, flash out from the serpent head ("She had a woman's mouth with all its pearls complete"). She could seem simultaneously to be

> some penanced lady elf,
> Some demon's mistress, or the demon's self.

Yet she is also pitiful, with her "melancholy eyes" that continue to "weep, and weep, that they were born so fair"; and when she confesses to Hermes that she is in love, she has the grace to blush. Her transformation, after he grants her wish, involves an excruciating pain before which she is completely helpless. Her mouth foams; her "eyes in torture fixed" are glazed and wide beneath their burned lashes.

> She writh'd about, convuls'd with scarlet pain:
> A deep volcanian yellow took the place,
> Of all her milder-moonèd body's grace;
> And, as the lava ravishes the mead,
> Spoilt all her silver mail, and golden brede:
> Made gloom of all her frecklings, streaks and bars,
> Eclips'd her crescents, and lick'd up her stars:
> So that, in moments few, she was undrest
> Of all her sapphires, greens, and amethyst,
> And rubious-argent: of all these bereft,
> Nothing but pain and ugliness were left.

Whatever else can be said about her, she is not essentially sinister. Aside from her own suffering, and her protective pity for the wood nymph, there is the fact that she intends anything but harm to the mortal she loves. There is little to suggest that she is dangerous except the early remark that she might seem the "demon's self" (though she could also be a "penanced lady elf"), the short reference to her "Circean head," and the fact that the foam of her mouth, while she shudders painfully through her transformation, is "virulent" as well as "sweet." Without her, of course, Lycius would not have ended as he did. But in both his commitment to her and his later inability to be satisfied, it is Lycius that is fundamentally responsible for the conclusion. Significantly she uses no magic arts to force him to love her (except that she understandably tries to convince him that she is a woman). He simply falls in love when he sees her. We can even infer that she is unable to force him to do so.

The whole development of her character is to underline the peculiar dependence on others of this gifted puzzling creature (both "wild and timid") who is capable otherwise of doing so much. She aspires (like art) toward reality without being entirely of it. Her dreams are of reality ("And sometimes into cities she would send / Her dream"); and here too she has something of the immortal ("Real are the dreams of gods"). If she can create illusion, she can also bring reality to sight, as she did with the wood nymph. Again like art (and this is not to say that she "represents" art; this is one element, though a large one, that enters into the conception), she is dependent on human recognition and response. Given this response, she can fulfill different—even conflicting—desires and demands, and do so with both innocence and clairvoyance, with beauty and unparalleled knowledge:

> A virgin purest lipp'd, yet in the lore
> Of love deep learnèd to the red heart's core:
> Not one hour old, yet of sciential brain
> To unperplex bliss from its neighbour pain.

Completely embraced, she can protectively muffle a lover from reality if he himself wishes it; and in the palace she constructs through artifice Lycius allows himself to become, in effect, a kept man. But she is powerless to prevent him from leaving it if he wishes to do so. Above all she is powerless to prevent him from bringing ruin on his own head—however eager she is for him not to do so—when he insists on regarding this palace as real in the same sense that the life he left behind is real. Nor, finally, can we be altogether confident that the palace *is* completely unreal. At least it is proved to be unreal only because—like Lamia herself—it cannot stand up against the penetrating eyes of Apollonius.

12

Because Lycius is sometimes identified with the poet, Lamia and the philosopher Apollonius are often contrasted as representing two alternative ways of life. They are said to mirror Keats's own divided commitment, on the one hand to poetry (or to love, seclusion, dream, and the like), and to philosophy on the other. The contrast, or possible aspects of it, may certainly enter into the picture. But not only is Keats's identification distributed among all the characters (with Lycius receiving the least sympathy) but, more important, it is involved in the course of the story itself, in the light of which all the characters reveal their limitations. Moreover, Lycius can hardly be said to be torn between Lamia and Apollonius; he wishes only to stay clear of the latter. Nor is the philosopher engaged in a struggle with Lamia to rescue his pupil. He is far more interested in solving a problem, though his diagnosis is to end by killing the pupil. Hence, as he walks calmly and unbidden to the marriage feast, looking sharply about,

> he laugh'd,
> As though some knotty problem, that had daft
> His patient thought, had now begun to thaw.

The plight of Lycius is just another problem to him; and though his laugh comes mainly from self-satisfaction in solving it (" 'twas just as he foresaw"), there is also a suggestion of unfeeling mockery at both Lamia and Lycius.

A far more fundamental contrast is that between the two mortals—Lycius and Apollonius—in their two extreme approaches to Lamia: the first completely absorbed in that side of her that he sees, and wants to see; the other regarding her merely as something to be seen through and then dismissed. It is their two attitudes of mind that sustain and destroy her. Altogether dependent on how she is viewed, she has the power to create for Lycius the palace and life of enchantment that he wants partly because his own eyes are constantly upon hers, where he also sees himself "mirror'd small in paradise." Conversely, at her first glimpse of Apollonius, she fears his "quick eyes." The turning point comes after Apollonius has entered the banqueting hall, and

> fix'd his eye, without a twinkle or a stir,
> Full on the alarmèd beauty of the bride.

As she begins to wither, Lycius cries out to Apollonius to "shut those juggling eyes, thou ruthless man," and then, as the philosopher continues to stare, Lycius turns helplessly to the guests:

> "Corinthians! look upon that gray-beard wretch!
> Mark how, possess'd, his lashless eyelids stretch
> Around his demon eyes! Corinthians, see!
> My sweet bride withers at their potency."
>
> .   .   .   .
>
>   The sophist's eye,
> Like a sharp spear, went through her utterly.

If the dreams of Lamia are—or can be—of reality, the reality of Lycius has become a dream. He has committed himself to the attempt to share passionately in the immortal (an aspiration that, in a different way, Keats had been testing and exploring throughout the "Grecian Urn") ; and, for a while, he appears to have what he wants ("Ah, happy Lycius!") . Lamia seems to offer a complete escape from time, and from the remorseless process by which pain and fatigue interpenetrate pleasure. Defying the flux of ordinary experience, she can not only isolate pleasures from "swift counterchange" with their unwanted opposites, pulling apart "their points of contact," but also unite them with other pleasures, ordinarily distinct:

> Intrigue with the specious chaos, and dispart
> Its most ambiguous atoms with sure art.

The "bewildering cup" she offers reminds us of that of "Fancy" in the rondeau: taking only the joys of spring, summer, and autumn, the freed Fancy can "mix these pleasures up / Like three fit wines in a cup." But there is another connection with the rondeau: the impossibility of keeping an emotion forever undiluted even if one can keep the object of it. That Lycius should think back after a while to the outside world and begin to wish—as Lamia apprehensively sees—something "more than her empery" is itself by no means fatal. There is nothing to prevent his being occasionally within the palace and occasionally without, though this would naturally have its own disadvantages. The real difficulty comes in the course of action on which he decides. First of all he will commit himself even more to Lamia, and wed her. At the same time he will bend reality toward this final and complete commitment: invite it openly to share as an active participant, and use it to reinforce this highly specialized experience. He has, in short, lost all ability to distinguish; illusion has passed into delusion. He goes ahead with his large public wedding feast; and Keats pauses briefly to present it with fluent gusto (he was after all—as he told Dilke in July—"an old Stager in the picturesque"). With blithe confidence, Lycius even assumes that Apollonius is swept up in the same enthusiasm. Taking his eyes for a moment from Lamia and "checking his love trance," he grasps a full cup of wine, turns to Apollonius, and starts to pledge him only to find the wrinkled face of the philosopher gazing, in sharp stare, at Lamia.

"I am convinced more and more," Keats wrote to Bailey this summer (August 14), "that (excepting the human friend Philosopher) a fine writer is the most genuine Being in the World." The philosophy in mind is one for facing and enduring reality, especially change and death, with "disinterested" openness to the diverse amplitude of fact, and with fully shared humanity. Apollonius, far from exemplifying this ideal, is limited to the reductive uses of analytic philosophy, the essence of which is to reduce a thing to certain elements and then to substitute the simple interpretation for the original complex reality. What is not susceptible of such reduction is merely denied. This is the point of the famous "rainbow" passage—famous because it has often been lifted from the context of the poem and championed or censured as an expression of anti-intellectualism. Actually it occurs when Keats, half jesting at the laurel-crown parties of Leigh Hunt in which he had once shared so eagerly, light-heartedly proposes different crowns for the characters of this near-comedy before the final scene is acted:

> What wreath for Lamia? What for Lycius?
> What for the sage, old Apollonius?

Upon the "aching forehead" of Lamia let there be hung a wreath of willow leaves, recalling Ophelia, and also the fern of "adder's tongue"; for the intoxicated Lycius, vine leaves from the thyrsus or staff of Bacchus, to help him sustain his illusion:

> and, for the sage,
> Let spear-grass and the spiteful thistle wage
> War on his temples. Do not all charms fly
> At the mere touch of cold philosophy?
> There was an awful rainbow once in heaven:
> We know her woof, her texture; she is given
> In the dull catalogue of common things.
> Philosophy will clip an Angel's wings,
> Conquer all mysteries by rule and line,

> Empty the haunted air and gnomèd mine—
> Unweave a rainbow, as it erewhile made
> The tender-person'd Lamia melt into a shade.

But Keats, though recalling the famous toast at Haydon's "immortal dinner," is unable to approach Apollonius with the mockery that flickers throughout his treatment of Lycius ("Had Lycius liv'd to hand his story down, / He might have given the moral a fresh frown"). In fact, Apollonius is given throughout an impressive dignity lacking in the others. So when Lamia—and we—first see him: uneasily she grasps the hand of Lycius

> as one came near
> With curl'd gray beard, sharp eyes, and smooth bald crown,
> Slow-stepp'd, and robed in philosophic gown.

The wedding guests, by contrast, are treated almost with contempt.[11] "The herd approach'd," gawking at the palace with "common eyes" of blank incomprehension, and then hurried in to carouse—"Save one"; and that one "look'd thereon with eye severe, / And with calm-planted steps walk'd in austere." Apollonius, it is true, is called a "sophist." The association is with the reductive spirit of denial of so many of the ancient sophists. Lycius, in fact, accuses Apollonius of this just before he dies: the gods will punish him for his continued, militant skepticism:

> for their long offended might,
> For all thine impious proud-heart sophistries.

There is indeed much that Apollonius cannot see. He can only see through. Put another way: Apollonius, like Lycius, sees only that for which he is looking, and each of them denies that for which he is not. Both, in short, are subjective in their approach to a reality—Lamia—far more complicated than either of them realizes. But as their limitations are dramatized, an essential difference in both degree and kind of subjectivity becomes undeniable. It is Apollonius who survives, not Lycius. If what he sees is only a part of the truth, a part with which much else that is true may seem to conflict, yet it is something that cannot be disregarded; whereas the approach of Lycius is vitiated from the beginning by the spirit of a more thoroughgoing and deliberate retreat. Keats was not writing *Lamia* to point this as a moral especially ap-

---

[11] In the original version, with open contempt and ridicule. See the discarded lines in *Letters*, II.158–159.

plicable to the future of poetry and the dangers it faced. But by the time he wrote the second part he had also started on the new *Hyperion.* There the poet—and all he represents—comes close to death because he has been a dreamer. He is saved in time only because he has begun dimly to see that the uses of the imagination for poetry and for dream must be "Diverse, sheer opposites, antipodes."

Shortly after *Lamia* was finished, Keats began to develop a fondness for it that has a certain poignance. It alone seemed to remain from this strenuous summer. For though the Induction to the revised *Hyperion* far excelled anything in *Lamia,* that new attempt at a "grand Poem"—an attempt limited to three or four preoccupied weeks—was even more a fragment than the first *Hyperion,* and it never occurred to him to publish it. Yet *Lamia* did much to lift his confidence. "I am certain," he told George (September 18), "there is a fire in it which must take hold of people in some way." He was thinking partly of its antisentimental bias. Whatever he wrote, there were to be no more *Isabellas,* with their "simplicity of knowledge" ("There is no objection of this kind to Lamia"). The sentimental was depressingly popular; but "I intend to use more finesse with the public." He was also reassured by the pace of *Lamia.* He was at last overcoming (though admittedly with some sacrifice) a difficulty that disturbed him about his narrative poetry—that it "doesn't cover its ground well."

In the winter, as he thought over the longer poems that might be included in the next volume—all of which seemed so remote from what he would have hoped to do with just a little more time —*Lamia* remained as at least a hint of what might have been done. In the title of the volume it was to be listed first: *Lamia, Isabella, The Eve of St. Agnes, and Other Poems.*

chapter xxi

The Close of the Fertile Year:
"To Autumn" and *The Fall of Hyperion*

✶֍֎֍֎֍֎֍֎֍֎֍֎֍֎֍֎֍

July to September, 1819

A THIRD of the final summer of Keats's writing had passed when Charles Brown appeared on July 22, full of his usual energy and ready to begin collaborating on their play, *Otho the Great*. The remaining two months were harassed by conflicting purposes and, in the last week or two, by further financial problems. To begin with, the greater part of three weeks was consumed by the play. There is something bizarre in the thought of a verse tragedy's being written in three weeks (or at least the bulk of it—the last four of its five acts); but Keats's dispatch shows his feeling of urgency. On September 10 bad news and appeals for help arrived from George; and from then until September 21, when he gave up the new version of *Hyperion*, the days were distracted by anxiety, by fruitless efforts to help George, and by the determination to turn to some other kind of work. This leaves little more than three weeks relatively free for other work. During that short time he took off a few days to write the second half of *Lamia* and tried to go on with the revised *Hyperion*, possibly writing most of it at this time; and on September 19 he composed the ode "To Autumn." Keats's active writing career is then essentially at an end.

2

When Brown arrived at the cottage where Keats and James Rice were staying in Shanklin, on the Isle of Wight, he brought along their congenial friend, John Martin.[1] The change was abrupt. "Sauntering Jack and idle Joe"—as Keats called himself and Rice —had been leading a melancholy but at least quiet life. In these suddenly crowded quarters Keats was naturally unable to work; something had to be done to entertain the visitors; and the in-

[1] Of the publishing firm of Rodwell and Martin (46 New Bond Street), and a friend also of Dilke and Reynolds.

valid Rice was as usual eager to throw himself into conviviality. In the small room that Keats and Rice used as a parlor, the four men spent their reunion, as Keats told Fanny Brawne, "playing at cards night and morning leaving me no undisturbed opportunity" even to write a short letter.

But after three days Rice and Martin left. With pent-up determination, Keats immediately returned to his "very abstract Poem" —the *Fall of Hyperion*—and spent a full day on it. Brown was presumably looking around the neighborhood. In another day or two they began work on *Otho the Great*. An energetic walker, Brown also persuaded Keats to spend more time out-of-doors. He himself would take along paper and pencils; he was a skillful if untrained artist. "The other day," Keats told Dilke (July 31), Brown "was sketching Shanklin church and as I saw how the business was going on, I challenged him to a trial of Skill—he lent me Pencil and Paper—we keep the Sketches to contend for the Prize at the Gallerry." This was undoubtedly the day when Brown made his drawing of Keats, probably the best likeness we have except for Haydon's life mask. Brown's granddaughter wrote the following account:

> Keats and my grandfather were out sketching together; when they came in Keats was a little tired, and he half-reclined in a couch or easy chair. My grandfather opened his portfolio and made this pencil copy. He was pleased with the result and kept it. Then it passed on to my father; and after his death my mother gave it to me.[2]

While the robust Brown again took off two days (August 1 and 2) in order to go "gadding over the country with his ancient knapsack," Keats snatched the opportunity to plunge into other work—presumably the *Fall of Hyperion*. Much as he liked Brown's company, Keats "regretted his return," he tells Fanny Brawne; "it broke in upon me like a Thunderbolt." Keats hoped before long to visit Fanny in London. But the visit would have to be brief; "for as I am in a train of writing now I fear to disturb it." Meanwhile he was constantly feeling the lack of a library. The thought of Winchester grew on him, especially the thought of its cathedral. Brown agreed to the move. Whatever the attractions of the scenery near Shanklin, "I shall give them a hearty good bye to exchange them for my Cathedral . . . I long to be off for Winchester for I

2 *Observer*, September 24, 1922. The drawing, which Brown had taken with him when he emigrated to New Zealand (1841), is now in the National Portrait Gallery in London. For discussion of other portraits of Keats, see Chapter VI, section 4.

begin to dislike the very door post[s] here—the names, the pebbles"; "the voice of the old Lady over the way"—a Mrs. Warder—was becoming "a great Plague." [3]

Keats was plainly driving himself hard. He would often continue to work throughout the night. Since much of the day had to be given over to *Otho,* with Brown sitting opposite and furnishing him the material to versify, we can assume that the *Fall of Hyperion* was now receiving the fatigued leavings of his time. One morning (August 6), he followed the night's work by beginning a letter to Fanny Brawne, when suddenly "Brown came down in his morning coat and nightcap, saying he had been refresh'd by a good sleep and was very hungry—I left him eating and went to bed too tired to enter into any discussions." By August 12, when they left for Winchester, they had almost finished the middle three acts of *Otho*—a total of about a thousand lines. Keats, working more independently, then wrote the final act during the first week or ten days that they spent in Winchester.

When we are tempted to try to make something out of the play, we should remember that Brown himself thought that the way the two of them wrote it was "curious." For Keats, until the last act, versified each scene with no knowledge of what was to come:

> I engaged to furnish him with the fable, characters, and dramatic conduct of a tragedy, and he was to embody it into poetry. The progress of this work was curious; for, while I sat opposite to him, he caught my description of each scene, entered into the characters to be brought forward, the events, and every thing connected with it. Thus he went on, scene after scene, never knowing nor inquiring into the scene which was to follow until four acts were completed. It was then he required to know, at once, all the events which were to occupy the fifth act. I explained them to him; but, after a patient hearing, and some thought, he insisted on it that my incidents were too numerous, and, as he termed them, too melodramatic. He wrote the fifth act in accordance with his own view. [4]

Though never performed until 1950,[5] *Otho* is by no means worse than the average tragedy written and produced at the time. Other reasons than quality operated against the acceptance of it: the two principal theaters were now and throughout the next year involved

---

[3] II.137–138, 142.
[4] Brown, pp. 54–55.
[5] At St. Martin's Theatre, London, on November 26. The reviews were naturally complimentary.

in bitter conflicts both within themselves and with each other; both were losing money; a rapid change in public taste was just beginning to take place.[6] Even so, the play, a conventional Gothic melodrama with Elizabethan ancestry, suffers from a complexity of presupposition that also imposed needless difficulties on Keats himself. Brown had something of a chess player's mind: he relished detail and liked to work out problems. Before the action of the play even begins, a bewildering array of incidents have taken place, none of which is very interesting but all of which have to be revealed early in the play in order for the action that follows to have any meaning.[7] It was apparently through Keats's own initiative that, as the play draws to a close, it focuses more on Ludolph —the character he hoped Edmund Kean would act—while some of the lesser characters that have cluttered the play are pushed very much into the background. The verse itself is not particularly wooden or undramatic, especially in the latter half. What we can say is that it is diluted—inevitably so, given the speed with which it was written and Keats's own lack of involvement. Naturally there are numerous Shakespearean echoes, and sometimes the verse itself attains a Shakespearean cadence and metaphor. As good an example as any are some lines that he quoted to George (September 27) as a specimen (the italics are Keats's own):

> Not as a Swordsman would I pardon crave,
> But as a Son: the bronz'd Centurion
> Long-toiled in foreign wars, *and whose high deeds*
> *Are shaded in a forest of tall spears,*
> *Known only to his troop,* hath greater plea
> Of favour with my Sire than I can have.

The good-humored docility with which Keats went ahead with the work, puzzling even Brown, indicates how much his real pre-

---

6 See Bernice Slote, *Keats and the Dramatic Principle* (1958), pp. 117–119, which also provides a detailed discussion of the play.

7 Ludolph, son of Otho, Emperor of Germany, had led an unsuccessful revolt because his father had refused to allow him to marry the unpleasant Auranthe, sister of Conrad, Duke of Franconia, and had chosen instead Erminia, Ludolph's cousin, to be his bride. Meanwhile the Hungarians have invaded Germany. Conrad, previously in disgrace for aiding Ludolph's rebellion, proves valuable in fighting the Hungarians, and has been restored to Otho's favor; and Ludolph, disguised as an Arab, has also performed heroically. Various other antecedent actions involving Erminia and Auranthe also have to be presupposed. The play then becomes essentially the tragedy of Ludolph. Otho, grateful for his son's part in the war, allows him to marry Auranthe. But the evil Auranthe betrays his love. Discovering this eventually, Ludolph goes mad; the guilty Auranthe commits suicide, and the tormented Ludolph dies of grief.

occupations were concentrated elsewhere. He wanted to oblige a friend to whom he owed a great deal, and who was convinced that the idea was a good one. The money Brown had lent Keats was apparently to be repaid by Keats from any profits the play might bring (according to Fanny Brawne they hoped to make as much as £200 apiece) ; [8] and Keats owed it to Brown to make this effort, whatever he may have thought of the project. Moreover, there was always the chance that Brown really knew the kind of thing that would appeal to actors and to the people who governed the theatrical world. He had not only had a play produced at Drury Lane —his comic opera *Narensky, or the Road to Yaroslaf,* which had run ten nights in January 1814—but he had received £300 for it, and, for whatever it was worth, a free lifetime admission to Drury Lane. Keats felt that he himself was in a poor position to judge the salability of anything. He had ended up, as he tells George a little later (September 17), in a "mire of a bad reputation which is continually rising against me":

> My name with the literary fashionables is vulgar—I am a weaver boy to them—a Tragedy would lift me out of this mess. And mess it is as far as it regards our Pockets—But be not cast down any more than I am. I feel I can bear real ills better than imaginary ones.

Still less did Keats feel qualified to weigh the unpredictabilities of theatrical taste. He was far from being the stage-struck youth he had been when, a year and a half before, he had felt so excited in going behind the scenes at Covent Garden. Still earlier he had assumed that the whole literary world, including Felton Mathew, shared in the "genius-loving heart." Throughout the autumn of 1817, the quarrels of Hunt and Haydon, the unexpected malice of the young Lockhart, the mannered and self-centered conversation of the minor writers he met at Horace Smith's, all left him in a state of "perplexity," and convinced him that the principal quality that "went to form a Man of Achievement especially in Literature & which Shakespeare possessed so enormously" was the ability to lose oneself in something more important. The writers at Smith's dinner party (December 1817), discoursing of "fashionables," talked of "Kean & his low company—would I were with that company instead of yours said I to myself!" By contrast the men of the theater had seemed vigorous, direct, and flexible. But,

[8] Brawne, p. 34.

possessed of so powerful a sympathetic imagination himself, Keats was quick to notice the limited mind and imaginative thinness of mere histrionic empathy, and the extent to which the theater exploits and encourages vanity as well as sympathetic identification. Of course, all this could be accepted with tolerance and gentleness; indeed, it had been accepted thus for a long time. But Keats was tired, and working against enormous odds; he was also unwell —more unwell than he knew; and moments of fatigued irritation were becoming more frequent. Except for Edmund Kean himself, the whole group of London actors depressed him. "The Covent Garden Company," he tells his sister (August 28), "is execrable— Young [Charles Mayne Young] is the best among them and he is a ranting coxcombical tasteless Actor . . . What a set of barren asses are actors!"

Certainly Brown was better qualified than himself to decide what would or would not do. And Keats could learn something from the exercise. One of his ultimate ambitions, as he told Bailey (August 14) was "to make as great a revolution in modern dramatic writing as Kean has done in acting"; and a revolution was badly needed. But with all his haste to make use of this summer while he was living on borrowed funds, and to go as far as he could before the autumn brought whatever new complications had been sown in "the wide arable land of events," he took it for granted that his own approach to the drama would have to be very gradual. Meanwhile, *Otho* was very much Brown's "child," as Keats said, and he himself was acting only as a "Midwife." If and when the day came that he made a serious start, he would have to work it out completely by himself; it would probably involve—as each new work of the past year and a half had involved—the simultaneous development of a new style. He had already developed a fairly new style for *Lamia,* and was in the process of forming still another for the *Fall of Hyperion.* In any case he would have to learn first how to handle narrative verse itself with some "dramatic skill." That, in fact, was the intervening step (for which *Lamia* was only a beginning)—a series of narrative poems during the next six years or so that would gradually "nerve me up to the writing of a few fine plays."

Out of loyalty to Brown Keats was reluctant not only to speak but probably even to think disparagingly of the work; and as he churned Brown's scenes into blank verse, he tried to join in

Brown's enthusiasm. But remarks keep slipping from him. "Brown and I," he tells Dilke when they are halfway through (July 31), "are pretty well harnassed again to our dog-cart. I mean the Tragedy which goes on sinkingly." He writes Fanny Brawne that he sees her "through the mist of Plots speeches, counterplots and counter speeches—The Lover [Ludolph] is madder than I am—I am nothing to him." Brown was delighted at Keats's willingness to work at the play so steadily. "Keats is very industrious," he wrote to Dilke as they neared the end of the fourth act (August 12). But the moments were increasing when Keats would become "obstinately monstrous." He would want to give the sedate Otho "a spice of drollery," and would argue for having "the princess blow up her hairdresser, for smearing her cheek with pomatum and spoiling her rouge. It may be more natural, as he observes, but so might many things." [9] Brown, indeed, was taking the play quite seriously, and, as soon as it was finished, set to work on a fair copy in his neatest hand—doing it, Keats told his sister, "in a superb style—better than it deserves."

When the play was finished (August 23), it is possible that Keats began the far superior *King Stephen,* of which about two hundred lines were written. More probably he began it in November.[10]

3

The move to Winchester (August 12) was an immense relief, though Keats's hope of finding a library there was disappointed. "The little coffin of a room at Shanklin," he tells Fanny Brawne

[9] Hampstead Keats, VIII.19–20.

[10] On September 5 Keats wrote Taylor "Since I finish'd [Otho] I have finish'd Lamia." In the thirteen days between August 23 and September 5 it is doubtful that even Keats—especially when this tired—could have written the entire second half of *Lamia,* continued his work on the *Fall of Hyperion* (for which he had little leisure after September 10), and also written very much of *King Stephen.* Brown, when he copied the fragment, headed it with the title, author, and date—the date in such a context indicating plainly when it was written: "King Stephen, a fragment of a tragedy, by John Keats Novr. 1819." No difficulty would have arisen except that in the memoir he wrote over twenty-one years later, when lack of strict precision in chronology was certainly forgivable, Brown said: "As soon as Keats had finished *Otho the Great,* I pointed out to him a subject . . ."; and then, after discussing the fragment, he adds, "This second tragedy, never to be resumed, gave place to 'Lamia' " (p. 56). Mr. Gittings advances no evidence to support his contention that "when Brown copied the fragment in the following November, he dated it, as so often, not with the date of composition but with the date of his copying" (p. 164). "As so often" may refer to Brown's date for the "Bright Star" sonnet, which Gittings also finds inconvenient.

four days after he and Brown have moved, "is changed for a large room—where I can promenade at my pleasure—looks out onto a beautiful—blank side of a house." Such a view was preferable to that "of the sea from our window at Shanklin"; it was ideal for what was most urgent to him now—his writing. In the same letter, which he describes as "flint-worded," he tells her that he has no leisure, nor is in a mood, to compose love letters. He has plotted out a full four months of intense work:

> Believe in the first Letters I wrote you: I assure you I felt as I wrote—I could not write so now—The thousand images I have had pass through my brain—my uneasy spirits—my unguess'd fate—all sp[r]ead as a veil between me and you . . . I would feign, as my sails are set, sail on without an interruption for a Brace of Months longer—I am in complete cue—in the fever; and shall in these four Months do an immense deal—This Page as my eye skims over it I see is excessively unloverlike and ungallant—I cannot help it—I am no officer in yawning quarters; no Parson-romeo—My Mind is heap'd to the full; stuff'd like a cricket ball—if I strive to fill it more it would burst.

He had plunged at once into the fifth act of *Otho,* trying to work at it a little more independently and to focus the action more on the main character. But principally he was trying to work on the "abstract" new *Hyperion.* In this he was becoming enormously involved—so much so that when he shortly gave it up he could hardly bring himself to discuss the matter except in the most tangential way.

When heavily fatigued he would sometimes try to shake into vividness his own image of himself as a writer, and sharpen his effort by identifying himself (to use Hazlitt's way of putting it) with that projected image. He had playfully told his young sister earlier in the year how he would like to read or work before a handsome painted window opening onto the Lake of Geneva ("and there I'd sit and read all day like the picture of somebody reading") ; and he had described to George the way in which he was writing his letter, one foot askew on the rug, and had suddenly wondered "in what position Shakespeare sat when he began 'To be or not to be.' " [11] Confused now with so many distracting purposes, but prodded by an almost desperate resolution ("I find I must buffet it"; "I must choose between despair & Energy—I

[11] See above, Chapter XVIII, section 4.

choose the latter") , he clutched at symbols and positions of calm, firmness, and dispatch. (One of his hopes, as he had told Sarah Jeffrey, was to learn to look on things with "the calmness of a Botanist.") He now tells George (September 17) that

> Whenever I find myself growing vapourish, I rouse myself, wash and put on a clean shirt brush my hair and clothes, tie my shoestrings neatly and in fact adonize as I were going out—then all clean and comfortable I sit down to write. This I find the greatest relief.

"My heart," he tells Fanny Brawne, "seems now made of iron"; he feels "as if I were at this moment engaged in a charge of Cavalry." The gestures of firmness and resolve keep recurring in the letters now. "The more I know what my diligence may in time effect," he writes Reynolds (August 24) , "the more does my heart distend with Pride and Obstinacy—I feel it in my power to become a popular writer—I feel it in my strength to refuse the poisonous suffrage of the public." If his health could stand it, he would be happy to live alone for the rest of his life. A few days later he tells Taylor of his conviction that the essence of health is "occupation" and effort. If one walked through a fever-ridden marsh slowly, apprehensive of the ague, one would be sure to catch it. But let Macbeth "cross the same path, with dagger in the air leading him on, and he would never have an ague or anything like it. You should give these things a serious consideration."

Then suddenly, in reaction, all the thought of iron resolution will disappear for a moment. "I should like now," he tells his sister (August 28) , to "promenade" with her around a garden:

> apple tasting—pear-tasting—plum-judging—apricot nibbling—peach sc[r]unching . . . and a white currant tree kept for company—I admire lolling on a lawn by a water-lilied pond to eat white currants and see gold fish: and go to the Fair in the Evening if I'm good.

4

Had it not been for the nagging problem of money, Winchester would have been ideal. The August weather had become hot and dry; his sore throat was disappearing; the air on the "dry chalky down" outside the city seemed "worth sixpence a pint." Autumn was close, but meanwhile the August days were long. For a time there would be "no chill'd red noses—no shivering—but fair Atmosphere to think in."

When they moved to Winchester, however, they had only a few pounds left of ready money. What property Brown had was locked up, and he had already been advancing money to Keats for months. Of the £230 Keats had lent various friends over the past year or two, nothing had yet been paid back. His letters in May and June asking for repayment had been very gentle and indirect; and the friends were needy, or thought they were needier than Keats, who was known to have inherited some money. Since Abbey was adamant in refusing to advance anything until the threat of a Chancery suit by Mrs. Jennings was settled, there was only one possible source—Keats's publishers, Taylor and Hessey. To approach them was acutely embarrassing. They had lost on *Endymion,* for which they had confidently advanced money while Keats was writing it. He had no choice but to nerve himself up to writing to John Taylor, whom he knew better than Hessey. He waited until he was out of what he called the "Claws" of the tragedy that he and Brown were writing. He wanted to be able to say that he had completed a work that might bring money. Then, as soon as the play was finished, he wrote at once to Taylor (August 23). He was always, as we have noticed, indirect in asking for advances. But so chagrined was he now, unable to forget for a moment how disappointed were Taylor's generous hopes for *Endymion,* that all his sympathetic awareness of another's character goes radically awry. The opening sentence, to this friend to whom he has not written for so long, begins with unintentional rudeness: "You will perceive that I do not write you till I am forced by necessity; that I am sorry for." It is not yet clear that he is asking for money. He tells Taylor that he will be abrupt; he will use a "business manner of wording." After mention of the possible Chancery suit, of debts owed him (he cannot bring himself to say how much, but can only speak of them as a "tolerable amount"), and of a play that he and Brown have "just finished," it is plain that Keats needs money. He starts to say darkly that he wishes to offer a "Bond." This is offered not because Taylor would ever expect a bond. Keats wants to offer this assurance because it will work against his own "too lax sensation of life." (The bond was to be offered by Charles Brown, who enclosed a statement that he would stand firmly behind any advance offered Keats.) The letter goes on: "I feel every confidence that if I choose I may be a popular writer." But "that I will never be"; he will not truckle. The thought of courting popularity dovetails with that of love and Fanny Brawne:

> I equally dislike the favour of the public with the love of a woman—they are both a cloying treacle to the wings of independence. I shall ever consider them (People) as debtors to me for verses, not myself to them for admiration—which I can do without. I have of late been indulging my spleen by composing a preface *at* them: after all resolving never to write a preface at all.

Taylor, in reading all this, will probably think "How a solitary life engenders pride & egotism." "True!" Keats exclaims. This pride and egotism will help him to "write finer things." The momentum picks up; and an extraordinary bitterness that he had long tried to muffle—if possible to sublimate and disarm by tolerance, by sympathy—breaks out. It is not merely the public of which he is thinking. He includes also the "commonplace crowd of the little-famous" who throng and jostle with each other, "playing the hypocrite," and for what?—"To beg suffrage for a seat on the benches of a myriad aristocracy in Letters." These awkward, strong expressions (awkward because they are so unhabitual) parallel the outburst in the *Fall of Hyperion,* which he was writing at or about the same time, and which he had the good sense to delete just after he had written it: the lines in which he says that, though he himself is condemned to "breathe death with them," it will be "life" to see all of these who have betrayed literature "sprawl before me into graves." Just so much, he tells Taylor, as he is humbled "by the genius above my grasp, am I exalted and look with hate and contempt upon the literary world."

Keats, after all this, forgot to mention any specific sum that he hoped Taylor and Hessey would advance. As he waited for an answer, another disappointment arose. For within only four or five days (on August 27 or 28), he and Brown heard that Edmund Kean was preparing to set off on an American tour. This, as he later told George, "was the worst news I could have had." Kean, he was convinced, was the only person who would be much interested in the play; the main character was planned specifically for him; and even if the play were accepted by others, only Kean could have made a success of it. For the moment Keats tries to speak lightly about it. "I had hoped to give Kean another opportunity to shine."

21. AMBLESIDE IN KEATS'S TIME

22. THE DRUID CIRCLE NEAR KESWICK

23. AILSA ROCK

24. EXTERIOR OF FINGAL'S CAVE, STAFFA

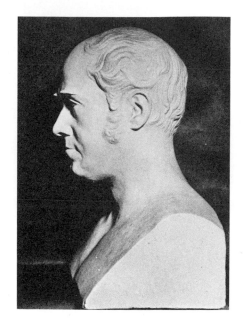

25. CHARLES BROWN IN 1828

26. WENTWORTH PLACE

27. THREE SCENES OF KEATS'S FAVORITE WALK IN WINCHESTER

*"I pass . . . the beautiful front of the Cathedral . . . some meadows . . .
the most beautifully clear river . . ."*

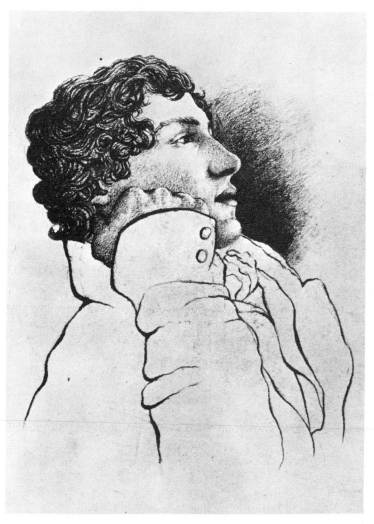

28. JOHN KEATS IN JULY 1819

29. MINIATURE OF FANNY BRAWNE

30. SILHOUETTE OF FANNY BRAWNE

31. THE PIAZZA DI SPAGNA IN KEATS'S TIME

32. KEATS ON HIS DEATHBED

He had not thought of publishing another volume of poetry until he had several substantial works from which to choose. But now the need was urgent. He would assemble a book immediately. The first thing to do, of course, was to finish *Lamia*. The *Fall of Hyperion* was a far more doubtful work: it would be much longer; what he could do with it was still very unclear; and even if it were eventually finished, it could never have the immediate popular appeal that he hoped *Lamia* might have. He at once concentrated on *Lamia* and wrote the second half by September 5. He then started to revise the *Eve of St. Agnes,* hoping it could be turned into something passable. Meanwhile, not getting an answer from John Taylor, he wrote him a shorter, calmer note, in which he is at least able to be more specific, though with great understatement, and say that he is "in want of a Month's cash—now believe me I do not apply to you as if I thought you had a gold Mine . . . Tell me you are not flush and I shall thank you heartily."

Keats was unaware that Taylor, who had not been well recently, had gone to stay with his father in Nottinghamshire. Keats's involved first letter had been forwarded to him. Taylor was naturally bewildered. How much did Keats really need—a few pounds, a hundred, or what? And the tone of the letter was disturbing. Keats knew only too well that the firm of Taylor and Hessey had lost money on his last publication. Yet now he was speaking of his pride and his scorn of public approval. The unwell Taylor sent the letter to Richard Woodhouse hoping that he could decipher it. Woodhouse's lengthy reply, which has endeared him to posterity,[12] tries to diagnose and explain what Keats meant by "pride." This is not mere personal pride. Keats is identifying himself (and very justifiably) with the tradition of letters. Of course the public is indebted to the poet for his verse, and not the poet to the public for approval. As for money, Woodhouse himself would like to advance £50 (he has absolutely nothing more that he can give at the moment) ; but it should be offered, for the sake of Keats's self-respect, from the firm of Taylor and Hessey: "Whatever People (say they) regret that they could not do for Shakespeare or Chatterton, because he did not live in their time, that I would embody into a Rational principle, and (with due regard to certain expediencies) do for Keats." But since Woodhouse's own means were severely limited, he was naturally uneager "to have the oats eaten

12 Printed in full, II.150–153.

by other cattle. I wish he could be cured of the vice of lending—for in a poor man, it is a vice." Woodhouse, since Taylor was in the country, then deposited £50 to Keats's credit with the firm of Taylor and Hessey. Hessey was to send only part of this at first (£30), holding the rest in reserve until there was a chance to see just what Keats really needed.

September 5 was a happy day. That morning he not only received the £30 from Hessey, which he felt to be a genuine expression of confidence in him from the firm, but he also got news that one of his friends had repaid a debt (£30, possibly £40); the letter had been sent to the wrong address. At the same time, Brown had been able to borrow another £30.[13] They had, all told, about £100, though most of it on loan. Keats's spirits rose immeasurably. All he needed now in order to "be a complete Midas" was to have someone send him "a pair of asses ears." Meanwhile *Lamia* was all finished. Brown was leaving in a couple of days for a three-week visit to his friends in Chichester and Bedhampton.[14] Keats, left to himself, would be able to find some time for the *Fall of Hyperion* before the autumn began.

5

His new feeling of jubilance was to last only five days. On Friday, September 10, a letter from George arrived announcing that

[13] William Haslam, who had borrowed the money from George, had addressed the letter, in a moment of absent-mindedness, to Chichester (where Keats had stayed with Brown the previous January); the letter had been lying in the post office there for three weeks. The friend from whom Brown borrowed his money may have been John Snook, Dilke's brother-in-law.

[14] It is sometimes assumed that Brown deceived Keats and went to Ireland for the purpose mentioned by Brown's son in a memoir written in 1890: "In August 1819 [actually it would have been during the three weeks from about September 7 to 30], when Brown left Keats at Winchester, he went over to Ireland and married Abigail Donohoo, a handsome woman of the peasant class; the marriage was performed by a catholic priest, and therefore not legal" (*KC*, I.lvi). Bodurtha and Pope argue persuasively against accepting this story (Brown, p. 108). See also Rollins' note, II.159. Brown probably told the story to his son, who would have appreciated the knowledge that there had been a marriage, even if illegal, before he was conceived (he was born July 16, 1820). Certainly Brown's liaison with Abigail O'Donaghue began before October 1819; and if Brown visited her in September, he could have done so in London. She was later a part-time servant at Wentworth Place, and may have already become so. It is she to whom Keats refers (January 15, 1820) when he says that "Our irish servant has plagued me this morning by saying that her Father in Ireland was very much like my Shakespeare only he had more color than the Engraving." Keats, as Bodurtha and Pope say, was by no means ignorant of Brown's relationship with her; but she did not come to live at Wentworth Place until after Keats left for Italy.

he had lost much—probably well over half—of the money he had brought with him from England. One thinks ahead to one of Keats's last letters (November 1, 1820): "Is there any news of George? O, that something fortunate had ever happened to me or my brothers!—then I might hope,—but despair is forced upon me as a habit."

George, traveling westward, had met John James Audubon, later to become famous as a naturalist. Chronically unsuccessful as a businessman (in the course of his career he bankrupted several partners, including his two brothers-in-law), Audubon became a good friend of the George Keatses and invited them to stay for a while in his log house at Henderson, Kentucky. Audubon radiated confidence. He had what appeared to be a flourishing grist and lumber mill at Henderson, though actually it was on the point of failing. He talked George into investing the greater part of his savings in a steamboat full of merchandise that could be sold down the river, in Memphis or New Orleans, at a high profit. The boat, to be sure, was not at Henderson: it was already proceeding south.

Audubon's Micawberlike optimism, his sheer incapacity to take anything but the most cheerful view, might not have been so persuasive to George in England. But frontier life was entirely strange to George; he was still only twenty-two; the long distance he had been traveling had intimidated him; and others were rushing about to invest in projects that they had never seen—that, because of the distances, they could not hope to see before investing. It then turned out that the boat into which George had put his money had at that very moment been at the bottom of the Ohio River.[15] Audubon may himself have invested in the boat (he

15 Stanley C. Arthur, *Audubon* (1937), pp. 91–92. The details are far from clear. George's letter has not survived, and Audubon understandably omits any mention of the matter in his journal. Kirk (Hampstead Keats, I.lxxvii–lxxxviii) assumed that George lost all the money he still had, one reason being that George had to borrow money for current expenses (and for his later trip to England in order to get his share of Tom's estate) from Audubon's brother-in-law, William Bakewell. But he seems to have invested in another boat, possibly at the same time, and this would explain why he had no ready funds. For George (June 18, 1820) tells John "I have an offer for the Boat which I have accepted, but the party who lives at Natchez (300 miles only near New Orleans) will not receive information that I have accepted his offer for some weeks" (II.295), and then later says he has not heard from the man though it was being offered for "only 500 dollars more than the sum she cleared me last year" (II.356). "Last year" would of course mean 1819. It is probably this boat, rather than that which had sunk, to which Keats refers on November 12, 1819: "Does the steam boat make any return yet?"

had his finger in several enterprises) and have been eager to have George take the investment off his hands. But this could have been because he needed the money at once and not because he knew the boat had sunk. George was convinced that he had been swindled. He was prepared to sue Audubon. But then Audubon's mill suddenly failed, and his creditors pounced on him. The hapless man was jailed for debt, and released only after he pled bankruptcy. (It was after this failure that Audubon, forsaking business, began to devote himself to the bird drawings for which he is remembered.)

George begged his brother to see Abbey at once. Letters to Abbey never seemed to bring any results. George was not now, as he had been earlier, simply asking for further money in order to get better placed. His situation was desperate. However little the Keats brothers thought they had inherited—and they had much more than Abbey ever let them know [16]—still they were aware that the money that would have come to Tom from their grandmother's estate amounted to £1,000 at the very minimum. They had not yet been able to touch it. For after Tom's death Abbey's first tactic, as we have noticed, was to hint darkly, and falsely, that all the children had to wait until the youngest, Fanny, was of age (1824). Keats at the time was "nearly confident 'tis all a Bam"— a hoax. Then in June Abbey had been able to fortify his obstructive stand by the vague threat of Mrs. Midgley Jennings, the widow of their uncle, to sue for the sum of which her husband had been allowed only to use the income (a threat that was completely idle; the decision had long since been made by the Chancellor). The whole matter seemed needlessly confusing and vague. The money was obviously there. At the very least could not Abbey advance as a loan some of what was due George from Tom's estate?

Keats left immediately on the night coach for London. It was a

[16] Leaving completely aside the money their grandmother had inherited directly from her husband and had made over to the children with Abbey as trustee, there was at the very least a further total by now of £4,000, counting the accumulated interest, from what had been left directly to the children by their grandfather and by their mother, and what had come to them on the death of their grandfather's sister (Mary Sweetinburgh). (See Appendix III.) None of this, which would have come to at least £1,330 for each of the three by 1819, was ever mentioned by Abbey. Moreover, none of it could have been threatened by the Chancery suit that Abbey used as subterfuge. If that suit had ever begun, it could at most have affected only the estate left by Mrs. Jennings herself; and the size of this estate, as we have seen, was itself never fully disclosed by Abbey.

twelve-hour trip. As soon as he arrived, at nine on Saturday morning, he went to Abbey's countinghouse in Pancras Lane. Abbey was not to be hurried. He needed time to collect his forces. He "appointed Monday evening at 7 to meet me," Keats wrote his brother, "and observed that he should drink tea at that hour." Keats gave him George's letter. "He really appeared anxious about it; promised he would forward your money as quickly as possible." Abbey would talk at once with his lawyer about the threatened Chancery suit.

There was nothing further that Keats could do but wait until Monday evening. He walked over to the bookshop of Taylor and Hessey in Fleet Street. Now more than ever he threw aside any thought of waiting until he had a good, selective volume to publish. He found Hessey and Woodhouse in the shop. When he burst in unexpectedly, he made it plain (said Woodhouse, writing to John Taylor) that he hoped to "publish the Eve of St. Agnes & Lamia *immediately;* but Hessey told him it could not answer to do so now." The reason for his journey to London, Woodhouse gathered, had to do with a Chancery Suit and an effort "to dissuade some old aunt from going into that Court." Keats could not bring himself to mention the painful news from George. Woodhouse was busy, but invited Keats to breakfast the next day; they could talk all morning; Woodhouse would then be leaving on the afternoon coach for Weymouth.

Keats left, wondering what else to do to kill the time until he saw Abbey on Monday evening. He had been away so long, and had been so completely absorbed in his work, that "London appeared a very odd place . . . I walk'd about the Streets as in a strange land." Most of his friends were away—Reynolds, the Dilkes, Taylor. "I had another strange sensation [;] there was not one house I felt any pleasure to call at." He could easily, of course, have gone out to Hampstead and seen Fanny Brawne. But he was afraid to do this: he was feeling very confused; he needed to come to some firm decisions about earning money and living cheaply. He went to Covent Garden, where he was able to get in "at half-price," and then "tumbled into bed."

The next day he showed up for breakfast at Woodhouse's rooms in the Temple. He broached the matter of a new volume. "I wondered," wrote Woodhouse to Taylor, "why he said nothing of Isabella: & assured him that it would please more" than the *Eve of St.*

Agnes. "He said he could not bear the former now. It appeared to him mawkish." They argued about this at length. Keats had brought along a new copy of the *Eve of St. Agnes:* the last three lines had been changed "to leave on the reader a sense of pettish disgust"; and he had made another change to make it clear that the union of the lovers (with Madeline half asleep) had been complete.[17] Woodhouse objected to this; it seemed needless and foolish. "He says he does not want ladies to read his poetry: that he writes for men . . . &c &c &c—and all this sort of Keats-like rhodomontade."[18] The two friends spent six hours together.

As Woodhouse left for the coach, Keats walked with him; they continued talking until they reached the coach door. Alone now, he thought what next to do. He called on the Wylies—Georgiana's mother and her two brothers, Henry and Charles—and stayed for dinner. He did not tell them about George's news. "I thought it better not. For better times will certainly come"; and why, he goes on to George and Georgiana, make them unhappy needlessly?

Then Monday morning arrived. Before taking the coach to Walthamstow to see his sister, he stopped in again at the shop of Taylor and Hessey in order to get paper and ink for a note to Fanny Brawne. He tells her he is in town because of a letter from George, but says only that "it is not of the brightest intelligence." He cannot see her now. "I love you too much to venture to Hampstead." It would not be a true visit. The letter may have been something of a shock to her. For he goes on, without giving any explanation or background: "really what can I do? Knowing well that my life must be passed in fatigue and trouble, I have been endeavouring to wean myself from you: for to myself alone what can be much of a misery?" He went out to see his sister, telling her at least something about George's situation; and in the afternoon he filled out time by seeing Rice and John Martin. Then he walked over to Abbey's rooms above the countinghouse for his appointment.

Abbey was prepared. Keats, so conveniently trusting about money in the past, was now plainly aroused; and if Abbey appeared too unsympathetic, Keats might, spurred on by George, be-

---

[17] See above, under the discussion of the poem in Chapter XVII, section 12.

[18] II.161–165. Keats later complained (August 1820) that women took "offence" at his poetry. The thought by this time was also partly a wish or hope; for, from 1818 until the end, he cringed at what he thought was the insipidity of his early poetry.

gin to think of taking legal action (as indeed Fanny Keats was to do when she became of age). To have his handling of the estate scrutinized closely was the last thing Abbey wanted. His procedure now was to disarm Keats by expressing strong but noncommittal sympathy. Certainly something must be done, and "as quickly as possible." He could not, it is true, advance any money out of his own pocket as a loan. He needed to keep fluid whatever he personally had in order to help protect the Keats children should the Chancery suit arise; and what if George should lose such a loan too? But Keats was sure that George's letter had "appealed home to him—He will not see the necessity of a thing till he is hit in the mouth." The trouble, Abbey mused, was that dark threat of a Chancery suit from Mrs. Jennings; but perhaps something could be done if he took strong steps at once (he "convinced me that he was anxious to bring the Business to an issue"), though dealing with lawyers was of course a complicated, time-consuming task. Keats must then have startled him by offering to remain in town "to be Abbey's messenger in these affairs"; but Abbey immediately "observed that by being himself the agent in the whole, people might be more expeditious."

Confident that he now had Keats well in hand, Abbey picked up a magazine where he had seen an extract from Byron's *Don Juan* attacking literary ambition ("What is the end of Fame? 'tis but to fill / A certain portion of uncertain paper"), and read it aloud. "Says he the fellow says true things now & then." "Mr. Abbey is to write me"—Keats trustfully tells George—"as soon as he can bring matters to bear." After leaving, Keats walked up Cheapside, then returned a way to drop some letters in the post, and ran into Abbey again. They strolled together for a few minutes through the Poultry as far as the hatter's shop in which Abbey had a part interest. Abbey again repeated the suggestion, made several times during the previous spring, that Keats should become a hatter.

He returned to Winchester on September 15. It would be another month before Brown's tenant for the summer, Nathan Benjamin, vacated the house in Hampstead. But Keats could not take any further advantage of Brown. He would have to get steady work, and this would mean living in town. The days now were haunted with the conviction that all the effort of the past year—of the past three years, in fact—must be suspended for an indefinite period.

6

Not long after he had first arrived at Winchester, Keats had found a favorite walk that he often took for an hour before dinner. He describes the first part of it in detail to George and Georgiana (September 21), knowing how homesick they were, four thousand miles away, for something that would remind them of England; and the ingenuous phrases of two years before, when he set off to begin *Endymion,* return now in the letters of his last sojourn in the English countryside ("the most beautiful streams about I ever saw"; "the most beautifully clear river"; the "whole Town is beautifully wooded") :

> Now the time is beautiful. I take a walk every day for an hour before dinner and this is generally my walk—I go out at the back gate across one street, into the Cathedral yard, which is always interesting; then I pass under the trees along a paved path, pass the beautiful front of the Cathedral, turn to the left under a stone door way— then I am on the other side of the building—which leaving behind me I pass on through two college-like squares seemingly built for the dwelling place of Deans and Prebendaries—garnished with grass and shaded with trees. Then I pass through one of the old city gates and then you are in one College-Street through which I pass and at the end thereof crossing some meadows and at last a country alley of gardens I arrive, that is, my worship arrives at the foundation of Saint Cross, which is a very interesting old place, both for its gothic tower and alms-square and for the appropriation of its rich rents to a relation of the Bishop of Winchester—Then I pass across St Cross meadows till you come to the most beautifully clear river—now this is only one mile of my walk.

The evenings were becoming cooler, and with them was the suggestion of the coming winter. But the days were still long.

The Sunday after he returned to Winchester from London, he took the same walk out to the St. Cross meadows along the small clear River Itchen (September 19). He mentions the walk in a letter to Reynolds two days later: 1819

> How beautiful the season is now—How fine the air. A temperate sharpness about it . . . I never lik'd stubble fields so much as now— Aye better than the chilly green of the spring. Somehow a stubble plain looks warm—in the same way that some pictures look warm— this struck me so much in my sunday's walk that I composed upon it.

The poem is the last of the great odes, "To Autumn."

It is because "To Autumn" is so uniquely a distillation, and at many different levels, that each generation has found it one of the most nearly perfect poems in English. We need not be afraid of continuing to use the adjective. In its strict sense the word is peculiarly applicable: the whole is "perfected"—carried through to completion—solely by means of the given parts; and the parts observe decorum (for no other poem of the last two centuries does the classical critical vocabulary prove so satisfying) by contributing directly to the whole, with nothing left dangling or independent. The "Ode to a Nightingale," for example, is a less "perfect" though a greater poem. The distinctive appeal of "To Autumn" lies not merely in the degree of resolution but in the fact that, in this short space, so many different kinds of resolution are attained.

Most of what Keats had developed in the structure of the ode stanza the previous April and May reappears effortlessly now (the poem seems to have been written very easily). There is only one new variation, simple but altogether appropriate: the ode stanza is given a more prolonged effect; and the prolonging of fulfillment is itself an intrinsic part of the theme of the ode.[19] Not only the formal structure but the whole conception of the odal hymn becomes transparent before its subject. The poet himself is completely absent; there is no "I," no suggestion of the discursive language that we find in the other odes; the poem is entirely concrete, and self-sufficient in and through its concreteness. But if dramatic debate, protest, and qualification are absent, it is not because any premises from which they might proceed are disregarded but because these premises are being anticipated and absorbed at each step. The result (in contrast to the "Nightingale" or the "Grecian Urn") is also a successful union of the ideal—of the heart's desire—and reality; of the "greeting of the Spirit" and its object. What the heart really wants is being found (in the first stanza, fullness and completion; in the second, a prolonging of that fulfillment). Here at last is something of a genuine paradise, therefore. It even has its deity—a

---

19 The basic ten-line stanza (a Shakespearean quatrain, followed by a Petrarchan sestet: *a b a b c d e c d e*) is now extended to eleven lines. The couplet, which he had wanted to avoid before, is brought back, and placed, not as a tag at the end, but just before the end (first stanza: *a b a b c d e d c c e*; the remaining two: *a b a b c d e c d d e*). The effect of the couplet, placed thus, is to sustain the approaching close at a momentary crest before the stanza subsides in the final line.

benevolent deity that wants not only to "load and bless" ("conspiring" with its friend, the sun), but also to "spare," to prolong, to "set budding more." And yet all this is put with concrete exactness and fidelity.

These resolutions are attained partly through still another one to which Keats's poetry has so often aspired: a union of process and stasis (or what Keats had called "stationing"). Each of the three stanzas concentrates on a dominant, even archetypal, aspect of autumn, but, while doing so, admits and absorbs its opposite. The theme of the first is ripeness, of growth now reaching its climax beneath the "maturing sun," as the strain of the weighty fruit bends the apple trees and loads the vines. The cells of the beehives are already brimming over. Yet growth is still surprisingly going on, as autumn and the sun conspire "to set budding more, / And still more, later flowers," and as the bees are deceived into feeling that summer will never end:

> Season of mists and mellow fruitfulness,
>   Close bosom-friend of the maturing sun;
> Conspiring with him how to load and bless
>   With fruit the vines that round the thatch-eves run;
> To bend with apples the moss'd cottage-trees,
>   And fill all fruit with ripeness to the core;
>   To swell the gourd, and plump the hazel shells
>   With a sweet kernel; to set budding more,
> And still more, later flowers for the bees,
> Until they think warm days will never cease,
>   For Summer has o'er-brimm'd their clammy cells.

If, in the first stanza, we find process continuing within a context of stillness and attained fulfillment, in the second—which is something of a reverse or mirror image of the first—we find stillness where we expect process. For now autumn is conceived as a reaper or harvester. Yet it is a harvester that is not harvesting. This benevolent deity is at first motionless, "sitting careless on a granary floor," or asleep on a "half-reap'd furrow," while its "hook / Spares the next swath and all its twinèd flowers"—spares not only the full grain but those new "later flowers" that are interlocking with it. Movement begins only in the latter part of the stanza. Even then it is only suggested in the momentary glimpses of the figure of the gleaner keeping "steady" its "laden head" as it crosses a brook; and autumn then stops again to watch the slow pressing of the apples into cider as the hours pass:

Who hath not seen thee oft amid thy store?
   Sometimes whoever seeks abroad may find
Thee sitting careless on a granary floor,
   Thy hair soft-lifted by the winnowing wind;
Or on a half-reap'd furrow sound asleep,
   Drows'd with the fume of poppies, while thy hook
     Spares the next swath and all its twinèd flowers:
And sometimes like a gleaner thou dost keep
   Steady thy laden head across a brook;
   Or by a cyder-press, with patient look,
     Thou watchest the last oozings hours by hours.

   There is a hint that the end is approaching—these are the "last oozings"—and the pervading thought in what follows is the withdrawal of autumn, the coming death of the year, and of course the familiar archetypal relevance of the association to our feelings of sequence in our own lives. But if the conception in the previous stanzas has been carried out partly through contrary images—fulfilled growth, while growth still continues; the reaper who is not reaping—the procedure now is almost completely indirect and left solely to inference. The personified figure of autumn is replaced by concrete images of life, and of life unafflicted by any thought of death: the gnats, the hedge crickets, the redbreast. Moreover, it is life that can exist in much the same way at other times than autumn. Only two images are peculiar to the season—the "stubble-plains," and the "full-grown lambs." The mind is free to associate the wailful mourning of the gnats with a funeral dirge for the dying year, but the sound is no more confined to autumn alone than is the "soft-dying" of any day; and if the swallows are "gathering," they are not necessarily gathering for migration:

   Where are the songs of Spring? Ay, where are they?
     Think not of them, thou hast thy music too,—
   While barrèd clouds bloom the soft-dying day,
     And touch the stubble-plains with rosy hue;
   Then in a wailful choir the small gnats mourn
     Among the river sallows, borne aloft
      Or sinking as the light wind lives or dies;
   And full-grown lambs loud bleat from hilly bourn;
     Hedge-crickets sing; and now with treble soft
     The red-breast whistles from a garden-croft;
      And gathering swallows twitter in the skies.

The resolutions we have been considering are formal: we have been thinking of the poem as a work of art. To document other considerations that enter would involve (as with every major poem Keats wrote) a recapitulation of much of his life. Yet, since this is the last great lyric that Keats wrote, we may mention three of the many preoccupations and ideals that reach back to the beginning. A principal one is stylistic. We could even start with the first poem he wrote—the "Imitation of Spenser," with its relative calm. We could then recall the lines in "Sleep and Poetry," and that early ideal of the dynamic caught momentarily in repose (poetry is "might half slumb'ring on its own right arm"); then the Elgin Marbles, and the various remarks on "intensity" ("Alcibiades, leaning on his Crimson Couch in his Galley, his broad shoulders imperceptibly heaving with the Sea"), and the marginal notes in *Paradise Lost*. This ideal of energy caught in repose pervades the imagery of the poem, and indeed the whole conception and "stationing" of autumn (perhaps the most successful example in English where this "stationing" is obtained with a concept as abstract as a season). A second preoccupation, more nakedly biographical though by no means unconnected with style, is the association of expectance, of waiting, with autumn: we recall that early sonnet, "After dark vapours," in which the almost sick anxiety of waiting for his first volume to appear becomes expressed in images and phrases that anticipate this final ode; and we think of the lines, when *Endymion* was begun in the spring, that leap forward to the thought of concluding it before autumn.

A third consideration, for which there is an equally long history (if the word "long" can be used of so short a life), is his inability to conceive fulfillment without a spring of promise still implicit within it. It may take the form of protest against the starkness of an end, as in those lines Keats wrote in December 1817, after finishing *Endymion* ("In a drear-nighted December"), voicing his envious thought of the bare branches that cannot remember their former green happiness (would that this were so, he goes on, with the human heart); or it may take the form of self-defeating affirmation and desperate hope, as in the "Grecian Urn" (with its "happy, happy boughs" that "cannot shed" their leaves). But the resolution to which he really aspires is that which touched home to him in reading Shakespeare's sonnets two and a half years before:

> When lofty trees I see barren of leaves,
> Which erst from heat did canopy the herd;—

a resolution ("gusto" or "intensity") whereby, as the mind conceives the present, the past and future are simultaneously incorporated in it, and the conception of the "greeting spirit" thus matches, in fidelity to fact, both the unfolding promise and the laden past that are a part of the very nature of the object it is attempting to greet and to rescue into consciousness.

7

These long, warm days, with only a "temperate sharpness" in the evenings, were almost finished. Moreover, a totally new life had to be started very shortly. No further delay was possible. He had probably been thinking since he returned from London on September 15 that he would have to abandon *Hyperion*—this effort that symbolized so much in his hope to be "among the English poets." Three days after the ode "To Autumn," he wrote to Reynolds (in the same letter where he described the warm stubble fields and his walk just before he wrote "To Autumn") that he had "given up Hyperion."

The writing of the first half of *Lamia* in the early summer may have suggested the new approach to *Hyperion,* to which Keats almost immediately turned for a week or two before Brown's arrival on July 22. Like so many poets, he found that the activity of writing one poem quickly suggested ideas for another in a different mode. A second poem, a second style, allowed him to pursue or develop what the formal limitations of the first poem prevented. The brisk narrative of *Lamia*, at least as he himself was handling it, brought much closer to the surface the whole tantalizing problem of illusion and reality; and yet, because of the demands of the story and the verse form, the poem also frustrated a more serious treatment of the subject.

Indeed, that simple word "illusion," as we have noted, had long since ceased to apply. With only a little reflection and honesty, we find ourselves turning from the small inlet that we usually agree to call "illusion" into the large, uncharted fluidities of reaction that make up most of human experience: we find ourselves turning, that is, to the endless swerve and mass of human aspirations, fears, envies, "Guesses at Heaven," interpretations of the past (informed, fanciful, or mixed)—indeed, all the pursuits that take their "reality and worth" so much from "the ardour of the pursuer." We pass, in short, to one of the ultimate problems of man: that of the self, and the ceaseless effort of the individual and of generations of individuals ("hungry generations," to use the phrase from the "Ode to a Nightingale") to come to terms with reality or to avoid it—the hungry effort to bring the self into harmony with such reality as we can glimpse ("truth") or to bend reality to the heart's desire, whether gently and tentatively (as the heart desires to do in the "Nightingale" and the "Urn") or drastically (as Lycius seeks to do in *Lamia*).

Keats's hope to come to some gradual understanding of all this, and of the elusive reality against which it plays, had found its polar guide in the ideal of "disinterestedness" that had so excited him when he read Hazlitt's *Principles of Human Action* a year and a half before. And his general psychological premise, as we have been noting, was also that of Hazlitt—a premise eminently capable of further grafting or development. The essence of it was the dependent, sympathetic, projective nature of the self (or of the imagination and all that the term may include). Even the most inveterate selfishness involves a detour: our imagination has to latch upon some fixed, limited (and often false) conception of ourselves and of our needs and security; and the images or abstractions with which the imagination becomes identified in such cases are just as much of the mind—the act involves just as much of a projection— as other sympathetic identifications more altruistic or more mentally nourishing and formative.[20] We could not, as Hazlitt said, "love" ourselves—our imagination could not "identify itself" with our own future interest—were we not equally capable of identifying ourselves with other interests.

The ideal of "disinterestedness" that had so forcibly struck the empathic young Keats was the developing use of the projective, assimilating mind for objects and purposes other than self, and with complete openness to whatever came. In his letter to George and Tom back in December 1817, he had used the cumbersome phrase "Negative Capability." Much had happened since then to darken the expanding circumference of his experience. More problems were constantly opening, more doors, "all leading to dark passages" unsuspected beforehand. The first *Hyperion* itself had demonstrated this. He had begun it with the eager premise that a meaning could be found to help us

20 See above, Chapter X, section 11.

> to bear all naked truths,
> And to envisage circumstance, all calm.

One possible meaning was that "first in beauty should be first in might." But was this really a "disinterested" diagnosis or just another aspiration of the heart, like those aspirations he later dramatized in the odes—an aspiration by no means false, and yet only a glimpse of one possible truth? Put another way, a central premise of the first *Hyperion* had been the widening of human consciousness throughout history. This growth, to be sure, brought its problems for many individuals, including himself. In fact, he himself had begun the first *Hyperion* under the shadow as well as the personal challenge of these problems. For epic "grandeur" may become "circumscribed" when we lack the "seeming sure points of Reasoning" that the great poets of the past seem to have possessed. He had admitted as much six months before he started *Hyperion;* and when he plunged into it prematurely, desperately needing something to distract him while he was nursing Tom, there had been a real struggle against the anxiety that little was left for the modern poet to do. Still, with some effort, he was able to regard this inhibition and anxiety as a result of his own immaturity. If certain kinds of traditional "grandeur" had to be sacrificed, there was other grandeur if one only had the eyes to see. There was the "grand march of intellect" itself, however painful the changes it brought to some through the growth in consciousness. But the poem, attempting to combine this confidence with epic simplicity, had encountered increasing obstacles. It was not that the idea of a "grand march of intellect" seemed impossible. It was rather that the concept seemed too simple. We can hardly help feeling that by the summer of 1819 Keats had really outgrown the first *Hyperion,* and that he was searching his way to a fundamentally different poem.

8

In the powerful fragment that he now wrote, anticipating much of what poetry was to do a century later, the interest that takes precedence over every other is the self as it tries to come to terms with reality. Other interests naturally joined or clashed. We can only guess their relative importance. For we are dealing, after all, with something even more fragmentary than the first *Hyperion,* and something that was only salvaged from his manuscripts thirty-five years after his death. Among the related interests that come to the surface, a few are especially prominent: the affirmation of the poet's solidarity with humanity, and also an uneasy sense of his difference; the isolation and at the same time the possibilities of further union that the developing imagination in general finds itself acquiring; the challenge to the poetry of the future to continue in something of the spirit of the great poetry of the past, and the temptations to betray that spirit. Any one of these may be taken up— and indeed each of them has been—as one corner of the blanket, so to speak. All proceed from the same premise, first suggested in the "Mansions of Life" letter and now built into the symbolic structure of the poem: as we extend the small clearing of our knowledge into the forest and "untrodden region" of the mind and of the unknown generally, the number of points at which we touch the unknown increases, and with it the number of questions.

Meanwhile formal considerations also added to the complexity Keats faced. In making his final try at the poem, he had already in hand an existing and very solid chunk of two and a half books of magnificent verse, at least a part of which he naturally wanted to use. This was already a large problem. Yet at the same time he was moving into a very different style.

As if in self-imposed challenge, the poem—which was to include a bitter attack on the whole conception of poetry as dream, retreat, or escape—is itself frankly cast as a dream vision. In short, the closest possible wrestle with the subject is promised, and one that will involve form itself. Contrasting extremes that interplay so rapidly in *Lamia* are here given a rooted strength as if in preparation for a more essential if precarious resolution. The *Purgatorio* of Dante, much on Keats's mind throughout the past few months, seemed especially appropriate in an exploration of the uses to which the imagination is, or can be, put—the imagination itself being "lost," as Keats had once said, "in a sort of Purgatory blind," helpless to find any clear-cut "standard law" in either heaven or earth. As has often been noted, Keats even catches something of the flavor of Dante's style, though he had barely begun the study of Italian, and knew Dante principally through the blank-verse translation of Henry Cary. The poem itself is purgatorial. We find ourselves looking back to the sonnet "On Sitting Down to Read *King Lear* Once Again," with its lines about the "fierce dispute / Betwixt damnation and impassioned clay." "Impassioned clay," as distinct from those whose "souls" are mere "clod," is inevitably subject to "vision." The range of this hunger and ceaseless activity of dream is suggested at the start of the poem:

> Fanatics have their dreams, wherewith they weave
> A paradise for a sect; the savage, too,
> From forth the loftiest fashion of his sleep
> Guesses at Heaven . . .
>
> .   .   .   .
>
> Since every man whose soul is not a clod
> Hath visions, and would speak, if he had lov'd
> And been well nurtured in his mother tongue.

If poetry differs, it is in only one way of which we can be confident —at least as a beginning premise: poetry can "tell" its dreams, and thus "save" them from oblivion—

> With the fine spell of words alone can save
> Imagination from the sable charm
> And dumb enchantment.

No other claim for poetry is made at this point. The test is simply whether the dream will be remembered:

> Whether the dream now purpos'd to rehearse
> Be Poet's or Fanatic's will be known
> When this warm scribe, my hand, is in the grave.

In the dream that follows, we have another use of the idea of stages of development that had so haunted Keats's imagination for the past three years. The poet first finds himself in a place that, like an Arcadia, seems to answer the heart's desire for freedom from process and from the separations imposed by the finitude of experience. Here are "trees of every clime": the forest of possibility is richly diverse. But this is also a garden in and of the mind. The arbor, the "trellis vines, and bells and larger blooms" are associated with that garden of the mind promised in the "Ode to Psyche,"

> With the wreath'd trellis of a working brain,
>   With buds, and bells, and stars without a name,
> With all the gardener Fancy e'er could feign.

We also have the first of the Biblical associations that continue to deepen throughout the poem (and with some novelty in Keats's writing) .²¹ For this is something of an Eden, but an Eden strangely used: the dreamer is very much a latecomer; this is a place where others have already been. Yet he is not a mere trespasser; he is free to avail himself of whatever is there. A "feast of summer fruits" is spread, as if in welcome. It is only on closer scrutiny that this feast is seen to be the refuse left by other visitors from an innocent, remote past—"refuse of a meal / By angel tasted or our Mother Eve," "empty shells" and other "remnants." But the promise of abundance is left, as Woodhouse had tried to reassure Keats the year before ("the wealth of poetry is unexhausted & is inexhaustible," whatever previous poets have drawn from it) :

> Still was more plenty than the fabled horn
> Thrice emptied could pour forth, at banqueting
> For Proserpine return'd to her own fields,
> Where the white heifers low.

This sacramental meal, suggesting union with the long-departed past, causes him to thirst, by contrast, for a cool and sober drink. No wine to reinforce the impression of Arcadia is desired. The thought is the reverse of the second stanza of the "Ode to a Nightingale." A frank, realistic acknowledgment of man's fleeting mortality is implied and indeed wanted. He takes this "transparent juice, / Sipp'd by the wander'd bee,"

> And, pledging all the Mortals of the world,
> And all the dead whose names are in our lips,
> Drank. That full draught is parent of my theme.

The drink and pledge prove unexpectedly potent. For something radically different suddenly replaces the first garden:

> I looked around upon the carvèd sides
> Of an old sanctuary with roof august,
> Builded so high, it seem'd that filmèd clouds
> Might spread beneath, as o'er the stars of heaven;
> So old the place was, I remember'd none
> The like upon the earth: what I had seen
> Of grey cathedrals, buttress'd walls, rent towers,
> The superannuations of sunk realms,
> Or Nature's rocks toil'd hard in waves and winds,
> Seem'd but the faulture of decrepit things
> To that eternal domèd monument.

²¹ Needless to say, some of these associations are as much with *Paradise Lost* as with the Bible itself.

9

The experience is that of a finite creature confronted with vastness ("straining at particles"—to go back to the letter of a few
months before—"in the midst of a great darkness"). Now, for the
first time in any of his longer poems, the imagery and tone begin
to move directly toward the religious and the sacramental. A
strong magnetic attraction toward the Biblical (both Hebraic and
Christian) is countered by a strenuous effort to universalize the
religious quest—or at least that part of the religious quest that approaches the "Burden of the Mystery" with awe, humility, and
fruitful (if tortured) puzzlement. In the fifty lines or so that follow, we find a coalescence of medieval Christendom, Judaism
(with echoes of Jacob's ladder, and the horned altar of Jehovah),
and Greek and Roman antiquity. Combining with them are suggestions of the Egyptian and Druidic religions. To the informed
and "disinterested" eye, even the by-products of man's constant
efforts to "guess at Heaven" remain in a potential present. The
paraphernalia—the robes, the draperies—that he sees about him
in a "mingl'd heap" are either

                    of dyed asbestos wove,
        Or in that place the moth could not corrupt,
        So white the linen.

No reductionism, no quick dismissal, is possible before these
poignant remains, from so distant a past, of man's attempt to penetrate the mystery of things. The poet turns from them with humility to the columns that extend above him as far as the eye can
see "ending in mist / Of nothing." The loneliness is the greater.
For in the east

                                    black gates
        Were shut against the sunrise evermore,
        Then to the west I look'd.

From now on, throughout the rest of what Keats writes in this
fragment, the twentieth-century reader is struck by images, assertions, indeed basic premises, that anticipate much that we associate with existentialism (no other major nineteenth-century poem
does this to the same extent). But we are also struck by the degree
to which this creative, self-earned effort stops short of the existential: not because of a lazy unwillingness to follow out the implica-

tions (these are only too starkly suggested) but because of the active presence of other considerations. To begin with, the intimidation of twentieth-century man before the vast spaces of possibility (in the physical universe or even in the swarm of man's own limited past on this planet) is here in solution: the Egyptian and Druidic—the line of columns "ending in mist," and the black gates that shut behind one, forbidding all return to the first garden, the first promise—illustrate the pull toward the abstract, the formal, the remote, and away from the warmly human. Symbolism, progressively developed in the odes, here becomes extreme and desperate. On the other hand, the debate with it, the protest, is put with frank, direct statement. That protest (from one point of view) comes from a "poor forked animal" (to use the phrase Keats adopts from *Lear*). We crawl, as Hamlet said, between Heaven and Earth. Moreover, the terror of this vast loneliness is the stronger because of the abyss that this protesting animal, so given to the hungers of both vision and fear, is carrying within itself: the undiscovered corridors within its own finite nature of "impassioned clay" match those that it encounters outside. We are indeed in a "labyrinth," both subjectively and objectively, as Keats had implied a year before in the letter about the "Chamber of Maiden-Thought"; and we ourselves create and add to the labyrinth.

In combination with the use of the remote and abstract as background is a new, sharply analytic consciousness of the body as an anatomical event both brief and complex. Thus, at the start, we find the narrator aware of his own hand as he writes, and thinking ahead to the cold that is to come. Whether the dream to follow be "Poet's or Fanatic's" will be known only "When this warm scribe, my hand, is in the grave." The image remained with Keats. He was later to use it in the lines found scrawled in the manuscript of the unfinished comic poem, *The Cap and Bells*: "This living hand, now warm and capable / Of earnest grasping, would, if it were cold / . . . I hold it toward you." Empathy is focused on the physical functions of the body: the tongue seeking to find syllables "about its roofèd home"; terror that makes the "heart too small to hold its blood"; the massive chill that rises from the pavement through the limbs "to put cold grasp / Upon those streams that pulse beside the throat"; the strained effort to penetrate the dark "chambers" of Moneta's brain—

                                        As I had found
A grain of gold upon a mountain's side,
And twing'd with avarice strain'd out my eyes
To search its sullen entrails rich with ore,
So, at the view of sad Moneta's brow,
I ached to see what things the hollow brain
Behind enwombèd: what high tragedy
In the dark secret Chambers of her skull
Was acting.

But elements we may associate with the existential—the inter-play of the oppressive feeling of vastness with the concentrated fo-cus on the brief, involved warmth of the body—are present not as an end result but as a vivid by-product of deepening experience. To begin with, they are suffused, and thus rescued from reduction-ism, by the growing sense of mystery. The imaginative strength that is able to discover them independently, through expansion of its own circumference of experience, is equally capable of retain-ing its openness to much else. In no case does it conclude that ev-ery further door before us is closed (its own experience of advance has been too genuinely earned), though the gates behind us may have swung shut. Indeed, the essence of the involved treatment of the next stage after the first garden is that it cannot remain for us even as a resting place. The mortal who has found himself in this place has only two alternatives: to "Rot on the pavement" en-tirely, or, by continuing to use the same restless capability of mind that has brought him here in the first place, to mount from this stark pavement.

10

Turning to the west, the dreamer faces in the distance a vast im-age, at the foot of which stands an altar. He approaches it slowly ("Repressing haste, as too unholy there") .[22] A flight of stairs leads up to the shrine, and beside the altar is a figure ministering to the sacrificial flame. The incense is "Maian"—a reminder of the frag-ment of the "Ode to Maia" of fifteen months before, with its thought of bards from a remote past ("O, give me their old vig-our . . . Rich in the simple worship of a day") . This early Maian incense, with its suggestion of a past long before that of "all the

---

[22] We can exaggerate the strictly autobiographical references. But it is impossible not to recall his dedicated conviction, in the months after the "Negative Capability" letter, that he must proceed slowly to what he had once called the "fane of Poesy": "For many years my offerings must be hush'd."

dead whose names are in our lips" whom the dreamer had pledged, brings (at first) a reassurance of health:

> When in mid-May the sickening East Wind
> Shifts sudden to the South, the small warm rain
> Melts out the frozen incense from all flowers
> And fills the air with so much pleasant health
> That even the dying man forgets his shroud;
> Even so that lofty sacrificial fire,
> Sending forth Maian incense . . .[23]

But the moment of reassurance is followed by the ominous message from the figure beside the flame:

> "If thou canst not ascend
> These steps, die on that marble where thou art.
> Thy flesh, near cousin to the common dust,
> Will parch for lack of nutriment,—thy bones
> Will wither in few years, and vanish so
> That not the quickest eye could find a grain
> Of what thou now art on that pavement cold."

The dreamer painfully tries to mount the steps. Coldness rises through the nerves of his feet, until it constricts the arteries of the throat, stifling the whole capacity for expression. To turn aside, or to stop, is unthinkable: "Slow, heavy, deadly was my pace." But the impetus of the first effort brings relief. As his "icèd foot" touches the lowest step, "life seem'd / To pour in at the toes." Mounting now with unexpected speed, he approaches the "hornèd shrine." Here the next trial is to begin: the horns of the shrine are like those grasped by the suppliant before Jehovah:

> "Holy Power,"
> Cried I, approaching near the hornèd shrine,
> "What am I that should so be saved from death?
> What am I that another death come not
> To choke my utterance, sacrilegious, here?"
> Then said the veilèd shadow: "Thou hast felt
> What 'tis to die and live again before
> Thy fated hour. That thou hadst power to do so
> Is thy own safety; thou hast dated on
> Thy doom." "High Prophetess," said I, "purge off,
> Benign, if so it please thee, my mind's film."

[23] The lines, partly suggested by the *Purgatorio*, also look back to the sonnet he wrote in January 1817 ("After dark vapours"), when, throughout those anxious weeks, he was waiting for his first volume to appear and was thinking ahead to a long future.

"None can usurp this height," returned that shade,
"But those to whom the miseries of the world
Are misery, and will not let them rest.
All else who find a haven in the world,
Where they may thoughtless sleep away their days,
If by a chance into this fane they come,
Rot on the pavement where thou rotted'st half."

Then follows the stark dialogue that seems to question the poet's very right to exist. There are "thousands" who "feel the giant agony of the world," who "Labour for mortal good." They can hardly be said to be reposing in the world in thoughtless sleep. Where are they, and why is the poet here alone?

"Those whom thou spak'st of are no visionaries,"
Rejoin'd that voice,—"they are no dreamers weak;
They seek no wonder but the human face;
No music but a happy-noted voice—
They come not here, they have no thought to come—
And thou art here, for thou art less than they—
What benefit canst thou do, or all thy tribe,
To the great world? Thou art a dreaming thing;
A fever of thyself—think of the Earth."

The distinction is central, though not for that reason conclusive. It echoes that implied in the long journal letter in March, a month before he wrote about the "Vale of Soul-Making." [24] Two other remarks also occur to us, written while he was working on the poem—the close repetition of phrasing suggesting how much the idea is on his mind. "I am convinced more and more every day that (excepting the human friend Philosopher) a fine writer is the most genuine Being in the world—Shakspeare and the paradise Lost every day become greater wonders to me" (August 14); "I am convinced more and more day by day that fine writing is next to fine doing the top thing in the world" (August 24).

The place, in short, is one to which only the "visionary" comes. If he is completely a "dreamer," and has strayed here by chance from his earthly repose, he "Rots on the pavement." If he has the power to climb from this pavement of paralysis and rapid disinte-

24 "I have no doubt that thousands of people never heard of have had hearts comp[l]etely disinterested." He then mentions Jesus and Socrates as examples of the ability to transcend self on behalf of the general human good. In contrast he himself is "young writing at random—straining at particles of light in the midst of a great darkness . . . Yet may I not in this be free from sin?" Perhaps poetry "is not so fine a thing as philosophy—For the same reason that an eagle is not so fine a thing as a truth" (II.80–81).

gration, the result (itself only another beginning) is a drastic encounter with oneself, with the entire past of man's effort, and with
the utmost demand on honesty and humility. These Keats tries
to suggest through the figure of "Moneta," his new version of
what, in the "Hymn to Pan," he had invoked as "Dread opener of
the mysterious doors / Leading to universal knowledge." He now
uses the Roman form of the name instead of the Greek Mnemosyne (goddess of memory and mother of the muses). No mere
guide or mentor, like Dante's Virgil or Beatrice, though something of their character and function is included in her own, she
is at once the repository of the tragic past—the laden memory "of
all the dead whose names are in our lips"—and also, as the Latin
name suggests, an "admonisher."

The Longinian intoxication with the ideal of the great art of
the past that had sustained Keats's remarkable development had
also, by the time *Endymion* was finished, led to the debate with
this ideal that we have been noticing. If he wanted desperately to
justify his own identity—and that of the poetry of the future—in
the light of that ideal, he also felt the need to dissociate them in
some details, to recognize inevitable and excusable differences. He
had swung back and forth. If, in February 1818, he had attacked
the confinement and egoism of modern poetry, when compared
with the ancient and Elizabethan, by May he was regarding the
modern approach as one that is destined to think more deeply
"into the human heart." If the following October he felt despondently that most of what poetry can do is already "exhausted" or
"forestalled," yet that same month he began his bold attempt in
the first *Hyperion* to combine the amplitude and grandeur of earlier poetry with the closer probe and exploration that are to be
the next task of poetry. Since *Hyperion* the debate had become
specialized, lyric, tentative: witness the credo in the "Ode to Psyche," with its hope to build in the "untrodden region" of the
mind, of "shadowy thought"; or the debate on the limits of art
that forms one theme of the "Ode on a Grecian Urn."

Meanwhile in the letters a suggestive premise for resolution had
begun, partly through a broadening of the whole frame of reference. Before the vast unknowable, even the greatest achievements
of past art, however noble, precious, even necessary, assume a less
intimidating stature. Something of the universality of context implied in the letter on the development of human "identity" and

the "Vale of Soul-Making" is suggested in the new figure of Moneta to whom the debate has shifted, or rather risen.

1 1

The encounter and dialogue with Moneta are those of the modern poet not merely with the accumulated achievement of the past, as represented by the mother and source of all the muses—of all man's arts—but also with the total accumulated experience of man, of which the arts themselves—even from the earliest days— are only one part. The encounter, in fact, is with a consciousness of the mysterious tragic destiny of man that reaches beyond the mortal into the vast "darkness" in which collective man is "straining at particles of light"; and when the "admonisher" at last lifts her veil,

> Then saw I a wan face,
> Not pined by human sorrows, but bright-blanch'd
> By an immortal sickness which kills not;
> It works a constant change, which happy death
> Can put no end to; deathwards progressing
> To no death was that visage; it had pass'd
> The lily and the snow; and beyond these
> I must not think now.

Before so formidable a figure the poet is forced to "resolve how to make use of the visionary capacity, what kind of poetry to write. He is alone . . . because in creating every artist is alone." [25] And what Moneta is saying is not an indictment of poetry but a challenge (unless the particular poet, either in genuine guilt or from mere timidity, construes it as a personal indictment of himself). One premise of the poem, after all—stated at the very start—is that

> every man whose soul is not a clod
> Hath visions, and would speak, if he had lov'd
> And been well nurtured in his mother tongue.

The poet, in other words, is—or can be—equivalent to those other benefactors of humanity who have "no thought to come" to this place. They each have "visions," and the poet's endowment of speech is no liability—the others "would speak" thus if they could. But in the direct benefactor the whole imaginative capacity to get

[25] David Perkins, *The Quest for Permanence*, p. 278.

beyond himself to "disinterestedness" and unselfish "Labour for mortal good" is implied by definition. In the poet, on the other hand, the habitual use of "vision" and his inevitable concentration on his art as art can always tempt him toward becoming a "visionary"—toward cherishing "vision" in and for itself, and in such a way that he begins to dwell in a separate and sealed world, as the "dreamer" Lycius, in *Lamia,* had tried to do.

Brought frankly into the open now is that deepening sense of the possible treacheries of art that we have detected in radically different ways in the "Ode on a Grecian Urn" and in *Lamia*—possible treacheries that seem inextricably meshed with the unique value and triumph of art. All this is implied by Moneta as something that has to be faced and answered—and, significantly, as something that *can* be faced and answered. The poet is "less" than the direct benefactors of humanity because he is here, in this spot —a purgatorial, transitional place—but he is not "less" if and when he is able to advance from it.

Quite understandably Keats had trouble in this part of the fragment: he was raising fundamental questions; he was writing in the presence of distractions and sharp anxieties; he was working on a timetable that would allow him only a few weeks for the entire poem; and hanging over him was the need to make a transition that would allow him to use as much of the first *Hyperion* as he could. Two difficulties in particular have needlessly complicated this passage that holds so much interest for all readers of poetry. First, Keats allows Moneta, in her condemnation of the "dreamer," to add that

> "every creature hath its home;
> Every sole man hath days of joy and pain,
> Whether his labours be sublime or low—
> The pain alone, the joy alone, distinct:
> Only the dreamer venoms all his days."

Now one of Keats's basic premises, deepening with every half year of his development, is the inseparability of joy and pain to the awake and honest consciousness (the Shakespearean "bittersweet" mentioned in the sonnet on *Lear*). The song of Apollo, representing the new poetry, the more discerning world to come, had made Clymene, in the first *Hyperion,* "sick / Of joy and grief at once"; in the yet undiscovered regions mentioned in the "Ode to Psyche," the branching thoughts will bring new pleasure and pain simultaneously; the interplay of joy and pain is used dramatically in the "Nightingale" and as a central theme in "Melancholy." Finally, Lamia's magic ability to "unperplex bliss from its neighbour pain" underlies much of the illusory happiness she inspires: it is exactly this divorce between joy and pain that the outright "dreamer," Lycius, craves most and believes he is finding.

Moneta's lines, in short, are a part of the challenge (not indictment) with which she is confronting the poet. The lines should not be strained at in isolation but should be viewed instead as something that the fragment left dangling—as a challenge to which the poem was presumably to develop an answer; the real question is the use to which the open consciousness of joy and pain is to be put. Indeed, we already have a hint that this question was to be posed dramatically. For Moneta, with mysterious irony, tells the poet that, in the experience ahead, he will be "Free from all pain, if wonder pain thee not." The implication is that he will be "free" from pain precisely because he *is* a dreamer—because the heavy weight of consciousness she bears will be to him only a mere "wonder." But of course it is not mere wonder that he experiences. Instead it is a fearful empathic sharing of misery exceeding anything he has yet suffered.

A more important difficulty is entirely created by ourselves. Keats, as Woodhouse noted, plainly intended to omit a passage of twenty-four lines (lines 187–210). Our desire to preserve the passage is understandable: the self-lacerating doubts in a poet of Keats's endowment, especially when he was on the point of developing in a new direction, have a magnetic interest. The difficulty comes when we forget that these lines are departing from the course of the poem—to some extent conflicting with it (as Keats himself saw)—and then attempt to use them as a means of explaining the context. Caught up in Moneta's indictment of the dreamer, Keats begins to apply it very personally to himself. He is a poet; can she be making a charge against poets in general?—

> "Majestic shadow, tell me: sure not all
> Those melodies sung into the world's ear
> Are useless: sure a poet is a sage;
> A humanist, Physician to all men.
> That I am none I feel, as Vultures feel
> They are no birds when Eagles are abroad.
> What am I then? Thou spakest of my tribe:
> What tribe?"

The response is put with ominous repetition:

> "Art thou not of the dreamer tribe?
> The poet and the dreamer are distinct,
> Diverse, sheer opposite, antipodes."

Forgetting momentarily that he has been saved (though very nar-
rowly), that he has only half rotted on the pavement, that indeed
unless he *is* saved for later developments the poem has nothing left
to tell, he takes it for granted that he is even now breathing death
with all the "mock lyrists" who have betrayed poetry into triviality and self-centeredness. He invokes Apollo, who is the bringer
of pestilence as well as the god of healing and of poetry:

> Then shouted I
> Spite of myself, and with a Pythia's spleen,
> "Apollo! faded! O far-flown Apollo!
> Where is thy misty pestilence to creep
> Into the dwellings, through the door crannies
> Of all mock lyrists, large self-worshippers,
> And careless Hectorers in proud bad verse?
> Though I breathe death with them it will be life
> To see them sprawl before me into graves."

This strong, personal digression is amputated.

The poet then humbly pleads to share in the knowledge that
this immortal "Shade of Memory" carries. She lifts her veil; and
in the face before him he reads both the remorseless accumulation
of suffering and also its transcendence. The Christian implications
here have been justly stressed. However unconsciously or inadequately, the symbolic rendering, through the figure of Moneta, of
the "Burden of the mystery" is parallel to Christ taking on himself
the sins of the world. Standing beside her, "Like a stunt bramble
by a solemn pine," the poet is granted his plea for more understanding. Knowledge grows within him (as it had in Apollo before Mnemosyne in the first *Hyperion*); but now it is a particular
quality of knowledge that is stressed—the immediate empathic
ability to

> take the depth
> Of things as nimbly as the outward eye
> Can size and shape pervade.

At every step, in what the poet now contemplates, the sympathetic involvement deepens:

> Without stay or prop
> But my own weak mortality, I bore
> The load . . .

However the poem might have developed in other ways, a central, even desperate interest is the formative use and direction of the "visionary" capacity: a use that would meet the challenging distinction drawn by Moneta between those whom the "visionary" imagination—the use of the imagination in art—has brought to this "pavement" and those "disinterested" benefactors of humanity whose identities have been directly merged in the concern for others.

12

But everything was working against the further development of the poem. Even if we disregard the lack of time and the acute personal anxieties crowding in upon Keats in early September, there is the fact that what he has written thus far, as a preface or frame for what could be salvaged from the first *Hyperion,* has evolved far beyond the possibilities that any reuse of the first fragment—however discreet—would permit. His whole procedure when making a fresh start worked against the continuation of poems left unfinished for more than a few months. This indeed is one of the most interesting qualities about him, especially to other writers. For he seems always to have needed the stimulus of a new style in order to get well started at anything. No poet of the last two centuries has so well exemplified, in his own habits of composition, that organic inseparability of style and subject to which we pay lip service as an ideal, though we often seem at a loss when we confront it concretely. There was nothing particularly wrong with the opening—or indeed the entire first two books—of the original *Hyperion.* But, in needing to begin afresh in order to acquire interest and momentum, he so enriched his new preface—his induction—that the former narrative could hardly fail to shrivel before it.

The story of the fallen Titans, even when used merely as a symbolic representation of the remorseless but ultimately beneficent development of consciousness, had disclosed liabilities. For two full books it had indeed seemed that objective epic grandeur could be attained before he turned to more specialized, and ultimately more inward, purposes. But when the point for the transition arrived, the problems had begun quickly to thicken. Now, in the new *Hy-*

perion, the reverse takes place. The problems involved in the poetic treatment of the growth of modern consciousness are now faced directly at the start. Because they had so teased him before, they had been given precedence in his own thinking at least since April, when he wrote the "Ode to Psyche." After he met them directly in his Induction—his first three hundred lines or so—his problem then was to go back to the earlier story and try to adapt and universalize it. Selecting here and there, making some changes in phrase, adding a few lines, he takes over about two hundred lines of the first version—just enough to lead to the introduction of Hyperion himself—and then the fragment stops. Whatever followed would, as he anticipated it, be focused on the tragedy of Hyperion (and the other Titans, of course) even more than was to have been the case in the first version. Hence the clear title: *The Fall of Hyperion.* The Apollo episode, as we have it in Book III of *Hyperion,* was forestalled. Some other use would probably have had to be made of Apollo.

The first *Hyperion* had come to a close partly because too much had been given the Titans: whatever happened afterwards had to be presented under the threat of anticlimax. Now the unwritten sequel (at least the sequel as it was newly considered a year later) was put with power and with a new idiom. But in the shift back to the earlier story, Moneta—particularized as a mere priestess attempting to keep alive the memory, the tragedy, of the Titans— begins to lose her universality. This was the old problem Keats had always faced, since the days at Guy's Hospital. In beginning the new adventure of a "long poem," he would put the best of what he could do at the start, hoping to continue and improve upon that first effort. If, after reaching as far as he could, he confronted an impasse, he would stop to get his bearings in the intervening months; and shorter or different poems—perhaps impossible otherwise—would result.

At least a few words may be permitted about the new versification of the fragment, which, like that of *Lamia,* though in so different a way, marks a deliberate departure from the rich, condensed style of the eight or nine months from the first *Hyperion* to the odes of April and May, 1819. We have already noticed something of the change in idiom: the conscious calm (which attains at its best a Virgilian mellowness); the quiet, sharp concentration of empathy on bodily functions that reminds us of the

Shakespeare of *Hamlet* and the other plays of that period; and, counterpointing with them, both the stretch to the abstract and formal in other imagery and, at the same time, the retrenchment to stark statement. A new delicacy interplays with the homely, the abstract, and the mellow. Mirroring all of these qualities, the versification avoids the packed, phonetic concentration of the poems from *Hyperion* through the *Eve of St. Agnes* to the odes.[26] The elaborate use of vowel interplay that we noticed earlier is almost as absent here as in *Lamia*. Keats seems to shun—as remarks in the letters of the time also suggest—whatever savors too much of conscious art. His yearlong attempt (in reaction to *Endymion*) to strengthen the foot, the caesura, the integrity of the line, is relaxed. A comparison of a few lines from the two *Hyperions* may suggest some of the differences. The first sample shows the firm masculine caesura (the caesura after an accented syllable), the medial full stops (marked xx) so common in Milton, and the sparing use of stress failure or pyrrhic feet. The lines in the *Fall,* as the second sample shows, are often weak-backed: a falling and colloquial rhythm is given through feminine caesuras, trisyllabic feet, and the frequent use of stress failure, either through outright pyrrhics or through a light, hovering accent (ι) instead of a firm beat:

> But horrors, (x) portion'd to a giant nerve,
> Oft made Hyperion ache. (xx) His palace bright
> Bastion'd with pyramids (x) of glowing gold,
> And touch'd with shade (x) of bronzed obelisks . . .
> (*Hyperion*, I.175–178)

> In neighbourhood of fountains, (x) by the noise
> Soft-showering in my ears, (x) and, by the touch
> Of scent, not far from roses. (x) Turning round,
> I saw an arbour (x) with a drooping roof . . .
> (*Fall of Hyperion*, I.22–25)

The looser, often prosaic blank verse of Cary's translation of Dante is apparent not as a model but as an encouragement. Of course, the lessons gained from the eight months between the first *Hype-*

---

26 A more detailed discussion of the versification is presented in my *Stylistic Development,* pp. 174–182.

rion and the odes have been absorbed. But the conscious effort for concentrated intensity of phrase (perhaps even Keats's interest in it) has somewhat waned. His own personal feeling now, like that of the poet in the fragment on finding that the eastern gates were shut against the sunrise, is that he needs a slow and sturdy patience. "I have of late been moulting," he tells Reynolds (July 11), "not for fresh feathers and wings: they are gone, and in their stead I hope to have a pair of patient sublunary legs." The stylistic interest for the moment has switched to three goals, none of which applies specifically, except in negative ways, to versification: he wants to work more toward the abstract, not as an end in itself but as an essential backdrop; he is in search of an idiom that probes more into the crevices of the analytic; he seeks the homely and directly sincere.

These different aims (or rather desires: the word "aims" implies leisure to reflect and deliberate) naturally conflicted. Add to them the larger conflicts opened by the new poem, and the result, when he faced the *Hyperion* of almost a year before, was bound to operate against his fluency. Indeed, it surprises us that the fluency should have been as great as it was.

13

Finally, on September 21, he definitely decided to give up the poem. So much hope and effort had been invested in the first *Hyperion,* and the surrender of it had cost him so much, that the disappointment he felt in abandoning the second was multiplied. He was by no means eager to talk about it in detail. Instead he focused on the fact that he had tried in the first poem to write in a Miltonic style, and that this was not what he now wanted to do. Hence his remark to Reynolds (September 21), which he more or less repeats in a letter to George three days later:

> I have given up Hyperion—there were too many Miltonic inversions in it [27]—Miltonic verse cannot be written but in an artful or

[27] In *Hyperion,* the inversion of noun and adjective ("palace bright") appears about once in every fourteen lines; in the *Fall,* only once in every thirty-three. Inversion of subject and verb ("There saw she") appears about once in every fifty-two lines in *Hyperion,* and in the revision less than a third as often. Meanwhile, as De Selincourt and others have pointed out, Keats adds a few new Miltonisms in the revision. With Keats's remark to Reynolds above, compare the letter to George (September 24), II.212. Reynolds did not have a copy of the *Fall,* only of the first *Hyperion;* and Keats, in suggesting that Reynolds look over the poem again, is referring

rather artist's humour. I wish to give myself up to other sensations. English ought to be kept up. It may be interesting to you to pick out some lines from Hyperion and put a mark × to the false beauty proceeding from art, and one ‖ to the true voice of feeling.

The explanation avoided numerous other and more essential complexities. So much else was pressing on him now. What could he say?

He put the poem aside, apparently for good. There is a certain poignance in hearing that, as the winter approached, he sometimes took it out again. "In the evenings, at his own desire," said Brown, Keats would go off alone to a "separate sitting-room," and there try to "remodel" Hyperion—a task his own critical judgment had told him was fruitless, or at least less valuable than making a new start. But by the winter of 1819 it was too late to make a fresh start.

---

to the first Hyperion. This does not mean, however, that he is implying to Reynolds that he is giving up only the first Hyperion; he is giving up the entire project (he refers to the Fall in other letters as Hyperion) .

Illness

✸⤍⊕⤍✸⤍⊕⤍✸⤍⊕⤍✸⤍⊕⤍✸⤍⊕⤍✸⤍⊕⤍✸⤍⊕⤍✸⤍⊕⤍✸⤍⊕⤍✸⤍⊕⤍✸⤍⊕⤍✸⤍⊕

Autumn and Winter, 1819

WHEN KEATS RETURNED to Winchester after seeing Abbey, it was
with the knowledge that he could no longer delay turning to other
work and not merely for his own sake but for that of George and
his family. The radical change he had been considering for months
was now being forced on him.

The strangeness of his life since he had left Guy's Hospital kept
coming home to him now—the ambitions and effort of the past
three years, all the moving about from place to place, the people
he had met, the unpredictable developments. He could feel rather
lucky to have been as free as he was during that time. "It strikes
me to night," he told Reynolds (September 21), "that I have led
a very odd sort of life—Here & there—No anchor—I am glad of
it." It was the day he decided to give up the new *Hyperion;* and
with that decision came a more general feeling of finality, a conviction that this whole relatively free period of his life was now
permanently over. At the same time the retrospection throughout
these days was suffused with a renewed feeling of the mystery of
time passing—its remorselessness as well as its promise. How
strange to think that, with every seven years, all the materials
within our bodies have completely changed! "Seven years ago it
was not this hand that clench'd itself against Hammond" back in
the Edmonton surgery to which he had come from Enfield only a
year before. "We are like the relict garments of a Saint: the same
and not the same: for the careful Monks patch it and patch it: till
there's not a thread of the original garment left, and still they show
it for St Anthony's shirt." Hence men who have become close
friends, and have then been separated for a number of years,

> afterwards meet coldly, neither of them knowing why—The fact is
> they are both altered—Men who live together have a silent moulding
> and influencing power over each other. They interassim[i]late. 'Tis

an uneasy thought that in seven years the same hands cannot greet each other again. All this may be obviated by a willful and dramatic exercise of our Minds towards each other.

2

Meanwhile, as autumn began to bring a "temperate sharpness" to the air, the thought of the coming winter kept recurring. He was often feeling rather chilly without any apparent reason. He had loved the hot August days ("no chill'd red noses—no shivering—but fair Atmosphere to think in") ; and what he liked most about the stubble fields now—as he told Reynolds after he wrote the ode "To Autumn"—was the warmth of their red-brown in the autumn sun: he liked this "better than the chilly green of Spring. Somehow a stubble plain looks warm in the same way that some pictures look warm."

As the twilight cooled rapidly, he would linger before the blacksmiths' shops in order to look in at the fire. "I should like a bit of fire to night," he wrote Woodhouse after going back to his rooms (September 21) : "one likes a bit of fire—How glorious the Blacksmiths' shops look now—I stood to night before one till I was very near listing for one."

That same night he wrote George: "Rest in the confidence that I will not omit any exertion . . . If I cannot remit you hundreds, I will tens and if not that ones." Nor should George continue to feel as bad as he did about the situation: Keats—typically English here as in so many other ways—himself considered it a relief to face "real" difficulties rather than "imaginary" ones.[1] The worst that could happen is that he may "have to perform a longer literary Pilgrimage." And there could be a gain. Writing less frequently, more slowly, he would read more. This meant, however, that he could not fulfill his promise to come and spend a full year with George in Kentucky in the near future. He did not have

---

[1] A remark he developed further two days later to Brown: "I assure you, I am as far from being unhappy as possible. Imaginary grievances have always been more my torment than real ones. You know this well. Real ones will never have any other effect than to stimulate me to get out of or avoid them. This is easily accounted for. Our imaginary woes are conjured up by our passions, and are fostered by passionate feeling: our real ones come of themselves, and are opposed by an abstract exertion of mind. Real grievances are displacers of passion. The imaginary nail a man down for a sufferer, as on a cross; the real spur him up into an agent."

many books of his own, and he wanted desperately not to be "out of the reach of Libraries." Moreover, what work could he himself do in that pioneer world when the pressing need at the moment was to earn money, and the businesslike George was himself having such difficulties? "How could I employ myself?" His feelings now differed in one radical way from that flurry of alternating hesitancy and determination last June when he had thought of signing up as a surgeon on an Indiaman or going to South America. He was more uneasy about his health than he wished to admit to anyone, including himself.

He had made up his mind what to do, and the night of September 21 and the entire next day were filled with letter writing—not only to Reynolds, Woodhouse, and George, but also to Charles Brown and Dilke. With all these letters he was trying to steel himself to the decision he had made, which was, as he told Woodhouse with attempted lightness, "to take up my abode in a cheap Lodging in Town and get employment in some of our elegant Periodical Works—I will no longer live upon hopes." To Brown, who had lent him so much money, he is franker. Keats has—he tells Brown —lived a "vicious life" of self-indulgence for a year, letting others support him through loans:

> Now I am going to enter on the subject of self. It is quite time I should set myself doing something, and live no longer upon hopes. I have never yet exerted myself. I am getting into an idle minded, vicious way of life, almost content to live upon others. In no period of my life have I acted with any self will, but in throwing up the apothecary-profession. That I do not repent of.

He will try to get employment in the newspapers or magazines, doing (with one provision) whatever hack writing is necessary:

> I will write, on the liberal side of the question, for whoever will pay me. I have not known yet what it is to be diligent. I purpose living in town in a cheap lodging, and endeavouring, for a beginning, to get the theatricals of some paper. When I can afford to compose deliberate poems I will.

Living in town rather than in Hampstead, he will have quicker access not only to publishing offices and to theaters—in case he is able to review plays—but also to books at the British Museum and other libraries. He adds another reason: the presence of Fanny

Brawne next door, if he lived at Wentworth Place, might distract
him from his resolution.[2]

It seems to Keats that, over the past year, he has "got into a habit
of looking towards [Brown] as a help in all difficulties. This very
habit would be the parent of [further] idleness and difficulties. You
will see it is a duty I owe myself to break the neck of it." He wants
whatever friends he has to approve of him "not for verses, but for
conduct." Hazlitt had helped Reynolds to get an article in the
Edinburgh Review. Keats will ask Hazlitt, "who knows the market
as well as any one, for something to bring me in a few pounds as
soon as possible. I shall not suffer my pride to hinder me." He cannot "continue a dead lump," which is what he has been hitherto.
The phrase remains in his mind as he begins a letter to Dilke,
spelling out his determination as if he were reading a lesson to
himself:

> Now an act has three parts—to act, to do, and to perform—I mean
> I should *do* something for my immediate welfare—Even if I am swept
> away like a Spider from a drawing room I am determined to spin—
> home spun any thing for sale. Yea I will trafic. Any thing but Mort-
> gage my Brain to Blackwood. I am determined not to lie like a dead
> lump.

The embarrassment in making this decision is acute. He is flying
in the face of an idealism about literature that for three or four
years has been healthful and formative in the highest degree, but,
in combination with the rather painful experiences of the past
year or so, has begun to carry with it a dark and confused suspicion
of commercial and periodical writing, especially for reviews, and
an association of it with the enemy—with the fashionable and in-
sincere, with all the innumerable uses of literature for vanity, flat-
tery, envy, and the like. He is fortunate that he has not had to
"venture on the common"—that is, become a literary street-walker
—before now. He was too simple-minded a year ago, but he has
now had a chance to become more sophisticated. "You may say I
want tact—that is easily acqui[r]ed." Anyone can quickly learn
"the slang of a cock pit in three battles," and he will soon be able

2 In the letters Brown prepared for his memoir, he conscientiously deleted the
names of most people still alive, especially (as he had promised her) of Fanny
Brawne. But the implication is plain: "I like x x x x x x x x x and I cannot help it.
On that account I had better not live there [in Hampstead]. While I have some immediate cash, I had better settle myself quietly" (II.177) .

to "shine up an article on any thing without much knowledge of the subject, aye like an orange." Then the bravado of what he considers to be his cynicism subsides. The truth is that he would really like to try some other work. But he is in a situation now where he feels he cannot: "I am fit for nothing but literature"; and as far as a livelihood is concerned, he can put "no trust whatever in Poetry —I don't wonder at it—the ma[r]vel is to me how people read so much of it." Since he will be living in town, "Should you like me for a neighbor again? Come, plump it out, I wont blush." If so, could Dilke find him a couple of cheap rooms in Westminster?

As always, after a decision that has involved intensive inner debate, his humor rises. But now it strikes us as a bit forced. The long letter to George written throughout these days (September 17 to 27) is filled with jokes and little comic sketches—the intention, of course, being to relieve himself ("I am glad you say you keep up your Spirits . . . still keep them up—for we are all young"). The same tone is found in his letter to the sedate Woodhouse (September 22), now vacationing with his family near Bath, the scene of much of Smollett's *Humphry Clinker*. "I think upon crutches," Keats tells him, after discussing the poems he has written, "like your folks in the Pump room"; and then suddenly (with "Have you seen old Bramble yet—they say he's on his last legs") he begins a comic continuation of *Humphry Clinker* about Matthew Bramble, his old maid sister, and her dog Chowder.

Nothing so typifies his need to get things into perspective, his instinctive effort to lighten or to reduce them to manageability, as some extemporaneous lines he writes in his letter to George burlesquing modern love and courtship. For in addition to whatever else the financial difficulties had brought, they had driven home to him the realization that marriage was impossible for a long time to come; and the thought of that indefinite future was naturally filled with apprehensions—about the possibility of Fanny's becoming weary of waiting, Mrs. Brawne's reactions, his own health. He is talking of his friend William Haslam. "A Man in love I do think cuts the sorryest figure in the world—Even when I know a poor fool to be really in pain about it, I could burst out laughing in his face." He begins his mock lines on the modern lover, "Pensive they sit, and roll their languid eyes / Nibble their toasts, and cool their tea with sighs." The thought is the contrast of modern courtship with all that we associate with medieval romance. He suddenly wearies of the burlesque. "You see I cannot get on without writing as boys do at school a few nonsense verses—I begin them and before I have written six the whim has pass'd." But the next day he fills his letter to George with a lengthy and tedious passage that he copies from Burton's *Anatomy of Melancholy* ("You will be very much amused"): "Every Lover admires his Mistress, though she be very deformed . . . a thin, lean, chitty face . . . her head still awry . . . a tan'd skin, a rotton carcass," and so on, with the abundant anatomical detail so typical of this lusty seventeenth-century prose. "There's a dose for you," he comments afterwards: he would like, he says, to have drawn on that long passage from Burton for a "speech in a Play."

Then the whole tone changes, with that "transparency" that Benjamin Bailey thought so typical of him, and we are reminded how young he actually was. Despite a development, a level of thinking, and an experienced courage that have made us feel that we are dealing with a mind—at once practical and sympathetically perceptive—ten or twenty years older, he was to become twenty-four in another month. Because of the politeness of some people he had met in London, he speculates wistfully, "I do think I must have been well spoken of," if not generally, at least "among sets."

3

Then, within merely a month, all this resolution—certainly as firm (indeed necessary) as any he had ever made—erodes with a speed, and accompanied by a suppressed desperation, without precedent in anything that has happened to him before. He concludes a short letter to Fanny Brawne on October 19 with a brief remark that startles us—taking for granted (as we have come to do by now) the habitual fortitude of this life, his capacity to take difficulties in his stride: "my mind is in a tremble, I cannot tell what I am writing."

The effort of the five months from late April to late September —the result of which gives Keats the rank that he has in the history of poetry—had drawn heavily on him in several ways. Not least had been the constant feeling that this was not at all the way to write poetry. He had hoped so much that he might at last be able to compose in a more "leisurely," a more thoughtful, spirit. The threat of a cruelly short timetable for this last effort before

turning to other work added a crippling inhibition to all the others that had been accumulating as he measured his intentions, and
his relatively naked resources, against ideals gleaned from what he
was learning of the greatest writing of two thousand years or more
—from the Greeks through Dante, Shakespeare, and Milton to the
present. Personal losses, money, and (in a way he could not permit
himself to dwell on) his own health had been adding one complication to another. "Nothing," as he allowed himself to say to
George a few weeks later (November 12), "could have in all its
circumstances fallen out worse for me than the last year has done,
or could be more damping to my poetical talent." And indeed it
did seem as though this autumn was bringing an unusually plen-
tiful harvest of distress, inhibition, complexity, and—though he
would naturally have resented the word—of fear.

Two weeks passed between those letters of resolution (September 21 and 22) and his return to London on October 8 or 9,
during which time Charles Brown rejoined him at Winchester.
Throughout these relatively silent two weeks, it is impossible not
to conclude that he began to feel very unwell. On October 10 he
had a visit of a few hours in Hampstead with Fanny Brawne—he
appears to have spent the night next door at Brown's—and it was
probably on this evening that he wrote the gentle, slightly elegiac
love sonnet, "The day is gone, and all its sweets are gone." He
went to Westminster the next morning, and the Dilkes showed
him the rooms they had found for him nearby at 25 College Street.
After moving into these rooms with some of his books, he then presumably walked over to Fleet Street during the next day or two
and inquired about positions writing for newspapers and magazines. He had not given up hope of employment when Joseph Severn, hearing of Keats's new decision to live and work in town,
called one evening at these new rooms. Something about Keats's
manner bothered him. He persuaded Keats to read some lines
from the poetry he had written during the last year. Like everyone else of the period, Severn was struck by *Hyperion*. But the
"very terms" that Severn used to praise this Miltonic poem "confirmed" Keats in his own feeling that the poem would not do:
Keats did not, he said, want to write a poem "that might have been
written by John Milton, but one that was unmistakeably by no
other than John Keats." The idiom and form were "too artificial,"
at least "for a prolonged strain." At all events Keats tried to exert

himself during this short visit. Severn came away with the impression that though the summer had "not wrought so much good" as he had expected, Keats seemed to be "in high spirits." [3]

But these first three or four days at 25 College Street, Westminster, were fruitless as far as Keats's real purpose was concerned. He did not find a position. Tramping the streets, in all probability, fatigued him enormously. He was feeling increasingly alone and helpless in the midst of this growing fatigue. Mrs. Brawne, noting his condition when he had made his visit a few days before, had asked him to come for a weekend of rest. On Friday, hoping to get better, he went out and stayed with the Brawnes till Sunday. Returning to Westminster, he put in a day or so either looking for positions or else lingering in his rooms, puzzled and frightened at the way he felt. He then (Tuesday, October 19) gave up his lodgings and went over to the Dilkes'. He was terribly shaken by his helplessness, his loneliness, his lack of any capacity to stand on his own feet. Where could he turn? That same afternoon he wrote to Fanny Brawne, referring to the "three days dream" of his weekend visit. "I was miserable last night—the morning is always restorative. I must be busy, or try to be so." As he had just told Mrs. Dilke, he would go back to Hampstead. How would Fanny feel at his living there? She means so much to him, and yet "I must impose chains upon myself—I shall be able to do nothing." It is in this letter that he says at the end: "my mind is in a tremble, I cannot tell what I am writing."

4

Within another two days he was back at Wentworth Place, living with Brown, and probably with more loss of self-confidence than at any other time in his life. After all his assurances to George, to others, and to himself ("Yea I will trafic"), he had failed to do a thing. He had even used up the £30 that Woodhouse had got Taylor and Hessey to pretend to advance. There was an excuse—more than an excuse. But it was too serious to dwell on or even admit: the possible implications were too disturbing. He could only freeze into reticence while he tried to get his bearings. Ready enough in the past to mention his sore throat and other ailments to a few of his friends, he now kept utterly quiet about his health. He either said nothing about his return to Hampstead, or

[3] Sharp, pp. 40–41.

else tried to make light of it, as when he informed his sister that the "petty attentions" a single man has to pay to "diminutive housekeeping" were a distraction down in Westminster. It was much more convenient to come back to Wentworth Place, where Brown had a maid who came in daily (a maid, as Keats already suspected, who was probably more than just a servant).

The change in Keats, throughout the past week or two, appalled Severn, who again dropped in at College Street, Westminster, in order to visit him, and then, finding Keats had returned to Hampstead, went out to see him there. Despite moments of gaiety and of his usual sympathy in speaking of others, Keats now

> seemed well neither in mind nor in body, with little of the happy confidence and resolute bearing of a week earlier; while alternating moods of apathetic dejection and spasmodic gaiety rendered him a companion somewhat difficult to humour. Yet not even then, in circumstances far more harassing than Severn had any idea of, was Keats otherwise than kindly and generous. "He never spoke of any one but by saying something in their favour, and this always so agreeably and cleverly, imitating the manner to increase your favourable impression of the person he was speaking of." [4]

There is little doubt that, from mid-September throughout the next month, the tuberculosis of the lungs that was to prove fatal to him had seriously begun (or suddenly moved into an active stage), bringing with it periods of immense fatigue and some fever. To this condition should be added the psychological effect of his own near conviction that he now had the disease, and the frustrating distress that it should be coming at this of all times, when he was almost penniless and facing such heavy demands. Keats's medical history has been carefully studied throughout the last forty years in the hope of dating the onset and stages of tuberculosis. The Victorians tended to assume that it began in the late winter of 1819–20, just before the severe hemorrhage Keats had on February 3, 1820. Because relatively little was known of Keats's life in September and October of 1819, the sentimental notion was spread that Keats abandoned any intention of doing other work (and even gave up writing poetry) because his attraction to Fanny Brawne sapped his will: that, like those lovers in his burlesque lines ("Pensive they sit, and roll their languid eyes"), he was content to give

[4] As with many of Severn's accounts, we have only the summary (p. 41) from his papers by William Sharp. Quotation marks signify direct quotations from Severn by Sharp.

up everything in order to go back to Hampstead and linger, as it were, near her doorstep. This impression, buttressed by remarks from the love letters, contributed to the legend of Fanny Brawne as an unfeeling flirt whose influence on Keats was unfortunate.

Beginning with Amy Lowell in 1925, the pendulum swung the other way. With what we must admit to be very limited medical support, she concluded that Keats's illness was dual: he had acquired laryngeal tuberculosis at least by the time that he was nursing Tom in Devonshire (March to May, 1818)—hence the sore throat; and tuberculosis of the lungs was only a later development, in the autumn and winter of 1819.[5] It was Miss Lowell's argument that gave rise to the impression, which still lingers, that Keats was ill with tuberculosis throughout the most important part of his creative career. This has since been effectively denied by Sir William Hale-White in what is certainly the most detailed and authoritative study of the subject.[6] If he really had tuberculosis of the larynx as well as of the lungs, then Keats, who knew anatomy, would have spoken not of a "sore throat" (which generally means the upper throat, the back of the mouth) but rather of the larynx itself.[7] More important, laryngeal tuberculosis is a very late—as well as rare—development: tubercle bacilli, coughed from the lungs, become caught in the larynx. But there is no history of such prolonged coughing—coughing throughout at least a year—before the appearance of the sore throat; and had tuberculosis of the lungs developed this far by the summer of 1818, when the sore throat suddenly began, Keats would never have been able to walk and climb as he did throughout the Scottish tour. Moreover, hoarseness and even loss of voice are typical in laryngeal tuberculosis, and Keats never showed any symptom of this sort. Finally, if Keats had had tuberculosis of the larynx, it would have become very pronounced in his last months. Far from this, his sore throat seems to have virtually disappeared during his last year of life.

---

5 Lowell, I.512–516; II.359.

6 *Keats as Doctor and Patient* (1938), esp. pp. 43–51. Walter A. Wells, *A Doctor's Life of John Keats* (1959) is more concerned with the psychological effect of Keats's disappointments, and, in its discussion of tuberculosis, focuses on Keats's final year. He does not go into the question of the sore throat, but appears to suggest a doubt that it was laryngeal tuberculosis since "laryngeal involvement is nearly always a late complication."

7 Similarly, all the references in Keats's letters, from late 1818 to late 1819, that suggest his relief and pleasure in swallowing cool drinks or fruits indicate that the discomfort is in the throat itself rather than in the larynx.

We forget how extraordinarily common recurrent sore throat was until the late nineteenth century (and also how much suffering was indirectly caused by trouble with teeth in northern countries, especially England). Chronic tonsillitis, catarrhal infection, or inflammation spreading from the teeth to the throat—an ailment less romantic than tuberculosis—was a far more probable cause of Keats's recurring sore throat. Hale-White, stressing the likelihood of an infection spreading from the teeth, reminds us that the first serious onset of the sore throat was accompanied by the severe toothache that Keats mentioned, together with his sore throat, in his letter to his sister (August 19, 1818)—"I have a confounded tooth ache . . . My tooth ache keeps on so that I cannot writ[e] with any pleasure."

Needless to say, the condition of which the sore throat was a symptom or result was one in which Keats's resistance was gradually lowered. He was not, as Sir William Hale-White points out, what was conventionally regarded as a tubercular type in the nineteenth century—as the thin, delicate Tom was: Keats's build, like his father's, was sturdy, and might by middle age be expected to be stocky. If George avoided infection while nursing Tom for a much longer time than had Keats by June 1818, it could be assumed that Keats was equally able to do so. But the violent cold he caught afterwards while walking through the bogs of the Isle of Mull in the summer of 1818, the possible tonsillitis that resulted, certainly the trouble with his teeth in August, the accumulated fatigue, had obviously weakened him when he returned to nurse Tom for a period of over three months (August 18 to December 1). No one at the time was aware that tuberculosis was contagious. The windows were shut, the air close. Throughout all these weeks, further harassed in other ways, Keats was next to Tom daily, and in a weakened condition, while Tom himself at this point was far more infectious than before. The probability is that Keats had caught tuberculosis of the lungs before December 1, and that it began moving into an active stage by early September, 1819.

5

Charles Dilke, seeing him before the return to Hampstead, had the impression that Keats's "whole mind & heart were in a whirl of contending passions—he saw nothing calmly and dispassionately." Meanwhile he was turning to Fanny Brawne with a desperation that could hardly have failed to startle her, much as she had become accustomed since July to the unexplained shifts of feeling in his letters. He now tried to arm her against the tone of his past letters, speaking of "the unpromising morning of my life," and how overready to suspect the worst in everything he had allowed himself to become. He wants her to know that he is turning to her now without the reservations he showed and felt before. But, in the very same letter (October 13—he had just moved into the rooms in College Street, Westminster) where he tells her this, and protests that "I have no limits now to my love," he goes on to say: "I could resist you till I saw you" on October 10, and even since then he has been trying to "reason against" his feelings. Six days later he tells her he will "impose chains" on himself, and then suddenly adds, with fatigue and a despair still unexplained to her, "I sho[u]ld like to cast the die for Love or Death."

It was during these weeks that he wrote at least three, possibly all, of the five poems addressed to Fanny Brawne or concerned directly with her.[8] There are the so-called "Lines to Fanny"—somewhat jumbled as well as tired and flat—openly expressing the same conflict of feelings as his letters to her:

> What can I do to drive away
> Remembrance from my eyes?
>
> .   .   .   .   .   .
>
> What can I do to kill it and be free
> In my old liberty?
>
> .   .   .   .
>
> How shall I do
> To get anew
> These moulted feathers, and so mount once more
> Above, above
> The reach of fluttering Love . . . ?

Dark references, possibly to America and George's misfortune there, then appear,[9] followed by the sudden transition to lines that remind us a little of the "Bright Star" sonnet:

---

[8] Omitting the lines "This living hand, now warm and capable," which may not have been addressed to her. (See below, section 9.)

[9] Where shall I learn to get my peace again?
To banish thoughts of that most hateful land,
Dungeoner of my friends, that wicked strand
Where they were wreck'd and live a wreckèd life.

O, let me once more rest
My soul upon that dazzling breast!
Let once again these aching arms be plac'd,
The tender gaolers of thy waist!
And let me feel that warm breath . . .

Then there are two Shakespearean sonnets (he had months before given up the sonnet form for serious writing; but the situation was very different now, and the form came easily) : the quiet sonnet we have already cited, "The day is gone," and its frantic, almost clutching opposite that begins "I cry your mercy—pity—love—aye, love! / Merciful love that tantalizes not."

A third Shakespearean sonnet that may possibly have been written now or during the early winter is the famous "Bright Star." [10] From the date affixed to the poem by Charles Brown, we know only that it was written in 1819; and it could perhaps have been written at any time during the year. During the later nineteenth century it was usually entitled "The Last Sonnet" because Keats wrote his revised (and distinctly improved) version of it on a blank page of his copy of Shakespeare's poems in early autumn, 1820, while he and Severn were on the boat to Italy. Since the earlier version and Brown's date of 1819 became known, different dates have been suggested, argued against, and resuggested—especially the early months of 1819 or July. In the absence of any real evidence in support of these dates, we are certainly justified in thinking that the months from October through December are equally plausible.[11] Certainly at no time before Keats's return to

---

[10] The first version is as follows:

Bright star! would I were stedfast as thou art!
Not in lone splendour hung amid the night;
Not watching, with eternal lids apart,
Like Nature's devout sleepless Eremite,
The morning waters at their priestlike task
Of pure ablution round earth's human shores;
Or, gazing on the new soft fallen mask
Of snow upon the mountains and the moors:—
No;—yet still stedfast, still unchangeable,
Cheek-pillow'd on my Love's white ripening breast,
To touch, for ever, its warm sink and swell,
Awake, for ever, in a sweet unrest;
To hear, to feel her tender-taken breath,
Half-passionless, and so swoon on to death.

[11] Colvin (p. 335) suggested the last week of February, 1819, because of a heavy snowfall which he thought might have suggested lines 7–8. Lowell (II.202–206) argued for mid-April on the ground that Keats was looking over letters he had sent Tom during the Scottish tour in which occur phrases that are echoed in the sonnet

Hampstead in October do his letters betray anything like the readiness to surrender other ambitions to love that this sonnet expresses. That surrender has been painful; and, whatever else may be said of the final line, we may note an implied desperation. The general tone before the end is admittedly calmer than some of the frenetic lines written this autumn (though the love sonnet "The day is gone" is also calm). But this is no argument. For however calm and assured his poetry often is, from the odes to the *Fall of Hyperion,* his reaction to Fanny Brawne (and that is what is really the essence of the problem) is far more divided, as indeed we have been noticing, before October than it is afterwards. Granted that none of this amounts to a genuine argument that the sonnet was composed now, the point is only that it could have been written as easily now as at other times. Nor does our quibbling help us in understanding Keats's life in 1819, or what distinguishes his poetic achievement in that year.

Whatever the date, we should note something about this sonnet that reminds us, in miniature, of the structure of two of the great odes—the "Nightingale" and, even more, the "Grecian Urn"—whether the poem was written as an anticipation or as an echo. It is that process of symbolic debate in which a dominant symbol or concept, after being postulated at the start, becomes the motif in a counterpoint of withdrawal, qualification, and partial return.[12] As so often before, a star is conceived as a metaphor not only of permanence but of a "disinterested" and fundamental order and repose. And this "stedfastness" of the star is enriched by further associations that the symbol engenders, or at least admits. For the loneliness, the disinterested "watching"—a "watching, with eternal lids apart"—is also that of a hermit, with the suggestions of a withdrawal that is ultimately religious in aim; and in such a patient, sleepless watch, the "morning waters" of the sea are conceived as "at their priestlike task / Of pure ablution round earth's human shores." And yet this symbol of detachment, which

---

(but this particular letter had been sent on to George months before). Gittings (pp. 25–26) followed Lowell in assuming Keats had just been looking at his letter of June 26, 1818, but pushed the date up to late October (just before Keats sent this letter on to George), and considered that it was really addressed to Isabella Jones. The argument does not seem convincing (see above, p. 359); nor does the argument of De Selincourt and Miss Ward for July 1819 (see above, p. 539).

12 See above, Chapter XIX, section 6. Here, as in discussing this subject in the odes, I am obligated to suggestive analyses in David Perkins, *The Quest for Permanence* (1959), esp. pp. 229–233.

would seem to answer so adequately the heart's desire (as the Grecian urn or the song of the nightingale at first seems to do in the
two odes) is not really completely adequate after all. The qualification of the symbol—the partial withdrawal from it—begins almost at once, though the negative is put wistfully, and with something of the envy with which the figures on the Grecian urn were
viewed:

> Not in lone splendour hung aloft the night;
> Not watching, with eternal lids apart,
> Like Nature's devout sleepless eremite.

The real desire, after all, is not what this symbol implies when it
is developed into genuine detachment. (We recall that, just before
he wrote the odes, he prefaced his sonnet "On Fame" with the
motto, "You cannot eat your cake and have it too.") What is
wanted, of course, is to rescue the heart into attaining those qualities of permanence and detachment that are denied to the human
being, but to attain this permanence and detachment without any
of the inevitable limitations: to be "still stedfast, still unchangeable," like the star, but not (to go back again to the "Grecian
Urn") to be "all breathing human passion far above." [13]

6

Returning to Hampstead, Keats tried desperately to compose
his mind. He had grasped at the notion, current at the time, that
animal food clouded the brain. He would stay clear of it, he wrote
his sister—he had neither the money to travel by coach to see
her, nor the energy to walk to Walthamstow—"I have left off
animal food that my brains may never henceforth be in a greater
mist than is theirs by nature." But he had another thought as
well. Consumptives were commonly—and very unfortunately—restricted to a vegetable diet. Keats of course knew this (Tom had
been kept on such a diet during his last year), and was blindly

[13] In addition to the four poems mentioned above, Keats may also have written
the "Ode to Fanny" ("Physician Nature! let my spirit blood") at some time between
October and December. The reference to "wintry air," suggesting November or December, is a point in favor of December. The occasion of the poem is Fanny's attendance at a dance, to which Keats is unable to go because of illness. Lowell and Colvin
date it the previous January or February. The flaccid verse, in a poem at least partly
serious, is unlike Keats at that time, and is more typical of the love verse now, especially the "Lines to Fanny." But with a poem of such quality we need not strain at
the date; and the poem could conceivably have been written as late as July or
August, 1820.

trying to take whatever steps he could think of in order to forestall the disease.

Brown was puzzled and distressed by Keats's state of mind: it was quite different from anything he had seen in Keats before: "his abstraction, his occasional lassitude," and above all "his assumed tranquillity of countenance gave me great uneasiness. He was unwilling to speak on the subject." Thinking that all Keats needed was to get back to work, Brown cast about for subjects that might interest him. Brown himself had just finished tidying up *Otho the Great,* and was about to send it to Drury Lane in the hope that someone there might at least be interested. And it was apparently at this time, though possibly he had first made the suggestion back in August, that he pointed out to Keats a subject for an English historical tragedy. In any case, it was now that Keats tried to do something about it. Brown told him that the historical tragedy might be laid

> in the reign of Stephen, beginning with his defeat by the Empress Maud, and ending with the death of his son Eustace, when Stephen yielded the succession to the crown to the young Henry. He was struck with the variety of events and characters which must necessarily be introduced; and I offered to give, as before, their dramatic conduct. "The play must open," I began, "with the field of battle, when Stephen's forces are retreating—" "Stop!" he said, "stop! I have been already too long in leading-strings. I will do all this myself." [14]

Throughout at least part of November—possibly during the first week or two—Keats tried to work on the play, writing three and a half short scenes (almost 200 lines). Tired though he was, he tried to be systematic in his preparation. He was using Holinshed's *Chronicles* as a basis. He also got hold of a copy of Selden's *Titles of Honor,* which, as J. L. Lowes suggested, he doubtless hoped to use as a reference book for feudal titles and customs.[15] He went carefully through a chapter on English titles, and started to make on the flyleaves a detailed index that he thought might be helpful. At the same time, as was always his habit, he tried to plunge ahead with an opening in order to create momentum and also with the hope that he might be able, in the process, to evolve or discover an appropriate style. The scenes have a briskness of pace and shift of action lacking in *Otho;* and the idiom is more colloquially vigorous, and at the same time is touched with an

14 Brown, p. 56.   15 See the discussion in Lowell, II.361–362.

occasional mellowness of phrase that reminds us of some of the passages in the *Fall of Hyperion*.

But he was not ready for a poetic tragedy, and he knew it: not ready, at least, unless he had several months to work on it and felt far better than he did now. To try to force things, as he was now doing, would produce at best a routine imitation of Shakespeare's earlier historical plays. "I have been endeavouring to write lately," he tells George, "but with little success." For the first time he makes the admission that he cannot write without "an untram- mell'd mind," and for this "I require a little encouragement." Within a few days he had put *King Stephen* aside, telling John Taylor (November 17) that he had "come to a determination not to publish any thing I have now ready written." The simplest and quickest way "to untether Fancy and let her manage for herself" would be with another narrative poem. He is thinking of a subject for a sort of historical romance having to do with the Earl of Leicester in Elizabeth's reign. Two or three such poems would help to develop "the little dramatic skill I may as yet have."

All this, however, would take a few weeks. For limited as the genre might be, he was determined to make the poem "a fine one." He would also need to borrow books from Taylor in order to soak himself in the subject.

7

Meanwhile Charles Brown, seeing that *King Stephen* had almost immediately failed as a project, had begun to encourage Keats to take up something as remote as possible from that play and indeed from anything else Keats had ever written—a satiric poem that would burlesque several things at once, including Byronic satire, the amours of the Prince Regent, his quarrel with his unhappy wife (which was common knowledge all over England), and the use of fanciful or supernatural "machinery" in poetry. The poem might easily make money: a few stanzas of anything Byron wrote were earning more from the publishers than Keats's entire output thus far. Moreover, it would take no time at all. Anyone with some fluency could write this sort of thing forever by simply (to use Johnson's phrase about Ossian) "abandoning his mind to it."

Keats was indeed pressed for money. Bills that had accumulated over the past several months could no longer be postponed. He had written urgently, and with only a tired echo of his usual embarrassment, to William Haslam for a loan of £30 (November 2). He had also gone over to the Surrey Institution, as he tells Severn, and submitted a poem to "have hung up for the Prize in the Lecture Room." The "most threatening" of the "many Rivals" there included "An Ode to Lord Castlereagh." Whatever the poem he submitted—probably the "Grecian Urn," since the "Nightingale" had already been published—it did not win the prize. Nor had Keats much hope that it would. Immediately after submitting the poem, he forced himself to call on Abbey, on November 11, and apparently secured a few pounds—the first money he had received from him in ten months. Abbey also used the occasion to tell Keats that he ought to try to enter the bookselling business. Not that Abbey was prepared to help in any concrete way. A month later, when he again told Keats that he should turn to other work, and this time mentioned tea brokerage—Abbey's own principal business—Keats was inclined to accept, and naturally thought Abbey would be willing to take him into his own concern. But "his mind takes odd turns. When I became a Suitor he became coy. He did not seem so much inclined to serve me."

If Keats wavered about trying the sort of poem Brown had in mind, it was only for a day or two. So helplessly in conflict were his own instincts about what to do that he was becoming amenable to almost any well-meant suggestion. The thought that such a poem would earn money was decisive. The least he could do was to make this effort for a few weeks: indeed what other choice had he? The money had to be earned, and he was not earning it in any other way. The result was the poorest of all Keats's poems, leaving aside the juvenile verses and the numerous impromptu ones: "The Cap and Bells: or The Jealousies"—an unfinished poem of almost 800 lines, written in the Spenserian stanza. Everything was against it: his health, anxieties about money, dejection because marriage was impossible for years to come, wavering confidence in the quality of his previous work, and, finally, lack of any real interest in the poem itself. It was "begun without a plan," said Brown, and they hoped that Keats would pick up ideas as he went along. But the whole conception of the thing was alien to him. Not that it was alien merely to what he had written thus far—his work for over a year had been the kind that was constantly opening new vistas, new considerations, new styles. But prolonged satire (as distinct from relief merely in satiric moments) is difficult for any empathic nature to sustain, however harassed by disappointments.

At the start, in conversation with Brown, ideas for such a poem naturally occurred to him. The Prince Regent—a far from admirable figure to any liberal—was already proving to be a fruitful source of satiric attack. And why not also include Byron himself, whom Fanny Brawne had admired in the past, and perhaps still did? The poem would be written under the pseudonym of one of Byron's feminine admirers—"Lucy Vaughan Lloyd," residing at Chin-a-Walk, Lambeth. Certainly the satiric hero of the poem, the Emperor Elfinan, is as much like Byron as the Prince Regent. In one place Keats (as Byron himself did with other poets) uses direct quotations for burlesque. He takes Byron's sentimental poem to Lady Byron, written two months after she left him ("Fare thee well! and if for ever, / Still for ever, fare thee well"). Elfinan, hopping in his insect way about the room, looks at his scorned fiancée, Bellanaine: "Poor Bell!" he says (using Byron's pet name for his wife, Annabel): " 'Farewell! and if for ever! Still / For ever fare thee well!'—and then he fell / A laughing!—snapp'd his fingers . . ." And some of the lines parody not only Byron but Keats himself. For in this puzzling fragment, the Byronic emperor is in love with a "Bertha Pearl" who lives in Canterbury. Keats is reintroducing, in an almost savage parody of his earlier work, the Bertha he had portrayed in the "Eve of St. Mark," dreaming gently over an illustrated manuscript book. In the "Cap and Bells," the emperor's henchman, Hum, gives him a mysterious old "legend-leavèd book," the sight of which is guaranteed to "drive Bertha to a fainting fit." In a murky desire to push aside the sentimentality of the "Eve of St. Agnes," he chose for the verse form the same Spenserian stanza, altogether inadequate for satiric poetry. This is one cause of the poem's failure. The slow, majestic pace of the stanza could have been turned to an opposite use only by an effort altogether single-minded in its hunger for burlesque.[16]

Throughout the last weeks of November and the first week or two of December, Keats churned out stanza after stanza. During the mornings, said Brown, "He wrote it with the greatest facility" —one morning, in fact, completing a total of twelve stanzas (108

[16] For a concise summary of sources, see Finney, II.733–736.

lines). Then, in the evening, "at his own desire, he was alone in a separate sitting-room." There he would try to adapt lines from the first *Hyperion* for the revision he had really given up in September. But when he turned to this poem, about which he cared so much, he could do little or nothing. In these weeks of November and December he recopied, with some change, only about fifty lines.

It was becoming colder with every day; and though he could ill afford it, "By the advice of my Doctor," he told his sister, "I have had a wa[r]m great Coat made and have ordered some thick shoes."

8

By the end of December, if not before, he had become engaged to Fanny Brawne. We can place the date between October and the end of December because of a passage in a letter that Fanny Brawne wrote to Keats's sister (May 23, 1821): George, she says,

is no favorite of mine and he never liked me so that I am not likely to say too much in his favor from affection for him, but I must say I think he is more blamed than he should be. I think him extravagant and selfish but people in their great zeal [Charles Brown] make him out much worse than that—Soon after your brother Tom died, my dear John wrote to him offering him any assistance or money in his power. At that time he was not engaged to me and having just lost one brother felt all of his affection turned towards the one that remained—George I dare say at first had no thoughts of accepting his offers but when his affairs did not succeed and he had a wife and one child to support, with the prospect of another, I cannot wonder that he should consider them first and as he could not get what he wanted without coming to England he unfortunately came—By that time your brother wished to marry himself, but he could not refuse the money.[17]

Keats's offer to render "any assistance or money in his power" came in his letter to George of September 21 ("Rest in the confidence that I will not omit any exertion . . . If I cannot remit you hundreds, I will tens and if not that ones."); and George's brief visit to England—by which time Keats himself "wished to marry" —took place in January.[18]

[17] Brawne, p. 33.
[18] Writing to Charles Brown, almost exactly ten years (December 29, 1829) after the Christmas of 1819, Fanny Brawne made the statement cited before (she was writ-

In any case, the engagement had been made by the end of the year. Fanny's mother was far from happy at the news when she at last learned of it. Among Dilke's papers his grandson found a note: "It is quite a settled thing between Keats and Miss ——. God help them. It's a bad thing for them. The mother says she cannot prevent it, and that her only hope is that it will go off." [19] But it is doubtful that Mrs. Brawne knew of it this early. The engagement appears to have been kept secret for some months.

9

At some time in December he jotted down a few lines of poetry —the last serious lines he was ever to write. The little fragment used to be thought of as something addressed to Fanny Brawne. The general feeling now is that the lines were a passage he might have intended to use in some future poem or play.

Whatever their intention, the lines were written on a blank space in the comic poem, "The Cap and Bells." He often thought by contrasts; and whatever was excluded by the tone and limitations of one work often began to clamor, to his instinctive sympathies, for equal justice, equal expression. He had apparently just written stanza 51, which included the little couplet done in needlework by the obdurate Bertha Pearl of Canterbury—

> Cupid I
> Do thee defy.

And when the stanza was finished—in this poem written so much against the grain—he appears to have stopped, and to have

---

ing out a first draft of her letter, and then deleted this particular remark) : "I was more generous ten years ago [December 1819]: I should not now like the odium of being connected with one who was working up his way against poverty and every sort of abuse." And in the same letter to Brown she again returns to this date of ten years before. (Mentioning the attacks on Keats, she writes: "I should be glad if you could disprove I was a very poor judge of character ten years ago and probably overrated every good quality he had." The letter, in the Hampstead Museum, is printed in *Letters of John Keats*, ed. M. B. Forman [4th ed., 1952], pp. lxii–lxiii.) Could it be that the remark so often misinterpreted as suggesting that the engagement took place on December 25, 1818–a date that, as we have seen, is almost impossible—could have involved a slip, and that she was really thinking of December 25, 1819? (The Brawnes and Keats met that Christmas at the Dilkes', and then presumably they had the latter part of the day free.) The remark was that made in a letter to Fanny Keats in December 1821: "I have to remember [Christmas day] three years ago was the happiest day I had ever then spent."

19 *Papers of a Critic*, I.11.

thought of something else. The space may have been left vacant a few minutes, a few days, indeed a month. But before trying to go on with the poem he wrote these lines:

> This living hand, now warm and capable
> Of earnest grasping, would, if it were cold
> And in the icy silence of the tomb,
> So haunt thy days and chill thy dreaming nights
> That thou wouldst wish thine own heart dry of blood
> So in my veins red life might stream again,
> And thou be conscience-calm'd—see here it is—
> I hold it towards you.

chapter xxiii

Adrift

January to August, 1820

MEANWHILE George Keats had become very restive. In early November he had received his brother's long letter from Winchester (September 17 to 27)—the letter in which Keats told of his hurried trip to London in order to see Abbey about the disaster of the Ohio River steamboat and about George's immediate need for money.

John, he could see, had been not only anxious but conscientious as well. He had been making visits to Abbey since May. He was ready to drop his own concerns and problems and to sacrifice himself in any way that might help. But the fact remained that Tom's estate (even as the Keats brothers underestimated it) came to at least £1000, and probably half again as much, and John was having no success in doing anything about it. And this final letter from Winchester, despite John's sense of urgency, was typically lacking in exact details. It was not until some years later that George learned how chronically dishonest and shifty Abbey had been; he was inclined now to interpret the vagueness and procrastination as partly a result of John's hopeless inability, when compared with the experienced George, to talk business with Abbey or the lawyers. George's need was so pressing that it was well worth the three months and £150 for a round trip if he himself could extract from Abbey his own share of Tom's estate. Even a mere £200, over and above the expenses of the trip, would go far in dollars in pioneer Kentucky. It was as much as a reasonably prosperous businessman could hope to earn there in a year. And the chances were that George could get double that amount. In the process he might also be able to clarify exactly what else remained, and thus do a service to his brother and sister as well as himself. He would simply have to settle the matter in person.

If George was to go to England, the sensible thing to do was to go at once. Leaving his wife and child in Louisville, he hurried eastward in late November, took a ship from New York, and arrived in London around January 7 to 9. Any letter he may have sent his brother would have arrived only a few days before, if indeed at all before, he himself did. (Few letters to Keats survive. Those still in his possession in the summer of 1820 he apparently burned before he left for Italy.)

2

The reunion was not only short but, as each of them looked back on it afterwards, sadly incomplete and even superficial. It was not what either would have expected. The hand we clasp, Keats had said months ago, is not the one we shook seven years before: even our bodies have completely changed. Though we can overcome this estrangement by a "wilfull and dramatic" exertion of the imagination—though it was only seventeen months since he and George had parted at Liverpool—yet so much had happened. George by now was preoccupied with his family, with the strange new pioneer world into which he had moved, and with his financial losses there. Quite understandably, John seemed to him in a far more comfortable position than the men among whom George had been living on the frontier. Here, in this safe and settled England, John appeared to be surrounded by cultivated friends. He may not have become prominent, but at least his poems were being published.

Keats, for his part, was timid about intruding in any way once George arrived. The year and a half that had passed were such that he could never begin to describe or suggest briefly to his brother what had happened, however close they had been in the past; and the last two months had been a frightening experience. His instinctive tendency was to avoid completely any talk of his own situation. "Altho' his reception of me was as warm as heart could wish," George told Dilke some years later, "he could not speak with his former openness and unreserve, he had lost the reviving custom of venting his griefs." He does not appear to have mentioned his engagement; as we have noted, he and Fanny were telling no one about it at the moment.

The brothers had little time together alone. George, to begin with, was staying for only two weeks or so. He had every good reason for wanting to leave for Liverpool around January 28 in order to catch a return boat for America: his family was waiting for him; his affairs at home were in very bad shape; his mind was filled with the thought of the next steps he had to take. Meanwhile he was staying with the Wylies—his wife's family—for he wanted to be in town, near Abbey. Keats, moreover, had no place of his own where George could be completely at home. There was an extra cot at Brown's place, and George slept there at least part of the time, but those rooms at Wentworth Place were not his brother's. And Brown, in all probability, had already begun to take a dislike to George (after Keats's death he was to become an inveterate enemy) : always suspicious about money and ready to fight with an outraged sense of justice about every penny, Brown assumed that the brief-visiting George was here to clean out the estate.

Keats, with his new "warm great coat" and his "thick shoes," hurried to London to dine with George and the in-laws as soon as George arrived (the dinner was at the home of Mrs. Millar, Georgiana's aunt, on January 9). But George was immediately afterwards swept up in social engagements. Excited by this brief visit to London after being in such a different world, George took his wife's mother to the theater the very next night, and then went to a dance at the Dilkes' the night after. Keats, who had said months before that he was through with dances and engagements of that sort, went with him, though he seems only to have lingered about in the corners. Thinking it would please George, who liked parties, Keats decided to give a dinner for him and some of their old friends; this took place on January 16, a week after George arrived. There was not much opportunity otherwise of seeing him; and it was rather an ironic commentary on the whole situation that, when the brothers were seeing so little of each other, this quasi-formal dinner had to be planned at all.

But Keats felt in no position to complain that George was bustling about on other matters. For within a few days George was able to get Abbey to come to terms of some sort, whereas Keats had been completely unsuccessful in doing so although he had made repeated efforts for months. He was content to sit on the sidelines. And why should George not throw himself into every social engagement he could? He had been away for a long time. Sitting out in Hampstead, it was as much as Keats could do to minimize his own difficulties, and try to think, with receptive interest, solely of George's affairs.

With Tom's estate settled to his satisfaction, George took the early morning coach for Liverpool on January 28, and secured return passage on a packet—the *Courier*—that left February 1. He did not even have time to see his sister Fanny while he was in London, but he wrote her a pleasant though hurried letter from Liverpool. Fanny's interest in George was to cool perceptibly henceforth.

3

In spare hours out at Hampstead George had copied many of Keats's poems in order to take them back to America. One was the "Ode to a Nightingale." That George should copy the ode in this wintry weather amused Keats. "It is like reading an account of the b[l]ack hole at Calcutta on an ice bergh." George also took back with him about £700. He did not at this time find out the complete amount to which he, John, and Fanny were entitled. He learned this much later, only after Fanny became of age and—tough-minded woman that she was, and with the pent-up frustration of ten years—immediately began to take firm legal steps against her former guardian.

The money George took back with him to America has caused endless dispute. How much of it was John's, granted to George as a loan when John himself was in desperate need? The controversy is full of murky charges that began three years after Keats's death. Brown, ready to believe the worst, thought for a while that the entire £700 really belonged to John. Later, after a detailed study of the matter, he changed the amount to £425. A few facts emerge. George persuaded—or he possibly frightened—Abbey into an immediate division of what Abbey led them to believe was Tom's complete estate: £1,100. By his own admission, George went back to Kentucky with £700. Why, from an estate of £1,100, should he be returning with an amount almost equal to two thirds? At first glance, it looks as though he departed with his own share and that of John (since Fanny definitely received her share). He later tried to explain. Bewildered at the charges he heard Brown was making, he wrote a long, defensive, and rather confused letter to Charles Dilke (April 10, 1824).[1] Of this £700, he says, a total of £160 was

---

[1] For George's letter, see *KC*, I.276–281, quoted in part in Appendix III, below. It is primarily with the details of this letter that Brown's still unpublished notes and his correspondence with Dilke are concerned (Keats Museum, Hampstead). Documentation of the complicated and ultimately unresolvable debate can now be covered

given him by Abbey, part of it as a gift, part as a loan, and another part presumably for a personal investment or speculation by Abbey. (George had not informed Keats of this. Try as he might to be cheerful, there were moments when Keats struck George as so depressed that George feared to let him know how little he really possessed. Instead he encouraged in John the belief that all the £700 was theirs.) [2] It is hard to imagine Abbey offering either a gift or a loan. He had refused to do so only a short time before ("You urg'd me," Keats had written George, "to get Mr. Abbey to advance you money—that he will by no means do"). But then George was here in person now. Obduracy on Abbey's part might have incited George to inquire a little more closely than he did into the family finances that Abbey, in order to hide his own use of the funds, purposely kept tangled and unclear. If the gift and loan were intended to keep George off his guard, they succeeded. As for the remainder of the amount, George claimed that he had left £300 with John when he had first sailed for America, in June 1818, and what he now took back with him from John (a total, he says, of only £170) was a partial repayment, although again he did not tell, or remind, John of this. "It was always my intention to keep him under the idea that I was in his debt." On the other hand, the brothers had kept no accounts for years of what had passed between them; and George, prophesying back in March 1818 that they would soon "be all at sixes and sevens," had spoken of his wish to calculate "the probable amount Tom and I are indebted to you."

When George sailed for America the second time, his brother was left with about £60 or £70 (at least £10 less than the amount necessary to pay his debts at that time).[3] George was probably as unaware of this as he was of the true state of Keats's health. And Keats, remembering his earlier promise to remit to George every

---

by referring to J. C. Stillinger's careful discussion in the *Keats-Shelley Journal*, XI (1962), 39–45.

     [2] "John himself was ignorant of the real state of his funds, it was so painful a subject and in our private communications he was so extremely melancholy that I always had to shew him the pleasing side of things; when I left London I had not courage to say that the 700£ I had obtained was not all ours by right; he therefore imagined it was, but he never thought and never could have informed any one of his Friends that the whole was his. I never considered it necessary to let him know the rights of it, since I did not intend to limit my remittances but by my means . . . it was always my intention to keep him under the idea that I was in his debt." (*KC*, I.278–279.)

     [3] *KC*, I.217–218, and Brawne, p. 33.

pound he could, and how completely he had failed to do anything the past three months, doubtless spoke optimistically of his own affairs and of his intention to turn soon to other writing.

When Keats the following August asked Abbey for some money to help him pay for the journey to Rome, Abbey's abrupt refusal included the remark: "You know that it was very much against my will that you lent your money to George." [4] This does not disprove the fact that George may have made a loan to John unknown to Abbey, of which the £170 could be regarded as a repayment. It only means that Keats had naively given Abbey a splendid excuse for turning down any request he might later make. [5]

Whatever the actual explanation, the brothers were indeed, as George had predicted, "all at sixes and sevens." It would have been unimportant now—as it had been unimportant during so many years before—except that each was in real need and neither was aware that there was still more money left to which they were entitled—a very sizable amount. Plainly George took with him at least £170 that Keats himself regarded as a loan to George; and probably Keats considered half of the extra £160 George really secured from Abbey as also his own (it being understood that Fanny's share was left in England). Needing money himself so badly, he naturally hoped that George would not take it too readily. Yet John had offered it, probably insisted on it. George had a family, and Keats had not. All the same, as Fanny Brawne reported, Keats brooded over it and finally said—it was as strong a condemnation as he could bring himself to make—"George ought not to have done this."

It was one of those situations where life, because of utterly unforeseen difficulties, harasses our altruism, however strong it is basically; and then one part of us insists on maintaining the older habits of generosity while another part, suffering in the new unpredictable circumstances, moves with hurt and surprise in the opposite direction. It is sad to know that Keats, in the trying months ahead, never wrote again to George; and we think back to

---

4 *Letters*, II.33.

5 Of little value as evidence is Abbey's admission to Brown (1822) that John lent George £350 to £400 (Brown's ms. letter to Dilke, September 6, 1824; see Stillinger, cited in note 1, p. 40), for he said three years later that George's explanation was correct (*KC*, I.285–286). Abbey seems to have been ready to agree to anything that would maintain a cloud of complexity to hide himself, sensing, as Fanny Keats approached her majority, that he would soon be called to account.

the long letters sent to him from the autumn of 1818 through the weeks at Winchester in September 1819. But of course Keats was not in a situation where he could write very much to anyone after February 1820. His average letter, from then until he was unable to write letters, was comparatively short.

4

Keats had tried, while George was in London, to pull himself up into active interest, frightened as he was about what was happening to himself. He at once—using those long evenings when George was going to the theater or paying social calls—made an effort to put together a cheerful journal letter to George's wife, for George to take with him when he left for America. It is filled with jokes, speculation, gossip. He tells of the Irish serving girl, Abigail O'Donaghue, who "piqued" him by saying that her father "was very much like my Shakespeare only he had more color than the Engraving." There are other, very different moments, as when he remarks on the "vapidness of the routine of Society . . . standing at Charing Cross and looking east west north and South I can see nothing but dullness." Georgiana had spoken of the dullness of Louisville society. But what of London and Hampstead? Keats is

> tired of the Theatres. Almost all the parties I may chance to fall into I know by heart—I know the different Styles of talk in different places: what subjects will be started how it will proceed, like an acted play, from the first to the last Act—If I go to Hunt's I run my head into many-times heard puns and music. To Haydon's worn out discourses of poetry and painting: the Miss Reynolds I am affraid to speak to for fear of some sickly reiteration of Phrase or Sentiment. When they were at the dance the other night I tried manfully to sit near and talk to them, but to no purpose, and if I had 't would have been to no purpose . . . At Dilkes I fall foul of Politics. 'T is best to remain aloof from people and like their good parts without being eternally troubled with the dull processes of their every day Lives.

Yet his old sense of humor returns, as he starts to play with the thought of the different characters of his friends Rice, Reynolds, and Thomas Richards, who attended the dinner he gave for George the night before. From them he turns to others, and finally to three entirely fictitious people, the last of whom, as A. C. Bradley said, sounds like someone invented by Falstaff:

I know three people of no wit at all, each distinct in his excellence. A. B, and C. A is the soolishest, B the sulkiest, C is a negative—A makes you yawn, B makes you hate, as for C you never see him though he is six feet high. I bear the first, I forbear the second I am not certain that the third is. The first is gruel, the Second Ditch water, the third is spilt—he ought to be wip'd up A is inspired by Jack o' the Clock—B, has been dull'd by a russian Sargeant, C—they say is not his Mothers true Child but that she bought him of the Man who cries 'young Lambs to sell.' T wang dillo dee.

"Twang dillo dee"—the phrase (signifying the twanging of a musical instrument at the end of a refrain) catches his fancy; and, a half dozen times, he continues to repeat and develop it in every kind of combination.

Then, after this long letter, he completely forgot to give it to George to take back with him. He had to post it. These days were filled with puzzlement, with thoughts of the hopes of the past, of the changes that life brings, of the whole "Burden of the Mystery" —the phrase that had meant so much to him for so long; and the "Burden" was greater now than any he had ever experienced before.

It was at some time during these days, probably the evening of the day George left, that Brown discovered that Keats was secretly beginning to take a few drops of laudanum—the extract from opium that Coleridge also took:

> He was too thoughtful, or too unquiet; and he began to be reckless of health. Among other proofs of recklessness, he was secretly taking, at times, a few drops of laudanum to keep up his spirits. It was discovered by accident, and, without delay, revealed to me. He needed not to be warned of the danger of such a habit; but I rejoiced at his promise never to take another drop without my knowledge; for nothing could induce him to break his word, when once given,—which was a difficulty.[6]

5

Suddenly, on February 3, six days after George had left for the boat at Liverpool, Keats had a severe hemorrhage in the lungs. He was just returning from London, sitting—as he so often did in order to save money—on top of the coach. Because a thaw had set in, he had forgotten to wear the heavy coat he had just bought the

6 Brown, pp. 63–64.

month before. He staggered into the house at eleven that night, said Brown, "in a state that looked like fierce intoxication."

> I asked hurriedly, "What is the matter,—you are fevered?" "Yes, yes," he answered, "I was on the outside of the stage this bitter day till I was severely chilled,—but now I don't feel it. Fevered!—of course, a little." He mildly and instantly yielded, a property in his nature towards any friend, to my request that he should go to bed. I followed with the best immediate remedy in my power. I entered his chamber as he leapt into bed. On entering the cold sheets, before his head was on the pillow, he slightly coughed, and I heard him say,—"That is blood from my mouth." I went towards him; he was examining a single drop of blood upon the sheet. "Bring me the candle, Brown; and let me see this blood." After regarding it steadfastly, he looked up in my face, with a calmness of countenance that I can never forget, and said,—"I know the colour of that blood;—it is arterial blood; —I cannot be deceived in that colour;—that drop of blood is my death-warrant;—I must die." I ran for a surgeon; [7] my friend was bled; and, at five in the morning, I left him after he had been, some time, in a quiet sleep.[8]

A week later he told Fanny Brawne: "On the night I was taken ill when so violent a rush of blood came to my Lungs that I felt nearly suffocated—I assure you I felt it possible I might not survive and at that moment though[t] of nothing but you—when I said to Brown 'This is unfortunate' I thought of you." With his future so apparently hopeless now, he refused to let their engagement imprison her, though as he afterwards let himself admit (she had refused to consider breaking the engagement for this reason), "I do not think I could bear any approach of a thought of losing you." Probably, as Sir William Hale-White suggested, Keats had already had a preliminary hemorrhage while he was on top of the coach; and as he coughed up the blood, "darkness had prevented his seeing it, but the taste of it made him fearful, hence the wild excited state in which he reached home." [9] It would have been like him not to mention it as he entered the house, still so uncertain of what it might have meant; and it would help to explain his docility in going to bed immediately.

---

[7] Apparently George Rodd, a nearby Hampstead surgeon (II.280n). Shortly afterwards, probably at the suggestion of Rodd and Dr. Sawrey, they called in a specialist, Dr. Robert Bree of Hanover Square (a Fellow of the Royal Society, now almost sixty years old, an authority on respiratory diseases; see Hale-White, *Keats as Doctor and Patient*, p. 74).

[8] Brown, pp. 64–65.

[9] *Keats as Doctor and Patient*, p. 52.

The treatment by George Rodd and later by Dr. Bree was of course the reverse of what would now be prescribed. Whenever Keats lost blood, they opened a vein in his arms and removed still more blood. He was put on a starvation diet that radically weakened him even further. The whole procedure, as Hale-White says, strikes the present-day physician as "horrible, and it was horrible." But bleeding, for almost any disease, had been a universal practice for three thousand years; and severe restriction of diet was especially common in the period from 1760 to 1830. Bree, as the weeks went on, was apparently unconvinced that Keats was suffering from tuberculosis of the lungs. He told not only Keats but Brown, to whom he might have been expected to divulge the truth, that Keats's illness was ultimately nervous and that the cure lay in rest—in avoiding any excitement and (after he learned more of Keats's life) any work on poetry. Brown took this advice literally, and discouraged Keats not only from writing poetry but even from seeing Fanny Brawne, whose presence, Brown and the doctors thought, added further excitement.

It is a measure of Keats's grasp at hope that he tried to subscribe to both the diagnosis and the remedy. Having lived closely with consumption in members of the family, he rightly suspected—perhaps most of the time he more than suspected—that he now had the same disease. But we find him clutching consistently at other alternatives. Above all, in obedience to Dr. Bree, he dropped any effort to write or even to think about poetry. From here until the end, poetry—much as he cared for it—was put completely aside except for some revising that he did later in the spring. Nor was there further talk about the attraction of death—about the rest, the forgetfulness, the "easefulness" of death. As he wrote James Rice (February 14) ten days after the hemorrhage:

> I may say that for 6 Months before I was taken ill I had not passed a tranquil day . . . The Beauties of Nature had lost their power over me. How astonishingly (here I must premise that illness as far as I can judge in so short a time has relieved my Mind of a load of deceptive thoughts and images and makes me perceive things in a truer light)—How astonishingly does the chance of leaving the world impress a sense of its natural beauties on us. Like poor Falstaff, though I do not babble, I think of green fields. I muse with the greatest affection on every flower I have known from my infancy—their shapes and coulours are as new to me as if I had just created them with a superhuman fancy—It is because they are connected

with the most thoughtless and happiest moments of our Lives—I have seen foreign flowers in hothouses of the most beautiful nature, but I do not care a straw for them. The simple flowers of our sp[r]ing are what I want to see again.

At first he was kept for a few days in a small bedroom at the back of the house. From the window, as he wrote his sister, "the grass looks very dingy, the Celery is gone, and there is nothing to enliven one but a few Cabbage Sta[l]ks." Then, on February 8, a sofa bed was made up for him in the front parlor, the parlor ordinarily used by Brown, and he could look out at the few people who were passing by—the two old maiden ladies from Well Walk whom he saw passing with their corpulent lap dog; the kindly David Lewis, whom he had known casually for two years, and who had been kind to Tom; an old French emigrant walking with his hands clasped behind his back, "his face full of political schemes"; an occasional gipsy and some "old women with bobbins and red cloaks." On February 9, which was a fair, warm day, he took a short walk in the garden, but he seems to have remained indoors the rest of the month, spending much of the time in bed.

6

The day after the hemorrhage, he wrote to Fanny Brawne (February 4) :

Dearest Fanny, I shall send this the moment you return. They say I must remain confined to this room for some time. The consciousness that you love me will make a pleasant prison of the house next to yours. You must come and see me frequently: this evening, without fail—when you must not mind about my speaking in a low tone for I am ordered to do so though I *can* speak out.

He did not know that she, and the whole Brawne family, were away all day, and hence he lay "looking for the Stage the whole afternoon." Finally, he had his note brought back from her door and added a postscript telling her of his hope that she would see him that night or the next morning.

From now until the middle of March he sent her a note every day or two (a total of twenty-two short letters, all of which she kept) . Would she see him this day, or, if not, the next? Would she "send me the words 'Good night' to put under my pillow"? And later: "Send me every morning a written Good night. If you come

for a few minutes about six it may be the best time." He hopes to
see her if she will be passing by the window. He tells her about his
physician's advice: "I am recommended not even to read poetry
much less to write it. I wish I had even a little hope." At times
there is a touch of bitterness: "The utmost stretch my mind has
been capable of was to endeavour to forget you for your own sake
seeing what a chan[c]e there was of my remaining in a precarious
state of health . . . I shall expect you tomorrow for it is certainly
better that I should see you seldom" (he is now, at the end of February, thinking of Bree's warning to avoid excitement). On a day
late in February he writes more fully:

> When I send this round I shall be in the front parlour watching
> to see you show yourself for a minute in the garden. How illness
> stands as a barrier betwixt me and you! Even if I was well—I must
> make myself as good a Philosopher as possible. Now I have had op-
> portunities of passing nights anxious and awake I have found other
> thoughts intrude upon me. "If I should die," said I to myself, "I have
> left no immortal work behind me—nothing to make my friends
> proud of my memory—but I have lov'd the principle of beauty in all
> things, and if I had had time I would have made myself remem-
> ber'd." Thoughts like these came very feebly whilst I was in health
> and every pulse beat for you—now you divide with this (may *I* say
> it?) "last infirmity of noble minds" all my reflection.[10]

There is another note, eloquent in its reserve: "I think you had
better not make any long stay with me when Mr. Brown is at home
—whe[n]ever he goes out you may bring your work. You will have
a pleasant walk today. I shall see you pass . . . Come round to my
window for a moment when you have read this. Thank your
Mother, for the preserves."

7

All these notes to Fanny, and also his short letters to his sister,
are filled with the precautions so typical of his readiness of sympathy, understandably a little subjective now (and we think back to
that impetuous phrase, as he was writing the *Eve of St. Agnes*—the
phrase he immediately struck out—"Put on warm Cloathing
sweet") : "You must be careful always to wear warm cloathing not
only in a frost but in a Thaw." "Mind my advice to be very careful to wear warm cloathing in a thaw." "Be very careful of open
doors and windows and going without your duffle grey." "Be very

10 II.263.

careful . . . this climate requires the utmost care." "You must not stop so long in the cold." "Why will you go out in this weather?" "If you travel outside," he tells Reynolds, "have some flannel aga[i]nst the wind."

If Dr. Bree was still uncertain whether his patient's illness was basically "nervous," his theory was confirmed—at least to his own satisfaction—by what happened on March 6. For after a month of confinement, and of trying with every hour to keep poetry—and everything else he cared about—out of his mind, he was suddenly taken (as Brown wrote Taylor) "with violent palpitations at the heart." Brown, "wretchedly depressed," immediately sent to London for Bree or else went himself. Bree could see nothing organic, in a young man so potentially rugged, to cause these "violent palpitations" of the heart. Keats's helpless struggle during these weeks to clarify his own thinking and feeling, and to cope with so large a challenge while all his resources seemed to have been pulled out from under him, would go far to explain, to the present-day physician, this sudden violence of heart palpitation. In the meantime Dr. Bree counseled Brown that Keats should be spared the "slightest circumstance" that might "create surprise, or any other emotion." If this were done, Bree gave "very favourable hopes." But the palpitations were to return, after Bree and others thought him better, in less than another two weeks.

Fanny Brawne immediately realized that Keats's illness had taken a more serious turn. He himself tried to make light of it. He can only think now in platitudes; he has become like old Justice Shallow, he implies. "Death must come at last; Man must die, as Shallow says." Joking at his helplessness, he says that he imagines her sitting in the "new black dress which I like so much," and that if only he were a "little less selfish," he would "run round and surprise you with a knock at the door. I fear I am too prudent for a dying kind of Lover. Yet there is a great difference between going off in warm blood like Romeo, and making one's exit like a frog in a frost."

The image put what was only too much in his mind, from here to the end: the enormous sense of anticlimax, after all the idealistic talk—his probable, perhaps inevitable, "exit like a frog in a frost." But he cannot let the letter end this way. Their notes back and forth had made him wonder, a few days before, "what would Rousseau have said at seeing our little correspondence" (though

"I would sooner have Shakespeare's opinion about the matter").
And he tries to end his present letter with a joke. Referring to
John Murray, the fabulously successful publisher of Byron, he
speaks again of "our correspondence (which at some future time
I propose offering to Murray)."

8

Meanwhile, in late February, long before the spring was ready
to come, he was thinking ahead to it. His thoughts also went back
to that spring two years before, which had been so infused with
the confidence in a new beginning—the beginning that followed
the "Negative Capability" letter, the meeting with Wordsworth,
the "Lines on Seeing a Lock of Milton's Hair," the sonnet "On
Sitting Down to Read *King Lear* Once Again."

Back then, two years before, the song of the early thrush had
seemed a poignant symbol of the promise of the year ahead. ("Aye,
on the shores of darkness there is light," he wrote in the sonnet
"To Homer" at about the same time: "And precipices show untrodden green; / There is a budding morrow in midnight.") This
had been the thought of the fine, gently brooding poem "What
the Thrush Said": the answer to come would be tentative (the refrain of the thrush was "O fret not after knowledge"—after certitude—"I have none") ; but the understanding would still come,
gradually, and with all the more "native" a fulfillment. "The
spring will be a harvest-time." But of course the autumn of 1818,
and the year that followed, had brought an altogether unexpected
kind of harvest. True enough, a part of that fulfillment was writing of a quality that was to establish a high-water mark for the
poetry of the next century and a half. But for Keats himself, the
outcome seemed hopelessly crossed and complicated, the fruition
deferred.

Now, in this present February, almost to the day, a thrush had
appeared across the field. And in a note to Fanny Brawne written
about February 24–26, a week or so before the heart palpitations
began, he asked her:

Do you hear the Th[r]ush singing over the field? I think it is a sign
of mild weather—so much the better for me. Like all Sinners now I
am ill I philosophise aye out of my attachment to every thing, Trees,
flowers, Thrushes Sp[r]ing, Summer, Claret &c &c aye [e]very thing

but you . . . That Thrush is a fine fellow I hope he was fortunate in his choice this year.

Then, as the days passed, the thrush seemed to come still closer to Wentworth Place. So poignant now were the associations that he felt he had to pull himself away from them a little. He tries to be playful. No, however the thrush might sing, he himself will not try to write anything now: "I will be as obstinate as a Robin, I will not sing in a cage." Then the heart palpitations begin. Why will Fanny go out in this treacherous weather? He continues to tell her to stay clear of cold draughts and open windows. "I am suspecting that window to be open." "Let me have another opportunity . . . I will not die without being remember'd."

Fanny naturally wants to know more precisely what has happened in this latest attack. Keats finally answers, but only in general terms. Dr. Bree has given him some medicine to keep down his racing pulse, though Keats finds he can do just as well without it. (Actually, his lungs, when the autopsy was performed a year later, were found to be entirely gone—the physicians wondered that he could have lived at all during his last month or two.) But what about her? "My dear girl do not make a joke of it: do not expose yourself to the cold."

Then he changes the subject (the reference to Clementi's is to the music publishers, who also sold musical instruments, at 26 Cheapside) :

> There's that Thrush again—I can't afford it—he'll run me up a pretty Bill for Music—besides he ought to know I deal at Clementi's.

9

When Keats talked to Taylor and others back in November about not publishing a volume for some time, he sincerely meant what he said. But much had happened since then; and the least he could do now was to try to put together a volume from what poems he had written since *Endymion*—since the new beginning of January 1818, over two years ago. For he was hardly able any longer to get other work and to let what he considered to be a really "mature" volume evolve slowly. His publishers, Taylor and Hessey, were more than willing. It was apparently they, in fact, who took the initiative. By the middle of March, Keats was revising *Lamia*. Shortly before this, the poet Bryan Waller Procter—

who wrote under the name of Barry Cornwall—asked Hunt to take him over to Hampstead and introduce him to Keats. Pleased by the visit, Keats was able without much effort to appear almost completely well (Procter speaks of his "resolute bearing"). Procter liked him enormously and saw him at least once or twice again, describing him as

> free from all affectation in manner and opinion. Indeed, it would be difficult to discover a man with a more bright and open countenance. He was always ready to hear and to reply; to discuss, to reason, to admit . . . I never encountered a more manly and simple young man.
> In person he was short, and had eyes large and wonderfully luminous, and a resolute bearing; not defiant, but well sustained.[11]

Though Keats told his sister on March 20 that he had again "been attack'd several times with a palpitation at the heart and the Doctor says I must not make the slightest exertion"—Keats is explaining why his note to her is so short—on March 25 he went to London in order to attend the showing of Haydon's "Christ's Entry into Jerusalem." The picture was at last finished, and Haydon had hired the large room at the Egyptian Hall in Piccadilly —a vast, barnlike structure with a façade supposedly in an Egyption style that had formerly housed the museum of William Bullock and was now available for renting. Tickets were issued, the attendance was large and distinguished, and Haydon was happy. Hazlitt was there—and both he and Keats, said Haydon, "were up in a corner, really rejoicing." More probably they were simply looking at the large gathering of people and speaking of it.

By April 27, Taylor and Hessey received the completed manuscript for the new and, as it proved, final volume of Keats's poems. Keats, for a while, thought it might be a good idea to put the *Eve of St. Agnes* first; Woodhouse, Taylor, and others had liked it, and he himself had lost all confidence in his own judgment. But finally *Lamia* was put first. All the sonnets were left out. Probably at Woodhouse's and Taylor's urging, the first *Hyperion* was included. Keats by now was far from eager to argue with anyone, and least of all with anyone he trusted. Any kind of possible sale was reason enough for whatever should be done. At the same time he was borrowing further from Brown, and was painfully chagrined at having to do so. But there was no alternative.

11 *Literary Recollections*, ed. R. W. Armour (1936), p. 104.

10

Keats was now up and walking about, and it was generally assumed that he was rapidly recovering. But a new problem was
arising as April passed—trivial enough ordinarily, but distressing
to Keats now in his general helplessness. Brown, with clocklike
regularity, was planning as usual to rent his place for the summer.
He could not be expected to be aware that Keats himself was
gravely ill when Dr. Bree was assuring them that the basis of
Keats's illness was nervous and that he would soon improve. In
any case Brown was short of money and needed to rent his place;
he counted on this as a regular part of his annual income. (Other
complications were developing. Abigail O'Donaghue was soon to
bear him a child, who might be born in June or July. Keats may
not have known this.) Determined to avoid being an encumbrance, Keats did everything he could to encourage the belief that
he was basically well, or almost so. For a while there was even some
talk, encouraged by the misguided Dr. Bree, that Keats should go
to Scotland with Brown.

Brown insisted on lending him enough to help him through the
next few weeks (though Brown himself had to borrow to do this),
and Keats, regretfully, accepted. But where was he to go? The
question racked him, though he did everything he could to prevent anyone from knowing how important and distressing a crisis
it was for him. To go back to the old rooms at Bentley's in Well
Walk was impossible: the place was haunted with the memory of
Tom's last months. There were perhaps other rooms in Hampstead
to be found. But was it a good idea to be near the Brawnes? Living nearby, alone, he would be wanting to come over constantly or
to have Fanny visit him; and he had no right to make such demands. Bree and Rodd, moreover, had kept telling him that he
must avoid any emotional excitement. Perhaps they were right,
and if he did as they said he might get well again. Counterpointed
with these thoughts was still another—altogether his own—about
which he never spoke except in the most indirect way: if he was
going to die within the next year (and there is little doubt that
some of the time he was convinced that this would happen), then,
in Stoic self-protection, he must try to cut himself off a little—try
to care less passionately about all that he dreaded most to lose.

He finally decided to leave Hampstead and to move to Kentish

Town, two miles away, until Brown's return at the end of the summer. Leigh Hunt, so actively present at the start of Keats's career, now appears again at its close. For Hunt himself was at this time living at Mortimer Terrace in Kentish Town. With his help, a sitting room and bedroom were found for Keats nearby, at 2 Wesleyan Place, for a weekly rent of twenty-one shillings. Keats's few belongings were moved over there on May 4, Brown paying the first week's rent in advance. The move called back to memory all the others that he had made. Then he went back to Hampstead and stayed with Brown for another two days. On May 6, Brown lent him £50 (he himself had been forced to borrow it at interest from a friend of theirs, Robert Skynner, a conveyancer in Cavendish Square). Then the two of them sailed on a smack at Gravesend and said good-bye, and Keats returned to London.

11

Alone in his new place at Kentish Town, he faced—as he had probably known beforehand he would have to face—an impossible situation. He needed to earn money, but he was helpless to do so. He needed to occupy his mind, but Dr. Bree and others had convinced him that it would be fatally short-sighted to return to the writing of poetry before he was well. Nothing, in short, that was necessary or even generally therapeutic to him as he now was could be resumed until he was better.

Keats stayed alone in these lodgings for seven weeks. He received a few calls from some of his friends. But many of his friends were away from London. Dilke, down in Westminster, was becoming more absorbed in politics, and his obsessive, suffocating interest in his son, which merely made his other friends laugh, now struck Keats as a little crazy. In any case, Kentish Town was a good distance from Westminster. Bailey was of course gone, Reynolds absorbed in law or going to Exeter to continue his courting, and Rice so unwell that one could see him only by going to him. Even had there not been some strain in their relationship, Haydon was far too ebullient to be pleasant company to a man as ill as Keats; and Haydon was altogether caught up in his own affairs. Brown had now left. Fanny Keats, the only remaining member of the family, was hopelessly shut off from him.

There was indeed no one left but Fanny Brawne, who called

frequently. True enough, he was engaged to her. But there was something ridiculous (as he now began to think of it) about the idea of this sprightly young woman, with so many other interests, tied to a man who was not only penniless but ill, probably fatally ill. He tried during the weeks that ensued to manage these thoughts, to reduce them to proportion. But this healthfully gregarious person was alone throughout most of every day—alone without the salutary outlet of work, and in a situation that was almost hopeless. All his capacity for empathy began to go awry. Inevitably he began to picture Fanny Brawne, the one person left to him, as enjoying herself in the company of other people. Every resource he could call on, in an effort to bring himself back to a sense of proportion, proved inadequate in these solitary hours, as week followed week. Hence the tone of the letters to Fanny Brawne—the very few letters (a total of four, leaving aside two short notes) between now and the time he left for Italy—so filled with frantic anxiety. It is these letters, considered apart from their context, that helped to create the impression either that Fanny Brawne was a chronic flirt or else that Keats was, in the later stages of this famous love affair, almost paranoid. Diagnoses and interpretations that beguile the diagnostician often avoid the obvious: one thinks of Johnson's hard-earned, contemptuous, and salutary phrase—"imagination operating on luxury."

Some time, perhaps a week or two, elapsed before Keats wrote Fanny a letter. He knows that she goes to town once in a while (usually just to shop or to call on Mrs. Dilke). "Your going to town alone, when I heard of it, was a shock to me—yet I expected it." And he underlines the next words: *promise me you will not for some time, till I get better.* She must confess—he goes on—that she likes the world of fashion, of idle chatter and affectation. If he and she ever marry, they "must not live as other men and women do—I cannot brook the wolfsbane of fashion and foppery and tattle." Then he sends another letter after a week or two. (The date is uncertain; Keats did not date these notes to Fanny, and her own replies were never preserved—he probably burned them, when he burned his other papers, before he left for Italy.) Fanny, possibly thinking of the Reynolds family, has said that friends of his laughed at her. Keats writes back:

> My friends laugh at you! I know some of them—when I know them all I shall never think of them again as friends or even ac-

quaintance . . . what a shame it is our Loves should be so put into the microscope of a Coterie. Their laughs should not affect you (I may perhaps give you reasons some day for these laughs, for I suspect a few people to hate me well enough, *for reasons I know of,* who have pretended a great friendship for me) when in competition with one, who if he never should see you again would make you the saint of his memory . . . I long to believe in immortality. I shall never be ab[le] to bid you an entire farewell. If I am destined to be happy with you here—how short is the longest Life—I wish to believe in immortality . . . Your name never passes my Lips—do not let mine pass yours—Those People do not like me . . . I am strong enough to walk over—but I dare not. I shall feel so much pain in parting with you again.

After he is told, on July 5, that he must go to Italy if he is to survive the coming winter, the cautions and anxieties he expresses become stronger. But they continue for only two more letters. By then he is confident that everything is over.

13

On June 22, seven weeks after he had moved to Kentish Town, he received an urgent letter from his sister to come out to Walthamstow and see her. He knew she had been having new troubles with Abbey and Mrs. Abbey, and he had already written her that he would do what he could, although he was far more helpless than he cared to tell her.

What could be this new trouble? It might be serious. Excited, he walked out shakily in order to get a coach, forgetting his anxiety about saving every penny. But as he waited for the coach, a gush of blood came from his lungs. He managed to get back to his lonely lodgings. What was he to do now? He obviously could not go to Walthamstow. Should he ask someone to get hold of Dr. Bree? But he had no further faith in Bree, who had assured him that there was nothing organically wrong.

When the bleeding subsided, he made his way over to Leigh Hunt's, the only place now left for him to go. Hunt himself was ill at this time with what was diagnosed as bilious fever. Keats, preoccupied with keeping himself under control, sank back into a chair, apparently saying nothing of the hemorrhage. Shortly afterwards, Shelley's friend Mrs. Maria Gisborne dropped by in order to see the Hunt family. She left an account in her journal. Mrs.

Hunt served tea—it was early in the evening—and "Mr. Keats was introduced to us." Mrs. Gisborne observed that "he had lately been ill also, and spoke but little." When he did speak, it was in so low a voice they could hardly hear. She and the Hunts began to talk of music, and of the difference between Italian and English singing.

Ill as he was, Keats's instinctive empathy was touched when Mrs. Gisborne mentioned that Carlo Farinelli

> had the art of taking breath imperceptibly, while he continued to hold one single note, alternately swelling and diminishing the power of his voice like waves. Keats observed that this must in some degree be painful to the hearer; as when a diver descends into the hidden depths of the sea you feel an apprehension lest he may never rise again. These may not be his exact words as he spoke in a low tone.[12]

When Keats returned that same night to his rooms in Wesleyan Place, the bleeding from the lungs started again. Thoroughly shaken by now, he asked the landlord or landlady to send for Dr. George Darling, who was John Taylor's personal physician, and whom Haydon had earlier urged Keats to consult (he was also the physician of Hazlitt and John Scott).

Dr. Darling, a man of superior intelligence, grasped the situation at once. Whatever Keats's possible chances, it was out of the question for him to continue to live alone in this way. Once again, as in that hopeful autumn of 1816, the Hunts took him in. He was moved over to their house in Mortimer Terrace the next day—into this feckless household, as cheerily chaotic as it had been years before, despite Hunt's own illness now. It was a strain on Keats, but at least he was not alone. Keats meanwhile wrote a short note to his sister to explain why he could not come to Walthamstow in answer to her urgent request: he had "a slight spitting of blood"; he is confident "there is nothing material to fear." Within a few days, Dr. Darling called in Dr. William Lambe, a specialist in consumption and a Fellow of the Royal College of Physicians. Dr. Lambe lived in the suburbs but maintained an office in what is now Theobald's Road, and was generous in helping patients without money. He was even more emphatic than Darling about the

---

[12] These and the following quotations from her journal are printed in *Maria Gisborne and Edward E. Williams . . . Their Journals and Letters*, ed. F. L. Jones (1951), pp. 36–37, 40, 44–45.

gravity of Keats's condition. He was convinced that Keats could not survive another winter in England.

While Lambe and Darling were deliberating how to put this to him, Keats wrote a short note to Fanny Brawne; "I endeavour to make myself as patient as possible. Hunt amuses me very kindly—besides I have your ring on my finger and your flowers on the table. I shall not expect to see you yet because it would be so much pain to part with you again." And he spent the next few days, as he tells her, "in marking the most beautiful passages in Spenser, intending it for you, and comforting myself in being somehow occupied to give you however small a pleasure."

It was while he was in the midst of doing this that Lambe and Darling told him—and presumably the Hunts—that his only hope was to leave for Italy by the end of the summer. The more benign climate might offer a chance. What they said suddenly jelled into conviction all of his accumulating suspicion that his life was coming to an end as certainly as had that of Tom: that there was to be nothing more of the career from which he had expected so much ("For many years my offerings must be hush'd," until he grew in "philosophy," in practical prudence, in psychological understanding of the human heart, in technical mastery) ; he was indeed to make an "exit" (to use the phrase he had written shortly before) "like a frog in a frost." Up in his room at Mortimer Terrace, while the noise of the Hunt family came up the stairs through the door, he wrote (July 5) one of the last two letters he was ever to send to Fanny Brawne:

> I am tormented day and night. They talk of my going to Italy. 'Tis certain I shall never recover if I am to be so long separate from you . . . I am literally worn to death, which seems my only recourse . . . When you were in the habit of flirting with Brown you would have left off, could your own heart have felt one half of one pang mine did . . . I *will* resent my heart having been made a football. You will call this madness. I have heard you say that it was not unpleasant to wait a few years—you have amusements—your mind is away . . . you can wait—you have a thousand activities—you can be happy without me. Any party, any thing to fill up the day has been enough . . . You do not know what it is to love—one day you may—your time is not come . . . Do not write to me if you have done anything this month which it would have pained me to have seen.

But the very same day he tried to write a reassuring letter to his sister. "For two or three days I have been getting a little stronger." His two physicians think it a good idea for him to spend this coming winter in Italy. "We have no recourse but patience."

He now retreated into complete silence most of the time, trying to adjust himself inwardly to the thought of this coming exile—for it was an exile to him as he now was. He was unable to make up his mind. He was easily swayed for moments—for days—though a strong protest would suddenly arise in him at other times. In any case he would write no further letters to Fanny Brawne. He would try not to see her. Brooding in this silent despair, trying to grasp at resolution, he determined to cut himself off from this and from almost everything. If he was to make his exit "like a frog in a frost," he would learn not to care. A week afterwards, the chatty—and curious—Mrs. Gisborne contrived to drop in again on the Hunts for tea (July 12). She learned from the Hunts that Keats was "under sentence of death from Dr. Lamb." He looked "emaciated" when he came down and joined them. "He never spoke."

14

Meanwhile, advance copies of the new volume, *Lamia, Isabella, The Eve of St. Agnes, and Other Poems*—in many ways perhaps the most remarkable single volume to be published by any poet during the past century and a half, if we leave aside collected works published by poets in their old age—were sent out. And on either Saturday, July 1, or Monday, July 3, the book was published. Keats, before the hemorrhage of June 22, had written Brown that he regarded the publication with "very low hopes . . . This shall be my last trial; not succeeding, I shall try what I can do in the Apothecary line."

His pride was cut when he saw the last sentence in a note written by Taylor or Woodhouse and printed in the book as an "Advertisement":

> If any apology be thought necessary for the appearance of the unfinished poem of HYPERION, the publishers beg to state that they alone are responsible, as it was printed at their particular request, and contrary to the wish of the author. The poem was intended to have been of equal length with ENDYMION, but the reception given to that work discouraged the author from proceeding.

Crossing out this passage in one of the gift copies, he wrote above it: "This is none of my doing—I was ill at the time," and then beneath the last sentence, "This is a lie." [13]

Within another month, the book began to get some commendatory reviews, beginning with one from Charles Lamb (in the *New Times*, July 19) and continuing through that of Francis Jeffrey in the *Edinburgh Review* for August [14] to others in September. But they were coming too late to make much difference. The reviews of Keats's two earlier volumes are altogether relevant to his biography, and are relevant, in a way, to his poetic development; but the reviews of the final volume are not. The subject of the reviews of this volume is part of another, more general topic: the beginning of Keats's posthumous reputation.[15]

He wistfully wrote Charles Brown (August 1820) that his book "has been very highly rated," though the sale of it had been slow. The sale was indeed slow, and through sheer bad luck. For the book was published at the very time that London and the London press were excited about the effort of George IV to pass a bill through Parliament ("The Bill of Pains and Penalties") that would free him from his wife, the Princess Caroline, who was now in London clamorously asserting her rights as Queen. George IV was trying to prove a case of adultery. The press was devoting all its space to every detail of the subject. Books of almost every sort suffered a sharp decline in sales throughout the summer.

15

Keats's principal thought was not the new book but rather how to get through the next few months, whether or not they were his last. If he had to go to Italy, could he manage it alone even if he

13 A gift copy to Burridge Davenport, a Hampstead neighbor. See the plate in Lowell, II.424.

14 Back on September 20, 1819, Keats had told George that the *Edinburgh Review* had been afraid "to touch upon my Poem [*Endymion*]—They do not know what to make of it—they do not like to condemn it and they will not p[r]aise it for fear . . . If on my next Publication they should praise me and so lug in Endymion—I will address [them] in a manner they will not at all relish." This was exactly what happened. Francis Jeffrey, whose Whig *Edinburgh Review* might ordinarily be expected to defend a liberal against *Blackwood's* and the Tory quarterlies, did procrastinate. Then, when he reviewed Keats's new volume (August 1820), he did "lug in" *Endymion* in the most complimentary way. Keats, needless to say, was too ill to carry out his threat, and would hardly have done so anyway.

15 For a general discussion of the reviews, see Hewlett, pp. 334–339.

could somehow raise the money? He was losing all confidence in his own ability to handle problems even from day to day. The thought of going to a foreign country in his present state, and, above all, of doing so completely without money, haunted him every hour.

With Hunt he once or twice took the coach out to Hampstead in order to see the familiar places he must soon leave. Near the house where he had lived with George and Tom, he suddenly displayed an emotion that surprised Hunt (however given to emotional expression himself, Hunt did not expect this from Keats) :

> The house was in Well Walk. You know the grove of elms there. It was in that grove, on the bench next the heath, that he suddenly turned upon me, his eyes swimming with tears, and told me he was "dying of a broken heart." He must have been wonderfully excited to make such a confession; for his was a spirit lofty to a degree of pride.[16]

At some other time, William Hone, the antiquary, also saw him "sitting and sobbing" at the end of Well Walk, holding a handkerchief before his face, and looking up at the Heath and surrounding houses, filled with associations of memory and hope.

In this distraught helplessness, a trivial accident—one that the Hunts could not possibly consider serious—caused him to leave the Hunts and go back to Hampstead in search of other lodgings. A messenger brought him a letter from Fanny Brawne. Mrs. Hunt at that moment was occupied with her children and asked the maid to take the letter to Keats. The maid was spiteful: she was to leave her job the next day. Deliberately dilatory, irritated by the additional housework caused by Keats, she handed Fanny Brawne's letter to the ten-year-old son of the Hunts and told him to deliver it to his mother after she left. The boy broke the seal. The letter contained nothing of importance. According to Mrs. Gisborne, who learned it from Mrs. Hunt's doubtless exaggerated account, Keats wept in helplessness and indignation. Whatever actually happened, he decided in a few hours to leave the Hunts and return to Well Walk, his and his brothers' old lodging. It was possibly sometime during this day (August 12) that he wrote Fanny Brawne what is apparently the last letter he sent her:

> I feel it almost impossible to go to Italy—the fact is I cannot leave you, and shall never taste one minute's content until it pleases

16 In Hunt's description of Hampstead in his *Wishing-Cap Papers* (1873) , p. 239.

chance to let me live with you for good . . . Mr. Dilke came to see me yesterday, and gave me a very great deal more pain than pleasure. I shall never be able any more to endure t[he] society of any of those who used to meet at Elm Cottage and Wentworth Place. The last two years taste like brass upon my Palate. If I cannot live with you I will live alone. I do not think my health will improve much while I am separated from you . . . I am sickened at the brute world which you are smiling with. I hate men and women more. I see nothing but thorns for the future—wherever I may be next winter in Italy or nowhere Brown will be living near you with his indecencies—I see no prospect of any rest. Suppose me in Rome—well, I should there see you as in a magic glass going to and from town at all hours, —— I wish you could infuse a little confidence in human nature into my heart. I cannot muster any—the world is too brutal for me —I am glad there is such a thing as the grave—I am sure I shall never have any rest till I get there At any rate I will indulge myself by never seeing any more Dilke or Brown or any of their Friends. I wish I was either in your a[r]ms full of faith or that a Thunder bolt would strike me.

When he reached Hampstead that night, he may have found the Bentleys all in bed at Well Walk and then gone over to the Brawnes', or more probably he stopped by at the Brawnes' on his way to Well Walk. In any case, seeing his feverish condition, Mrs. Brawne insisted that he stay with them for a while. He was to remain with them for a month, until a few days before he left for Italy.

The Voyage to Italy

✻⤳☉⤿✻⤳☉⤿✻⤳☉⤿✻⤳☉⤿✻⤳☉⤿✻⤳☉⤿✻⤳☉⤿✻⤳☉⤿✻⤳☉⤿✻⤳☉⤿✻⤳☉⤿✻⤳☉⤿✻⤳☉

August to November, 1820

AT THE SMALL HOUSE of the Brawnes, by now fairly crowded, Keats tried to get a grip on himself. The next morning after he arrived, he wrote to John Taylor (August 13) : "This Journey to Italy wakes me at daylight every morning and haunts me horribly. I shall endeavour to go though it be with the sensation of marching up against a Battery." If the thing had to be done, the "first step" was to find out how much it would cost. Could Taylor get hold of some people who would know about this, and give him an estimate of the expense of a trip to Italy and of a year's stay there?

The "first step," however necessary, could also seem hopeless. How, indeed, was he to go to Italy when he had no money at all and, with every week, was becoming physically more helpless? The next day, brooding over the trip, he sent Taylor what he thought would serve as a will.[1] Then, embarrassed as he was to turn again to Charles Brown for help, he wrote to tell him of the situation (August 14) . Brown, traveling about Scotland, did not receive the letter for some time.

Not hearing from Brown, Keats a week later girded himself to write to Abbey. This was always a heavy, unpleasant chore to him, while to George dealing with Abbey was an exciting game. Abbey's last entrance in the life of Keats was true to form as he wrote from his countinghouse in Pancras Lane:

> I have yours of Sunday and am exceedingly grieved at the contents—You know that it was very much against my will that you lent your money to George . . .

[1] In case of my death this scrap of Paper may be serviceable in your possession.
All my estate real and personal consists in the hopes of the sale of books publish'd or unpublish'd. Now I wish *Brown* and you to be the first paid Creditors—the rest is in nubibus—but in case it should shower pay my Taylor the few pounds I owe him.
My Chest of Books divide among my friends—

(Letters, II.319.)

Bad debts for the last two years have cut down the profits of our business to nothing, so that I can scarcely take out enough for my private expence—It is therefore not in my power to lend you any thing— [2]

Meanwhile the generous Shelley, hearing of Keats's condition, wrote him from Italy. Would Keats care to come and stay with the Shelleys? A combination of pride and tired fatalism appears in Keats's answer, which he also tried to make thoughtful and courteous. He indeed—he tells Shelley—has to go to Italy, though, as he is now, he approaches it (as he had already said to Taylor) a little "as a soldier marches up to a battery." But he cannot accept Shelley's kind offer. He is "prevented by a circumstance I have very much at heart to prophesy" (perhaps, in this vague excuse, he is thinking of his probable death). And he at once changes the subject to poetry. Shelley, in his own letter, had offered some friendly criticism of Keats's writing. In the same spirit Keats refers to Shelley's *Cenci,* which he has just read:

> There is only one part of it I am judge of; the Poetry, and dramatic effect, which by many spirits now a days is considered the mammon. A modern work it is said must have a purpose, which may be the God—*an artist* must serve Mammon—he must have "self concentration" selfishness perhaps. You I am sure will forgive me for sincerely remarking that you might curb your magnanimity and be more of an artist, and "load every rift" of your subject with ore. The thought of such discipline must fall like cold chains upon you, who perhaps never sat with your wings furl'd for six Months together.

He can hardly help being amused that, in the position he is now in, he is so ready with advice: "Is not this extraordina[r]y talk for the writer of Endymion? whose mind was like a pack of scattered cards—I am pick'd up and sorted to a pip."

2

The August days were passing. Keats had still not heard from Brown. Who could go with him, if anyone? And where was the money to come from? He had another hemorrhage in late August. John Taylor, hearing about this, decided to act, though his own firm was going through a difficult period and sales were generally slow. Within the next three weeks he made a very generous arrangement, which in effect canceled all Keats's debts to Taylor and

[2] II.331.

Hessey and left him with a surplus of £180. The copyright of *Endymion* was bought outright for £100, and that of the *Poems* (1817) and the new *Lamia* volume for a second £100. After deducting the advances Taylor had given him, starting back in 1817, when he began *Endymion,* this left £30. Should the firm ever realize more than this from the sale of these works, the surplus would be credited to Keats. At the same time the firm would arrange to have £150 put to his credit in Rome as a new advance for whatever else he might write and publish with Taylor and Hessey.[3]

It is now that Joseph Severn enters the Keats story more prominently. Taylor had made arrangements for Keats to sail to Naples on the *Maria Crowther,* a small brig of 127 tons leaving on September 17. It was far more common at that time than it is now for a man seriously ill to live alone, and even to take care of himself alone. But it was plain to Taylor, Woodhouse, and William Haslam that Keats could not go to Italy by himself.

Four days before the boat was to sail, Haslam, who was himself clearly unable to go (his business kept him in London; his wife was expecting a child) , dropped in on Joseph Severn. No one considered Severn the ideal companion for this purpose, but he was at least free to make the journey. As an aspiring artist he might be interested in the trip to Rome, a place that every painter naturally hoped to visit. He had won the gold medal of the Royal Academy for his picture "Una and the Red Cross Knight in the Cave" (or "The Cave of Despair"—"You had best put me into your cave of despair," Keats had told him some months before) . Why should not Severn, while abroad, paint another picture and submit it for the traveling fellowship awarded by the Academy? If he won it he could remain in Rome and continue his study there for another three years. Severn left two accounts of his talk with Haslam, the briefer and more probable of which is as follows:

> Haslam said to me, "As nothing can save Keats but going to Italy, why should *you* not try to go with him, for otherwise he must go alone, and we shall never hear anything of him if he dies. Will you go?" I answered, "I'll go." "But you'll be long getting ready," he added; "Keats is actually now preparing. When would you be ready?" "In three or four days," I replied, "and I will set about it this very moment."[4]

[3] Taylor assumed that £200 would before long be sent from George, and that Keats would not need the full sum that he and Hessey advanced. (See *KC,* I.218.)

[4] Sharp, p. 48. In his other account he states that he was asked just before the

He called on Sir Thomas Lawrence, and got from him an introduction to the Italian artist, Antonio Canova. He also collected
£25 from a woman who owed him this amount for a miniature,
and in other ways made preparations.

But when the moment came to leave, he had a rather painful
scene with his father, who was neither mentally nor physically
well. Altogether opposed to the trip, his dejected father rose from
his armchair, according to Severn, and, standing in the doorway
as the son tried to pass, "struck me to the ground." Severn left
with "agitation and trembling nerves"—a state that was apparently
to become more familiar to him in the months ahead.[5] And since,
from here to the end of Keats's life, we depend so much on Severn's accounts of what happened, we may note the tone of gentle
hysteria—gentle because the character of this man was gentle,
though also timid and very easily alarmed. In some respects Severn is no more reliable than Haydon. Each was what we should
call an honest man—indeed a good man—unless we began to elim-
inate most of humanity from consideration. But neither Haydon
nor Severn had a very firm purchase on fact, although this lack
showed itself in radically different ways. Haydon saw what a
strong, inventive imagination might see or want to experience.
More than most people, he lacked the emotion ordinarily called
fear. Severn's tendency to exaggerate (and occasionally to dramatize) floated more easily over the waves of daily experience. If
nothing distressing was obvious, then he himself was not distressed; he was hopeful. But if a trouble arose—a trouble of which
Haydon might well be oblivious—alarm spread instantly through
Severn's frame. To recognize this, to take it for granted, helps us
to interpret what this kindly if slight man tells us of Keats's last
months.

3

Meanwhile Keats had said good-bye to the Brawnes, not wishing
to delay the pain of it until the last minute, and had gone down to
London to stay at Taylor's lodgings before getting on board the
brig.

---

boat sailed, and replied that he could be ready "if I can have six hours." We now
know, from Haslam's letter to Taylor (II.333), that Severn had five days to prepare
for the trip.

[5] Sharp, pp. 50–51.

After his unhappy scene with his father, Severn hurried to the wharf on the south side of the river, just across from the Tower, from which the *Maria Crowther* was to sail (Sunday morning, September 17). At the wharf were waiting Keats, Taylor, Haslam, and some others whom Severn does not specify. The boat was far from inviting. It was a very small merchantman, intended almost solely for freight, and it was poorly equipped for passengers. Severn, scurrying about the boat, noted that there was only one "little Cabin with 6 beds and at first sight every inconvenience." As their friends were asked to leave the boat, Keats had to go and find his bewildered companion and bring him to the boatside in order to say good-bye. The boat moved down the tide to Gravesend, arrived there at noon, and lay to for the rest of the day. The Captain, Thomas Walsh, intended to leave Gravesend that night. But weather in the channel was unfavorable, and they had to spend most of the next day (Monday, September 18) at Gravesend, waiting for the weather to improve.

Throughout these two days Keats succeeded in maintaining the appearance of pleasure and even high spirits, and indeed kept it up for another two weeks. Severn, beginning a short journal to send William Haslam, wrote on the first evening that "Keats seemed happy" throughout the whole day.[6] In fact, Keats actually "cracked his jokes at tea and was quite the 'special fellow' of olden time." Severn almost began to look on the trip as something of a lark. A Mrs. Pidgeon had joined the boat at the same time as Keats and Severn. She now presided over the little tea table. But that first afternoon Keats also persuaded Severn to go ashore at Gravesend and buy some medicines for him (there were hardly any aboard), and to get in particular a bottle of laudanum. The laudanum was apparently unused by Keats during the boat trip; but the fact that he wished to have it suggests something of his state of mind. Severn also, at Keats's request, bought a few dozen apples and biscuits. When Severn returned, he found Keats "full of his waggery."

That evening, as the boat lay to at Gravesend (September 18), Charles Brown was, ironically, passing Keats on the way to London. Alarmed by the letters he had finally received while tramp-

---

[6] The following quotations from Severn's account of the voyage are from the letters printed by Rollins, II.338–344, 353–355, and from the excerpts from Severn's papers in Sharp, pp. 54ff.

ing through the Scottish Highlands, Brown had at once hastened
to Dundee and got a vessel. As Brown's boat came up the estuary,
it also stopped off Gravesend, waiting for the change of tide. The
two boats, as Brown later said, were little more than a stone's
throw from each other.

4

At Gravesend a young woman of about eighteen—a Miss Cotterell—boarded the *Maria Crowther* for Italy. This "very sweet girl,"
as Severn described her, was apparently dying of consumption;
and the effect on Keats was unfortunate. Months before—as when
Keats went with his ill friend, James Rice, to the Isle of Wight, in
the hope of beginning *Lamia*—he had come to the point where
the illness of another person pressed on his imagination constantly,
bringing back to him that terrible autumn when he was living
daily with Tom from August until Tom's death on December 1,
1818.

His sympathy was immediately caught by this frail, wraithlike
young woman, and all the more because of the remarkable courage she showed. Miss Cotterell, moreover, had unfortunately
reached that state where the invalid is humanly tempted to compare notes, and she did this throughout the trip, with a great deal
of curiosity about Keats. When Severn first saw her—a "mere
shadow" but "very agreeable and ladylike"—she "looked hesitat-
ingly [as she walked on board] at Keats and myself and inquired
which was the dying man." Her opening question was a shock.
Most invalids, as Severn wrote in his journal letter to Haslam, like
to think they are worse off than others—he cited his mother's rage
when she was crossed in any argument of this sort. But this young
woman (who died in Naples a couple of years later) was the reverse; and so was Keats. "She insists on [being] better than Keats
—and Keats feels she is certainly worse than himself." The extent
to which Keats's adhesive empathy was caught by this young
woman—naturally complicating the voyage for him when he
hoped, and indeed needed, to turn his mind away from illness—is
shown by his own admission, in a letter to Mrs. Brawne (October
24) as the boat lay quarantined in the Bay of Naples, five weeks
after he had sailed:

> It has been unfortunate for me that one of the Passengers is a
> young Lady in a Consumption—her imprudence has vexed me very

much—the knowledge of her complaint—the flushings in her face, all her bad symptoms have preyed upon me—they would have done so had I been in good health. Severn now is a very good fellow but his nerves are too strong to be hurt by other people's illnesses—I remember poor Rice wore me in the same way . . .

During all these weeks, the little group was penned up in the small cabin except when some or all of them could go out on deck. One tier held berths for Keats and Severn; the second tier was for Captain Thomas Walsh and presumably the mate, though of course they were rarely in the cabin during the day; and in the third, provided with a curtain that could be drawn, were Mrs. Pidgeon and Miss Cotterell. Of the four passengers, the two who were physically well seem to have been especially disconcerted by the lack of comforts, probably because more serious matters were not occupying their minds. Mrs. Pidgeon, whom Severn calls a "brute," seems to have resented the company as well as the surroundings, and to have been completely indifferent to Miss Cotterell's condition. We could discount Severn's own remark had not Keats himself taken an "aversion" to her and apparently imitated or described her with a "bustling wit." Brown, after talking with friends (John Snook and his wife) who saw Keats when the boat came tacking westward and stopped for a while at Portsmouth harbor, told Taylor: "He likes one of the Ladies"—Miss Cotterell—"and has an aversion for the other whom he ridicules with all the bustling wit of a man in saucy health."

Severn, unprepared for this confinement, unprepared for the seriousness of Keats's own condition (he had started the voyage with the belief that a trip to Italy would completely restore Keats to health), wrung his hands, attempted to exert himself, and began gradually to rise to the unexpected demands. He hurried about the cabin and tried to help; and it is with a little self-drama that he describes the conflicting embarrassments of what was, after all, a very new situation for him. "You will like to know," he tells Haslam,

> how I have managed in respect to self—I have had a most severe task —full of contrarieties—what I did one way—was undone another— the lady passenger though in the same state as Keats—yet differing in constitution required almost every thing the opposite to him—for instance if the cabin windows were not open she would faint and remain entirely insensible 5 or 6 hours together—if the windows were open poor Keats would be taken with a cough (a violent one—

caught from this cause) and sometimes spitting of blood—now I had this to manage continually for our other passenger is a most consummate brute—she would see Miss Cotterell stiffened like a corpse; I have sometimes thought her dead—nor ever lend [her] the least aid —full a dozen times I have recovered this Lady and put her to bed— sometimes she would faint 4 times in a day yet at intervals would seem quite well—and was full of spirits—she is both young and lively —and but for her we should have had more heaviness—though much less trouble.—She has benefited by Keats advice—I used to act under him—and reduced the fainting each time.[7]

5

The weather, after they got out into open water, had become very bad. So small a brig had no alternative but to tack, and to start moving around to the southern coast of England before going down through Gibraltar. A full two weeks were to pass before the voyage really got under way.

On September 19 they were just off Dover, and the brig began tossing in the heavy sea. The two invalids, Keats and Miss Cotterell, kept their composure for a while, "but poor me!"—writes Severn—"I began to feel a waltzing on my stomach at breakfast." He quickly lost his breakfast; and after a while "Miss Cotterell followed me—then Keats who did it in a most gentlemanly manner." Later Miss Cotterell fainted, and Keats, ill in his tossing berth, continued to dictate what to do for her. The storm increased as they tacked toward Brighton. The trunks rolled back and forth across the cabin, and the water passing over the ship poured into the cabin from the skylight. Severn staggered up from his berth and then immediately "fell down from my weakness and the rolling of the ship—Keats was very calm." So the day passed, with the passengers all "pinn'd up in our beds like ghosts by day light—except Keats was himself all the time." By the next day, with the weather a little better but with the boat still tacking, the passengers in the small cabin were exhausted. Severn, completely shaken by the last two days, appears optimistic about the invalids: "Keats is without even complaining," he writes in a tone of continued wonderment, "and Miss Cotterell has a colour in her face." Meanwhile the anxious Severn records, with an attempt to regain his own confidence, that Keats "brags of my sailorship   he says could

7 II.354–355.

I have kept on my legs in the water cabin—I should have been a standing Miracle."

The boat continued to hug the southern coast, waiting for favorable winds, and on one or two occasions Captain Walsh let the passengers go ashore for a while. On September 28, by which time the boat had moved over to Portsmouth harbor, Keats and Severn landed and spent that day and night at nearby Bedhampton—at the home of John Snook (Dilke's brother-in-law), where Keats had written most of the *Eve of St. Agnes*. Here again he just missed seeing Charles Brown.[8] He and Severn also went ashore when the *Maria Crowther* lay becalmed off the Dorset coast. "For a moment he became like his former Self. He was in a part that he already knew"; and he showed Severn some of "the splendid caverns and grottos with a poet's pride."[9] Returning to the ship, he wrote down on a blank page of Shakespeare's *Poems* the "Bright star" sonnet, making a few improvements in phrase.

6

On September 30, the boat lay off the Isle of Wight, at Yarmouth.

The Isle of Wight was haunted by associations with the career in which so much hope and effort had been invested. This was where the first really great effort had begun three and a half years before—the "long Poem" that was to be written (if only as a preparation, a large and demanding exercise) under the aegis of Shakespeare. Now, as the boat lay at anchor, Keats poured out his feelings in a letter to Brown. He was becoming afraid that before long he "might become too ill to write at all." He apologizes for what might seem a dispirited tone; they have been tossed around at sea for a full two weeks without making any headway. Then he becomes very direct: "The very thing which I want to live most for will be a great occasion of my death. I cannot help it. Who can help it? Were I in health it would make me ill, and how can I bear it in my state?" In all probability he is speaking of the writing of poetry, which he had put aside with Spartan resolution months be-

[8] Brown (p. 72), returning from Scotland and not finding Keats, had gone down to Chichester, where he was staying with the older Dilkes. (Brown's house was still being rented to his summer tenants.)

[9] Either at Lulworth Cove or more probably Holworth Bay (see Gittings, *The Mask of Keats* [1956], p. 84).

fore. One thinks back to the "Ode on Indolence"—that last figure of the three that passed before him, "maiden most unmeek . . . my demon Poesy." We are also free to assume, indeed the incurably sentimental are quick to assume, that he refers to Fanny Brawne. Yet he introduces her into the letter in a separate way, later on:

> I think without my mentioning it for my sake you would be a friend to Miss Brawne when I am dead. You think she has many faults—but, for my sake, think she has not one— —if there is any thing you can do for her by word or deed I know you will do it. I am in a state at present in which woman merely as woman can have no more power over me than stocks and stones, and yet the difference of my sensations with respect to Miss Brawne and my Sister is amazing.

"When I am dead"—the phrase starts out from the letter. It is the first really open admission. Meanwhile he goes on: he finds himself no longer thinking very much of George and Georgiana in America. But at the "thought of leaving Miss Brawne," he has

> the sense of darkness coming over me—I eternally see her figure eternally vanishing. Some of the phrases she was in the habit of using during my last nursing at Wen[t]worth place ring in my ears—Is there another Life? Shall I awake and find all this a dream? There must be we cannot be created for this sort of suffering.

Severn, who knew nothing of this letter and the feelings expressed in it, was struck by the extent to which Keats daily seemed to be recovering "that elasticity of mind and spirit . . . characteristic of both the man and the poet." Certainly Keats—from now until almost the end (indeed from the spring of 1819 until the end: in a sense perhaps from the beginning) —was exemplifying that extraordinary capacity which we so often find among the English at their best, and perhaps more frequently than among most other peoples, to grow calmer as emergency increases and demand deepens. We have noted how frequently Keats himself distinguishes between the reactions to "real" and "imaginary ills" ("the imaginary nail a man down for a sufferer . . . the real spur him up into an agent"),[10] and among his parting words to his sister was the remark that, however exasperating her dealings with Abbey, the difficulties were still the sort that "tempt you to employ your imagination on them, rather than endeavour to dismiss them

10 See, e.g., II.113, 181, 186, 210, 329–330.

entirely." The capacity to feed upon "imaginary ills," but with a restlessness and anticipation kept below the surface, can result in a chronic sense of dissatisfaction, hesitations of will—even the "English melancholy" that fascinated Voltaire and Stendhal because it often seemed to arise when the problem involved nothing more than the choice of pleasures, or inner conflicts having to be debated in comfort or safety, without direct external challenge. But as demands strike more sharply, frivolity and querulousness evaporate; the saving integrity or wholeness that Goethe prized in many Englishmen—a bracing shake of the inner self toward unity and health—asserts itself; and the result is a new release of unpredicted energy and also, at times, a confident and refreshed calm.

All this is very much a part of Keats, who in so many ways exemplifies the English character as richly as any other poet since Shakespeare. To illustrate would be to summarize once again much of his life. Even the phrases that recur from the rather flighty Severn are typical: "he cracked his jokes at tea"; "my wit would have dropped in a moment but for Keats plying me"; Keats loses his own breakfast, but only "in the most gentlemanly manner"; everyone is sick one night, but Keats is "not even looking pale"; Severn, as the sea rushes in, falls to the floor, but "Keats was very calm"; Keats and Miss Cotterell are full of high spirits, whereas Severn and the other healthy passenger are exhausted; Keats cheers up the fainting Severn by saying complimentary things about Severn's growing gift for "sailorship."

7

At last, around October 2—a full two weeks after the boat had left the wharf at London—favorable winds appeared, and the *Maria Crowther* sailed out of the Channel past Land's End and down toward Gibraltar. A bad storm arose in the Bay of Biscay. For three days it seemed that the boat might be lost. All this time the four passengers had no help and little food, and the sea kept coming into the cabin. Keats tried to keep up the spirits of the others, and "even managed to indulge in his old habit of punning." As the storm waned, he began to read the shipwreck canto from Byron's *Don Juan*. Severn had apparently brought the poem along with him, and related the following incident twenty-five years later, possibly with some expansion:

Keats threw down the book and exclaimed: "this gives me the most horrid idea of human nature, that a man like Byron should have exhausted all the pleasures of the world so completely that there was nothing left for him but to laugh and gloat over the most solemn and heart-rending scenes of human misery; this storm of his is one of the most diabolical attempts ever made upon our sympathies, and I have no doubt it will fascinate thousands into extreme obduracy of heart—the tendency of Byron's poetry is based on a paltry originality, that of being new by making solemn things gay and gay things solemn." [11]

Off Cape St. Vincent, there was a dead calm of sea and wind; and as they floated near a large Portuguese man-of-war (the *San Josef*), which was also becalmed, they were startled by a shot sent immediately above the cabin. What had happened was that the *San Josef* had at first signaled the *Maria Crowther,* and then, when no one answered (Thomas Walsh, the captain, was below, shaving himself), it fired a warning shot. Walsh ran up to the deck. As the *San Josef* drifted closer, a voice hailed them in English: the man-of-war was looking for pirates and wanted to know if the English boat had seen any.[12]

As they passed the straits of Gibraltar early one morning, the African coast stretched before them golden in the haze. On deck, in a sort of reclining chair, "Keats lay entranced, and with a look of serene abstraction on his face." The mass of Gibraltar itself, as they looked back on it suffused by the morning sun, seemed like a "vast topaz." From now until they came into the Bay of Naples, the sea was easy and the weather genial. Severn sat on deck and painted a water color. He was confident that Keats was immensely improved—that Keats was as happy and cheered as Severn himself was once the heavy tossing weather was finished. "I perceived great changes in Keats for the better."

But actually—now that the immediate dangers of the sea were past, and the port in sight—Keats's reserve of effort seemed to diminish or disappear for a while. Within two days after they had passed into the gentle Mediterranean, "blood came from his stomach, with fever at night and violent perspiration." So the days passed until they came into the Bay of Naples on October 21. Severn was intoxicated by the beauty of the panorama before them—

11 Colvin, p. 496.
12 Later they learned that the boat was trying to intercept vessels going to the aid of Spain, then in a state of civil war started by Don Carlos who was attempting to get the crown (Sharp, p. 58).

the bay, the ships, the terraced gardens and vineyards, and beyond them the great majestic cone of Mt. Vesuvius, emitting its "writhing columns of smoke, golden at their sunlit fringes." Keats, roused by the scene, stared at it "with so sad a look in his eyes, with, moreover, sometimes, a starved haunting expression that bewildered me."

8

Of course Severn was bewildered, and of course there was a "starved haunting expression" on Keats's face now. The Cockney youth had read of the Bay of Naples long before he used to walk over to Enfield along the country lane from the Edmonton surgery. The verse letter to Clarke, written in that first trial of hope in Margate back in 1816, had spoken of this place. And then, in the first of the odes—the fragment of an "Ode to Maia"—there was the promise to recapture the treasured past, to rescue it for living imaginations, while at the same time looking ahead to the modern exploration of the human heart ("May I sing to thee / As thou wast hymnèd on the shores of Baiae?"—seeking to revive the "old vigour" of the classical world, while also pushing forward into the uncleared forest and future of the arts). Looking at the scene before him now of this place so long imagined, so personally felt, he froze into quietness, and with the starved look that so puzzled Severn. In the days that followed, as the boat still kept in the harbor, Severn concluded something was seriously wrong; but "so excruciating was the grief that was eating away his life that he could speak of it to no one."

It turned out that the *Maria Crowther* had to be held in quarantine for ten days. For the authorities at Naples had just heard that a small typhus epidemic existed in parts of London, and this boat from London therefore had to be watched and checked. Severn and Mrs. Pidgeon, eager to get ashore, soon became bored and finally frustrated. Miss Cotterell was now too ill to think much about the situation one way or another. But Keats, rousing himself, kept talking throughout the first day or two about "the classic Scenes he knew so well." He tried to put aside the thought of this voyage as the end of all that he most cared about, and "made live again" those scenes he had so often imagined—"that old antique world when the Greek galleys and Tyrhenian sloops brought northward strange tales of what was happening in Hellas and the mysterious East." Even Miss Cotterell seemed to breathe a fresh hope from this talk, as Keats himself, in this quarantined vessel and beset with convictions that all his hope and effort were over, seemed to Severn "to breathe an inspiration from these lovely scenes."

9

Meanwhile men in small boats came up to the side of the *Maria Crowther,* hoping to sell peaches, figs, and melons. An English fleet was anchored in the Bay. Seeing the British flag on the *Maria Crowther,* a half dozen men, commanded by a Lt. Sullivan, rowed over in a small boat. By boarding the *Maria Crowther,* they violated the laws of quarantine, and therefore they had to stay on the boat. But Lt. Sullivan and his men enjoyed the enforced idleness. In fact Sullivan "made himself quite at home." This proved a help to Keats. For Keats, by this time, was understandably beginning to exhaust his capacity to interest the others by trying to describe the classic associations of the Bay of Naples (all of them now crossed with a finality he could never even begin to express—would not want to express, could not let himself dwell on). The challenge to his ready sympathy provided by a new person, a new demand, was such that Keats, said Severn, suddenly "became much better, and indeed revived to be almost like himself."

Shortly afterwards the passengers had still another visitor, the brother of Miss Cotterell (Charles Cotterell, now a member of a banking firm in Naples). Learning how much Keats had done to help his sister during the voyage, Cotterell was "unbounded in his direct kindness to Keats and myself," wrote Severn, and arranged to have brought to the passengers all the fresh food that he could —fresh fruit, chicken, and fish. "All kinds of chaff went on, and Keats was not behind Mr. Cotterell or Lieutenant Sullivan in witty puns and remarks." Keats was later to admit, in his last letter to Brown (November 30), that while they were quarantined he "summoned up more puns, in a sort of desperation, in one week than in any year of my life."

But as the boat lay in quarantine, Keats—who had written to no one for weeks—also wanted to try to tell somebody what this long journey was like, this journey that had been affecting him hourly in so many ways for so many weeks. He could not bring himself to write directly to Fanny Brawne now. He was convinced this was the end. Instead he wrote to her mother to tell her briefly what had happened, thus writing to Fanny vicariously. They have reached Naples, he tells her, and now lie in quarantine. The sea air has helped, but this was counterbalanced by confinement most of the time in the stifling little cabin.

> Give my love to Fanny and tell her, if I were well there is enough in this Port of Naples to fill a quire of Paper—but it looks like a dream—every man who can row his boat and walk and talk seems a different being from myself . . . I am—at this moment I am suffering from indigestion . . . O what an account I could give you of the Bay of Naples if I could once more feel myself a Citizen of this world.

He sends his regards to the Dilkes, and signs the letter. But of course the letter is really meant for Fanny, though he cannot write to her directly. What could he say? How could he begin to tell her all that he had been feeling during these weeks? He hastily wrote his last direct message to her by adding a postscript, with no explanation: "Good bye Fanny! God bless you."

10

For still another week the boat remained in quarantine. Then the passengers were finally allowed to go ashore, on October 31.

It was Keats's birthday; and he was going ashore, to a coast about which he had imagined so much and for so long, on the day that he reached the age of twenty-five. Keats and Severn got rooms at the Villa di Londra, in the vico S. Giuseppe—by far the simplest of the three hotels where Englishmen generally stayed in Naples. In fact, as compared with the others, it was hardly a hotel at all. It was listed at the time as only a *trattoria* (that is, a light restaurant), with some furnished rooms for transients.[13] From this *trattoria,* with its few rooms, Keats wrote to Brown the next day (November 1). And in his letter he poured out the accumulated feelings of six weeks—of the whole voyage, of the long delay along the English coast because of the weather, of the long quarantine that followed the trip, of all this time that he had tried to get out of himself, had tried to help Miss Cotterell, had been "full of his

[13] The principal hotel was the Grand Bretagne (276 della Riviera di Chiaia), and after that a *locanda,* the Isole Britanniche, near the Piazza Vittoria. For this information, and for information about the Villa di Londra, I am indebted to Signor Gino Doria, Chairman of the Art Galleries of Naples and Campania.

waggery," and had talked—heartbreakingly—of the classic scenes
before them in the Bay of Naples:

> I am well enough this morning to write to you a short calm let-
> ter;—if that can be called one, in which I am afraid to speak of what
> I would the fainest dwell upon. As I have gone thus far into it, I
> must go on a little;—perhaps it may relieve the load of WRETCH-
> EDNESS which presses upon me. The persuasion that I shall see her
> no more will kill me. I cannot q—— [Brown here makes a note: "He
> could not go on with this sentence, nor even write the word 'quit,'
> —as I suppose. The word WRETCHEDNESS above he himself
> wrote in large characters."] My dear Brown, I should have had her
> when I was in health, and I should have remained well. I can
> bear to die—I cannot bear to leave her. Oh, God! God! God! Every
> thing I have in my trunk that reminds me of her goes through me
> like a spear. The silk lining she put in my travelling cap scalds my
> head. My imagination is horribly vivid about her—I see her—I hear
> her . . . My dear Brown, what am I to do?

What could he do? "I will endeavour to bear my miseries patiently." He thinks of his sister, for whom he has felt so much responsibility. He has not written to her; he cannot write to anyone
else for the time being. Will Brown therefore write to her at Abbey's, and tell her that he has heard from her brother? Finally,

> Is there any news of George? O, that something fortunate had
> ever happened to me or my brothers!—then I might hope,—but de-
> spair is forced upon me as a habit. My dear Brown, for my sake, be
> her advocate for ever. I cannot say a word about Naples; I do not
> feel at all concerned in the thousand novelties around me. I am
> afraid to write to her. I should like her to know that I do not for-
> get her. Oh, Brown, I have coals of fire in my breast. It surprised me
> that the human heart is capable of containing and bearing so much
> misery.

Keats showed little to Severn of what he was really feeling. Severn, for his part, wrote cheerfully to William Haslam that they had
a room above the *trattoria* that looked out to Vesuvius: "Keats has
become calm—and thinks favorably of this place." The weather is
"cold—wet and foggy." It was while Severn was saying this that
Keats was writing his letter to Brown. The next day, wrote Severn, Keats seemed "much recover'd." In fact "he made an Italian
pun today." A copy of Richardson's *Clarissa Harlowe* had been
brought along by Severn. Keats read the nine small volumes of it
rapidly while they were staying in the Villa di Londra. Severn naturally wanted to see the city, and Keats went with him to a per-

formance at the San Carlo theater. The sentries present at the performance depressed Keats. This was new to his experience. He told Severn he wanted to hurry along to Rome. He did not wish to be "buried" among a people so politically abject.

The very next day Keats again received a letter from the generous-hearted Shelley. But their plans were fixed. They wanted to go at once to Rome, where, in the English colony, there was a physician who was expecting Keats; and Keats, after arriving in Naples, had written ahead to him.

Rome and the Last Months

November 1820 to February 1821

CHARLES COTTRELL held a small farewell dinner party for Keats and Severn on November 6 or 7. However Keats felt, he was determined to attend, and during it, said Severn, made "a special effort and was very entertaining."

The next day they started for Rome in a *vettura*—a small hired carriage. So slow was their progress along the bad roads and so beautiful was the season that Severn got out of the carriage and walked beside it most of the time until they reached the outskirts of Rome. And when the wild flowers were profuse, he would pick some of them and put them into the little carriage. Keats had now "become very listless, and seldom seemed even relatively happy." The effort he had made throughout the seven weeks' trip had exhausted him. The constant jolting of the carriage caused him great discomfort, and the food—for they were trying to travel very cheaply —was execrable. Still there were moments when Keats would look up with the old self-forgetfulness—moments when "a fine prospect opened before us," or when the odor of the growing plants was brought to them in a strong breeze, or when Severn "literally filled the little carriage with flowers." Then, a week after they had left Naples, they came into the Campagna—the large plain around the city of Rome—and saw a cardinal, with two footmen in livery, shooting birds. The sight fascinated Severn and Keats. This country seemed to contrast vividly with England. They entered Rome by the Lateran Gate, and came immediately upon the Colosseum, so different in its setting then, surrounded by small cottages, covered with ivy—a vast ruin on what was still the outer edge of a small city (a city of about 130,000, less than a twelfth of its present population, and covering less than a quarter of the present area).

Meanwhile (November 8) George Keats had been writing his

brother from Louisville. "Again, and Again I must send bad news." For his second or remaining steamboat (the first being the one lost on the Ohio) , he has not yet found a buyer. His new lumber mill has not been finished in time to bring the returns he had hoped to forward to Keats. Every day he is in the woods, "superintending the felling of Trees and cutting saw-logs." He also has a new firm set up: "Geo. Keats & Co." His partners are accomplished ironworkers. Money will soon be forthcoming. Keats never received the letter. It came to Hampstead (probably in early January, 1821) as Keats lay dying in Rome. The letter was sent from Louisville a week after Keats had written to Brown: "Is there any news of George? O, that something fortunate had ever happened to me or my brothers!—then I might hope,—but despair is forced upon me as a habit."

2

Back in August, at the suggestion of Dr. Darling, Taylor and Hessey had written about Keats to a young Scottish physician in Rome, Dr. James Clark (later Sir James Clark) .[1] After the *Maria Crowther* reached Naples, Keats wrote ahead to Dr. Clark to say he had arrived and to ask his help in finding lodgings. Clark, then a man of thirty-two, was kindly and shrewd. He liked music, and had a good library of musical scores. He seems to have tried beforehand to find out something about his new patient. In order to be as near as possible to Keats, Clark secured for him and Severn an apartment of two small but pleasant rooms, just vacated by an English doctor, in a house (No. 26) across the street from where he himself lived in the Piazza di Spagna. These famous rooms, together with two others that adjoin them, now contain the library of the Keats-Shelley Memorial House, to which five or six thousand visitors come each year.[2]

The area around the Piazza di Spagna, a favorite residence for foreigners and especially for the English, was one of the most pleasant in Rome. It was relatively quiet, for it lay at what was then the very northern edge of the city. In the center of the Piazza stood the boat-shaped fountain by Pietro Bernini; and throughout much of

1 He returned to London in 1826, and became, in time, physician to Queen Victoria, who made him a baronet in 1837. He retired from practice in 1860, and died ten years later at the age of eighty-two.

2 For help with much of the material in this chapter, I am indebted to Signora Vera Cacciatore, the Curator of the Keats-Shelley Memorial House.

the day, and especially during the night, the constant play of water could be heard by the inhabitants of the surrounding houses. The great stairs (the English were later to call them the "Spanish Steps") that swept up from the Piazza to the church of the Trinità dei Monti, as well as the two houses (Nos. 23 and 26) on each side of the foot of the steps, had been built in the 1720's, a gift of the French government. Immediately north of the church of the Trinità, the countryside began. No. 26, at the right-hand side of the stairs, had been a lodging house for years; and of the next ten houses, all were completely given over to apartments and rented rooms except for No. 30, the shop of a saddle maker, and No. 33, a stable for coaches and horses.

The landlady of No. 26, Anna Angeletti—a woman of forty-three who originally came from Venice—has been rather brusquely treated. For Severn, timid by nature and uneasy lest she discover the nature of Keats's illness—which could admittedly have serious consequences—lived in dread of the "old Cat," as he once called her. A friendlier as well as ampler description is given in the diary of the peripatetic Rev. Robert Finch, who had stayed in the house in 1815. Looking for an apartment, Finch "called on Signor Vasi, who has a magazine of books and engravings here" (most of the shops in and near the Piazza "belong to print-sellers, and Artists in Mosaic") ; and Vasi then

> directed me to his niece, Signora Angeletti, with whom I have fix'd my abode. It is No. 26, Piazza di Spagna at the corner of the steps leading up to the church of Santa Trinita del Monte, and I pay 19s. a week for four rooms, elegantly furnish'd. The neatness, which distinguishes every thing about the Signora, is truly charming; and is rare in this country. Her husband has been for some years in Portugal, and has quite neglected her. She is a lively, smart, handsome little woman, and has two nice daughters, who scarcely appear younger than their mother. She has much taste for the fine arts, & draws and engraves.[3]

From the thorough census taken each February or March by the Vatican, we can fill out the picture a little more, and also learn something of the other lodgers at the time Keats and Severn lived there. Anna's husband, Alessandro (also an engraver) , died sometime earlier in 1820 (he had probably returned by then to Rome) . Of the two daughters, Lucrezia appears to have married and left

---

[3] Bodleian Mss. Finch e.15, f.60 and 63; e 16, f.60. Cf. Elizabeth Nitchie, *The Reverend Colonel Finch* (1940) , pp. 47-48.

home in 1819, at the age of twenty-one. Virginia, five years younger, married in 1820, but remained in the house with her husband, Nicolo Palmieri. Signora Angeletti, her daughter and son-in-law, and a serving woman lived in the back rooms of the first two floors. Thomas Gibson, an elderly Englishman, occupied the front rooms of the first floor. Immediately above him were Keats and Severn—Keats's room was on the corner facing the Spanish Steps. On the third floor a young Irishman of twenty-five, James O'Hara, lived in one apartment, and an Italian army officer of twenty-seven, Giuseppe d'Alia, in the other.[4]

The rent was unexpectedly high for Keats and Severn—probably around £8.5 a month (or about £41 in present-day money).[5] This did not include the cost of food. They had been told that prices generally were lower than in England. But they were living in a rather fashionable district where the average tenant was far better off financially than they. The two young men were the only people in the house, for example, who lacked a personal servant.[6] But the place was well furnished, as Finch says. After Finch left, Signora Angeletti referred specifically in a letter to the rooms that Keats and Severn later took. She was writing to thank Finch for recommending her place to a Mr. Brown, whose arrival she was awaiting. She then goes on: "as the second floor . . . is vacant, I thought I would furnish it as nicely as possible for visitors, and there is now comfortable accommodation for two friends or a family." One of Finch's friends who later stayed there spoke with pleasure of the "festoons of Roses & the Carpeted floors," and the roses are doubtless those that can still be seen on the ceilings of the second floor.[7] According to the census, Anna Angeletti continued to own the house until 1825. She then sold it, moved with her daughter and son-in-law to a fourth-floor apartment in No. 29, and within three years had either died or left Rome.

[4] "Stato dell'Anime (S. Andrea delle Fratte)," in the *Archivio Segreto Vaticano*.

[5] For his four rooms in 1815, Finch paid "19s a week" (the "s" refers to scudi, not shillings). If we assume that, for their two rooms, Keats and Severn paid at least half that, the amount would have come to £8.12 (or 43 scudi) a month for them both. Hence Severn's remark to Taylor (*KC*, I.184) that lodging cost £4.16 a month probably refers to the amount that they each paid. This would be slightly less than the average rent for rooms in the Piazza di Spagna, which, said Finch, tended as a rule to run from a minimum of 20 piastres monthly, presumably for one room, to about 70.

[6] Gibson had a French valet, Jean Montbrun, and O'Hara and d'Alia each had Italian manservants.

[7] Joanna Richardson, *The Times*, February 2, 1953.

Dr. Clark immediately did all that he could to help his new patient. But so shattered did Keats seem to him, and in such a number of ways, that for a while Clark felt unable to make a diagnosis.
He began to wonder whether the basic trouble was not some disease of the stomach—even of the heart—rather than of the lungs.
Consumptives were always coming to Italy—he had seen any number of them—but they were usually attenuated, frail, withdrawn.
This was by no means the case with Keats, ill as he was. It seemed
that some fearful nervous complaint was shaking him.

It catches our interest that so intelligent a man as Clark should
have begun to speculate in the same way that Rodd and Dr. Bree
had done months before. There were, of course, no physical tests
for tuberculosis. The lungs could be almost completely destroyed,
and the physician might conceivably be unaware of it until an autopsy. What was happening was that, in Keats's protest against the
disease that was killing him, he was not at all behaving, to Clark's
mind, as consumptives generally seemed to do. To begin with, the
alarm Keats felt at the frustration of hopes that had been a part of
him since adolescence was so strong that it cut through the familiar temptations of the late consumptive to fatigue and ennui.
At the same time, Keats was instinctively trying to muffle this very
alarm through still another effort. Even if we leave aside the strain
on him that had begun in the summer and autumn of 1818—that
had begun with the sore throat during the Scottish tour, had been
sharpened during the three months Tom was dying, and had continued throughout the next year—even if we leave that year aside,
the alternations of apprehension and determination that became a
daily occurrence in the autumn of 1819, after he had given up the
hope of writing poetry, tried to find other work, and then been
forced to give that up too, had taken a heavy toll on what physicians in a later generation were to call the sympathetic nervous
system. A vivid proof was that violent "palpitation of the heart"
months ago, in late February and March, when, as he lay trying
desperately to put poetry, ambition, and Fanny Brawne out of his
mind, suddenly an early thrush had appeared, bringing back to
him those weeks after the "Negative Capability" letter and their
vista of a new beginning ("There's the thrush again—I can't afford it—he'll run me up a pretty Bill for Music"). There was
nothing organically wrong with his heart, as Bree had said; and
Dr. Clark, like Dr. Bree, was unfamiliar with this strong a protest,

a protest that was also suppressed and therefore intensified (as Clark began to guess) by a manly reticence. "Noble," in fact, was the word that Clark began to use about his patient. On November 27, a week after Keats arrived, Clark wrote a tentative statement to an agent of Taylor and Hessey's firm:

> The chief part of his disease, as far as I can yet see seems seated in his Stomach. I have some suspicion of disease of the heart and it may be of the lungs, but of this say nothing to his friends as in my next I shall be able to give you something more satisfactory. His mental exertions and application have I think been the sources of his complaints—If I can put his mind at ease I think he'll do well—get Mr Taylor or some of his friends to write him. I'm afraid the Idea of his expenses operates on his mind and some plan must be adopted to remove this if possible. The truth is, having come abroad for the purpose of restoring his health, every thing must be done to favor the ch[ange] of climate— . . . he's too noble an animal to be allowed to sink without some sacrifice being made to save him. I wish I were rich enough his living here should cost him nothing. He has a friend with him who seems very attentive to him but between you & I is not the best suited for his companion, but I suppose poor fellow he had no choice. I fear much there is something operating on his mind—at least so it appears to me—he either feels that he is now living at the expence of some one else or something of that kind.[8]

3

Though Clark forbade Keats to go sightseeing, confident that it would excite him too much, he encouraged him to walk around the neighborhood. The Pincian Hill, immediately north of the Spanish Steps, was a favorite promenade for both Romans and visitors. There, within a few days, Keats and Severn met a young English army officer who also had consumption, Lt. Isaac Marmaduke Elton of the Royal Engineers (he died in Switzerland about two and a half years later).[9] Clark thought it would help Keats's

---

[8] *KC,* I.172.

[9] On their walks they frequently met the notorious Pauline Buonaparte, sister of Napoleon and wife of the Prince Borghese (from whom she lived apart in the nearby Villa Paulina): "Canova had just done a nude statue from her, which we went to see, and thought it 'beautiful bad taste.' It was Keats gave this statue its lasting name, 'The Æolian Harp.' But among other virtues which distinguished this eminent lady was a quick eye for a handsome figure and fine features, and hence it came about that she cast languishing glances upon Lieutenant Elton each time we encountered her. At last this so jarred upon Keats's nerves, though he thankfully acknowledged that he was not the attraction, that we were obliged to go and take our walk in another place. Elton gladly enough acquiesced, for, as I have said, he too was con-

chest and stomach if he rode horseback a little. A horse was therefore hired at a cost that seemed exorbitant (£6 a month); and when the weather permitted, Keats rode at a snail's pace for an hour or two, often in the company of Lt. Elton. Occasionally he would walk slowly down the Corso for a short distance from the house, looking at the shops.

But with every day, he was finding it more difficult to leave the room at the corner of the Spanish Steps. As soon as he had arrived in Italy, he had insisted on using some of the little money he had in order to buy a few Italian books, including a volume of Alfieri. He was determined to continue learning the language, and was by now, ill as he was, reading it rather easily. He also began to think about music, possibly because of the encouragement of Dr. Clark. Could a piano be found? From Signora Angeletti they rented one at seven scudi a month (about 28 shillings at the rate of exchange they were receiving, and about £7 a month at present values). Dr. Clark lent them volumes from his musical library, and among them several scores of Haydn. While Severn played them on their rented piano, Keats, striving desperately to concentrate, would try to follow each note. As passage followed passage, he could sometimes forget other things and rejoice in the possibilities of freedom and spontaneity that music could provide. "This Haydn," he said happily once while Severn was playing, "is like a child for there is no knowing what he will do next." Moments like this encouraged Severn immensely. But others plunged him into an abyss of despondency. And at the same time Severn was naturally beginning to think of his own future. He had no other choice. He had apparently been able to pay his own fare to Italy, but most of his expenses were now being paid from the money Taylor and Hessey had advanced Keats. Haslam and other friends had encouraged Severn to take this trip. He might, they said, with all of Rome before him, find stimulus and momentum to paint a picture that would win him three years on a Royal Academy fellowship.

Though Dr. Clark looked a little askance at Severn, he felt the pathos of the whole situation. If Severn's gifts seemed mild and his character a little flighty—perhaps too flighty to make him "suited for [Keats's] companion" in an emergency like this—yet he was "attentive" and well-meaning. Alone in this comparatively well-

---

sumptive, and shunned all excitements; and to be with us was a pleasure, for he was quite alone in Rome." (Sharp, p. 82.)

to-do English colony, he had no money, and his situation was certainly likely to become worse rather than better. Clark at once went to see John Gibson, the well-known English sculptor living in Rome, and told him of Severn. Gibson, a large-natured man, was extraordinarily kind to Severn, who called on him just as the famous English connoisseur, Lord Colchester, was also entering the studio. Shrinking back, Severn was about to leave when Gibson came forward, seized him by the arm, and brought him in with Lord Colchester. Throughout the whole visit, Gibson deliberately showed as much attention to Severn as to Lord Colchester. "I thought, 'if Gibson, who is a great artist, can afford to do such a thing as this, then Rome is the place for me.' Indeed, the act, slight as it may seem, was like sunshine to me."

Keats, hearing the story immediately afterwards, was delighted at Gibson's conduct and his readiness to help a poor and unknown artist. This, as Keats told Severn, was a "treat to humanity." People so free from littleness were (he increasingly felt) rare enough to surprise one. Moreover, if Severn had been worried about his own future and about what to do in Rome, so was Keats, always quick to think of another's situation, and anxious from the beginning lest Severn, because of a feeling of responsibility to Keats, fail to use this opportunity to get started on his own. A strong vicariousness appears in his urgent advice to the timid Severn as soon as they settled in their new rooms at the Piazza di Spagna. "Now, he urged, it was most expedient that I should lose no time in contending with my artistic enemies, and to confront them before they could do me further harm." Keats never, said Severn, "even mentioned" the *Blackwood's* attack. But on one occasion, as Severn continued to delay starting on his own work, Keats began to talk of the frightening omnipresence of envy. He divulged the story of a dinner at which William Hilton, the painter, and others had attacked Severn for having won the Academy award, whereupon Keats, after expressing his indignation at this smallness, had "abruptly left." As Keats referred to this incident now, "with his ready sympathy he placed himself in my position" and became "much agitated." His strong reaction, said Severn, reminiscing about it long afterwards, "was a marvellous contrast to his charming manner when he was tranquil. Yet though thus ever ready to speak of my small worries, he said little of his own." [10] At

10 Sharp, pp. 65–66.

Keats's urging, Severn began to make some preliminary sketches for an historical painting with eight figures, which he had discussed with Sir Thomas Lawrence and John Gibson, "The Death of Alcibiades."

4

Meanwhile food was presenting something of a problem. Within three weeks or so, when they were worrying more about money and Keats was becoming very ill indeed, Severn tried to do some of the cooking, as he tells Charles Brown (December 17) in one of his more distressed moments: "These wretched Romans have no Idea of comfort—here I am obliged to wash up—cook—& read to Keats all day—added to this I have had no letters yet from my family—this is a damp to me for I never knew how dear they were to me." But frequently, especially at the start, food was brought up from the tiny restaurant or *trattoria* that the landlady had recently opened downstairs; she may have found it difficult to supervise, since it was very soon abandoned.[11] The dinners that were sent up got progressively worse, though they were paying a full crown—about twenty-two shillings in present-day money. Admiring a resolution he himself lacked, Severn was delighted when Keats finally took the matter into his own hands. In his old age, Severn described the incident in detail. When the porter came in one day with the basket and began to lay out the dinner, Keats rose, and "smiling roguishly," he

> opened the window, which was over the front steps, and taking up each dish one after the other he quietly emptied the contents out of the window and returned the plate to the basket—and thus disappeared a fowl, a rice pudding, cauliflower, a dish of macaroni, &c. This was all done to the amusement of the porter and the padrona. He then quietly but very decidedly pointed to the basket for the porter to take away, which he did without demur. "Now," said Keats, "you'll see, Severn, that we'll have a decent dinner;" and sure enough in less than half-an-hour an excellent one came, and we continued to be similarly well treated every day. In the account, more-

11 The *trattoria* was in No. 27 (which occupies one half of the ground floor of the house, the other half consisting of the hall and stairway of No. 26). Early in 1820 the Angelettis were still renting No. 27 to a plaster molder. The *trattoria* was therefore opened sometime between then and the time Keats arrived. The food may have been as poor as Severn says; for the *trattoria* was closed by February 1821, when No. 27 is listed, in the "Stato dell'Anime" in the Vatican Archives, as vacant. In 1824 Signora Angeletti seems to have turned the house into a *pensione* for transients, and No. 27 was once again used as a *trattoria* and general kitchen for them.

over, the padrona was discreet enough not to charge for the dinners thrown out of the window.[12]

As November came to a close, Keats wrote to Charles Brown the last letter he was to write anyone—at least it is the last that survives; and we can assume that almost anything he wrote at this time would have been kept. He had been in Rome now for two weeks, and he had less than three months to live. He begins (November 30) :

> My dear Brown,
> 'Tis the most difficult thing in the world to me to write a letter. My stomach continues so bad, that I feel it worse on opening any book,—yet I am much better than I was in Quarantine. Then I am afraid to encounter the proing and conning of any thing interesting to me in England. I have an habitual feeling of my real life having past, and that I am leading a posthumous existence. God knows how it would have been—but it appears to me—however, I will not speak of that subject . . . I am so weak (in mind) that I cannot bear the sight of any hand writing of a friend I love so much as I do you. Yet I ride the little horse,—and, at my worst, even in Quarantine, summoned up more puns, in a sort of desperation, in one week than in any year of my life. There is one thought enough to kill me —I have been well, healthy, alert &c, walking with her—and now— the knowledge of contrast, feeling for light and shade, all that information (primitive sense) necessary for a poem are great enemies to the recovery of the stomach. There, you rogue, I put you to the torture,—but you must bring your philosophy to bear—as I do mine, really—or how should I be able to live? Dr Clarke is very attentive to me; he says, there is very little the matter with my lungs, but my stomach, he says, is very bad. I am well disappointed in hearing good news from George,—for it runs in my head we shall all die young.

Severn, he goes on, is well, "though he leads so dull a life with me." Would Brown write to George and "tell him how I am, so far as you can guess." And would Brown also, he ends, write

> a note to my sister—who walks about my imagination like a ghost— she is so like Tom. I can scarcely bid you good bye even in a letter. I always made an awkward bow.
>
> God bless you!
John Keats

5

Then on December 10, a week and a half after Keats wrote this final letter, he had a fearful hemorrhage, vomiting blood and sink-

12 Sharp, p. 67.

ing back with the haunted look of which Severn speaks. Dr. Clark came at once and, not knowing what else to do, drew still more blood from Keats's arm.

After four days had passed, Severn found a moment in which to begin a letter to Brown,[13] stating that this relapse was "most unlooked for" (Severn had been confident that Keats was "convalescing"). But Severn suddenly had to put aside the letter he had just begun. Keats was becoming much worse. Finally, another three days later, at four in the morning, Severn again had a free moment; and in the room next to Keats, he tried to take up for Brown the story of what had been happening:

> Not a moment can I be from him—I sit by his bed and read all day —and at night I humour him in all his wanderings. he has just fallen asleep—the first for 8 nights, and now from mere exhaustion. I hope he will not wake until I have written this, for I am anxious beyond measure to have you know this worse and worse state—yet I dare not let him see I think it dangerous.—I had seen him wake on the morning of this attack, and to all appearance he was going on merrily and had unusual good spirits—when in an instant a Cough seized him, and he vomited near two Cup-fuls of blood.—In a moment I got Dr Clarke, who saw the manner of it, and immediately took away about 8 ounces of blood from the Arm.

Keats was "much alarmed" at the appearance of the blood ("black and thick in the extreme"):

> He rush'd out of bed and said "this day shall be my last"—and but for me most certainly it would. At the risk of losing his confidence I took every destroying mean from his reach, nor let him be from my sight one minute. The blood broke forth again in like quantity the next morning—and the doctor thought it expedient to take away the like quantity of blood—this was in the same dismal state, and must have been from the horrible state of despair he was in.

The ninth day after the hemorrhage, there was still

> no change for the better—five times the blood has come up in coughing, in large quantities generally in the morning—and nearly the whole time his saliva has been mixed with it—but this is the lesser evil when compared with his Stomach—not a single thing will digest —the torture he suffers all and every night—and best part of the day —is dreadful in the extreme—the distended stomach keeps him in perpetual hunger or craving—and this is augmented by the little nourishment he takes to keep down the blood—Then his mind is worse than all—despair in every shape—his imagination and memory

[13] II.361–363.

present every image in horror, so strong that morning and night I tremble for his Intellect.

All of his past kept coming back to him now, in a constant round of despair as he looked before him with "staring glassy eyes": "O he will mourn over every circumstance." For a while his mind especially returned to his sister, virtually imprisoned by Abbey out at Walthamstow. Would Severn write and ask Mrs. Brawne and Mrs. Dilke to go and visit her?

He was put on a starvation diet—a little bread and milk and an occasional mouthful of fish. Clark's thought was to check the flow of blood by drastically limiting Keats's food. As a result, said Severn, "Every day he raves that he will die from hunger—and I was obliged to give him more than allowed—You cannot think how dreadful this is for me—the Doctor on the one hand tells me I shall kill him to give him more than he allows." In general, Dr. Clark "will not say much—although there is no bounds to his attention." Clark was coming over four or five times a day. Once he himself "went all over Rome for a certain kind of fish, and got it— but just as I received it from Mrs C[lark] delicately prepared, Keats was taken by the spitting of blood," and was as ill as he had been the night of December 10.

So it continued, with a slight improvement just after Christmas; and occasionally Keats went out-of-doors for a short while into the sunshine. But on January 3 Dr. Clark again wrote to Taylor and Hessey, and spoke of the constant bleeding from the lungs. Keats is now "in a most deplorable state":

> His stomach is ruined and the state of his mind is the worst possible for one in his condition, and will undoubtedly hurry on an event that I fear is not far distant and even in the best frame of mind would not probably be long protracted. His digestive organs are sadly deranged and his lungs are also diseased—either of these would be a great evil, but to have both under the state of mind which he unfortunately is in must soon kill him. I fear he has long been governed by his imagination & feelings & now has little power & less inclination to endeavour to keep them under. I feel much interested in the poor fellow indeed—it is most distressing to see a mind like his (what it might have been) in the deplorable state in which it is. His friend Mr Severn is most attentive to him. Were Christianity of no use but to give tranquillity to the sick bed it were the greatest blessing on earth.[14]

14 II.366–367.

Money, moreover, had once again become a painful problem. The letter of credit for £150 that Taylor and Hessey had given Keats was to the famous banking house of the Messrs. Torlonia. Stendhal later described them as "the bankers of all the English who came to Rome," from whom "they make enormous profits in changing pounds sterling for Roman scudi or crowns"; and Stendhal went on to speak of the indignation of the rich English lords after their dealings with "the cold and tranquil banker," Prince Alessandro Torlonia.[15] However Torlonia may have dealt with the English aristocracy (Stendhal implies that he used to placate such clients by holding large dinners and balls) , his firm gave Keats a very favorable rate of exchange.[16] But Torlonia could offer this favorable rate only if a large sum were drawn. He also reminded Keats that there was a fee for each transaction—that one large transfer would be cheaper than repeated small ones.

Hence, on Torlonia's advice, Keats had drawn a total of £120 the day he had arrived in Rome (November 15) , and he had then deposited it in the bank in Italian money. But Taylor and Hessey were completely unprepared for this. They had assumed that Keats would be drawing only small sums at a time, and were meanwhile expecting George Keats to send John money at any moment. As soon as they received the bill for £120, they at once wrote to Torlonia to stop further payment. Torlonia did so. When Severn heard that Torlonia had stopped payment, he became frantic. How were they to live? He implored Dr. Clark, who had begun to advance money from his own pocket, to write to Taylor and Hessey. Severn felt that a letter from Clark would be received with more understanding than one from himself. Clark did write, and the letter produced an immediate effect.

No sooner did Taylor get this news than he at once began to raise a subscription for Keats, in the meantime writing to Torlonia to resume payment. Five friends and acquaintances at once sent £10 apiece. Woodhouse jotted down the names, and does not mention his own probable contribution (£50)—of which we can guess from a letter of Taylor to his father.[17] Finally the Earl Fitz-

15 *Promenades dans Rome,* ed. Caraccio (1938) , I.195.

16 For £120, Torlonia gave him 552 scudi. See the bank account published in *KSMB,* No. 2 (1913) . This is a cost of only four shillings per scudo. Theoretically the rate was five.

17 Woodhouse Ms., Morgan Library. See *KC,* I.207. The five subscribers of £10 each were Rice, John Percival (a friend of Taylor's at Oxford) , William Hilton, Peter Dewint, and Joseph Bonsor (*KC,* I.235) .

william, whom Taylor knew well, sent £50. But this total of £150 was collected only in early February; it would take another three weeks for news of it to arrive; and Keats was dead by the end of the month. Meanwhile Charles Brown had written to Severn that he was convinced that much of Keats's unhappiness was owing to the way "George has treated him. I sit planning schemes of vengeance upon his head." Brown had also told Mrs. Brawne of the latest news he had received from Severn. Fanny Brawne, he said, was aware of what was happening: "I understand she says to her mother, 'I believe he must soon die, and when you hear of his death, tell me immediately. I am not a fool.' " Fanny was trying to meet this situation "with great firmness, mournfully but without affectation."

6

Severn, at Keats's request, had in the meantime himself written to Mrs. Brawne (January 11). He was unable to make the letter reassuring. Severn was thoroughly frightened by now, with everything converging on him, and his tone reminds us a little of George's remark about "the complaining Severn":

> For Three weeks I have never left him—I have sat up at night—I have read to him nearly all day & even in the night—I light the fire, make his breakfast & sometimes am obliged to cook—make his bed and even sweep the room. I can have these things done, but never at the time when they ought & must be done—so that you will see my alternative—What enrages me most is making a fire I blow—blow— for an hour—the smoke comes fuming out—my kettle falls over on the burning sticks—no stove—Keats calling me to be with him—the fire catching my hands & the door bell ringing—all these to one quite unused and not at all capable—with the want of every proper material come not a little galling— [18]

Then there was the new fright of money. Needless to say, he had now given up all thought of working on his picture, though, unless he submitted a painting by the following summer, he had no chance of competing for the Royal Academy's traveling fellowship. (It is pleasant to know that he did complete the picture, received

[18] *KC*, I.189. This is one of the passages that particularly irritated Isabella Jones when Taylor showed her Severn's letters to himself, Mrs. Brawne, Haslam, and Brown. "I never saw so much egotism and selfishness displayed under the mask of feeling and friendship," she writes; and she ridicules Severn's undeniable tendency to dramatize his sufferings (such as his attempt to light the kettle—"what enrages me most is making a fire . . . my kettle falls") while Keats was in the condition that he was. (See her letter to Taylor, printed in Gittings, pp. 231–233.)

the fellowship, married very well, and lived a relatively happy life until his death at the age of eighty-six.) [19]

To complicate matters still further, Signora Angeletti had guessed the nature of Keats's illness, and, as she was required to do, had informed the police. If English medicine still doubted that tuberculosis was contagious, Italian physicians did not; and it was now a law in Rome, in fact in most of Italy, that everything in a room occupied by a consumptive must be burned after his death. The problem was that Keats wanted desperately to have a change of scene, to get out of his small bedroom for a while, and move into the next room—a somewhat larger room used as a kind of parlor, vestibule, and emergency kitchen, where Severn also slept. Dr. Clark, too, thought this a good idea. But in this larger room were the newly hired piano, Severn's few painting materials, the books they had bought, a sofa, and other furniture. These would all be burned later if it were known that Keats had been moved into the room. The property was worth at least £150. How could Keats be moved into it without the landlady's knowing it—and, at the same time, without Keats's knowing anything of the difficulties and complications?

Severn tried to think of a ruse. This gentle optimist lacked cunning, but he realized that the important thing was to keep Signora Angeletti and her servant from entering while Keats was in the larger room. His mind filled with terrors and the unpredictabilities of the future, himself penniless in Rome and in a situation he had never expected, the desperate Severn first of all blocked up the door by moving furniture before it, piling one thing on another. This had to be done silently in order not to arouse the curiosity of anyone, including Keats. To know the reason for all this deception, and of the situation that Severn would be in after

---

19 The fellowship (awarded him in November 1821) brought him £130 annually for three years, and his travel expenses to Rome were refunded (Sharp, p. 113). He remained in Italy for several years more, securing the Countess of Westmorland as patroness and marrying her ward, Elizabeth Montgomerie (1828), daughter of the late General Archibald, Lord Montgomerie. The Countess of Westmorland strongly disapproved of the marriage. ("I make a point," Severn told his sister a couple of years after Keats's death, "never to know anyone who is not superior to me in fortune or ability, or some way or other, that I may still be raising myself and improving, even in moments of pastime.") Of Severn's six children, three became known as artists, Walter, Arthur, and Ann (the wife of Sir Charles Newton). After twenty-one years in Rome, Severn returned to England (1841) and continued his painting. Then, at the age of sixty-seven, he returned to Rome as British consul, and died some eighteen years later (1879). For a summary of his later years, see *KC*, I.cxxxvi–cxxxviii.

his death, would have distressed Keats beyond measure. "The greatest difficulty was in keeping all from him." When Severn had moved the furniture as quietly as possible, he made up a bed on the sofa, opened the door to Keats's room, and slowly carried Keats in to it. Severn had gone without dinner while making these arrangements, and told Keats that, while he himself was out dining, a servant had come in and arranged the room for this purpose. He believed that Keats "half suspected" what had happened. But Keats, whatever his suspicions and thoughts, now remained silent. He did not embarrass Severn with questions.

7

By the middle of January Keats was again so ill that Dr. Clark put him on an allowance of "a single anchovy a day, with a morsel of bread." The thought again was to give him so little sustenance that the lungs would not bleed profusely. But the lungs did bleed again, and this "threw Keats back to the blackest despair."

Keats now expected, he told Severn, a death that might drag on for months; and at least some of his anxiety was for Severn, who had come with him on so hopeless a journey. But he had planned ahead for this. He had a "foreseen resource"—the bottle of laudanum he had persuaded Severn to buy at Gravesend. He wanted it now. Severn was appalled. Then Keats began to "claim it as his own and his right." If he was going to die, why should he not be allowed to die speedily? Keats continued to argue:

> As my death is certain, I only wish to save you from the long miseries of attending and beholding it. It may yet be deferred, and I can see that you will thereby be stranded through your lack of resources, and that you will ruin all your prospects. I am keeping you from your painting, and as I am sure to die, why not let me die now?

The argument continued intermittently throughout the day. Then Keats began to rage helplessly at Severn: he had long ago, he said, foreseen

> this fatal prospect—the dismal nights—the impossibility of receiving any sort of comfort—and above all the wasting of his body and helplessness—these he had determined on escaping—and but for me—he would have swallowed this draught 3 Months since—in the ship—he says 3 wretched months I have kept him alive—and for it—no name —no treatment—no privations can be too bad for me.[20]

20 Sharp, p. 84, and II.372.

After two days of bitter contention, Severn turned to Dr. Clark and confided all that had happened. Severn, for his part, was ready to surrender the bottle of laudanum. Clark quietly took it away with him. Keats then became "silent and resigned," but the next day Keats looked searchingly at Clark as he entered, and asked, "How long is this posthumous life of mine to last?"

8

The moments were increasing when, as Severn wrote, despite that "exquisite sensibility for every one save his poor self," Keats —who by now had virtually lost both lungs, and was in addition almost starving—began forgivably to wonder what he had done amiss.

He had even begun to wonder whether the attempt to help others over the years had brought on this state: "all his own means & comfort expended upon others—almost in vain—he would contrast with his present suffering—and say that all was brought on by them—and he was right." [21]

This turning against sympathy, in the need to find some explanation, is the most distressing single thing about the death of Keats. Had there been some terrible mistake of emphasis, of concern? He needed an answer as the round of helpless questioning continued, every few minutes, throughout these long weeks. Here was Severn, himself giving up so much in order to help a dying man; and what would be his reward?—to be left penniless and helpless in Rome. And, in Keats's own experience, that total commitment of the heart and imagination to all that could be suggested by the word "sympathy" (that word of which Hazlitt— whose writing was one of the three things in the age to "rejoice at"—had been so fond) : had it imposed an impossible toll on him, biologically or physically, and had there even been something morally askew about it, something that did not fit at all into the frame of things?

Certainly that commitment to sympathetic openness, that commitment to what is outside the prison house of oneself, had been naive at first—in the Enfield days, and later during the time at Guy's Hospital (so filled with the thought of the "genius-loving heart"). Of course it had been naive then, and even after it had

21 *KC*, I.188.

been lifted to another level, even after Haydon had helped to increase his intoxication with the ideal of greatness and, for over a year, Keats had saturated himself with Shakespeare. But then, in the year that followed, his attempt to understand—to think more "into the human heart" and its context—had qualified and developed the nature and predicament of that commitment. The great poems of 1819 (and the unrivaled letters of 1818 and 1819) had been new and far more informed attempts to understand the "Burden of the Mystery," the "Vale of Soul-Making." But were these too a little silly and excessive? It was certainly a concept or approach at complete variance with the way in which the Lockharts and Giffords of the world got through life. And where were they now? Probably succeeding. He could not let himself think about it: he could only urge Severn to battle against the enemies that Severn—that any good man—would face.

But if the whole procedure was wrong, then what of the Christian religion itself? Of course everything depended on the avenue by which you approached Christianity. Yet the maxims, the great injunctions, were the same: He who loses his life shall find it; Love thy neighbor as thyself; It is more blessed to give than to receive. Needless to say, he was hardly in a situation now where he could think clearly. He had been speculating brilliantly, at another level, in the spring of 1819, when he wrote at length to George about the "Vale of Soul-Making." No one could have said that those speculations had been cheaply won. But now, in something close to delirium, starved and without even enough oxygen in his lungs, he would keep protesting to Severn. (The prolonged lack of oxygen, as we now know, is by itself a cause of the most severe mental depression.) "He says the continued stretch of his imagination has already killed him." Any thought of all of his friends in England is just "another load"; "he will not hear" of them. To think of them is to become apprehensive about their future; and this at once becomes for him a still increased "load of care for the future." He lay there, said Severn, with no hope —with nothing—"to feed his voracious imagination."

Severn was shaken enough even to see "all that fortitude and as it were—bravery of mind," so habitual to Keats, now deserting him and leaving him in the midst of a mere "wreck of ideas without purpose." But there had also been a frightful moment, a couple of days before Christmas, when Keats had become almost completely paranoid in his exhaustion, and had begun to suspect that he had been poisoned long ago in London. In a rather fragmentary letter to Taylor (December 24) that still survives, Severn writes that very recently "his dreadful state of mind turns to [per]secut[ion and some]times even murder—he is now [the next few words are missing] . . . was administered to him by an individual in London." [22] (He could have been thinking of William Gifford, possibly even some of his own friends.) Yet this was only for a moment. And meanwhile Severn tells Taylor that, despite this unexpected and violent suspicion, "Yet every one is struck with him and interested about him," though even this attention Keats is able to "turn to persecution." On Christmas Eve, as he lay in bed staring glassily at the ceiling, he suddenly turned to Severn and said: "I think a malignant being must have power over us—over whom the Almighty has little or no influence." He could not accept the Bible completely. But was there not some other book? He had always trusted books. "I feel the horrible want of some faith—some hope—something to rest on now—there must be such a book."

William Haslam had written Severn that he wanted more details. Where was the daily journal Severn had promised? Severn wrote back. He mentioned the problem of money. They had nothing. But, above all,

> This noble fellow lying on the bed—is dying in horror—no kind hope smoothing down his suffering—no philosophy—no religion to support him—yet with all the most [g]nawing desire for it—yet without the possibility of receiving it.—It is not from any religious principles I feel this—but from the individual sufferings of his mind in this point—I would not care from what source—so he could understand his misfortunes—and glide into his lot—O! my dear Haslam this is my greatest care—a care that I pray to God may soon end.

Severn at last was in a state where he wanted Keats's struggle to end. Keats was now talking in a way that really shook Severn.

> For he says in words that tear my very heartstrings—"miserable wretch I am—this last cheap comfort—which every rogue and fool have—is deny'd me in my last moments—why is this—O! I have serv'd every one with my utmost good—yet why is this—I cannot understand this"—and then his chattering teeth. [23]

22 *KC*, I.180.   23 *KC*, I.181; *Letters*, II.368.

"I cannot understand this." He had been trying to understand for the past year, trying—and indeed feeling that he was slowly succeeding—when the greater poetry began two and a half years before. In a sense, he had been trying to understand from the beginning. Back at the time when the Hunt family had taken him in and he had stayed there happily overnight, on the sofa in their cottage at Hampstead, there had been those lines in "Sleep and Poetry" as he lay anticipating the future, in which he had thought of advancing gradually to

> a nobler life,
> Where I may find the agonies, the strife
> Of human hearts.

And, from the time of the first great effort, when he had gone off alone to the Isle of Wight four years before, he had been coming back to *King Lear* and the questions it posed to life. Thus the whole thing had continued to deepen, through the great odes of April and May, 1819, to those lines he had written in the new *Hyperion* as autumn had begun that same year ("Who am I that should be so saved from death?"). But now the situation was different even from those haunted days in Winchester, when he had tried to start a new style and a new conception of writing in the *Fall of Hyperion* (for which there were so few days—two or three weeks constantly punctuated with other demands): when he had stood in the chilly evenings before the fires of the blacksmiths, and when he had written his final ode, "To Autumn," thinking of the warm afternoon colors of the stubble fields—so much better than "the chilly green of Spring." He was then beginning, despite all the liabilities and despite the lack of time, to reconsider that whole use of the self (morally, or in art, or in anything else) which is the primary concern of our moral and inner life.

All this was over now. He was lying penniless, convinced that this was the end, in a small room on the northern edge of a Rome he could not even get to see. "I cannot understand this." Keats would no longer read the letters sent to him. "He has made me put by 2 unopened," wrote Severn, "they tear him to pieces." One was a letter from Fanny Brawne and another was from his sister. Beside him was a small box in which he kept his special possessions. "He made me put [the letters] into his box unread." Later he asked Severn to bury them with him.

And he was through with books, as he lay there feebly expectorating, "with the approaches to a diarrhoea by laxity and gripping of the bowels." "He cannot bear any books"—even the few Italian books he had so recently bought and tried to read, still hoping to learn the language in such time as remained. Books were associated, and had been from the beginning, with all that was immortal. As such, they were now completely remote, a hopeless contrast with the way in which he was ending—an end after so little had been done. Less distressing (he was now quoting *Lear* for the last time) were things about him that frankly "smelled of mortality."

9

Everything Keats knew about medicine heightened the frightful experience of these last weeks. The sweat, the blood from the lungs, the inability to take food, the constant hunger, Dr. Clark's expectation that a wasting diarrhoea was about to begin, were all noted and even anticipated by Keats. "Keats sees all this—his knowledge of anatomy makes it tenfold worse at every change—every way he is unfortunate."

For a month or so, Keats had often been thinking back to those few weeks at Oxford with Benjamin Bailey, when he was finishing *Endymion,* reading the Bible and Hazlitt's *Principles of Human Action,* and continuing to reread and think about Shakespeare. Bailey had always loved Jeremy Taylor: he had tried to woo one of the Reynolds girls, as Keats once said jokingly, with a volume of Taylor under one arm and the Bible under the other. Keats was still confident that "there must be such a book" as to bring him "some faith—some hope—something to rest on now." Could Severn find a copy of Jeremy Taylor? Severn tried but could not.

Finally, as the days passed and Keats became worse, Severn turned to Dr. Clark, who himself looked around Rome and found a volume of Jeremy Taylor, containing both *Holy Living* and *Holy Dying,* and Severn began to read from it to Keats every evening. Keats "heard me read to night," Severn tells Haslam (January 15) : "This is a treasure—and came when I thought it hopeless—Why may not other good things come?—and even money?" And sometimes Keats asked Severn to read him a little from other books they had with them—Mme. Dacier's translation of Plato, some pages from Maria Edgeworth's novels, *Pilgrim's Progress,* and *Don Quixote.* It was within another few days (January 25–26) that he could no longer "bear any books." But generally, from now until the end, he would turn to Severn and ask him to read for a while from Jeremy Taylor.

However dreadful these weeks were, Severn (long after they were over) recalled that Keats had still "never quite lost his cheerful and elastic mind." These moments stood out in Severn's memory like "the flickering rays of the sun in a smothering storm." Going on with this account written in later years, Severn found himself wondering whether "these bursts of wit and cheerfulness were called up on set purpose—were, in fact, a great effort on my account. I could perceive in many ways that he was always painfully alive to my situation, wholly dependent as I was upon my painting." [24]

Even as Keats entered his final month, Severn was struck by the extent to which this "elastic" capacity of heart and interest was still alive. For there, much of the time, lay Keats "desiring his death," as Severn wrote on January 25–26, "with dreadful earnestness—the idea of death seems his only comfort." (Severn, who had rarely been out of their rooms the past six weeks, and had often sat up for three nights together, suffered now from complete "heaviness of mind—no power of thinking." This challenged man was indeed rising to the occasion in ways neither he nor anyone else had expected.) But Keats, even on his deathbed, was continually changing ("the strangeness of his mind every day surprises me—no one feeling or one notion like any other being"). Only a few days before this, he had been through with sympathy—through with idealism, with books, with concern of any sort. But suddenly there was a quiet moment when he became his former self, and there was a return of that "sensibility for every one save his poor self." He looked closely at the exhausted Severn, who, if he had been gradually rising to the demand of the occasion, was now feeling ill and numb. "At my altered appearance today Keats is much alarmed—he has talked it over—and proposing having a nurse for me." The nurse was found. "I am afraid she won't do." For Keats kept "wanting to say something or have something done every minute in the day." But the nurse remained, or, if not this one, another; for one was

[24] Sharp, p. 69.

present the night Keats died. An English artist, William Ewing, also dropped by frequently now and helped Severn.

Keats became more actively alive as he forgot himself in sympathy for the bewildered companion who had come with him to Rome and was now exerting himself so much. Severn, he said, could have endured his delirious demands—of which Keats had some memory—only because of religious faith. "I now understand how you can bear all this—'tis your Christian faith." Ashamed at what he himself may have been saying over the past month, he tried to lift himself into clarity and determination. "Here am I, with desperation in death that would disgrace the commonest fellow."

10

Near the end of the month, as he lay asleep early in the morning (January 28, 3:00 A.M.), Severn made a drawing of him, writing underneath the date and hour, and the words "Drawn to keep me awake—a deadly sweat was on him." This is the famous sketch now in the library of 26 Piazza di Spagna.

Time after time, when Dr. Clark came over, Keats would continue to look at him "with his large increasing hazel eyes for as his face decreased his eyes seemed to enlarge and shine with an unearthly brightness." Each time, rousing himself to a determined resignation, he would say quietly to Dr. Clark, "How long is this posthumous life of mine to last?" And though his eyes always had, said Severn, an "abstract expression," it was plain from what followed that Keats—with his old readiness to identify himself with another—"knew well all that was passing in the Doctor's mind, although the latter was unable to venture a word." This went on for a week. Clark, convinced that it was too late to do anything to help Keats, had relaxed his restrictions on diet. But by now Keats could retain very little food, and confined himself to some milk—about a pint a day. Severn one day tried to make Keats some coffee—something of a luxury at that time—and Keats, in a kind of somnambulistic fatigue, threw it away twice. But when Severn made the coffee a third time, Keats pulled himself up from the petulance of exhaustion, saw quickly the pathos of Severn's efforts to help, and was filled with shame. "He was deeply affected"; he "was sure my endurance of his 'savageness' arose from my long prayers on his behalf."

Severn, completely exhausted, was by now often falling asleep late at night. Since Keats would frequently wake in the dark, Severn connected a thread from the base of one candle to another. Awakening, Keats saw one candle sputter out and then a flame pass over to the top of another. "Severn! Severn! here's a little fairy lamplighter actually lit up a second candle."

As he lay in his corner room next to the Spanish Steps, listening night after night to the constant play of water in the fountain outside, the words kept coming back to him from a play of Beaumont and Fletcher (*Philaster*): "all your better deeds / Shall be in water writ." Finally, a week or two before he died, he told Severn he wanted no name upon his grave, no epitaph, but only the words "Here lies one whose name was writ in water." Severn's promise was only half fulfilled. For the epitaph was to be sentimentally embellished by Brown and Severn (against the stern opposition of John Taylor) in language that not only betrayed the spirit of Keats's request but did it in a way that would have caused him excruciating embarrassment. (Brown later regretted his impetuousness, thought he and Severn had been guilty of a "sort of profanation," and wished that what they had added could be erased.) [25] As Keats looked by the hour at the stylized festoons of roses on the ceiling above him, his mind also went back to simple English flowers. A few days before he died, as he thought of the grave, he said he could feel "the daisies

[25] Severn, who during the spring of 1821 had made a design for the tombstone ("A delicate Greek lyre with half the strings broken—signifying his Classical Genius—left unfinished by his early death"), hesitated to carry out Keats's request about the wording, and wrote Brown for advice. Brown ("swayed," as he later said, "by a very natural feeling at the time") argued that an epitaph was regarded as the act not of the deceased but of the friends of the deceased. He would agree to omitting Keats's name, since Keats had felt so strongly, but otherwise suggested that, beneath Severn's emblem of the broken lyre, they put: "This grave contains all that was mortal of a young English poet, who, on his death-bed, in bitter anguish at the neglect of his countrymen, desired these words to be engraved on his tombstone: 'Here lies one whose name was writ in water.'" (Sharp, p. 112.) Taylor, he added, had opposed both Severn's emblem and also "any words except what Keats himself desired." In the final phrasing Severn altered the words "in bitter anguish at the neglect of his countrymen" to "in the bitterness of his heart, at the malicious power of his enemies." Brown later regretted ever having made the suggestion, and when Severn (1836) began to think of raising funds to build a monument to Keats in the Protestant Cemetery, he wrote to him: "If a dying friend, a good man, leaves strict orders for the wording of his epitaph, he should be obeyed, if good faith is in the world. I have repented of my fault, and must repeat what I said to you in Rome, 'I hope the government will permit the erasure of every word, with the exception of those words to which he himself limited his epitaph.'" (Sharp, p. 178.) Severn did not try to change the epitaph.

growing over me." He asked Severn to pay a visit to the place where he would be buried, and Severn hurried out to see the Protestant Cemetery. Keats "expressed pleasure at my description of the locality"—the Pyramid of Caius Cestius on the edge of the cemetery, the grass and flowers ("particularly the innumerable violets . . . Violets were his favorite flower"). Frequently he held in his hand a little present that Fanny Brawne had given him—a small, oval, white carnelian. It was the only tangible thing left to remind him of their engagement; for he would still not have her letters opened. Words struck home to him too powerfully.

11

Finally, two weeks before he died, that brief desperate resentment of books, and of the murderous "stretch of the imagination" that they, and all they symbolized, had brought to him, completely evaporated.

Now, on the contrary, he wanted to have books close to him—as many as possible. Severn had just become reconciled to Keats's talk "of the quiet grave as the first rest he can ever have" when suddenly this "great desire for books came across his mind." However puzzled at this changeability, Severn tried to do something as Keats kept calling for more and more books to be near him. "I got him all the books on hand." He was of course unable to read. But hour after hour, for three full days, the mere presence of these books acted on him (to use Severn's word) as a "charm."

Then he became very quiet, taking it for granted that death would come within a week. "He was calm and firm at its approaches," in fact he was calm and firm "to a most astonishing degree." "Last night," wrote Severn to Haslam on February 22, "I thought he was going—I could hear the Phlegm in his throat—he told me to lift him up in the bed—or he would die with pain." Dr. Clark had just told Severn that the end would come at any moment. "Did you ever see any one die?" Keats asked Severn. The reply, of course, was "No." "Well then I pity you poor Severn—what trouble and danger you have got into for me—now you must be firm for it will not last long." Keats himself became altogether "firm," said Severn, now that everything was about to conclude. Severn, for his part, had not been able really to believe that this life was indeed over, despite his experience of the last several weeks. In fact only a day or two before he had written home to his sister Maria a letter full of gossip and pleasant chatter.

The end was indeed near. Throughout Friday, February 23, the English nurse Clark had engaged remained with them; for Severn was by now exhausted from lack of sleep. Then, around four in the afternoon, as Severn told Brown,

> the approaches of death came on. "Severn—I—lift me up—I am dying—I shall die easy—don't be frightened—be firm, and thank God it has come!" I lifted him up in my arms. The phlegm seemed boiling in his throat, and increased until 11, when he gradually sunk into death—so quiet—that I still thought he slept.[26]

Either Severn or more probably Dr. Clark arranged for a man to come on Saturday to take casts of the face, hand, and foot; and what was almost certainly the death mask survives in copy.[27] Then on Sunday Dr. Clark, a Dr. Luby, and an Italian surgeon "opened the body," as Severn later told John Taylor. "They thought it the worst possible Consumption—the lungs were intirely destroyed—the cells were quite gone." The physicians "could not conceive by what means he had lived these two months."

Arrangements were also being made for a funeral and burial early Monday morning, February 26. Non-Catholics were ordinarily required to bury their dead at night, though permission was frequently given for funerals early in the morning. Early on Monday morning, before daylight, the little funeral procession started for the Protestant Cemetery. Several Englishmen attended —Dr. Clark and Dr. Luby, the artists William Ewing and Richard Westmacott, an architect, Ambrose Poynter, and perhaps three or four others. An English chaplain, the Rev. Mr. Wolff, read the funeral service. By now it was nine o'clock. Immediately afterwards, Dr. Clark had the gravedigger "put turfs of daisies upon the grave." "This," he said, "would be poor Keats's wish— could he know it."

---

[26] *KC*, II.94. Severn had written a first draft of this before he sent his letter to Brown. In it, he had recorded Keats as saying "Severn—S—lift me up . . ." (the "S," of course, being an abbreviation for "Severn"). We can assume that the earlier version is closer. (*KSMB*, No. 1 [1910], 42f.)

[27] Presumably a man named Gherardi, the mask maker for the artist Canova, took the casts. For discussion of the death mask see esp. Hewlett, pp. 383–384, and Gittings, *The Mask of Keats* (1956), pp. 1–4, both of whom reproduce photographs of it.

12

Meanwhile, in Hampstead, Fanny Brawne was considering how to tell Keats's young sister, confined to Abbey's house out at Walthamstow, that the end of her brother's life was near.[28] George, several thousand miles away in Kentucky, had not yet received news to make him realize that the situation was as bad as it had been for months.

Early the following summer Charles Brown distributed Keats's books among his friends, as Keats had himself requested before he left England. Brown wanted to do this with cool, deliberate thought.[29] For these books were of course the only property Keats was confident he had, and they had meant so much to him in other ways. In order to buy them, he had practiced a severe economy in every way except in lending money to friends.

Brown had to make an effort to carry out this request conscientiously or even to turn to it at all. He was altogether shaken. Indeed, the hold Keats had taken on almost everyone who ever knew him proved to be permanent; and fifteen years later, trying to write his short memoir of Keats in the "most plain unvarnished way," the rough, virile Brown was to find himself (as he confided to Leigh Hunt), "oppressed, all the while, by a headache,—uncommon for me—or I was crying like a child." Nor, when he tried still later to go through his manuscripts of Keats's poems to help Monckton Milnes, in the preparation of the Milnes biography, could he choose what should be sent to Milnes for publication and what not. Before leaving for New Zealand in 1841—by then it was twenty years after the death of Keats— Brown finally, in desperation, bundled off to Milnes everything he had that was written by Keats: he himself could not make a choice; and, though it was "against all reason . . . Call it nervousness, if you will," yet whenever he turned to the task it seemed

28 It was said by Gerald Griffin, the novelist, that the young Spaniard, Valentin Llanos y Gutierrez, who was interested in England and English writers, had visited Keats occasionally and now dropped by three days before he died. Later in the year, Llanos left Rome in order to visit England. Apparently with a letter of introduction from Severn, he called on Fanny Brawne and Fanny Keats. A few years later, he and Fanny Keats were married (March 30, 1826).

29 He pointedly omitted two people, Haydon and George Keats, and for much the same reason: Haydon had pressed Keats for a loan, and George had accepted one, when Keats could not afford it. This Brown could not forgive. Otherwise the eighteen people who received books (KC, I.259–260) represented everyone who had been personally close to Keats from 1816 on.

as though Keats were "sitting by my side, his eyes seriously wandering from me to the papers by turns, and watching my doings." What still frustrated Brown—what indeed continued to press on the minds of everyone who had known Keats—was how "to do justice to his fame." That concept of "justice" was always at the forefront of their thoughts whenever he came to mind. To each of them Keats represented a deeply human and a fundamentally moral mind—capacious, honest, and, in the process of its development, also acquiring a gift of expression that could be compared only with the greatest writers. To all of them, therefore, however different in temperament from Keats or from each other, the recognition of what Keats was—of what he valued and of what he himself typified—was fundamentally a moral need: it was inextricably tied up with their faith in the general possibilities of justice that life offered or withheld.

In distributing Keats's books, Brown sent only one to Benjamin Bailey—whom he scarcely knew—though to other friends he sent many. But he added something else to that one book (*Auctores Mythographi Latini*), and, simply because his acquaintance with Bailey was so slight, he probably did this only because Keats himself, before leaving England, had said something to him. It had been Bailey who had first introduced Keats to all that Keats meant by the word "philosophy": introduced him also to the greater poetry of Wordsworth, to a poetry that was "thinking more into the human heart" and thus coming closer to "the Burden of the Mystery"—introduced him, above all, to a more philosophic conception of what was to become his polar ideal of "disinterestedness" and to the creative use of the selfless potentialities of the moral imagination. As Bailey wrote long afterwards from far-off Ceylon (almost thirty years after Keats's death), the present Brown sent was "a fine old engraving of Shakespeare."

It was, of course, the engraving of Shakespeare for the frame of which Georgiana, knowing what the picture meant to Keats, had woven the homely little tassels before she and George had left for America. It was the picture that he had found back in the rooming house in the Isle of Wight, when he had left his brothers to go off on his first great "trial of Invention" four years before he died, and that Mrs. Cook, the old landlady, later insisted he take with him when he left. Allowed by her to remove it from the hallway just after he arrived and to put it above his small shelf of books, as he prepared to begin that first long work, he had written happily to Haydon: "I remember your saying that you had notions of a good Genius presiding over you—I have of late had the same thought . . . Is it too daring to fancy Shakespeare this Presider?"

Appendices

✻⇢◈⇢✻⇢◈⇢✻⇢◈⇢✻⇢◈⇢✻⇢◈⇢✻⇢◈⇢✻⇢◈⇢✻⇢◈⇢✻⇢◈⇢✻⇢◈⇢✻⇢◈

I. Family Origins

Sir Sidney Colvin assumed (pp. 3–4) that the name Keats derived from ME "ket," "kete," meaning bold or gallant. Less romantic and far more probable is the assumption that the name (the genitive of "Keat" or "Keate," analogous to the genitives, "Williams," "Edwards," or "Jones"; related names being "Keit," "Keyte," "Kett," "Ketts," "Kyte," etc.) comes from OE "c̄yte" (a hut or shed for cattle or sheep), the name probably denoting a herdsman. Other possibilities are that it was originally a nickname for "Christopher" ("Kitt," "Kitts"), or, less probably, a genitive of "Kate," as the name "Maggs" is possibly the genitive of "Mag" ("Margaret"). Given the uncertainties, one can perhaps sympathize with the puzzled question of the old lady in the Victorian story who, on hearing the poet's name, asked, "What are Keats?"

The name, though uncommon, is at least more frequently found in Cornwall than elsewhere, but rather as "Keat" or "Keate" than in what is presumably the possessive form, "Keats." A Cornish correspondent of the name informed Sir Sidney Colvin a half century ago that many of the rural Cornish who formally signed documents as "Keat" still colloquially used the possessive form, "Keats." Among the literally scores of thousands of names that make up the *Cornwall Parish Registers,* there are few instances of the form "Keats" (though any number with the name "Keat"), and none at all in the marriage registers for years (1740–1776) during which the parents of Thomas Keats would presumably have married.

The largest concentration of people bearing the name "Keat" in the eighteenth and early nineteenth centuries appears to have been at St. Teath, near Camelford, in Cornwall. The St. Teath marriages that are reconcilable with the probable date of the marriage of the parents of Thomas Keats are those of John Keat (m. June 9, 1774)—possibly the son of John Keat (m. February 4, 1748)—and Thomas Keat (m. January 29, 1759). All are listed in "St. Teath," *Cornwall Parish Registers,* I.128–131. Since his widow or mother-in-law gave his age as about thirty when he died (April 16, 1804), we can assume Thomas Keats was born somewhere around 1774–1776. (Mrs.

Keats or Mrs. Jennings may not have been quite accurate; even close friends were uncertain of the year in which John Keats, the poet, was born.) The line of John Keat (m. 1748) and John Keat (m. 1774) seems more promising as a possible background than any other—the first as the possible grandfather and the second as the possible father of Thomas Keats. To the objection that St. Teath is not very close to Land's End, we can remember that our authority for Land's End, Fanny Keats, probably knew next to nothing of Cornwall. To a Londoner anything in Cornwall could understandably seem near Land's End, perhaps the one spot in Cornwall known to all Englishmen of the time. There is only one occurrence of the name, as far as I know, in the marriage registers of any of the parishes closer to Land's End that would coincide with the probable marriage of Keats's grandparents. This is in Madron (Penzance) on June 7, 1767: "Shilson Keate, blacksmith, & Ursula Stokes of Pz. [Penzance]" ("Madron," *Cornwall Parish Registers* XII.51).

A final though remote possibility is suggested by a conjecture of Sir Sidney Colvin's, which was generally accepted until Professor Willard Pope's discovery of the approximate age of Thomas Keats at his death ruled out the possibility (*TLS*, December 22, 1932, p. 972). Colvin found that a "Thomas Keast" was born in St. Agnes in 1768, and wondered whether, on reaching London, the name could have been changed ("a somewhat similar phonetic change is that of Crisp into Cripps"). Assuming that Thomas Keats was recorded as "Keast" (a purely Cornish name, but rare even in Cornwall, and not apparently a cognate; a more probable explanation would be that the recorder unintentionally transposed the letters), we could forget the St. Agnes entry mentioned by Colvin and move directly to Land's End itself. For in the St. Sennen parish registers ("St. Sennen," *Cornwall Parish Registers*, III.109) is the marriage of "Thomas Keast of Phillack, and Bridget Wallis," on January 7, 1775.

In addition to the speculations sketched above there are three other possibilities. Two of Keats's friends, Dilke and Brown, believed that Thomas Keats came from Devonshire. Second, Mr. John Keats of Philadelphia tells me his branch of the family believes that his ancestor—a brother of Thomas Keats—came to the United States from Wales. Keats, of course, is by no means a Welsh name. It would have been common enough for a Cornishman to have crossed the channel to Wales, where work was more available, and then to have left Wales later for America. Finally there is Thomas Hardy's belief that Thomas Keats came from Dorsetshire. In his youth Hardy knew a family named Keats living a few miles from Dorchester. They were "hauliers"—that

s, they kept horses for hire—and they bore, felt Hardy, a facial resemblance to John Keats and his family. Moreover, they were related to a
family of the same name that lived near Lulworth, a place with which
Severn said Keats was familiar. Hardy's speculation is fully presented
by Miss Lowell (I.6–7), and developed further by Robert Gittings,
The Mask of Keats (1956), pp. 79–87.

II. *The Length of Keats's Apprenticeship*

The date Keats left Enfield and the length of his apprenticeship
with Hammond have always been disputed. The reasons for questioning the dates followed above (that Keats left Enfield after the midsummer term of 1811, and was apprenticed for only four years) are put by
H. W. Garrod (pp. lxxix–lxxx). These, as I see it, come down to the
following: (1) Clarke, in a letter to Milnes of December 20, 1846 (*KC,*
II.169), states that Keats "went to Hammond's the summer of 1810."
(2) Brown (p. 41) states "After the usual term of years with Mr. Hammond [the usual term being five years], he became a student at Guy's
Hospital." (3) The school prize (Bonnycastle's *Introduction to Astronomy*) that Keats received in 1811 could possibly have been given him
for independent work, as a sort of part-time pupil, after he left school.
(4) In the Register of Apothecaries' Hall, the form (printed in Lowell,
I.154) mentions that Keats is "of full age," and states that he has served
a five-year apprenticeship with Hammond.

The only real problem, to my mind, is that raised by the last point,
and this does not seem to me serious. Garrod's four arguments can be
balanced by the following considerations: (1) Clarke had just written
for Milnes a brief summary of Keats's life in which he said "He left
school at 14, and served a four-years apprenticeship to a medical gentleman" (*KC*, II.148). This statement represents Clarke's immediate
and probably best recollection. Then Milnes obviously upset Clarke by
asking him whether indeed this was a four-year apprenticeship, since
five years was the norm. Clarke's reply, in which occurs the statement
to which Garrod refers, wavers with confusion, apologizes for his poor
memory for dates, and makes an error in one of the two dates he says
he "knows." The letter begins: "I have the most fatal memory with regard to dates. It always was so with me. I used annually to incur my
mother's displeasure because I forgot the precise date of my father's
birth. Your letter has therefore put me to my wits' trumps, and I can

only guess at the precise points you require in Keats's life. For instance;
I know that he was born in 1796 [actually, of course, 1795]; and that
at age 14 he went to Hammond's the summer of 1810. He was bound
to be with him 5 years." The final sentence does not state that Clarke
believed he filled out the term, but was only "bound." Significantly, a
few lines later, he states that it would "seem that Hammond had released him from his apprenticeship before his time; *and I have some
vague recollection that such was the case* [my italics]," then appears to
change his mind once again, and finally ends by saying that he fears
his help "will prove to be most limping." (2) In Brown's two short
paragraphs that summarize Keats's life from his birth to his entrance
at Guy's Hospital, there are actually more errors than true statements
of fact. Brown's reliability begins at the point when he got to know
Keats. In the remark, "After the usual term of years with Mr. Hammond," the word "usual" is probably incidental and not meant with
literal precision. (3) The Bonnycastle book bears much the same inscription that the earlier prize did ("Assigned as a reward of Merit to
Master John Keats at Mr. Clarke's Mids. 1811"). Keats, as Clarke said,
carried off the first prize in each term during his last year and a half
at school. The Ovid, definitely given after Keats left, simply says "John
Keats, emer. 1812"—"emer." presumably being, as Colvin says (p. 16),
"for *emeritus,* a boy who has left school." We are not certain, of course,
that the astronomy book was given him while he was still at school;
but the probability is so strong that the burden of proof is on the other
side. (4) The statement on the Apothecaries' register that he had
served as apprentice for the usual five-year term is probably routine;
the important thing that the register was designed to certify was the
examination; and Sir William Hale-White saw nothing unusual in this
procedure. (The certificate, after all, states that Keats was "of full age,"
and yet he was not of full age until three months later. The wording
was mechanical: it simply meant that he would not receive the diploma
or be licensed to practice until October 31). Again the entry in the
Apothecaries' register states that Keats was "6 months at Guy's and
St. Thomas's"; but we know he had already been there for almost ten
months. The mention of merely his first six months' term was probably
conventional, or routine, like that of the ordinary five-year term of the
apprenticeship. Finally, however unreliable Abbey himself may have
been about the reason why Keats left Hammond early, or about the
date of his conversation with John (see above, p. 42), Abbey took it
for granted that Keats did leave Hammond before the five-year term
was completed. So much continues to point to the four-year term that
we are justified in accepting it until there is conclusive evidence to
the contrary.

III. The Keats Children's Inheritance *

1

The ambiguities in the will left by Keats's grandfather John Jennings are immediately apparent even to the layman. Both his will and that of Mrs. Jennings (July 31, 1810) are in Somerset House. Excerpts from the first are printed by Miss Hewlett (pp. 375–376). The account of the suit brought by Frances Keats Rawlings in 1805 and the decisions of the court are printed in Francis Vesey, Jr., *Reports of Cases . . . in the High Court of Chancery . . . 1789 to 1817* (1827), XII.39ff., reprinted in *English Reports, Chancery* (1903), XIII.209–212. The bequests in the will of John Jennings are phrased as follows:

(1) "After all my just debts shall be duly paid and my funeral Expenses discharged, I give and bequeath to my wife Alice Jennings two hundred pounds per year being part of the monies I now have in Bank Security entirely for her own use and disposal together with all my household furniture and effects of what nature or kind soever that I may be possessed of at the time of my decease." Mrs. Jennings naturally wondered about the capital. Though her husband did not mention it, he does state that the income is "entirely for her own *use and disposal.*"

(2) An opposite difficulty arose in the next bequest. "I give and bequeath to my son Midgley John Jennings two thousand pounds that I have in East India stock and one thousand nine hundred pounds being part of the monies that I have in Bank Security called The New Fives." Though this was an outright bequest of £3,900,** the father was presumably thinking that the son would be using only the income. For the bequest, he goes on, is "for [Midgley's] use during his natural Life and if he should die without Issue I then give and bequeath to his widow if living at the Time of his Decease the sum of £500 and the remaining part to return to my family." Even if Midgley died with issue, it was not clear whether the actual capital was payable to his child or children.

(3) "I give and bequeath to my Daŭr Frances Rawlins wife of William Rawlins of Saint Stephens Coleman Street fifty pounds per year during her natural Life and after her Decease the same to be equally divided amongst my Grandchildren Sons and Daughter of the said Frances Rawlins, that is to say John Keats George Keats Thomas Keats and Frances Keats." The bequest does not mention capital. But the sense is presumably that, whereas their mother was to be allowed only

---

* Readers are again referred to the detailed analysis that has since appeared in Mr. Gittings' *The Keats Inheritance* (1964).

** Actually only £2,900 (see above, p. 14, n. 11a).

the use of the income, the capital would be distributed to her children after her death. There is no suggestion that the youngest must be of age before the older ones receive their share.

(4) "I give and bequeath to my aforesaid four Grandchildren one thousand pounds to be equally divided amongst them as they become of age with the accumulating Interest thereon and in case either of them should die before they come of age I then wish that the same may be equally divided amongst the Survivors." A possible ambiguity, of course, lies in the phrase, "as they become of age." [1] But there is no real basis for the general belief that the children were not legally entitled to receive any of their inheritance—and that would include the present bequest—until they had reached twenty-one (though Abbey, abusing his position as trustee, could have decided on his own not to distribute until then that part of the money left by Mrs. Jennings herself). It is plain that the children were simply unaware of the existence of the additional £1000 bequest—and also of the bequest to their mother cited above—until George discovered it and asked for a settlement (1823–24), by which time both Tom and John were dead. The sense of the phrase, "*as* they become of age," suggests that each, on becoming twenty-one, is to receive one fourth. Significantly, when Mrs. Jennings, her son, and her daughter all sought clarification of the will in May 1806, neither the Court nor the participants in the suit thought it necessary even to raise the question. After the death of Mrs. Jennings, there was no one except Abbey who could have brought the matter to the attention of the Keats children and advised them to ask for clarification from the Court of Chancery provided any clarification was needed. Nor did Abbey inform himself—or, if he knew, inform the chil-

---

[1] Sir Sidney Colvin, Miss Lowell (who mistakenly thought [I.27] the children were given £1,000 apiece), and later writers, except for Miss Hewlett, assumed that all the children had to be of age before any division could be made. (This would have been in June 1824, when Fanny became twenty-one—more than three years after John Keats died.) They may possibly have made the inference from a statement in a letter of Dilke to Milnes, December 28, 1846 (*KC*, II.175), that Keats "could not enforce a division before his Sister attained the age of 21." Dilke had nothing to do with Fanny Keats's finances until 1824, when she became of age. She then tried to force Abbey to relinquish her share of the grandmother's bequest and of the estates of John and Tom Keats, and asked help of Dilke, who then served her as a trustee. In all probability, Dilke is referring only to the money left by Mrs. Jennings—not the direct bequest to the children from her husband. (The sum of £1,500 apiece, which he says he thinks they were due to receive—he got the information from George twenty-two years before [see below, n. 3]—suggests he is thinking not of the bequest discussed above but of the grandmother's estate.) Though Mrs. Jennings did not in her will state that the children must all wait until twenty-one, Abbey as trustee and guardian could have done as he liked *unless* he was challenged. If Dilke after all these years is recalling the direct bequest from Jennings himself, he would have nothing to go on except Abbey's explanation for his failure as trustee to ask for the distribution at an earlier time.

dren—of the money left untouched by their mother.

(5) "I give and bequeath to my Sister Mary Sweetingburgh . . . thirty pounds per year as long as she shall live." On her death (1813), the capital (£1,000) was divided between the trustees of the Keats children and the executors of the estate of Midgley Jennings.

(6) Six minor bequests then follow, of £5 each: to the three children of his sister, Mary Sweetingburgh—Charles Sweetingburgh, Betsy Cousins of Lothbury, and Sarah Boswell of Walworth; "to Thomas Baxter of Kensington the sum of five pounds and likewise to his wife five pounds"; and to "Henry Nash of Penn Street Bucks the sum of five pounds."

The executors of the will were Charles Danvers of Upper Thames Street, Midgley Jennings, and the widow.

2

A residue was left after all bequests. Whatever the amount, it was enough to justify concern. Within a short time after Jennings' death, Mrs. Rawlings and her husband brought the suit that they both hoped might clarify matters. The following stands, as stated in the Chancery reports, were taken.

Frances Rawlings claimed that her father "died intestate as to the residue of his personal estate; and claiming accordingly in the right of *Frances Rawlings,* as one of the next of kin with the dependents, *Midgley John Jennings* and *Alice Jennings.*"

Midgley, for his part, "claimed the interest and dividends of the *East India* Stock and Bank Annuities under the Will; and submitted the question whether the capital of those funds will upon his death without issue sink into the residue of the testator's personal estate, or not; and whether on his death, leaving issue, the said capital will or will not belong, and become payable to . . . such issue; and insisted that *Alice Jennings* is not entitled to the capital of the stock, which will produce £200 *per annum;* but is entitled only to the sum of £200 *per annum* for her life." He also claimed a share of the undisposed residue.

Mrs. Jennings claimed that she was entitled not only to the sum of £200 a year for life but to the capital of such stock as would produce it. She also claimed the whole undisposed residue of the personal estate as passing to her under the heading of "effects."

On July 29, two months later, the Court decided the following, after beginning with the remark, "This Will is very obscure": (1) Mrs. Jennings was entitled "to the absolute interest in so much Capital Stock as will produce to her £200 a-year." The total given her proved to be more than was necessary to bring in £200 annually. It seems to have amounted to about £7,364.[2] (2) The claim of Mrs. Rawlings for a portion of the undisposed residue was not allowed. The residue was split between her mother and brother. (3) Midgley's request for clarification of his bequest—what would happen if he should die with issue—was deferred until the matter should actually arise.[3] (4) Later, the sum of £1,666.13.4 (Thomas manuscript notes, Hampstead) was set aside by the Court for the annual income of £50 to Mrs. Rawlings, the capital to pass to her children at her death.

3

The amount that the Keats children could expect to inherit may be estimated as follows:

(1) There is the sum of £7,364 or so received by Mrs. Jennings from her husband. Whatever was given Midgley's children in the deed of settlement (now lost) to which her will refers, it was probably not much.[4] We may assume (with Miss Hewlett) that the amount set aside for the Keats children came to about £6,500 (or £1,625 apiece). This is not far from George Keats's estimate (£1,500) in his letter to Dilke of April 10, 1824—an estimate probably conservative because of the peculiarly defensive purpose of the letter (see note 6, below). As far as the children knew, until two years after the death of John Keats and five after the death of Tom, this sum was all that they possessed, except in so far as they may have known of (2) and (3) below as further and separate additions to their grandmother's trust.

(2) Added to this amount put in trust in July 1810 was the total of £1,690.12 that was transferred to Alice Jennings in 1811 from the estate of her late son Midgley.

(3) Of the £1,000 of which Jennings allotted the income to his sister, Mary Sweetingburgh, £500 went to the trustees of the Keats children after her death (1813). This with accumulated interest would have amounted to £545 by 1817.

[2] Ralph Thomas, a solicitor investigating the Chancery records in the 1880's, found that Alice Jennings received the following (Thomas ms. notes, Keats Museum, Hampstead): £4,170.11.4 in consols, £2,420.16.3 in other investments, and £772.12.6 cash. This total of £7,364 may well have included her half of the "residue" (mentioned above) that the court divided between her and Midgley; or, if not the entire half, that portion of it (probably the £772.12.6 in cash) not tied up in real estate, furnishings, and personal property. Mr. Gittings, taking into account the value of the stocks at the time she received them, has put the total value as of that date at about £8,809 (*The Keats Inheritance*, p. 32).

[3] His three (possibly four) children were born between 1806 and 1809; he died at some time between late November 1808 and February 20, 1809. In the "Order of 26 July 1811, of the Lord High Chancellor," a total of £1,690.12 was transferred to the estate of Alice Jennings (Thomas ms. notes, Keats Museum).

[4] That Alice Jennings accepted (and kept) that half of the sum which Midgley had originally received from his father, and which Chancery awarded her in 1811, indicates her confidence that his family was already better provided for than the Keats children. Midgley's family, as we have observed, was not poorly off; his widow and her own family presumably had some money of their own.

(4) By 1817, when John Keats became twenty-two, the sum of £1,666 received by their mother presumably amounted to about £1,900 through accumulated interest.

(5) The bequest of £1,000 from John Jennings to be divided among the children "as they become of age" would have amounted with accumulated interest to almost £1,400 by 1817. Our estimates of interest may be low. For we know that when George Keats discovered the existence of (4) and (5) in 1823, the combined sums came to about £4,800.

(6) There was the further sum of £200 owed to Frances Keats Rawlings as arrears on her annuity and for maintenance allowed to her children till she died (see above, Chapter I, section 8, item 4), which still lay unclaimed in Chancery in 1888.

In short, if none of the capital had been spent, a total of about £12,235 (or £3,059 apiece) could be assumed to be the property of the Keats children in 1817, a year after John Keats became twenty-one. The question then arises how much capital was used. George later claimed that neither he nor Tom exceeded before 1818 their shares of the income of their grandmother's estate (about £60 apiece annually, according to Brown).[5] But, trying to justify himself against the charge that he had borrowed heavily from John, he told Dilke that John, before he came of age, had been advanced about £1,000. It is quite possible that George exaggerates.[6] But even if we deduct this £1,000, together with the £500 Abbey placed in Keats's account in June, 1818, Keats would still have been entitled to £1,559 that he never received (if we include the sums in Chancery not under Abbey's control).

[5] Brown ms., Hampstead. This would fit our estimate if we assumed 3.7 per cent of £1,625—no. (1) above. But, if we assume Abbey also allowed them the income and (2) and (3) above, the interest would be less than 2.6 per cent.

[6] In addition to the apprenticeship-fee of 200 guineas paid to Hammond, which Mr. Gittings (see above, p. 30, n. 7) convincingly shows to be appropriate and probable, George mentions another £170 for the expenses at Guy's Hospital. It is at least possible to question whether, in addition, John spent £160 annually for himself and Tom, while George (who led a far more active social life) lived within his £60 income. The letter is designed to prove to Dilke that George did not take £700 of John's money when he returned to America in January 1820; and the procedure is to try to prove that John could not even have had that much. It is this letter from George that so infuriated Brown, and to which Brown compiled a detailed refutation. Dilke sided with George. Hence the bitter Dilke-Brown quarrel. Professor J. C. Stillinger, after a detailed analysis of the Brown papers, argues persuasively that Brown has proved his case ("The Brown-Dilke Controversy," *Keats-Shelley Journal*, XI [1962], 39–45).

George's account to Dilke is as follows (*KC*, I.276–278): "Thro' a relation of Mr. Taylor's [John Taylor] now living at Cincinnati I heard that he had been informed that I had brought away £700 of John's money: to show that it was impossible that he could be in possession of that sum clears me to that large amount, leaving it possible that I may have taken all he had . . . John and I left school at the same time he immediately paid 200 Guineas and expences to be bound to a Surgeon and during his apprenticeship spent more than the interest of his money. I was

If we look at the picture after Tom's death (December 1, 1818), and add a third of Tom's potential estate of £3,059, Keats's total resources starting with 1819 (from which time until his death he was in such need) were not far from £2,580.

In only one way could our estimate be too high in any significant degree: that is, in the very unlikely event that Alice Jennings, in her deed of settlement, had not assigned the bulk of her estate to the Keats children but had divided everything she possessed equally among not only them but also among Midgley's four children. In this case the resources of each of the four Keats children would have been about £2,075.[7] Deducting the possible £1,500 used by Keats himself from capital, but adding a third of Tom's £2,075, he was still entitled to £1,267 that he never received (or at least four or five times that amount in present-day values).

Abbey's duplicity is therefore incontestable. As far as the money is concerned over which he himself had control, he probably was unable to resist the temptation to invest it in enterprises in which he was personally involved, doling out to the children about £60 apiece as their annual income. Certainly as soon as Fanny Keats became twenty-one, and she, Dilke, and later on her husband began seriously to press Abbey, it turned out that there was little or nothing of the estate left by Mrs. Jennings in the original investments or those she had requested the trustees to make;[8] and Abbey was ultimately forced to mortgage and then sell his Walthamstow property (*More Letters and Poems of*

---

with my Guardian at no expense: between the time of John's leaving the Surgeon and his coming of age, he and Tom (who had been with Mr. Abbey and left him) spent 3 times their income, to make up a considerable part of which I pd when I became of age, besides the various sums John had to pay for dressership and Fees, books and instruments which Mr. A. advanced for him: thus you see my Brothers' property rapidly diminishing and mine stationary. . . . Now sum this up presuming £1500 was the amount each of us possessed. Suppose with the *premium* £200 to Mr. Hammond and *apprenticeship* fees £30, *dressership* £50 and other *hospital* fees £50, *books* £20 and surgical *instruments* £20, and the *current* expenses £160 per an. (Tom being with him) between the time of getting his indentures untill he was of age, nearly 4 years, he spent £1000, a most moderate calculation, he had but £500 left to lend £175 which he informed me he did and spend at least £200 per annum untill I started to America, almost 2 years, when I left him with nearly £300."

[7] Adding (1), (2), and (3) above, the total trust of Alice Jennings would come to about £9,600 (or £1,200 for the eight children). Then, for the Keats children alone, nos. (4), (5), and (6) would total an additional £3,500 (or £875 apiece). But against this possibility are first, the weight of opinion from those closest to the family; second, the fact that Alice Jennings did insist on taking the amount the Court awarded her from Midgley's estate—no. (2) above; and third, most conclusively, the threat of Midgley's widow in 1819 to sue for the return of (2).

[8] Her will requests the Trustees to invest in "The Parliamentary Stocks, funds, or securities of Great Britain and to stand possessed thereof . . . for the benefit of my Grandchildren."

the Keats Circle, pp. 4–5). As for the other money—that which lay in Chancery, and should have come to the children directly from their mother and grandfather—there is no accounting for his action. He could not touch it himself. Possibly, having made his own way upward (the sort of man Dickens burlesques in the figure of Bounderby in *Hard Times*), he felt it good for youth to feel the pinch of need. Just as possibly he may have intended to disclose its existence later as a surprise, when Fanny became twenty-one, in order to divert them from clamoring for the capital of Alice Jennings's estate. We can only speculate.

4

The purchasing power of these sums in terms of the present-day pound—the pound for the first fifteen years since World War II—may be roughly estimated if we multiply them by five, and this despite the general inflation (1800 to 1820) because of the Napoleonic Wars. Aside from the lack of specific indices (except for textiles and certain food prices), the principal difficulty in trying to arrive at an estimate is the enormous change in consumption habits. People buy such different things, including different food. Leaving aside the cost of labor in preparing food, the general impression is that food has increased about two and a half times in price.[9] But labor, of course, has increased many more times than that; and far more labor now enters into the cost of food by the time it is bought by the consumer. Domestic service can hardly be compared (a serving girl worked for the Wordsworths two or three hours a day, did not live in, and was paid two shillings a week). No really adequate information exists on rents. We can only try to glean what we can from memoirs, letters, and diaries. Rents in general, however, averaged far less than one-fifth the present price. Wordsworth rented Alfoxden for £23 a year. Abbey, for his rather pretentious house in Walthamstow, paid a yearly rent of £82 before he bought it. A moderate-sized house (six or seven rooms)

---

[9] Using the available indices, food prices increased 2.4 times and textiles trebled between 1820 and 1953 (Augustus Sauerback, "Prices of Commodities and Precious Metals," *Journal of the Statistical Society,* XLIX [1886], 581–649; Board of Trade, *Report on Wholesale and Retail Prices,* London [1903] p. xxxiv; *The Economist,* Wholesale Price Index, CV [1927], 977; CLXVII [1953], 693). Since the indices vary as far as their composition and weights are concerned, splicing them is a rather artificial procedure. On the inflation generally of the years 1800 to 1820, in relation to the twenty years before and the thirty years following, see N. J. Silberling, "British Prices and Business Cycles, 1779–1850," *Review of Economic Statistics,* V (1923), 223–261, especially pp. 254–255.

could be built for about £150 or £200. Finally, despite all our estimates, we repeatedly find instances where people, though by no means "passing rich with forty pounds a year," like Goldsmith's clergyman of the generation before, were at least able to live on that amount in 1800–1820, and in a way we should now think appropriate to seven or eight times that amount. Much, however, depends on the economic level of the group being considered. Changes in diet, for example, have been far more radical in the lower and lower-middle economic groups than in those above. The floor, in short, has risen much more than the ceiling. So with rents: the man living very modestly received more per pound, in comparison with his economic counterpart today, than those of higher income. In considering the financial resources of the Keats family, we are probably being quite conservative if we regard a pound as equivalent to five at the present time.

Index